LAW AND THE PUBLIC DIMENSION OF HEALTH

London • Sydney

LAW AND THE PUBLIC DIMENSION OF HEALTH

Edited by
Robyn Martin, BA, LLB, MURP
Professor of Law, University of Hertfordshire
and
Linda Johnson, LLB, MPhil, PhD
Formerly Senior Lecturer in Law, University of Hertfordshire

Cavendish Publishing Limited

London • Sydney

First published in Great Britain 2001 by Cavendish Publishing Limited,
The Glass House, Wharton Street, London WC1X 9PX, United Kingdom
Telephone: +44 (0)20 7278 8000 Facsimile: +44 (0)20 7278 8080
Email: info@cavendishpublishing.com
Website: www.cavendishpublishing.com

British Library Cataloguing in Publication Data

Martin, Robyn
Law and the public dimension of health
1 Public health laws, international
I Title II Johnson, Linda
341.7'65

ISBN 1 85941 652 7

Printed and bound in Great Britain

CONTRIBUTORS

Dr Yutaka Arai-Takahashi was formerly a Lecturer in Law at the University of Hertfordshire and now lectures at the University of Kent, Canterbury. His research interests are international human rights law, humanitarian law and comparative public law. He has published in a range of European journals on issues of human rights and is currently preparing for publication a book on *The Margin of Appreciation Doctrine and the Principle of Proportionality in the Jurisprudence of the European Convention on Human Rights*, to be published by Hart/Intersentia.

Dr Sylvie Da Lomba undertook her undergraduate law study in France before completing her postgraduate research in Glasgow. Her research interests lie in the fields of international law, European law and human rights, and more particularly in the area of refugee and asylum law which was the subject of her PhD research. She is a Lecturer in Law at the University of Hertfordshire.

Gill Korgaonkar is a Principal Lecturer in Law at the University of Hertfordshire. Her research interests are in the area of health law and in particular issues of mental health.

Dr Linda Johnson was formerly Senior Lecturer in Law at the University of Hertfordshire, and has lectured at the University of Hong Kong. She now lives in Shanghai where she pursues her particular research interest in health law in China. She has also published on issues of law and gender, and criminology.

Professor Robyn Martin is Professor of Law at the University of Hertfordshire, and has taught at the University of Hong Kong and the University of Bristol. Her research interests lie in tort, law and gender and public health law, and she has published widely in these areas. Her most recent book was (with Allen, D and Hartshorne, J) *Damages in Tort* (2000, Sweet & Maxwell).

Stephanie Pywell is a PhD student at the University of Hertfordshire and will shortly take up a post as research editor with ILEX Tutorial College. Her research interests lie in issues of vaccine damage (which is the subject of her PhD research) and passive smoking, and she has published on both of these topics.

Professor Diana Tribe is Dean of the Faculty of Law, University of Hertfordshire. She has published on issues of telemedicine, medical law and legal education.

Dr Mark Wilde was formerly Lecturer in Law at the University of Hertfordshire and now lectures at Brunel University. His research interest lies mainly in the field of environmental liability in the UK, the EC and the US. His most recent articles have looked at environmental and health risks associated with electromagnetic fields and GM crops. He is currently completing a book on environmental liability.

CONTENTS

TABLE OF CASES

TABLE OF STATUTES

TABLE OF INTERNATIONAL LEGISLATION

TABLE OF TREATIES AND CONVENTIONS

TABLE OF PROTOCOLS

TABLE OF STATUTORY INSTRUMENTS

EU Directives and Regulations

INTRODUCTION

Robyn Martin and Linda Johnson

This is a book about law and public health, but not about public health law as it has been traditionally understood. The book does not focus on statutory measures for the containment of disease (although they are referred to when relevant). Nor does it focus on national powers and duties and the implementation of national policies on health harms (although these are referred to as well). Rather, it is recognised that public health regulation and the use of law as a tool for the attainment of public health operate at global, regional, national and personal levels, just as responsibility for health lies on international, regional and national bodies and on the individual citizens who are the subjects of health.

Aims

The aims of this book are threefold. The first is to define public health as distinct from private health or medicine so that a body of public health law can be identified, with a view to evaluation of that law as a mechanism to support the attainment of health. The identification of public health and public health law must recognise that public health cannot be isolated from the political, cultural, economic and social environment in which it operates.

The second aim is to explore the spectrum of legal relationships inherent in public health. This will take into account a consideration of the relationships which citizens of the world have with their local environment, with other citizens, with the political State and as citizens of an increasingly globalised world. The legal relationships between agents of public health, government and non-government, at national, regional and international levels will also be relevant.

The third aim of this book is to examine the legal framework of particular issues of public health from a global perspective, recognising that these public health concerns and public health initiatives are influenced by law at many levels. The delineation of the different strands of law and regulation is important for any examination of the role of law in determining, supporting or inhibiting health.

Themes

Across the chapters of this book, several themes emerge. Perhaps the first and foremost is the importance of binary classifications. The public/private division is a binary that has long engaged philosophers in the context of physical space,[1] political space,[2] working space,[3] racial space,[4] gender space[5] and body space.[6] English law, uniquely within the European region to which it now politically and legally belongs, has preserved a divide between private and public law, a division echoed with some qualification in commonwealth and north American jurisdictions. This separation of public and private law has not always been logical or practical,[7] and in England at least it is now being challenged by the Human Rights Act 1998, introducing the Convention for the Protection of Human Rights and Fundamental Freedoms into English domestic law. Health provision has seen a similar divide between medicine and public health. While it might seem to the disinterested onlooker that the practice of medicine, characterised by the individual doctor/patient relationship, should operate as a subset of an all-embracing policy of public health, the politics of medicine both within Britain and elsewhere have been such that public health has become a branch of the practice of medicine. It is certainly the case that law has engaged with the practice of medicine and has reached an (uneasy) compromise with the medical profession on power to control the physical body and the morality of citizens. However, law has paid scant attention to matters of public health on the premise that public health is more properly accountable to politics and economics and so falls outside the domain of law. The tensions between private and public law, and between medicine and public health, are examined both generally and in relation to particular issues of health throughout this book.

Another binary inherent in health and medicine, as well as in law, is that of the normal/other. In medicine, medical science determines for us the normal body, normal bodily function, normal bodily behaviour and normal emotional behaviour. Failure to fit the category of medical normal is more than descriptive; it carries with it an assumption that medical treatment is

---

1 Eg, Mumford, L, *The City in History*, 1961, Harmondsworth: Penguin.

2 Eg, the work of Plato and Aristotle on theorising the citizen and the public domain; Plato, *The Republic*, Lee, D (trans), 2nd edn, 1974, London: Penguin; Aristotle, *The Politics*, Sinclair, T (trans), 1962, London: Penguin. See also Simms, M, 'Women and the secret garden of politics: preselection, political parties and political science', in Grieve, N and Burns, A, *Australian Women*, 1994, Melbourne, OUP.

3 Eg, Yeandle, S, *Women's Working Lives*, 1984, New York: Tavistock.

4 For a discussion on public versus private discrimination see Karlst, K, *Law's Promise, Law's Expression*, 1993, New Haven: Yale UP, Chapter 4 and Bell, D, 'Aboriginal women, separate spaces and feminism', in Gunew, S, *A Reader in Feminist Knowledge*, 1991, London: Routledge.

5 Eg, Eisenstein, Z, *The Radical Future of Liberal Feminism*, 1981, New York: Longman; MacMillan, C, *Women, Reason and Nature*, 1982, Oxford: Blackwell; Richards, J, *The Sceptical Feminist: A Philosophical Enquiry*, 1982, Harmondsworth: Penguin.

6 Eg, Grbich, J, 'The body in legal theory', in Fineman, M and Thomadsen, N, *At the Boundaries of Law*, 1991, New York: Routledge. See also Cheah, P, Fraser, D and Gribch, J (eds), *Thinking Through the Body of the Law*, 1996, St Leonards, NSW: Allen & Unwin.

7 Eg, in the context of the law of nuisance, in relation to some judicial review applications, and particularly in relation to hearings to determine in advance the legality of medical treatment, such as in *Re F* [1990] 2 AC 1 and *Airedale National Health Service Trust v Bland* [1993] AC 789.

required to convert the other into normal. The normal medical body has traditionally been male, such that women's gynaecological and childbirth functions fall into the category of other, warranting medical interference. Western medicine has characterised the normal body as European such that behaviours, practices, and body behaviours of ethnic minorities can fall outside the medical normal. Public health by its nature deals not with the individual and individual idiosyncrasies, but with average health, mean health and health profile. The role of surveillance in public health practice has worked to identify clusters of persons as normal and so to be left alone, and clusters of persons as other, prone to illness, and as such the target of public health promotion. The law colludes in these divisions, making distinctions to facilitate medical and public health interference with those classified as other. The law's distinction between capacity and incapacity in relation to consent, for example, enables the practice of medicine to operate where individuals resist subsumption into the normal. Women who opt for natural childbirth contrary to medical advice have had the capacity device used to override their choice.[8] The law supports forcible detention and exclusion of persons with a notifiable disease,[9] and fails to support children who might suffer harm as a result of a mass vaccination campaign.[10] The law supports divisions between human rights which are entitled to prioritised protection and those which are less protected,[11] and between citizens who are entitled to health protections and those who are less entitled.[12]

A second theme to emerge is the recognition within public health theory of changing approaches in science and sociology to causes of ill health. Traditional public health focused on removal of sources of disease from the social environment, treating the person as the innocent victim of the dangers of nature. Modern public health is characterised by an understanding of the dynamic of relationships between people, States and nature, and of the health dangers arising from the modern industrialised technological world, such that there has been a shift from prevention and cure as the province of public health to the containment of risk of the activities of people. While this shift has been much examined in public health commentary, it has not been reflected, or indeed recognised, in public health law. Public health law at all levels, but most commonly at national level, remains grounded in the identification of statutory nuisances as sources of public health harm. Examination of the inadequacies of law in the provision of a framework for the 'new' public health is a prominent theme across the book.

8 See, eg, *Tameside and Glossop Acute Services Trust v CH* [1996] 1 FLR 762.

9 Public Health (Control of Disease) Act 1984.

10 See Chapter 10 by Stephanie Pywell.

11 See the discussion on first and second generation human rights in Chapter 5 by Yutaka Arai-Takahashi.

12 See Chapter 6 by Sylvie Da Lomba.

A related theme is the perpetuation of positivism in the context of both health and law. The body is an object to be observed and treated in medicine, and populations are bodies to be observed and manipulated within public health. Science has interpreted lifestyle in a positivistic way, and whilst medical science has incorporated extra-corporal factors into health, it has continued to look for system breakdown in the determination of health risk in the same way that early medicine focused on diagnosis of bodily breakdown in the determination of illness. The ideal picture of an holistic public health has been colonised by medical science and has been reduced to a check list of risk factors which can be administered by medical professionals. Within health, physical and engineering science have driven public health policy despite exhortations from international and domestic public health commentators to take a more overarching and contextual approach to health. This is reflected in public health law, particularly domestic public health law across jurisdictions. Public health law is embedded with scientific reductionism, and works only to preserve the physical status quo from interferences from physical threats of harm. There is no normative approach to be found in domestic public health law, identifying factors which go to good health and providing a framework for working towards health ideals. International public health law has recently begun to incorporate notions of rights into definitions of health that introduce normative thinking, and the refashioning of domestic law in this way is discussed.

Examination of the role of the State and the individual, and their respective responsibilities for health, also recurs throughout these chapters. Public health law and practice have proceeded on the assumption of the authority of the State, and the obligation of citizens to subjugate themselves to that authority when it is exercised for the benefit of the population. That State authority is now being challenged from above and below. From above, the increasingly important power and influence of regional and international authorities in public health law for the benefit of the regional or international environment has caused domestic governments to reconsider both health law and practice. This is taking place in an environment where global threats (global warming, poverty, AIDS, pollution, immigration) are major public health concerns that cannot be efficiently addressed from a national standpoint. At the same time, attitudes of individuals to State authority are evolving as understandings of rights in the context of health are developed, such that interventions in the private lives of individuals, families and communities by the State must be justified as infringements of rights. These understandings of rights are taking place in a changing social environment which is increasingly multi-cultural, increasingly fluid, and increasingly educated. The individual is no longer the grateful recipient of the commodity of health from the State, but rather an agent of health, and responsibility for the attainment of health must be negotiated between State and citizen. It is also the case that the notion of citizenship is evolving. Relationships between individuals and States, and between individuals and global health concerns, have developed as a result of access to health information (the Internet, for example), international trade, freedom of travel and population movement, leading to individuals seeing themselves as having allegiance to ideas, beliefs and values that are not constrained by frontiers.

Finally, the relationship of the person to the natural world is examined in relation to the dynamic between the environment and health. Is health important because ill health represents a flaw in the overall environment, or is the environment important because a healthy environment is an important dictator of health? A similar dilemma is apparent in health law. Environmental law and public health law are inextricably entwined, particularly at domestic level, but it is not clear whether this is so because regulation of industry and polluting activities is necessary for the protection of the environment, or because regulation of the environment is essential for the protection of health. Traditional public health law places public health as subservient to the environment and much so called public health legislation is, in fact, aimed at the environment. The relationship between health and environment is examined in several contexts within these chapters.

Contents

The book begins with an examination by Linda Johnson of the province of public health. She follows the philosophy of public health through history, placing shifts in understanding of public health in their wider social and epistemological contexts. She examines the complex individual as the focus of public health regulation and surveillance, and the emergence of risk containment as the primary public health objective so as to characterise a 'new' public health that operates beyond national boundaries. The significance of the body, particularly identity, is incorporated into her analysis.

In the second chapter, Robyn Martin continues to chart the boundaries of public health definition by examining those factors which dictate the state of a population's health and those factors which have influenced public health practice. Issues such as the influence of culture, the restraints of religion, politics and economics, the relevance of socio-economic status and gender, the role of the media in determining perceptions of health, and the environmental context of health, are examined. The chapter also considers the importance of ethical public health practice and recognises that some more effective public health methodologies might be denied us by the imposition of ethical constraints. The chapter concludes by stressing that the indicators of health can no longer be confined by national boundaries and that the more serious detriments to public health are increasingly global threats requiring global solutions. Issues of culture, politics, economics, religion, environment and even ethics are rarely universal, compounding the difficulties of determining global health policies. Awareness of these constraints is essential to negotiating international agreement on approaches to health such that moves to improve the health of one population do not serve to displace health threats to other populations.

From this more general discussion of the nature of public health, the book moves to consider the detailed legal framework of the practice of public health. Robyn Martin begins in Chapter 3 by determining what law falls within the classification of public health law, and examines four components of the public health law of England and Wales: the legislative framework of health protection, public health enforcement mechanisms, the role of public and private law in the protection of health and, finally, the legal framework of the provision of health services. Several weaknesses in law as a tool for the protection of health emerge. One is the reliance on statutory nuisance as a determinant of public health harm, in ignorance of changing scientific and sociological approaches to the causes of ill health. Another is the classification of public health as an element of the environment rather than a desirable in its own right, with the consequence that health is protected by law as a spin-off from protection of the environment. A third weakness is the clumsiness of the patchwork of accumulated statutory law pertaining to public health, such that an outsider would be hard put to determine the law on a particular public health issue. A similar weakness lies in the accumulation of law that provides the legal framework of health provision, a body of law representing a range of differing political and sociological approaches to health protection. A need for reform of the law is identified, prompted by such factors as the introduction of recognised rights into English law, the influence of European and international law, changing public attitudes to health risks and health provision, and awareness of the importance of a concerted global approach to many health concerns.

Yutaka Arai-Takahashi then examines the role of international health law and the World Health Organisation (WHO) in the regulation of public health. He looks to define international public health law and to determine its sources. He considers the role of the International Health Regulations, and examines the law making powers of the WHO. The weakness of the WHO in using the powers assigned to it are well recognised, and the chapter goes on to consider the possibility of establishing international supervisory and dispute settlement mechanisms to strengthen the role of international public health law, concluding that there are opportunities for reconceiving international law and its enforcement mechanisms to make it a powerful force in the protection of health. In Chapter 5, Yutaka Arai-Takahashi then goes on to consider the role of rights in the protection of health. International human rights documents are examined to determine the extent to which rights are recognised, and the extent to which recognition of rights enables enforcement of those rights. Traditional distinctions between categories of rights have resulted in the prioritising of some rights over others, and it is inevitably the case that health rights, which fall outside the classification of civil and political rights, are relegated to a secondary position in rights rankings. This chapter criticises these distinctions and proposes an approach to health rights which promotes health to a level of importance equal to that of other essentials to a free and stable society.

From these discussions of the general legal framework, the book progresses to examination of particular issues of public health. Sylvie Da Lomba considers the legal protection of the health of one group of particularly vulnerable people, refugees. The various categories of refugee are identified and the implications of such categorisation for health are examined. Mechanisms of international law for protection of refugees are explored, and while international law is recognised as being the most appropriate forum for the determination of refugee matters, it is concluded that weaknesses in the law as it stands leave many refugees unprotected. Robyn Martin and Linda Johnson look then at population control as a component of public health policy and, in particular, fertility control. The relationships between population control and fertility control, fertility control and health, fertility control and reproductive rights, and reproductive rights and public health are explored. Law has been used in this context not to protect reproductive rights, but to inhibit reproductive freedoms, particularly in relation to access to contraception, compulsory sterilisation and access to abortion. Domestic law tends to reflect traditional cultural and religious views on women's sexual freedom to the detriment of reproductive health. Any protection of reproductive rights is likely to emerge from international law, and it is essential that reproductive rights gain specific recognition in international human rights documents.

The issue of infectious diseases is examined by Linda Johnson, building on the international framework of law on infectious disease covered in the earlier chapter on the role of international law. This chapter explores the nature of disease, looking particularly at those diseases not containable by vaccination, and considers the approaches of populations and States to disease and the implications of disease for public health. The continuing and changing threat to health presented by infectious diseases has meant that contemporary disease is less amenable to traditional medical and legal strategies. Law has a role to play in public health responses in this context, but it is as yet a much underused tool.

Mark Wilde considers public health in the context of protection of the environment, identifying an anthropocentric bias in the determination of international environmental law. Particular environmental hazards with health implications are examined. As with other areas of international law, questions of enforceability are vital, and these are discussed in the context of the environment. It is concluded that national self-interest as a determinant of the direction of environmental regulation has proved inhibitive in achieving international agreement on environmental protection measures, and that firm political commitments to a healthier environment are essential.

Stephanie Pywell then looks at the legal framework of mass vaccination. While many infectious diseases are threats across jurisdictions, the law governing vaccination has developed at national level. The role of ethics and law, and the domestic administrative framework of vaccination in England and Wales, are examined. The chapter gives an outline of the risks of infectious diseases common in the West and considers the vaccination schedules in relation to these diseases. The risk of vaccine damage and the law's response to vaccine damage are explored in relation to the risks of disease. The issue of vaccination raises the difficult question of when an individual should be required by the State to undertake a health risk for the benefit of the wider public health, and the role of the State in that risk exercise. Recognition of the risk, a risk suppressed by Western governments in the interest of the attainment of 'herd immunity', is a first step in the determination of distributive justice in the context of public health.

Gill Korgaonkar considers the treatment of mental health in international, European and domestic law. Determination of what constitutes a mental disorder is problematic, and alternative approaches are discussed. Mental health is an area where the introduction of rights arguments is likely to prove effective in challenging domestic laws on detention and treatment, and the chapter explores the role of rights in this context, particularly in relation to discrimination, which is a significant feature in attitudes to the mentally ill. English domestic mental health law is set for a barrage of challenge after the introduction of the Human Rights Act 1998, and the face of domestic mental health law is likely to change significantly in the near future. This domestic position is placed in the wider global context in this chapter.

Finally, Diana Tribe looks at significant new public health tools, telemedicine and e-health. Technological development will change not only the methodology, but also the culture of public health practice, and could prove an effective mechanism for working towards equity in global public health provision once problems of the 'digital divide' are overcome. However, use of technology for the purposes of health provision across international borders has legal implications. This chapter explores the potential legal pitfalls of the use of telemedicine in a range of situations, including the promulgation of medical treatment to support remote and under-resourced health services, and the use of e-health records as a system of health surveillance.

The direction of public health law

Understandings of health have changed, and are continuing to change. These changes are challenging the prioritising of the role of medicine in the production of health. On the domestic front, health services and the legal framework which supports them are striving to retain authority over factors affecting health which go beyond the medical. The many recent government documents on health have assumed that the particular targeted health problems can be resolved by medicine, regardless of the causes of ill health. Extraneous causes of ill health such as diet, exercise, stress, smoking, and drug taking are reduced to treatment issues, and it is to the practising medical profession rather than to public health sociologists that the government turns for solutions to these wider health problems.

The result has been the extension of the authority of medicine such as to validate inquiry by medical professionals into non-medical aspects of patients' lives. This is in fact a form of surveillance, but not public health surveillance. The tension between medicine and public health has not been alleviated by shifts in public health, nor by new understandings of ill health. Medicine continues to move into the public health domain, weakening the authority and reach of public health.

Yet, the problems faced by contemporary public health practitioners are increasingly beyond the medical. Issues such as the ownership of knowledge essential to health improvement, ownership of genetic information and techniques, for example, plague the implementation of public health programmes. It is politics and economics that will determine whether scientific knowledge can be used for public health purposes, and the medical profession will have little say or control over how health practice develops. It is equally politics and economics which now decide the direction of health research, the priorities of health research and the application of health research, as well as the availability of health improving drugs and vaccines and the availability of health personnel. Major public health developments such as the mapping of the human genome have relied heavily on public funding[13] and the funding of industry.[14] The implications of genetic information for patients and populations will be determined not by doctors, but by the influence of insurance companies and of drug companies on governments.

A cynical view might be that medical practice and the success of medicine has been the cause of some major public health concerns. The age to which people can live is increasing, and it is predicted that a baby born in 2000 could have a life expectancy of 130 years.[15] This advancing age expectancy can be attributed in part to improved medical services, but the economic consequences of an economically unproductive elderly population could be

13 Such as through the Sanger Centre, jointly set up by the Medical Research Council and the Wellcome Trust.

14 Such as the American company, Celera.

15 This was the finding of a Swedish study published in the journal *Science*, and reported in (2000) *The Times*, 29 September.

catastrophic. While people may live to the age of 130, they will not necessarily be competent or able for the last third of their lives, and will require protection and care from a public health service. Similarly, advances in medicine have reduced mortality from stroke or brain injury, but the result is an increasing population of chronically ill persons needing intensive health care. While the most seriously disabled and incompetent will be cared for within the system of medical provision, a larger proportion will fall outside increasingly restrictive definitions of the domain of medicine and will fall within the wider domain of public health responsibility.

Given that it is not medicine, but politics and economics that will dictate public health responses to contemporary health crises, the role of law is increasingly important in providing a regulatory framework for public health practice. Law is needed both to empower governments, public authorities and public health practitioners in exercising public health responsibilities, and in protecting individuals from intrusions into their rights and their private space by public health activities.

Yet, as is identified throughout this book, public health law as it stands, particularly domestic public health law, but to some extent also public health law at regional and international level, is singularly ill equipped to provide the legal framework which will be required for implementation of a 'new' public health. Public health officials are working within a legal framework that is a century old in its jurisprudence. Public health practices are vulnerable to challenge under emerging human rights laws and arguments, but no attempt has yet been made to provide legal underpinning for the work that will be required of public health authorities in addressing contemporary public health problems.

This book has done no more than identify where the legal weaknesses may lie. It is another project altogether to attempt reform of public health law, and indeed while academic commentary may explore legal solutions, any law that is implemented must work within the political and economic framework of the government in power, and within the capacity of public health services. Modern governments across the world are grappling with identification of public health policies that protect national interests, but at the same time recognise the wider role of individuals and States in the protection of global public health. To determine public health policies without the inclusion of lawyers and legal scholarship in the process would be counter-productive. Law can be an invaluable tool in the implementation of policy, just as it can be a valuable tool in the disruption of policy by those who oppose it, and the role of law in the future of public health will be essential.

CHAPTER 1

DEFINING PUBLIC HEALTH

Linda Johnson

INTRODUCTION

Constructing boundaries, discriminating and differentiating is the work of all academic and professional disciplines. Law and medicine are complex in the divisions and categorisations they employ, but so too are sociology, anthropology, history, mathematics and the natural and applied sciences. In pursing academic study or professional achievement, actors do not only adopt their disciplines' categorisations through their work and the language they use. They also actively participate in the construction and perpetuation of those categories. Acting out the world as if it were as defined within one's discipline is a creative and sustaining activity with a strong tendency towards solidifying the status quo. The categorisation of health into public and private domains has affected not only medicine and how it is practised, but has also affected how health and its administration has been regulated. Yet categorisations are not immutable. They are not firm boundaries imposed by one powerful group to constrain others. They are constructed within particular social, economic, cultural, political contexts and, as such, are susceptible ultimately to change.

This chapter examines how the differentiations between public and private health have been made and sustained, and argues that the process is a complex one. In order to appreciate the significance of the categorisations used in medicine and in law (and how those categorisations are now in a state of flux), it is necessary to examine contextual considerations that range from the changing role of the state to changes in the nature of disease. How the individual is perceived, the nature of individual responsibility and the relationship between the State and the individual are all relevant aspects of the categorisations of public and private health. For law to effectively regulate the provision of health care, it sustains, reinforces and adjusts existing definitions sometimes invisibly and sometimes controversially. In doing so, it lends support to recategorisations which in the particular context are within a range of tolerance.[1] It is argued in this chapter that the

1 See the development of this idea in relation to queer theory, Stychin, C, *Law's Desire: Sexuality and the Limits of Justice*, 1995, London: Routledge. See also Butler, J, *Bodies that Matter: The Discursive Limits of 'Sex'*, 1993, New York: Routledge.

range of tolerance for adjusting definitions of public and private health has expanded as the dominant paradigm within the practice of medicine has moved from cure to containment of risk.[2]

THE SIGNIFICANCE OF CATEGORISATION

The use of categorisations is a means of simplification and has been viewed as a desirable and necessary tool to bring clarity and certainty to the governance of a complex world. The legal philosopher Philip Allott, for example, writes:

> A legal relation is heuristic because it simplifies actual reality for computational purposes. Actual reality, as it presents itself in human consciousness, is infinitely complex, uncertain and dynamic. In order to make legal relations operationally effective, as instruments of social transformation, they must exclude much of actual reality.[3]

The division between public and private health has a substantial history and whilst the underlying distinction between focusing on the individual and focusing on the population has remained, how these emphases have been conceived has altered over time. The meaning of 'the individual' has been interrogated and the relationship between the individual and the State has been reassessed with the emergence of internationalisation and globalisation. Ideas about identity, consumerism, surveillance, the environment and risk have all had an impact upon how categories are interpreted and reconceived. The individual is no longer viewed as a single, self-contained entity but is recognised as reflexive: constructed by a complex web of meaning produced by the world in which we live.[4] There is a range of interpretations in the literature on health as to what is significant within this 'world': culture, race, gender, ethnicity, the economy, social structures and development have all been seen as defining, alone or in combination.

---

2 Beck, U, *Risk Society: Towards a New Modernity*, Ritter, M (trans), 1992, London: Sage. On risk and law, see Baldwin, R (ed), *Law and Uncertainty: Risks and Legal Processes*, 1997, Berlin: Kluwer.

3 Allott, P, 'The International Court and the voice of justice', in Lowe, V and Fitzmaurice, M (eds), *Fifty Years of the International Court of Justice*, 1995, Cambridge: CUP, p 17, at pp 19–20.

4 The movement away from conceiving 'we' in terms primarily, if not solely, of national loyalty is amply discussed in Spiro, PJ, 'New global communities: nongovernmental organisations in international decision-making institutions' (1995) 18 Washington Quarterly 45, cited in Franck, TM, *The Empowered Self: Law and Society in the Age of Individualism*, 1999, Oxford: OUP, pp 78–79: '... [it] is becoming increasingly difficult to use the word 'we' in the context of international affairs ... Dramatically multiplied transnational contacts at all levels of society have not only resulted in greater awareness of the global context, but have also created new commonalities of identity that cut across national borders and challenge governments at the level of individual loyalties.' See also Elkins, DJ, *Beyond Sovereignty: Territory and Political Economy in the Twenty-first Century*, 1995, Toronto: Toronto UP.

Lawyers commonly divide the world into a web of binary oppositions: legal/illegal, criminal/civil, statute/case law, public law/private law, international/domestic, applicant/defendant. Each side of the binary gives the other meaning, and together they provide the boundaries of the world according to law. Medicine has a similar format: body/mind, public health/private health, disease/health, disease/illness, reactive/preventive, hospital medicine/general practice, medicine/complimentary medicine, traditional/alternative, doctor/quack. It is these constructed boundaries that define any discipline's distinctiveness. Sociology has from its beginnings drawn a boundary between the natural world and the social world.[5] Within the social realm, it has developed and applied a range of paradigms to social life. Those paradigms have categorised and analysed identified groups, each made distinct from the other through this process. Class, race, religion, ethnic origins, culture, location, age, education, employment have all been used to confirm Otherness. Within medical sociology, it is these paradigms that define illness, leaving disease to the biomedical realm.

The division between the natural and the social has outlined distinctions between public and private health. The concern for a healthier environment, central to contemporary ideas about public health, is distinctly social and economic. Armstrong[6] has identified four regimes dominating the development of public health: quarantine, sanitary science, social medicine and the 'new' public health. What distinguishes this current regime is its response to nature. Previous regimes have viewed nature as producing dangers or hazards that must be removed from the social. Germs, parasites, viruses were the focus of early interventions, with the later addition of regulations to facilitate industrialisation.[7] The 'new' public health is set apart by its focus on harms and hazards produced by man's interference with nature. Dangerousness is in this regime not inherent in nature itself, but reflects a spoiling of nature, a product of modernity itself.[8]

These distinctions are of overarching significance as they are not mere conveniences or even tools, but they constrain how issues and ideas are understood, formulated and imaged. That is not to say that all lawyers, doctors and sociologists accept and reinforce the distinctive boundaries of

---

5 Max Weber, considered to be the founder of the discipline, drew definite, indisputable distinctions between nature and culture, scientific method and sociological method. Weber, M, *Economy and Society: An Outline of Interpretative Sociology*, 1979, Berkeley: California UP; Gerth, HH and Wright Mills, C (eds), *From Max Weber: Essays in Sociology*, 1991, London: Routledge.

6 Armstrong, D, 'From clinical gaze to a regime of total health', in Beattie, A *et al* (eds), *Health and Wellbeing: A Reader*, 1993, London: Macmillan.

7 McQueen, D, 'Thoughts on the ideological origins of health promotion' (1989) 4(4) Health Promotion 339–42.

8 This argument follows the work of Beck and Giddens on the reflexivity of modernity. See Beck, U, *Risk Society: Towards a New Modernity*, Ritter, M (trans), 1992, London: Sage; Giddens, A, *The Consequences of Modernity*, 1990, Cambridge: Polity.

their disciplines, but that those boundaries persist despite challenge. More significantly, ideas defining disciplines are not merely academic abstractions but are political, affecting whom gets what, when and how. Legal historical research, for example, on women and law, has demonstrated how unstated assumptions about gender have determined outcomes. In one famous early 20th century case, a woman was not treated as a person for the purpose of being elected to office, but was treated as a person for the purpose of being prosecuted for holding that office illegally.[9] At that time, it was considered unnatural for a woman to occupy public office. A middle class woman belonged in the private sphere and working class women belonged in the factory. These ideas determined the interpretation of 'person' and when the ideas began to be challenged the law adapted its interpretation.

The significance of categorisation then goes well beyond the boundaries of the discipline itself, affecting the way ideas and problems are perceived and prompting appropriate methods of resolution. The binary opposition of public health and private care has persisted for centuries, but the interpretation of what those categories signify has shifted over time and place. This shift in meaning has important implications for the future scope of public health law and will form the focus of this chapter. In order to understand the current constructions of the term public health, it is necessary to step outside of legal interpretations and examine the analyses within the sociology of health and health policy. If future legal regulation is to effectively interpret and apply 'new' public health policy, knowledge of other ways of thinking about public health is essential. Assumptions and divisions within legal regulation can constrain and undermine those policies by integrating emerging redefinitions into constructed categories that are based upon other paradigms. The scope for law within public health and critique of public health law is also limited by confining problems and solutions within particular registers of categorisation.

REINTERPRETING CATEGORIES

The process of interpretation and reinterpretation of categories is usually slow and reactive to changes in reality which make existing categorisations no longer tenable. It has been argued elsewhere,[10] for example, that the

9 The Persons Case discussed by Sachs, A and Hoff-Wilson, J, *Sexism and the Law: A Study of Male Beliefs and Legal Bias in Britain and the United States*, 1978, Oxford: Martin Robinson.

10 See Featherstone, M *et al* (eds), *Global Modernities*, 1995, London: Sage; Featherstone, M (ed), *Global Culture: Nationalism, Globalization and Modernity*, 1990, London: Sage; Santos, B de Sousa, *Toward a New Common Sense: Law, Science and Politics in Paradigmatic Transition*, 1995, London: Routledge; Held, D and Thompson, JB (ed), *Social Theory of Modern Societies: Anthony Giddens and His Critics*, 1989, Cambridge: CUP.

demise of communism and the collapse of states into warring 'neo-nations', coupled with the rise of supranational institutions has finally called into question dependence upon the nation and the State as identity-defining categories.[11] The Grotian view of the international order as a collectivity of sovereign States has become untenable as powerful supranational and transnational organisations, such as the World Bank, and supranational institutions, such as the UN, have become key actors in the international system. International relations has a rigid Vattelian base fostering the idea that an individual's identity flows from citizenship, yet there has been a proliferation of transnational non-governmental organisations participating in international forums.[12] Multinational corporations, global religions, the Red Cross, Amnesty International and transnational media organisations all have influence on global governance.[13] The result is whilst the individual is seen as indirectly participating in the international system through State representatives, territorial boundaries are no longer effective in determining who is effected by international decision making.[14]

It is this order of change that demonstrates the arbitrariness of categorisations developed in particular historic, political, social, cultural contexts. Michel Foucault in his *The Order of Things: Archaeology of the Human Sciences*[15] gives the example of an archaic Chinese definition of the word animal to demonstrate this:

> (a) belonging to the Emperor, (b) embalmed, (c) tame, (d) sucking pigs, (e) sirens, (f) fabulous, (g) stray dogs, (h) included in the present classification, (i) frenzied, (j) innumerable, (k) drawn with a very fine camel hair brush, (l) et cetera, (m) having just broken the water pitcher, (n) that from a long way off look like flies.

As he points out, this definition has a clear imprint of the culture, place and time in which these ordering categories were created. Within another set of variables, the definition is unsustainable, the categories cease to be adequate to impose the order necessary for language and governance. Beyond this, the way the categories are constructed entails a process of discriminating

---

11 Frank, TM, *The Empowered Self: Law and Society in the Age of Individualism*, 1999, Oxford: OUP.

12 Elkins, DJ, *Beyond Sovereignty: Territory and Political Economy in the Twenty-first Century*, 1995, Toronto: Toronto UP, p 7.

13 Some recent writers have argued that the creation of a more transnational civil society has produced a cosmopolitan world order bolstered by international rights in which the cosmopolitan citizen has a legitimate identity. See Binnie, J, 'Cosmopolitanism and the sexed city', in Bell , D and Haddour, A (eds), *City Visions*, 2000, Harlow: Pearson Educational; Isin, E and Wood, P, *Citizenship and Identity*, 1999, London: Sage; Beck, U, 'The cosmopolitan perspective: sociology of the second age of modernity' (2000) 51 British J of Sociology 79.

14 Held, D, *Democracy and the Global Order*, 1993, Cambridge: Polity, p 8.

15 Foucault, M, *The Order of Things: An Archaeology of the Human Sciences*, 1972, London: Tavistock, p xv, cited by Franck, TM, *The Empowered Self: Law and Society in the Age of Individualism*, 1999, Oxford: OUP, p 4.

and differentiating which sets off one category from another and renders them as 'other' by the observer. Each category takes on a meaning, which is then reproduced and legitimated through use, analysis, redefinition, impacting upon that particular category, but also the other categories surrounding it.

THE PUBLIC HEALTH/PRIVATE HEALTH DISTINCTION

Public health is a distinction from private health and the law has adopted that distinction, concentrating its application on private health, particularly the doctor/patient relationship. Medical sociology and medical practice have also treated that distinction as one worth making. Public health has, since at least the 19th century, been treated as the other, with private medicine dominating as 'real medicine'. According to Singer and Underwood, medicine in European civilisations has had at least two distinct phases: the Hippocratic tradition (around 600BC for at least 800 years) and rational, ultimately scientific medicine (from about 1400BC).[16] These periods were separated by a long period of religious intolerance of scientific healing, but both drew distinctions between holistic and reductionist approaches to health.

The writings of Hippocrates, although considered an atheist, make frequent reference to two goddesses of health from the Minoan belief system, Hygiea and Panacaea.[17] The former is used to signify the belief that health can be maintained by adopting what was considered a healthy or reasonable lifestyle. Panacaea on the other hand symbolised healing through knowledge of medications made from plants or the earth.[18] In Minoan beliefs, the two were intimately connected, often seen as sisters, but Hygiea always subservient to the superior knowledge of Panacaea.[19] Hippocrates drew upon both, seeing diet, the environment, the patient and the healer as contributors to health, proposing preventative and interventionist approaches to treatment.

Rationalist in approach, Hippocrates was committed to diagnosis and treatment based upon what the physician himself learnt from seeing and listening to the patient. His medical judgement was used to determine whether the four 'humors' of the body, black bile, yellow bile, blood and

16 Singer, C *et al*, *A Short History of Medicine*, 1962, Oxford: Clarendon.

17 Jones, W, *Hippocrates and the Corpus Hippocraticum*, 1945, Oxford: OUP, Vol III, pp 192–224.

18 Waldron, H, *The Medical Role in Environmental Health*, 1978, Oxford: OUP.

19 Dubos, R, 'Mirage of health', in Davey, B *et al* (eds), *Health and Disease: a Reader*, 2nd edn, 1995, Buckingham: OU Press, pp 4–10.

phlegm, were in balance.[20] As with other naturalistic[21] systems of disease causation, like Ayurvedic medicine in India (assessing the balance of three 'doshas': bile, phlegm and wind) and traditional Chinese medicine (assessing the equilibrium of yin and yang), the physician's role was to restore balance, rather than isolate a cause.[22]

Aristotle was also a rationalist and advanced the study of medicine with his writings on ethics, logic and biological observation. Under the more religious Roman Empire, the intellectual endeavour to acquire knowledge through the senses was gradually replaced by a firmer belief in celestial power and semantic analysis. The dominance of the spirit world (in the form of deities, ancestors, evil spirits or human agents such as sorcerers and witches) over the mortal has, across a range of societies, provided an explanation for events outside of man's control. In most examples, however, there remains recognition of disease caused within the mortal realm, such as burns, overeating and falls.[23] If the disease is the result of offending the spirit world, there may be a ritual appeasement, if caused by evil entering the body, a witch doctor or shaman would be required, and if a product of a spell, a counter-spell may be necessary. The expertise needed for diagnosis and treatment in this type of personalised system is of the spirit world rather than of the effected body, yet the relationship between healer and the individual is still an essential component.

Beliefs about disease causation continued as a varied combination of personalistic and naturalistic factors well into the 18th century, with the general understanding that health was individualistic, influenced by each person's particular circumstances.[24] Whilst the rise of rational medicine has been linked to the Renaissance period in the 15th century, studies have shown that progress was intermittent and the practice of medicine continued to be imbued with received wisdom of the age. It was only with relaxation in the church's attitude to human dissection and the development of an anatomical atlas that clinical knowledge about abnormality provided new ways of seeing disease.[25]

---

20 Chadwick, J and Mann, W (eds), *The Medical Works of Hippocrates*, 1950, Oxford: Blackwell Scientific.

21 The terminology used to identify these approaches to disease comes from Foster, G and Anderson, B, *Medical Anthropology*, 1978, London: John Wiley.

22 Morgan, M *et al* (eds), *Sociological Approaches to Health and Medicine*, 1985, London: Routledge, pp 12–13.

23 For example, see Hamnett, M and Connell, J, 'Diagnosis and cure: the resort to traditional and modern medical practitioners in the North Solomons, Papua, New Guinea' (1981) 15 Social Science and Medicine 480–98.

24 Jewson, ND, 'Medical knowledge and the patronage system in nineteenth century England' (1975) 83 Sociology 309–64.

25 Jones, L, *The Social Context of Health and Health Work*, 1994, London: Macmillan; Naidoo, J and Wills, J, *Health Promotion Foundations for Practice*, 1994, London: Bailliere Tindall.

The epistemological shift came with the assumption of a system-based model and the reductionist methodology necessary for scientific inquiry.[26] Seeking out the cause of system failure drove the natural sciences[27] and later the social sciences. Within medicine it linked specific causes with diseases by confining the range of variables in ill health to those operating within the system under scrutiny, the body. Diseases came to have specific names, be linked to the presence of specific pathogens and to be seen as universal. Patients were examined and tested to match their condition to identified disease categories in order to locate the appropriate treatment. Hospitals were built as part of the 'great incarcerations' programme of the industrial revolutions that also spurned factories, prisons, asylums and schools to house and manage the urban working classes. It was in the hospitals where the 'medical model' became firmly established[28] and became the locus for the development of the profession and its myriad specialisms. It was also in the hospital where most research into the practice of medicine has been done and where ideas about the nature of medical knowledge, the doctor-patient relationship and the centrality of the body have been explored.[29]

Scientists began to see nature within a mechanical paradigm from the 17th century. This approach taken by Galileo, Descartes and Newton was followed by biologists, seeing the individual as a sum of parts.[30] This methodology was key to the development of biomedicine as positivism as it allowed for concentration on ill health (breakdown of the mechanism), seeing the body as the locus of the problem and as the site for treatment and for the development of universal, elementary laws as pathology. The essential reductionism and materiality of scientific inquiry was contained within biomedicine as a way of seeing.

26 Antonovsky, A, *Health, Stress and Coping*, 1985, San Francisco: Josey Bell; Antonovsky, A, *Unravelling the Mystery of Health*, 1987, San Francisco: Josey Bell.

27 Kuhn, TS, *The Structure of Scientific Revolutions*, 2nd edn, 1970, Chicago: Chicago UP.

28 Three key developments made it possible for medicine to become a more scientific process: the discovery of anaesthesia by John Snow, developments in knowledge of the chemistry relating to Sulpha drugs and later antibiotics to minimise pot-operative infections and technologies to provide more accurate diagnoses. MacDonald, TH, *Rethinking Health Promotion: A Global Approach*, 1998, London: Routledge, pp 1–10.

29 Atkinson, P, *Medical Talk and Medical Work*, 1995, London: Sage, pp 31–36.

30 McKeown, T, 'A historical appraisal of the medical task', in McLachlan, G and McKeown, T, (eds) *Medical History and Medical Care*, 1971, London: OUP; McKeown, T, *The Role of Medicine: Dream, Mirage or Nemesis?*, 1979, Oxford: Blackwell.

THE BODY

Ill health was imaged within the body and the clinical gaze, as described by Foucault,[31] allowed modern medicine to read localised signs and symptoms to identify the cause within the body. This detailed scrutiny or panopticism, surveillance and monitoring of the body produced a discrete, passive, individualised body as the object of medical science.[32] Armstrong in his detailed Foucauldian analysis of 20th century medical knowledge summarises this view of political anatomy:

> The modern body of the patient, which has become the unquestioned object of clinical practice, has no social existence prior to those same clinical techniques being exercised upon it. It is as if the medical gaze, in which is encompassed all the techniques, languages and assumptions of modern medicine, establishes by its authority and penetration an observable and analysable space in which is crystallised that apparently solid figure – which has now become as familiar – the discrete human body.[33]

Armstrong goes on to argue that the gaze has continued to fall upon the body, defining it as an individual entity, but the development of specialisms and technologies has produced a multiplicity of images of the human body.[34] The bedside is no longer the place where the actual body becomes intelligible.[35] Jewson has seen these technological developments as marking a new era, Laboratory Medicine, characterised by the increased objectification of the body and the loss of identity of the sick patient.[36] Data

---

31 Foucault, M, *The Birth of the Clinic: An Archaeology of Medical Perception*, 1976, London: Tavistock. The sociological literature has tended to adopt the rather exaggerated distinction that Foucault drew in this study between pre- and post- revolutionary medicine in Paris and apply it to the slightly later development of clinical medicine in Britain. See Turner, B, *Medical Power and Social Knowledge*, 1987, London: Sage; Nettleton, S, *Power, Pain and Dentistry*, 1992, Buckingham: OUP. For a more critical approach to the homogeneity of clinical medicine, see Armstrong, D, *Political Anatomy of the Body: Medical Knowledge in Britain in the Twentieth Century*, 1983, Cambridge: CUP; Bury, MR, 'Social constructionism and the development of medical sociology' (1986) 8 Sociology of Health and Illness 137–69 and Nicolson, M and McLaughlin, C, 'Social constructionism and medical sociology: a reply to MR Bury' (1987) 9 Sociology of Health and Illness 107–26.

32 Lupton, D, *Medicine as Culture: Illness, Disease and the Body in Western Societies*, 1994, London: Sage.

33 Armstrong, D, *Political Anatomy of the Body: Medical Knowledge in Britain in the Twentieth Century*, 1983, Cambridge: CUP, p 2.

34 Lynch, M, 'The externalised retina: selection and mathematization in the visual documentation of objects in the life sciences', in Lynch, M and Woolgar, S (eds), *Representation in Scientific Practice*, 1990, Mass: MIT, pp 153–86.

35 That is not to say that the bedside is no longer the locus for significant interaction, but that interrogation of the body is no longer tied to it. See Atkinson, P, 'Discourse, descriptions and diagnoses', in Lock, M and Gordon, D (eds), *Biomedicine Examined*, 1988, Dordrecht: Kluwer.

36 Jewson, N, 'The disappearance of the sick-man from medical cosmologies: 1770–1870' (1976) 10 Sociology 225–44.

collected from the body is scrutinised and interpreted through a range of processes and by a range of personnel. These processes are often complex and uncertain, requiring reflexive expertise.[37] The individual patient is the product of gazes mediated by available knowledge and social construction. Physical reality is no longer the object of medicine. The object is a composite of interpreted results of disembodied fragments:[38]

> With the growth in medical technology and super-specialities, the panoptic gaze has focused on an even more detailed analysis of the body. Thus at the same time as the community gaze constructs identities and relationships, the Panopticon produces ever more discrete and individualised bodies.[39]

Armstrong has identified the significance of the advent of hospital medicine at the end of the 18th century as lying in the relationship it drew between symptom, sign and illness.[40] Medical practice had been concerned with hearing and examining the patient to identify the distinctive cluster of symptoms that enabled the physician to name and treat the disease. Hospital medicine went a stage further by linking the symptoms with an underlying pathological lesion within the body. It was this which made the hospital as the locus for medical practice essential, and which facilitated increasingly complex forms of investigation of the body. Whilst the body became segmented, Armstrong maintains the relationship between symptom, sign and illness has continued. The body remained the focus for the diagnosis and treatment of the disease: illness, like individuality, was sited within the atomised body. Armstrong does, however, see as a significant shift the growth of what he calls Surveillance Medicine. By this he means medicine which addresses the health of populations rather than targeting the ill individual, medicine that problematises the normal by seeing populations perpetually at risk of ill health.[41]

---

37 Detailed studies of some specialisms demonstrate this. See Atkinson, P, 'Discourse, descriptions and diagnoses', in Lock, M and Gordon, D (eds), *Biomedicine Examined*, 1988, Dordrecht: Kluwer (haematologists); Pasveer, B, 'Knowledge of shadows: the introduction of X-ray images in medicine' (1989) 11 Sociology of Health and Illness 360–81 (X-rays); Daly, J, 'Innocent murmurs: echocardiography and the diagnosis of cardiac normality' (1989) 11 Sociology of Health and Illness 99–116 (echocardiography); Yoxen, E, 'Seeing with sound: a study of the development of medical images', in Bijker, WE *et al* (eds), *The Social Construction of Technological Systems*, 1990, Cambridge, Mass: MIT, pp 281–303 (ultrasound). See, also, work on histological staining and the production of biomedical reality in microscopy. Conn, HJ, *Biological Stains: A Handbook on the Nature and Uses of the Dyes Used in the Biological Laboratory*, 7th edn, 1961, Baltimore: Williams and Wilkins.

38 Lynch, M, *Art and Artifact in Laboratory Science*, 1985, London: Routledge.

39 Armstrong, D, *Political Anatomy of the Body: Medical Knowledge in Britain in the Twentieth Century*, 1983, Cambridge: CUP, p 111.

40 Armstrong, D, 'The rise of surveillance medicine' (1995) 17(3) Sociology of Health and Illness 393–404.

41 *Ibid*, p 395.

EARLY PUBLIC HEALTH MEASURES

Risk of ill health certainly underlay early public health measures in Britain. The role of contagion in the spread of disease had been known since the second Bubonic Plague of 1660[42] and had led to quarantine regulations in Venice as early as the 14th century. As the Industrial Revolution and the various Enclosure Acts created increasing urban poor populations, the risk of epidemics grew. Edwin Chadwick and other public health reformers championed the need for national action to improve sanitation so as to protect the urban bourgeoisie from disease rooted in the poor.[43] Miasmatism, popular during the 18th and 19th centuries, saw disease as resulting from marshes and swamps producing airborne substances that produce fever, and although the theory was wrong, it nevertheless supported measures which had a positive effect on the health of the population.[44] Clean water, efficient sewerage disposal and drainage had a far more significant impact on the nation's health than clinical interventions[45] and these public health measures reached their peak in the mid-19th century. Vaccination and inoculation programmes were also used in the early 20th century to address the problem of epidemics amongst the poor. It has been argued, however, that this is more an example of preventative medicine treating the individual than a measure properly described as public health, even where it is sponsored by the State.[46]

René Dubos has defined public health as concerning itself with social organisation, ways of life.[47] Public health workers examine the interplay between social and environmental factors and health with the aim of managing a problem identified as posing a health threat to the community. This definition is certainly applicable to early public health interventions. Factory reform measures and measures addressed to child health also fall

---

42 Chave, SP, 'The origins and development of public health', in *Oxford Textbook of Public Health*, Vol 1, 1986, Milton Keynes: OU Press.

43 *Ibid.*

44 Tesh, S, *Hidden Arguments: Political Ideology and Disease Prevention Policy*, 1988, New Brunswick: Rutgers UP.

45 Powles, J, 'On the limitations of modern medicine' (1973) 1 Science, Medicine and Man 1–30. There is convincing evidence that improved housing and working conditions had a far greater impact on health than clinical interventions and sanitary reforms combined. McKeown, T, *The Role of Medicine: Dream, Mirage or Nemesis?*, 1979, Oxford: Blackwell.

46 Turshen, M, *The Politics of Public Health*, 1989, London: Zed, pp 52–54 and Brubaker, BH, 'Health promotion: a linguistic analysis' (1983) 5 Advances in Nursing Science 1–14. Compare, eg, MacDonald, TH, *Rethinking Health Promotion: A Global Approach*, 1998, London: Routledge, pp 21, 27–30 and Tannahill, A, 'What is health promotion?' (1985) 44 Health Education Journal 21–29, who both see health promotion as including disease prevention.

47 Dubos, R, *Man, Medicine and Environment*, 1968, Harmondsworth: Penguin, p 82.

within this domain: the former managing the industrial environment and the latter managing the environment within which a child should be permitted to grow.[48] They are concerned with issues outside of the body and whilst they had an impact on individuals, their focus was environmental.

At the time of the advent of germ theory[49] in the 1880s, British public health was clearly differentiated from the practice of clinical medicine. The Clinic, first established in France during the late 1700s, had thrived on the widespread vision of science as a positive good and the development of the medical profession had institutionalised medical knowledge as power.[50] Living and working conditions had been improved and the fear of contagious diseases subsided. The work of public health on the other hand had remained within local government and the powers of Medical Officers of Health, appointed following the Public Health Act 1848, had successively been reduced, subjecting public health measures to the filter of medical authority.[51] Germ theory, the first biomedical theory on disease, saw diseases as caused by germs invading the body, rather than being linked to extra-corporeal conditions. Specific germs were linked to particular diseases as in more recent times specific genes have been linked to particular conditions.[52] Diseases were typified as self-contained and short-lived and

48 Armstrong, D, 'The rise of surveillance medicine' (1995) 17(3) Sociology of Health and Illness 393–404.

49 Robert Koch and Louis Pasteur identified bacterial and viral agents as causative of disease and the reductionism of scientific method erroneously saw a simple direct relationship between cause and effect. Such a relationship could not, for example, explain why the contemporary cholera epidemic in Zanzibar devastated the local African population by claiming 20,000 to 30,000 of its number but affected none of the 60 European colonisers living on the same small island. Davies, J, 'James Christie and the cholera epidemics of East Africa' (1959) 36 East African Medical Journal 1–6, cited in Turshen, M, *The Politics of Public Health*, 1989, London: Zed, p 20.

50 The development of medicine as a profession and the implications of this for the status of clinical medicine and its practitioners have been the subject of extensive sociological enquiry. See, eg, Johnson, TJ, *Professions and Power*, 1972, London: Macmillan; Turner, B, *Medical Power and Social Knowledge*, 2nd edn, 1995, London: Sage. Some have argued that the preoccupation with medicine as a profession within the discipline has produced an inaccurate picture because of reductionism and its over-emphasis on culture as deterministic of knowledge and behaviour. Atkinson, P, *Medical Talk and Medical Work*, 1995, London: Sage.

51 See Chapter 3 herein by Robyn Martin on domestic regulation of public health. For a detailed discussion of this era of public health and its regulation, see Hart, J, *A New Kind of Doctor*, 1988, London: Merlin.

52 Current views on the human genome have moved away from the idea that individual genes or collections of genes can be identified as causes of disease, towards a more multifactorial approach which takes into account environment and lifestyle. In this context knowledge about genes is more of an aspect of risk assessment than an indicator of certain ill health although there are exceptions to this such as Tay Sachs, haemophilia and cystic fibrosis. For discussion, see Brownsword, R *et al* (eds), *Law and Human Genetics: Regulating a Revolution*, 1998, Oxford: Hart.

curable by the elimination, avoidance or rendering harmless of identifiable agents.

This understanding of disease not only confirmed the body as the only relevant site in disease causation, but also confirmed biomedicine as the cure for alleviating disease. As a theory it was attractive to the medical profession, to governments anxious to contain public spending and to industrialists anxious to minimise interference with their economic freedom.[53] It was a product of its time, confirming the individual as a self-contained entity and man armed with science having mastery over his environment.[54] Developments within surgery and the production of pharmaceutical antibiotics kept fears of disease at bay and it was only after the Second World War that it became evident that germ theory was inadequate to explain the chronic diseases that became the leading causes of death in industrialised societies.

Concentration on the body and germ theory duly had an impact on public health as well as clinical medicine. Quarantine regulations, for example, adopted the germ theory model in seeing disease as an aggressor, a foreign invader which could be turned away at the borders of a state to protect the health of its population. The biological model of seeing an entity as a sum of its parts was pervasive. Sanitary engineering and public works became the stuff of public health, reliant upon engineering expertise. Health in the workplace concerned itself with the safety of machinery and systems of work. Ideas of biological determinism dominated the study of behaviour, reducing 'disordered' behaviour to physical, psychosocial or biochemical processes within the body.[55]

THE VIEW OF THE INDIVIDUAL

Western law and medicine developed as professions within the same historical context. The idea of the individual as the locus for ill health had its parallel in law, with the individual as the locus for rights, duties and responsibilities. Both medicine and law had their foundations in early history. The Hippocratic Oath and Plato's concept of justice were developed as positions to adopt in the practice of these necessary social structures. The maintenance of health and the provision of justice were seen as falling

53 Berliner, H, *A System of Scientific Medicine: Philanthropic Foundations in the Flexner Era*, 1985, New York: Tavistock.

54 Hobsbawn, E, *The Age of Capital 1848–1875*, 1975, New York: Charles Scribner, p 258.

55 There is a well developed critique of this in the contexts of crime and deviance and mental health. See, eg, Cohen, S and Scull, A (eds), *Social Control and the State*, 1983, Oxford: Robertson.

within the realm of man's control and this position came to be reasserted much later in the Enlightenment period, when scientific method provided a framework for the development of specialist knowledge based on observation rather than experience.

The development of the State as an entity beyond the individual and the God-given power of a ruler spawned philosophy harking back to Plato and Socrates to establish and define the significance of the individual. The individual as source of State power was clothed in a variety of garbs, but was consistently male, rational and a possessor of free will. The individual was divided out from the collective, and the collective in dominant Western 18th and 19th century thought, was a group of individuals, not a shared community,[56] contained within national boundaries.[57]

Republicanism and a reaction against fealty obligations to another individual underscored the view of the individual that dominated during the Enlightenment period. The American and French Revolutions and the constitutional history of England provided an alternative form of relationship of governance. Citizens of the State owed loyalty to each other and were bound together by common ideals to form a State. Citizens were imaged as acting out of free will, constrained only by reason. Nationalisms were created or fostered to provide support for these new States,[58] France, Italy and America in particular, but the ideals to which they ascribed were seen as being derived from logic or common sense, capable of universal application, and implicit in the nature of man.[59] The German romantic view of nationalism came to the fore in the late 19th century, where illusion to a shared history and shared kinship, rather than allegiance to a set of values, was the binding force.

It is this latter view of nationalism which dominated the 20th century nation-State[60] and which is now defended against transnationalism. Yet

56 Obviously, there were significant communitarian theorists in this period, most notably Karl Marx. The point here is not that communitarianism did not exist as a theory, but that the liberal State which dominated Western society adopted a model of society which placed considerable value on the individual, thereby closing down holistic approaches.

57 The significance of containment within national boundaries has been explored in, eg, Stychin, C, 'New Labour, new "Britain"?: constitutionalism, sovereignty, and the nation/State in transition' (1999) 19 Studies in Law, Politics and Society 139; Darian-Smith, E, *Bridging Divides: The Channel Tunnel and English Legal Identity in the New Europe*, 1999, Berkeley: California UP. Border control has had continuing links with the body, disease and public health measures from quarantine regulations to the discourse on AIDs and the European response to CJD. See Smith, AM, *New Right Discourses on Race and Sexuality*, 1994, Cambridge: CUP.

58 Hobsbawn, EJ, *Nations and Nationalism since 1780*, 2nd edn, 1992, Cambridge: CUP; Schulze, H, *States, Nations and Nationalism*, trans Yuill, W, 1996, London: Blackwell.

59 Kant, I, 'On perpetual peace' (1795), in Reiss, H (ed), *Kant's Political Writings*, 2nd edn, Nisbet, H (trans), 1990, Cambridge: CUP.

60 Gay, P, *The Cultivation of Hatred: The Bourgeois Experience, Victoria to Freud*, 1995, London: Fontana.

Kant's view of the State, linking citizens together through the intellect (shared values or ideals) rather than through blood (race, ethnic, spatial history) was not so constrained. He envisaged movement towards a global community, with the State as an essential building block in a process towards a federalist ideal of humanity, rather than as an ethnocentric unit to be defended against dilution. This view provided a framework for the advancement of internationalisation through, for example, shared ideals contained in human rights instruments after the Second World War. Both sought to preserve the freewill of the individual against the tyranny or determinism of an omnipotent State, prioritising a concept of individual autonomy within a particular understanding of a set of ideals preserving the community.

Unlike some communitarian views, however, Kant saw the State as defining identity. It was for him the shared values represented in the State that demanded loyalty and could not be dismantled and replaced by other social structures. Individual virtue lay in a universalised respect for those values, so that an individual acts only in accordance with those values and does nothing to prevent others from acting similarly. This view of the individual allowed autonomous choices constrained only by allegiance to shared ideals, rather than to group interests and has been increasingly prioritised in recent years over Benthamite ideals of acting to produce the greatest good for the greatest number. It is this utilitarianism, however, that has largely justified public health measures, such as vaccination programmes and confinement of those with contagious diseases.

The liberal individualist viewpoint has been used extensively to support, for example, the growing body of human rights provisions and the provision of individual choice within and beyond the marketplace. The constraints placed upon the individual in the choices she makes has been the subject of extensive and prolonged debate and there is frequent reassessment of the balance that should exist between the rights of the individual, the State and the group.[60a] This reassessment has been frequent and controversial within international institutions, transnational organisations, states and academic debate and the literature that has emerged is complex, blurring the boundaries between concepts elaborated in simpler forms of society, such as autonomy, utilitarianism, communitarianism and rights.

Professor Michael J Sandel,[61] for example, has argued against liberal individualism on the basis of a State's civic republican virtues. In his view,

60a For a full discussion, see Franck, T, *The Empowered Self: Law and Society in the Age of Individualism*, 1999, Oxford: OUP.

61 Sandel, MJ, *Democracy's Discontents*, 1996, Cambridge, Mass: Belknap Press of Harvard UP. Other examples of communitarian critique can be found in MacIntyre, A, *After Virtue: A Study in Moral Theory*, 1981, London: Duckworth; Williams, B, *Ethics and the Limits of Philosophy*, 1985, London: Fontana; Taylor, C, *Philosophy and the Human Sciences: Philosophical Papers*, 1985, Cambridge: CUP, Vol II.

American law and society have overemphasised personal entitlements so as to undermine the common good. His analysis locates two theories as competing with each other: liberalism protecting the individual from the State and civic republicanism reposing rights in the community. The increasing emphasis on individual-liberalism, he argues, has overwhelmed the State, making it incompetent in its role in socialising its citizens to support measures designed for purposes other than personal gain. Professor Robert Clinton,[62] looking at indigenous peoples, argues that a dichotomy between individual rights and group rights is unhelpful, as individual rights only have meaning in the context of the relationships that individuals have. To him, the unconnected individual is a peculiarly Western concept and it is 'membership in the family, kinship and associational webs of the society'[63] which cause rights to exist. An individual is never simply that, but is always located in a relational context. Both of these approaches are particularist, harking back to more traditional forms of society and are referred to as communitarianism because of their desire for law to protect group interests above other interests.

Individualism, on the other hand, sees persons engaging in associations and affiliations out of choice. Loyalties emerge out of overlapping self-interest or shared values and are always contingent. Of course, choice is always dependent upon opportunity and the perceptions of the individual and even Kant sees autonomy as necessarily constrained by rationality. Since Freud, notions of absolute autonomy have been difficult to argue. The idea that we control our own lives free from influences conscious or unconscious is no longer sustainable.[64] Professor Jennifer Nedelsky argues that in exercising autonomy, an individual is always constrained by their context and the relationships she has with others.[64a] The need to preserve or enhance relationships has a significant and necessary impact upon how choices are perceived, assessed and exercised. Those relationships may be with another individual, a group or the State, and each individual will reside within a matrix of relationships affecting choice. Acting out of concern for these relationships, consciously or not, is clearly distinct from being compelled to act in the interests of defined groups or the State, and allows for changing and multi-layering of affiliations.

62 Clinton, RN, 'The rights of indigenous peoples as collective group rights' (1990) 32 Arizona Law Rev 739.

63 *Ibid*, p 742.

64 Chodorow, NJ, 'Towards a relational individualism: the mediation of self through psychoanalysis', in Heller, TC *et al* (eds), *Reconstructing Individualism*, 1986, Stanford UP, p 197.

64a Nedelsky, J, 'Law, boundaries and the bonded self', in Post, R, *Law and the Order of Culture*, 1991, Berkeley: University of California; 'Reconceiving autonomy: sources, thoughts and possibilities' (1989) Yale Journal of Law and Feminism 7; 'A relational approach to citizenship', in Beiner, R and Norman, W (eds), *Canadian Political Philosophy: Contemporary Reflections*, 2000, Toronto: OUP.

The individual she perceives is very different from Sandel's figure of the 'deontological self,' an atomised, rational, self-interested man. Both, however, are engaged in the ongoing critique of idealised conceptions of the person, autonomy and reason found in Universalist ethics. With Nedelsky, the aim is to reconceive autonomy,[65] whereas the communitarian agenda, prevalent particularly in American literature of the 1980s, is to shift the focus away from the individual. The tension between the interests of the individual and those of the community is ongoing within the health arena and is central in the development of the 'new' public health. I shall argue that the individual has remained the focus of public health, but has been reconfigured and not subsumed to the interests of 'the community'.

The modernist emphasis on individualism and reason (as opposed to traditional ideas of society based upon religion, mysticism and community) brought along with it a belief in ultimate truth and the capability of scientific method to allow objective observation of reality. Scientific method was not confined to natural science and mathematics,[66] but was extended to physical and social problems within societies.[67] The positivist search was for causes, to apply cures and eradicate or minimise problems. The fallacy of this idea of knowledge of the world through trained observation lies at the heart of Michel Foucault's much discussed genealogy and is a central limb of the ensuing 'postmodernist' critique. Through postmodernism, reality lost its certainty and was seen as necessarily contingent, ambiguous and open-ended.[68] There is no truth behind distinctions and categorisations; there are only different ways of seeing, particular interpretations. The order of the day became deconstruction and identification of complexity as opposed to the reductionism of scientific inquiry.

SHIFTS IN PUBLIC HEALTH

Parallels have been drawn between these developments in approaches to knowledge and shifts in the significance of public health in national and international health care systems, particularly in relation to health promotion.[69] Not only has the growth of community health programmes

65 The preservation of Kantian universalism whilst redefining the concepts it uses is not confined to Nedelsky's work. Perhaps the best know attempts at such reconstruction are Rawls, J, *Theory of Justice*, 1971, Cambridge, Mass: Harvard UP; Dworkin, R, *Taking Rights Seriously*, 1977, London: Duckworth and the abstract work of Onora O'Neill, such as *Towards Justice and Virtue: A Constructive Account of Practical Reasoning*, 1996, Cambridge: CUP.

66 Kuhn, TS, *The Structure of Scientific Revolutions*, 2nd edn, 1970, Chicago: Chicago UP.

67 Lyotard, JF, *The Post-modern Condition: A Report on Knowledge*, Bennington, G and Mascum, B (trans), 1984, Manchester: Manchester UP.

68 Featherstone, M, 'In pursuit of the post-modern: an introduction' (1988) 5 Theory, Culture and Society 195–215.

69 Kelly, MP *et al*, 'The four levels of health promotion: an integrated approach' (1993) 107 Public Health 319–26.

promoted a broader approach to the factors affecting health, the holism and subjectivity underlying health promotion has encouraged and fed upon the deconstruction of medical models. Redefining disease as an expression of medical power, emphasising the significance of expertise and professionalism rather than truth in the determination of ill health,[70] politicising health issues with rights-speak and communities defining their own health needs all have a resonance with the philosophy of *difference*.

A brief survey of definitions of health within the international arena exemplifies this. The World Health Organisation in 1946 defined health in its constitution as a 'complete state of physical, mental and social wellbeing'.[71] This in itself seemed to reject any distinction between science and morality: health was a subjective issue produced through a combination of all aspects of life, not a determination made by experts on the absence of disease. In 1974, Marc Lalonde, the Canadian Minister for Health, produced an important document called *A New Perspective on the Health of Canadians*, in which he defined a concept of 'the health field' and included in it human biology, environment, lifestyle and the health care facilities available.[72] He weighted each component equally and considered health of the individual as intrinsically linked to the society in which she lived. Lalonde's intention was to dilute the control of the medical profession and biomedicine over health issues[73] and, whilst this aim was not realised in 1974, his document did form the basis of the WHO's strategies for health[74] outlined at the Alma Ata conference in Russia in 1978.[75]

It was here that the WHO advocated primary health care as an effective strategy for achieving its Health for All by the year 2000 initiative[76] by providing health promotion, prevention, curative and rehabilitative services.[77] All signatory States were to provide these on the basis that

70 On medical power and its relationship to professionalism see the extensive work of Brian Turner, eg, *Medical Power and Social Knowledge*, 2nd edn, 1995, London: Sage.

71 WHO, *Constitution of the World Health Organisation*, 1946, New York: WHO, first principle.

72 Lalonde, M, *A New Perspective on the Health of Canadians*, 1974, Ottawa: Information Canada.

73 Hancock, T, 'Lalonde and beyond: looking back at *A New Perspective on the Health of Canadians*' (1986) 1 Health Promotion International 93–100. The context in which Lalonde produced his report is particularly interesting. As Hancock points out, health in Canada is a predominantly provincial issue and there was no mechanism for Lalonde's federal report to be implemented. It has been argued that Lalonde's concerns for a more public health oriented approach were principally fiscal concerns. Parish, R, 'Health promotion: rhetoric or reality', in Bunton, R *et al* (eds), *The Sociology of Health Promotion: Critical Analyses of Consumption, Lifestyle and Risk*, 1995, London: Routledge pp 13–23 at pp 16–17.

74 WHO, *Alma Ata Declaration*, 1977, No 6, Copenhagen: WHO.

75 Naidoo, J and Willis, J, *Health Promotion Foundations for Practice*, 2nd edn, 2000, London: Harcourt.

76 WHO, *Primary Healthcare: Report of the International Conference on Primary Healthcare at Alma-Ata, USSR, September 6–12*, Geneva: WHO/UNICEF.

77 Little, C, 'Health for all by the year 2000: where is it now?' (1992) 13 Nursing and Healthcare 198–201.

citizens were holistic beings, affected by all aspects of their environment and social life, with rights and duties to individually and collectively participate in the preservation and promotion of their health. States had a duty to consider the health implications of all aspects of their activities and a responsibility for the health of their population. The purpose of the agreement was for States to enable their citizens to make healthy choices, rather than to determine citizens' actions in the name of health. The enterprise appeared to be to empower citizens to lead healthy lifestyles by promoting and facilitating individual, community and national self-determination.[78] It was implicit within this approach that health is a matter of politics; that science does not produce political answers but produces one type of information relevant, but not conclusive of health.

The Ottawa Charter for Health Promotion in 1986,[79] to which Britain was also a signatory, reproduced a framework defined by Jake Epp, the Canadian Minister of National Health and Welfare.[80] He perceived health promotion as an approach to health care, 'the process of enabling people to increase control over and to improve health'. Unlike the earlier Lalonde approach, Epp emphasised that many influences on health fell outside the control of individuals and community groups. Without the prerequisites to health being met by society, the political initiative to promote health could not be grasped by citizens or communities. These prerequisites were peace, shelter, education, food, income, sustainable resources, a stable ecosystem, social justice and equity. In 1988, a further document produced in Adelaide[81] indicated a consensus that it was necessary for States to have explicit regard for the health and equity implications of all aspects of public policy, and should be accountable for the health impact of policy decisions. Social welfare, agriculture, economics, housing and education were all aspects of government having an impact on health.

ENHANCED INDIVIDUALS?

This broadening and bureaucratisation of health based upon an agenda to empower the citizenry as individuals and as community groups is, it has been argued, part of the new politics.[82] By formulating statements which require State action to facilitate the rights, duties and responsibilities of its

78 Naidoo, J and Willis, J, *Health Promotion Foundations for Practice*, 2nd edn, 2000, London: Harcourt.

79 WHO, *Ottawa Charter for Health Promotion*, 1986, Canada: WHO.

80 Epp, J, 'Achieving health for all: a framework for health promotion' (1986) 77 Canadian Journal of Public Health 393–430.

81 WHO, *The Adelaide Recommendations: Healthy Public Policy*, 1988, Copenhagen: WHO.

82 Stevenson, HM and Burke, M, 'Bureaucratic logic in new social movement clothing: the limits of health promotion research' (1991) 6 Health Promotion International 281–96.

citizens for health, international forums have implicitly, and on occasion explicitly, critiqued the modernist idea that science and scientific method, combined with a developed bureaucratic system, can solve the problem of a nation's health. Enhancing the position of the individual in her relationship with the State, as with the proliferation of individual rights and rampant consumerism, is part of a general enhancement of autonomy and choice. Health has become an issue for issue-based politics and resolution requires more than national politics, delegitimating state power. Responsibilities for health are decentralised to individuals or communities and supra-State organisations like the WHO have legitimate authority.

Yet the literature on health promotion[83] in Britain has viewed this movement with scepticism.[84] First, the movement from experts' control of health to lay control has been illusory. The Government's White Paper *The Health of the Nation*[85] left the responsibility for public health education and the promotion of healthier lifestyle firmly in the hands of the National Health Service. Individual responsibility for health was reiterated in the document by incorporating behaviour change and surveillance of individual's behaviour into the payment system for general practitioners. Limitations were placed on the relevance of economic and social conditions to health by setting national targets for behaviour change without reference to class, poverty or other indicator of economic status.[86] The document selected five key areas[87] to target as the basis of this national health improvement strategy: coronary heart disease and stroke, cancers, mental illness, HIV/AIDS and sexual health, and accidents. Each issue was given a particular course of action to allow the targets to be met, all of which revolved around education and promoting individual responsibility for lifestyle change, particularly improving diet, increasing exercise, reducing

---

83 Modern health promotion involves promotion of a positive state of health, public participation and an awareness of social, economic and ecological, as well as behavioural influences, on health. It has been seen as a political activity with local, national and global perspectives. It has been linked to empowerment of health consumers and public health professionals and to the transformation of social and economic structures damaging to health. As such, modern health promotion and the 'new' public health have been treated as interchangeable concepts. See MacDonald, TH, *Rethinking Health Promotion: A Global Approach*, 1998, London: Routledge; Naidoo, J and Willis, J, *Health Promotion Foundations for Practice*, 2nd edn, 2000, London: Harcourt; Seedhouse, D, *Health Promotion: Philosophy, Prejudice and Practice*, 1996, London: John Wiley; Buchanan, D, *An Ethic for Health Promotion*, 2000, Oxford: OUP.

84 Davies, JK and Kelly, MP (eds), *Healthy Cities: Research and Practice*, 1993, London: Routledge.

85 Department of Health, *The Health of the Nation: A Strategy for Health in England*, 1992, London: HMSO.

86 *Ibid*.

87 The Green Paper that proceeded it contained 16 key areas and included the elderly, pregnant women, child health and alcohol. The five were chosen on the grounds of greatest need and the scope for cost-effective improvements to health.

smoking and alcohol consumption. It included no real proposals to tackle pollution, poverty, poor housing or homelessness.[88]

Secondly, the paradigms used in relation to health have remained essentially positivist.[89] Just as medical discourse has viewed the body as an object to be observed, diagnosed and treated, statements by the international community see ill health as causally linked to a breakdown in effective State and international systems. Just as a surgeon removes an infected part of the body to return it to health, the WHO has seen the removal of poverty, malnutrition and pollution as cures. The paradigm is still one of a faulty system where diagnosis and treatment will produce a cure.[90]

Turshen[91] has identified four theories underlying public health in the post-war period, all of which she explains as being centred on the individual, rather than upon social organisation. Her argument is that when multifactorial causes of disease were postulated they could have included both individualised and broader social, economic and political solutions, but instead preventative, environmental, lifestyle and genetic responses remained firmly within an individualistic frame of reference. The example she gives is of responses to malaria.[92] Germ theory led the pharmaceutical industry to search for a substance that would kill the parasite in its human host or to eradicate mosquitoes, the insect vector for the parasite. Lifestyle theorists aimed to alter individual's behaviour in mosquito infested areas to protect themselves from contact by using mosquito nets. Gene theory underlay research on resistance in parasites and mosquitoes to chemical agents whilst environmental approaches sought to deprive mosquitoes of their habitat by draining areas of stagnant water. She argues that as research has shown the disease is correlated with economic development, improved housing and reduced migration, a social organisation response could have been more effective than this range of etiological approaches.

The fallacies within positivism, revealed by postmodernist approaches to knowledge[93] have not been removed from the way health is thought about.[94] In fact, the use of health as a positive concept, as something to be

88 For a discussion of the problems within *The Health of the Nation* document see the four month series of articles and letters in the British Medical Journal between July and October 1991.

89 Clarke, JN, 'Feminist methods in health promotion research' (1992) 83 Canadian Journal of Public Health 54–57.

90 See Antonovsky, A, *Unravelling the Mystery of Health*, 1987, San Francisco: Josey Bass.

91 Turshen, M, *The Politics of Public Health*, 1989, London: Zed.

92 *Ibid*, pp 56–57, 156–75.

93 See Seidman, S and Wagner, DG, *Post Modernism and Social Theory*, 1992, Oxford: Blackwell.

94 Similar criticisms have been made in, for example, the sociology of crime and deviance where sociological approaches have continued to identify crime as the product of a failure within the body, the mind or the social environment of the offender. Even approaches that have taken a more radical view have continued to search for [contd]

valued as a fundamental good, rather than as an indication of the absence of disease, has compounded the search for causes. By seeing health as fashionable, as something we should all have, not only commodifies health[95] but also raises the issue of blame where health is not assured. The individual citizen is a victim, acted upon by the social system to her detriment. The system operates in a faulty manner to cause health disadvantages to certain groups and the individual is imaged as the passive recipient, rather than a political actor with free will.[96]

REDEFINITION OF HEALTH AS REFLEXIVE OF WIDER SOCIAL CHANGE

This apparent paradox in the image of the individual within the health promotion sphere is problematic but not necessarily surprising. Anthony Giddens in his contemporary social theory has examined the continuing relationship between free will (or agency) and determinism (or structure) in the modern world.[97] Using his views, it is possible to see the 'new' public health as representative of wider social change associated with late modernity. Existing social structures are not in the process of being supplanted, but are in a state of flux and redefinition. In the health care field, movements away from reliance upon diagnosis and cure were apparent in the 1970s in a range of European countries and the United States. As the major causes of death had become chronic degenerative disorders rather than contagious diseases, policy makers increasingly drew links between lifestyle and health. In 1976, the Department of Health and Social Security produced a major policy document *Prevention and Health: Everybody's Business*, in which it sought to reorient health care towards preventative medicine and individual responsibility for health. A massive collection of policy documents followed on the topic of health promotion within the health service. Canada, the United States, Ireland and Hungary similarly showed a political commitment to a new vision of public health in the face

94 [contd] causes of crime, but have looked at systems beyond the individual, such as the economic, patriarchy and power. See Sumner, C, *The Sociology of Deviance: An Obituary*, 1994, Buckingham: OU Press.

95 On commodification of public health, see Lefebvre, C, 'Social marketing and public health intervention' (1988) 15 Health Education Quarterly 3.

96 Crawford, R, 'Individual responsibility and health politics', in Conrad, P and Kern, R, *The Sociology of Health and Illness: Critical Perspectives*, 1986, New York: St Martins.

97 Giddens, A, *The Consequences of Modernity*, 1980, Cambridge: Polity; Giddens, A, *Modernity and Self-identity: Self and Society in the Late Modern Age*, 1981, Cambridge: Polity.

of expensive health care systems which were failing to produce dramatic improvements in their nation's health.[98]

By addressing lifestyle, the concept of health was broadened, so as to bring a vast array of information into view. Yet the position of the individual remained at centre stage. Just as in other areas of social and political organisation, the consumer became the significant social unit within health care,[99] supported by liberal ideology and technological changes within a medical profession increasingly concerned with problem-solving approaches to treatment. This extended view of health is reflective of changes within the practice of medicine itself. Expanding knowledge and technologies have provided medicine with an extended dominion over life through transplantation, genetic manipulation, fetal screening and chemical enhancements, whilst responsibility for life has abated. Risk factors within lifestyle fall outside of the ambit of medicine: transport choices, diet, fitness, work choices and environments, family relationships and obligations, social life and sex life can all intervene. Health workers share responsibilities with the patients themselves, educators, employers, family members, the voluntary sectors and communities.

Movements in public health have also been linked to shifts in the way Western populations have been segmented beyond class differentiations.[100] Marketing strategies have employed a range of lifestyle categories, as has sociological research. Counter-cultures demonstrate movement towards lifestyle politics by platforming shared values which cut across traditional ideological divisions: ecological, peace, sexual liberation, anti-racist and disabled rights movements all reveal agendas promoting new cultural identities:[101]

> Stressing individual responsibility and self-reliance, the integrated totality of the material, the mental and the spiritual, the counter-cultures offered alternative ideologies of the present and visions of the future rooted in a transformation of environmental ethics and a repersonalisation of political choices. Ideologically they served to break down existing boundaries between production and consumption, work and home, public and private and to promote new cultural identities based on shared experiences, goals and values.[102]

---

98 Parish, R, 'Health promotion: rhetoric or reality', in Bunton, R *et al* (eds), *The Sociology of Health Promotion: Critical Analyses of Consumption, Lifestyle and Risk*, 1995, London: Routledge, pp 13–23.

99 Featherstone, M, 'Lifestyle and consumer culture' (1987) 4 Theory, Culture and Society 55–70.

100 Willis, P, *Common Culture*, 1990, Milton Keynes: OU Press.

101 The connections between these lifestyle differentiations and developments in health care was drawn by O'Brien, M, 'Health and lifestyle: a critical mess?', in Bunton, R *et al*, *The Sociology of Health: Critical Analyses of Consumption, Lifestyle and Risk*, 1995, London: Routledge, pp 191–205.

102 *Ibid*, p 199.

This group politics has also reinforced and been reinforced by the breakdown of boundaries between the local and the global. As a strong globaliser, Giddens maintains that the importance of national boundaries and nation States is rapidly declining and we are moving swiftly towards economic and social interdependencies.[103] His theory of structuration sees social structures as having a continuing impact on human behaviour.[104] Individuals operate within the limits allowed by their knowledge of the world, structures inherent in language and discourse constrain human action through the common sense, taken-for-granted assumptions they produce.[105]

Unlike social theories concerned with the relationship between powerful structures and the individual, Giddens sees these constraints as being generated internally so that an exercise of choice or agency is always constrained by what the actor is capable of perceiving as possible.[106] Actions that push the limits contribute to developments within the discourse, allowing the individual to be an active participant in changing the very structures that constrain. In his analysis, structure and agency have an intimate relationship rather than being viewed as opposing poles of a political spectrum. There are clear comparisons here between Giddens' view of the individual and that of Nedelsky outlined earlier.

The debate over individualism and structure has a significant literature within sociological and social policy theory. The central theme, if such a thing can be distilled from the wide range of theoretical positions that come within the rubric of structuralism, is that moves to promote health and prevent ill health have been inadequate because of their failure to focus on the material conditions of life. That is, health and ill health must be seen holistically, and promoting individual responsibility without attending to such fundamental concerns as poverty, unemployment, discrimination, class and the environment does nothing to improve health.[107] Promoting individual responsibility does, however, perpetuate inequalities and

---

103 For a discussion of Giddens' complex analysis of globalisation, see Held, D and Thompson, J (eds), *Social Theory of Modern Societies: Anthony Giddens and his Critics*, 1989, Cambridge: CUP. For an alternative view on globalisation, see Santos, B de Sousa, *Toward a New Common Sense: Law, Science and Politics in Paradigmatic Transition*, 1995, London: Routledge.

104 Giddens, A, *Modernity and Self-identity: Self and Society in the Late Modern Age*, 1981, Cambridge: Polity.

105 Kelly, MP and Charlton, B, 'The modern and the postmodern in health promotion', in Bunton, R *et al* (eds), *The Sociology of Health Promotion*, 1995, London: Routledge.

106 For an analysis of Giddens' work in the context of health promotion, see Kelly, MP *et al*, 'Healthy cities: a modern problem or a post-modern solution', in Davies, J and Kelly, M (eds), *Healthy Cities: Research and Practice*, 1993, London: Routledge.

107 Doyal, L, *The Political Economy of Health*, 1979, London: Pluto; Townsend, P *et al* (eds), *Inequalities in Health: The Black Report and the Health Divide*, 1988, Harmondsworth: Penguin.

necessarily results in victim blaming.[108] Whilst the rhetoric of health promotion after Alma-Ata appears to encompass both changes to the political-social-economic structures and the lifestyles of individuals,[109] it is argued that the emphasis remains firmly on the individual.[110] Community groups, for example, have been found to have very little power to bring about change and have been colonised by State health care structures.[111]

The centrality of individual lifestyle to health has important connotations for how the individual is viewed. In one sense, the idea of what is a healthy lifestyle can be seen as negative because it represents the racist, sexist, homophobic perceptions of advantaged sectors of Western society (white, middle-class, able-bodied).[112] In another, it has been examined as a method of reinforcing and perpetuating existing discrimination by attacking the 'unhealthy lifestyles' of already marginalised groups, for example, the targeting of homosexuals and drug users as the groups responsible for the spread of HIV/AIDS.[113] In a wider sense, the promotion of a healthy lifestyle can also impact upon perceptions of those with ill health, making them even less tolerable to healthy society.[114]

These sociological critiques of health promotion and public health have argued that movements towards a 'new' public health have not displaced existing structures in society. The individual whilst centred in the rhetoric of health promotion and health education has been defined according to the values of conservative liberalism, rather than as an empowered activist.

---

108 See, eg, Gostin, L, 'The future of communicable disease control: toward a new concept in public health law' (1986) 64 Millbank Quarterly 1; Brandt, AM, *No Magic Bullet: A Social History of Venereal Disease in the United States since 1880*, 1985, Oxford: OUP.

109 See above discussion of the WHO statements on the State's role in health.

110 Beattie, A, 'Knowledge and control in health promotion: a test case for social policy and social theory', in Gabe, J *et al* (eds), *The Sociology of the Health Service*, 1991, London: Routledge.

111 See *ibid*; Farrant, W, 'Addressing the contradictions: health promotion and community health action in the United Kingdom' (1991) 21(3) International Journal of Health Services 423–39; Yen, L, 'From Alma Ata to Asda – and beyond: a commentary on the transition in health promotion services in primary care from commodity to control', in Bunton, R *et al* (eds), *The Sociology of Health Promotion*, 1995, London: Routledge, pp 24–37. Yen discusses how the short lived New GP Contract of 1990 included funded health promotion clinics which tended to reflect professional ideas of what the community wanted, but had to be attractive to the public to sustain funding.

112 See, eg, Wilton, T, *Engendering AIDS: Deconstructing Sex, Text and Epidemic*, 1997, London: Sage.

113 Patton, C, *Last Served? Gendering the HIV Pandemic*, 1994, London: Taylor & Francis; Kayal, PM, *Bearing Witness: Gay Men's Health Crisis and the Politics of AIDS*, 1993, Boulder, CO: Westview.

114 This type of argument has been explored in relation to genetic screening for disability and in the literature on media representations of disability as the potential negative outcome of failures to protect health.

Tamsin Wilton[115] in her gender analysis of health promotion material on HIV/AIDS demonstrates how homophobic, sexist assumptions have been reproduced and reinforced within an individualistic health discourse of victim blaming which facilitated the resurrection of classic free market liberalism:

> Health education, as an institutional activity, follows pre-existing unidirectional circuits of power, rather as an electric charge flows round a circuit board. In so doing it both conforms to and reasserts the hegemony of the structural and institutional networks whereby power is differentially assigned and enacted.[116]

IDENTITY AND PUBLIC HEALTH

The unintended consequences of the 'new' public health have also been explored in the context of identity. The idea that identities are constructed is well established.[117] As discussed above, the advent of hospital medicine constructed the identity of the patient as the three-dimensional site for the diagnosis and treatment of disease. Separated from the rest of the population by being designated sick, as opposed to one of the healthy mass, her body contained disease. The 'new' public health constructs a very different identity. The healthy and the sick are no longer delineated, populations are at risk and the aim is containment of risk. Health as a positive value is something that we all desire and seek to attain, but is elusive and multi-faceted. It is a comparative, not an absolute value. Health can exist alongside illness within the body and the existence or absence of symptoms is part of an assessment of risk, rather than the outward signs of an inward lesion.

In his work on surveillance medicine, Armstrong[118] has developed this idea of identity in the context of mechanisms within the community to map risk factors within populations. Many of these mechanisms are invasive, touching many aspects of lifestyle such as diet, exercise, social life, family life, sexual activity, travel and work.[119] Legislation on reproductive technologies, abortion, contagious diseases, childcare and those with mental

115 Wilton, T, *Engendering AIDS: Deconstructing Sex, Text and Epidemic*, 1997, London: Sage.

116 *Ibid*, pp 40–41

117 See, eg, Stychin, C, *Law's Desire: Sexuality and the Limits of Justice*, 1995, London: Routledge. See, also, Butler, J, *Bodies that Matter: the Discursive Limits of 'Sex'*, 1993, New York: Routledge.

118 Armstrong, D, *Political Anatomy of the Body: Medical Knowledge in Britain in the Twentieth Century*, 1983, Cambridge: CUP; Armstrong, D, 'Public health spaces and the fabrication of identity (1993) 27(3) Sociology 393–410; Armstrong, D, 'The rise of surveillance medicine' (1995) 17(3) Sociology of Health and Illness 393–404.

119 Nettleton, S, *Power, Pain and Dentistry*, 1992, Buckingham: OU Press; Nettleton, S, *The Sociology of Health and Illness*, 1995, Cambridge: Polity.

disabilities has all been seen as illustrative of increased surveillance of the body.[120] These mechanisms are not confined to the Clinic, but are now dispersed beyond the health care worker/patient relationship into the supermarket, the fitness market and the high street.[121] On his analysis, the movement towards State involvement in producing a healthier nation is more effective in its surveillance than it is in altering health profiles of sections of the population whose health is most at risk, namely the poorer and more deprived.

Others, such as Featherstone,[122] have emphasised consumption and its impact upon identity. Bourdieu[123] in the 1980s wrote about identity as a composite of consumables: people see themselves and others in relation to what they have, how they live, where they live and the opportunities available to them in the marketplace. Sociologists of health[124] have used this paradigm to argue that healthiness of lifestyle is yet another consumable implicating identity. This has an effect not only upon the identity of those leading a healthier life, but has a negative impact upon those who are perceived as failing to reduce the risks to their health. Research on advertising has been particularly instructive in this regard. Exhortations to wear seat belts and to not drink and drive have been linked to the threat of disablement. Text declaring that being falling down drunk may mean never being able to walk again, accompanied by a photograph of a wheelchair is a graphic representation of disability as personal tragedy rather than as a social construct,[125] reinforcing negative images of wheelchair users and attributing blame to the individual rather than to social organisation.[126]

The stress within the 'new' public health on community involvement has also been seen as having implications for identity. To some, this has impacted in a positive way, seeing the involvement of community organisations and bottom-up groups as a movement away from passivity

---

120 For a discussion of this, see Turner, B, *Regulating Bodies: Essays in Medical Sociology*, 1992, London: Routledge.

121 Nettleton, S and Bunton, R, 'Sociological critiques of health promotion', in Bunton, R *et al* (eds), *The Sociology of Health Promotion*, 1995, London: Routledge, pp 41–58, p 49.

122 Featherstone, M, *Consumer Culture and Postmodernism*, 1991, London: Sage; Featherstone, M, 'The body in consumer culture', in Featherstone, M *et al* (eds), *The Body: Social Process and Cultural Theory*, 1991, London: Sage.

123 Bourdieu, P, *Distinction: A Social Critique of the Judgement of Taste*, 1984, London: Routledge.

124 Bunton, R and Macdonald, G, *Health Promotion: Disciplines and Diversity*, 1992, London: Routledge; Grace, VM, 'The marketing of empowerment and the construction of the health consumer' (1991) 21 International Journal of Health Services 329–43.

125 Wang, C, 'Culture meaning and disability: injury prevention campaigns and the production of stigma' (1992) 35 Social Science and Medicine 1093–102, cited by Nettleton, S and Bunton, R, 'Sociological critiques of health promotion', in Bunton, R *et al* (eds), *The Sociology of Health Promotion*, 1995, London: Routledge, pp 41–58, at pp 45–46.

126 Lupton, D, *Medicine as Culture: Illness, Disease and the Body in Western Societies*, 1994, London: Sage.

and towards a more proactive vision of the individual's role in their own health.[127] Others have charted the failure of the Government's investment in the 'new' public health to live up to the rhetoric of community involvement.[128] This failure has been linked to the upsurge of individualism in the 1970s and to the enduring interests of capitalism:[129]

> How else can one explain a public health rhetoric which argues that social conditions affect health outcomes and then, in turn, argues that the appropriate solution is to eat better, exercise more, drink less and give up smoking?[130]

Identity has also been examined in terms of the discrimination inherent within the 'new' public health.[131] Inequalities caused by class, race, gender, poverty and culture were not acknowledged by The Department of Health's *The Health of the Nation* despite the exhortation to egalitarianism contained in the WHO strategy *Health for All*. Failure to recognise these inequalities has allowed sexism and racism to remain within health strategies and, at the same time, has attributed value to a type of lifestyle outside the experience of the least healthy.[132]

From a global perspective, the universalising of a healthy identity has been further problematised. Ideas about empowerment within public health and their individualistic interpretation have been seen as inherently eurocentric and irrelevant to cultures and communities with different historical, political and economic conditions. Emphasis on the written word

---

127 Beattie, A, 'Knowledge and control in health promotion: a test case for social policy and social theory', in Gabe, J *et al* (eds), *The Sociology of the Health Service*, 1991, London: Routledge; Bunton, R and Macdonald, G, *Health Promotion: Disciplines and Diversity*, 1992, London: Routledge.

128 Baum, F and Sanders, D, 'Can health promotion and primary health care achieve Health for All without a return to their more radical agenda?' (1995) 10(2) Health Promotion International 149–60; Walt, G, *Health Policy: An Introduction to Process and Power*, 1994, London: Zed Books.

129 Turshen, M, *The Politics of Public Health*, 1989, London: Zed; Farrant, W, 'Addressing the contradictions: health promotion and community health action in the United Kingdom' (1991) 21(3) International Journal of Health Services 423–39; Doyal, L, *The Political Economy of Health*, 1979, London: Pluto.

130 McQueen, D, 'Thoughts on the ideological origins of health promotion' (1989) 4 Health Promotion 339–42, cited by Nettleton, S and Bunton, R, 'Sociological critiques of health promotion', in Bunton, R *et al* (eds), *The Sociology of Health Promotion*, 1995, London: Routledge, pp 41–58, at pp 45–46.

131 See, eg, Thorogood, N, 'Caribbean home remedies and their importance for black women's health care in Britain', in Abbott, P and Payne, G (eds), *New Directions in the Sociology of Health*, 1990, London: Falmer; Douglas, J, 'Developing anti-racist health promotion', in Bunton, R *et al* (eds), *The Sociology of Health Promotion*, 1995, London: Routledge, pp 70–77; Doyal, L, *What Makes Women Sick? Gender and the Political Economy of Health*, 1995, Basingstoke: Macmillan.

132 Whitehead, M, *The Health Divide: Inequalities in Health in the 1980s*, 1982, London: Health Education Council; Plant, M, *The Risk Takers*, 1992, London: Routledge.

as education,[133] the assumption of the abnormality of particular socio-sexual practices[134] and the representation of Western health science as neutral[135] have all been shown as having a negative effect on improving health in non-Western countries. Some have gone so far as to argue that although the *Health for All* initiative is valuable in emphasising the need for a global approach to health, it is so imbued with eurocentric notions as to be invalid:

> ... our psychological insights into the necessary preconditions for the development of empowerment, on which health promotion is based, are so strongly eurocentric as to possibly render them invalid if applied outside the first-world context. Unless and until that problem is addressed and resolved, health promotion will languish on the vine as a compelling intellectual and social argument with no means of being applied.[136]

Whilst there are different emphases within the health identity literature, all are broadly concerned with analysing reflexivity in the context of medicine as risk assessment and it is this movement rather than any movement towards communitarianism which seems to underlie the 'new' public health. Whilst the relationship between health and risk is not in itself new, Beck[137] has influentially argued that risk has become pivotal in what has been styled as late modernity. In modern society, deregulation in the market, the erosion of family and kinship, increasing reliance on State institutions created a precarious social environment. The production of wealth and the institutionalisation of science, Beck argues, intensified and dispersed risks as they became impersonal, hidden from view and global.

RISK AND PUBLIC HEALTH

In the public health context, risks changed from inadequate sanitation to genetic imperfection, from smog to BSE, from disease to all aspects of lifestyle. Environmental risks are a key example of Beck's risk society as they threaten everyone regardless of status (what he calls democratic risks),[138] they require expertise to detect (greenhouse gases, radiation) and they present a huge danger. In the risk society, power is reorganised around

133 Airhihenbuwa, CO, 'Health promotion and the discourse in culture: implications for empowerment' (1994) 21 Health Education Quarterly 345–53, cited in MacDonald, TH, *Rethinking Health Promotion: A Global Approach*, 1998, London: Routledge.

134 Wilton, T, *Engendering AIDS: Deconstructing Sex, Text and Epidemic*, 1997, London: Sage.

135 Berry, J, 'On cross-cultural compatibility' (1969) 4 International Journal of Psychology 119–28.

136 MacDonald, TH, *Rethinking Health Promotion: A Global Approach*, 1998, London: Routledge, p 43.

137 Beck, U, *Risk Society: Towards a New Modernity*, Ritter, M (trans), 1992, London: Sage.

138 *Ibid*, p 36.

scientific knowledge to measure and organise risk on a global scale.[139] Risks are not, therefore, simply a surface effect of modernisation, but affect social organisation. He sees knowledge altering relationships between the consumers of risk and those who define and provide public images of risks.[140] Global risks erode the significance and boundaries between nation States and empower global and transnational institutions. New groups are formed to respond to risks, organised across previous divisions and across frontiers. Positive ideas about growth and expansion have, in a risk society, been replaced by ideas of containment and management of risk.

Beck's analysis, like that of Giddens', is a useful tool for examining current debates within public health. Beck specifically addresses the issue of chronic diseases and medicine's technological capacity to diagnose, but also its incapacity to effectively treat these conditions. He refers to the changes medicine has made to reproduction as a 'noiseless social and cultural revolution'[141] because of the largely unrestricted alterations it made to the family and to ideas of personhood. This capacity of medical science to produce and test innovations within its own professional spheres is the victory of the clinic, bolstered by the burgeoning global need for such innovation within risk society. The progress of medical science and the impact of it on notions of the *individual*, is also reflective of Beck's individualisation theory.[142] He sees the individual as the significant social unit, with social classes fragmented by changes in employment patterns and opportunities. The individual has become the site for inequalities, requiring new and increasingly complex responses by government.

Turner[143] has responded to Beck's analysis by questioning the novelty of his approach and the historical distinctions he draws. The history of contagious diseases[144] shows that epidemics were globalised through trade and travel, they were invisible as no one understood their cause or epidemiology and they did massive, often democratic, damage to populations. Lifestyle has been shown as relevant to the distribution of disease across social classes in the 19th century. These criticisms, however, fall short of negating the usefulness of Beck's approach to understanding changes within public health. What is perhaps more significant in Turner's critique is his questioning of Beck's assertion of the decline of regulation and standardisation in risk society. By pointing to research on McDonaldization,

139 Beck, U, *Risk Society: Towards a New Modernity*, 1992, London: Sage, pp 23–24.

140 *Ibid*, p 46.

141 *Ibid*, p 207.

142 Beck, U, 'The debate on the "individualization theory"' (1994) 3 Soziologie 191–200, cited in Turner, B, *Medical Power and Social Knowledge*, 2nd edn, 1995, London: Sage, p 223.

143 Turner, B, *Orientalism, Postmodernism and Globalism*, 1994, London: Routledge.

144 McNeill, WH, *Plagues and People*, 1976, Harmondsworth: Peregrine.

Turner argues that although there is uncertainty produced by proliferating global hazards there is a corresponding push to maintain predictability in everyday life:

> As the macro social and economic environment becomes more unstable and uncertain, then new systems of surveillance and government would be put in place to provide some control and regulation over the environment both social and natural.[145]

Turner makes the link here with Castel's work on government by surveillance in France.[146] Castel argues that government control of dangerousness has moved from confining a dangerous individual to using preventative strategies to avoid dangerousness.[147] This is reflected in the use of preventative strategies in medicine,[148] but also in the eventual demise of the doctor/patient relationship and the new role of health care workers as health strategists. The focus of medicine, he argues, will become less about identification of symptoms in individual patients and more about the profiling of populations. He concludes that this process will dissolve the individual into a composite of risk factors that are defined and managed through surveillance.

CONCLUSION

What emerges is not a Utopian view of society advancing towards a communitarian model where public health regulation is a response to community led health initiatives. Nor is public health regulation likely to be the product of a global free market within which autonomous individuals should escape all but minimal regulation. The idea of the individual has become far more complex than envisaged by Kant, but the individual remains the focus of regulation. Part of that complexity is the production of identity, an important aspect of surveillance as it raises the complexity of self-surveillance and its embodied mediation as part of the regulatory framework.[149] The increasing significance of risks to health, their definition

---

145 Turner, B, *Medical Power and Social Knowledge*, 2nd edn, 1995, London: Sage, p 226.

146 Castel, R, 'From dangerousness to risk', in Burchell, G *et al* (eds), *The Foucault Effect: Studies in Governmentality*, 1991, London: Harvester Wheatsheaf, pp 281–98.

147 See, also, Lupton, D, who has theorised public health as a strategy of governance in *The Imperative of Health*, 1995, London: Sage.

148 The obvious example is cancer screening, although seeing this as a preventative measure is only one of a range of interpretations. See Howson, A, 'Embodied obligation: the female body and health surveillance', in Nettleton, S and Watson, J (eds), *The Body in Everyday Life*, 1998, London: Routledge.

149 Nettleton, S, *Power, Pain and Dentistry*, 1992, Buckingham: OU Press; Nettleton, S, 'Wisdom, diligence and teeth: discursive practices and the creation of mothers' (1991) 13 Sociology of Health and Illness 98–111.

and management, is reflective of wider moves in industrialised society. Developments in medical science and in the changes in the hazards to health facilitate and promote increased surveillance, particularly in a context where health is perceived to be a desirable but limited resource. The medical profession, through medical science, has continued to clothe itself with expertise appropriate to the identification and management of risk.

The emerging framework for the development of a 'new' public health is global, but on a national level remains restrained.[150] The scope for domestic legal regulation has on one level expanded as ideas about public health have moved its concerns beyond health protection. The traditional public health approach, using legal, political and fiscal measures to protect and prevent ill health was based upon images of the individual and of hazards to health which are being reconstructed. Public health has a broader role as surveillance medicine, addressing itself to populations and man-made hazards. This role has emerged in the context of broader changes within social organisation that have brought individuals within systems designed to manage and contain risk.

The role that domestic law can play within surveillance medicine is largely dependant upon the limits of persuasion and self-surveillance brought about by other social mechanisms, such as the media, health education and consumerism. Limitations will also come from the nature of law itself, such as its reliance upon the written word, the imprecision of language and effectiveness based upon enforcement. As the individual, although reconstructed, remains the effective social unit in Western countries, human rights will necessarily be important in a regime of surveillance. The global nature of this 'new' public health, coupled with the mass destructive nature of contemporary hazards, such as pollution, food-borne diseases and emerging and re-emerging contagious diseases, also offers opportunities for extended international and transnational legal regulation. As with domestic legal regulation, however, the scope for legislation will always depend upon the complex of contextual issues within which law is identified as an appropriate response.

150 The reasons for this restraint are complex, rooted in the social developments outlined in this chapter but also clearly related to economic and structural concerns. See Parish, R, 'Health promotion: rhetoric and reality', in Bunton, R *et al* (eds), *The Sociology of Health Promotion*, 1995, London: Routledge, pp 13–23.

CHAPTER 2

CONSTRAINTS ON PUBLIC HEALTH

Robyn Martin

INTRODUCTION

However the boundaries of public health responsibility are drawn, and however public health responsibility is allocated, there will always be externalities constraining public health practice. Awareness of these externalities will assist in the formulation of public health objectives and strategies. It would not be possible to include in a definition of public health all of the factors which affect public health, or the definition would read something like a treatise on the meaning of life, and would be for all practical purposes useless. Nevertheless, it is important to identify issues which will influence the public health profile of societies. This chapter will assess these constraints.

Law plays an important role in regulating the interaction between factors external to public health, and public health itself, through the regulation of activities and behaviours. The extent to which legal regulation of activities which are not directly health related can be driven by health needs is controversial and dependant on the recognition of public health as a primary social goal. Law also plays an important role in determining the framework of powers of public bodies acting with public health objectives. The enforceability of duties, powers and rights in relation to public health is dependent on legal recognition and regulation. The detail of the involvement of international, regional and national law in the attainment of public health will be considered in subsequent chapters.

CULTURAL CONSTRAINTS ON PUBLIC HEALTH

A society, or a cultural group within a society, is made up of the individual members of that group but amounts to more than the sum of its parts. The commonality of behaviour, beliefs, custom, language and perception creates a reality that is more concrete than an accumulation of individual beliefs and behaviours. The result is a 'social legacy which individuals acquire from their group, a kind of blueprint for all of life's activities'.[1] Studies of urbanisation[2] suggest that permanent settlements of heterogeneous people can develop, for survival, subcultures of commonality to enable organisation of what would otherwise be an unstructured collection of individuals deteriorating into chaos. Cultural identity is not limited to homogeneous peoples with commonality of background and customary practices, although greater social cohesion within society will be relevant to the state of that society's health.[3] Nor is it limited to jurisdiction or geography; several different age or social cultures might co-exist, operating different behaviour practices and subject to different cultural influences.

Recognition of particular social groups is problematic, and not always separable from ethnic origin, socio-economic status, employment and family make-up. A range of qualitative and quantitative analytical identification techniques has been tried, and the methodologies of group selection lay any generalisations open to criticism.[4] But disagreement tends to lie in the drawing of social space boundaries and not in recognition of the importance of cultural characterisation as a constraint on health populations, quite apart from the influence of physical and economic environments. The beliefs and behaviour of individuals feed into the make-up of a cultural group, but equally the culture feeds back into the beliefs and behaviours of its constituents. Customary cultural patterns of health behaviour impact on both the health of individual members and on the profile of the community's health. Cultural values impose socially acceptable roles and functions, and much of what we classify as disease or illness depends on recognition that the condition inhibits the capacity to perform a social role.[5] As Illich noted, 'Each person's health is a responsible performance in a social script ... Body-sense is experienced as an ever-renewed gift of culture'.[6]

If we accept that public health for all is a positive objective, not simply an absence of disease, then the dynamics of a cultural group will play a part in achieving that positive state. Classification of health and illness is evaluative, with health considered a universal good. Ill health threatens the productivity and stability of society. The evaluation process will incorporate what is valued both within the culture itself, putting pressure on members to behave in culturally acceptable ways, and in relationships with those outside the culture. Much has been written on how this interaction might

1 Hannay, D, *Lecture Notes on Medical Sociology*, 1988, Oxford: Blackwell Scientific, p 120.

2 Eg, Wirth, L, 'Urbanisation as a way of life' (1938) 44 American Journal of Sociology 3; Beshers, J, 'Urban social structure', in Stewart, M (ed), *The City*, 1972, Harmondsworth: Penguin.

3 See Wilkinson, *Unhealthy Societies: The Afflictions of Inequality*, 1996, London: Routledge.

4 Yen, I and Syme, S, 'The social environment and health: a discussion of the epidemiologic literature' (1999) 20 Annual Review of Public Health 287.

5 For more on this, see Parsons, T, *The Social System*, 1951, London: Routledge.

6 Illich, I, *Limits to Medicine*, 1976, London: Marion Boyars, p 129.

work. Durkheim's early study of suicide practices[7] identified group behaviours that helped to explain variations in suicide rates. These group behaviours became independent of the individuals in the group, such that when individuals moved on, new members were socialised into the behaviour pattern. Other studies attribute disease patterning to cultural group dynamics,[8] consider the effect of the cultural support network on the chronic nature of disease[9] and look at cultural baby care practices in relation to infant mortality.[10]

Acknowledgment of the existence of disease and recognition of the symptoms of disease may be culturally determined. Obesity is considered a public health risk in Western societies, but may be desired as an attribute of health and beauty elsewhere. Low blood pressure, not considered a particular health risk in Britain, is taken very seriously in other parts of Europe. Statistics for public health surveillance purposes show serious incidences of hypotension in much of Europe with no incidence in Britain, where low blood pressure is not recognised as indicative of disease. Doctors in each jurisdiction will tend to read the medical literature of their own jurisdiction and so their culture of medical learning will be reinforced. The result is that medical concerns within one society, and communicated to the public through public health education, might be considered low priority in another.[11]

Symptoms of a pathology which are common enough within a social group to be considered normal, will not be recognised as symptoms of ill health until they fall into the range of abnormal.[12] Until members of the social group are prepared to seek medical treatment for their health concerns, their illness experiences will not be recognised as a health issue, because accounts of a society's health are almost universally based on medical surveillance and not on patients' story-telling of their own health assessment. Medical data on the prevalence of disease may not recognise that some cultural groups are reluctant to report to doctors.[13]

---

7 Durkheim, E, *Suicide: A Study in Sociology*, 1951, London: Routledge.

8 Eg, McKewan, B, 'Protective and damaging effects of stress mediators' (1998) 338 New England Journal of Medicine 171.

9 See, eg, Mar, T *et al*, 'Chronic diseases. Selection in the social network' (1998) 8 European Journal of Public Health 286.

10 Eg, Sudden Infant Death Syndrome; see van Steenbergen, J, 'Ethnicity and childhood mortality in the Netherlands' (1999) 9 European Journal of Public Health 205.

11 See Field, M, 'Comparative health systems and the convergence hypothesis', in Powell, F and Wessen, A, *Health Care Systems in Transition*, 1999, Thousand Oaks: Sage.

12 Eg, a Glasgow study which found a high proportion of chronic bronchitis in a group which did not consider the occurrence of cough and phlegm as evidence of ill health; see Hannay, D, *Lecture Notes on Medical Sociology*, 1998, Oxford: Blackwell Scientific, Chapter 3.

13 Beurger's disease (narrowing of the arteries and veins) was once considered prevalent amongst Eastern European Jewish men because of the circumstances in which [contd]

Reactions to, and expression of, pain and distress may be dictated by what is culturally accepted behaviour in the circumstances.[14] Willingness to consult doctors or undergo hospitalisation, and willingness to discuss intimate body functions, differ from culture to culture. Expectations of treatment methods even within Western scientific medicine may be culturally influenced. Antibiotics and painkillers would normally be administered by suppository in France, and by injection or tablet in Britain. The approach of doctors to patients and the doctor/patient relationship will vary markedly from culture to culture, as will the degree to which medicine is regarded as a science rather than an art.[15] Responsibility for health is also cultural. A society which places responsibility for health onto the individual will recognise fewer public health concerns than a society which regards health as a community or government responsibility, although allocation of responsibility can be manipulated for economic and political purposes. Responsibility for initiating screening for example will affect the success of treatment for cancer.[16]

Cultural attitudes to the body will affect health behaviour. The reluctance of the people of Japan to accept organ transplantation stems from cultural beliefs which reject recognition of brain death, which respect the wishes and beliefs of the wider family structure to the detriment of autonomy and informed consent, and which recognise sacrilege of the body.[17] Even within Europe, there are differing attitudes to both cadaver and live organ donation which public health arguments have been unable to sway.[18] The issue of xenotransplantation raises even more complex cultural

13 [contd] these sufferers sought medical help. See discussion in Scrambler, G, 'Illness behaviour', in Patrick, D and Scrambler, G (eds), *Sociology as Applied to Medicine*, 1986, Bailliere's Concise Medical Textbooks: Bailliere Tindall.

14 See, eg, Zborowski, M, 'Cultural components in response to pain' (1952) 8 Journal of Social Issues 16; Pilowsky, I and Spence, N, 'Ethnicity and illness behaviour' (1977) 7 Psychological Medicine 447; Beecher, H, *Measurement of Subjective Responses*, 1959, New York: OUP; Good, M *et al*, *Pain as Human Experience*, 1992, Berkeley: California UP.

15 Payer, I, *Medicine and Culture: Varieties of Treatment in the United States, England, West Germany and France*, 1988, New York: Henry Holt.

16 See Rohlfs, I *et al*, 'The role of sociodemographic factors in preventative practices. The case of cervical and breast cancer' (1999) 9 European Journal of Public Health 278.

17 See Shin Ohara, 'The brain death controversy: the Japanese view of life, death and bioethics' (1997) XXV(2) Japan Foundation Newsletter XXV, August; see, also, the Organ Transplants Act 1997 (No 104) which introduces limited circumstances in which transplants may be carried out. Ohara comments that this legislation is acceptable to the Japanese people because 'Japanese Society, with its insistence in acting in unison, prefers decisions to be made by the national government, and the issue of brain death is no exception' at p 2; see also Nudeshima, J, 'Obstacles to brain death and organ transplantation in Japan' (1991) 338 The Lancet 1063; Yamauchi, M, 'Transplantation in Japan' (1990) 301 BMJ 507.

18 See, eg, Mason, J and McCall Smith, R, *Law and Medical Ethics*, 5th edn, 1999, London: Butterworths, Chapter 14; Price, D, 'Living organ transplantation in Europe: re-evaluating its role' (1998) 5 European Journal of Health Law 19; Kennedy, I *et al*, 'The case for "presumed consent" in organ donation' (1998) 351 The Lancet 1650; [contd]

concerns about the sacrosanct nature of the body.[19] Cultural attitudes to food will also be significant. The olive-oil based diet of Mediterranean communities is considered a contributory factor to longer life expectancies,[20] while French products made from unpasteurised milk[21] and cultural market shopping practices[22] and the English adoption of 'junk' food[23] create public health risks. Teenage eating patterns also have health implications.[24] Societies that place value on particular body shapes, for example, breast size or thinness, will experience increased health risks resulting from efforts to achieve cultural body acceptability.[25] The complex psychological relationship between beauty and health associates culturally unattractive physical presentation of the body with attribution of the negative quality of ill health.[26]

Membership of a social group will affect relationships with others outside the group to the detriment of health. Studies of discrimination and segregation[27] suggest not only inequitable access to health resources, but also low self esteem and stress from the social stigma of membership. Relationships with health care providers can also be influenced by preconceptions about membership of the social group. Assumptions made about the sexual behaviour, pain tolerance, work ethic and hygiene practices

---

18 [contd] Taylor, R, 'Opting in or out of organ donation' (1992) 305 BMJ 1380; Eaton, S, 'The subtle politics of organ donation: a proposal' (1998) 24 JME 166.

19 Fox, M and McHale, J, 'Regulating xenotransplantation' (1997) 147 NLJ 139; Downie, R, 'Xenotransplantation' (1997) 23 JME 205.

20 For example, statistics presented in the WHO's *World Health Report 1995* on average life expectancy showed higher expectancy in Greece, Italy, Spain and France than in Britain; see Busfield, J, *Health and Health Care in Modern Britain*, 2000, Oxford: OUP; see, also, debate on 'Why mortality from heart disease is low in France' (2000) 320 BMJ, 22 January; Tunstall-Pedoe, H, '*Autres pays, autres moeurs*: theories on why the French have lesser heart disease than the British' (1988) 297 BMJ 1559.

21 See Desenclos, J-C *et al*, 'Large outbreak of salmonella enterica serotype paratyphi B infection caused by a goats' milk cheese, France, 1993: a case finding and epidemiological study' (1996) 312 BMJ 91.

22 See commentary by Dorozynski, A, 'Seven die in French listeria outbreak' (2000) 320 BMJ, 4 March,

23 See Elliott, V in (2000) *The Times*, 2 June, commenting on the Food Standards Agency *National Diet and Nutrition Survey*.

24 See the report by O'Connell, A, 'Teenagers' cola linked to broken bones' (2000) *The Times*, 15 June, on research carried out by Dr Grace Wyshak of the Harvard School of Public Health on the correlation between drinking carbonated drinks and bone fractures.

25 See Angell, M, 'Evaluating the health risks of breast implants: the interplay of medical science, the law and public opinion' (1996) 330 New England Journal of Medicine 1697.

26 See, eg, Gilman, S, *Picturing Health and Illness: Images of Identity and Difference*, 1995, Baltimore: John Hopkins UP.

27 EG, Krieger, N *et al*, 'Racial discrimination and blood pressure: the CARDIA study of young black and white adults' (1996) 86 American Journal of Public Health 1370 [Medline]; Polednak, A, 'Trends in US urban black infant mortality, by degrees of residential segregation' (1996) 86 American Journal of Public Health 723 [Medline].

of patients from particular cultures can influence diagnosis and treatment of disease, access to treatment services such as contraception, abortion or treatment for drug addiction, as well as recording of disease prevalence.[28] Public health measures have targeted social groups on the basis of characterisation of cultural practices common to the group[29] and indeed have been known to use public health powers to prejudice racial and social groups.[30]

Equally important is the culture of health care provision. Where the medical profession occupies a position of dominance and social status, as in Britain and North America,[31] then society will accord to doctors the power to determine aspects of patient's lives beyond treatment of disease. So, for example, doctors in Britain have the power to determine suitability for work or social welfare benefits, the power to determine suitability for parenting,[32] the power to determine the need for a woman to undergo an abortion[33] and the power to make decisions about matters such as withdrawal of life supporting treatment[34] or treatment of a child patient against the wishes of the child's parents.[35] Access to health resources is dependent on acceptance of and submission to medical power. Other health care providers such as nurses or paramedics, while they may be trained and skilled, cannot make such decisions.

Recognition of ill health and of the causes of ill health are reliant on medical diagnosis of illness and cause, and the patient's story of illness or perception of causes of illness carries comparatively little weight. Reports of the local community of the effects of water pollution at Camelford which led eventually to litigation[36] and vindication of the complainants, were disregarded as a product of public hysteria by the Clayton Committee which was set up to investigate the public health risk:

---

28 See Turner, B, *Medical Power and Social Knowledge*, 1995, London: Sage, Chapter 11.

29 See Lupton, D, *Medicine as Culture*, 1994, London: Sage, Chapter 2.

30 In the case of *Jew Ho v Williamson* (1900) 103 F 10 (Cal), a Chinese citizen of San Francisco successfully challenged quarantine laws for bubonic plague which operated only against Chinese citizens; see also Shepardson, L *et al*, 'Racial variations in the do-not-resuscitate orders' (1999) 14(1) J Gen Med 15.

31 See Turner, B, *Medical Power and Social Knowledge*, 1995, London: Sage; MacDonald, K, *The Sociology of the Professions*, 1995, London: Sage.

32 Under s 13(5) of the Human Fertilisation and Embryology Act 1990, it is the responsibility of the treating doctor, when treating a woman, to take into account 'the welfare of any child who may have been born as a result of the treatment (including the need of that child for a father), and of any other child who may be affected by the birth'.

33 Under s 1 of the Abortion Act 1967, the doctor may take into account in the decision whether to provide abortion services 'the pregnant woman's actual or reasonably foreseeable environment'.

34 *Airedale National Health Service Trust v Bland* [1993] 1 All ER 821.

35 As in the case of the separation of conjoined twins, *Re A (Children) (Conjoined Twins: Medical Treatment)* [2000] 4 All ER 961.

36 *AB v South West Water Services Ltd* [1993] 1 All ER 609.

> In our view it is not possible to attribute the very real current health complaints to the toxic effects of the incident, except inasmuch as they are the consequence of the sustained anxiety naturally felt by many people.[37]

The explanations given by professionals were given significantly greater weight despite widespread and convincing evidence from lay witnesses. The language of health in a culture where doctors are given special authority will reflect the medical experience of health to the detriment of the patient experience.[38] This is particularly relevant to determination of public health concerns and priorities. Health challenges which attract medical attention, such as AIDS and infertility, may not in fact represent the real public health concerns of the people.[39] The World Health Organisation envisages that 'health developments in communities are made not only for, but with and by the people',[40] but the determination of public health priorities is distorted by the greater weight attributed to medical perceptions of health need. The lay perception of the body and the relationship of the body with the natural and built environment may differ from scientific theories and may indeed be unfettered by traditional medical teachings.[41]

The relationship of doctors to other health care providers will also have wider implications for public health. To what extent do midwives have input into policy making for pregnancy and childbirth? What recognition is given to non-invasive or alternative treatments for chronic illnesses? What role can be played by other practitioners of healing such as acupuncturists, chiropractors, homoeopaths or osteopaths? Access to non-standard health treatments is dependent on recognition of the validity of those treatments by the dominant health practitioners, and so power balances amongst providers of health care will affect access to information about, and access to funding for, treatments which patients might seek. Parents who have opted for alternative healing for their children have been challenged by doctors in the courts, and in many cases the child has been made a ward of court to allow the medical treatment to go ahead,[42] with the possible exception of

---

37 Department of Health, *Water Pollution at Lowermoor North Cornwall: Second Report of the Lowermoor Incident Health Advisory Group* (Professor Dame Barbara Clayton), 1991, London: HMSO; for a commentary on this incident, see Williams, G and Popay, J, 'Lay knowledge and the privilege of experience', in Gabe, J *et al*, *Challenging Medicine*, 1994, London: Routledge.

38 Williams, G and Popay, J, 'Lay knowledge and the privilege of experience', in Gabe, J *et al*, *Challenging Medicine* 1994, London: Routledge.

39 Percy-Smith, J and Sanderson, I, *Understanding Local Needs*, 1992, London: Institute for Public Policy Research.

40 WHO, *Health for All*, 1985, Copenhagen.

41 See, eg, the work by Emily Martin on immunology: Martin, E, *Flexible Bodies: Tracking Immunity in American Culture* 1994, Boston: Beacon; and Martin, E, 'Immunology on the street: how non-scientists see the immune system', in Nettleton, S and Watson, J (eds), *The Body in Everyday Life*, 1988, London: Routledge.

42 See, eg, *Healthcare Otago Ltd v Holloway-Williams* [1999] NZFLR 792; *Re C (HIV Test)* [1999] 2 FLR 1004.

cases where the parent is him or herself a health professional who has chosen to reject treatment.[43]

There has been an increasing public interest in alternative medicine techniques.[44] The success of scientific medicine in reducing mortality from life threatening conditions has resulted in an increase in the numbers suffering from chronic illness of variable severity. Scientific medicine has been less successful in dealing with long term incapacity, and sufferers have turned to therapies which combine both physical and psychological healing approaches.[45] Practitioners of alternative medicines, as they develop academic and public credibility, challenge both the superiority of scientific western medicine and the status of doctors. Doctors have met this threat to their authority with attacks on alternative medicine in medical literature[46] and in the media. Funding for research on alternative medicine practices has been limited in an environment when allocation of funding is medically influenced, with the result that scientific support, even if it could be established, is inhibited.[47] Where there has been recognition of alternative techniques, as in the case of acupuncture, Western doctors have incorporated acupuncture skills into scientific medical practice, rather than to recognise trained acupuncturists as professionals in their own right. Availability of alternative treatments, and of information about them, is stifled by medical dominance. Given the risks of some scientific medical practices,[48] non-inclusion of alternative practitioners cannot be entirely justified by arguments based on risk and must at least in part be attributable to medical response to encroaching practices. In societies where doctors play a less status conscious role, for example, in France, even where legal restrictions on the practice of medicine are strict, there has been greater recognition of the value of alternative medicine techniques.[49]

It is also relevant here to consider the way in which health care is provided. In a system where the patient pays for medical treatment, even where that payment is reimbursed through a public or private insurance

43 See, eg, *Re T (Wardship: Medical Treatment)* [1997] 1 FLR 502.

44 See Sharma, U, *Complimentary Medicine Today: Practitioners and Patients*, 1992, London: Routledge.

45 Bayliss, R, 'The National Health Service versus private and complimentary medicine' (1998) 296 BMJ 1457.

46 Eg, British Medical Association, *Report of the Board of Science and Education on Alternative Therapy*, 1986 London, BMA; Bagenal, F *et al*, 'Survival of patients with breast cancer attending the Bristol Cancer Health Centre' (1990) 336(2) The Lancet 606.

47 Saks, M, 'The alternative to medicine', in Gabe, J *et al*, *Challenging Medicine*, 1994, London: Routledge.

48 Gould, D, *The Medical Mafia*, 1987, London: Sphere.

49 Bouchayer, F, 'Alternative medicines: a general approach to the French situation', in Lewith, G *et al*, *Complementary Medicine and the European Community*, 1991, Saffron Walden: CW Daniel, cited in Saks, M, 'The alternatives to medicine', in Gabe, J *et al*, *Challenging Medicine*, 1994, London: Routledge.

scheme,[50] the patient has contractual or quasi-contractual rights to demand service of merchantable quality. However, in such a system there is the risk that market forces will dictate access to treatment services over which the provider has power. Where the health service is State provided, the patient as the recipient of a welfare service is dependent on access to that welfare provision by the doctor, and has limited choice of services. But in such a system the doctor might be an employee, and so less able to make autonomous treatment decisions.[51] The relationship of health care providers to the funding system will be important in determining who makes policy decisions on access to treatment, on the balance between hospital and primary care, and on where health resources are concentrated. The move in Britain to introduce an internal market to health provision[52] and the managerial structures recommended in the Griffiths Report in 1983[53] were intended in part to reduce medical control of the health service. It is questionable whether this has been successful and doctors still play a significant role in the determination of health policy, even more so since the recent reforms made by the Labour Government which focus on clinical governance rather than competition.[54]

In Britain, as in many other Western countries, there remains an overall faith in the integrity and competency of the medical profession to determine the direction of health care provision and to shape the health profile of British society.[55]

Arguments about the relevance of culture to health care, while still important, are gradually being eroded by increased globalisation of health issues. Technological advances in communication and travel, increased movement of populations and labour forces, and the movement to consider health from the wider European or international perspectives will all work to destabilise identifiable cultural groups. It may become more difficult, and more irrelevant, to talk about cultural attitudes in the face of economic and political forces which represent far wider interests. Nevertheless, there are signs of backlash in which populations which identify with particular cultural heritage or which respect particular cultural values are fighting to preserve identity, by encouraging the use of minority languages, by resisting mass immigration, by downsizing and by rejecting imported foodstuffs in favour of local, seasonal, organic and 'slow food' products. Preservation of

---

50 As, for example, in Australia and France.

51 Hunter, D, 'From tribalism to corporatism: the managerial challenge to medical dominance', in Gabe, J *et al* (eds), *Challenging Medicine*, 1994, London: Routledge.

52 National Health Service and Community Care Act 1990.

53 *Report of the NHS Management Inquiry*, 1983, London: DHSS.

54 For further discussion on this point, see Busfield, J, *Health and Health Care in Modern Britain*, 2000, Oxford: OUP.

55 Hunter, D, 'From tribalism to corporatism: the managerial challenge to medical dominance', in Gabe, J *et al*, *Challenging Medicine*, 1994, London: Routledge.

cultural identity requires regulation of any behaviour which compromises cultural norms, and cultural influences on health must still be considered in the making of public health policy.

RELIGIOUS CONSTRAINTS ON PUBLIC HEALTH

Religion and the treatment of the body have always been interconnected. Spiritual and moral good assume regulation of, and punishment to, the body. The notion of sin is inseparable from ideas about appropriate use of the flesh. The language of medicine is not unrelated to the language of religion and equally regards the body as something to be regulated according to the beliefs and teachings of the practitioner. 'Malady' and 'malignant', for example, derive from the Latin *malus*, meaning evil, and the classification of a sufferer of disease as a patient introduces religious overtones of passive compliance.

Early medical knowledge was not the province of doctors but of both religious men and apothecaries, with treatments for bodily illnesses incorporating both physical and spiritual cures.[56] Religious attitudes to behaviours such as masturbation and homosexuality have influenced medical approaches to the causes of and treatments for conditions which were considered retribution for sinful behaviour.[57] Bodily functions such as menstruation have been interpreted as the incompleteness and incapacity of the body.[58] Natural disasters and epidemics are interpreted as punishments for the sins of society. Even responses to pain can be dictated by religious attitudes to the purpose of pain and its relationship to health and happiness.[59] Good physical health continues to be seen as a product of good spiritual health. Serious ill health (cancer for example) and physical incapacity (such as infertility) carry with them a stigma that defies scientific analysis.[60]

Religion now plays a lesser but still visible role in medical issues in developed countries and the doctor's role extends beyond physical medicine. Through the giving of a placebo to the patient, the doctor exercises a power no different from that of a spiritual healer. Religious leaders are consulted and speak authoritatively on the ethics of medical

56 Park, K, 'Medicine and society in medieval Europe', in Wear, A (ed), *Medicine in Society: Historical Essays*, 1992, Cambridge: CUP.

57 Clatts, M and Mutchler, K, 'AIDS and the dangerous other: metaphors of sex and deviance in the representation of disease' (1989) 10 Medical Anthropology 105.

58 Kern, S, *Anatomy and Desire: A Cultural History of the Human Body*, 1975, Indianapolis: Bobbs-Merrill.

59 Illich, I, *Limits to Medicine*, 1976, London: Marion Boyars, p 147.

60 Sontag, S, *Illness as Metaphor*, 1989, New York: Anchor.

procedures ranging from infertility treatment to treatment withdrawal. Ethics committees and government bodies established to advise on medical procedures will generally include religious representation.[61] Religious groups claim the standing to be heard in legal disputes about treatment.[62] Religious arguments are raised with authority in debates about euthanasia, AIDS, contraception, transsexualism, organ transplantation, and force feeding of anorexics and hunger strikers.[63]

We may no longer look to religion for healing to the extent that we once did, but it has been argued[64] that rather than taking full personal responsibility for our bodies and souls, we have transferred our allegiances to the medical profession, looking to doctors to define secular sin and to provide solutions for our physical, emotional and social problems. The new sins are coveting food, alcohol, tobacco and drugs, failure to exercise and unsafe sexual practices. As self-flagellation once expressed extreme religious piety, atoning for individual or societal sin, so modern self-flagellation takes the form of self-starving. This is about more than a desire for beauty. It is also about self control, rejection of excess, pursuit of purity[65] and perfection[66] and societal normality.[67] Body piercing and tattooing are about alternative cultural conformity as well as dissatisfaction with wider values and ability to conform to those values. More serious self-harming such as cutting (regular shallow cutting of the wrists), castration and amputation (body dysmorphic disorder)[68] are responses to secular sin, parallel to the sort of religious extremism which prompts self-immolation or self-crucifixion. The prevalence of self-harming, particularly amongst adolescents, suggests that in this context there are issues about health to be resolved which go well beyond individual psychiatric illnesses, and that

61 Eg, the Warnock Committee (Committee of Inquiry into Human Fertilisation and Embryology) which reported in 1984; the Human Fertilisation and Embryology Authority constituted under the Human Fertilisation and Embryology Act 1990.

62 Eg, *Airedale NHS Trust v Bland* [1993] 2 WLR 316; *Re A (Children)* [2000] 4 All ER 961.

63 See Hanafin, P, 'D(en)ying narratives: death, identity and the body politic' (2000) 20 Legal Studies 393.

64 See, eg, Foucault, M, *The Birth of the Clinic*, 1973, London: Tavistock; and Turner, B, *Medical Power and Social Knowledge*, 1995, London: Sage.

65 Turner, B, *The Body and Society: Explorations in Social Theory*, 1984, Oxford: Blackwell; Lupton, D, *Medicine as Culture*, 1994, London: Sage; Dresser R, 'Article and commentary on Anorexia Nervosa: feeding the hunger artists: legal issues in treating Anorexia Nervosa' [1984] Wis L Rev 297, excerpted in Bridgeman, J and Millns, S, *Feminist Perspectives on Law*, 1998, London: Sweet & Maxwell.

66 Halmi, K *et al*, 'Perfectionism in Anorexia Nervosa: variation by clinical subtype, obsessionality, and pathological eating behaviour' (2999) 157 (11) Am J Psychiatry 1799.

67 Orbach, S, *Hunger Strike: The Anorectic's Struggle as a Metaphor for our Age*, 1993, London: Penguin.

68 See commentary on non-therapeutic amputations carried out at Falkirk and District Royal Infirmary: (2000) *The Guardian*, 1 February.

addressing concepts of physical shape normality and health sinning is a public health concern.

Religion, both in its traditional and in its modern secular form, is also responsible for other-harming. Female genital mutilation in its varied forms is practised in conformity with cultural and religious requirements among some African and Middle Eastern societies. Objections to FGM practices were first raised by Christian missionaries as part of a wider agenda of Western religious challenge to traditional beliefs. The practice is prohibited in Britain[69] though not completely repressed, and the sociological, anthropological and legal debate about the legitimacy of female circumcision practices continues.[70] The debate about male circumcision is more recent and is illustrative of the fusion of religious and medical ideas about body regulation. Although common in Third World societies, male circumcision is also central to the tenets of Judaism, a mainstream Western religion, and became incorporated into scientific medical beliefs about hygiene and appropriate body shape such that baby boys in many Western jurisdictions[71] were almost routinely circumcised until the 1960s.

Only more recently as scientific doubt has been cast on the health benefit arguments surrounding circumcision has the debate turned to the wider socio-legal question of the legitimacy of invasive treatments on non-consenting children. It is questionable whether any non-therapeutic treatments on children unable to consent, from cosmetic surgery to organ donation,[72] can be supported, but people of religious conviction continue to argue that their religious beliefs justify the imposition of irreversible medical treatment on the bodies of others.[73] Ironically, there are now suggestions that circumcision may provide some limited protection against the contraction of the HIV virus, with the result that members of African tribal groups who have been religiously opposed to circumcision are now being encouraged by Western doctors to circumcise in the fight to reduce AIDS mortality.[74] Tribal leaders are concerned that the imposition of routine circumcision will impinge on tribal cultural identity and religious beliefs.

---

69 Prohibition of Female Circumcision Act 1989.

70 Bibbings, L, 'Female circumcision: mutilation or modification?', in Bridgeman, J and Millns, S (eds), *Law and Body Politics: Regulating the Female Body*, 1995, Aldershot: Dartmouth.

71 Eg, in North America and Australia.

72 Price, D and Garwood-Gowers, A, 'Transplantation from minors: are children other people's medicine?' (1995) 1 Contemporary Issues in the Law 1; Mumford, S, 'Bone-marrow donation – the law in context?' [1997] CFLQ 305.

73 See the judgment of the Court of Appeal in *Re J (A Minor) (Specific Issue Orders: Muslim Upbringing and Circumcision)* [2000] 1 FLR 571; see also Bridge, C, 'Religion, culture and conviction – the medical treatment of young children' [1999] CFLQ 1.

74 Szabo, R and Short, R, 'How does male circumcision protect against HIV infection?' (2000) 320 BMJ 1592.

Public health policy can be hampered by religious objection, particularly in relation to matters of sexual health. The Catholic Church has been influential in inhibiting access to contraception and abortion services in much of Latin America and Eastern Europe with consequences for the health of women.[75] The fight against AIDS and education on safe sexual practices has been countered by religious and cultural objection to the use of condoms. Religious attitudes to homosexuality have helped to stigmatise sexually transferable diseases. In extreme cases, religion has justified refusal of life saving blood transfusion[76] or the refusal of interventionist medical treatment. In other cases, religious conviction has called for extraordinary medical treatment beyond that which would normally be administered.[77] Religious attitudes cannot be ignored in the structuring of public health measures, although the weight to be accorded to individual religious beliefs in a predominately secular society will always be problematic.

POLITICAL CONSTRAINTS ON PUBLIC HEALTH

Public health is just one of many societal concerns. All public functions must compete for public resources, and the priorities that dictate hierarchies of public spending will be determined in part by the political agenda and economic strategies of the governing political party. There can be no simple correlation between political philosophy and health care agenda, but public health commentary has identified in the macro political framework some commonalities. Studies of the relationships between political philosophy of a jurisdiction and other administrative and regulatory systems have noted similar correlations.[78]

Political philosophies having as their objective a capitalist economy in which the requirements of economic strength take priority will favour limited public spending on health and encourage individual self-sufficiency and individual responsibility for health and health costs. In this political environment there tends to be resistance to recognising societal causes of ill health such as environmental pollution or industrial disease because this would incur public funding or regulation of industry. Health must compete in a market economy and is a commodity to be traded against other

75 Doyal, L, *What Makes Women Sick*, 1995, London: Macmillan.

76 Eg, *Re T* [1992] 4 All ER 649.

77 *Re C (Medical Treatment)* [1998] 1 FLR 384.

78 See, eg, Cioffi, J, 'Governing globalisation? The State, law and structural change in corporate governance' (2000) 27 Journal of Law and Society 572, where correlations between political stance and regulation of both labour and corporate enterprise and examined.

commodities, with cost an ever-present bottom line.[79] The extent to which the politics of a nation is committed to market maximisation will influence the type of healthcare system the government is prepared to support.[80]

Where the political agenda favours enterprise development, the protection of the workforce is a priority. When there are competing health needs, a political triage would support allocating health spending priority to those who can get quickly back into the workforce and contribute to economic development. Rationing of healthcare resources using cost-effectiveness as a premise will tend to result in a health care system that disadvantages the non-productive and runs contrary to ideas on distributive justice. An example is the QALY (Quality Adjusted Life Years) which was developed by economists as a tool to determine funding priorities in the context of health[81] and which supports health spending on those with the longest and highest quality survival rate.[82] Spending is more likely to focus on treatment of illness than maintenance of health[83] in part because looking at maintenance of health will raise wider questions of societal causes of ill health and health care inequalities, and creates greater expectations of health provision. Spending will be more concentrated on treatment of traumatic injury and illness, getting people back to work, than in long term care for chronic disease or care of the elderly. The Oregon Experiment, an attempt by the State of Oregon to set up a template for health care rationing, prioritised treatment for short term illness and injury (such as pneumonia, peritonitis and foreign body in the throat) over more long term and chronic illnesses (cancer, terminal stage AIDS, varicose veins, bronchitis).[84] Treatment emphases in such a climate will be on technology and invasive surgery (heart surgery[85] and hysterectomy[86] are significantly more likely to be

---

79 For a detailed discussion of capitalism and illness, see Turner, B, *Medical Power and Social Knowledge*, 1995, London: Sage, Chapter 9.

80 See Anderson, O, *The Health Services Continuum in Democratic States: An Inquiry into Solvable Problems*, 1989, Ann Arbor: Health Administration Press.

81 See Newdick, C, *Who Should We Treat?*, 1995, Oxford: Clarendon; Carr-Hill, R and Morris, J, 'Current practice in obtaining the Q in Qalys: a cautionary note' (1991) 303 BMJ 699; Nord, E, *Cost-value Analysis in Health Care: Making Sense Out of QALYS*, 1999, Cambridge: CUP.

82 For a critique of the Qaly, see Jones, I and Higgs, P, 'Putting people before logic' (1990) 31 Health Service Journal 814.

83 This has been a common criticism of President Clinton's failed health care agenda for the United States: see Mechanic, D, 'Lessons from abroad: a comparative perspective', in Powell, F and Wessen, A (eds), *Healthcare Systems in Transition*, 1999, Thousand Oaks: Sage.

84 Honigsbaum, F, *Who Shall Live? Who Shall Die? Oregon's Health Financing Proposals*, 1992, London: King's Fund College Papers.

85 Vadya, E *et al*, 'A decade of surgery in Canada, England and Wales and the US' (1982) 117 Archives of Surgery 846, cited in Baggott, R, *Health and Health Care in Britain*, 1998, London: Macmillan.

86 McPherson, K *et al*, 'Regional variations in the use of common surgical procedures: within and between England and Wales, Canada and the USA' (1981) 15A Social Science and Medicine 273.

recommended in the US than in the UK, for example) with the result that illness is over-diagnosed and unnecessary treatments administered.[87] This will be exacerbated by a political system that facilitates litigation by patients when treatments are unsuccessful.

It has been argued[88] in favour of this approach to health care that the introduction of market principles leads to greater economic efficiency in health care spending, and that the element of competition inherent in the market place both increases productivity, and stimulates initiative and dynamism. A market based system is likely to facilitate patient choice as to doctor and place of treatment, and choice is a factor in the trust relationship between patient and doctor which contributes to the healing process. Enabling patients to 'shop around' in conjunction with fees for service also prompts doctors to be more responsive to patients and provides an incentive for high standards of service. It was such arguments that supported a movement towards a more market approach to health care in parts of Europe in the 1980s, including Margaret Thatcher's reorganisation of the National Health Service embodied in the National Health Service and Community Care Act 1990. Such moves were part of responses to wider economic and philosophical concerns about the involvement of the State in direct provision of services ranging from transport to education, and increased privatisation of health services was characteristic of health service reforms in many parts of the world[89]. Privatisation moves may have been prompted by burdensome State health costs, such that State-owned facilities could be sold off to private purchasers in order to raise State revenues, but it cannot be doubted that at the time there was political support for relieving over-stretched public services of tasks which were thought could be more productively administered by the private sector.[90] There was also in Britain, as has been commented: '... in the Conservative Party a streak that remains hostile to the "socialist" NHS; one that believes State spending even on health should be cut, wishing to see the service replaced largely by private care with the State subsidising only the poor.'[91] The distancing of the State from direct regulation of health care is dependent on the self-regulation and autonomy of the medical profession, which takes responsibility for maintaining health care standards.

---

87 The Audit Commission, *Improving Your Image: How to Manage a Radiology Service More Effectively*, 1995, London: HMSO suggested that 20% of X-rays were unnecessary with a cost to the NHS of £60 million per year; Winslow, C *et al*, 'The appropriateness of performing coronary artery bypass surgery' (1988) 260 JAMA 505 suggest that a significant proportion of heart surgeries were inappropriate.

88 See discussion in Figueras, J *et al*, 'Introduction', in Saltman, R *et al*, *Critical Challenges for Health Care in Europe*, 1998, Buckingham: OUP.

89 See Barker, C, *The Health Care Policy Process*, 1996, London: Sage, Chapter 13.

90 Walt, G and Gilson, L, 'Reforming the health sector in developing countries: the central role of policy analysis' (1994) 9(4) Health Policy and Planning 353.

91 Timmins, N, *Guide to the NHS Debate*, 1988, Oxford: The Alden Press.

An example of a market based health economy is that of the United States. Three quarters of the hospital facilities in the US are privately owned, and increasingly the financing of health facilities is profit led.[92] The majority of medical practitioners operate privately for a fee. The majority of the population takes out private insurance to cover medical costs, although approximately 40 million people have no insurance.[93] The State manages health care schemes such as Medicaid and Medicare for the poor, the elderly and the disabled, but these schemes are limited in their coverage[94] and in their application, leaving many without protection and dependant on the charity of public hospitals. Reform of the health care system has been a keen political issue, and access to health care remains a serious concern. For all this, the US spends more of its gross domestic product (13.7%) on health, higher than any other country, yet in the WHO analysis ranking world health care systems, it ranked only 37th out of 191 WHO Member States.[95] Health systems in which private enterprise plays a significant role tend to result in the poorest access to health care for those most in need of it. Even within the National Health Service, access to health care is 'post coded', not only for non-essential treatment such as fertility treatment but also for casualty beds and cancer treatment.[96]

More socialist political policies are less likely to perceive health as a market consumable and are more likely to assume that the State is the most efficient and appropriate body to oversee public services, recognising the role of the State in protection of its weakest and most vulnerable members. Disease avoidance, achieved by addressing social ills such as poverty, the environment and housing, is more likely to be the focus of attention than medical treatment.[97] Marx in particular was concerned by the implications of exploitation of the workforce and the concentration on accumulated profits, on the poverty and health of the working populace.[98] Marx attributed the inequalities in access to health care and the disparate vulnerability to infection and disease to the class system that was inherent in capitalism. More recently critics of health care provision have linked the application of market principles to health care with inequalities of access. A

---

92 See Baggott, R, *Health and Health Care in Britain,* 1998, London: Macmillan.

93 See Hellander, I *et al,* 'The growing epidemic of uninsurance: new data on the health insurance coverage of Americans' (1995) 25(3) International Journal of Health Services 377.

94 See Baggott, R, *Health and Health Care in Britain,* 1998, London: Macmillan, p 108.

95 World Health Organisation, *World Health Report 2000: Health Systems: Improving Performance,* 2000.

96 'Success rests on screening' (2000) *The Times,* 14 July.

97 Deacon, B, 'Medical care and health under socialism' (1984) 14(3) International Journal of Health Services 453.

98 Navarro, V, *Class Struggle, the State and Medicine,* 1978, Oxford: Martin Robinson; Macdonald, K, *The Sociology of the Professions,* 1995, London: Sage; Doyal, L, *The Political Economy of Health,* 1979, London: Pluto.

State-socialist system, the Soviet Union, for example,[99] would regard the health of its citizens as a collective or community asset, such that the treatment of an individual citizen results in a communal benefit. The State in a more socialist system is likely to provide health care as a public service, to own health care facilities and to employ health workers directly. The medical profession is unlikely to be autonomous and will be State controlled, and doctors will not command the status they hold in a capitalist system. Of course, inequalities in access to health care exist in socialist countries too. Health systems within socialist States differ, and studies of health care systems in socialist States suggest that the reality falls far below the ideals such that the overall health profile of populations in such States is below that of many Western European States.[100]

An example of a Western health care system which has retained some aspects of the private market but leans more towards the socialist model is that operated in France.[101] The system is funded by the State social security administration from taxes. A high proportion of health costs across the population are funded by the State, with the remainder frequently reimbursed by private insurance arrangements with non-profit making insurers. Treatment for many serious illnesses, such as cancer, is fully funded. A high proportion of hospital facilities are State owned and hospital staff are employed by the State. General practitioners operate privately but their fees are regulated by the State. Such a scheme is expensive,[102] resulting in high levels of taxation, and there have been unsuccessful attempts to sanction doctors' health spending[103] as a result of financial pressures.[104] Inequalities in access to health care have not been eradicated even here,[105] but the French health system is highly regarded. In the WHO league table of health systems, France ranks first[106] despite comparatively lower health spending than many other jurisdictions (9.8% of its gross domestic product).

The British health care system envisaged in its inception universal access to health care, free at the point of delivery. These objectives have largely

99 See Baggott, R, *Health and Health Care in Britain*, 1998 London, Macmillan.

100 Deacon, B, 'Medical care and health under State socialism' (1984) 14(3) International Journal of Health Services 453.

101 See Baggott, R, *Health and Health Care in Britain*, 1998, London: Macmillan, p 108.

102 See commentary by Dorozynski, A, 'French health costs rising rapidly' (2000) 321 BMJ, 2 September.

103 See commentary by Dorozynski, A, 'France abandons fines to control health costs' (1999) 318 BMJ, 9 January.

104 Bach, S, 'Managing a pluralist health system: the case of health care reform in France' (1994) 24(4) International Journal of Health Studies 593.

105 Turner, S, *Medical Power and Social Knowledge*, 1995, London: Sage, p 193.

106 World Health Organisation, *World Health Report 2000: Health Systems: Improving Performance*, 2000, and see commentary by Kmietowicz, Z, 'France heads WHO's league table of health systems' (2000) 320 BMJ 1687, 24 June.

been preserved, although the extent and quality of health care coverage have varied over the years. Britain spends just over 6% of its gross domestic product on health care[107] and is ranked 18th in the WHO league tables of health systems. The autonomy and status of the medical profession in Britain has been protected, and any challenges to the profession have come from the patients themselves, by means of litigation and consumer groups. No government regardless of leaning has attempted to disband the National Health Service, although the reorganisation effected by the Conservative Governments in the late 80s and early 90s introduced some principles of the marketplace into the supply and provision of health resources, a form of quasi-privatisation by the back door.[108] Recent developments in organisation of the National Health Service following the election of the Labour Government[109] have served to dismantle some of the internal market and have introduced measures[110] and enforcement bodies[111] to enable the Government to intervene in the regulation of the medical profession, significantly challenging its autonomy. The State will play a more direct role in determining best clinical practice, clinical effectiveness and cost effectiveness. These changes have been in part directed by concern at clinical standards and pressures of escalating health costs,[112] but they are also consistent with somewhat more left-leaning political philosophy and a recognition that Britain competes poorly with much of Western Europe on infant mortality,[113] life expectancy and cancer treatment tables.[114] Within Britain, the political preferencing of the south east of England over other regions, particularly during the Thatcher Government,[115] has also contributed to geographical inequalities of health provision. Current British

107 For critiques of NHS funding, see, eg, Harrison, A *et al*, 'Funding the NHS: can the NHS cope in the future?' (1997) BMJ 139; Dixon, J *et al*, 'Funding the NHS: is the NHS underfunded?' (1997) 314 BMJ 58; Harrison, A *et al*, 'Funding the NHS: is the NHS sustainable?' (1997) 314 BMJ 296; Culyer, J, *Economics and Public Policy: NHS Research as a Public Good*, 1998, York: University of York Centre for Health Care Economics.

108 See discussion in Jacobs, J, 'Lawyers go to hospital' [1991] PL 255.

109 See Department of Health, *The New NHS: Modern, Dependable*, 1997, Cm 3807.

110 Such as Clinical Governance, evidence-based medicine and the statutory duty of quality imposed by the Health Act 1999, s 18(1).

111 Such as the National Institute for Clinical Excellence, and the Commission for Health Improvement.

112 See Davies, A, 'Don't trust me, I'm a doctor: medical regulation and the 1999 NHS reforms' (2000) 20 OJLS 437.

113 Busfield, *Health and Health Care in Modern Britain*, 2000, Oxford: OUP.

114 Berrino, F *et al*, *Survival of Cancer Patients in Europe: the Eurocare Study II*, 1999, Lyons, IARC Scientific Publication No 151.

115 Following the economic philosophies of Milton Friedman and Friedrich von Hayek, Mrs Thatcher took the view that 'Opportunity means nothing unless it includes the right to be unequal', believing that society as a whole would, over time, benefit from the riches by the raising of minimum standards; see Timmins, N, *The Five Giants: A Biography of the Welfare State*, 1996, London: Fontana, Chapter 20.

political philosophy, described as 'the third way',[116] professes a communitarian approach, underpinned by redistribution of quality of life resources, while respecting and protecting individual rights and autonomy, but these aims are potentially difficult to reconcile.

Despite differences in political philosophy underlying health care systems, across the developed world there are nevertheless some identifiable common features of modern health care provision which transcend all political philosophies. While the content of health policies might differ, the importance of health as a national and international concern is now readily accepted across boundaries and included in government statements of intent. Responsibility for the provision, management and monitoring of health resources either directly, or indirectly through regulation of the private sector, is common to all stable governments. Acceptance of external causes of ill health (occupational disease, pollution, food products, etc) is also widespread with concomitant acceptance of some responsibility for limiting the effects of these national and global causes. Recognition of issues of justice in the context of access to health resources is also, in the theory if not in the practice, an articulated policy of contemporary governments. Even the most capitalist of regimes would not be prepared to allocate health resources entirely on an ability to pay, recognising that need is a valid objective in any health care system, and even the most socialist of regimes recognise that funds for health care are not open-ended, and that some restrictions must be placed on health spending in the interests of other calls on the public purse. Scientific medicine and the increasing adoption of medical technology is also common to most modern health systems, and almost universally alternative medicine philosophies have been forced into the sidelines of health care.

It is inevitable that health care philosophies across the developed world will become more customised. Global access to web based health information, comparative literature on health care ethics, increased movement of medical staff across jurisdictions, telemedicine and e-health, international responses to infectious diseases and the increasing role of the World Health Organisation will all serve to familiarise health policy makers and politicians with developments and ideas from around the world. The technology inherent in modern medical care serves to standardise medical knowledge, minimising subjective and individual diagnoses and treatments, transforming medical questions into technical problems and raising expectations of minimum, accurate screening and treatment. Governments are well aware of international health league tables and sensitive to poor

116 Giddens, A, *Third Way: The Renewal of Social Democracy*, 1998, London: Polity.

ratings on life expectancy, infant mortality, waiting lists[117] and success in the treatment of cancers. Improvement in these politically sensitive areas of health provision is a common promise in political manifestos regardless of politics. What is more, governments across the developed world are facing common threats to their health populations[118] such as AIDS, increased longevity, increased level of chronic illness resulting from improved life saving techniques and the escalating costs of developing medical technology. At the macro political level, there is sensitivity to international criticism of the ethical basis of distribution of health care provision in individual nation-States. Nevertheless, each State is likely to develop its own unique system of health care reflecting in part its own particular blend of politics, and the health care system of one jurisdiction is unlikely ever to be appropriate for wholesale importation into another.[119] As has been noted in another context: '... national political institutions remain powerful and distinctive determinants of political economic adjustment. Globalisation does not determine the form of national institutions any more than nations govern globalisation.'[120]

Given this globalisation of health concerns, international politics plays an important role in determining co-operation in relation to public health measures. Despite a professed awareness of the importance of addressing major threats to public health such as the environment, nuclear hazards, AIDS and other infectious diseases in a co-ordinated and co-operative way, there is little evidence of any real willingness to compromise State political and economic interests for the benefit of international strategies. The most powerful political and economic nations dominate discussions on health issues as on other issues and continue both to protect their own interests (such as polluting industries) and to press the blame and responsibility for health threats on to poorer nations (as is the case with the response of the First World to AIDS). Economic embargoes, such as the United States' embargoes of Cuba and Iraq, include embargoes on food supplies, medicines, hospital equipment and medical information, and result in an undermining of public health. Despite over-production of foodstuffs in the developed world, children in poorer countries still starve. The ability to produce routine medicines easily and cheaply has been a boon to the First

117 Spurgeon, P *et al*, point out that Britain fares badly in an international comparison on cancer patient's survival rates in 'Waiting times for cancer patients in England after general practitioners' referrals: retrospective national survey' (2000) 320 BMJ 838; Warden, J, 'UK waiting lists grow longer' (1998) 316 BMJ 1625.

118 See Wessen, A, 'The comparative study of health care reform', in Powell, F and Wessen, A, *Health Care Systems in Transition* 1999, Thousand Oaks: Sage.

119 Taylor-Goodby, D, 'The future of health care in six European countries: the views of policy elites' (1996) 26(2) International Journal of Health Studies 203.

120 Cioffi, J, 'Governing globalisation? The State, law and structural change in corporate governance' (2000) 27 Journal of Law and Society 572, p 600.

World drug industry, but has not benefited much of the world's most needy population. Over-reluctance to interfere with internal political turmoil even where atrocities are committed (such as the reluctance of the UN to intervene in Rwanda) combined with over-willingness to intervene in internal politics when First World national interests are threatened (for example, where oil supply might be affected) have left civilian populations devastated and contributed to public health disasters. The availability of cheap and unregulated labour forces in poorer nations has enabled wealthier nations to exploit Third World labour for their own economic advantage, heedless of the health consequences of working conditions which would be intolerable in the First World. Third World commercial debt resulting from the lending practices of First World institutions, particularly during the boom period of the 1970s, now means that health spending in poorer countries is secondary to debt repayment and industrial development.[121] The technology and scientific expertise of the industrialised nations has only served to increase the health disparity amongst the world's populations.

It is at the European level that harmonisation and co-operation in matters of health are most likely. As the European Union increasingly turns its attention to health, with directives bringing Member States into line with overall European objectives, health will become less and less a national issue for members and more a European issue. The introduction of the European Convention on Human Rights and Fundamental Freedoms into UK domestic law[122] will further standardise rights of access to health provision. Given the disparity of health service across Europe, it will be interesting to see the extent to which citizens of Member States will seek, or be granted, access to the health services of other Member States. France and Belgium already provide cheap and accessible alternatives to private medical treatment in England[123] and there is pressure to extend these opportunities to NHS patients.[124] European Union competition rules support trans-European access to medical treatment and it may not be long before patients look for treatment, particularly of a specialist nature, far wider afield.

Of course, even at the micro level, politics will play a part in public health provision. In the 2000 American election, the articulated policies of Gore and Bush on abortion, gun control and capital punishment were significant to the vote. Health provision played a major part in the 1987

121 World Bank, *World Development Report 1990: Poverty*, 1990, New York: OUP.

122 Human Rights Act 1998.

123 The British Cardiac Patients Association suggests that bypass operations are one-third cheaper in France and Belgium than in the UK; (2000) *The Independent on Sunday*, 17 December.

124 The East Kent Health Authority has asked the Department of Health to relax guidelines to allow patients to receive NHS treatment in France and Belgium; (2000) *The Independent on Sunday*, 17 December.

British elections, with both the Conservative and Labour parties including in their manifestos policies on health spending, health coverage and health access, and continues to be an election issue. Issues of public health can be emotive, especially where public health measures threaten religious or cultural values, and democratic politics are bound to include in their platforms promises which appeal to sections of the voting population. More worryingly, the policies of some governments include interests that are directly detrimental to public health, such as the pro-apartheid regime in South Africa in which violence and inequitable access to health resources were endemic to the process of government.[125] The choice of government can thus be significant for the direction of any public health reforms.

It must also be remembered that politics is itself subject to influence and that doctors are by virtue of their individual status and their membership of a powerful profession, in a position to contribute to both policy and law. Moran and Wood point out[126] that the political resources of the medical profession include positive public image, communication and research skills, membership of powerful and politically active bodies (such as the BMA) which defend the interests of doctors, and the powerful sanction of non co-operation with policies they oppose. Doctors are well represented in Parliament and on government bodies, especially those with a health brief. The views of doctors are given weight and respect not always accorded to other individuals[127] giving doctors as a profession and as individuals particular purchase in the determination of political policy.

ECONOMIC CONSTRAINTS ON PUBLIC HEALTH

It is stating the obvious to point out that public health provision will be constrained by the budgets allocated to it both at policy making and implementation levels. At policy level, the funding available for public health will in part be dictated by political priorities. But even within governments there will be competing pressures in relation to the funding of public services, and there will be public and media pressures to attend to other equally pressing needs such as social welfare, police, education and transport. Unforeseen events such as wars, natural disasters, train crashes, meningitis outbreaks and upsurges in crime will at different times force governments to push available funds around from one cause to another, not always in accordance with strategic funding plans.

---

125 See Nadasen, S, *Public Health Law in South Africa*, 2000, Durban: Butterworths.

126 Moran, M and Wood, B, *States, Regulation and the Medical Profession*, 1993, Buckingham: OUP.

127 See Sheldon, S, 'Who is the mother to make the judgment' [1993] 1 Feminist Legal Studies 3.

More complex are the economic pressures that dictate allocation of funds within the health system. Attempts made by economists to devise techniques for health resources on economic efficiency principles, such as the QALY and the Oregon Experiment discussed above, have been criticised for reinforcing societal inequalities. Nevertheless, a health system which is economically inefficient is also open to criticism.

Questions of economic efficiency will be relevant at various points in the spectrum of health provision. Firstly there is the question of determining which treatments to fund and which to exclude completely from funding. This dilemma applies not only to the funding of controversial treatments such as infertility treatment, tattoo removal, transgender surgery[128] and viagra,[129] but also to potentially life saving drugs such as tamoxifen for the treatment of breast cancer, AZT and Diflucan for the treatment of AIDS, Ribavirin for Hepatitis C, Aricept for Alzheimer's Disease and zanamivir (Relenza) for the treatment of influenza. There will also be disagreement as to whether the system should fund only treatments which have been proved to be effective, or whether it should also fund novel or heroic treatments which may be expensive but which may only have a small chance of succeeding.[130] This dilemma is compounded by the fact that routine life saving treatments often develop from knowledge gained from extraordinary or novel processes. Then there is the question of ranking those treatments which everyone agrees should be included in coverage. Should a health service spend large amounts of money treating one child with leukaemia, when that child might not survive despite the treatment, or with the same funds vaccinate a million children against meningitis? Should an expensive screening programme which will save only a few lives operate to the detriment of more hospital beds or more effective treatments of less serious conditions?[131] And, lastly, at what level of safety should a health service operate? Given sufficient staff and sufficient resources, we have the skills and technology to prevent, cure or treat most modern illnesses. If doctors are given the time and resources to run every test, take time with patients, work short shifts and prescribe every available treatment, the survival and recovery rates of those with disease and injury would be far higher than it is, but this could only be achieved at a cost. It is the determination of what cost we as a society are prepared to pay which must be evaluated.

One way of determining the balance between what we are prepared to pay for effective health provision and the risks we are prepared to take is to apply an economic analysis. This might take the form of cost-benefit analysis

128 *North West Lancashire HA v A and D* [2000] 1 WLR 977.

129 'Resource allocation' (1999) 6 Medical Law Monitor 1.

130 Such as the case of Jamie Bowen: *R v Cambridge HA ex p B* (1995) 23 BMLR 1.

131 See, eg, Hakama, M and Pukkala, E, 'Effectiveness of the public health policy for breast cancer screening in Finland' (1997) 314 BMJ, 22 March.

in which economic values are attached to the costs and benefits of health measures, a sort of economic utilitarianism. Factors that we consider worthwhile, such as incentives for positive health behaviour or deterrents from negative health behaviour, can be built into the equation. Health economics has produced sophisticated studies in order to determine the optimal point at which a society might choose to stop funding particular types of health care, the point at which the marginal cost of producing one unit of health care is equivalent to the marginal benefit derived from it. Such policies have attracted criticism in that they assume that the benefits of health care are measurable, and in that they are unable to accommodate principles of distributive and corrective justice.[132] It is argued that there are values that should override economic efficiency, such as the value to the community as a whole of protecting its most vulnerable members, the 'feel good' factor of living in a society which values health, prevention of the distress which results from illness, and the learning curve which is attached even to what are currently considered to be economically inefficient treatments. The application of economic models to health provision has also been criticised[133] as inappropriate in that the relationship between the powerful doctor with unique access to health resources, and the docile patient who must comply to gain access, is not one where market choice can operate. Moreover, doctors or health institutions are not necessarily able to choose whether or not to treat, as professional norms as much as economic considerations may determine the treatment.[134]

The application of economic theory to resource allocation inevitably involves a 'top down' approach, starting with the funding available and developing formulae governing the distribution of that money. An alternative approach is the 'bottom up' approach, where a calculation is made of what resources are needed and negotiations for funding begin from there. The recognition of need as a primary determinant in a health care system has been an important development particularly in those jurisdictions in which health provision is publicly funded. Identifying what constitutes need is difficult, and strategies have developed to factor in variables such as age, employment, ethnicity, and deprivation, based on either an ecological analysis (area of residence)[135] or individual data.[136]

132 Judge, K and Mays, N, 'Allocating resources for health and social care in England' (1994) 308 BMJ 1363; Sheldon, T and Carr-Hill, R, 'Weighting in the dark: resource allocation in the new NHS' (1993) 306 BMJ 403.

133 Arrow, K, *Social Choice and Justice*, 1983, Cambridge: Harvard UP.

134 Turner, B, *Medical Power and Social Knowledge*, 1995, London: Sage.

135 Eg, the British approach; see Carr-Hill, R *et al*, 'Allocating resources to health authorities: development of methods for small area analysis and use of inpatient services' (1994) 309 BMJ 1046; Smith, P *et al*, 'Allocating resources to health authorities: results and policy implications of small area analysis of use of inpatient services' (1994) 309 BMJ 1050.

136 Eg, the Swedish approach; Diderischen, F and Spetz, C-L, *Need Based Planning in Health Care*, 1987, Stockholm: National Board of Health Care and Social Welfare, [contd]

Assessing need will itself be subject to debate. As more urgent needs are satisfied, expectations rise such that there will always be gaps between need and provision. Busfield[137] gives the example of hip replacement surgery. Before the development of hip replacement techniques in the 1970s, sufferers from hip complaints experienced pain and disability, but because there was no health remedy, they did not acknowledge a need for surgery. It was the development of the remedy which created the need for treatment. Of course, even an ideal calculation of need will be subject to political constraints (such as, in Britain, the political consequences of moving significant amounts of public funding from the south to the north, or from the suburban areas to inner city and rural communities) and economic constraints. Economic considerations constrain not only public health spending, but also other public spending which might have a knock-on effect for public health. Funding cuts for research into BSE at the Neuro-Pathogenesis Unit in Edinburgh significantly delayed the understanding of the relationship between BSE and new variant CJD, for example.[138] A needs approach does not help balance funds between health and other competing public services. But at least a needs based approach makes apparent where gaps in provision lie, gaps which are often disguised in a policy based on economic efficiency, and can thus provide useful support for claims that health care as a whole is under-funded. This is particularly pertinent in Britain where a comparatively small proportion of gross domestic product is devoted to health provision.[139]

These debates are not limited to First World countries, although developing economies often do not have the luxury of ranking non-life saving treatments. Arguments about cost-effectiveness have become more intense with the development of expensive medical technology,[140] particularly physical and genetic screening programmes. The possibility of ownership of the rights to genetic processes, such as the BCRA2 gene for breast cancer, will make economic arguments all the more integral to debates about allocation of resources. Demographic forecasts threaten an escalation of health care costs, with an increasingly large proportion of elderly people per population as modern medicine becomes a victim of its own success. Health expectations rise with health successes, and the disparity in health provision between First World and developing countries, combined with greater awareness of disparity as a result of access to foreign media, takes economic arguments about the funding of health out of the

---

136 [contd] cited in Diderischen, F *et al*, 'Resource allocation to health authorities: the quest for an equitable formula in Britain and Sweden (1997) 315 BMJ 875.

137 Busfield, J, *Health and Health Care in Modern Britain*, 2000, Oxford: OUP, p 144.

138 (2000) *The Times Higher Education Supplement*, 27 October.

139 Judge, K and New, B, 'UK health and health care in an international context', in Harrison, A (ed), *Health Care UK 1995/96*, 1996, London: King's Fund.

140 Abel-Smith, B, 'The escalation of costs: how did we get there?', in *Health Care Reform: The Will to Change*, 1996, Paris: OECD.

national arena and places them firmly in the context of international economic strategies.

Much public health regulation involves placing limits on the economic freedom of industry with consequent financial detriment to private enterprise, a detriment which can be fatal to the emerging industrial sector of some nations. At the same time there seems to be little willingness to regulate industry in the developed countries which impinges on the public health of poorer nations. Tobacco companies actively encourage the sale of tobacco products, and manufacturers of infant formula milk have created a market for their products in areas where breast feeding was traditional, operating advertising practices which would not be acceptable in the developed world.[141] Trade and finance agreements between First World and developing countries are potentially a powerful tool for addressing the major determinants of ill health, and to consider public health apart from the economic context of the provision of health resources is unworkable. The concern is that in global debate on issues of public health, the determination of policy will be dominated by, and for the benefit of, countries with the financial clout.

SOCIO-ECONOMIC CONSTRAINTS ON PUBLIC HEALTH

One of the major failures of modern public health systems is the inequality of access to health within societies. This inequality exists regardless of the political and economic framework of the system, but appears to be exacerbated by the application of market principles to health care provision. In Britain, the creation of the National Health Service in 1948 was intended to provide equality of access to all citizens regardless of geography, class or financial status. In 1980, the Black Report[142] revealed that considerable inequalities still existed, and more recently commentators[143] have identified continuing, and possibly increasing,[144] inequalities in the distribution of health resources within Britain. Differentials from region to region and class

141 WHO has criticised British American Tobacco for using 'dirty tricks' in attempting to undermine anti-smoking campaigns: (2000) *The Times*, 3 August.

142 Department of Health and Social Security, *Report of the Working Group on Inequalities in Health*, 1980, London: HMSO.

143 Townsend, P *et al*, *Inequalities in Health (The Black Report)*, 1988, Hammondsworth: Penguin; Benzeval, M *et al*, *Tackling Inequalities in Health*, 1995, London: King's Fund; Barker, C, *The Health Care Policy Process*, 1996, London: Sage; Busfield, J, *Health and Health Care in Modern Britain*, 2000, Oxford: OUP.

144 Benzeval, M *et al*, *Tackling Inequalities in Health*, 1995, London: King's Fund; Shaw, M, *The Widening Gap: Health Inequalities and Policy in Britain*, 1999, Bristol: Policy.

to class can be found in mortality rates, life expectancy, hospital beds, general practitioner coverage, cancer survival rates and access to services such as infertility treatment. Some of these equalities in provision can be attributed to cultural and political constraints as discussed above, but the effects of poverty and the social environment must also be considered.

The relationship between poverty and health is complex.[145] Wealth relativity will be relevant – the perception of adequacy in housing and material possessions will be influenced by what others in the same social group possess. Clearly inadequate diet, poor housing, and lack of heating[146] will be contributing factors, but deprivation has other characteristics. Areas of poverty tend also to foster crime and violence, which limit socialisation and freedom of movement. Fear of the consequences of poverty, especially combined with debt, can lead to health damaging stress. Absence of life choices and lack of control lead to depression. Depression results in lack of will to prepare balanced meals and repair deterioration in housing. Poverty and unemployment have a symbiotic relationship, and unemployment is a contributory factor in socialisation and depression.[147] There is also a relationship between poverty and smoking and alcohol consumption, with consequences for health.

Class and socio-economic status in Britain tend to be measured across six hierarchically ranked socio-economic groups measured according to the occupation of the head of the household. When health indicators across these groups are compared, it becomes clear that members of the lower groups fare poorly. Members of the lowest group experience nearly double the mortality rate of members of the highest group,[148] and life expectancy for a member of the highest group is seven years higher than for a member of the lowest group. Infant mortality is significantly higher in the lower groups.[149] Weight and height are related to household income.[150] Members of the lower groups are more likely to work in unhealthy working environments.[151] Families with children, particularly single parents and the aged, are disproportionately represented in the lower income groups,[152] and

145 See Barker, C, *The Health Care Policy Process*, 1996, London: Sage.

146 Lawlor, D *et al*, 'Investigation of the association between excess winter mortality and socio-economic deprivation' (2000) 22 Journal of Public Health Medicine 176.

147 Blackburn, C, *Poverty and Health: Working with Families*, 1991, Milton Keynes: OU Press.

148 Barker, C, *The Health Care Policy Process*, 1996, London: Sage.

149 Baggott, R, *Health and Health Care in Britain*, 1998, London: Macmillan.

150 Der, S *et al*, 'The relationship of household income to a range of health measures in three age cohorts from the West of Scotland' (1999) 9 European Journal of Public Health 271.

151 Blane, D *et al*, 'Research note: social class differences in lifetime exposure to environmental hazards' (1998) 20 Sociology of Health and Illness 532; Busfield, J, *Health and Health Care in Modern Britain*, 2000, Oxford: OUP.

152 Benzeval, M *et al*, *Tackling Inequalities in Health*, 1995, London: King's Fund.

socio-economic status is particularly important in the determination of health in the aged[153] and in children.[154]

Geography is also relevant to health, not only because of the economic profile of residents, but also because of comparative health spending. A breast cancer patient in the East Surrey Health Authority has a 20 per cent higher chance of survival than a patient in the North Staffordshire Health Authority. Figures issued for 1998 and 1999 by the NHS Executive [155] on cancer survival showed higher survival rates in the south of England than in the north. Deaths from lung cancer and heart disease are highest in Manchester,[156] where the life expectancy for men is four years below the national average. There are wide regional variations in both access to abortion and access to safer methods of abortion.[157]

In other Western countries, similar correlations exist between socio-economic status and health. Studies of health profiles in Europe have identified higher rates of chronic illness amongst those with lowest incomes,[158] as well as higher mortality rates[159] and higher infant mortality rates.[160] Women in lower income groups are less likely to take advantage of screening opportunities and therefore have higher cancer mortality.[161] Middle class people generally have healthier diets.[162] North American studies have identified higher mortality rates[163] and higher morbidity rates[164] in lower income groups. Studies have also found that sustained

153 Breeze, E *et al*, 'Inequities in health. Socio-economic status and transition in status in old age in relation to limiting long-term illness measured at the 1991 census. Results from the UK longitudinal study' (1999) 9 European Journal of Public Health 265.

154 Aber, L *et al*, 'The effects of poverty on child health and development' (1997) 18 Annual Review of Public Health 463.

155 (2000) *The Times*, 14 July.

156 (2000) *The Times*, 19 February, based on research by the King's Fund for the Channel 4 programme *The Sick List: The NHS from Best to Worst*, 20 February 2000.

157 (2000) *The Times*, 2 February.

158 Blaxter, M, 'A comparison of measures of inequality in morbidity', in Fox, J (ed), *Health Inequalities in European Countries*, 1989, Aldershot: Gower.

159 Reijneveld, S and Gunning-Schlepers, L, 'Age, socio-economic status and mortality at the aggregate level' (1994) 48 Journal of Epidemiology and Community Health 146.

160 Elmen, H, 'Infant mortality: social inequality in a Swedish city' (1993) 3 European Journal of Public Health 237.

161 Rohlfs, I *et al*, 'The role of socio-demographic factors in preventative practices. The case of cervical and breast cancer' (1999) 9 European Journal of Public Health 278.

162 Hupkens, C *et al*, 'Social class differences in food consumption. The explanatory value of permissiveness and health and cost considerations' (2000) 10 European Journal of Public Health 108.

163 Pappas, G *et al*, 'The increasing disparity in mortality rates between socio-economic groups in the United States 1960 and 1986' (1993) 329 New England Journal of Medicine 103.

164 Rice, D, 'Ethics and equity in US health care' (1991) 21 International Journal of Health Services 637.

economic hardship leads to poorer physical, psychological functioning[165] and that children in low income groups are more likely to have drug dependant mothers.[166] A large scale Australian study[167] demonstrated that demography, socio-economic status and environment were serious risk factors for the determination of health.

Significant differentials in health can of course also be found within developing countries. Interestingly, in countries where the socio-economic differential is lowest, health indicators suggest that the overall standard of health is high even though the average income is low. Barker[168] gives the examples of China and Sri Lanka, where life expectancies are as high as in many wealthier countries, suggesting that in a more egalitarian society, prices of basic goods will not be determined by what the rich can afford to pay, and that personal control over lifestyle may have a psychological effect on health. Not only is the absolute value of the resources available relevant to health expectation, but also the relative value in relation to others within the same society. Inequality in distribution of wealth within a society hits twice, once in the material deprivation, and again in the psychological and social consequences of feeling deprived.

GENDER CONSTRAINTS ON PUBLIC HEALTH

Women's biology appears to work both for them and against them. If life expectancy tables are any indication of health profile then women fare well. In Britain, the life expectancy for a woman is some five years greater than for a man[169] across social classes, with even greater differential in some other European countries. Men are more likely to take on dangerous jobs, more likely to go to war and more likely to become involved in acts of violence, all of which make them more vulnerable to premature death. At the same time, women's reproductive biology makes them more vulnerable to illness and injury. In times and places of scarcity, women are more likely to be poor, work longer hours,[170] be inadequately fed and be more subject to domestic

165 Lynch, J, 'Cumulative impact of sustained economic hardship on physical, cognitive, psychological and social functioning' (1997) 337 New England Journal of Medicine 1889.

166 Haack, M, (ed), *Drug-Dependant Mothers and Their Children: Issues in Public Policy and Public Health*, 1997, New York: Springer.

167 National Health Strategy, *Enough to Make You Sick: How Income and Environment Affect Health*, 1992 National Health Strategy Research Paper No 1, Department of Health, Housing and Community Services, Canberra.

168 Barker, C, *The Health Care Policy Process*, 1996, London: Sage, citing Murray, C and Chen, L, ' In search of a contemporary theory for understanding mortality change' (1993) 25 Social Science and Medicine 773.

169 Hattersley, L, 'Expectation of life by social class', in Drever, F and Whitehead, M, *Health Inequalities*, 1997, London: Stationery Office.

170 See Lewis, J, *Women in Britain Since 1945*, 1992, Oxford: Blackwell.

violence. Women are more likely to suffer incapacity in later life[171] and appear more likely to suffer mental ill health.[172] If morbidity is a measure of health profile, then women fare poorly.

However, it is now recognised that biology plays a rather minor part in explanations of mortality and morbidity and that cultural assumptions and attitudes to women, as well as the attitudes and behaviours of women, go a long way to accounting for differentials in men's and women's health patterns.[173] If this is so, then those differentials are far from inevitable, and addressing the cultural factors that contribute to health profiles may have the consequence of improving the health of both men and women. Much has been written about the health effects of women's traditional roles in European and developing world societies[174] and about religious and cultural attitudes to the control of women's 'leaky'[175] and 'abnormal' bodies.[176] There has also more recently been a considerable body of commentary examining the assumptions of medical science and its practitioners which potentially distort recognition, diagnosis and treatment decisions in relation to women,[177] examining the way women perceive and respond to their own health, and supporting recognition of women's narratives of their own health.[178] Women's presumed reproductive role still dominates medical accounts of women's health. There is a paucity of literature on men and health, probably because much of the existing critique has arisen from the application of emerging feminist theory, but similar analysis could potentially explain flaws in the profile of male health.[179]

171 Aber, S and Ginn, J, *Gender and Later Life: A Sociological Analysis of Resources and Constraints,* 1991, London: Sage.

172 Morgan, M *et al, Sociological Approaches to Health and Medicine,* 1985, London: Routledge.

173 See, eg, Waldron, I, 'Trends in gender differences in mortality: relationships to changing gender differences in behaviour and other causal factors', in Allendale, E and Hunt, K, *Gender Inequalities in Health,* 2000, Buckingham: OUP.

174 See, in particular, Doyal, L, *What Makes Women Sick,* 1995, London: Macmillan; Lupton, D, *Medicine as Culture,* 1994, London: Sage.

175 Shildrick, M, *Leaky Bodies and Boundaries: Feminism, Postmodernism and (Bio)ethics,* 1997, London: Routledge.

176 See, eg, Turner, B, *Medical Power and Social Knowledge,* 1995, Thousand Oaks: Sage; Smart, C, 'Disruptive bodies and unruly sex: the regulation of reproduction and sexuality in the nineteenth century', in Smart, C (ed), *Regulating Womanhood: Historical Essays on Marriage, Motherhood and Sexuality,* 1992, London: Routledge.

177 See, eg, Bendelow, B and Williams, J, 'Natural for women, abnormal for men: beliefs about pain and gender', in Nettleton, S and Watson, J, *The Body in Everyday Life,* 1988, London: Routledge.

178 Popay, J and Groves, K, 'Narrative in research on gender inequalities in health', in Annandale, E and Hunt, K, *Gender Inequalities in Health,* 2000, Buckingham: OUP.

179 See as an example, Watson, J, 'Running around like a lunatic: Colin's body and the case of male embodiment', in Nettleton, S and Watson, J, *The Body in Everyday Life,* 1988, London: Routledge.

In the context of public health, it is essential that decisions relating to the funding and operation of health services address the health needs of women, and are not based on an assumption that women's needs are the same as men's. Women's involvement in policy making in politics and the executive is comparatively recent, and women are still proportionately poorly represented in senior policy making bodies, not only within Britain but worldwide.[180] Women have also been traditionally excluded from the practice of medicine, and even now that women are well represented in the medical student body, they are far less well represented in senior medical practice and management.[181] Although women constitute a high proportion of the overall health force, the areas of practice dominated by women (nursing, midwifery and other para-medical services) have little political clout in the determination of important health issues. Even in the context of 'women's health' matters such as childbirth and contraception, the male dominated medical profession has successfully challenged traditional midwives such that male ideas about appropriate treatment have dominated. The gendering of roles within health provision, based on assumptions about nurturing skills, and the consequences for the valuing of those roles and for recognition in the policy making process, have been often noted.[182] It is not surprising then that both within the institutional framework of macro health policy as well as within the micro level of individual medical treatment, the needs of women have not been fully recognised.

Given that many of the causes of women's ill health are embedded in the roles and activities women undertake, the constraints of gender lie not so much within the framework of health provision but across the governmental and cultural spectrum. As Doyal has commented:

> ... traditional epidemiological methods have to be turned on their head. Instead of identifying diseases and then searching for a cause, we need to begin by identifying the major areas of activity that constitute women's lives. We can then go on to analyse the impact of these activities on their health and well being.[183]

In many Third World countries, the status of women remains governed by traditional attitudes with detrimental consequences for the health profile of the female, and child, populations. Even within the First World, gender continues to be a contributory factor in relation to issues ranging from

180 United Nations, 'The world's women 1970–1999: trends and statistics', in *Social Statistics and Indicators*, 1991, Series K, No 8, New York: UN.

181 Doyal, L, 'Changing medicine? Gender and the politics of health care', in Gabe, J *et al*, *Challenging Medicine*, 1994, London: Routledge.

182 See, eg, Witz, A, *Professions and Patriarchy*, 1992, London: Routledge; Davies, C, *Gender and the Professional Predicament in Nursing*, 1995, Buckingham: OUP.

183 Doyal, L, *What Makes Women Sick*, 1995, London: Macmillan, p 21.

decisions on research funding,[184] policies on routine treatment of women's conditions and illnesses[185] to medical control of sexual behaviour, and the constraints of gender cannot be ignored in determination of public health policy either nationally or internationally. The employment structure in medical practice disadvantages women with families, and many areas of speciality still operate within a male dominated culture that inhibits women's medical careers. Until women have a full hearing in the determination of health policy at all levels, it is unlikely that public health provision will begin to address the particular health needs of women, and given women's importance within the family unit, health provision will be continue to be inadequate in determination of the health of the population as a whole.

MEDIA CONSTRAINTS ON PUBLIC HEALTH

The relationship between the public and the health care system will be very much influenced by media coverage. Proportionately few members of society have had close dealings with the health service outside the General Practitioner's surgery, perhaps a short hospital stay or a visit to the local hospital Casualty Department. Those few who have suffered serious long term illness or injury will have had sufficient experience of health provision to make their own informed judgments, but others will rely on media portrayal to judge how well they are served by their health system. There is now significant media coverage of health issues, much of it challenging received medical opinion. The media therefore has considerable power and, with it, considerable responsibility to present a balanced account of health provision. Of course, horror stories make better reading and viewing, and there has been sustained media coverage of undiagnosed meningitis, false diagnoses of cancer, treatment waiting lists and negligent, reckless and callous doctoring. In response, television series such as *Children's Hospital*[186] emphasise medical success stories, raising expectations that a children's casualty department provides friendly, efficient and professional treatment in a welcoming environment. It is in fact medicine rather than health that attracts media attention and, in particular, the treatment of life threatening conditions, medical disasters, and the treatment of babies and children. Treatment of the chronic injuries of the aged, provision of out-patient

184 Annandale, E and Hunt, K, 'Gender inequalities in health: research at the crossroads', in Annandale, E and Hunt, K, *Gender Inequalities in Health*, 2000, Buckingham: OUP.

185 See Hann, A, *The Politics of Breast Cancer Screening*, 1996, Aldershot: Avebury.

186 BBC1.

services, health education and preventative medicine make less exciting viewing.

Medical soaps and dramas also colour our view of medical treatment and medical practitioners, but again, the emphasis is on medicine and not health. This can work to undermine recognition of health as a public concern. Bury and Gabe point out that:

> The representation of health and medicine as essentially technical issues effectively reinforced the individualistic approach to health, offering a 'dominant ideology' suggesting that health and medicine were essentially about pharmaceutical and technical progress.[187]

Doctors in medical dramas are portrayed as authoritative, benevolent, knowledgeable and effective,[188] and the white coat is used as a symbol of this authority reinforcing mainstream scientific medicine.

Media entertainment can perform an educative function. Williams and Bendelow[189] examined the sources of children's understanding of cancer and the way dramas aimed at children and young teenagers bring anxieties about health and illness into mainstream debate. Issues such as hair loss and socialisation problems arising as the result of leukaemia, for instance, have been dealt with in ways that reassure and normalise the effects of illness. Other studies[190] confirm that television plays an important role in suggesting solutions and sources of help for health concerns.

Even entertainment in which a health message is not intended can influence health attitudes. Research on smoking by women in American films[191] showed that actresses on film smoked twice as much as women in real life, and smoked significantly more than male actors in film. Representations of body shape and behaviour in art[192] and in music videos create expectations of culturally acceptable shape and behaviour. The Internet is an increasingly important source of entertainment and health information.[192a]

A more direct source of health information is contained in magazines. These are generally aimed at an identifiable group – teenagers, sexually

---

187 Bury, M and Gabe, J, 'Television and medicine', in Gabe, J *et al*, *Challenging Medicine*, 1994, London: Routledge; see also Karpf, A, *Doctoring the Media*, 1988, London: Routledge.

188 *Ibid*, Karpf.

189 Williams, J and Bendelow, G, 'Children's beliefs about health, cancer and risk', in Nettleton, S and Watson, J, *The Body in Everyday Life*, 1998, London: Routledge.

190 Eg, Oakley, A *et al*, 'Health and cancer prevention; knowledge and beliefs of children and young people' (1995) 310 BMJ 1029.

191 Research by I Kawachi in American Journal of Public Health, cited in (2000) *The Times*, 3 March.

192 Blaikie, A and Hepworth, M, 'Representations of old age in painting and photography', in Jamieson, A *et al*, *Critical Approaches to Ageing and Later Life*, 1997, Buckingham: OUP.

192a See, eg, Wootton, J, 'The quality of information on women's health on the Internet' (1997) 6(5) J Women's Health.

active singles, mothers-to-be, parents and the over-50s. As a result, the health information offered is more specific and explicit. The success of the magazine concept is such that our images of ourselves are very much shaped by the quasi-scientific information presented in this form.[193] Photographs illustrate perfect health in the form of young, thin, beautiful people. There is pressure on readers to conform to the pictorial representation of health, but the recommended solutions (diets, breast implants, excessive exercise, surgery) may themselves be causes of ill health. Not all advice given in magazines is well researched or accurate, and the underlying motivation remains entertainment for the purpose of boosting magazine sales. In a review conducted by Whelan[194] of 10 popular magazines published in July and August 1992, it was noted that the health advice given was 'a distortion of scientific reality, but also that the disinformation about health is sponsored (through advertising)...'. While the bulk of health advice given related to diets and environmental threats to health, the bulk of the advertising and of celebrity stories focused on smoking and alcohol as positive activities which would improve lifestyle. Whelan commented, 'the role of cigarette advertising revenues in the "filtering" of stories with bad news about smoking cannot be underestimated'.

Advertising is as important as media content in sending out health messages. Advertising images often undermine positive health behaviour and counter health education,[195] as is recognised in the regulation of tobacco advertising. Advertisements for junk food, fizzy drinks,[196] alcohol and sweets, much of it aimed at children and teenagers, suggest that happiness and physical pleasure can be easily purchased. Meanwhile low fat and low cholesterol food products, cosmetics, cleansing and exercise products sell the idea of the body as a commodity in a consumer culture[197] in which health can be bought and sold. As Lupton points out, 'The slippage between food as medicine and medicine as food in such advertisements is significant'.[198] The power of advertising is now being harnessed by public

193 See, eg, Hepworth, M and Featherstone, M, 'The male menopause: cultural reconstruction', in Nettleton, S and Watson, J, *The Body in Everyday Life*, 1998, London: Routledge; Featherstone, M, 'The body in consumer culture', in Featherstone, M and Turner, B, *The Body: Social Processes and Cultural Theory*, 1991, London: Sage.

194 E Whelan, President of the American Council on Science and Health, reported in (1992) *The New York Times*, 8 September.

195 Townsend, J, 'The burden of smoking', in Benzeval, M *et al*, *Tackling Inequalities in Health*, 1995, London: King's Fund.

196 Research by Dr Grace Wyshak, reported in Archives of Paediatrics and Adolescent Medicine, suggests that teenagers who drink large quantities of cola are more likely to suffer broken bones as a result of the adverse effect of phosphoric acid in the drinks on calcium metabolism and bone mass, cited in (2000) *The Times*, 15 June.

197 See Lupton, D, *Medicine as Culture*, 1994, London: Sage, Chapter 2.

198 *Ibid*, p 41.

health advocates. The Department of Health has used media advertising in its AIDS campaign, public interest groups use advertising on issues such as the prevention of cot death, and advertising has been used in advocacy for road safety and the prevention of domestic violence.

Beyond the entertainment sector, media journalism now takes a serious interest in health politics. It has been suggested[199] that this has come about in part because we increasingly see health as a commodity such that the rising costs of health provision make health funding issues economically and politically controversial. The media interest in health has been exploited by governments[200] and by critics of government policy, and through the media pressure groups have been able to engage public interest such as to engineer changes in policy.[201] Media documentaries and advertising are now being used openly to confront health issues by advocates of wide ranging approaches to public health,[202] and the role of the media in informing the public health debate is increasingly important.

ETHICAL CONSTRAINTS ON PUBLIC HEALTH

No matter how highly a society might value the health of its population, other moral values will come into play when health strategies are devised. The public health of a society might well be improved by killing or exiling every carrier of infectious disease, by aborting all babies carrying a health defect, by restricting freedoms or forcing treatment on non-consenting patients, but our ethics will limit what can be done.

A crude utilitarian or consequentialist approach would suggest that how we should act is determined by the extent to which we can achieve the greatest happiness for the greatest number, and indeed much health rationing is underlined by utilitarian principles. But even so, we would not sanction the cultivation of body organs from a friendless, unemployed criminal even to save the lives of 10 deserving and meritorious patients in need of transplant if the donation process involved letting the donor die unnecessarily. Rather, most modern societies accept that there are some principles of medical ethics which must be heeded. These include such absolute principles as non-maleficence, the duty not to intend harm to a

---

199 See Kellerher, D *et al*, 'Understanding medical dominance in the modern world', in Gabe, J *et al*, *Challenging Medicine*, 1994, London: Routledge.

200 Klein, R, *The New Politics of the NHS*, 1995, London: Longman.

201 Walt, G, 'Implementing health care reform: a framework for discussion', in Saltman, R *et al*, *Critical Challenges for Health Care Reform in Europe*, 1998, Buckingham: OUP.

202 Eg, 'Australian TV airs "right to die" advert' (1999) *The Guardian*, 16 March.

patient, which overrides all other treatment norms,[203] and more relative principles such as the duty of beneficence (the duty to do good), confidentiality and respect for autonomy. Most societies would also support the public health objective of distributive justice such that health resources are allocated equitably and impartially. More recently, arguments about patients' rights, particularly the right to health, have complicated arguments about health ethics.

It is the determination of the hierarchy of relative norms of ethics that has given rise to difficulty and debate in the context of medical treatment and public health. If a woman in labour chooses to reject the medical advice that she must undergo caesarean surgery in order to save the life of her baby, should the treating doctor be governed by respect for the patient's autonomy or duty to do good to the mother and child?[204] To what extent should the law sanction quarantine, compulsory reporting of infectious disease, vaccination, water fluoridation, abortion or euthanasia, all of which raise competing ethics principles? These same ethics principles will place limits on the research that can be carried out to determine the causes of ill health,[205] in the management of health services[206] and in the funding of health resources. Much traditional public health containment is predicated on control of individuals and populations, and the increasing recognition of arguments based on rights and autonomy has forced public health practice to move towards public health education and promotion, rather than restriction, as health measures.

A particular concern in the administration of public health is health surveillance. Foucault[207] first identified in the development of public health institutions and policies, the focusing of the medical gaze on particular social groups and individuals such that the surveillance of these subjects was justified by the collation of health information. The greater the knowledge obtained from surveillance, the greater the power differential between health provider and patient, and so the greater the control over the subjects of surveillance. The more intimate knowledge the health provider has of our non-medical lives (diet, lifestyle), the easier it is to direct life style choices.[208] The more the patient is seen in the context of a group health

203 Subject to the doctrine of double effect; see Beauchamp, T and Childress, J, *Principles of Biomedical Ethics*, 1994, Oxford: OUP.

204 *St George's Healthcare NHS Trust v S* [1998] 3 WLR 673.

205 See Kimmel, A, *Ethics and Values in Applied Social Research* 1988, London: Sage

206 See Dracopolou, S, *Ethics and Values in Health Care Management*, 1998, London: Routledge.

207 Foucault, M, 'The politics of health in the eighteenth century', in Rainbow, P, *The Foucault Reader*, 1984, New York: Pantheon.

208 Bunton, R, 'More than a woolly jumper: health promotion as social regulation' (1992) 3 Critical Public Health 4.

profile, the less relevant the individual characteristics of the patient and the more the patient's health becomes a matter of statistical risk.[209] The potential conflict between surveillance on the one hand and confidentiality, autonomy and informed consent on the other remains an issue, and guidelines on public health practice acknowledge the problems arising from this conflict.[210]

Public health advocacy can also give rise to ethics concerns. Impartiality, neutrality, scientific objectivity and fairness are ethical virtues essential to the management of public health, while advocacy necessitates the enthusiastic promotion of a particular position to the exclusion of other views. For example, in relation to the smoking/lung cancer debate, public health campaigners will find themselves locked into battle with tobacco companies such that neutrality becomes non-viable. Any public health campaign or advocacy will be conducted in the context of prevailing social and cultural ideologies and policies. Public health advocacy risks political partiality, especially when practised by a government health department. Feminist critiques of health promotion have identified assumptions about women which result in placing on them a disproportionate responsibility for health care,[211] and any institutional racism in society is likely to be reflected in public health approaches as it is with other public services.[212] Much early public health research has also been criticised for racial and sexual bias in the subject group or in the interpretation of research results.

Medical perceptions and attitudes to disability and to sufferers of particular types of illness and disease may also shape public health promotion. Campaigns which draw attention to the consequences of censured behaviour (dangerous driving, unsafe sex, non-vaccination), pointing out the horrors of being confined to a wheelchair, being disabled and being chronically ill, reinforce the stigma of disability and illness and devalue the lives of those who live with those conditions.[213] The frustrations of medical scientists in not being able successfully to cure can be translated into rejection of responsibility, with consequent passing of responsibility to patients who may be living in a social and physical environment that

---

209 Nettleton, S and Bunton, R, 'Sociological critiques of health promotion', in Bunton, R *et al*, *The Sociology of Health Promotion*, 1995, London: Routledge; Castel, R, 'From dangerousness to risk', in Burchell, C *et al*, *The Foucault Effect: Studies in Governmentality*, 1991, London: Harvester Wheatsheaf.

210 Eg, the International Epidemiological Society, 'Guidelines on ethics for epidemiologists' (1990) 19 International Journal of Epidemiology 226; World Medical Association: Declaration of Helsinki, Helsinki, June 1964 as amended.

211 Daykin, N and Naidoo, J, 'Feminist critiques of health promotion', in Bunton, R and Nettleton, S, *The Sociology of Health Promotion*, 1995, London: Routledge.

212 Douglas, J, 'Developing anti-racist promotion strategies', in Bunton, R and Nettleton, S, *The Sociology of Health Promotion*, 1995, London: Routledge.

213 Wang, C, 'Cultural meaning and disability: injury prevention campaigns and the production of stigma' (1992) 39 Social Science and Medicine 1093.

constrains patient choice. Public health promotions on issues such as obesity, domestic violence, cervical cancer, lung cancer and AIDS have all at some time taken victim-blaming approaches. Public health funding, such as for abortion, contraception or sex education may be influenced by attitudes to marriage and sexual behaviour.

Another ethics concern is the sponsoring of health promotion and research. Where research is funded or administered by a drug company or a political or quasi-political body, a conflict of interest arises which may not always be made clear in the dissemination and application of the research results. Where public health promotion, health facilities and health technology are provided by one wealthy country for the benefit of another, poorer nation, there is the risk of paternalism or ethics imperialism,[214] whereby the dominant cultural ideologies of the wealthier nation are imposed by virtue of economic power without reference to cultural relativism. Health practices which are no longer supported in wealthier countries, such as smoking or feeding babies with formula milk, and unacceptable health resources such as drugs which have failed stringent western safety standards, may be imposed on vulnerable populations who have no choice but to accept what is offered.

There has for a long time been an awareness of the role of ethics in the context of both individual medical treatment and in health research. The importance of ethics in the wider context of public health advocacy and public health management has been less frequently addressed,[215] but it is increasingly clear that any health activity which is not based firmly on principles of ethics will be flawed.

ENVIRONMENTAL AND CATASTROPHIC CONSTRAINTS ON PUBLIC HEALTH

Both the natural and the man-made environment will influence health and dictate public health strategies. Excessively cold climates and excessively hot climates will pose health risks.[216] Environments subject to natural predators, for example, mosquitos, ticks, sandflies and midges, will pose risks of viral illnesses such as malaria, plague, encephalitis, dengue fever and yellow

214 Angell, M, 'Ethical imperialism? Ethics in international collaborative research' (1988) 319 New England Journal of Medicine 1081; Last, J, 'Ethics and public health policy', in Wallace, R *et al*, *Public Health and Preventative Medicine*, 1993, Stamford: Appleton & Lange.

215 Though see Bradley, P and Burls, A, *Ethics in Public and Community Health*, 1999, London: Routledge.

216 See Kilbourne, E, 'Illness due to thermal extremes', in Wallace, R *et al*, *Public Health and Preventative Medicine*, 1998, Stamford: Appleton & Lange.

fever. Impure water and food supplies are responsible for typhoid fever, shigellosis, cholera, new variant CJD and similar diseases. Wild and domesticated animals can transmit rabies, anthrax. brucellosis and other viruses. Occupational exposure to toxic environments and to industrial chemicals can lead to diseases such as asbestosis, lung disease, silicosis, lead and arsenic poisoning and chemical poisoning. Everyday living in modern societies potentially gives rise to health threats from electromagnetic radiation (microwave ovens, cell phones, power transmission lines),[217] nuclear power stations, traffic fumes, tobacco smoke, sick building syndrome,[218] job stress[219] and hospital-acquired infection.[220]

Given sufficient resources much of the effects of these environmental threats are preventable. Adequate heating and cooling will counter hypothermia and heat stroke. Adequate sewage disposal, water filtration, hygienic food preparation and regulation of the use of pesticides and food additives will significantly lessen the risks of diseases spread by food and water. Effective vaccination programmes can minimise the effects of insect transmitted disease in vulnerable environments, as it has done for diseases that previously threatened Western societies such as measles, poliomyelitis and diphtheria.[221] Regulation of industry, of fuel production and of tobacco use will reduce modern environmental hazards. The cause and effect relationship in relation to most of these environmental risks is well understood. The environmental consequences are predictable, and the solutions are available, but always at a cost. That cost is not only a monetary cost, but also a cost to freedoms of movement and enterprise.

The dilemma of public health strategists is how much in the way of funding and regulation will society be prepared to concede to achieve a safe living environment. Where there is a direct environmental threat to an identifiable population, that population may be willing to pay a high price for safety, but where the threat is more diffuse, or where the main benefits will be derived by another geographical or social population, it is more difficult to persuade societies or governments to expend the necessary costs. The challenge for environmentalists is to balance strategies for protection of

---

217 The relationship between cancer and power lines is disputed; see UK Childhood Cancer Investigators, 'Childhood cancer and residential proximity to power lines' (2000) 83 British Journal of Cancer 1573.

218 Thorn, A, 'Case study of a sick building. Could integrated biopsychosocial perspective prevent chronicity?' (2000) 10 European Journal of Public Health 133.

219 Houtman, I *et al*, 'Job stress, absenteeism and coronary heart disease European co-operative study' (1999) 9 European Journal of Public Health 52.

220 'Unclean hospitals killing 5,000 a year' (2000) *The Times*, 17 February; 'Hospitals that make us ill cost the NHS £1 billion a year' (2000) *The Times*, 19 January.

221 Although there is debate about the role of vaccination in the reduction of some disease, and argued that other factories, such as prosperity and sanitation, have contributed significantly to reduction in mortality and morbidity as well as incidence of disease. See Chapter 10 by Stephanie Pywell on vaccination.

the environment with the sustainable development required to maintain thriving populations. And the challenge for other policy makers, in areas of industry or transport, for example, is to balance the benefits, including the health benefits of employment and transport access to facilities, with the adverse health consequences of enterprise. At national policy level and beyond, health, environment and enterprise have traditionally been operated with minimal integration and it is only more recently, as European influences begin to bite,[222] that there has been recognition within Britain of joint and overlapping responsibilities.[223]

Other threats to public health are not so predictable. Natural phenomena such as earthquakes, tidal waves, drought, bush fires and typhoons not only kill directly, but create living environments which are uncontrollable without massive investment of resources. War clearly threatens the health of engaged military forces, but war also poses both physical health risks, such as food shortage, medicine shortage and polluted water, and psychological health risks to civilian populations. The emergence of new bacteria, and the decreasing effectiveness of antibiotics poses problems that modern medicine is not yet equipped to face. And changes in societal health behaviour such as drug use, work behaviour and food consumption, often in response to other social pressures, create new and changing public health concerns.

No public health strategy can be set in stone. Global warming will alter living environments in ways that we cannot yet predict. Whereas many other catastrophic environmental risks tend disproportionately to affect developing nations and so are of only indirect concern to the Western world, the effects of global warming will be indiscriminate.[224] The response of any one nation will contribute to consequences for the world as a whole. Similarly, AIDS, which was once considered to be an African problem, now knows no borders and strategies based on closing barriers, with responsibility lying on African governments to contain the disease, are no longer viable. Such public health risks necessitate a global approach to health strategies, and have prompted a growing awareness of the importance of approaching public health from a co-ordinated, transnational standpoint. However, any such approach will be constrained by the political, economic and cultural factors discussed above.

222 See Bruce, N *et al*, 'Health transport and the environment: does European and UK policy support effective joint action?' (1999) 9 European Journal of Public Health 251.

223 Department of the Environment/Department of Health, *United Kingdom National Health Action Plan*, Cm 3323, 1996, London: HMSO; UK Government, *Our Healthier Nation – A Contract for Health*, Cm 3852, 1998, London: The Stationery Office.

224 See, eg, 'Cold, not global warming, bigger threat to Europeans' (2000) 321 BMJ 650, p 670.

CONCLUSION

Common to the constraints discussed in this chapter has been the influence of globalised threats to health, whether at political, economic, cultural, or environmental level. It is now no longer appropriate to consider health from a local or national perspective, nor to continue to focus on health treatments without addressing the causes of ill health. We must now take into account that the nature of human interaction has changed and 'that boundaries, whether spatial (territorial), temporal (time) and cognitive (thought processes) are being redefined'.[225] Recognition of globalisation in the context of health has resulted in a resurgence of interest in public health, which has in the last 50 years been marginalised by a focus on medical technology and the provision of medical treatment.

Globalisation is about more than acknowledging that threats to a nation's health might come from other populations; it also requires recognition that the economic and environmental practices of all nations may pose threats beyond national boundaries and may contribute to global patterns of climate change, migration, spread of disease and health and safety standards. This does not mean abandoning local and national health strategies in favour of international regulation of health, but rather placing domestic health strategies in a context of global health awareness. Much of the legal framework of health provision and protection must be formulated at national level, given the limited powers of enforcement at international law. It is important that the policy makers responsible for preparation and administration of that legal framework are sensitive not only to intra-jurisdictional constraints, but also to the health consequences of national policy for the health of the world's populations.

225 Lee, K, 'Globalisation and the need for a strong public health response' (1999) 9 European Journal of Public Health 249.

CHAPTER 3

DOMESTIC REGULATION OF PUBLIC HEALTH: ENGLAND AND WALES

Robyn Martin

DEFINING PUBLIC HEALTH LAW

The role of domestic law in public health is complex. Given the range of factors that determine health, the laws which impinge on public health will themselves be various. Very little law is completely divorced from health. Criminal law has implications for the harm which results from crime; laws on the workplace, transport, the building industry, education or discrimination look to health and welfare; laws on negligence and contract have as objectives safety standards and deterrence; even laws regulating financial transactions will have consequences for health. Categorising that body of law which regulates public health is therefore as difficult as the task of defining public health.

Definitions of public health law taken from other jurisdictions[1] focus on public health legislation. This would be inappropriate in a discussion of English domestic law, which additionally includes a body of common law enabling individuals to use law in the pursuance of public health objectives. Public health is not a commodity to be distributed by the State. Contemporary public health philosophy recognises that individuals take some responsibility for their own health and for behaviour that infringes the health of others, and that health involves rights as well as obligations. This chapter will assume that public health law is that body of law which can be used as a tool in the provision, protection and promotion of the health rights of the population.

Four components of public health law will be examined: first, the legislative framework of health protection, secondly, public health enforcement mechanisms, thirdly, the role of public and private law in the

---

1 Eg, in the American context, Gostin defines public health law as 'the study of the legal powers and duties of the State to ensure the conditions of the people to be healthy ... and the limitations on the power of the State to constrain autonomy ...': Gostin, L, 'Public health law in a new century, Part I' (2000) 283 JAMA 2837; Bidmeade and Reynolds define public health law in Australia as 'any area of legal regulation which affects the maintenance and improvement of the health of individuals in a community': Bidmeade, I and Reynolds, C, *Public Health Law in Australia: Its Current State and Future Directions*, 1997, Canberra: Commonwealth of Australia.

enforcement of health rights and the achievement of public health objectives, and fourthly, this chapter will consider the legal framework of the provision of health services and the maintenance of public health.

THE LEGISLATIVE FRAMEWORK OF HEALTH PROTECTION: THE PUBLIC HEALTH ACTS AND PARALLEL LEGISLATION

English law in 2001 contains a maze of Public Health Acts and secondary legislation which purport directly to address health protection. This legislation has proved insufficient as a framework for even the most limited definition of public health, and so the Public Health Acts are complemented by a further volume of legislation regulating matters such as pollution, disease, animals, waste and housing.

Government control of matters of public health can be traced back to laws on repairs of sewers in 1225.[2] From that time, legislation was passed in response to individual health concerns (adulteration of food, radiation, epidemics, child labour) within the domain of police powers rather than of public health. The role of medical officers in advising governments on health concerns did not develop until the late 18th century, and the first legislative use of the term 'public health' was in the Public Health Act 1848. Britain's leadership in the industrial revolution had resulted in environmental health dangers more acute than in other less densely populated and less industrialised nations, requiring more co-ordinated control of industrial activity. Early English public health legislation became a model for public health regulation in other jurisdictions.[3]

The Public Health Act 1875 was the first legislation to address national public health concerns. The Act applied to England and Wales, but not to London until 1963.[4] Power to control health hazards was assigned to local level through urban and rural sanitary boards, districts and authorities, and although the Act provided template subsidiary legislation in an attempt to standardise health protections, it provided for little central control. Parallel to the early Public Health Acts, other statutes regulated isolated health

2 9 Hen III, c 15 and 16; see Warren, M, *A Chronology of State Medicine, Public Health, Welfare and Related Services in Britain 1066–1999*, unpublished, 2000, Faculty of Public Health Medicine: Royal College of Physicians.

3 Eg, in Australia; see Bidmeade, I and Reynolds, C, *Public Health Law in Australia*, 1997, Canberra: Commonwealth of Australia.

4 London Government Act 1963, s 40; see the Local Government Act 1972, Sched 14 for application of the Public Health Acts to London.

threats in an uncoordinated way.[5] The 1875 Act itself was followed by a series of amendment Acts, parts of which remain in force, including the Public Health Act 1875 (Support of Sewers) Amendment Act 1883, the Public Health Acts Amendment Acts 1890, the Public Health Acts Amendment Act 1907 and the Public Health Act 1925.

The assumption behind all early public health legislation was that contagious disease was spread through waste, refuge and poor drainage, and the legislative focus was on controlling these causes by classifying sources of disease as statutory nuisances. As medical science developed greater understanding of causes of ill health, so the legislation added to the list of sources of nuisance. Statutory nuisance had its origins in legislation with a public health objective, and the continuing importance of the old public health Acts for the purposes of determining statutory nuisance has inhibited the development of statutory nuisance for other purposes, such as an environmental protection mechanism.[6] There was no co-ordinated umbrella approach to maintenance of health so that the various public health and other Acts combined to create a patchwork of public health regulation. Legislative containment of one health risk created other threats to health. For example, attempts by the Alkali Acts[7] to control atmospheric pollution prompted industries to dispose of alkali waste in liquid form into water supplies,[8] and refuse removal and drainage in aid of disease prevention resulted in the dumping of offending materials. The correlation between public health and nuisance control underpins all the public health Acts, and public health as the prevention of environmental threats to health as they are recognised by science continues to shape legislative responses to public health.

In the context of contemporary public health law, the foundation of public health legislation is the Public Health Act 1936 which gives relevant local authorities power to intervene in the case of specified nuisances which are 'prejudicial to health'.[9] Section 343(1) of the Act defines prejudicial to

5 Eg, the Public Health (Water) Act 1978; the Contagious and Infectious Diseases (Animals) Act 1978; the Disease Prevention (Metropolis) Act 1883; the Housing of the Working Classes Act 1885; the Infectious Disease (Notification) Act 1889; the Prevention of Cruelty, and Protection of, Children Act 1889; the Public Health (London) Act 1891; the Factory and Workshop Act 1901; the Public Health (Regulation as to Food) Act 1907; the Coal Mines Regulation Act 1908; the Public Health (Prevention and Treatment of Disease) Act 1913; the Milk and Dairies Act 1914; the Public Health (Tuberculosis) Act 1921; the Mental Treatment Act 1930; the Town and Country Planning Act 1932; and the Pharmacy and Poisons Act 1933.

6 See comments by Bell, S and McGillivray, D, in *Environmental Law*, 2000, London: Blackstone.

7 Alkali Act 1863, Alkali Act 1874 and Alkali etc Works Regulation Act 1906.

8 Bell, S and McGillivray, D, *Environmental Law*, 2000, London: Blackstone, p 10.

9 Eg, s 25 covers sanitary conveniences prejudicial to health, s 48 looks to drainage which is prejudicial to health, and s 81 deals with animals which are prejudicial to health.

health as meaning 'injurious, or likely to cause injury to, health'. This has been interpreted as distinguishing poor health from injury such that a nuisance which presents danger of injury is not necessarily prejudicial to health. An accumulation of building materials which may have been dangerous, but which was not likely to contribute to the spread of disease, was not considered to be prejudicial to health,[10] and a steeply built staircase was held not to be prejudicial to the health of a tenant with a back problem.[11] More recently, the House of Lords has further limited the meaning of prejudicial to health. In *Oakley v Birmingham CC*,[12] the layout of a house (the nearest washbasin to the toilet was the kitchen sink, creating risk of cross-infection) was held not to be prejudicial to health within the meaning of s 79(1)(a) of the Environmental Protection Act 1990, because there was no particular feature which in itself was prejudicial to health in that it was a source of infection or disease. It has been suggested that the reasoning in the decision was based on the policy of limiting the burden of expenditure on landlords,[13] but the effect has been to limit protection of health to containment of disease for the purpose of a large number of public health statutes.

The Public Health Act 1936 provides authorities with powers that go beyond the protection of health. Activities may also be controlled under the Act when they constitute a nuisance. No definition of nuisance is provided in the statute, but it is recognised that 'a nuisance coming within the meaning of the Public Health Act 1936 must be either a public or private nuisance as understood by common law'.[14] This raises two points of interest: first, the meaning of common law nuisance and its relevance to health, and secondly the relevance of private as distinct from public nuisance in the context of legislation dedicated to public health.

A nuisance at common law includes both damage to land and things on land,[15] and interference with the enjoyment of land.[16] Common law nuisance is a land protecting tort concerned with the value of land to persons with legal interest in land title, and there has long been resistance to expansion of the tort from protection of purely proprietary rights to protection of personal interests.[17] Common law nuisance is also limited to escapes (noise, smoke, vibrations) from land within one title to land within

10 *Coventry CC v Cartwright* [1975] 1 WLR 845.

11 *R v Bristol CC ex p Everett* [1999] Env LR 587.

12 (2000) unreported, 30 November.

13 See Baker, A, 'Statutory nuisance redefined' (2000) 122 SJ 1142.

14 *National Coal Board v Thorne* [1976] 1 WLR 543, *per* Watkins J.

15 *St Helen's Smelting Co v Tipping* (1865) 11 HL Cas 642.

16 *Harrison v Southwark and Vauxhall Water Co* [1891] 2 Ch 409.

17 See, eg, *Hunter v Canary Wharf* [1997] AC 655.

another, and provides no remedy where harm results on the land containing the nuisance. The inclusion of nuisances which present no health risk in legislation purporting to focus on public health suggests a primitive correlation between maintenance of health and defective premises in the hope that improvements will, causally or coincidentally, result in improvement in health.

The difficult distinction between public and private nuisance parallels the distinction between public health and private medicine. As public health can include both the profile of health as well as an accumulation of threats to the health of individuals, so a public nuisance might be either an interference with some public right[18] or an accumulation of private nuisances.[19] An interference with the land rights of a single land owner, or even a group of individual land owners,[20] does not fall within public nuisance. The public nature of public nuisance has made it inappropriate for individual personal injury claims. It has been suggested that the tort of negligence is the better form of action in the case of harm to individual persons and that 'personal injury cases should altogether be excluded from the domain of nuisance'.[21]

The inclusion of public nuisance in public health legislation is difficult enough to justify given that nuisance is more about land rights than health. The inclusion of private nuisances suggests that public health legislation is in reality no more than a collection of laws on statutory nuisance with incidental relevance to public health.

English public health legislation does not have as its primary focus the promotion of health, nor does it particularly address the causes of ill health. The concern is with inadequate premises, on an understanding that ill health results from identifiable bodies escaping from a physical source. This understanding dates from scientific identification of germs in relation to disease, and early 20th century public health became the containment of germ producing sources. The Public Health Act 1936 does no more than identify different types of premises that are thought should be subject to control,[22] and has actually served to prevent challenges to harmful activities

---

18 Eg, the blocking of a public right of way on a river: see *Rose v Miles* (1815) 4 M & S 101; or a road: see *Hubbard v Pitt* [1976] QB 142.

19 Eg, when a whole neighbourhood suffers from an escape of a substance that interferes with enjoyment of land: see *AG v PYA Quarries* [1857] 2 QB 169.

20 See *Halsey v Esso Petroleum* [1961] 1 WLR 683; *Gillingham BC v Medway Dock Co Ltd* [1993] QB 343.

21 *Hunter v Canary Wharf Ltd* [1977] AC 655, *per* Lord Goff; see also Newark, F, 'The boundaries of nuisance' (1949) 65 LQR 480.

22 Eg, sanitary conveniences, drains, water wells and cisterns.

by implying that compliance with the Act constitutes a defence to any common law action in nuisance or *Rylands v Fletcher*.[23]

Much of the Public Health Act 1936 has now been subsumed into the Environmental Protection Act 1990 which is aimed at the protection of the environment (defined as air, water and land)[24] rather than protection of the person. Harm is defined to mean 'harm to the health of living organisms or other interference with the ecological systems of which they form part and, in the case of man [*sic*], includes offence caused to any of his senses or harm to his property'.[25] The relationship between environment and health is complex. Is public health important because of the way it affects the world's environment, or is the environment important because of its consequences for public health? Public health legislation has prioritised the environment, and issues of health are addressed in this context.

Following the 1936 Act came a series of Acts either amending or extending the provisions of the 1936 Act,[26] or operating in parallel to public health legislation,[27] until the next major attempt at addressing public health in the Public Health Act 1961. This is neither a replacement nor a consolidation, but rather a further addition to the collection of public health legislation. The Act reflects no change in approach, continuing to add individual sources of nuisance such as roller skating rinks and derelict petrol tanks, without questioning the nuisance/public health correlation. Further statutes followed covering public lavatories,[28] fire precautions,[29] pollution control,[30] sports safety,[31] refuse disposal,[32] and local government powers in relation to public health,[33] all on the statutory nuisance model.

The final piece of legislation dedicated specifically to public health is the Public Health (Control of Disease) Act 1984, incorporating and expanding on disease provisions in the Public Health Act 1936. The philosophy of the 1984 Act makes some concession to developments in epidemiological science in that the Act no longer addresses only the physical sources of

---

23 In *Smeaton v Ilford Corporation* [1954] Ch 450, the Public Health Act 1936, s 31 provided a complete defence to an action in relation to sewage under *Rylands v Fletcher*.

24 Environmental Protection Act 1990, s 1(2).

25 *Ibid*, s 1(4).

26 The Public Health (Drainage of Trade Premises) Act 1937.

27 Such as the Prevention of Damage by Pests Act 1949 and the Local Government (Miscellaneous Provisions) Act 1953.

28 Public Lavatories (Turnstiles) Act 1963.

29 Fire Precautions Act 1971.

30 Control of Pollution Act 1974.

31 Safety of Sports Grounds Act 1975.

32 Refuse Disposal (Amenity) Act 1978.

33 Local Government (Miscellaneous Provisions) Act 1976; Local Government (Miscellaneous Provisions) Act 1982.

disease, but looks also to people as disease carriers. Five notifiable diseases[34] are identified which give rise to reporting obligations and powers of compulsory testing and exclusion. The legislation complies with the common law requirement of consent to treatment, providing only exceptionally for forcible removal and detention and not at all for forcible treatment. The Act makes no provision for funding or facilities for treatment of disease, or for right of access to treatment.

Since the 1984 Act, there have been other statutes which more or less directly pertain to public health[35] and which respond to particular public health crises. An example is the Food Standards Act 1999, passed in response to the Government White Paper on food safety[36] prepared after the considerable media attention given to food scares (salmonella in eggs, listeria in cheese). The stated aim of the legislation is to restore public confidence in food and to protect public health in relation to food, but once again the focus is on containment of sources of food infection.

The sum total of domestic public health legislation is a collection of *ad hoc* responses to particular threats to health as they are identified by science or public outrage, supported by a body of statutory instruments which are revoked as crises fade from public attention.[37] These *ad hoc* responses do not always take account of other responses such that legislation overlaps, or displaces rather than solves the health threat. The common feature of all the public health legislation is that it deals not with health, nor with the causes or consequences of ill health, but with individual identified nuisances. The majority of legislation continues to have as its objective the control of the physical sources of nuisance or control of activities that might result in nuisances. Some of the public health Acts actually say very little about public health. Health measures are tagged onto law aimed at protection of the environment, diluting the importance of health law and shaping health law in the mould of environmental law. Whereas there has been some co-

34 Cholera, plague, relapsing fever, smallpox and typhus. Section 16 of the Act provides powers to local authorities to direct that other diseases be notifiable.

35 Eg, the Building Act 1984, which provides, s 1(1)(a), for 'securing the health, safety, welfare and convenience of persons in or about buildings'; the Food and Environment Protection Act 1985, which covers a range of disparate issues, not all of which relate to public health, the Fire Safety and Places of Sport Act 1987, the Environment and Safety Information Act 1988, the Environmental Protection Act 1990, the Radioactive Material (Road Transport) Act 1991, the Water Industry Act 1991, the Noise and Statutory Nuisance Act 1993, the Clean Air Act 1993, the Environment Act 1995, the Dogs (Fouling of Land) Act 1996, the Noise Act 1996, the Pesticides Act 1998, the Road Traffic Reduction (National Targets) Act 1998, and the Pollution Prevention and Control Act 1999.

36 *The Food Standards Agency: A Force for Change*, Cm 3830, 1998, London: HMSO.

37 Eg, the Food Protection (Emergency Prohibition) (Oil and Chemical Pollution of Salmon and Migratory Trout) Order 1996 SI 1996/856, and the Food Protection (Emergency Prohibitions) (Oil and Chemical Pollution of Salmon and Migratory Trout) (Revocation) Order 1996 SI 1996/1212.

ordination and integration of legislation relating to protection of the environment, there has been no overall assessment and restructuring of legislation on health.

Public health legislation is negative in its approach, tackling issues detrimental to health and assuming health to be an absence of disease, rather than positive in working to create a healthy physical and social environment. The body of legislation includes statutes over a century old, drafted at a time of a very different understanding of the causes of ill health, while health sociology and health science have moved on to sophisticated explanations of health behaviour. There may be good political and economic reasons for persisting with a simplistic disease approach to public health. Containment of disease is relatively cheap and politically uncontroversial. It does not recognise poverty, inequality, class, race, gender and geography as determinants of health and so does not raise potentially expensive and fraught questions about distributive justice in the allocation of health resources. By relying on unsophisticated science and ignoring sociological causes of ill health, the law is able to propose simple and inexpensive measures in answer to complex health problems. The most common manifestations of serious ill health today are not cholera, smallpox or infection from drains and refuse, but cancer, heart disease and stroke, AIDS and drug abuse. Little in the existing public health legislation addresses these conditions.

The inadequacy of domestic public health law and policy has been recognised. The Acheson Committee Report[38] on public health noted that there was no clear understanding of the role and responsibilities of public health officials, and that this resulted in part from the complexity and incoherence of public health legislation. Further research on public health resulted from this report[39] and there is ongoing consideration of possible solutions,[40] but public health policy continues to focus on containment of disease rather than to address health. This jurisdiction is not alone in inheriting public health laws which no longer reflect health risks in the modern world. Other countries are in the process of their own overhaul of law[41] in recognition that law has a powerful part to play in facilitation of a population's health.

38 Acheson, D (Sir), *Public Health in England: The Report of the Committee of Inquiry into the Future Development of the Public Health Function*, 1988, London: HMSO.

39 Department of Health, *Review of Law on Infectious Disease Control: Consultation Document*, 1989, London: Department of Health.

40 Department of Health, *First Meeting of the Communicable Disease Strategy Group*, 1999, London: Department of Health, press release.

41 See Bidmeade, I and Reynolds, C, *Public Health Law in Australia: Its Current State and Future Directions*, 1997, Canberra: Commonwealth of Australia; Opeskin, B, 'The architecture of public health law reform: harmonisation of law in a federal system' (1998) 22 Melbourne UL Rev 338 (Australia); Gostin, L, 'Public health law in a new century'(2000) 283 Journal of the American Medical Association 2837 and 2979 (US).

Working from the present legislation and looking for appropriate amendment to the law can only constrain public health thinking. Statutory nuisance as the foundation of public health protection is no longer workable, and modern public health legislation needs to address maintenance of health through the creation of health standards. It is impossible to categorise and criminalise all behaviour which prejudices health in the modern industrial world. The creation of crimes and torts which make actionable any behaviour which impinges on accepted health standards moves the focus from the negative (limitation on activities) to the positive (recognition of health values), from individual actors to the community, from medicine to public health. Public health law must now recognise that health is not a luxury that is secondary to the requirements of economic and industrial enterprise, but a primary right belonging to each and every member of the community. A body of public health law which approaches the maintenance of health from the position of the subject of health rather than the object of health protection will accommodate recognition of the right to health.

PUBLIC HEALTH ENFORCEMENTS: MECHANISMS FOR PROTECTING PUBLIC HEALTH

An approach to public health based on control of sources of public health threats requires mechanisms of enforcement. Public health is dependent on 'the power of the State to preserve itself; the right of societal self-defence',[42] and any exercise of power must be subject to constitutional limitations. One of the primary purposes of a government in organised society is to protect the health, welfare and security of its people[43] and, reciprocally, individuals are obliged to subordinate themselves to government powers constitutionally exercised for the welfare of the community. The community has a stake in the health of its members for the economic prosperity and security of the community, and communal measures exercised by government ensure the collective goods essential to health.[44]

42 Richards, E *et al*, 'Public health law', in Wallace, R (ed), *Public Health and Preventive Medicine*, 1988, Stanford: Appleton and Lange. See also Richards, E, 'The jurisprudence of prevention: society's right of self-defence against dangerous individuals' (1989) 16 Hastings Constitutional LQ 329.

43 Tobey, J, 'Public health and the police power' (1927) 4 New York UL Rev 126.

44 Gostin, L, 'Public health law in a new century' (2000) 283 Journal of the American Medical Association 2837, p 2838.

Enforcement mechanisms may apply at individual level (such as detention of infected persons), at corporate level (by regulating the operations of the industry) and at national level (through taxation to fund health services, through regulation of health practitioners, through public services in, for example, water fluoridation). Enforcement mechanisms may take the form of a power, where there is discretion as to enforcement, or, more rarely, a duty to enforce without discretion. Rarely does public health law operate in a positive way to support activities and behaviour which contribute to the maintenance of public health.[45]

Injunctions and abatement notices

An injunction is a judicial tool used in anticipation of a public health harm, to prevent a continuing harm, or, more rarely, to require action in pursuance of a public health objective. An abatement notice is a notice served by a local authority requiring either the cessation of the harm, or steps to redress a harm. Both tools are important public health enforcement measures and are frequently used.

Injunctions have been sought, for example, to force removal of structures built on land contrary to planning laws,[46] to prevent the publication of material which would be detrimental to the health and welfare of patients,[47] to prevent pig farming methods prejudicial to health,[48] to force the removal of rubbish and decaying food under the Public Health Act 1936,[49] to evict gypsies from council land under the Public Health Act 1936,[50] and to force a local authority to comply with conditions in the construction of sewage works.[51] An injunction is usually granted pursuant to a statutory jurisdiction,[52] but an injunction may also provide an equitable remedy unattached to statute for the prevention of either a common law harm such as a private nuisance, or a crime such as public nuisance.

45 Eg, the Clean Air Act 1993, s 26, allows a local authority to make grants to assist an owner or occupier of premises subject to a smoke order to adapt property so as to reduce the consequences of smoke. The Building Act 1984, s 106 proposes powers of compensation for a person who has suffered damage as a result of the exercise of the authority's powers in relation to building works. The Public Health (Control of Disease) Act 1984 provides for compensation to any person who has sustained damage as a result of measures carried out under the Act.

46 See, eg, *Aylesbury Vale DC v Miller* (1999) unreported, where an injunction was granted against the owner of a gypsy caravan.

47 *Broadmoor Special HA v R* [2000] 1 WLR 1590.

48 *Vale of White Horse DC v Allen* [1997] Env LR 212.

49 *Wyre Forest DC v Bostock* [1993] Env LR 235.

50 *Bradford MBC v Brown* (1986) *The Times*, 18 March.

51 *AG v Wellingborough UDC* (1974) 72 LGR 507.

52 Eg, Protection from Harassment Act 1997; Environmental Protection Act 1990; Building Act 1984.

An injunction has the advantage of speed. Courts will hear applications quickly and can award the injunction to take effect immediately, before any real damage is done. The breach of an injunction amounts to a contempt of court, which is more serious than most statutory offences and can be punished with imprisonment. However, the award of an injunction is discretionary, although in the case of serious continuing nuisances an injunction is fairly readily granted unless it would cause extreme harm to either the person on whom it was imposed or to the public at large.[53] Where injunctions are not specifically allowed by statute, challenge to the injunction can result in an award of costs, and where an interim award has been made, damages against the claimant. An application for an injunction can be made at the same time as other remedies are sought, such that the injunction is an additional rather than a last resort remedy.[54]

Abatement notices must be authorised by statute. Powers and duties to issue abatement notices for removal of threats to health abound in public health statutes, particularly in relation to removal of statutory nuisances.[55] Failure to comply with an abatement notice constitutes a criminal offence and so legal aid may be granted to defend.[56] Prosecution operates on the criminal burden of proof, beyond reasonable doubt, whereas actions for an injunction at common law operate on the civil law burden of proof, on the balance of probabilities. Occasionally, an abatement notice will recognise a reasonable excuse for failure to comply[57] and the authority then has the burden of establishing that the excuse was not reasonable on an objective test of reasonableness.[58] Some provisions for an abatement notice also specify acceptable defences for failure to comply,[59] or acceptable grounds of appeal against the notice.[60] Judicial review may be sought in challenge of an

53 See *Aylesbury Vale DC v Miller* (1999) unreported, where the injunction was suspended for 12 months because of the hardship which would result to the owner of land.

54 *Hammersmith LBC v Magnum Automated Forecourts Ltd* [1978] 1 WLR 50; *Lloyd's Bank v Guardian Assurance* (1987) 35 BLR 34.

55 Statutes which contain such powers include the Public Health Act 1936; the Public Health Act 1961; the Control of Pollution Act 1974; the Public Health (Control of Disease) Act 1984; the Building Act 1984; the Environmental Protection Act 1990; the Clean Air Act 1993; the Noise Act 1996; the Party Wall etc Act 1996. Statutes which contain duties include the Environmental Protection Act 1990, s 80; the Public Health Act 1936, s 45; the Building Act 1984, s 64.

56 *R v Inner London Crown Court ex p Bentham* [1989] 1 WLR 408.

57 Eg, the Environmental Protection Act 1990, s 80(4): 'If a person on whom an abatement notice is served, without reasonable excuse, contravenes or fails to comply with ...'

58 See Bell, S and McGillivray, S, *Environmental Law*, 5th edn, 2000, London: Blackstone.

59 Eg, Environmental Protection Act 1990, s 80(7): '... it shall be a defence to prove that the best practicable means were used to prevent, or to counteract the effects of, the nuisance'.

60 Eg, Buildings Act 1984, s 70: 'Among the grounds on which an appeal may be brought ... are that it is not reasonably practicable to comply with the notice ... that the person against whom that appellant has a cause of action ought to contribute towards the expense of executing the works ...'

abatement notice,[61] but where the statute gives a right of appeal, judicial review will only exceptionally be granted where public health and safety were at risk.[62]

The abatement notice is the most common mechanism for removal of statutory nuisances and is the most effective procedure for minor health infringements. However, abatement is slow to enforce and requires a high burden of proof for conviction. It is not uncommon to use injunctions for more serious public health concerns in addition to the abatement notice.

Offences punishable by fine

Many public health statutes lay down offences which are punishable by fine calculated according to a standard scale.[63] Some statutes create an offence subject to a fine, but do not specify the level of the fine, and in such cases the fine must be within the offender's capacity to pay.[64] Some statutes impose an initial fine and then impose a further fine for continued non-compliance.[65] Prosecution for an offence punished by fine is a criminal prosecution, and offences may be subject to summary jurisdiction or indictment as specified in the legislation.

Powers of entry, detention and exclusion

Many public health statutes allow an authority to enter premises to remove a threat to health.[66] Some powers of entry are limited to 'reasonable hours',[67] or with notice,[68] or to particular hours of the day,[69] or entry by specified persons.[70] Statutes passed after the Second World War began to

---

61 *R v Falmouth and Truro Port HA ex p South West Water Ltd* [2000] 3 WLR 1464.

62 [2000] 3 WLR 1464.

63 Eg, the Party Wall etc Act 1996, s 16 imposes a fine not exceeding level 3 on the standard scale; the Noise Act 1996 and the Clean Air Act 1993 impose fines according to specified scales.

64 *R v Churchill (No 2)* [1967] 1 QB 190.

65 Eg, Building Act 1984, s 3.

66 Eg, Public Health (Control of Disease) Act 1984, ss 61 and 50; Building Act 1984, s 95; Food Standards Act 1990, s 9; Clean Air Act 1993, s 56; Noise Act 1996, s 10.

67 Building Act 1984, s 95; where the occupier is a business, any time in which the premises are open for business purposes is reasonable.

68 The Public Health (Control of Disease) Act 1984, s 61(2), requires 24 hours' notice.

69 The power to enter a canal boat under the Public Health (Control of Disease) Act, s 50, is limited to 'any time between six o'clock in the morning and nine o'clock in the evening'.

70 It is not always specified in legislation who has the power of entry; eg, the Prevention of Damage by Pests Act 1949, s 22(2), empowers 'anyone duly authorised by the Minister or local authority'.

use this mechanism more widely, when it was accepted that greater public intrusion on private life could be justified for the public good,[71] and it is only recently in an era of human rights that such powers have been questioned.

The significance of statutory powers of entry is that they can be exercised for the purposes of protecting health without a warrant, giving public health officials broader powers than the police, justified by the duty of the State to preserve the health of the public. The need to obtain a warrant for every search and entry would greatly increase both cost and delay, with detrimental consequences to health. Courts are not in a position to determine the validity of an application to search for the purposes of the many public health Acts, and it is more efficient to leave those scientific judgments to the responsible officers. Refusal of entry is a criminal offence, in which case the relevant officer will need to gain a warrant authorising entry from a Justice of the Peace,[72] and an offence will have been committed giving rise to a fine.[73] Some statutes authorise entry onto property without permission where there is serious risk to health.[74]

More rarely, there may be detention of persons who present a public health risk. Under the Public Health (Control of Disease) Act 1984 a Justice of the Peace may, on the written advice of an authorised medical practitioner, order that someone reasonably believed to be suffering from or carrying a notifiable disease be medically examined,[75] removed to a hospital,[76] or detained.[77] There is no equivalent provision requiring the person to be treated. These provisions also apply to a person with AIDS.[78]

The Public Health (Control of Disease) Act also contains powers of exclusion. Children suffering from or carrying a notifiable disease can be excluded from school[79] and from places of entertainment,[80] and workers may be prevented from attending their place of work.[81] A person with or carrying a notifiable disease cannot use public laundries[82] or libraries.[83]

---

71 See Paine, P, 'Powers of entry to private property' (2000) 144 SJ 850.

72 See, eg, Public Health (Control of Disease) Act 1984, s 61(3).

73 See, eg, *ibid*, s 63.

74 Eg, the Fire Services Act 1947, where there is an actual or suspected fire and entry is required to rescue person, property or to make the building safe. Where there is no fire, the powers cannot be used for other purposes: *Sands v DPP* [1990] Crim LR 585.

75 Public Health (Control of Disease) Act 1984, s 35.

76 *Ibid*, s 37.

77 *Ibid*, s 38.

78 Public Health (Infectious Disease) Regulations 1988, reg 5.

79 Public Health (Control of Disease) Act 1984, s 21.

80 *Ibid*, s 23.

81 *Ibid*, s 20.

82 *Ibid*, s 24.

83 *Ibid*, s 25.

It is possible that powers of entry, detention and exclusion may now be challenged under the Human Rights Act 1998 incorporating the European Convention for the Protection of Human Rights and Fundamental Freedoms, which seeks to balance individual rights and public interests. Article 8 of the Convention provides that everyone has the right to respect for private and family life, subject to intrusions necessary in the interests of public safety, for the protection of health or morals, or for the protection of the rights and freedoms of others. There must be proportionality between legitimacy of the authority's objectives and interference with private rights, and only in the absence of proportionality will the Act enable a challenge to powers.

Registration and licensing powers

An effective, although administratively expensive and cumbersome, enforcement tool in the context of public health is the licensing of activities which are potentially hazardous to health. Licensing of an activity permits revocation of the licence when terms and conditions are not met. Licensing is only effective for commercial activities where revocation of the licence has a financial sting, and in relation to recognition of professional status where revocation has career implications.

There are many and diverse examples of licensing as a control mechanism in the health context. Doctors, for example, are licensed to practise through the General Medical Council in accordance with the Medical Acts 1993 and 1988 and the Medical (Professional Performance) Act 1995, which require a register of medical practitioners[84] and provide powers of erasure and suspension from the register[85] where conditions of professional conduct are not met. The provision of private health care was until recently regulated under the Registered Homes Act 1984,[86] which required registration of residential care homes[87] (administered by the local authority) and nursing homes and mental nursing homes[88] (administered by the health authority), subject to conditions. A more comprehensive and

84 Public Health (Control of Disease) Act 1984, s 2.

85 *Ibid*, s 36.

86 As amended by the Registered Homes (Amendment) Act 1991.

87 Registered Homes Act 1984, s 1018.

88 *Ibid*, ss 23–36; see also the Nursing Home and Mental Nursing Home Regulations 1984 SI 1984/1578.

consistent regulatory system for private health care has now been established, subject to an independent regulator, the National Care Standards Commission, and with the involvement of the Commission for Health Improvement and the National Institute for Clinical Excellence.[89]

A licensing authority operates for the manufacture, testing and marketing of medicinal products under the Medicines Act 1968[90] 'to promote public health and safety'.[91] The Food Standards Agency[92] has powers of registration and licensing of food premises,[93] and power to prohibit an individual or business from selling food where there is a risk to health.[94] Acupuncture, tattooing, ear-piercing and electrolysis require registration with the local authority under the Local Government (Miscellaneous Provisions) Act 1982.[95]

Another important licensing authority is the Human Fertilisation and Embryology Authority, established under the Human Fertilisation and Embryology Act 1990. The Authority has licensing powers in relation to both infertility treatment services and embryo research and has the power to impose licence conditions in accordance with the provisions of the Act. Research with implications for public health is regulated and monitored by the Authority, and the threat of licence revocation is a powerful regulatory tool.

Licensing of activities which pose health risks represents a trade-off between the private interests of the individual or business operating the activity, and the wider public benefit of community health. Activities subject to licence tend not to be those likely to cause a direct, serious harm, but those which contribute to an environment of potential or unidentifiable risks to health. So there is less justification for serious infringement of economic rights and freedoms. The licensing compromise, with the discretion in the regulatory agency, allows for flexibility and is more acceptable to industry. Licensing also has the advantage of operating prospectively rather than retrospectively, in that the person applying for authorisation or licence must meet the conditions before the licence is issued.

---

89 Care Standards Act 2000. See *Regulating Private and Voluntary Health Care: A Consultation Document*, 1999, London: HMSO; *The Government's Response to the Health Committee's Fifth Report on the Regulation of Private and Other Independent Healthcare*, 1999, London: Department of Health.

90 See, also, the Health and Medicines Act 1988; Dentists Act 1983; Dentists Act 1984.

91 *R v DHSS ex p Organon Laboratories* [1990] 2 CMLR 49, *per* Mustill LJ.

92 Food Standards Act 1999.

93 *Ibid*, s 19.

94 *Ibid*, s 11.

95 Local Government (Miscellaneous Provisions) Act 1982, ss 14 and 15 give powers of inspection of cleanliness and qualifications.

Prohibition orders

A prohibition order is an order executed by a body authorised by statute, or by a court pursuant to statute, prohibiting certain specified activities and behaviours. The prohibition notice may apply to a single activity, or might be open ended until specified steps are taken to remedy any stated health risk. The order might be in the nature of an emergency order that is then revoked or amended by a further order. Many statutes provide powers to impose prohibition orders.[96]

The Food Standards Act 1990 provides for a prohibition order imposed by a court on a person convicted of a food offence. The enforcement authority is required to serve the prohibition order and fix a copy of the order on the outside of the premises. After an outbreak of *E coli* 0157 food poisoning, such a prohibition order was placed on a cheese production company. Hearing a challenge to the order,[97] the Court of Appeal found that the order was posted in the interests of public health, and was proportional to the nature of the risk. The Food Standards Act also contemplates emergency control orders and regular use is made of this power to deal with serious emergency threats to health.[98]

A prohibition notice is a significantly more powerful public health tool than an abatement notice or fine. The consequence of a prohibition order can be the closing down of a business or livelihood. The appeals provisions against such notices are therefore spelled out fully in the legislation.[99] The penalty for failing to comply with a prohibition notice is also more stringent and can result in imprisonment, either as laid down by statute[100] or as contempt of court. Prohibition notices tend only to be authorised where the risk to public health is identifiable, direct and imminent, justifying an infringement of individual rights and benefits.

---

96 Eg, Prevention of Damage by Pests Act 1949, s 14; Fire Precautions Act 1971, s 10; Control of Pollution Act 1974, s 23; Safety of Sports Grounds Act 1975, s 10; and Public Health (Control of Disease) Act 1984, s 42.

97 *R v Secretary of State for Health ex p Eastside Cheese Co* (2000) 55 BMLR 38.

98 Eg, the Food Protection (Emergency Prohibitions) (Paralytic Shellfish Poisoning) (No 6) Order 1995 preventing fish or scallops from being fished from a designated area, and the Food Protection (Emergency Prohibitions) (Oil and Chemical Pollution of Salmon and Migratory Trout) Order 1996 preventing salmon or trout from being fished from a designated area.

99 See, eg, Environmental Protection Act 1990, s 15; Building Act 1984, s 102.

100 See, eg, Environmental Protection Act 1990, s 23(3).

THE ROLE OF COMMON LAW IN PUBLIC HEALTH

Statutory remedies provide mechanisms for bodies with responsibility for public health. Individuals wishing to protect their own health must turn to common law, which has traditionally included both public and private law. However, the distinction between public and private law is particularly inappropriate to public health. Public health may mean in some contexts the accumulated health of individuals, and in other contexts the profile of a nation's health. There will be circumstances when only a few will suffer a public health harm, and those individuals can pursue their own private remedies. At other times, when the threat is to the health of the community, a more public legal challenge to the health threat is called for. However the remedy is framed, it is still focused on procuring a public right and benefit.

Private law remedies

There is a range of common law actions within the law of tort which enable individuals to bring actions in their own right and on their own instigation when their health is at risk.

Breach of statutory duty

Some statutes specifically allow an individual to bring a civil action where there has been breach of a duty laid down by statute.[101] These statutes envisage civil liability against the creator of the harm, rather than against public bodies responsible for regulating and monitoring harmful activities. Other statutes make clear that an individual has no right of civil action in relation to harm sustained from breach of statute.[102] Still others remain silent as to right of civil action.

In some circumstances, it is possible for a claimant to argue that a statutory duty, as opposed to a power, gives rise to a common law claim for breach of statutory duty. Such actions may be brought not only against the creator of the harm, but also against a public body with responsibility to protect against harm. It is for the court to determine whether on a true

---

101 Eg, Control of Pollution Act 1974, s 88; Environmental Protection Act 1990, s 73(6); Consumer Protection Act 1987; Electricity Act, s 39(3); Petroleum Act, s 23. In *Blue Circle Industries v Minister of Defence* [1998] 3 All ER 385 a landowner was able to sue under the Nuclear Installations Act 1965, ss 7–10 for damage to land from radioactive materials. In *Bygraves v Southwark LBC* [1990] CLY 1640, a child housed by the council in a damp and mouldy flat was able to sue under the Defective Premises Act 1972, s 4, for the asthma which resulted.

102 Eg, under the Fire Safety and Places of Sport Act 1987, s 37; Guard Dogs Act 1975, s 5(2); Medicines Act 1968, s 133.

construction of the statute, the words imply such a private right of action. Where legislation is designed to protect an identifiable class of persons, such as in employment health and safety legislation,[103] the courts have been ready to imply a civil right. Where the statute is intended to protect the health of the public at large,[104] or where the statute is regulatory or administrative in nature,[105] a civil right is less willingly applied. In *X v Bedfordshire CC*,[106] the House of Lords found that children who had suffered abuse as a result of a breach by the local authority of a duty to protect them, could not claim for breach of statutory duty because the relevant statutes established a social welfare system for the public at large. Breach of statutory duty was confined to limited and specific duties and did not apply to general administrative functions imposed on public bodies.

If all public health legislation were dedicated to public health, then *X v Bedfordshire CC* would preclude any private enforcement of statutory duties under these Acts. Actions for breach of public health duties have generally been unsuccessful.[107] However, public health legislation includes provisions on nuisance, which have given rise to successful civil claims.[108]

More significantly in relation to threats to health which fall into the category of environmental hazards regulated under EC law, the EC White Paper on Environmental Liability[109] proposes an EC Directive on civil liability for environmental damage, reflecting the 'polluter pays' principle. This would cover damage to person and property as well as significant harm to specific environments, with serious environmental hazards attracting strict liability and less serious hazards attracting fault liability.

---

103 The Health and Safety at Work Act 1974, s 47(1)(a), recognises civil liability in relation to health and safety regulations, but not in relation to general duties imposed by the Act.

104 See *Cutler v Wandsworth Stadium* [1949] AC 398, where a statute making it an offence to exclude bookmakers from a dog-racing track was held to be for the benefit of the public at large and so provided no right of civil action.

105 As in *R v Deputy Governor of Parkhurst Prison ex p Hague* [1992] 1 AC 58, where a prisoner was unable to bring a civil action based on a statute establishing an administrative legal structure.

106 [1995] 2 AC 633; see also *O'Rourke v Camden LBC* [1998] AC 188, where a released prisoner failed in an action under the Housing Act 1985 in relation to the failure of the local authority to house him.

107 See, eg, *Issa v Hackney LBC* [1997] 1 All ER 956, where children who suffered ill health after being inadequately housed contrary to Part III of the Environmental Protection Act 1990, which incorporates the relevant provisions of the Public Health Act 1936, failed in their claim because the Public Health Act was found not to confer a private right of action.

108 See, eg, *Read v Croydon Corp* [1938] 4 All ER 631, which allowed a claim to a ratepayer as a member of an identifiable class under the Waterworks Clauses Act 1847 in relation to impure drinking water; and *Sandwell MBC v Bujok* [1990] 1 WLR 1350, where a neighbour brought proceedings under the Public Health Act 1936, s 99 (now repealed) in relation to premises in a poor state of repair.

109 2000, COM(2000)66.

Even now, protection of public health comes about because of its association with harm to the environment rather than for its own sake.

Negligence

Anyone who has suffered a public health harm as a result of negligence will have a claim for damages in the tort of negligence. It is often the case that claims are brought not only for compensation, but also in pursuance of the wider tort objectives of deterrence and education of public health risks. Many claims have been brought successfully in relation to industrial disease,[110] but these have been primarily employees suing in employers' liability where the courts have, as a question of policy, been sympathetic. Claims outside the area of employment have been less successful, either on the point of duty to take care of the claimant's health, or more commonly because the claimant could not establish any causal relationship between the defendant's behaviour and the damage. So in *Loveday v Renton*[111] the claimant failed in an action for brain damage which he claimed resulted from the pertussis vaccine,[112] and in *Reay v British Nuclear Fuels*[113] the claimants failed to establish that exposure to radiation caused a predisposition to cancer.

The problems of duty and causation make actions for non-traumatic injury and slowly deteriorating health more difficult than for traumatic injury cases.[114] This is even more so in the case of mental harm. English jurisprudence is much more attuned to compensation for injury than to risks to health.[115] Were public health to become a genuine political and social concern, the policy components of negligence law would enable the law to adapt to include recognition of ill health as a recognised harm.

There are also two particular procedural problems that arise in litigation for deterioration of health as distinct from injury. Time limitations for commencing legal action imposed by the Limitation Act 1980 can expire

110 Eg, *Bonnington Casting Ltd v Wardlaw* [1956] AC 613, in which the claimant was awarded damages for pneumoconiosis from inhalation of silica dust at work; and *McGhee v National Coal Board* [1972] 3 All ER 1008, in which the claimant was compensated for dermatitis from coal dust. In *Sparrow v St Andrews Homes* (1998) unreported, 21 May, it was accepted that an employer owes a duty of care to provide a smoke-free working environment where it was foreseeable that an employee's health would suffer from passive smoking.

111 [1990] 1 Med LR 117.

112 Although see *Best v Wellcome Foundation* [1994] 5 Med LR 81, where such a claim, in unusual circumstances, succeeded.

113 [1994] 5 Med LR 1.

114 For an examination of the approaches of law to differing types of injury and ill health see Allen, D, Hartshorne, J and Martin, R, *Damages in Tort*, 2000, London: Sweet & Maxwell, Chapter 2.

115 See Stapleton, J, *Disease and the Compensation Debate*, 1986, Oxford: OUP.

before the full implications of the damage to health and its cause are understood. This has been a difficulty in the tobacco litigation. In *Hodgson v Imperial Tobacco*,[116] patients suffering lung cancer instituted a group action against a tobacco manufacturer, but some members of the group were statute-barred because they had failed to commence proceedings within three years of knowledge of their cancer. They applied to have the time limitation disapplied under s 33(1) of the Limitation Act, but failed because the potential litigation would be both expensive and have limited chance of success. The court also held that to disapply the time bar would only encourage more cancer sufferers to attempt legal action against the tobacco manufacturers for damages.

The second problem is that English law has not fully recognised the class action which enables patients in other jurisdictions to join together to strengthen their case and save costs.[117]

Public health cases have had very limited success and, in most cases, any payout has been by way of settlement or *ex gratia* payment rather than as a result of successful legal action: for example, the litigation on thalidomide, HIV infection from blood transfusions,[118] damage from contraceptive devices, drug damage[119] and sufferers of Creutzfeldt-Jakob disease from human growth hormone[120] and BSE have all encountered substantive and procedural obstacles in their claims for compensation.

Nuisance, Rylands v Fletcher *and trespass*

Nuisance and *Rylands v Fletcher* are both essentially land protecting torts, but will allow compensation for harm to the person when that harm arises out of an infringement of land rights.

Private nuisance allows persons who have a legal interest in land[121] to sue for damages or to seek an injunction against anyone who creates or adopts a nuisance. A nuisance is a substantial interference with the beneficial enjoyment of land, including harm to property and person, and the nuisance must result from an escape of some harmful thing from the property of another. Anyone who sustains a harm to health, or whose health is threatened, can sue to prevent the harmful activity[122] even where the

116 (1999) unreported, 9 February.

117 See Allen, D, Hartshorne, J and Martin, R, *Damages in Tort*, 2000, London: Sweet & Maxwell.

118 See *Re HIV Litigation* (1990) 41 BMLR 171.

119 Eg, Opren, Debendox; see *Davies v Eli Lilley* (1987) 137 NLJ 1181 on the *Opren* litigation.

120 See *The Creutzfeldt-Jakob Disease Litigation* (1997) 41 BMLR 157.

121 *Hunter v Canary Wharf* [1997] 2 All ER 426.

122 Eg, see *Halsey v Esso Petroleum Co Ltd* [1961] 1 WLR 683, where the plaintiff sued in nuisance for harm done by oil smuts; and *Bone v Seale* [1975] 1 All ER 787, where smells from pig farming were challenged.

activity or land use causing the nuisance had been given planning approval.[123]

Public nuisance has two forms: an interference with a public right of way such as harm done by activities on a public road, or a nuisance which is so widespread that it would be unreasonable to expect an individual to bear the financial cost of challenging it.[124] Before the development of public health legislation providing criminal penalties and powers of enforcement for statutorily defined nuisances, public nuisance played an important role in the control of activities threatening public health. Most potential public nuisances are now covered by statute and there have been few recent cases in public nuisance.[125]

Rylands v Fletcher[126] is a tort which enables a claim for damages for the storage of dangerous substances which escape causing harm. Only extraordinary uses of land, where the quantity, manner and place of storage are exceptional, will qualify. The tort has the potential of providing a mechanism for individual challenge of major public health and environmental threats,[127] and the extraordinary or 'non-natural' use requirement enables courts to manipulate the scope of the tort on policy grounds.

The tort of trespass may provide a remedy in certain cases.[128] The advantage of a trespass action is that the complainant does not need to have suffered any damage to bring the action. The fact of the trespass is itself enough.[129] The trespass must, however, be direct in that it passes spatially and temporally straight from the trespasser to the claimant. So oil spillage from a tanker which drifted slowly to shore and polluted the claimant's property was not held to be sufficiently direct,[130] but sewage released into a river so that the force of the flowing river brought it straight up onto the claimant's land was a trespass.[131]

---

123 *Wheeler v Saunders Ltd* [1995] 2 All ER 697.

124 *AG v PYA Quarries* [1965] 2 QB 169.

125 Though see *AB v South West Water Services Ltd* [1993] 1 All ER 609, where a contaminated water supply amounted to a public nuisance, and *Wandsworth LBC v Railtrack plc* (2000) EGCS 104, in which pigeons roosting under a railway bridge were held to be a public nuisance even though the bridge owners had done nothing to encourage the pigeons. By not removing the nuisance, Railtrack had adopted it.

126 (1866) LR 1 Ex 265.

127 See *Cambridge Water Co v Eastern Counties Leather plc* [1994] 2 WLR 53.

128 Eg, *Cook v Minion* [1979] JPL 305, where an owner of land succeeded in trespass in relation to a sewer laid by the local authority across his land.

129 See *League Against Cruel Sports v Scott* [1985] 2 All ER 489.

130 *Esso Petroleum v Southport Corporation* [1956] AC 218.

131 *Jones v Llanwrst UDC* [1911] 1 Ch 393.

Unfair dismissal

Employment law also provides protection against unhealthy working environments. In *Masiak v City Restaurants*,[132] a restaurant chef who was dismissed when he refused to cook chicken which was a health hazard to customers claimed unfair dismissal under the Employment Rights Act 1996. The Employment Appeals Tribunal took into account European law in relation to health[133] to find that the chef was entitled to consider the health of the public in his decision whether to obey an employer's orders. An employee forced to work in an office where other employees smoked sued successfully for unfair dismissal when her employer failed to find her a working environment which did not compromise her health.[134]

Public law remedies

Public law enables individuals to challenge the decisions and activities of public bodies. Unlike private law, which usually requires an individual to have suffered a harm to have status to sue, public law mechanisms allow individuals affected by decisions of public bodies to challenge those decisions without the need to prove harm. Public law is not concerned with whether the public body has acted in the most appropriate way or made the best decision, but rather with whether the public body has acted appropriately and in accordance with procedural requirements. Public law cannot be used to reopen substantive arguments, but only to question the way in which the decision was made or the action carried out. In the context of health care decisions, the most commonly used mechanism is judicial review, seeking either a declaration that a decision was not properly made, or an injunction restraining a public body from continuing with an activity or implementing a procedure. The court may also grant an order of certiorari to quash an administrative decision that fails to comply with procedural requirements,[135] a prohibition order to prevent a statutory authority from exercising its power, or an order of mandamus forcing a statutory body to carry out its statutory duty.

132 [1999] IRLR 780.

133 Directive 89/391.

134 *Waltons v Morse v Dorrington* (1997) IRLR 488.

135 Eg, *R v Merton, Sutton and Wandsworth HA ex p Perry* (2000) unreported, 31 July, in which applicants were successful in an action to quash a decision by the health authority to move patients out of a long-stay hospital into community care because the health authority had failed to take into account in their decision some material considerations such as promises made to residents, and statements of policy. A similar, but unsuccessful, application was made in *R v Barking and Dagenham LBC ex p Marie Lloyd* (2000) unreported, 31 July.

Judicial review has been used to challenge health resource allocation decisions. In *R v Secretary of State for Social Services ex p Hincks*,[136] patients waiting for orthopaedic treatment challenged a decision not to go ahead with the building of a new hospital wing on the grounds that the Secretary of State was in breach of his duty under the National Health Service Act 1977.[137] The Court of Appeal found that the duties of the Secretary of State to provide health services had to be read in the context of the resources available, and the question of resources was a political and economic decision of the government in power and not of the court. Other such claims have been similarly unsuccessful. In *R v Secretary of State ex p Walker*,[138] the parents of a baby in need of heart surgery failed to obtain a declaration that a further decision to postpone surgery because of staff shortages was unreasonable. The Court of Appeal applied the public law *Wednesbury*[139] principle of unreasonableness, such that a declaration would be granted only where the decision was so unreasonable that no reasonable body could have decided in that way. A declaration was similarly refused in the challenge by Jamie Bowen of the refusal by Cambridge AHA to offer her further cancer treatment.[140]

However, judicial review was used successfully to challenge a decision by the North Derbyshire HA not to fund treatment with the drug beta-interferon for a patient with multiple sclerosis.[141] The Authority had placed a blanket ban on prescribing the drug on grounds of expense, in contravention of a public statement by the Secretary of State that no effective clinical treatment would be excluded from NHS provision as a matter of principle, and in contravention of a circular[142] issued by the NHS Executive requesting that beta-interferon be made available for treatment of multiple sclerosis. The treatment refusal was considered in the light of this wider background, and it was held that any departure from NHS policy had to be justified with clear reasons. Application for judicial review was also successful in *North West Lancashire HA v A, D and G*[143] in the case of a challenge by a group of transsexuals of a blanket decision not to provide

---

136 (1980) BMLR 93.

137 'It is the Secretary of State's duty to continue the promotion in England and Wales of a comprehensive health service designed to secure the improvement ... in the prevention, diagnosis and treatment of illness', s 1; 'It is the Secretary of State's duty to provide throughout England and Wales, to such extent as he considers necessary to meet all reasonable requirement, hospital accommodation ...', s 3.

138 (1992) 3 BMLR 32; see, also, *R v Central Birmingham HA ex p Collier* (1988) unreported, 6 January on similar facts, but where the urgency of the operation was greater. This claim also failed.

139 *Associated Provincial Picture Houses v Wednesbury Corporation* [1948] 1 KB 223.

140 *R v Cambridge AHA ex p B* (1995) 23 BMLR 1.

141 *R v North Derbyshire HA ex p Fisher* [1977] 8 Med LR 327.

142 Executive letter EL (95)97.

143 [1999] Lloyd's Rep Med 399.

transgender surgery. The Court of Appeal accepted that rationing priorities were necessary where resources were limited, but held that there must be clear and rational health funding policies which are subject to exception for an individual meritorious case.

Judicial review has been used to challenge provision of social services under the Chronically Sick and Disabled Persons Act 1970,[144] to challenge decisions by the Advertising Standards Authority and the Independent Reviewer of the Advertising Standards Authority on unsubstantiated health claims in advertising of health products,[145] to challenge eviction of gypsies,[146] to challenge an abatement notice issued under the Environmental Protection Act 1990,[147] and to challenge a refusal by a local authority to exercise its power under the Road Traffic Regulation Act 1984 to restrict traffic where there was a danger to the public.[148]

In *R v Secretary of State for Health ex p United States Tobacco International*,[149] the manufacturer of snuff sought judicial review of a decision by the Secretary of State to make regulations under the Consumer Protection Act 1987 banning snuff, after research had indicated a link between oral snuff and cancer. The declaration was granted on grounds of procedural unfairness because the applicant should have been given an opportunity to respond to a major change in policy. However, arguments based on economic hardship to the applicant would not have outweighed public health interests. In *R v Hammersmith Hospitals NHS Trust ex p Olantunji Reffell*[150] a foreign visitor applied unsuccessfully for judicial review of a decision to charge him for non-emergency medical treatment. It was held that the hospital had acted within its discretion under the National Health Service (Charges to Overseas Visitors) Regulations 1989. In *R v*

144 *R v Gloucester CC ex p Barry* (1997) 36 BMLR 69. The challenge was unsuccessful because the decision was dictated by limited resources. However, see the dissenting judgment of Lord Lloyd, who argues that resource arguments do not make the claimant's needs disappear.

145 *R v Advertising Standards Authority ex p Matthias Rath* (2000) unreported, 6 December. The claim was unsuccessful because the claimants had access to the advertising guidelines of the British Code of Advertising and Sales Promotion. The decisions of the bodies were necessary for the protection of health in that the advertisements were misleading, and so the rulings did not contravene the freedom of expression components of Art 10.2 of the European Convention on Human Rights.

146 *R v Essex CC ex p Curtis* (1992) 24 HLR 90. The application was unsuccessful because the authority had not acted with perversity or unreasonableness.

147 *R v Falmouth and Truro Port HA ex p South West Water* [2000] 3 All ER 306. The application was successful because the abatement notice was invalid within the powers provided by the Act.

148 *R v Greenwich LBC ex p W (A Minor)* [1997] Env LR 190. The application failed because on a true interpretation of s 14 of the Act, the authority only had such powers where the risk of harm was caused directly by vehicles or pedestrians.

149 [1992] 1 All ER 212.

150 (2000) unreported, 16 July.

Secretary of State for Health ex p Wagstaff,[151] relatives of the deceased patients of Dr Harold Shipman successfully challenged a decision by the Secretary of State that the independent inquiry into the doctor's practice should be held in private. Relatives had not been consulted on whether they desired privacy. Prisoners who objected to prison rules on the service of meals in cells successfully challenged a decision by the prison governor in *R v Governor of HM Prison Frankland ex p Russell*.[152]

Judicial review may also result in an injunction to restrain continuing action. In *R v Humberside FHSA ex p Moore*,[153] two chemists applied to the Humberside FHSA to establish a chemist's shop in a village. The GPs in the village, who had been authorised to provide pharmaceutical services, successfully sought an injunction restraining the FHSA from considering the chemist's application without taking into account their representations. Other such applications have been sought to require the local authority to divert a sewer from a claimant's property,[154] and to stop an NHS trust from housing adult mental patients in a neighbouring house.[155] In *R v Secretary of State for Health ex p Imperial Tobacco Ltd*,[156] tobacco companies unsuccessfully sought an interim injunction to prevent the government from implementing a European Directive banning tobacco advertising,[157] arguing that the legal validity of the Directive was questionable.[158]

Judicial review is more likely to provide an appropriate remedy where a group of people is affected rather than an individual. Legal aid is rarely available for judicial review actions[159] and the losing side is likely to be responsible for costs unless the court considers that the case was brought in the public interest.[160] The time limits for seeking judicial review are short; any claim must be made 'promptly'[161] and any unjustified delay is likely to result in refusal to hear the application.

151 (2000) unreported, 20 July.

152 (2000) unreported, 10 July.

153 [1995] COD 343.

154 *Weaver v Yorkshire Water Authority* [1981] CLY 2874. The application failed on the grounds that the Water Act 1973, s 16 already provided the applicant with a civil remedy.

155 *Brown v Heathlands Mental Health NHS Trust* (1996) 31 BMLR 57. The injunction was not granted, as public law was an inappropriate remedy for enforcing private rights in land.

156 (2000) unreported, 7 December.

157 Directive 98/43/EC.

158 It was held by the House of Lords that the relevant law governing the award of the injunction was European law rather than national law, since the issue was common to other European States.

159 *R v Legal Aid Area No 8 (Northern) ex p Sendall* [1993] Env LR 167.

160 As in *R v Secretary of State for the Environment ex p Greenpeace Ltd* [1994] Env LR 401.

161 CPR Ord 53, r 4(1).

Any applicant seeking judicial review must also establish standing to make the application. Where the applicant's health is put directly at risk, this is not a problem, but where judicial review is being sought for a more general threat to public health, standing becomes an issue.[162] A recognised interest group which has gone on record as committed to a particular cause may have standing even if individual members of the group are not at particular risk,[163] and an increasing number of patient groups[164] have formed to challenge health decisions and research funding. Such groups may well be able to use public law remedies in a concerted way to place limits on the powers of public health bodies.

The fusion of public and private law

Nowhere has the private/public law distinction become more blurred than in the area of public health. In a series of treatment cases beginning with *Re F*,[165] the legality of medical treatments has been challenged before the treatment is carried out, in a form of action which has no parallel in matters other than health. In *Re F*, the issue was the legality of sterilisation of an adult woman with severe mental disabilities. A declaration that sterilisation without consent could be lawful was made, and the principles embodied in *Re F* were then formalised into a Practice Note from the Official Solicitor[166] setting out guidelines for seeking a declaration in relation to non-consensual sterilisation. Similarly, in *Airedale NHS Trust v Bland*,[167] where the family and doctors of a patient in a persistent vegetative state asked for authorisation to withdraw life sustaining treatment, the withdrawal was authorised, and the case paved the way for a series of cases on withdrawal of treatment,[168] culminating in a Practice Note regularising the form of application.[169] Competent patients have also been able to seek a declaration

162 See *R v North West Leicestershire DC ex p Moses* (2000) unreported, 12 April, where an individual challenge to the extension of an airport runway was not considered because the applicant lived too far from the airport to be directly affected. However, see also *Gillick v West Norfolk and Wisbech HA* [1986] AC 112, where the mother of teenage girls was allowed to challenge a government circular which envisaged contraceptive treatment of teenage girls without their parents' consent.

163 Eg, Greenpeace was recognised as having standing in relation to a challenge to the thermal oxide processing plant at Sellafield; see *R v Inspector of Pollution ex p Greenpeace Ltd No 2* [1994] 4 All ER 329.

164 Eg, the Justice Awareness Basic Support Group (JABS), which is challenging some infant vaccinations such as MMR on the grounds that the health risks of vaccination have not been sufficiently researched.

165 *Re F (Mental Patient: Sterilisation)* [1990] 2 AC 1.

166 Practice Note: Official Solicitor: Sterilisation [1996] 2 FLR 111.

167 [1993] 1 All ER 821.

168 See *Frenchay Healthcare NHS Trust v S* [1994] 2 All ER 403; *Swindon and Marlborough NHS Trust v S* [1995] 3 Med LR 84; *Re D* (1997) 41 BMLR 81; *Re H* (1997) 38 BMLR 11.

169 [1996] 2 FLR 375.

that treatment could not be administered without their consent,[170] so creating precedent guidelines for doctors and hospitals as to when treatment can be legally administered. As a result of individual claims by patients, the patient's family and/or treatment staff, a more general legal framework for health provision is developed. These cases have been significant in their contribution to public health law.

Another area of overlap between public and private law is action by individuals against public bodies for failure properly to exercise public powers. Although there have been some successful claims framed in the tort of negligence,[171] other cases have rejected any duty of care in relation to exercise of a power on policy grounds.[172] Many such actions have been brought in circumstances that would normally have been appropriate for an application for judicial review, resulting in an 'interface of public and private law obligation'.[173] Public bodies are already constrained by political and administrative accountability such that subjecting them to further private accountability may inhibit their effectiveness.

Where a claim in negligence is based on failure to exercise a power, the courts have approached the claim as if it were an application for judicial review. In *X v Bedfordshire CC*,[174] which considered five separate actions against public bodies, one claim was by children who sought damages for the failure of the local authority to take them into care. The public law principle of *Wednesbury* unreasonableness was applied – were the actions of the authority so unreasonable that they fell outside its discretion?

Where the claim relates to a positive exercise of a power, courts have used the third, policy, component of the three stage test for determination of duty of care[175] to find that policy rules against a duty. In another claim in *X v Bedfordshire CC*, a child complained that she had suffered harm from being taken unnecessarily into care. It was held that for reasons of policy, it would be inappropriate and impracticable to hold psychologists and social workers liable in negligence for decisions they had made in pursuance of their powers. Actions against the Crown Prosecution Service for time served in remand by prisoners,[176] against the Health and Safety Executive for unnecessarily closing down a business,[177] and against a local authority in

170 *Re T* [1992] 4 All ER 649.

171 Most notably in *Anns v Merton LBC* [1977] 2 All ER 492, where an action succeeded for failure of the local authority to exercise powers under the Public Health Act 1936.

172 See, eg, *Murphy v Brentwood DC* [1990] 2 All ER 908; *X v Bedfordshire CC* [1995] 2 AC 63.

173 *Per* Lord Nicholls, *Stovin v Wise* [1996] AC 923, p 928.

174 [1995] 2 AC 633.

175 The three stages are determination of foreseeability of harm, determination of proximity between claimant and defendant, and determination of whether the actions of the defendant were fair, just and reasonable; *Caparo v Dickman* [1990] 2 AC 605.

176 *Elguzouli-Daf v Commissioner of Police* [1995] QB 335.

177 *Harris v Evans* [1998] 1 WLR 1285.

relation to sexual abuse of a child by foster parents[178] also failed on policy grounds. Where the public body has carried out its day to day operations in a negligent way, such as where a child was taken into care but badly treated by the local authority,[179] there has been no difficulty with the imposition of a duty of care.

The use of policy to protect public bodies against action by private individuals does not, however, accord with the European Convention on Human Rights. In *Osman v UK* [1999] 1 FLR 193, the family of a man murdered by a stalker took their case against the police to the European Court of Human Rights after domestic law held that police had an immunity in the exercise of police powers. The European Court held that everyone has the right to have a claim relating to civil rights heard by the court,[180] and that right was violated by an assumption of immunity.[181] The European Convention has now been incorporated into domestic law by virtue of the Human Rights Act 1998, and as a result recent cases have accepted that public bodies may be liable to individuals in the exercise of their powers. In *Phelps v Hillingdon LBC*,[182] a child sued her education authority for failing to diagnose her dyslexia. The Court of Appeal denied a right of action on the policy grounds that imposition of a duty of care would make the job of educational psychologists more difficult, and because limited education resources would be wasted in defending future claims. The case went to the House of Lords on appeal, where such policy arguments were found not to deny a duty. Similarly, in *W v Essex CC*[183] the House of Lords overturned the finding of the Court of Appeal that a local authority should be immune for policy reasons from civil action in relation to the placing of a foster child. However, it remains the case that some actions and decisions of public bodies are not justiciable[184] and it will fall to future courts to determine criteria as to where a duty of care may lie.

The Human Rights Act 1998

As well as influencing the direction of English law, the Human Rights Act, which came into force in October 2000, provides remedies of its own in challenging the decisions of bodies exercising public functions. Section 6(1) of the Act provides that it is unlawful for a public authority to act in a way

178 *H v Norfolk CC* [1997] 1 FLR 384.

179 *Barrett v London Borough of Enfield* [1999] 3 WLR 79.

180 Under the European Convention on Human Rights, Art 6(1).

181 English courts have not responded enthusiastically to *Osman*. See the comments of Lord Browne-Wilkinson in *Barrett v London Borough of Enfield* [1999] 3 WLR 79.

182 [2000] 4 All ER 504.

183 [2000] 2 WLR 601.

184 See *Scott v Gloucestershire CC* [2000] 3 All ER 364.

incompatible with a Convention right and in interpretation of the Convention, courts must take into account previous decisions of the European Court of Human Rights.[185] The Act allows for both judicial review and private law claims and the court may grant relief to include damages, declarations and injunctions.[186]

Article 2 of the Convention provides that everyone's right to life shall be protected by law. This imposes on the State, and agencies of the State such as a health authority or public hospital, a positive duty to protect the life of citizens. Failure to provide adequate health resources, failure to set up cancer screening programmes, failure to provide particular life saving drugs, or failure to warn of genetic or other health risks may amount to breach of rights.[187] The unsuccessful judicial review claims challenging failure to provide health resources may need to be reviewed in the light of Article 2. Positive medical treatment such as infant vaccination which may carry a health risk, or non-medical circumcision, might fall within the Act. The treatment withdrawal cases may also be challenged as a breach of the right to life, especially where relatives do not support the medical application for withdrawal.[188] Anti-abortion arguments based on Art 2 are unlikely to be successful as the right has been interpreted as not applying to a foetus.[189]

Article 3 provides that no one shall be subjected to torture or degrading and inhuman treatment. Failure to provide proper medical treatment might fall within this article,[190] as might treatment such as leaving patients on trolleys in hospital corridors, performing unnecessary medical treatment, causing unnecessary pain, treating patients in a humiliating way, or performing experimental medical treatment.[191]

Article 5 provides that everyone has the right to liberty and security, with exceptions including the lawful detention of persons for the prevention of the spreading of infectious diseases, detention of persons of unsound mind, alcoholics, drug addicts or vagrants. Powers of detention under the Public Health (Control of Disease) Act 1984 and under the National

---

185 Human Rights Act 1998, s 2.

186 *Ibid*, s 8(1).

187 In *LCB v UK* (1999) 27 EHRR 212, it was held that the failure of the government to warn that exposure of a child's father to radiation might prejudice the child's health could potentially give rise to a breach of Art 2. On the facts, there was no breach, as the causal links between radiation exposure and cancer were not sufficiently known at the time.

188 In *Re G* [1995] 2 FCR 46 the patient's mother objected to withdrawal of life sustaining treatment, but withdrawal was authorised on the grounds that it was ultimately a medical decision.

189 *Paton v UK* (1980) 19 DR 244; *H v Norway* (1992) 73 DR 155.

190 See *Tanko v Finland* (Case 2364/94) (1994) unreported.

191 See *X v Denmark* (1983) 32 DR 282.

Assistance Act 1948[192] are probably protected by this exception. However, common law on the detention of persons with mental illness is likely to require review to avoid contravening Art 5.[193]

Under Art 8, everyone has the right to respect for his family and private life, with the exception of the exercise of the law as necessary in a democratic society in the interests of public safety and the protection of health and morals. This may have implications for medical confidentiality and medical records, as well as for the right to express one's sexuality, for example by changing sex. This article may also impose obligations on residential units to protect residents from harm.[194] However, protection of family life has not been held to give rise to a right to State funded fertility treatment or to adoption, or to the right to marriage for transsexuals or same-sex couples.[195]

Article 14, which prohibits discrimination, may have implications for allocation of resources and funding of research. Discrimination on grounds of age in relation to access to screening, priority for transplant services, withdrawal of treatment and DNR orders may breach Art 14. Funding of research for causes of disease for one sex, such as coronary heart disease in men, may also constitute a breach.

The application of the Human Rights Act to public health will warrant a rethinking of many public health policies. Any intrusion on the rights of individuals must be proportional to the public benefit obtained. Much public health law has developed on the assumption that individual rights will always be subject to public benefit, and as this jurisdiction has had no constitutional statement of rights, rights-based arguments in challenge of public health policies have been difficult to support. The Human Rights Act will now allow individuals to frame arguments based on recognised rights, and public bodies will need to justify intrusion to uphold public health practices.

192 Section 47 allows for the detention of an aged, infirm, incapacitated or seriously ill person who is not receiving proper care.

193 See Chapter 11 by Gill Korgaonkar.

194 In *X v Netherlands* (1985) 8 EHRR 235, the failure to protect a mentally handicapped woman from sexual assault was found to breach Art 8.

195 See *X v UK* (1997) 24 EHRR 143.

THE LEGAL FRAMEWORK OF PUBLIC HEALTH SERVICES IN ENGLAND AND WALES: HEALTH PROVISION, HEALTH PROMOTION AND HEALTH SURVEILLANCE

Early provision of medical services in England and Wales was professionally controlled and offered on a private or a charitable basis. The present English health care system, establishing publicly provided health services, was introduced in 1948 by the National Health Service Act 1946. This Act envisaged three faces of health provision: primary care services, hospital services and community care services, and that division continues to characterise domestic health provision.

The foundation for the modern NHS is the National Health Service Act 1977. Section 1 of this Act provides that it is the duty of the Secretary of State:

> ... to continue the promotion in England and Wales of a comprehensive health service designed to secure the improvement –
>
> (a) in the physical and mental health of the people of those countries, and
>
> (b) in the prevention, diagnosis and the treatment of illness
>
> and for that purpose to provide or secure the effective provision of services ...

The services anticipated by s 3 of the Act include, to such extent as the Secretary of State considered necessary to meet all reasonable requirements,[196] hospital accommodation, other accommodation for health purposes, medical, dental, nursing and ambulance services, facilities for expectant and nursing mothers and young children, facilities for the prevention, diagnosis and treatment of illness, and the care of persons suffering from illness and aftercare services. Other duties specified in s 5 include provision of contraceptive services and medical monitoring of school children.

Reorganisation of the health service was introduced by the National Health Service and Community Care Act 1990 which now stands alongside the 1977 Act to provide the legal framework of health provision. Motivations for the changes brought about by the 1990 Act were both financial and political; financial in response to increases in cost to the service,[197] and political in response to prevailing political philosophy which favoured greater independence of public services.[198] The 1990 Act, following the

---

196 And subject to the financial resources available to him, *R v Secretary of State for Social Services, West Midlands RHA and Birmingham AHA ex p Hincks* (1980) 1 BMLR 93, *per* Lord Denning MR.

197 Resulting from expansion in the public perception of what constitutes medical treatment, from expensive medical technology and from escalation in clinical litigation.

198 See Chapter 2 by Robyn Martin.

Government White Paper *Working for Patients*,[199] introduced an internal market to NHS provision, simulating within a public service the behaviour and competition of private enterprise in order to improve efficiency of output. The principles that the health service should be funded mainly from taxation, that treatment should be free at the point of delivery,[200] and that access to treatment should be based on need, were preserved.

More significant than the details of the restructuring introduced in the 1990 Act was the new market philosophy that permeated the changes. The NHS was no longer presented to the public as a public service, but rather as a quasi-private service. The consequence was that patients no longer felt they had to be grateful and uncomplaining about the charitable service they were offered, and began to expect merchantable quality as for any other contracted service. Expectations of standard were raised, and reinforced by the Patient's Charter, which formally introduced to patients the language of rights. The internal market approach to organisation of health services changed once and for all patient attitudes to the NHS, and the financial savings made by greater efficiency and competition within the service were more than balanced by the increased costs of litigation by dissatisfied patients.[201]

The National Health Service and Community Care Act 1990, as its name suggests, placed much greater emphasis on community care than previous legislation. The Act incorporated recommendations of the Government White Paper *Caring for People, Community Care in the Next Decade and Beyond*.[202] Anyone in need of community services has a right to request to have that need assessed for entitlement to services,[203] and the availability of able voluntary (family) carers is taken into account. However, unlike medical services provided within the NHS, community care services provided by the local authority need not be provided free of charge, and the authority can recover the cost of services on a means tested basis.

The distinction between health and social services means that social services are excluded from the premise of publicly available care, free at the point of delivery. This is significant in the context of the changing nature of medical treatment. While it was once the case that patients were, on the whole, either cured by medical treatment or died, modern medicine is more

199 Cm 555, 1989.

200 Subject to the Road Traffic (NHS Charges) Act 1999, which allows some recoupment of the cost of treating victims of road accidents from persons legally responsible for the injuries, and the NHS (Charges to Overseas Visitors) Regulations 1989 SI 1989/306.

201 See Harpwood, V, 'The manipulation of medical practice', in Freeman, M and Lewis, A (eds), *Law and Medicine Current Legal Issues*, 2000, Oxford: OUP, Vol 3.

202 Cm 849, November 1989. Proposals included accommodation for the physically and mentally incompetent, support for the disabled in the community, care for the elderly, and plans outlining treatment of the chronically ill. See also the Chronically Sick and Disabled Persons Act 1970.

203 National Health Service and Community Care Act 1990, s 47.

likely to result in the survival of patients who are not, and cannot, be cured. Cancer patients and patients with heart disease can survive for many years with their disease. Patients severely disabled by accident or stroke may have a long life expectancy during which they hope to resume some normal life. The need for community care is very much greater now than it was at the establishment of the health service, and indeed the balance of need between treatment of traumatic injury and disease, and treatment of chronic injury or disease, has begun to weigh more heavily in favour of the latter. It is ironic, then, that it is this greater health need which has been removed from the funded agenda.

Most treatment now provided by the NHS is for individual medical treatment, while those issues of health which fall within the wider domain of public health are no longer NHS priorities and are regarded as primarily the responsibility of social services, charities and the family. At the same time, there has been concern at the breaking down of the traditional family structure, and this is particularly the case in relation to the three-generation family. Care of the elderly is no longer seen as a duty within the family, and yet it has been eased out of the responsibility of the health service and left to float among other government and non-government organisations. The National Health Act 1977 requires that health authorities co-operate with local authorities 'in order to secure and advance the health and welfare of the people',[204] but criteria for determination of which authority is finally responsible for the individual chronically ill person is not clear.

A classification of a treatment as medical brings it within the responsibility of the NHS and is provided free of charge. A classification of the treatment as social care means that it will be means tested and charged for. Guidelines issued by the NHS Management Executive to district health authorities[205] in 1992 distinguished between general and specialist nursing care such that general nursing care was to be purchased by social services while health services would be prepared to pay for specialist nursing care, and guidelines issued in 1995[206] further delineated the two. The distinction is not always obvious. In *White v Chief Adjudication Officer*,[207] Ralph Gibson LJ, considering the status of hospital care for a group of long term mentally ill patients, said:

> I acknowledge that if the provision of nursing care by professionally trained nurses in an institution is minimal, as for example only rarely expected to be required, such an institution may not be a hospital. In this case, however, the 14 patients are mentally ill. They require appropriate nursing for and because of their illness ... I would hold that Forest Lodge is a hospital ...

204 National Health Service and Community Care Act 1990, s 22.

205 (1992) HSG (92) 50.

206 (1995) HSG (95) 8.

207 (1994) 14 BMLR 68.

The Court of Appeal looked at the distinction again in *R v North and East Devon HA ex p Coughlan*[208] and excluded some nursing care from the responsibility of the NHS, but only that nursing care required in the way of care and attention which genuinely falls within s 21 of the 1990 Act. The simplistic distinction between general and specialist nursing care was rejected as idiosyncratic: '[t]here can be no precise legal line which can be drawn between those nursing services which are and those which are not capable of being treated as included in such a package of care services'.[209] The issue is not always easily resolved, especially in the case of elderly patients slipping into senility, and it remains unclear how the lay term 'illness' is to be separated into medical illness and community illness other than on administrative, political and financial grounds.

The 1990 NHS and Community Care Act reflected the political philosophy of the government in power at the time. One of the consequences of the 1990 Act was greater patient dissatisfaction with the NHS, and the new Labour Government in 1997 was quick to address the public image of the health service, issuing a series of Government White Papers with ambitious titles,[210] followed by the Health Act 1999 introducing further restructuring of services. The Health Act, along with the National Health Service (Primary Care) Act 1997, provides a significantly greater role for primary care in the provision of health services.[211] In conjunction with the National Health Service (Private Finance) Act 1997, the Health Act also enables private financing and ownership of public hospitals, and a number of plans have been approved. Plans for similar private financing of primary care are being considered.[212] The line between primary and secondary care which underpinned earlier NHS legislation is no longer clearly drawn, and it is now the case that hospitals may in some circumstances provide primary care treatment and vice versa.[213]

The Health Act inserts into s 28 of the 1977 Act a provision making clear that where the functions of a local authority 'have an effect on the health of

208 [1999] Lloyd's Rep Med 306.

209 *Per* Sedley LJ.

210 *A First Class Service: Quality in the New NHS*, White Paper, 1999, London: HMSO; *The New NHS: Modern and Dependable*, Cm 3807, 1999; *Designed to Care*, Cm 3811, 1999; *Putting Patients First*, Cm 3841, 1998.

211 GPs are now members of primary care groups and may become members of primary care trusts with responsibility for their own funds. It will be possible under the new 'pilot' arrangements for GPs to form a private limited company with shares owned by those engaged in the NHS. See Newdick, C, 'The NHS in private hands? Regulating private providers of NHS services', in Freeman, M and Lewis, A (eds), *Law and Medicine Current Legal Issues*, Vol 3, 2000, Oxford: OUP.

212 *The Government's Expenditure Plans 1999–2000*, Cm 4203, 1999, London: Department of Health; see Newdick, C, 'The NHS in private hands? Regulating private providers of NHS services', in Freeman, M and Lewis, A (eds), *Law and Medicine Current Legal Issues*, 2000, Oxford: OUP, Vol 3.

213 National Health Act 1977, s 28E, as amended by the Health Act 1999.

any individuals', an NHS body may make payments to the local authority for services. Similarly, a local authority may make payments to the NHS. This at least gives some protection to patients requiring community, rather than medical care. The power to pass funding between authorities is only a power, but it facilitates a more co-ordinated approach to the treatment of a person who needs to move between community and medical care. The Act does not, however, resolve the question of who is responsible for the person who is not in need of traumatic medical treatment, but who moves between residential, nursing and medical care. This issue remains one of the weaknesses of contemporary health legislation.[214] The 1999 Government Report, *With Respect to Old Age: Long Term Care – Rights and Responsibilities*,[215] addressed funding of long term care on the premise of 'the importance of shared responsibilities between the individual and the State',[216] recognising the confusion and inefficiency in current law and practice. 'Modernisation' of the system was proposed, recommending that long term care should be split between living costs, housing costs and personal care. A National Care Commission is to monitor demographic trends, spending, transparency and accountability. In line with the Report, the Government has promised to invest an extra £900 m in care to facilitate changes in responsibility between health and social services.[217] Meanwhile, the Care Standards Act 2000 imposes on private health care and nursing homes standards of health provision which are subject to monitoring and enforcement.

A further matter included in the Health Act 1999 in response to patient complaints about quality of service is enforcement for clinical governance mechanisms. The Act imposes on NHS trusts and primary care trusts a statutory duty of quality[218] parallel to the common law duty of care, requiring trusts to establish plans for monitoring and improving health care in accordance with principles of clinical governance.[219] Mechanisms such as evidence-based medicine, audit and risk management strategies will

---

214 See Newdick, C, *Who Should We Treat? Law, Patients and Resources in the NHS*, 1995, Oxford: Clarendon; and Henwood, M, *Through a Glass Darkly: Community Care and Elderly People*, 1992, London: King's Fund.

215 Sutherland, S (Sir), *With Respect to Old Age: Long Term Care – Rights and Responsibilities*, Report by the Royal Commission on Long Term Care, 1999, London: HMSO.

216 Point 11, Introduction.

217 Health Secretary Alan Milburn, *NHS Plan Sets Out Radical Programme of Reform* 'The NHS plan: a plan for investment. A plan for reform', press release, September 2000.

218 'It is the duty of each Health Authority, Primary Care Trust and NHS Trust to put and keep in place arrangements for the purpose of monitoring and improving the quality of health care which it provides to individuals': s 18.

219 'A framework through which the NHS organisations are accountable for continuously improving the quality of their services and safeguarding high standards of care by creating an environment in which excellence in clinical care will flourish.' *A First Class Service: Quality in the New NHS*, White Paper, 1999, London: HMSO.

implement quality control. Guidelines on best practice will be issued by the National Institute of Clinical Excellence,[220] a special health authority responsible to the Health Secretary overseen by the Commission of Health Improvement.[221]

The quality provisions of the Health Act focus on issues of clinical treatment rather than health in any wider sense. The sorts of activities subject to control will be medical technologies (screening, communications, PRODIGY),[222] prescriptions (drugs, rationing) and treatments (diagnosis, treatment effectiveness). There is, however, reference in the Health Act 1999 and in government papers to improving the health of the population beyond the administration of medical treatment. All doctors will be required to participate in the four national confidential inquiries[223] to enable fully representative national standards on causes of death to be formulated. The National Institute for Clinical Excellence will be responsible for national service frameworks on particular aspects of health care[224] in which professional standards will be set and monitored. The Commission for Health Improvement is to provide national leadership and to conduct national reviews of health care services. More significantly, the Government Green Paper *Our Healthier Nation*[225] proposes tackling the root causes of avoidable illness beyond the medical and into the social (poverty, geography, inequality, smoking, diet, drugs). Much of the paper, as with other proposals, is in the language of rhetoric ('Connected problems require joined-up solutions'),[226] but there is for the first time a recognition that health and medical treatment are not identical. Access to medical treatment may be necessary for health, but it is not sufficient.

The Health Act 1999 is, in reality, primarily a Clinical Treatment Act, but it is not impossible, following the Green Paper, that we could one day see a genuine Health Act providing a legal framework for a service committed to public health.

220 Established under the National Institute for Clinical Excellence (Establishment and Constitution) Order 1999 SI 1999/220.

221 For a detailed account of the workings of these bodies see Harpwood, V, 'The manipulation of medical practice', in Freeman, M and Lewis, A (eds), *Law and Medicine Current Legal Issues*, 2000, Oxford: OUP, Vol 3.

222 'Prescribing rationally with decision support in general practice study', computer software program giving prescription advice.

223 Monitoring death resulting from surgery, suicides, maternal deaths and neo-natal deaths.

224 The four areas presently covered are mental health care, care of the elderly, diabetes and coronary heart disease.

225 Cm 3852, 1998.

226 Point 1.12.

CONCLUSION

Domestic public health law, and responsibility for public health implementation, is fragmented. Public health legislation has developed as a collection of responses to individual health risks as they are recognised by health science, focused almost exclusively on the biological causes of disease to the exclusion of social causes. The body of public health law is composed of a complex and uncoordinated patchwork of technical rules aimed at individual sources of health risk, and representing a sociological and scientific approach to public health that is outdated. Enforcement of public health law falls to a wide range of disparate public bodies, and to the willingness of individuals and pressure groups to bear the costs of instituting legal action to protect public health interests. Public health legislation says little about most major contemporary public health concerns, in part because contemporary causes of ill health do not fit easily into the category of statutory nuisance. As public health legislation has not moved on from early 20th century nuisance jurisprudence, it has not been able to accommodate ill health that results from lifestyle. The nuisance premise of public health legislation is no longer workable. A new approach to the legal framework of maintenance of public health based on health standards, focusing on the right to health of the population rather than on premises and activities which threaten health, is long overdue.

The legal framework of health provision is also complex and uncoordinated and consists of a number of statutes, standing side by side, but reflecting very different political and social philosophies. Responsibility for the long term management and care of ill health, as distinct from treatment of traumatic injury and disease, falls through gaps in the legislative net. Responsibility for health promotion and maintenance lies at the fringes of health provision, resulting in a legislative structure more attuned to medical treatment than to public health.

The health of the community must ultimately be the responsibility of government, and the government has authority to enact and enforce laws that serve to maintain health subject to individual rights. The nature and extent of that responsibility will be dependent on public perception of health risks and public acceptance of the subjugation of private interests to the public good. Public attitudes can be influenced by public health education, and responsible public health advocacy is necessary to achieve a balance between State intrusion for public benefit on the one hand, and private economic and social rights on the other. The legal framework which supports both public interference and private rights needs to reflect that balance, or a surfeit of challenging litigation will result making laws ineffective and inefficient. Public health law and the agenda behind it must be clear, logical and comprehensible to the population to reach a public consensus in pursuit of public health. Domestic public health law as it stands fails to meet these requirements, and so does not fulfil its potential as a public health tool.

Several factors will serve to force change to the domestic legal framework of public health. The introduction into domestic law of the European Convention on Human Rights will enable individuals to challenge laws which unjustifiably intrude on private rights. More co-ordinated legal responses to public health threats at international and European level will increasingly filter down into domestic law. Changing public attitudes to health risks, recognition of individual responsibility for health behaviour, patient rights, increased public awareness of health issues from the media and internet, and changes in the doctor/patient power relationship, will result in greater public participation in health policy. Individuals are no longer prepared to accept government assurances that public health measures are 'for your own good', as the public response to the MMR vaccine illustrates.[227]

There is a political awareness that domestic public health law does not effectively serve the health of the nation. Repeal and replacement of all domestic law on public health is a mammoth and daunting task. Before it can begin, there must be a co-ordinated domestic health policy so that the law can effectively implement public health objectives and initiatives. Preparation of that policy has begun, but is in its infancy, and it has been hindered by lack of public health scholarship in this jurisdiction. What is important is that any new public health law framework reflects contemporary philosophy on the causes of ill health, and is aimed at protection of the public from health risks rather than limiting the consequences of health hazards.

227 There has been a significant drop in take-up of the trivalent measles, mumps and rubella vaccine despite government safety assurances. Media coverage of the concerns of both health researchers and of public interest vaccination groups has resulted in individuals determining the risk/benefit of the vaccination for themselves. See Chapter 10 by Stephanie Pywell.

CHAPTER 4

THE ROLE OF INTERNATIONAL HEALTH LAW AND THE WHO IN THE REGULATION OF PUBLIC HEALTH

Yutaka Arai-Takahashi

INTRODUCTION

Article 55 of the United Nations (UN) Charter states that the promotion of 'higher standards of living' and 'solutions of international ... health, and related problems' is one of the primary objectives of the UN. Representatives of 61 States signed the WHO Constitution in July 1946 at the International Health Conference in New York. In April 1948, the World Health Organization (WHO) began its function as a specialised agency of the UN replacing its predecessor, the Health Organization of the League of Nations (HOLN), which existed during the inter-war period. Today, the WHO is one of the largest specialised agencies with six regional offices, more than 190 Member States and an annual budget of more than $800 m.[1]

While the WHO is not the sole organ tackling issues of health at an international level,[2] its 'directing and co-ordinating' role in global health as

1 As to the WHO and its approach to international law, see Allin, N, 'The AIDS pandemic: international travel and immigration restrictions and the World Health Organization's response' (1988) 28 VJIL 1043; Bélanger, M, 'The future of international health legislation' (1989) 40 International Digest of Health Legislation (IDHL) 1; Fidler, D, 'Return of the fourth horseman: emerging infectious diseases and international law' (1997) 81 Minnesota L Rev 771; 'The future of the World Health Organization: what role for international law?' (1998) 31 Vanderbilt J Trans L 1079; 'International law and global public health' (1999) 48 Kansas UL Rev 1; Fidler, D, *International Law and Infectious Diseases*, 1999, Oxford: OUP; Fluss, S, 'International public health law: an overview', in Detels, R *et al* (eds), *Oxford Textbook of Public Health*, 3rd edn, 1997, New York: OUP, p 371; Forrest, M, 'Using the power of the World Health Organization: the International Health Regulations and the future of international health law' (2000) 33 Colum JL and Social Problems 153; Godlee, F, 'WHO in crisis' (1994) 309 BMJ 1424; 'WHO reform and global health – radical restructuring is the only way ahead' (1997) 314 BMJ 1359; McCarthy, B, 'The World Health Organization and infectious disease control: challenges in the next century' (2000) 4 DePaul Int'l LJ 115; Sharp, W, 'The new World Health Organization' (1947) 41 AJIL 509; Taylor, A, 'Making the World Health Organization work: a legal framework for universal access to the conditions for health' (1992) 18 AJIL Med 301; 'Controlling the global spread of infectious diseases: toward a reinforced role for the international health regulations' (1997) Hous L Rev 1327; Vignes, C, 'The future of international health law: WHO perspectives' (1989) 40 International Digest of Health Legislation 16. See also 'International legal developments in review: 1997, public international law, international health law' (1998) 32 International Lawyer 539.

2 Other main specialised agencies dealing with health issues include the Food and Agriculture Organization (FAO) and the United Nations Environmental Program (UNEP).

envisaged in its Constitution undoubtedly makes it the central focus of any appraisal of the nature and role of international health law.[3] Article 1 of the Constitution describes the primary objective of the WHO as 'the attainment by all the peoples of the highest possible level of health'. The Preamble of the Constitution defines health as 'a state of complete physical, mental and social well-being and not merely the absence of disease or infirmity'. It also takes cognisance of a human rights approach to health, asserting that '[t]he enjoyment of the highest attainable standard of health is one of the fundamental rights of every human being without distinction of race, religion, political belief, economic or social condition'. It is worth noting that the right to the highest attainable standard of health as formulated in this provision has been adopted as the definition of the right to health in other international human rights treaties.[4]

THE INSTITUTIONAL ORGANISATION OF THE WHO

The WHO consists of three main organs. The World Health Assembly (WHA), consisting of delegates of Member States, forms the supreme decision making body of the WHO. It meets in Geneva every May to discuss proposals and programmes in response to global health issues. Its legislative function includes the power to make two types of binding rules – treaties (or agreements)[5] and regulations[6] – and it additionally has the function of devising non-binding rules such as recommendations, principles and guidelines.

Secondly, the Executive Board is the administrative arm of the WHO, comprising 32 individuals technically qualified in the field of health. Membership is determined by Member States on three year terms. The Board meets at least twice a year with a main meeting in January and a second shorter one in May, just after the Health Assembly. The principal tasks of the Executive Board are to give effect to the decisions and policies of the WHA and to provide it with technical advice and expertise.

3 WHO Constitution, Art 2.

4 See, eg, the International Covenant on Economic Social and Cultural Rights (ICESCR) 1966, Art 12 ('the right ... to the enjoyment of the highest attainable standard of physical and mental health'). Compare also the African Charter on Human and Peoples' Rights 1981, Art 16(1) ('the right to enjoy the best attainable state of physical and mental health') as well as the Additional Protocol to the American Convention on Human Rights in the Area of Economic, Social and cultural Rights, or the Protocol of San Salvador, Art 10(1) ('the enjoyment of the highest level of physical, mental and social well-being').

5 WHO Constitution, Art 19.

6 *Ibid*, Art 21.

The third principal body is the Secretariat, headed by the Director General and staffed by about 3,800 health and other experts working at the Geneva headquarters and six regional offices.[7] The Director General is appointed by the World Health Assembly on nomination by the Executive Board. As with other international organisations and with the United Nations itself, election of both the Executive Board and the Director General is highly politicised, determined more by the political weight, interests and rivalry of Member States than personal merits of the candidates. The election of the current Director General, Dr Gro Harlem Bruntland in 1998, bridging the traditional divide between Western industrialised countries in the North and developing countries in the South, raised the hope that she would put an end to the political and financial scandals which plagued the WHO under the leadership of the previous Director General.[8]

WHAT IS INTERNATIONAL HEALTH LAW?

International health law may be defined as the body of public international legal instruments aimed at the protection and enhancement of human health.[9] Fidler summarises the inherently interdisciplinary nature of international health law:

> Just as domestic public health law cannot be easily contained within a single legal area, international law relating to health spreads across virtually every aspect of international relations. In short, 'international health law' goes far beyond what WHO may adopt under its international legal powers and involves diverse international legal regimes developed in different contexts by different international and nongovernmental organizations.[10]

The origin of international health law can be traced to the European diplomatic initiative in the 19th century to regulate quarantine and control

---

7 The six regional offices are the Regional Office for Africa (AFRO), Regional Office for the Americas/Pan American Health Organization (AMRO/PAHO), Regional Office for South East Asia (SEARO), the Regional Office for Europe (EURO), the Regional Office for the Eastern Mediterranean (EMRO) as well as the Regional Office for the Western Pacific (WPRO). There are other research-related offices, such as the Centre for Health Development in Kobe (WCK), the International Agency for Research on Cancer (IARC) and the Onchocerciasis Control Programme (OCP). Further, the WHO has offices in Washington and at the UN, OAU and EU.

8 In this respect, many commentators refer to the internal politics surrounding the previous Director General, Dr H Nakajima, who was supported by the coalition of Asian and African countries against a candidate nominated by Western nations. However, under his leadership there were a number of financial scandals. See Godlee, F, 'WHO in crisis' (1994) 309 BMJ 1426.

9 Bélanger, M, 'The future of international health legislation' (1989) 40 International Digest of Health Legislation 1, p 1.

10 Fidler, D, 'International law and global health' (1999) 48 Kansas UL Rev 1, p 39.

of infectious and communicable disease. The concern of European powers of the time was not, however, to tackle universal health problems, but rather to prevent the spread to Europe of contagious diseases considered as originating from outside Europe such as cholera and yellow fever. The underlying rationale was to safeguard Europeans, as opposed to other 'non-civilised' people in Asia and Africa, from infections at the height of European imperialism and colonial exploitations. There was also need for international regulation of national measures of quarantine in order to minimise the restrictive effect of national prohibitions on international trade and travel. The most important measure consisted of a series of international sanitary conventions between 1892 and 1938. The first International Sanitary Conference was held in Paris in 1851 and adopted an aborted treaty, 'a convention and regulations designed to bring some uniformity into quarantine practice'.[11] It was only in 1892 that the first successful international treaty, the International Sanitary Convention applicable to cholera, was adopted, paving the way for a further treaty on measures against plague in 1897. A parallel move in the Americas to devise international treaties to counter infectious disease yielded the Inter-American Sanitary Convention, first adopted at the Inter-American Sanitary Conference in Washington, DC in 1905.[12] Just as in the European context, this initiative was primarily motivated by the US to defend itself against microbial invasion from its Southern 'non-civilised' Latin American countries. As regards international agreements on infectious disease control adopted between 1898 and 1938, it has been observed that '[w]hile WHO has been accused of focusing too little on international law, international relations immediately prior to World War II were plagued by too much international health law'.[13]

Such diplomatic and law making efforts prompted European and North American States to appreciate the need for permanent institutions to conduct surveillance of international sanitary conventions. The first decade of the 20th century saw the establishment of two permanent international health organisations, the International Sanitary Bureau (Washington DC, 1902)[14] and L'Office International d'Hygiène Publique (OIHP) (Paris, 1907). After the First World War, the institutionalisation of international health law culminated in the establishment of the Health Organization of the League of

11 This treaty did not, however, come into force: Fidler, D, 'The future of the World Health Organization: what role for international law?' (1998) 31 Vanderbilt J Trans L 1079, pp 1083–84.

12 This treaty was replaced by the 1924 Pan-American Sanitary Code.

13 Fidler, D, 'The future of the World Health Organization: what role for international law?' (1998) 31 Vanderbilt J Trans L 1079, p 1083.

14 This was later renamed the Pan-American Sanitary Bureau and then the Pan-American Sanitary Organization, and it was a predecessor of the Pan-American Health Organization (PAHO), which today serves as the WHO's Regional Office for the Americas.

Nations (HOLN) (Geneva, 1919) as an umbrella organ of the League of Nations. Since then, the significance of OIHP has been overshadowed by HOLN. As well as institutions dealing with human infectious disease control, the international community created the International Office of Epizootics (Paris, 1924) to cope with animal diseases.[15]

The end of the Second World War and the creation of WHO did not mark a complete watershed in the history of international health law, evidenced by the fact that the International Health Regulations (IHR) prepared by WHO incorporated the main provisions of the previous international sanitary conventions.[16] After all, as Sharp notes, WHO owes its operational effectiveness to the considerable expertise and experience of its precursors in health matters.[17] However, Bélanger points out that there exist three characteristics of modern international health law which distinguish it from earlier international regulation of health.[18] First, contemporary international health law is truly global in nature, with both international organisations and non-governmental organisations involved in its formation and implementation. Secondly, its principal emphasis is positive action such as vaccination, immunisation and other preventative mechanisms in developing countries. Thirdly, the potential of modern international health law is enhanced by the extensive scope of WHO's 'quasi-legislative' power to regulate any matters falling within its competence. Matters falling within the scope of international health law are diverse, ranging from the traditional control of communicable diseases to social and occupational issues such as alcoholism, tobacco consumption, narcotics, occupational disease, and accident.[19] Yet, whether this potentially wide ambit of regulatory power has been actually exercised is another matter, and will be examined below.[20]

One can attribute this conceptual shift in the nature of international health law to evolution of modern international relations. The independence and growing assertiveness of developing countries in Asia and Africa have dramatically changed the geopolitical landscape of international relations since the Second World War, injecting new dynamism and diverse value

15 Fidler, D, 'The future of the World Health Organization: what role for international law?' (1998) 31 Vanderbilt J Trans L 1079, pp 1084–85. See also the treaties designed to co-ordinate international action on plant diseases: the 1878 Convention between Austria-Hungary, France, Germany, Portugal and Switzerland Respecting Measures to be Taken Against *Phylloxera Vastatrix* (153 Consol TS 247) and the International Convention for the Protection of Plants 1929 (126 LNTS 305).

16 Bélanger, M, 'The future of international health legislation' (1989) 40 International Digest of Health Legislation 1, p 2.

17 Sharp, W, 'The new World Health Organization' (1947) 41 AJIL 509, p 511.

18 Bélanger, M, 'The future of international health legislation' (1989) 40 International Digest of Health Legislation 1, pp 2–3.

19 *Ibid*, p 4.

20 See p 134.

systems into what used to be a Eurocentric international law. The emphases of newly independent States on the principle of self-determination, on people's rights and on the new international economic order, have significantly influenced the progressive development of treaty making in areas such as international environmental law, economic law and the law of the sea. In the area of health, preference for second generation human rights, namely social, economic and cultural rights, has been central to strengthening the status of the right to health both in practice and in academic discourse.[21]

Another explanation for this conceptual shift may be provided by a distinct feature of post Second World War international relations, the expansion of intergovernmental and non-governmental organisations and their political force in the field of global health. Technological innovation and improved communications have facilitated closer liaison and co-operation between national organs and civic groups across borders, and have led to an emerging sense of common values within a global civil society in the area of health.[22]

If one accepts WHO's broad definition of health, international health law can be identified in other domains of law such as human rights, labour, trade, environment, medicine and consumer protection law. Multiple treaties concluded by international organisations other than WHO include health-related matters essential for the physical and mental integrity of individuals. Among them, the International Committee of the Red Cross (ICRC), one of the oldest international organisations, has been actively involved in development of international humanitarian law touching on health and sanitary matters during warfare,[23] as well as in training of doctors and other health personnel in peace time.[24]

21 The so called 'generations of human rights' consist of three types of human rights: civil and political rights as the first generation of human rights, economic, social and cultural rights as the second generation, and the rights of peoples (such as the right of self-determination and the right to development) as the third generation. However, it is not desirable to draw a rigid line between generations of human rights, as they must be deemed as 'indivisible and interdependent and interrelated': the Vienna Declaration and Programme of Action 1993, I, para 5.

22 Fidler, D, 'The future of the World Health Organization: what role for international law?' (1998) 31 Vanderbilt J Trans L 1079, p 1119.

23 The foremost important achievements of the ICRC include the adoption of the four Geneva Conventions 1949 (Geneva Convention I for the Amelioration of the condition of the Wounded and Sick in Armed Forces in the Field; Geneva Convention II for the Amelioration of the Condition of Wounded, Sick and Shipwrecked Members of Armed Forces at Sea; Geneva Convention III Relative to the Treatment of Prisoners of War; and Geneva Convention IV Relative to the Protection of Civilian Persons in Time of War) as well as the two Geneva Protocols 1977 (Geneva Protocol I Additional to the Geneva Conventions of 12 August 1949, and Relating to the Protection of Victims of International Armed Conflicts; and Geneva Protocol II Additional to the Geneva Conventions of 12 August 1949, and Relating to the Protection of Victims of Non-International Armed Conflicts).

24 The ICRC's annual training course, the 'HELP' (Health Emergency in Large [contd]

Assertiveness in law making powers can be seen in the initiatives of international and regional organisations in pursuance of human rights in the context of health. The International Covenant on Economic, Social and Cultural Rights (ICESCR), adopted under the auspices of the UN in 1966, guarantees the right to health under Art 12, obliging States to take concrete measures to enhance citizens' health. At regional level, the Council of Europe incorporated the right to health in its European Social Charter 1961 and, more recently, adopted the Convention for the Protection of Human Rights and Dignity of the Human Being with regard to the Application of Biology and Medicine (Convention on Human Rights and Biomedicine) in 1997. Human rights approaches to health can be seen in other regional human rights treaties, such as the African Charter on Human and Peoples' Rights 1981[25] adopted under the Organization of African Unity, and the Additional Protocol to the American Convention on Human Rights in the Area of Economic, Social and Cultural Rights 1988 (Protocol of San Salvador),[26] drafted under the auspices of the Organization of American States.

Moreover, as the BSE crisis and the outbreak of foot and mouth disease in Europe demonstrate, issues of international health are closely intertwined with those of international trade. The primary purpose of the trade system developed under the General Agreement on Tariffs and Trade (GATT) (1947) was to promote free trade in goods through reduction or elimination of trade barriers. The adoption of the Final Act of the Uruguay Round and the Marrakesh Agreement Establishing the World Trade Organization (WTO) 1994 has considerably enlarged the regulatory scope of the GATT/WTO regime, encompassing such diverse issues as trade in services and intellectual property. The GATT system does not prevent contracting parties from adopting measures pursuant to public health and environmental policies. But, once implemented, by virtue of the national treatment requirement of Art III, such measures must treat imported like products no less favourably than domestic goods.[27] If policy objectives based on public health cannot be achieved in a manner compatible with

---

24 [contd] Population) organised in tandem with the WHO and Geneva University's Faculty of Medicine, attracts a number of doctors and other health staff from all over the world to broaden their expertise and knowledge in such areas as planning, epidemiology, nutrition, sanitation, infectious diseases, emergency, training of local personnel, co-ordination of health programmes and the protection of war victims: Russbach, R, 'The International Committee of the Red Cross and health' (1987) 260 Int Rev Red Cross 513, p 520.

25 African Charter on Human and Peoples' Rights, Art 16.

26 Protocol of San Salvador, Art 10.

27 Correa, C, 'Implementing national public health policies in the framework of WTO agreements' (2000) 34 Journal of World Trade 89, p 91; Jackson, JH, *The World Trading System – Law and Policy of International Economic Relations*, 2nd edn, 1997, Cambridge, Mass: MIT Press, p 233.

Art III, States can invoke Art XX(b) to make exceptions to the general requirements embodied in GATT on the condition that an exceptional measure does not constitute 'a means of arbitrary or unjustifiable discrimination ... or a disguised restriction on international trade'.[28] However, public health concerns of States are not adequately addressed under Art XX. The principle of proportionality enjoins a State relying on Art XX to choose the least trade restrictive measure available, and this requirement would often tip the balance in favour of free trade,[29] leaving national governments with 'little room to design and implement public health measures'.[30]

Of special importance to public health issues is the Uruguay Round Agreement on Sanitary and Phytosanitary Measures (SPS Agreement), which deals with measures to protect human, animal or plant life or health from micro-organisms and pests, as well as from risk arising from additives, contaminants, toxins or disease-causing organisms in foods, beverages or feedstuffs. Under Art 2.2 of the SPS Agreement, a Member State may introduce measures to protect human and animal life or health based on 'scientific principles'. If there is a scientific justification, or if it is determined to be appropriate in harmony with the risk assessment, a State can also, as guaranteed in Art 3.3, adopt a measure which results in a higher level of protection than would be achieved by international standards. The public health objectives are reinforced by the incorporation of the precautionary principle in Art 5.7, enabling States to take a provisional SPS measure on the basis of available information, even where relevant scientific evidence is insufficient. A notable advantage of employing the GATT/WTO system is its mandatory third party adjudication and appellate review, 'a historically unique "legalization" of international relations',[31] and its unitary dispute settlement procedure for trade disputes arising from GATT and most of the Uruguay Round codes, including the SPS Agreement. Not adopted under the GATT/WTO regime, but a source of potential conflict with the SPS Agreement, is the Cartagena Biosafety Protocol, which was adopted in 2000

28 Article XX reads as follows: 'Subject to the requirement that such measures are not applied in a manner which would constitute a means of arbitrary or unjustifiable discrimination between countries where the same conditions prevail, or a disguised restriction on international trade, nothing in this Agreement shall be construed to prevent the adoption or enforcement by any contracting party of measures ... (b) necessary to protect human, animal or plant life or health.'

29 This can be demonstrated in the *Thai Cigarette* case, where the GATT panel found that least trade restrictive alternative than an import ban of cigarettes imposed by Thailand would be available to pursue public health objectives: *Basic Instruments and Selected Documents*, 37th Supp 200; Correa, C, 'Implementing national public health policies in the framework of WTO agreements' (2000) 34 Journal of World Trade 89, p 93.

30 *Ibid*, p 96.

31 Petersmann, E-U, 'How to promote the international rule of law? Contributions by the World Trade Organization Appellate Review System' (1998) 1 Journal of International Economic Law 25, pp 33–34.

in response to growing concern among consumers over the commercialisation of genetically modified organisms (GMOs) or living modified organisms (LMOs), including most notably transgenic seeds.[32]

Some may see the development of a body of regional health law, the involvement of other branches of international law with public health issues and other institutional authorities as a threat to the unitary and effective operation of international health law.[33] Yet this is inevitable, given that health cannot be examined in isolation. Operational effectiveness of international health law should not be considered to be compromised by the overlap of different regulatory regimes. It is against this backdrop that WHO needs to assume a leadership role and co-ordinate national and international health-related treaties and regulations, setting standards and allocating functions as appropriate.

SOURCES OF INTERNATIONAL HEALTH LAW

The sources of international health law must be evaluated in light of those of public international law. According to Art 38 of the Statute of the International Court of Justice, custom, treaties and general principles of law constitute the primary sources of international law. There also exist subsidiary sources such as judicial decisions and international publicists' views. Given the paucity of international judicial decisions on issues of health, any endeavour to obtain insight into the nature of international health law will need to focus on primary sources of law.

There exist two requirements in order for custom to be identified as international law: there must exist a general and consistent State practice over time; and State practice must be accompanied by a legal sense of obligation to abide by the rule of custom (*opinio juris*).[34] Customary international law normally denotes general international law, and as such it is binding on all States except for those which persist in objecting to

---

32 As to a critical evaluation of the Cartagena Protocol from the perspectives of international economic law, see Eggers, B and Mackenzie, R, 'The Cartagena Protocol on Biosafety' (2000) 3 Journal of International Economic Law 525; Phillips, P and Kerr, W, 'The WTO versus the Biosafety Protocol for Trade in Genetically Modified Organisms' (2000) 34 Journal of World Trade 63; Qureshi, A, 'The Cartagena Protocol on Biosafety and the WTO – co-existence or incoherence?' (2000) 49 ICLQ 835; Schoenbaum, T, 'International trade in living modified organisms: the new regimes' (2000) 49 ICLQ 856.

33 Bélanger, 'The future of international health legislation' (1989) 40 International Digest of Health Legislation 1, p 4.

34 The necessity of the *opinio juris* was reconfirmed in the *North Sea Continental Shelf* cases, ICJ Rep, 1969, 3, para 72.

formation of the customary rule.[35] Just as with treaties, customary norms are based on the consensual undertaking of Sovereign States.

As regards treaties, the Vienna Convention on the Law of Treaties 1969 has codified most pre-existing customary rules governing the formation and implementation of treaties.[36] A treaty is a written agreement between States, between States and international organisations, or between international organisations themselves, and must be governed by international law.[37] The binding obligation of a treaty will not arise for a signatory State until the latter ratifies it by way of constitutional arrangements in national law, and a treaty will come into force only after a defined number of States have ratified it. States unable or unwilling to accept all obligations arising from the treaty can opt out of some provisions by attaching reservations at the time of signing, ratifying or acceding to the treaty.[38] Where treaties are silent on the permissibility of reservation, States may make only those reservations that are not of general character and not incompatible with the object and purpose of the treaty.[39] This requirement codifies the pre-existing customary rule and hence is applicable even to those States not parties to the Vienna Convention. The fact that there is no specific judicial or quasi-judicial machinery set up for settling 'disputes' as to failure of Member States to comply with WHO regulations or other legal instruments, and that the International Court of Justice is not invested with compulsory jurisdiction to adjudicate compatibility questions, means that questions of compatibility are mostly left to the discretion of Member States.

With respect to general principles of law, there are divergent views as to their meaning and status, but the prevailing opinion is to classify general principles as either general principles of (national) law or general principles of international law.[40] Classification as general principles of international law will not only overlap with customary norms, but some general principles may be considered as elevated to *jus cogens* in the hierarchy of sources of international law.[41] Classification as general principles of national

---

35 The persistent objector rule was recognised by the opposing parties in the *Anglo-Norwegian Fisheries* case, ICJ Rep 1951, p 116; Brownlie, I, *Principles of Public International Law*, 5th edn, 1998, Oxford: OUP, p 10.

36 For a thorough examination of the law of treaties, see Brownlie, I, *Principles of Public International Law*, 5th edn, 1998, Oxford: OUP, Chapter XXVI; Sinclair, I, *The Vienna Convention on the Law of Treaties*, 2nd edn, 1984, Manchester: Manchester UP.

37 Vienna Convention on the Law of Treaties 1969, Art 2(1)(a).

38 *Ibid*, Art 19.

39 This compatibility test was confirmed in the advisory opinion of the International Court of Justice in the *Reservations to the Convention on Genocide* case (1951) ICJ Rep 15, and incorporated into the Vienna Convention on the Law of Treaties, Art 19.

40 Brownlie, I, *Principles of Public International Law*, 5th edn, 1998, Oxford: OUP, pp 15–19.

41 Albeit in a circular manner, the Vienna Convention on the Law of Treaties, Art 53 defines *jus cogens* as 'a peremptory norm of general international law ... accepted and recognized by the international community of States as a whole as a norm from [contd]

law means that principles are construed so as to refer to national norms, procedural or substantive, including *res judicata* and standards of evidence.

One of the most striking features of international health law is that while treaty making efforts have been minimal or dormant over the last 50 years, indeed since the establishment of the WHO, prior to the outbreak of the Second World War there existed an abundance of international sanitary conventions and treaties dealing with diseases affecting animals and plants. Between the 1890s and 1930s, treaties played a crucial role in developing detailed rules for containing the spread of infectious disease[42] and to minimise their impact on trade and traffic. It is notable that from the outset, international health law has owed much of its derivation to treaties, and custom has played a minimal or, at most, a theoretical role. When the first International Sanitary Convention was drafted, there existed no customary rules on notification or minimum interference with commerce.[43] In contrast, other areas of international law have relied on customary rules as the main source of law, and the International Law Commission has made significant headway over the last half century, codifying existing customs and accomplishing a progressive development of international law under the auspices of the United Nations.

Even assuming that treaties have served an almost exclusive role in the formation of international health law, there remains the question as to whether customary international law has evolved from the provisions of treaties or from the International Health Regulations (IHR). In the *North Sea Continental Shelf* cases[44] and the *Nicaragua (Merits)* case,[45] the International Court of Justice recognised the co-existence of customary rules and treaties covering the same ground. In the former decision, the ICJ upheld the possibility that some treaty provisions might generate customary norms even over a short period of time. The ICJ's ruling furnished two provisos: first, there must exist 'a very wide and representative participation' in the treaty at hand and, secondly, the treaty must include the participation of 'States whose interests were specially affected'.[46] One may infer from this

41 [contd] which no derogation is permitted and which can be modified only by a subsequent norm of general international law having the same character'. For critical analysis of this concept, see Sztucki, J, *Jus Cogens and the Vienna Convention on the Law of the Treaties*, 1974, Vienna: Springer.

42 The sources of infectious diseases are the four types of agent: bacteria, viruses, parasites and fungi: Fidler, D, 'Return of the fourth horseman: emerging infectious diseases and international law' (1997) 81 Minnesota L Rev 771, p 776; and McCarthy, B, 'The World Health Organization and infectious disease control: challenges in the next century (2000) 4 DePaul Int'l LJ 115, p 118.

43 Fidler, D, *International Law and Infectious Diseases*, 1999, Oxford: OUP, pp 98–104.

44 *North Sea Continental Shelf* cases (1969) ICJ Rep 3, para 73.

45 *Military and Paramilitary Activities in and against Nicaragua (Merits)* (1986) ICJ Rep 14, paras 174–79.

46 *North Sea Continental Shelf* cases (1969) ICJ Rep 3, para 73.

that a number of rules provided in the IHR might suffice as customary norms in view of the quasi-universal participation of States in the WHO. However, it is still necessary to overcome a paradox discerned by Baxter: where a treaty governing matters not formerly covered by customary norms enjoys a wide participation of States, identifying emerging customary rules in that area would be difficult, because States may simply be acting in conformity with obligations flowing from the treaty without evidencing any *opinio juris*.[47] Fidler[48] concludes that it is intractably difficult to identify, outside the obligations emanating from international sanitary treaties and the IHR, any *opinio juris* of States in relation to such requirements as the notification duty and principle of minimum interference with trade. Frequent instances of non-compliance with International Sanitary Conventions and IHR militate against the possibility that those requirements be regarded as candidates for customary rules.[49]

THE WHO AND ITS LEGAL INSTRUMENTS: SOURCES OF MODERN INTERNATIONAL HEALTH LAW

Treaties

The WHO is empowered to adopt three types of legal instrument. Firstly, under Art 19 of the WHO Constitution, the WHA is authorised to make conventions or agreements concerning 'any matter within the competence of the Organization'. This fairly broad treaty making capacity is based on a two-thirds majority vote of the WHA, and entry into force of the treaty is subject to ratification by each Member State. Under Art 20, Member States are required to take necessary action to implement treaties or agreements within 18 months after their adoption by the WHA. All States ratifying a WHO treaty must submit an annual report to the Director General detailing action taken as well as progress in the health and well being of populations. This is a standard supervisory procedure akin to those of international human rights monitoring bodies dealing with economic, social and cultural rights.[50] Presumably, WHO treaties are dealt with in this way owing to the social and economic nature of their obligations, which are treated as having

47 Baxter, R, 'Multilateral treaties as evidence of customary international law' (1965) 41 BYIL 275, pp 298–300.

48 Fidler, D, *International Law and Infectious Diseases*, 1999, Oxford: OUP, pp 98–109.

49 *Ibid*, p 104.

50 For critical analysis of the Committee on Economic, Social and Cultural Rights, see Alston, P, 'The Committee on Economic, Social and Cultural Rights', in Alston, P (ed), *The United Nations and Human Rights, A Critical Appraisal*, 1992, Oxford: Clarendon.

not an immediate effect, but as susceptible to the 'progressive realization' approach.[51]

Regulations

The second type of legal rule binding on Member States is regulation. The power to make this innovative legal instrument is provided in Art 21 of the WHO Constitution, which assigns to the WHA five specific fields in which regulations may be adopted:

(a) sanitary and quarantine requirements and other procedures designed to prevent the international spread of disease;
(b) nomenclatures with respect to diseases, causes of death and public health practices;
(c) standards with respect to diagnostic procedures for international use;
(d) standards with respect to the safety, purity and potency of biological, pharmaceutical and similar products moving in international commerce; and
(e) advertising and labelling of biological, pharmaceutical and similar products moving in international commerce.

In 1998, the WHO's Executive Board approved recommendations from a special group that by way of amendment of the WHO Constitution, the regulatory power under Art 21 be extended to cover any matter falling within the functions of the WHO.[52] As Fidler notes, this would result in the duplication of the power to formulate binding rules, as Art 19 already provides the same general treaty making power.[53]

The WHO has so far designed only two regulations under Art 21(a) and (b). An Expert Committee on International Epidemiology and Quarantine was established to draft regulations. The first outcome was WHO Regulations No 1 on the nomenclature of diseases and causes of death (the Nomenclature Regulations). The second regulations were the International Sanitary Regulations in 1951,[54] replacing the previous International Sanitary Conventions. These Regulations dealt with diseases susceptible to quarantine, such as plague, cholera, yellow fever, small pox, louse-borne

51 See, eg, ICESCR, Art 2(1), which provides that: '[E]ach State Party ... undertakes to take steps ... to the maximum of its available resources, with a view to achieving progressively the full realization of the rights recognized in the present Covenant.'

52 World Health Organization, Review of the Constitution and Regional Arrangements of the World Health Organization: Report of the Special Group, WHO Doc EB101/7, 14 November 1997; Review of the Executive Board Special Group, WHO Doc EB101.R2, 22 January 1998.

53 Fidler, D, 'The future of the World Health Organization: what role for international law?' (1998) 31 Vanderbilt J Trans L 1079, p 1092.

54 5 WHO 5/H35/2 (1983).

typhus, and louse-borne relapsing fever. Subsequent to the amendment of these Regulations in 1969, they have been renamed the International Health Regulations (IHR), excluding louse-borne typhus and relapsing fever. The fundamental principle underlying the second Regulations is to ensure maximum security against international spread of disease with minimum interference with world traffic and trade.[55]

Just as with treaties, regulations are binding on Member States. However, there are several distinct features inherent in the regulations. First, they are adopted by way of non-rejection, and are not subject to the complex procedure of ratification normally required for treaties. As a corollary, one advantage of regulations is that they can be adopted instantly and hence are more answerable to issues arising in the field of health, where medical science and technology are in constant evolution.[56] Secondly, under Art 22, regulations adopted pursuant to Art 21 will automatically come into force for each WHO Member State unless a State clearly informs the Director General of its intention to opt out by way of reservations or rejection within a fixed period of time. The presumption of the obligatory nature ascribed to regulations is a 'unique' procedure in international law, representing a clear departure from the normal rules governing treaties.[57] These innovative legal instruments may be explained by the reflection of the founders of the WHO that the traditional *ad hoc* treaty approach was not adequate to address global health issues in the modern age.[58]

Recommendations

The third type of legal instrument is the recommendation as provided in Art 23. Over the last 50 years, the WHO has preferred to follow an approach based on recommendations rather than on binding instruments in the form of treaties or regulations.

As Vignes notes, the WHO has also adopted provisions that are not recommendations in the strict legal sense. These other 'soft' law rules include guidelines, action plans, principles and codes of practice, drawn up

55 See, eg, International Health Regulations (1969) (IHR), Foreword, para 2.

56 Vignes, C, 'The future of international health law: WHO perspectives' (1989) 40 International Digest of Health Legislation 16, p 17.

57 Fidler, D, 'The future of the World Health Organization: what role for international law?' (1998) 31 Vanderbilt J Trans L 1078, pp 1087–88; Taylor, A, 'Controlling the global spread of infectious diseases: towards a reinforced role for the International Health Regulations' (1997) Hous L Rev 1327, p 1345. See, also, Sharp, W, 'The new World Health Organization' (1947) 41 AJIL 509, p 525.

58 Fidler, D, 'The future of the World Health Organization: what role for international law?' (1998) 31 Vanderbilt J Trans L 1079, p 1088.

by expert committees.[59] There has developed a body of provisions applied by health authorities across the world, such as the International Code of Marketing and Breast-milk Substitutes, and the Expanded Programme on Immunization.[60] While recommendations and other soft law rules do not have any binding effect on Member States,[61] they command considerable respect among physicians and health services, and are widely considered as a 'standard guide' to practice,[62] or even as a body of 'quasi-binding' rules.[63] An example is the Global Programme on AIDS, comprising principles and measures for the prevention of HIV infection, the criteria for screening for HIV and methods of sterilisation and disinfection as well as encouragement of national AIDS control programmes.[64] Another illustration is the WHO's ambitious Health for All Campaign initiated pursuant to the Declaration of Alma-Ata, or 'Health for All by the Year 2000', which was adopted at the International Conference on Primary Care at Alma-Ata in 1978. The Alma-Ata Declaration emphasised universal primary health care, and this action plan has been influential on programmes designed by the UNICEF, World Bank and other international organisations.

INTERNATIONAL HEALTH REGULATIONS (IHR)

Overview of the IHR

The IHR, the second series of regulations drafted by the WHO, represent the most important health law instrument, with their purpose of ensuring 'the maximum security against the international spread of diseases with a minimum interference with world traffic'.[65] All WHO Member States except for Australia are parties to the IHR, although some countries have attached reservations to certain provisions. The health regulations are governed by the law of treaties subject to certain modifications. Article 94 of the IHR

59 Vignes, C, 'The future of international health law: WHO perspectives' (1989) 40 International Digest of Health Legislation 16, p 18.

60 This Code was originally proposed as a regulation, but instead adopted as a form of recommendation: Tomasevski, K, 'Health rights', in Eide, A, Krause, C and Rosas, A (eds), *Economic, Social and Cultural Rights – A Textbook*, 1995, Dordrecht: Martinus Nijhoff, p 134.

61 For critical analysis of the so called 'soft law' see Van Hoof, GJH, *Rethinking the Sources of International Law*, 1983, Deventer: Kluwer, pp 187–89.

62 Taylor, A, 'Making the World Health Organization work: a legal framework for universal access to the conditions for health' (1992) 18 AJL Med 301, p 317, n 111.

63 Vignes, C, 'The future of international health law: WHO perspectives' (1989) 40 International Digest of Health Legislation 16, p 18.

64 *Ibid*.

65 Foreword, IHR.

requires certified true copies of the IHR to be delivered by the Director General to the Secretary General of the UN for registration in accordance with Art 102 of the UN Charter.

The IHR create legal obligations on Member States in three main fields: the requirement of notification and epidemiological information as governed in Part II; requirements relating to health organisations at national ports, airports and other frontier posts in Part III; and a number of detailed legal duties imposed on Member States to take health measures and to follow procedures in relation to individuals, goods and means of transportation as listed in Part IV. Part V encompasses specific measures that may be applied by national authorities in relation to three specific diseases regulated by the IHR: cholera, including cholera due to *eltor vibrio*, plague and yellow fever. Article 1 of the IHR defines these diseases as 'diseases subject to the Regulations', termed as 'quarantinable diseases' prior to the 1969 amendments. The question whether the minimum interference principle of the IHR is also applicable beyond those diseases is a matter of debate.[66] Allin[67] refers to the WHO's reliance on Art 81 of the IHR[68] to declare that 'no country bound by the Regulations may refuse entry into its territory to a person who fails to provide a medical certificate stating that he or she is not carrying the AIDS virus'.[69] This can be regarded as a departure from the strict textual interpretation, but one isolated incidence cannot alter the view that there exists no customary rule requiring States to report outbreaks of infectious disease *in general*.

With respect to the notification obligations, each State health administration must report to the WHO within 24 hours after the first case of a disease subject to the IHR in its territory. It has also to notify the WHO of any infected area within the subsequent 24 hours. The reporting duty of the national health authority is extended to confirmation of the notified disease promptly by laboratory methods, subject to available resources.[70] The IHR impose on the reporting State an obligation to supplement information as to source and type of disease, number of cases and death toll, conditions affecting the spread of disease, and prophylactic measures

66 Taylor, A, 'Controlling the global spread of infectious disease' (1997) Hous L Rev 1327, p 1349.

67 Allin, N, 'The AIDS pandemic: international travel and AIDS restrictions and the World Health Organization's response' (1988) VJIL 1043, pp 1055–56.

68 IHR, Art 81, inserted in Part VI dealing with health documents, provides that: '[n]o health document, other than those provided for in these regulations, shall be required in international traffic.'

69 (1985) 60 Weekly Epidemiological Record 311.

70 IHR, Art 3.

adopted.[71] In relation to health organisations, the IHR set out rules on sanitary conditions, health personnel and services to be maintained at ports, airports and national frontier posts,[72] as well as conditions of issue of health certificates (Deratting Certificates and Deratting Exemption Certificates), including their periodic review by the WHO.[73] As Taylor notes, the IHR's emphasis on border control is based on the outmoded and even mistaken assumption that infectious disease can be contained within national boundaries.[74] This is reinforced by the argument based on 'globalisation of public health' that the traditional dividing line between national and international public health is anachronistic at a time when rapid spread of infectious diseases, facilitated by technological and transportation development, exposes the impotence of Sovereign States in protection of their citizens' health.[75]

Finally, as for health measures applicable to individuals, means of transportation, goods, cargo, baggage and mail, Taylor[76] describes three general governing principles: any measures prescribed in the IHR must be the maximum measures exercised;[77] any health measure must 'be initiated forthwith, completed without delay, and applied without discrimination';[78] and there must be free movement of persons and free *pratique* of ships and aircraft.[79] While the second principle is generally straightforward, the first and third require further examination.

The first principle is fundamental to the IHR's primary objective of maximum security against international spread of disease with minimum interference with world traffic and trade. The IHR require a national health authority to issue free of charge to a carrier a certificate specifying any applicable measures and reasons for applying the measures.[80] The first principle is reminiscent of the proportionality test inherent in European

71 IHR, Art 5.

72 *Ibid*, Arts 14, 18 and 22.

73 *Ibid*, Arts 17, 20–21.

74 Taylor, A, 'Controlling the global spread of infectious diseases: towards a reinforced role for the International Health Regulations' (1997) Hous L Rev 1327, p 1347. See also Forrest, M, 'Using the power of the World Health Organization: the International Health Regulations and the future of international health law' (2000) 33 Colum JL and Social Problems 153, p 163.

75 Fidler, D, ' International law and global public health' (1990) 48 Kansas UL Rev 1, p 9.

76 Taylor, A, 'Controlling the global spread of infectious diseases: towards a reinforced role for the International Health Regulations' (1997) Hous L Rev 1327, p 1344.

77 IHR, Art 23.

78 *Ibid*, Art 24.

79 *Ibid*, Arts 27 and 28.

80 *Ibid*, Art 26. A similar certificate must also be issued, upon request, to any traveller, consignor, the consignee and the carrier.

Community law[81] and international trade law based on the GATT/WTO system,[82] which requires that States choose means the least burdensome for free trade. In particular, the notion of proportionality assumes a key interpretative function under the Agreement of the Application of Sanitary and Phytosanitary Measures (SPS),[83] as evidenced in the *Beef Hormone* case.[84]

As for the third principle, the IHR guarantee free movement of a person under surveillance as well as free *pratique* of a ship and aircraft.[85] Free *pratique* refers to freedom of a ship to enter a port, disembark and commence operation, or of an aircraft, after landing, to disembark and commence operation.[86] Restrictions on free *pratique* cannot be authorised for diseases other than those governed by the IHR. However, Art 28 of the IHR provides the possibility of derogation from this general rule in cases of emergency.[87] This can open the way for States to impose excessive and unreasonable restrictions on trade and traffic without having to register a reservation and hence to undergo the process of WHA approval. The absence of a supervisory and enforcement system in which the legality of measures exercised pursuant to Art 28 can be scrutinised is a serious defect of the IHR. Forrest observes that '[u]ntil a mechanism is in place to compensate for unnecessary economic losses incurred because of required disease reporting, countries may not immediately provide information on major outbreaks, undermining the IHR's purpose of mitigating global disease spread'.[88]

81 Strictly, the first principle of the IHR emulates the second limb of the three pronged proportionality principle in Community law, which consists of the suitability test, the necessity (the least restrictive alternative or LRA) test, and the proportionality test in a narrow sense: de Búrca, G, 'The principle of proportionality and its application in EC law' (1993) 13 Yearbook of European Law 105.

82 Eg, see GATT 1947, Art XX, which calls for the notion of 'necessity' when allowing exceptions from general obligations in the GATT for various public purposes.

83 SPS Agreement, Art 2(1) provides that '[m]embers have the right to take sanitary and phytosanitary measures necessary for the protection of human, animal and plant life or health', while the second paragraph of this provision requires that SPS measures be 'applied only to the extent necessary to protect human, animal or plant life or health'. For the examination of scientifically justified sanitary and phytosanitary measures pursuant to this provision under the GATT/WTO system, see Fidler, D, *International Law and Infectious Diseases*, 1999, Oxford: OUP, 146–52.

84 In this respect, see the *European Communities, Measures Concerning Meat and Meat Products (Beef Hormones)* case, WTO Doc WT/DS 26/AB/R and WT/DS48/AB/R, Appellate Body Report, 16 January 1998, paras 250 and 252.

85 IHR, Arts 27 and 28.

86 IHR, Art 1.

87 IHR, Art 28 reads as follows: 'Except in case of an emergency constituting a grave danger to public health, a ship or an aircraft, which is not infected or suspected of being infected with a disease subject to the Regulations, shall not on account of any other epidemic disease be refused free pratique by the health authority for a port or an airport; in particular it shall not be prevented from discharging or loading cargo or stores, or taking on fuel or water.'

88 Forrest, M, 'Using the power of the World Health Organization: the International Health Regulations and the future of international health law' (2000) 33 Colum JL and Social Problems 153, p 167.

Legal character of the IHR

The IHR entail a number of features not shared by treaties. In relation to the 'unique' nature of the contracting out procedure,[89] it must also be emphasised that the rules relating to reservations differ considerably from those of treaties. First, the Vienna Convention on the Law of Treaties is silent on how to evaluate the validity of reservations entered by contracting parties, except for requiring their compatibility with the object and purpose of a treaty. This question is left to other State parties to the treaty, and reservations are regarded as having been accepted by States that have raised no objection to them within 12 months after notification of the reservation, or by the date on which consent to be bound by the treaty was expressed, whichever is later.[90] In contrast, Art 88 of the IHR provides that a reservation to the IHR 'shall not be valid unless it is accepted by the World Health Assembly', and until that acceptance, the IHR shall not enter into force with respect to a reserving State.[91] The second difference is the effect of unaccepted reservations on the IHR, especially the principle that incompatible reservations make the entire regulations inapplicable to the reserving State. There exist two possibilities in international law as to the effect of an illegal reservation on a treaty: either the treaty provision to which the reservation is formed applies in full to the reserving State; or the consent of the State to the treaty as a whole ought to be considered as invalid so that it is not a party to the treaty.[92] On one hand, there is a tendency in international human rights law to follow the first approach, severing invalid reservations from a provision and obliging the reserving State to comply with it.[93] On the other, the IHR's approach approximates to the second possibility. If the WHA considers that the reservation 'substantially detracts from the character and purpose' of the IHR, the reservation is not considered as valid. The invalidity of a reservation leads to the consequence that the IHR's entry into force in the reserving State is suspended until that reservation is withdrawn. It must be added that even if the invalid reservation is not withdrawn and the IHR do not enter into force in the reserving State, the State remains bound by the earlier International Sanitary Conventions, Regulations and other agreements.[94] To subordinate

89 Taylor, A, 'Controlling the global spread of infectious diseases: towards a reinforced role for the International Health Regulations' (1997) Hous L Rev 1327, p 1345.

90 Vienna Convention on the Law of Treaties 1969, Art 20(5).

91 IHR, Art 88(1).

92 Shaw, M, *International Law*, 4th edn, 1997, Cambridge: CUP, pp 647–48. For a discussion on this issue, see Schabas, W, *Genocide in International Law – The Crimes of Crimes*, 2000, Cambridge: CUP, pp 534–38.

93 See, eg, *Belilos v Switzerland*, European Court of Human Rights, Judgment of 29 April 1988, Series A, No 132; *Loizidou v Turkey (Preliminary Objections)*, European Court of Human Rights, Judgment of 23 March 1995, Series A, No 310.

94 IHR, Arts 86 and 88(5).

the question of validity of reservations to majority voting of representatives of Member States is a bold approach aimed at curbing abuse of the right to form reservations.[95] It can also be regarded as an attempt to preserve the entrenched character of the IHR, which purports to achieve maximum State participation with minimum doubtful reservations.

The IHR are, at times, mistakenly considered as having only recommendatory force on the basis of the frequency of non-compliance with their obligations.[96] States are reluctant to report outbreaks of infectious disease for fear of triggering other nations to adopt restrictive measures detrimental to its trade and tourism. Yet, failure to report to the WHO will only exacerbate an infected State's economic interest by invoking suspicion among other nations and prompting excessive protective measures. Taylor comments on problems arising from self-reporting of Member States without sanction:

> Since WHO traditionally has relied upon government self-reporting as the sole source of information and does not utilize any mechanism to encourage national compliance with the reporting procedures ... non-reporting has resulted in gaps in the international surveillance system and has left WHO in a position of being unable to officially inform other States of disease outbreaks widely reported by the international press.[97]

Instances where nations reluctantly report outbreaks of disease only after coverage by the global press[98] illustrate the vulnerable nature of the IHR reporting procedure, and national distrust in calculation of the cost benefit of non-compliance with the IHR requirements. As Chen, Evans and Cash emphasise, one must depart from this traditional conceptual paradigm based on the zero-sum notion, as health should be postulated as a global 'public good', which is 'positive-sum': one person's good health does not detract from another's.[99]

---

95 See, also, UN Convention on the Elimination of Racial Discrimination 1966, Art 20(2), which allows a two-thirds majority vote to invalidate a reservation.

96 Allin notes the instances of the seventh cholera pandemic, which started in South Asia in 1960. In this case, the failure of some States to report the outbreak of cholera in their countries led to the imposition of restrictive measures by other States: Allin, N, 'The AIDS pandemic: international travel and immigration restrictions and the World Health Organization's response' (1988) 28 VJIL 1043, pp 1050–51.

97 Taylor, A, 'Controlling the global spread of infectious diseases: towards a reinforced role for the International Health Regulations' (1997) Hous L Rev 1327, p 1349.

98 See, eg, the 1991 plague outbreak in India.

99 Chen, L, Evans, T and Cash, R, 'Health as a global public good', in Kaul, I, Grunberg, I and Stern, M (eds), *Global Public Goods – International Cooperation in the 21st Century*, 1999, New York: UNDP and OUP, p 294.

Revision of the IHR

Revision of the Regulations is currently under way since the WHA resolution (WHA 48.7) of May 1995, and the target date for submission to the WHA is May 2004.[100] The purpose of this revision is to 'develop Regulations which will be applicable to the epidemiology of communicable diseases and to international traffic in the 21st century'.[101] Changes in patterns of disease origin and transmission, coupled with frequent non-compliance with the existing notification requirement, have finally persuaded the WHO to start revising the outmoded IHR. The new IHR will set out basic provisions and principles, and attach specific technical details in a series of annexes. The expert group has already recommended several points that require attention. They propose that the IHR's role should be expanded beyond reporting of three infectious diseases, and suggest a reporting obligation of defined syndromes of urgent international importance.[102] An objective of a pilot study begun in early 1998 was to 'evaluate proposed notification criteria and case definitions of the notifiable syndromes'. The first provisional draft designates six notifiable syndromes: hemorrhagic fever, respiratory, diarrhoeal, neurological, jaundice, and other. While all the hemorrhagic fever syndromes require immediate reporting, others will be subject to this regime only if they are of 'urgent public health importance'.[103] Forrest considers that a syndromic reporting approach may overcome problems of identifying emerging diseases by applying common groups of symptoms, provided that the health infrastructure of nations is sufficiently co-ordinated.[104] An interim review has concluded that syndromic reporting, though valuable in national contexts, does not prove appropriate in the regulatory framework mainly because of difficulties with reporting syndromes in the field test, and the failure to link syndromes to preset rules for control of spread. It is not clear whether the syndromic reporting approach has been entirely abandoned or not.[105]

The second notable aspect underlying revision is that the WHO intends to integrate the revised IHR with ongoing WHO programmatic activities to strengthen both effective prevention against epidemic disease and epidemic control.[106] As suggested by several commentators, the IHR should furnish

100 (2001) 76 Weekly Epidemiological Record, No 8, 23 February 2001, p 63.

101 (1999) 74 Weekly Epidemiological Record, No 30, 30 July 1999, p 252.

102 *Ibid*.

103 Draft IHR, Annex III; Forrest, M, 'Using the power of the World Health Organization: the International Health Regulations and the future of international health law' (2000) 33 Colum JL and Social Problems 153, p 168.

104 *Ibid*.

105 (2001) 76 Weekly Epidemiological Record, No 8, 23 February 2001, p 62.

106 Taylor, A, 'Controlling the global spread of infectious diseases: towards a reinforced role for the International Health Regulations' (1997) Hous L Rev 1327, p 1351.

detailed guidelines for detecting emergent diseases early, given that many countries lack sufficient resources to devise their own health laws.[107] The WHO's 'global alert and response network' has been operational since 1997 to provide co-ordinated mechanisms for epidemic alert and response and to maintain global public health security. The WHO is investigating the possibility that this network could supply information on non-communicable diseases and environmental, chemical or nuclear risks, and that a 'decision tree' may be set up in countries to determine whether a public health risk is of urgent international concern and, if so, what public health measures are to be adopted. It is proposed that the revision of the IHR should include the effective use of this network and its 'decision tree' as a supplementary source of information on public health risks of urgent international importance, quite apart from the country reports system.[108]

THE WHO'S INABILITY TO USE ITS LAW MAKING POWER

The WHO's wide ranging law making powers and institutional independence, established in 1948 after the havoc of the Second World War, raised expectation that this new international health organisation would act as a leading organ on issues of global health. Yet, for more than half a century, the WHO's power has lain dormant, with the adoption of no single treaty or agreement and with the drafting of only two regulations. The WHO has also been criticised for its 'almost total lack of interest' in contributing to the ICESCR's implementation procedures with respect to the right to health.[109] Nor has any serious amendment of health regulations been undertaken in response to global challenges presented by resurgence of eradicated diseases such as malaria and tuberculosis, or emergence of newly recognised pathogens and new types of infectious disease.[110] Even the HIV/AIDS pandemic since the late 1980s has not prompted the WHO to take specific enforceable regulatory steps[111] or to add HIV to the list of diseases subject to the IHR. Serious microbial threat from the re-surfacing of

107 Forrest, M, 'Using the power of the World Health Organization: the International Health Regulations and the future of international health law' (2000) 33 Colum JL and Social Problems 153, p 159.

108 (2001) 76 Weekly Epidemiological Record, No 8, 23 February, pp 62–63.

109 Alston, P, 'Out of abyss: the challenges confronting the new UN Committee on Economic, Social and Cultural Rights' (1987) 9 HRQ 332, p 367.

110 Taylor refers to HIV/AIDS, Legionnaires' disease, Lyme disease, toxic shock syndrome, hepatitis C virus, virulent new strains of *E coli*, and hantavirus pulmonary syndrome: Taylor, A, 'Controlling the global spread of infectious diseases: towards a reinforced role for the International Health Regulations' (1997) Hous L Rev 1327, p 1333.

111 On this issue, see Allin, N, 'The AIDS pandemic: international travel and immigration restrictions and the World Health Organization's response' (1988) 28 VJIL 1043.

microorganisms is particularly linked with their antibiotic resistance, and experts have warned of the evolution of multi-drug resistant tuberculosis (MDR-TB) with the MDR-TB bacilli resistant to available antibiotics.[112]

There can be no panacea for global pandemics, as these are associated with structural problems such as poverty, poor sanitation, and deterioration in maintenance of water and sewage in many developing countries. Partially accountable for microbial adaptation and drug resistance may be global breakdown in 'public health infrastructure' such as laboratories for surveillance and diagnosis.[113] Failure of the IHR to respond to novel infection and re-emerging disease seriously hampers the effectiveness of the IHR and risks widening the gap between the public health concerns of individual nations and the WHO's global strategy.

While the achievements over the last half century of the WHO in eradicating and eliminating epidemic and endemic infectious diseases across the world, most notably smallpox, are impressive, many commentators both within and outside the WHO have questioned the unwillingness of the WHO to rely on legal and regulatory mechanisms to promote and enforce public health programmes. This is in stark contrast to the abundance of international sanitary conventions adopted before the Second World War. Some critics attribute the WHO's inertia in utilising its treaty making powers to a political factor inherent in international organisations: the WHO, just as with other international organisations and indeed the UN itself, is plagued by bureaucracy, and technocrats hesitant to pursue a bold and confrontational approach to health against the will of sovereign Member States.

One way of explaining the non-legal approach of the WHO is to look at the professional background and composition of WHO staff members. It is often pointed out that most staff working in WHO are trained in medicine and health-related fields, and are not fully cognisant of international law. Taylor attributes the WHO's apathy to a law-based approach to 'the organizational culture established by the conservative medical professional community that dominates the institution'.[114] Fidler argues that the WHO's antipathy towards international law stems from the tendency of medical specialists to regard global health problems as better addressed through application of medical and technical resources. With this entrenched

---

112 Forrest, M, 'Using the power of the World Health Organization: the International Health Regulations and the future of international health law' (2000) 33 Colum JL and Social Problems 153, p 158.

113 Taylor, A, 'Controlling the global spread of infectious diseases: towards a reinforced role for the International Health Regulations' (1997) Hous L Rev 1327, p 1335.

114 Taylor, A, 'Making the World Health Organization work: a legal framework for universal access to the conditions for health' (1992) 18 AJL Med 301, p 303. See, also, Fidler, D, 'The future of the World Health Organization: what role for international law?' (1998) 31 Vanderbilt J Trans L 1079, p 1099.

professional ethos among WHO staff, emphasis has been placed on the attempt to eradicate, rather than control, infectious disease through universal vaccination and immunisation.[115] However, the WHO, despite its passive role in international law making, has annually compiled and published a voluminous digest of national and international health legislation, suggesting that WHO officials have some knowledge and appreciation of the significance of international law.

A further explanation might lie in an argument applicable to all international organisations: any attempt to adopt and enforce binding legal instruments would prove counterproductive in face of the power balance between national sovereignty and the mandate of international organisations. To enforce treaties and agreements is dependent on the goodwill of Member States, which vie for sovereign power and are unwilling to compromise it. The WHO's financial resources depend on contribution, with its budget comprising 'assessed contributions' from Member States and associate members.[116] The politicisation of international organisations is evidenced by the US and UK withdrawal from the ILO and UNESCO in the 1980s and the US failure to pay its UN contribution. Those adhering to this view propose that rather than binding and obligation-based law, political tools of persuasion and co-operation would be the better alternative. A non-coercive approach based on voluntary compliance, which leaves it to the discretion of Member States to determine the extent and conditions of adoption of specific measures, would be more effective in ensuring compliance with the WHO's framework programme.[117]

A third and relatively more convincing argument is that binding treaties require an unnecessarily lengthy process of adoption, ratification and entry into force and hence cannot, in a timely manner, address health issues arising in an environment of technological development.[118] Article 19 of the WHO Constitution provides that adoption of conventions or agreements requires a two-thirds majority of the Health Assembly, and their entry into force would be delayed for several years, depending on the readiness of each Member State to initiate its constitutional procedure of ratification.

These arguments have their merits, but cannot justify the WHO's negative attitude to binding rules compared with that of other international

---

115 Godlee, F, 'WHO's special programmes: undermining from above' (1995) 310 BMJ 178, p 181; Fidler, D, 'The future of the World Health Organization: what role for international law?' (1998) 31 Vanderbilt J Trans L 1079, p 1101.

116 Taylor, A, 'Making the World Health Organization work: a legal framework for universal access to the conditions for health' (1992) 18 AJL Med 301, p 341, n 264.

117 Fidler, D, 'The future of the World Health Organization: what role for international law?' (1998) 31 Vanderbilt J Trans L 1079, p 1102.

118 Vignes, C, 'The future of international health law: WHO perspectives' (1989) 40 International Digest of Health Legislation 16, p 17.

organisations such as the International Labor Organization (ILO), the United Nations Environment Programme (UNEP) and the International Maritime Organization (IMO),[119] all of which are actively involved in regulation of health issues such as the health conditions of workers, environmental protection and prevention of marine pollution. The WHO's reticence marks a striking contrast to the ILO's bold approach to the enhancement of workers' rights, with an inventory of human rights treaties scrupulously regulating health and sanitary requirements and conditions for workers,[120] along with consideration of the special needs of women and children, and the indigenous population.[121] The ILO has developed an auditing procedure whereby an independent technical committee ascertains a Member State's compliance with ILO standards, and these findings are then subjected to a 'public hearing' at the Conference Committee on the Application of Conventions and Recommendations.[122]

Another contrast may be drawn with international environmental law, where treaties have set ambitious objectives to tackle such issues as acid rain, ozone depletion, global warming and the threat to biodiversity. As Fidler notes, neither health issues nor environmental concern in the modern world can be countered by a State's unilateral effort, but rather call for well co-ordinated international action setting common standards and guidelines to be fulfilled in domestic law.[123] The world community's anger over the decision of the US President not to ratify the Kyoto protocol on climate change illustrates the danger inherent in unilateralism of the only remaining superpower in subordinating environment and health issues of global concern. The interrelated nature of global health and international environment concern makes the dearth of law making endeavour of the WHO all the more striking.

REINFORCING THE ROLE OF INTERNATIONAL HEALTH LAW

Two strong arguments support a more assertive commitment by the WHO to formation and enforcement of international law. By their nature, health

119 The IMO was also crucial for encouraging the States to adopt the International Convention on Oil Pollution Preparedness, Response and Cooperation 1990: Taylor, A, 'Making the World Health Organization work: a legal framework for universal access to the conditions for health' (1992) 18 AJL Med 301, p 334.

120 See, eg, the ILO Convention Concerning Occupational Safety and Health and the Working Environment.

121 See, eg the ILO Convention Concerning Indigenous and Tribal Peoples in Independent Countries, 1989.

122 Taylor, A, 'Making the World Health Organization work: a legal framework for universal access to the conditions for health' (1992) 18 AJL Med 301, p 337.

123 Fidler, D, 'The future of the World Health Organization: what role for international law?' (1998) 31 Vanderbilt J Trans L 1079, p 1098.

issues cannot be effectively addressed on a national basis, but require co-ordination among nations. This was the primary reason why European States and the US adopted international sanitary conventions to resolve problems of infectious disease in the 19th century. The diversification and complexity of health issues confronting modern industrialised countries necessitate better international co-operation and assistance.

The growing interdependence of health matters with other global issues such as trade and environment calls for closer co-ordination among States, international organisations and non-governmental organisations (NGOs). The return of previously eradicated infectious disease and the alarming spread of AIDS cannot be separated from underlying political, economic and social problems such as poverty, civil war, rapid urbanisation and pollution.[124] The development programme prescribed by the World Bank and the IMF, premised on economic efficiency, has been blamed for a reduction in health and welfare spending in many developing countries. This highlights the need for a more structural and holistic approach to global health, with closer liaison among international organisations. As Godlee notes, the WHO's active consultation with the World Bank and IMF in the design and implementation of development programmes could mitigate the health impact of financial and economic programmes on developing countries.[125]

One example of successful co-ordination and potential synergy between the WHO and other international organisations can be seen in health measures adopted in the area of international trade law. The WHO has participated in an informal session of the Committee on Sanitary and Phytosanitary Measures (SPS Committee) of the World Trade Organization (WTO), and the revised draft of the IHR has been provided to the Committee since 1998. Since almost all members of the SPS Committee are Member States of the WHO, there is awareness of the need to resolve any potential conflict between the IHR and the SPS Agreement.[126] Discussions to explore 'potential areas for synergy' are said to be taking place between the secretariats of the two organisations, and the revised IHR emphasise WHO's closer engagement with the WTO's task of settling disputes arising in the area of public health.[127] Adoption of the WTO's dispute settlement procedure, with the benefit of SPS Committee and the Codex Alimentarius

---

124 Fidler, D, 'The future of the World Health Organization: what role for international law?' (1998) 31 Vanderbilt J Trans L 1079, p 1102.

125 In this respect, however, Godlee considers that while the World Bank's emphasis on economic growth and efficiency is detrimental to the WHO's programme based on equity and universal primary care, the WHO must be blamed for its lack of leadership and the Member States' reluctance to co-operate: Godlee, F, 'WHO reform and global health – radical restructuring is the only way ahead' (1997) 314 BMJ 1359, p 1359.

126 (2000) 75 Weekly Epidemiological Record, No 29, 21 July 2000, p 235.

127 WHO, A 52/9, 1 April 1999, para 11.

Commission expertise,[128] may offer an appropriate response to questions of compliance with the IHR in relation to excessive measures.

Cross-organisational co-ordination, coupled with wide participation of NGOs in the deliberations of international organisations, are essential for establishing an international regime designed to address the diverse health issues of the modern world. Both the regime theory[129] and liberalism[130] in international relations lend theoretical support to the importance of establishing a common framework. Through the creation of working groups and a common set of rules, this loosely linked 'global health regime' would serve to enhance the effective enforcement of international law and its compliance among the nations.[130a]

TOWARDS THE ESTABLISHMENT OF AN INTERNATIONAL SUPERVISORY MECHANISM AND DISPUTE SETTLEMENT

There have been proposals aimed at limiting the temptation of States to violate the IHR. One approach would be to strengthen the existing State reporting system. Of the various approaches to international surveillance, the State reporting system is the most common, requiring Member States to inform any action they have taken and headway achieved in implementing treaties. The effectiveness of this approach is enhanced by a system of independent fact finding, and critical review by a supervisory body.[131] The WHO Constitution itself adopts State reporting under Arts 61 and 62. As Taylor suggests, this reporting system could be transformed into an effective supervisory procedure if accompanied by critical review of State reports by the WHO. An alternative may be the reconstruction of the State reporting system provided in Art 13 of the IHR on infectious disease, into a general

128 The Codex Alimentarius Commission was established by the resolution adopted in the Eleventh Session of the Conference of FAO in 1961 and by the resolution of the Sixteenth World Health Assembly in 1963.

129 Krasner defines international regimes as 'sets of implicit or explicit principles, norms, rules, and decision-making procedures around which actors' expectations converge in a given area of international relations': Krasner, S, 'Structural causes and regime consequences: regimes as intervening variables' (Spring 1982) International Organization 1, p 3. For a critical analysis of the creation of regimes in the area of international environmental law, see Franck, T, *Fairness in International Law*, 1995, Oxford: OUP, p 358.

130 See, eg, Slaughter, A, 'International law in a world of liberal states' (1995) 6 EJIL 503; and 'The real new world order' (Sept/Oct 1997) 76 Foreign Affairs 183.

130a See Fidler, D, 'The future of the World Health Organization: what role for international law?' 31 Vanderbilt J International Law 1079, pp 1118–20.

131 Taylor, A, 'Controlling the spread of global infectious diseases: towards a reinforced role for the International Health Regulations' (1997) Hous L Rev 1327, p 1357. See the ILO's auditing procedure: Leary, V, 'Lessons from the experience of the International Labour Organization', in Alston, P (ed), *The United Nations and Human Rights: A Critical Appraisal*, 1992, Oxford: Clarendon, pp 595–602.

duty of reporting any infectious disease.[132] In all cases, it is essential that the IHR furnish detailed criteria for reporting obligations and specify what constitutes excessive measures in breach of the IHR. This would prevent States from broadly construing the IHR to justify inappropriate measures.[133]

Many experts suggest that international supervisory systems should be introduced on a model similar to that currently practised by other international human rights bodies. The international supervisory mechanism is increasingly recognised as the most effective way to strengthen compliance with international legal obligations. Successful experience in other international organisations, including UNESCO, OECD, and UNEP in monitoring States' implementation of international commitments, is instructive for the WHO.[134] There are also more drastic suggestions. Allin proposes that the revised IHR should incorporate a system of sanctions for non-compliance in order to strengthen enforcement.[135]

The existing IHR envisage that any dispute as to interpretation and application will be referred to the Director General for settlement and, failing this, the dispute can be submitted to the 'appropriate committee' or even to the International Court of Justice.[136] This procedure has never been used,[137] and a number of commentators stress the need for establishing a monitoring mechanism within the WHO to deal with questions and disputes relating to the IHR. As Fidler points out,[138] Art 56 of the revised IHR provides for the establishment of a 'Committee of Arbitration' to which any State or the Director General may refer a question or dispute,[139] and the Committee's decision would be final and binding on the parties to the dispute.[140] This dispute settlement procedure would be strengthened by any sanctions that the WHA might be authorised to impose on a recalcitrant State.[141] If adopted, this would mark a clear shift from the current situation

132 Taylor, A, 'Controlling the spread of global infectious diseases; towards a reinforced role for the International Health Regulations' (1997) Hous L Rev 1327, p 1360.

133 *Ibid*, p 1356.

134 *Ibid*.

135 Allin, N, 'The AIDS pandemic: international travel and immigration restrictions and the World Health Organization's response' (1988) 28 VJIL 1043, p 1063.

136 IHR, Art 93.

137 Fidler notes that this procedure was used only once before 1974, but no IHR dispute has ever been brought before the ICJ: Fidler, D, *International Law and Infectious Diseases*, 1999, Oxford: OUP, p 69, n 87.

138 *Ibid*, p 77.

139 IHR Provisional Draft, Art 56(1).

140 *Ibid*, Art 56(3).

141 *Ibid*, Art 56(4). As to the examples of sanction, Fidler refers to the possibility of suspension of voting privileges and services under 'exceptional circumstances' as stipulated in the WHO Constitution, Art 7: Fidler, D, *International Law and Infectious Diseases*, 1999, Oxford: OUP, p 77, n 143.

in which, despite widespread violations of the Regulations, the WHO finds itself powerless or simply reluctant to take action or to publicise instances of non-compliance.

Another significant step towards greater reliance on international law is the WHO's attempt to request that the International Court of Justice provide advisory opinions on matters of health which fall within the scope of the WHO.[142] However, this suffered a setback when the ICJ rejected the WHO's request for an advisory opinion in the *Legality of the Use of Nuclear Weapons* case.[143] The Court was confronted with the question raised by the WHO:

> In view of the health and environmental effects, would the use of nuclear weapons by a State in war or other armed conflict be a breach of its obligations under international law including the WHO Constitution?

The Court interpreted narrowly the scope of the WHO's competence and ruled, by 11 votes to 3, that WHO was not competent to address the question of the legality of nuclear weapons in international law with special regard to their health impact.[144]

CONCLUSION

The WHO seems now to have finally and slowly awakened from its inertia and is moving in the direction of adopting its first ever treaty, the proposed International Framework Convention for Tobacco Control.[145] The approach taken is based on the framework treaty, which has been used in international environmental law. This approach is instructive in persuading States to agree on broadly stated goals and to adopt domestic measures on a

142 The Statute of the International Court of Justice, Art 65(1) provides that: '[t]he Court may give an advisory opinion on any legal question at the request of whatever body may be authorized by or in accordance with the Charter of the United Nations to make such a request.'

143 'Legality of the use by a State of nuclear weapons in the armed conflict' (request by the World Health Organization) (1996) ICJ Reps 66. See, also, the second request made by the UN General Assembly: 'Legality of the use by a State of nuclear weapons in the armed conflict (request by the General Assembly) (1996) ICJ Reps, p 226.

144 'Legality of the use by a State of nuclear weapons in the armed conflict' (request by the World Health Organization) (1996) ICJ Reps, p 66. In contrast, as regards the second request made by the General Assembly, the Court found that the General Assembly had the competence to do so and examined the merits of the case. For critical examination of these cases, see Akande, D, 'Nuclear weapons, unclear law? Deciphering the *Nuclear Weapons* advisory opinion of the International Court' (1997) 68 BYIL 165; 'The competence of international organizations and the advisory jurisdiction of the International Court of Justice' (1998) 9 EJIL 437.

145 World Health Assembly, Res WHA 49.17, 26 May 1996. For the issue of Tobacco Control in international law, see Taylor, A, 'An international regulatory strategy for global tobacco control' (1996) 22 Yale J Int'l L 257.

progressive basis, leaving to separate protocols the more difficult task of setting manageable targets in specific areas.

The recent tendency of international human rights law to assign economic, social and cultural rights to a complaint-based procedure[146] provides an opportunity to re-conceive the nature of international health law and search for a workable solution to issues of non-compliance. To set up a 'Committee of Arbitration' as its supervisory body could be a salutary move for the WHO towards enhanced reliance on international law, approximating the position of international health law to that of international human rights law. Closer co-ordination among international organisations and revision of the IHR, investing WHO with increased power in dispute settlement and enforcement, would present a brighter future for international health law. These proposals, if implemented, would enable WHO to make a valuable contribution to enhanced world health standards and to lead a global mission in the challenges posed by microbial evolution and resurgence of eradicated disease.

146 See, eg, the collective complaint system established under the European Social Charter: the Additional Protocol to the European Social Charter Providing for a System of Collective Complaints, Art 1 (1995).

CHAPTER 5

THE RIGHT TO HEALTH IN INTERNATIONAL LAW – A CRITICAL APPRAISAL

Yutaka Arai-Takahashi

INTRODUCTION

As with a number of other human rights, the discourse on the right to health has gained both theoretical momentum and practical value over the last 50 years.[1] This coincides with the dynamic development of an international human rights movement since the end of the Second World War, and the adoption of international human rights instruments safeguarding rights of an economic, social and cultural nature, which are often classified as 'second generation' human rights. Despite its obscurity of definition and scope of application, the right to health has been fully anchored both in the institutionalised framework and the academic debate on human rights.

The practical utility and methodological validity of employing the language of human rights in the public health sphere is demonstrated by Gostin and Lazzarini, who propose a 'human rights impact assessment' for public health decisions. The human rights approach, as opposed to a utilitarian or market-oriented approach, serves 'to replace decisions based on irrational fear, speculation, stereotypes, or pernicious methodologies with reasoned, scientifically valid judgments'.[2]

This chapter will examine guidelines on the protective ambit of the right to health. It will then defend the argument that certain aspects of the right to health, just as with other types of economic, social and cultural rights, should be deemed justiciable and susceptible to the process of binding judicial or quasi-judicial decision making.

---

1 For the right to health in general, see Jamar, S, 'The international human right to health' (1994) 22 Southern UL Rev 1; Leary, V, 'Implications of a right to health', in Mahoney, K and Mahoney, P (eds), *Human Rights in the Twenty-first Century – A Global Challenge*, 1993, Dordrecht: Martinus Nijhoff, p 481; Toebes, BCA, *The Right to Health as a Human Right in International Law*, 1999, Antwerp: Intersentia; Tomasevski, K, 'Health rights', in Eide, A, Krause C, and Rosas A (eds), *Economic, Social and Cultural Rights – A Textbook*, 1995a, Dordrecht: Martinus Nijhoff, p 125; 'The right to health for people with disabilities', in Degener T and Koster-Dreese Y (eds), *Human Rights and Disabled Persons, Essays and Relevant Human Rights Instruments*, 1995b, Dordrecht: Martinus Nijhoff, p 131; and Willis, FM, 'Economic development, environmental protection, and the right to health' (1996) 9 Georgetown Int'l Envt'l L Rev 195.

2 Gostin, LO and Lazzarini, Z, *Human Rights and Public Health in the AIDS Pandemic*, 1997, New York: OUP, p 66.

THE RIGHT TO HEALTH IN INTERNATIONAL HUMAN RIGHTS LAW

The right to health as a part of economic, social and cultural rights

The right to health is generally classified as an economic and social right and guaranteed in international human rights instruments. Within the framework of the United Nations (UN), the Universal Declaration of Human Rights (UDHR) embraces not only civil and political rights, but also some economic, social and cultural rights. Articles 22 and 25 safeguard the right to social security and the right to a standard of living adequate for health and well being. The UDHR has been adopted as a General Assembly resolution and hence, strictly, lacks binding force in international law. Yet, a number of provisions embodied in the UDHR have evolved into customary international norms, and as such they are binding on all States. The question remains whether the provisions dealing with economic and social rights have generated rules of customary law.

Search for a 'harder' and more reliable source must turn to a treaty of universal character, namely, the International Covenant on Economic, Social and Cultural Rights (ICESCR) 1966.[3] The controversy surrounding the rift between first and second generation rights has led the UN Commission of Human Rights to draft two separate international bills of rights. Classic civil and political rights, such as freedom of expression and freedom from torture, derive their conceptual validity and force from the natural law theory prevailing in 18th century Europe's Age of Enlightenment. Their subsequent development has been based on libertarian and *laissez-faire* political theory, the fundamental tenet of which is that classic human rights are of negative character, demanding States not to interfere with the liberty and private autonomy of individual persons. On the other hand, economic, social and cultural rights are conceived as requiring States to undertake obligations of a positive nature, and to provide citizens with services and

3 For critical analysis of the ICESCR, see, *inter alia*, Alston, P, 'Out of the abyss: the challenges confronting the new UN Committee on Economic, Social and Cultural Rights' (1987) 9 HRQ 332–81; 'The Committee on Economic, Social and Cultural Rights', in Alston, P (ed), *The United Nations and Human Rights – A Critical Appraisal*, Oxford: Clarendon, 1992, pp 473–509; Alston, P and Quinn, G, 'The nature and scope of States Parties' obligations under the International Covenant on Economic, Social and Cultural Rights' (1987) 9 HRQ 156–229; Arambulo, MK, *Strengthening the Supervision of the International Covenant on Economic, Social and Cultural Rights: Theoretical and Procedural Aspects*, 1999, Antwerp: Intersentia; Craven, MCR, *The International Covenant on Economic, Social and Cultural Rights – A Perspective on its Development*, 1995, Oxford: Clarendon; Leckie, S, 'The Committee on Economic, Social and Cultural Rights: catalyst for change in a system needing reform', in Alston, P and Crawford, J (eds), *The UN Human Rights Monitoring System in Action*, 2000, Cambridge, CUP.

facilities in education, work, social security, and health. This conceptual difference was reflected in the decision of the UN Commission on Human Rights to adopt two separate treaties in 1966: the International Covenant on Civil and Political Rights (ICCPR) and the ICESCR. While the majority of the so called 'third world' countries and those belonging to the communist camp strongly advocated the ICESCR, most Western countries were hesitant to recognise that these rights were immediately enforceable. Some States even expressed doubt as to whether the rights could be classified as 'human rights', preferring to regard the ICESCR provisions as aspirational or moral claims at best.

This theoretical division has a bearing on the effect of rights guaranteed in the ICESCR as well as on its enforcement system. In contrast to the ICCPR, the ICESCR is not immediately binding, but subordinated to the principle of 'progressive realisation' as provided in Art 2. This means that treaty provisions are intended to acquire full realisation of rights only 'progressively', 'to the maximum of its [a State's] available resources'.[4] Exceptions to this principle are envisaged only in two circumstances. First, there is the requirement of non-discrimination on the ground of race, sex, religion or other grounds in Art 2, along with that of equality between men and women in the enjoyment of the ICESCR rights embodied in Art 3. Secondly, there is the obligation 'to take steps' as laid down in Art 2(1).[5] These requirements are regarded as immediately binding on States. In particular, the terms 'ensure' or 'guarantee' employed in non-discrimination and equality provisions connote stronger operative force and effect than the term 'recognize'. It is also possible to deem the non-discrimination obligation as representing a part of customary international law.[6]

---

4 See the General Comment made by the Committee on Economic, Social and Cultural Rights:

> The concept of progressive realization constitutes a recognition of the fact that full realization of all economic, social and cultural rights will generally not be able to be achieved in a short period of time ... Nevertheless, the fact that realization over time, or in other words progressively, is foreseen under the Covenant should not be misinterpreted as depriving the obligation of all meaningful content. It is on the one hand a necessary flexibility device, reflecting the realities of the real world and the difficulties involved for any country in ensuring full realization of economic, social and cultural rights. On the other hand, the phrase must be read in the light of the overall objective, indeed the *raison d'être*, of the Covenant which is to establish clear obligations for States parties in respect of the full realization of the rights in question.

General Comment No 3 (1990): The Nature of States Parties Obligations (Art 2, para 1 of the Covenant), Committee on Economic, Social and Cultural Rights, 5th Session, *Economic and Social Council, Official Records*, 1991, Supplement No 3, Annex III, para 9, E/1991/23, E/C 12/1990/8.

5 General Comment No 3 (1990): The Nature of States Parties Obligations (Art 2, para 1 of the Covenant), Committee on Economic, Social and Cultural Rights, 5th Session, *Economic and Social Council, Official Records*, 1991, Supplement No 3, Annex III, E/1991/23, E/C 12/1990/8, paras 1–2.

6 Jamar, S, 'The international human right to health' (1994) 22 Southern UL Rev 1, p 25.

Chapman points out the conceptual and methodological complications of the principle of progressive realisation:

> The progressive realization benchmark assumes that valid expectations and concomitant obligations of States Parties under the Covenant are not uniform or universal, but instead relative to levels of development and available resources. This necessitates the development of a multiplicity of performance standards for each enumerated right in relationship to the varied social, developmental, and resource contexts of specific countries.[7]

This difficulty in identifying the progressive and relative standards in different segments of society is exemplified by the need to disaggregate into categories such as gender, race, socio-economic or linguistic groups and urban/rural divisions.[8] Supporters of this principle did not view it as 'an escape hatch' to lessen State obligations, but as a necessary compromise to take into account varied economic circumstances.[9]

The weaker force ascribed to the provisions of the ICESCR is supported by textual differences. While ICCPR provisions are formulated in an affirmative and unconditional way such as 'Everyone ... shall have the right ...', ICESCR provisions state only that 'the States Parties ... recognize or undertake to ensure ...'. The term 'recognize' was chosen to lessen the operative force of the provisions and to entrust to States a broader ambit of discretion.[10] Obligations on States with respect to rights 'recognized' can be described as the combination of 'obligations of result' and 'obligations of conduct'.[11]

Weaknesses inherent in the ICESCR can be identified in the extent of obligations flowing from the general clause of Art 2. It is questionable whether the duty of States to ensure the full realisation of rights 'by all appropriate means, including particularly the adoption of legislative measures', implies that States are required to incorporate the Covenant into domestic law. Incorporation and direct application in national law would be ideal for individuals, but commentators suggest that such obligation cannot

7 Chapman, AR, 'A "violations approach" for monitoring the International Covenant on Economic, Social and Cultural Rights' (1996) 18 HRQ 23, p 31.

8 *Ibid*, p 33.

9 Alston, P and Quinn, G, 'The nature and scope of States Parties' obligations under the International Covenant on Economic, Social and Cultural Rights' (1987) 9 HRQ 156–229, p 175.

10 Toebes, BCA, *The Right to Health as a Human Right in International Law*, 1999, Antwerp: Intersentia, p 293.

11 This is explicitly stated in the General Comment No 3 (1990), The Nature of States Parties' Obligations (Art 2, para 1 of the Covenant): *Committee on Economic, Social and Cultural Rights, Report on the Fifth Session, Economic and Social Council, Official Records*, 1991, Supp No 3, E/1991/23, E/C 12/1990/8, para 1 *et seq*.

be derived from the text of Art 2.[12] Nor is it supported by the drafting record.[13] Another deficiency in Art 2 of the ICESCR is that as compared to a comparable general clause in Art 2 of the ICCPR, there is no explicit reference to judicial or other forms of remedy.[14]

The reduced operational effectiveness of the rights safeguarded in the ICESCR can be confirmed by their monitoring. There is no individual or inter-State complaint mechanism as with that operating under the ICCPR and its First Optional Protocol. The States Parties to the ICESCR are only required to submit reports to the Committee on Economic, Social and Cultural Rights on any national legislative and other measures taken to give fuller effect to the rights guaranteed in the ICESCR.

The absence of justiciability and remedies enforceable by a supranational body does not prevent economic, social and cultural rights from being seen as human rights, as these procedural safeguards are not preconditions of a human right.[15] It is simplistic to maintain that civil and political rights are free from any resource conditionality and that the duties of States are satisfied once they abstain from interference with citizens' private autonomy.[16] Indeed, many civil and political rights require national authorities to adopt action to give full effect to their realisation, as with the right to a fair trial, which would remain hypothetical without the effective operation of judicial institutions. There is also growing reluctance to deploy the artificial division between first and second generation human rights. Instead, the emerging consensus seems to be that all human rights are 'universal, indivisible and interdependent and interrelated'.[17]

---

12 Alston, P and Quinn, G, 'The nature and scope of States Parties' obligations under the International Covenant on Economic, Social and Cultural Rights' (1987) 9 HRQ 156–229, p 166.

13 *Ibid*.

14 The preparatory work suggests that various States' proposals to incorporate references to judicial remedies were rejected on the ground that the rights listed in the ICESCR were not justiciable: UN Doc E/CN 4/SR 236 (1951); Alston, P and Quinn, G, 'The nature and scope of States Parties' obligations under the International Covenant on Economic, Social and Cultural Rights' (1987) 9 HRQ 156–229, p 170.

15 Jamar, S, 'The international human right to health' (1994) 22 Southern UL Rev 1, p 14.

16 Alston, P and Quinn, G, 'The nature and scope of States Parties' obligations under the International Covenant on Economic, Social and Cultural Rights' (1987) 9 HRQ 156–229, p 172. In this regard, see Van Hoof, GJH, 'The legal nature of economic, social and cultural rights: a rebuttal of some traditional views', in: Alston, P and Tomasevski, K (eds), *The Right to Food – From Soft to Hard Law*, 1984, Utrecht: SIM, p 97.

17 Vienna Declaration and Programme of Action 1993, I, para 5. See also the Preamble to the European Social Charter (revised) (1996), which refers to 'the need ... to preserve the indivisible nature of all human rights, be they civil, political, economic, social or cultural'.

The right to health in the ICESCR

Issues relating to interpretation and application

The right to health is not an entitlement to individual good health,[18] but ensures that States provide citizens with certain conditions essential for achieving good health. Article 12(1) of the ICESCR provides that '[t]he States Parties to the present Covenant recognize the right of everyone to the enjoyment of the highest attainable standard of physical and mental health'. The highest attainable standard of health depends on resource allocation and on evolving social perception of what constitutes a healthy lifestyle.[19] The provision enumerates four steps to give effect to the protection of the right to health. States must act to enhance the welfare of children in general, such as reduction in stillbirth rate and infant mortality, and the health development of the child. States must take measures to improve environmental and industrial hygiene. They must prevent and treat epidemic, endemic, occupational and other diseases. Contracting States must also strive to optimise health services. There remains the question whether these four areas are exhaustive. Given that human rights treaties are of a law-making character as opposed to a contracting treaty as understood in traditional international law, and that they purport to give fuller effectiveness to their guarantee, it is essential that wide ranging and socially evolving matters affecting health be encompassed within Art 12.[20]

It is possible to consider that a number of rights enumerated in the Universal Declaration of Human Rights have become customary law principles. If one accepts that the right to health could, for all the ambiguity surrounding its definition and the scope of application, be regarded as a customary international law norm, all States, including those that have yet to ratify the ICESCR and other treaties guaranteeing the right to health, would be bound to accord effect to this right by adopting legislative or other appropriate action. Judge Weeramantry, in his dissenting opinion in the advisory opinion by the International Court of Justice (ICJ) on the *Legality of the Use of Nuclear Weapons*, took the view that State duties in relation to health can be recognised as binding international law. He assimilated State obligations in respect of the right to health to environmental obligations,

18 Taylor, AL, 'Making the World Health Organization work: a legal framework for universal access to the conditions for health' (1992) 28 Am JL & Med 301.

19 Willis, FM, 'Economic development, environmental protection, and the right to health' (1996) 9 Georgetown Int'l Envt'l L Rev 195, p 202.

20 In the General Comment No 14, the Committee on Economic, Social and Cultural Rights has enunciated that States Parties' obligations enumerated in Art 12(2) are 'illustrative, non-exhaustive examples': Committee on Economic, Social and Cultural Rights, General Comment No 14, 22nd Session, 2000, UN Doc E/C 12/2000/4; (2001) 8 IHRR 1, para 7.

suggesting that the States owe an obligation *erga omnes* to all members of the international community.[21] As Toebes observes,[22] it is regrettable that in that case the ICJ based its finding on the principle of prohibition of use of force under the UN Charter and humanitarian law in general, avoiding a potentially meaningful discourse on the human rights approach to health.[23]

Another important facet of the right to health under the ICESCR is that by virtue of Art 2(1), there are obligations to furnish other States with international assistance and co-operation in the economic or technical field. As Taylor observes, this means that although the duty on a State to implement the right to health is primarily directed toward the individual,[24] emerging international health challenges such as the HIV/AIDS pandemic translate the right to health from an individual right into a group right or a right of peoples.[25] The obligation flowing from the right to health embraces international solidarity, calling on each State to facilitate access to essential health facilities, goods and services in other countries or to supply necessary aid.[26]

---

21 ICJ, *Legality of the Threat or Use of Nuclear Weapons*, Advisory Opinion, 8 July 1996 (1996) ICJ Reps, Dissenting opinion of Judge Weeramantry; Toebes, BCA, *The Right to Health as a Human Right in International Law*, 1999, Antwerp: Intersentia/Hart, p 176.

22 Toebes, BCA, *The Right to Health as a Human Right in International Law*, 1999, Antwerp: Intersentia, pp 177–78.

23 The Court concluded that:

> ... the threat or use of nuclear weapons would generally be contrary to the rules of international law applicable in armed conflict, and in particular the principles and rules of humanitarian law;
>
> However, in view of the current state of international law, and of the elements of fact at its disposal, the Court cannot conclude definitively whether the threat or use of nuclear weapons would be lawful or unlawful in an extreme circumstance of self-defence, in which the very survival of a State would be at stake.

Operative para 2E, General Assembly Opinion (1996) ICJ Reps, p 266: the opinion of the Court was split evenly by seven to seven with the decision made by the casting vote of the President. Those judges who favoured the ruling include President Bedjaoui, Judges Ranjeva, Herczegh, Shi, Fleischhauer, Vereshchetin and Ferrari Bravo. The dissenting judges were Vice President Schwebel and Judges Oda, Guillaume, Shahabuddeen, Weeramantry, Koroma and Higgins.

Compare this with the General Comment 6(16)d of the UN Human Rights Committee, which pointed out that '[e]very effort ... to avert the danger of war, especially thermonuclear war, and to strengthen international peace and security would constitute the most important condition and guarantee for the safeguarding of the right to life': General Comment 6(16)d (general comment on Art 6 of the ICCPR (right to life)), General Assembly Official Records, Thirty-seventh Session, Supplement No 38 (A/37/38).

24 Taylor, AL, 'Making the World Health Organization work: a legal framework for universal access to the conditions for health' (1992) 28 Am J L and Med 301, p 311.

25 Note that while Art 16 of the African Charter on Human and Peoples' Rights categorise the right to health as primarily based on an individual citizen, it also requires the State Parties to take measures to protect the health of their population.

26 The Committee on Economic, Social and Cultural Rights, General Comment No 14, 22nd Session, 2000, UN Doc E/C 12/2000/4; (2001) 8 IHRR 1, para 39.

RESTRICTIONS ON THE RIGHT TO HEALTH UNDER THE ICESCR

Article 4 of the ICESCR[27] sets out three criteria for restrictions on rights, including the right to health, to be considered lawful. Restrictions must be 'determined by law', be 'compatible with the nature of [the] rights' restricted and seek solely the legitimate 'purpose of promoting the general welfare in a democratic society'.

Principle 56 of the Limburg Principles stipulates that restrictions 'compatible with the nature of the rights' require that a limitation shall not be interpreted or applied so as to jeopardise the essence of the right concerned.[28] The third criterion suggests the principle of proportionality, requiring States to choose 'the least restrictive alternative' among limitations available.[29] This accords with the second limb of the proportionality test developed under European Community law.[30]

In contrast to the ICCPR, ECHR, ACHR and the ESC, the ICESCR does not include a derogation clause applicable in cases of war or other national emergency.[31] Alston and Quinn argue that three factors may explain this deliberate absence. First, the nature of economic, social and cultural rights, which are regarded as more prone to restriction in time of war or other emergency; secondly, the existence of a general and potentially extensive limitation clause laid down in Art 4, unlike the approach followed in the ICCPR; and thirdly, the 'flexible and accommodating nature' of the general obligation stipulated in Art 2(1) of the ICESCR.[32]

---

27 This provision reads as follows:

> The States Parties to the present Covenant recognize that, in the enjoyment of those rights provided by the State in conformity with the present Covenant, the State may subject such rights only to such limitations as are determined by law only in so far as this may be compatible with the nature of these rights and solely for the purpose of promoting the general welfare in a democratic society.
>
> ICESCR, Art 4.

28 The Limburg Principles 1987, Principle 56. The Limburg Principles on the nature and scope of the obligations of States Parties to the International Covenant on Economic, Social and Cultural Rights were proposed by a group of distinct experts in human rights law at the meeting in Maastricht on 2–6 June 1986, which was convened by the International Commission of Jurists, the Faculty of Law, University of Limburg, and the Urban Morgan Institute for Human Rights, University of Cincinnati; (1987) 9 HRQ 122.

29 The Committee on Economic, Social and Cultural Rights, General Comment No 14, 22nd Session, 2000, UN Doc E/C 12/2000/4; (2001) 8 IHRR 1, para 29.

30 For critical examination of the proportionality principle under EC law, see de Búrca, G, 'The principle of proportionality and its application in EC law' (1993) 13 YBEL 105.

31 This is also the case with the Protocol of San Salvador.

32 Alston, P and Quinn, G, 'The nature and scope of States Parties' obligations under the International Covenant on Economic, Social and Cultural Rights' (1987) 9 HRQ 156–229, p 217. In this respect, the comparative study of the implementation of the ILO Conventions may provide an insightful guidance as regards the treatment of economic, social and cultural rights at the time of national emergency. See, eg, the *Greek* [contd]

THE COMMITTEE ON ECONOMIC, SOCIAL AND CULTURAL RIGHTS

The ICESCR did not originally have a supervisory body of its own, but rather the implementation of rights were examined by the Working Group within the UN Economic and Social Council, which consisted of 15 governmental representatives of Member States. It was only in 1987 in response to the inadequacies of the Working Group that the Council decided to delegate its responsibilities under the ICESCR to a Committee comprising 18 independent experts who serve in their personal capacity.[33] Committee sessions proceed on the basis of a 'constructive dialogue' on issues arising from State reports. States are required to submit a report within two years of the Covenant's entry into force, detailing the progress in implementing ICESCR rights, and thereafter submit a report every five years.[34] The tasks of the Committee include the design of an effective system for monitoring States' performance in the field of economic, social and cultural rights.[35]

THE RIGHT TO HEALTH IN OTHER UN-BASED HUMAN RIGHTS TREATIES

There are other specific treaties designed to ensure the rights of particularly vulnerable segments of the society such as racial minorities, women, children and refugees. Such treaties recognise the right to health as essential,[36] supplying to individuals vehicles to supplement the core provision of Art 12 of the ICESCR.[37]

---

32 [contd] case, 'Report of the Commission Appointed under Art 26 of the Constitution of the International Labor Organization to Examine the Complaints concerning the Observance by Greece of the Freedom of Association and Protection of the Right to Organise Convention 1948 (No 87), and of the Right to Organise and Collective Bargaining Convention 1949 (No 98)' (1971) 54 Int'l Labor Org Official Bull 25 (special supplement) 1, Chapter 5.

33 Alston, P, 'The Committee on Economic, Social and Cultural Rights', in Alston, P (ed), *The United Nations and Human Rights – A Critical Appraisal*, 1992, Oxford: Clarendon, p 473.

34 Toebes, BCA, *The Right to Health as a Human Right in International Law*, 1999, Antwerp: Intersentia, p 91.

35 Alston, P, 'The Committee on Economic, Social and Cultural Rights', in Alston, P (ed), *The United Nations and Human Rights – A Critical Appraisal*, 1992, Oxford: Clarendon, p 489.

36 However, no treaty was adopted to deal with discrimination against the mentally ill, the disabled or persons with communicable diseases. The UN General Assembly adopted the Declaration on the Rights of Mentally Retarded Persons in Resolution 2856 (XXVI) of 20 December 1971 and the Declaration on the Rights of Disabled Persons in Resolution 3447 (XXX) of 9 December 1975, but both are, as General Assembly resolutions, not intended to be binding on Member States.

37 While the ICESCR is not equipped with a 'violation approach' to the [contd]

Article 24 of the Convention Relating to the Status of Refugees (Refugees Convention) 1951 protects the right to social security of refugees.[38] Similarly, Art 28 of the Convention on the Protection of the Rights of All Migrant Workers and Members of their Families 1990 provides for the right of equal access of migrant workers to medical care.[39]

A number of health-related rights are incorporated in the Convention on the Elimination of Racial Discrimination 1966. Article 5 of the Convention provides: 'State Parties undertake to prohibit and to eliminate racial discrimination in all its forms and to guarantee the right of everyone, without distinction as to race, colour, or national or ethnic origin, to equality before the law,' with respect to 'the right to public health, medical care, social security and social services.'

Insufficient attention to the causes of women was partially addressed by the adoption of the Convention on the Elimination of All forms of Discrimination against Women (CEDAW) in 1979. Article 12 of CEDAW proscribes sex discrimination in the area of health care, especially with respect to access to health care services.[40] This provision is supplemented by other health-related rights of women in particular contexts. Article 10 secures the equal rights of men and women in education and vocational opportunities, and refers to the obligation on States to ensure equal access to specific educational information, including information and advice on family planning. Article 11 guarantees equal rights in relation to employment opportunities, with special requirements for the concerns of women. Article 11(e) requires States to ensure to women social security in

---

37 [contd] supervision of its rights, the Racial Discrimination Convention allows individuals or groups of individuals to submit complaints to the Committee on the Elimination of Racial Discrimination under Art 14. Similarly, the absence of a comparable provision authorising the complaint system in the CEDAW was remedied by the adoption of the Optional Protocol in 1999.

38 See Chapter 6.

39 Article 28 of the Convention reads as follows:

Migrant workers and members of their families shall have the right to receive any medical care that is urgently required for the preservation of their life or the avoidance of irreparable harm of their health on the basis of equality of treatment with nationals of the State concerned. Such emergency medical care shall not be refused to them by reason of any irregularity with regard to stay or employment.

Convention on the Protection of the Rights of All Migrant Workers and Members of Their Families 1990.

40 CEDAW, Art 12 provides as follows:

1 States Parties shall take all appropriate measures to eliminate discrimination against women in the field of health care in order to ensure, on a basis of equality of men and women, access to health care services, including those related to family planning.

2 Notwithstanding the provisions of paragraph 1 of this article, States Parties shall ensure to women appropriate services in connexion with pregnancy, confinement and the post-natal period, granting free services where necessary, as well as adequate nutrition during pregnancy and lactation.

cases of sickness, invalidity and old age, and the right to paid leave, while Art 11(f) guarantees the right to health and safety in employment, including safeguarding of the function of reproduction. This is reinforced by Art 11(2)(d), which obligates States to provide safeguards for pregnant women in harmful types of work. Article 14(b) applying to rural women obliges States to ensure equal access to adequate health care facilities, including information, counselling and services in family planning.[41]

Among the UN human rights treaties, the most effective guarantee of health is in the Child Rights Convention (CRC). Article 24 guarantees the right of the child to the enjoyment of the highest attainable standard of health and to facilities for the treatment of illness and rehabilitation of health. This provision is more thoroughly drafted than Art 12 of the ICESCR, listing specific measures that States are bound to implement. These include target reduction in infant and child mortality, provision of necessary medical assistance and health care (with emphasis on the development of primary health care), care for disease and malnutrition, prenatal and post-natal health care for mothers, dissemination of information on child health and nutrition, promotion of breast-feeding, and preventive health care. Commentators note that the influence of the WHO on the drafting of this provision was crucial for inserting reference to primary health care and information concerning breast-feeding.[42] The third paragraph specifically requires States to take necessary steps to abolish traditional practices prejudicial to the health of children. There has been controversy as to whether this provision should have expressly referred to traditional practices harmful to children, including female genital circumcision or mutilation.[43] Despite the omission of express reference to such practices, the Committee on Economic, Social and Cultural Rights has repeatedly admonished States to adopt measures to eradicate them or to prevent third parties from coercing women to undergo them.[44]

---

41 See Chapter 7.

42 Leary, V, 'Implications of a right to health', in Mahoney, K and Mahoney, P (eds), *Human Rights in the Twenty-first Century – A Global Challenge*, 1993, Dordrecht: Martinus Nijhoff, p 489.

43 The UK's proposal to refer to female genital circumcision was opposed by the delegation of Senegal, which emphasised prudence when discussing issues involving differences in cultural values: Toebes, BCA, *The Right to Health as a Human Right in International Law*, 1999, Antwerp: Intersentia, p 58.

The Committee on Economic, Social and Cultural Rights has, however, expressed profound concern about the prevalence of this practice in some countries: the Committee on Economic, Social and Cultural Rights Report on the Tenth and Eleventh Sessions, *Economic and Social Council Official Records*, 1995, Supplement No 3, E/1995/22, E/C 12/1994/20, para 351 (as to Mali).

44 The Committee on Economic, Social and Cultural Rights, General Comment No 14, 22nd Session, 2000, UN Doc E/C 12/2000/4; (2001) 8 IHRR 1, paras 22, 35, and 51. See, also, the World Health Assembly resolution, WHA 47.10, 1994, entitled 'Maternal and child health and family planning: traditional practices harmful to the health of women and children'.

Outside the UN-based treaties, the International Labor Organization (ILO) has played an assertive role in codifying a number of significant treaties involving health-related rights of workers. The most notable achievements are in relation to the protection of occupational health, as exemplified by the Social Policy Convention and the Convention on Maternity Protection.[45] Discourse on health-related rights in a different dimension can be seen in ILO Convention No 169 Concerning Indigenous and Tribal Peoples in Independent Countries. Article 25 of this Convention requires States to ensure the 'highest attainable standard of physical and mental health' of the indigenous and tribal population, while stressing the need to take into account their cultural and traditional preventive care, healing practices and medicines.[46]

The Council of Europe

The European Social Charter

The position of the Council of Europe on economic, social and cultural rights mirrors the conceptual dichotomy that plagued the drafting of the ICCPR and the ICESCR. Under the auspices of the Council of Europe,[47] while the European Convention on Human Rights has been supplemented by the First Protocol 1952 entailing rights to property and education, two rights of economic and social nature, the full impetus for guaranteeing many economic and social rights had to await the adoption of the European Social

---

45 ILO Maternity Protection Convention (revised) 1952; and ILO Social Policy (Basic Aims and Standards) Convention 1962.

46 Article 25 of the Convention lays down as follows:

1 Government shall ensure that adequate health services are made available to the peoples concerned, or shall provide them with resources to allow them to design and deliver such services under their own responsibility and control, so that they may enjoy the highest attainable standard of physical and mental health.

2 Health services shall, to the extent possible, be community-based. These services shall be planned and administered in co-operation with the peoples concerned and take into account their economic, geographic, social and cultural conditions as well as their traditional preventive care, healing practices and medicine.

3 The health care system shall give preference to the training and employment of local community health workers, and focus on primary health care while maintaining strong links with other levels of heal care services.

4 The provisions of such health services shall be co-ordinated with other social, economic, and cultural measures in the country.

ILO Convention Concerning Indigenous and Tribal Peoples in Independent Countries (ILO Convention No 169) 1989.

47 Note, also, that while the right to health as such is not expressly guaranteed, issues of public health are fully governed by Art 152 of the EC Treaty (as amended by the Amsterdam Treaty), which ensures a high level of human health protection in the definition and implementation of all Community policies and activities.

Charter (ESC) in 1961.[48] Article 11 of the ESC[49] stipulates that measures must be taken in order to ensure the right to protection of health. These measures are to achieve three objectives: the removal of the causes of ill-health, the provision of advisory and educational facilities, and the prevention of epidemic, endemic and other diseases. As Toebes notes, while this provision has the advantage of referring to advisory and educational facilities in matters of health, no mention is made of child health, occupational health and environmental health.[50]

Reference to individual responsibility in matters of health should not be construed to suggest that States have only secondary duties. The right to health is complemented by two other related rights, the right to social and medical assistance in Art 13, and the right to safe and healthy working conditions guaranteed in Art 3. Article 13 embodies the obligation of States to ensure that any person who is without adequate resources and unable to secure such resources under a social security scheme be granted adequate assistance, and, in case of sickness, necessary care.

The absence of a complaint-based supervisory mechanism under the ESC has now been remedied by the adoption of the Additional Protocol to the European Social Charter Providing for a System of Collective Complaints (Collective Complaints Protocol) of 1995, which came into force in 1998. Under the amended ESC, national employers and trade union organisations as well as social rights NGOs can bring complaints before the European Committee of Social Rights (which was called the Committee of Independent Experts till 1999, the committee established under Art 25 of the 1961 ESC).[51] While still not allowing individual complaints, this Protocol has opened the way for a collective complaint system that is significant for

48 This chapter deals with the European Social Charter adopted in Turin in 1961 by the Council of Europe, the international organisation which is based in Strasbourg and equipped with the European Court of Human Rights for supervising the European Convention on Human Rights 1950. The European Social Charter should not be confused with the European Community Charter on Fundamental Social Rights of Workers, which was adopted by the European Parliament in Strasbourg in 1989 and is often called 'European Social Charter' as well.

As regards the European Social Charter 1961, see Harris, DJ, *The European Social Charter*, 1984, New York: Virginia UP; 'Lessons from the reporting system of the European Social Charter', in Alston, P and Crawford, J (eds), *The UN Human Rights Monitoring System in Action*, 2000, Cambridge: CUP, Chapter 16; Brillat, R, 'A new Protocol to the European Social Charter Providing for Collective Complaints' (1996) EHRLR 52.

49 The European Social Charter was revised in 1996 to incorporate the rights recognised in the amended European Social Charter and the rights guaranteed by the Additional Protocol of 1988 as well as to add new rights. Article 11 of the ESC is left largely unaltered except for the addition of the phrase 'as well as accidents' added to the end of para 3. At the time of writing in July 2001, only 11 States are parties to the revised ESC.

50 Toebes, BCA, *The Right to Health as a Human Right in International Law*, 1999, Antwerp: Intersentia, p 69.

51 See, eg, *International Commission of Jurists v Portugal (No 1 of 1998)*, 9 September 1999, ECSR (2000) 7 IHRR 525 (as to the right of children and young persons to protection in the work place, ESC, Art 7).

the advancement of economic and social rights, reinforcing the argument that aspects of economic, social and cultural rights are justiciable and capable of judicial enforcement.

The State reporting system established under the ESC is more complicated than in the ICESCR Committee or other UN treaty-based reporting procedure. According to Art 21, States are required to submit to the Secretary General of the Council of Europe a report at two-yearly intervals, explaining the application of the provisions of Part II of the Charter. Under Art 20, States are obliged to consider themselves bound by at least five of the core articles enumerated in Part II: Arts 1, 5, 6, 12, 13, 16 and 19.[51a] While the right to health under Art 11 is not granted this privileged status, rights to social security and social and medical assistance are.[51b] States are also required to recognise that they are bound by other provisions in Part II. The ESC entrusts the task of examining State reports to the European Committee of Social Rights (the previous Committee of Independent Experts), which prepares a report containing its conclusions.[52] The report is then transmitted to the Governmental Committee, which in turn draws up a report for the Committee of Ministers. Finally, the Secretary General of the Council of Europe transmits to the Parliamentary Assembly the reports of the European Committee of Social Rights (the previous Committee of Independent Experts) and of the Governmental Committee as well as the resolutions of the Committee of Ministers.[53] On the basis of these three documents, the Parliamentary Assembly decides whether recommendations should be adopted. With the entry into force of the Additional Protocol, it is now possible for international or national organisations of employers and trade unions, as well as non-governmental organisations, to bring complaints of 'unsatisfactory application' of the Charter.[54]

The ESC envisages wider restrictions on the right to health than the ICESCR. Article 31 of the ESC allows lawful restrictions to be made, provided that restrictions are 'prescribed by law', are 'necessary in a democratic society' and pursue a legitimate objective 'for the protection of

51a Under Art A(1) of the revised ESC (1996), the 'core articles' are extended to include Arts 7 and 20 and the States are enjoined to consider themselves bound by six of the core articles.

51b Under Art A(1) of the revised ESC (1996), Art 11 remains as a 'non-privileged' provision, but the right of children and young persons to protection in Art 7 is now included in the 'core articles'.

52 ESC, Art 24, as amended by Protocol Amending the European Social Charter 1991.

53 ESC, Art 29, as amended by Protocol Amending the European Social Charter 1991.

54 Additional Protocol to the European Social Charter Providing for a System of Collective Complaint 1995, Art 1. According to Art 1(b), international non-governmental organisations having consultative status with the Council of Europe are granted the right to submit complaints. Further, by virtue of Art 2(1), the State Parties can declare at any time that they will recognise the right of a national non-governmental organisation within its jurisdiction to do so.

the rights and freedoms of others or for the protection of public interest, national security, public health, or morals'.

These limitations correspond to those developed under the jurisprudence of Arts 8–11 of the ECHR.[55] Under Art 30, the ESC also permits States to derogate from the obligations in time of war or public emergency. Three conditions must be met in order to invoke lawful derogation: derogating measures must be proportionate to the exigencies of the situation; they must be consistent with other obligations under international law; and there is a duty to notify the Secretary General of the Council of Europe of such measures and the reasons therefor.

THE CONVENTION ON HUMAN RIGHTS AND BIOMEDICINE

The need to safeguard human dignity in response to progress in biomedical research prompted the Council of Europe to adopt the Convention for the Protection of Human Rights and Dignity of the Human Being with Regard to the Application of Biology and Medicine (the Convention on Human Rights and Biomedicine) in 1997.[56] The Convention underscores the need for 'free and informed consent' to any intervention in health.[57] It guarantees access to information about health, and stipulates conditions for genetic tests and scientific research, organ and tissue removal from living donors for transplantation purposes, as well as the prohibition of financial gain and disposal of parts of the human body. Article 3 of the Convention ensures that States shall take measures to provide 'equitable access to health care'. An enhanced need for protecting the right to privacy is evidenced by the Convention's express recognition of the right to health information of an individual under Art 10. Restrictions on this right are allowed only in 'exceptional cases' in the interests of the patient. With respect to the human genome, Art 12 of the Convention provides that predictive genetic tests can be performed only for health purposes or for scientific research linked to health purposes, and that they require appropriate genetic counselling.

According to Art 26, States cannot place restrictions on the exercise of rights and protections afforded by the Convention other than as are 'prescribed by law and are necessary in a democratic society in the interest of public safety, for the prevention of crime, for the protection of public health or for the protection of the rights and freedoms of others'.

55 Harris, DJ, O'Boyle, M, and Warbrick, C, *Law of the European Convention on Human Rights*, 1995, London: Butterworths, Chapter 8.

56 For a discussion of the issues around human dignity raised by the cloning debate see Robertson, JA, 'Liberty, identity and human cloning' (1998) 76 Texas L Rev 1371, and on human dignity and genetics, see Brownsword, R *et al* (eds), *Law and Human Genetics: Regulating a Revolution*, 1999, London: Hart.

57 Convention on Human Rights and Biomedicine 1997, Art 5.

States are required under Art 30 of the Biomedicine Convention to submit reports on implementation of the Convention when requested by the Secretary General of the Council of Europe. The European Court of Human Rights can furnish advisory opinions on legal questions concerning interpretation. The parties entitled to request advisory opinions are limited to the government of a party, and the Steering Committee on Bioethics established in accordance with Art 32, membership of which is restricted to representatives of the parties to the Convention.[58] One positive feature of the Convention is that, unlike the ECHR and ESC, it is open to signature and ratification by the European Community as well,[59] hence extending the protective scope of the Convention to any Community-based action and contributing to the shaping of Community public health policies.

THE ORGANIZATION OF AMERICAN STATES

Within the framework of the Organization of American States (OAS),[60] the impetus to recognise economic, social and cultural rights was seen as early as in 1948 when the OAS adopted the American Declaration of the Rights and Duties of Man. Article XI of the American Declaration provides that '[e]very person has the right to the preservation of his health through sanitary and social measures relating to food, clothing, housing and medical care, to the extent permitted by public and community resources'. However, as with the Universal Declaration of Human Rights, the American Declaration was not intended to be a binding document.[61]

The approach of the OAS to the regional bill of rights bears some resemblance to that of the Council of Europe. The OAS gave priority to the treaty dedicated to civil and political rights, the American Convention on Human Rights 1969 (ACHR), with only a general clause for the protection of

58 Convention on Human Rights and Biomedicine 1997, Art 29.

59 *Ibid*, Art 33. See, also, the European Convention on the Exercise of Children's Rights 1996, Art 22(1), another treaty devised by the Council of Europe, which allows the European Community to accede to that Convention. In this context, note that the European Court of Justice expressly rejected the possibility that the European Communities could accede to the ECHR: Opinion 2/94 on Accession by the Community to the ECHR [1996] ECR I-1759.

60 See, also, the OAS Charter itself, which implicitly recognises a number of economic, social and cultural rights. Art 43(a) and (b) of the Charter refers to the 'right to material well-being' and healthy working conditions: Charter of the Organization of American States, 30 April 1948 (1994) 33 ILM 981.

61 However, the Inter-American Commission and Court of Human Rights recognised that a certain normative value must be given to the American Declaration: the Advisory Opinion of the Inter-American Court of Human Rights of 14 July 1989 (OC-10/89), Inter-American Court of Human Rights, Series A, Judgments and Opinions, No 10.

economic, social and cultural rights provided in Art 26. It is only since the OAS adopted the Additional Protocol to the American Convention on Human Rights in the Area of Economic, Social and Cultural Rights (Protocol of San Salvador) in 1988 that economic, social and cultural rights have been recognised. Article 10 of the Protocol secures the right to health in a detailed manner, reflecting the co-ordinated assistance provided by the Pan-American Health Organization.[62] It characterises health as a 'public good' and requires States to take measures in six specific areas: primary health care; extension of health services to all individuals; universal immunisation against the principal infectious diseases; prevention and treatment of endemic, occupational and other diseases; education of the population on the prevention and treatment of health problems; and satisfaction of the health needs of the highest risk groups and the poor. The emphasis on primary health care and on the needs of the poor is of special importance to the region where poverty in the societal structure is inimical to full entitlement to healthy living conditions.[63] There is a symbiotic link between human health and environment in Art 11, which guarantees 'the right to live in a healthy environment and to have access to basic public services', and requires States to promote the protection, preservation and improvement of the environment.

It is generally understood that as in the case of the ICESCR, rights embodied in the Protocol of San Salvador do not have immediately enforceable effect, but are susceptible to the progressive realisation benchmark.[64] The Protocol does not envisage a complaint mechanism as in the ACHR, but implementation relies rather on the State reporting system, which emulates the original reporting system of the ICESCR prior to the establishment of the Committee on Economic, Social and Cultural Rights.[65] According to Art 19 of the Protocol, States undertake to submit to the Secretary General of the OAS periodic reports on the progressive measures adopted to ensure due respect for rights. The Secretary General transmits the reports to the Inter-American Economic and Social Council and the Inter-American Council for Education, Science and Culture, both of which

62 Leary, V, 'Implications of a right to health', in Mahoney, K and Mahoney, P (eds), *Human Rights in the Twenty-first Century – A Global Challenge*, 1993, Dordrecht: Martinus Nijhoff, p 489.

63 *Ibid*. Reference to the need to establish primary health care can also be found in the UN Convention on the Rights of the Child 1989, Art 24(2)(b) and the African Charter on the Rights and Welfare of the Child 1990, Art 14(2)(b) and (j).

64 The scope of State obligations under Art 1 of the Protocol is reduced to an ostensibly modest degree. The States are required to adopt necessary measures 'to the extent allowed by their available resources, and taking into account their degree of development, for the purpose of achieving progressively and pursuant to their internal legislation'.

65 This original reporting system is provided in the ICESCR, Art 16.

subsequently issue annual reports containing a summary of the information and recommendations appropriate to States in respect of certain rights.[66]

The exception to this general procedure is that the system of individual petitions operating in the ACHR can apply to trade union rights in Art 8 and the right to education in Art 13, with the consequence that both the Inter-American Commission on Human Rights and the Inter-American Court of Human Rights may condemn State Parties for violation of these rights.[67] This may not represent any fresh approach to economic and social rights in an international perspective, as freedom of association including the right to form trade unions, and the right to education, are guaranteed under the ECHR and its Protocol I, enabling the European Court of Human Rights to supervise their implementation. Nevertheless, that the right to strike is expressly recognised as a right capable of judicial enforcement is significant to the enhancement of economic, social and cultural rights in general.

The Inter-American Commission on Human Rights has power to monitor State compliance with both the American Declaration on the Rights and Duties of Man and the American Convention on Human Rights. In the *Yanomami Indians* case, the Commission found that highway construction in the Amazon was a violation of the right to the preservation of health and to well being specifically provided in Art XI of the American Declaration.[68] While the Commission's opinions are not binding, their impact on the shaping of jurisprudence in economic, social and cultural rights exerts a considerable influence on national practice and policy.[69]

THE ORGANIZATION OF AFRICAN UNITY

In contrast to the approach of the Council of Europe and the OAS, the African Charter on Human and Peoples' Rights safeguards a substantive number of economic and social rights relevant to health and treats them as capable of violation-based supervision by monitoring bodies. Article 16 of the African Charter is inspired by Art 12 of the ICESCR and deploys a similar definition of the right to health, guaranteeing 'the right to enjoy the

---

66 Protocol of San Salvador 1988, Art 19.

67 Individual complaint procedures are provided in ACHR, Arts 44–51 and 61–69.

68 Annual Report of the Inter-American Commission on Human Rights (1984–85), Resolution No 12/85, 5 March 1985, Case No 7615 (Brazil); Reprinted in Buergenthal, T and Norris, RE, *Human Rights, The Inter-American System, Pt 3, Cases and Decision*, 1986, Dobbs Ferry, New York: Oceana, p 213.

69 Toebes, BCA, *The Right to Health as a Human Right in International Law*, 1999, Antwerp: Intersentia, p 184. Note that specific economic, social and cultural rights are not guaranteed by the ACHR, and hence that they do not form the *ratione materiae* of the Inter-American Court of Human Rights.

best attainable state of physical and mental health'. The primary emphasis of the African States is on 'medical attention' of the sick. The African Charter allows individuals and NGOs to submit complaints to the African Commission on Human and Peoples' Rights on behalf of victims under the heading 'Other Communications' in Art 55. The African Court of Human and Peoples' Rights, which will be established subsequent to the coming into force of the relevant protocol, will not allow individuals direct access, but the Commission or States whose citizen claims to be a victim of a breach of rights can act on their behalf.[70]

THE SYMBIOSIS OF THE RIGHT TO HEALTH WITH OTHER ECONOMIC AND SOCIAL RIGHTS

The right to health is conceptually or practically interwoven with other economic, social and cultural rights, such as the right to work,[71] food, clothing, housing,[72] education[73] and social security.[74] That the protective scope of the right to education can be extended to an individual entitlement to education on nutrition, prenatal or post-natal care suggests that other stand-alone economic and social rights have considerable bearing on health.

THE RIGHT TO HEALTH IN THE CIVIL AND POLITICAL RIGHTS CONTEXT

In the context of human rights, health is not limited to individual violations of the right to health. International jurisprudence reveals that applicants are successfully claiming violations of their civil and political rights with respect to a range of health-related issues. These include compulsory medical treatment,[75] conditions of prisoners or detainees requiring special medical and psychiatric needs and treatment,[76] disclosure of confidential medical

70 Protocol on the Establishment of an African Court on Human and Peoples' Rights 1998, Art 5.

71 See, eg, ICESCR, Art 6.

72 See the right to an adequate standard of living guaranteed in *ibid*, Art 11.

73 Eg, *ibid*, Art 11.

74 Eg, *ibid*, Art 9.

75 See, *inter alia*, *Herczegfalvy v Austria*, Judgment of 24 September 1992, A 242-B; 15 EHRR 437.

76 See, eg, *Henry and Douglas v Jamaica*, Communication No 571/1994, UN Doc CCPR/C/57/D/571/1994; (1997) 4 IHRR 387, para 9.5. Note also the case of *D v UK*, where the European Court of Human Rights found that the intended deportation of a drug courier, dying of AIDS, to St Kitts would, if implemented, violate Art 3 of the ECHR on the ground that there were insufficient medical facilities for his care and treatment: judgment of 2 May 1997, 24 EHRR 423.

data of patients[77] access to information on health[78] or environment,[79] the impact of pollution[80] as well as other forms of environmental damage to human health. Important issues of medical ethics may be raised with respect to the disclosure of personal medical data in breach of privacy.[81]

The absence of a supervisory mechanism based on an individual complaint system in most human rights treaties guaranteeing economic, social and cultural rights has prompted individuals and NGOs to rely on the complaint systems of civil and political rights treaties to advance their arguments. There is an increasing tendency of such supervisory bodies as the European Court of Human Rights and the UN Human Rights Committee to uphold health-related claims on the basis of civil and political rights provisions such as the prohibition of torture or other forms of ill-treatment, the right to life, as well as freedom of privacy and family life. With respect to Art 6 of the ICCPR, which guarantees the right to life, the Human Rights Committee has stressed that the expression 'inherent right to life' cannot be interpreted in an isolated manner, but rather requires States

77 See the judgment of the European Court of Human Rights in *Z v Finland*, Judgment of 25 February 1997, 25 EHRR 371 (disclosure of an HIV status of an applicant, whose husband was tried on the ground of attempted manslaughter in relation to his various sexual offences). Note also *Andersson v Sweden*, Judgment of 27 August 1997, 25 EHRR 722 (the decisions of a psychiatrist to disclose a patient's medical information to welfare authorities for the purpose of determining her fitness to raise a child); and *MS v Sweden*, Judgment of 27 August 1997, 28 EHRR 313 (a women's clinic's disclosure of the applicant's medical recording, including her abortion, to the Social Insurance Office for determining industrial injury).

78 See, in this regard, the *McGinley and Egan v UK*, which concerned the complaint of the denial of access to health information in relation to nuclear tests on Christmas Island. The Court ruled as follows:

> Where a Government engages in hazardous activities ... which might have hidden adverse consequences on the health of those involved in such activities, respect for private and family life under Art 8 requires that an effective and accessible procedure be established, which enables such persons to seek all relevant and appropriate information.

McGinley and Egan v UK, Judgment of 9 June 1998, 27 EHRR 1, para 101.

79 *Guerra and Others v Italy*, Judgment of 19 February 1998, 26 EHRR 357. This is a landmark decision in the sense that when finding a violation of Art 8, the Court recognised the positive obligations incumbent on the State to inform the citizens of any environmental or health hazard caused by private factories.

80 In this regard, see the European Court of Human Rights' decision in *López Ostra v Spain*, Judgment of 9 December 1994, A 303-C.

81 The European Convention for the Protection of Individuals with Regard to Automatic Processing of Personal Data, Art 6 provides that '[p]ersonal data revealing racial origin, political opinions or religious and other beliefs, as well as personal data concerning health or sexual life, may not be possessed automatically unless domestic law provides appropriate safeguards'.

to assume positive obligations such as adopting steps to curb infant mortality, to increase life expectancy and to eliminate malnutrition and epidemics.[82]

THE NORMATIVE CONTENT OF THE RIGHT TO HEALTH

Delineating the protective scope of the right to health

Providing a workable and meaningful definition of the right to health calls for careful examination of approaches to health of international human rights monitoring bodies and international organisations. As Toebes observes, health is a highly subjective experience, and is not susceptible to measurement by objective standards.[83] The definition of health adopted in the Preamble of the WHO Constitution is a breakthrough for human rights discourse on health.[84] Nevertheless, as Leary notes, the WHO's failure to assume a leading and assertive role in regulating health, and actively to participate in the implementation procedures of international human rights instruments, has severely compromised any endeavour to ascertain the normative scope of this essential right.[85]

Despite the dynamic attitude to health of human rights monitoring bodies, the proliferation of health concepts in human rights discourse needs to be addressed. To delineate the right to health is necessary for providing clearer and more predictable guidelines on its scope of application. Toebes has attempted to identify two essential components of the right to health: the right to health care, and what she describes as the right to 'underlying health conditions'. The latter concept is understood to encompass health issues such as clean drinking water, adequate sanitation, sufficient

82 General Comments of the Human Rights Committee under the ICCPR, Art 40, para 4, General Comment 6(16)d (Art 6), *General Assembly Official Records: Thirty-Seventh Session*, Supplement No 38, A/37/40, para 5.

83 Toebes, BCA, *The Right to Health as a Human Right in International Law*, 1999, Antwerp: Intersentia, p 20.

84 *Ibid*, p 36.

85 Leary critically comments on the little contribution that the WHO made to the conceptualisation of the right to health.

> The reality remains that the WHO, with the exception of the recent work concerning the monitoring of the Children's Convention, has shown little interest in defining the content of a right to health as an international human right. The Organization undertakes little normative activity and has not been greatly interested in the normative activity of other organizations with regard to health issues.

Leary, V, 'Implications of a right to health', in Mahoney, K and Mahoney, P (eds), *Human Rights in the Twenty-first Century – A Global Challenge*, 1993, Dordrecht: Martinus Nijhoff, p 491.

nutritious food, environmental health, occupational health, access to health-related information and harmful traditional practices.[86] While admitting that significant overlap exists between the right to health and other rights, such as the right to life, education, adequate living standards, and physical integrity and privacy, Toebes proposes that the right to health be postulated as a 'repository' for every aspect touching on health.[87]

The Committee on Economic, Social and Cultural Rights has categorised the right to health secured in Art 12 of the ICESCR as 'an inclusive right', consisting not only of the entitlement to 'timely and appropriate health care', but also of the entitlement to the 'underlying determinants of health'. This embraces such issues as 'access to safe and potable water and adequate sanitation, an adequate supply of safe food, nutrition and housing, healthy occupational and environmental conditions, and access to health-related education and information, including on sexual and reproductive health'.[88] The Committee emphasises that the entitlement to both health care and the underlying determinants of health basically entails four essential elements: public health facilities, goods and services must be available in sufficient quantity within a Member State (availability); health facilities, goods and services must be physically accessible and economically affordable to everyone without discrimination (accessibility); all health facilities, goods and services need to respect medical ethics and be sensitive to cultural and gender requirements (acceptability); and, finally, health facilities, goods and services must be scientifically and medically appropriate and of good quality (quality).[89]

LEGAL OBLIGATIONS ON STATES

These disaggregated elements of an individual's entitlement to health correspond to the specific obligations incumbent on States. The Committee takes the view that the right to health, as with other human rights, places three types of obligation on States: obligations to respect, to protect and to fulfil. The obligation to respect accords with the traditional conceptualisation of civil and political rights, suggesting that States should abstain from interfering directly or indirectly with the enjoyment of the right to health. This requires States to refrain from denying or limiting equal

86 Toebes, BCA, *The Right to Health as a Human Right in International Law*, 1999, Antwerp: Intersentia, pp 254–58.

87 *Ibid*, p 259.

88 The Committee on Economic, Social and Cultural Rights, General Comment No 14, 22nd Session, 2000, UN Doc E/C 12/2000/4; (2001) 8 IHRR 1, para 11.

89 *Ibid*, para 12.

access to health services to prisoners or detainees, minorities, asylum seekers and illegal immigrants, and from obstructing traditional preventive care, healing practices and medicines. It also enjoins States to abstain from 'unlawfully' polluting air, water and soil, for instance, through industrial waste from State-owned facilities; from testing or using nuclear, biological or chemical weapons releasing substances harmful to human health; and from impeding access to health services as a punitive measure during armed conflict.[90] The obligation to protect means that States are required to take action to prevent third parties from interfering with the Art 12 guarantee. This includes a responsibility on States to ensure that harmful or traditional practices do not impinge on the healthy development of girls or obstruct access to pre- and post-natal care and family planning.[91] The obligation to fulfil requires States to adopt appropriate legislative, administrative, budgetary, judicial, promotional and other measures to realise fully the right to health. In turn, this obligation further consists of three specific elements: the obligation to facilitate, requiring States to adopt positive measures capable of assisting individuals and communities to enjoy fully the right to health; the obligation to provide a specific right guaranteed in the ICESCR when individuals or groups are unable to realise that right themselves for reasons beyond their control; and the obligation to promote, calling on States to undertake actions that create, maintain and restore the health of citizens.[92]

THE RIGHT TO HEALTH CARE

As Bismarck's introduction of the world's first compulsory social insurance in 1883 suggests, the development of public health in the national laws of European States predates the recognition of human rights concepts.[93] Health care is a broad notion embracing health services in relation to disease prevention, health promotion, therapeutic services and rehabilitation.[94] The WHO's attitudes to health care as a human right are mixed, revealing a shift from its initial negative position to a more assertive stance. As Tomasevski observes, at the drafting stage of Art 12 of the ICESCR, the WHO was

90 The Committee on Economic, Social and Cultural Rights, General Comment No 14, 22nd Session, 2000, UN Doc E/C 12/2000/4; (2001) 8 IHRR 1, paras 33–34.

91 *Ibid*, para 35.

92 *Ibid*, paras 36–37.

93 Tomasevski, K, 'Health rights', in Eide, A, Krause, C and Rosas, A (eds), *Economic, Social and Cultural Rights, – A Textbook*, 1995a, Dordrecht: Martinus Nijhoff, p 131.

94 Willis, FM, 'Economic development, environmental protection, and the right to health', (1996) 9 Georgetown Int'l Envt'l L Rev 195, p 199.

reluctant to support the proposed obligation on States to ensure access to medical care on the ground that the Organization did not wish to oblige States to adopt any particular measure of medical care. The WHO's advocacy for health care at that juncture was restricted to maternal and child care, and it was only in 1978 that it set the Health for All Strategy and explicitly advanced the need for providing primary health care for all.[95]

One of the most material aspects of health care may be the establishment of primary health care. In its Declaration of Alma-Ata, the WHO defined primary health care as:

> Essential health care based on practical, scientifically sound and socially acceptable methods and technology made universally accessible to individuals and families in the community through their full participation and at a cost that the community and country can afford to maintain at every stage of their development in the spirit of self-reliance and self-determination ... It is the first level of contact of individuals, the family and community with the national health system bringing health care as close as possible to where people live and work, and constitutes the first element of a continuing health care process.[96]

As Taylor notes, the Declaration's emphasis was not limited to basic medical care, but extended to the need for securing underlying health conditions, including the promotion of food supply and proper nutrition; basic sanitation and safe water; provision of essential drugs; maternal and child care; the dissemination of information on health; prevention and control of locally endemic disease; appropriate treatment of common diseases and injuries; and immunisation against major infectious diseases.[97]

UNDERLYING HEALTH CONDITIONS AND ECONOMIC DEVELOPMENT

The concepts of economic development and environmental protection are closely intertwined with the right to health, furnishing preconditions for 'the highest attainable standard of health'.[98] The notion of sustainable

95 Tomasevski, K, 'Health rights', in Eide, A, Krause, C and Rosas, A (eds), *Economic, Social and Cultural Rights, – A Textbook*, 1995a, Dordrecht: Martinus Nijhoff, pp 128–29.

96 Declaration of Alma-Ata, Art VI, in WHO, *Primary Health Care: Report of the International Conference on Primary Health Care*, 1978, pp 3–4; Taylor, AL, 'Making the World Health organization work: a legal framework for universal access to the conditions for health' (1992) 28 Am J L and Med 301, pp 314–15.

97 *Ibid*, Declaration of Alma-Ata, Art VII, pp 4–5; *ibid*, Taylor, pp 314–15.

98 Willis, FM, 'Economic development, environmental protection, and the right to health' (1996) 9 Georgetown Int'l Envt'l L Rev 195, p 212.

(economic) development offers double-edged, ambivalent consequences. The allocation of resources to public health and the development of a health infrastructure, including better sanitary and hygiene systems, contribute to the prevention of infectious disease, as well as reduction in infant mortality. In contrast, as Willis observes, States prioritise their economic development at the expense of the environmental health of their own population, minorities or the indigenous population.[99] The Committee on Economic, Social and Cultural Rights has called on States belonging to international financial institutions, such as the IMF and the World Bank, to 'pay greater attention to the protection of the right to health in influencing the lending policies, credit agreements and international measures of these institutions'.[100]

THE MINIMUM CORE AND JUSTICIABILITY OF THE RIGHT TO HEALTH

The minimum core of obligations

Indispensable to the disaggregating analysis of economic, social and cultural rights is the search for the 'minimum core' of rights. In the General Comments on the general obligations in Art 2, the Committee on Economic, Social and Cultural Rights has fleshed out the minimum core obligation to 'an obligation to ensure the satisfaction of at the very least minimum essential levels of each of the rights'. Furthermore, 'a State Party in which any significant number of individuals is deprived ... of essential primary health care ... is, *prima facie*, failing to discharge its obligations under the Covenant. If the Covenant were read in such a way as not to establish such a minimum core obligation, it would be largely deprived of its *raison d'être*'.[101] On comparative examination of international human rights jurisprudence, the WHO's Primary Health Care Strategy in the Alma-Ata Declaration, and the Programme of Action of the International Conference on Population and

99 See, eg, the case of *Yanomami Indians of Brazil*, Resolution No 12/85, 5 March 1985, Case No 7615 (Brazil); reprinted in Buergenthal, T and Norris, RE, *Human Rights, The Inter-American System*, Pt 3, Cases and Decisions, 1986, Dobbs Ferry, New York: Oceana, p 213.

100 The Committee on Economic, Social and Cultural Rights, General Comment No 14, 22nd Session, 2000, UN Doc E/C 12/2000/4; (2001) 8 IHRR 1, para 39.

101 General Comment No 3 (1990), 'The nature of States Parties obligations' (Art 2, para 1 of the Covenant), *Committee on Economic, Social and Cultural Rights, Report on the Fifth Session, Economic and Social Council Official Records*, 1991, Supplement No 3, Annex III, 83, para 10.

Development,[102] the Committee proposes six obligations as the minimum core content of the right to health. These include:

(a) to ensure the right of access to health facilities, goods, and services on a non-discriminatory basis, especially for vulnerable or marginalized groups;

(b) to ensure access to the minimum essential food which is nutritionally adequate and safe, to ensure freedom from hunger to everyone;

(c) to ensure access to basic shelter, housing and sanitation, and an adequate supply of safe and potable water;

(d) to provide essential drugs, as from time to time defined under the WHO Action Programme on Essential Drugs;

(e) to ensure equitable distribution of all health facilities, goods and services;

(f) to adopt and implement a national public health strategy and plan of action, on the basis of epidemiological evidence, addressing the health concerns of the whole population; the strategy and plan of action shall be devised, and periodically reviewed, on the basis of a participatory and transparent process; they shall include methods, such as the right to health indicators and benchmarks, by which progress can be closely monitored; the process by which the strategy and plan of action are devised, as well as their content, shall give particular attention to all vulnerable or marginalized groups.[103]

The Committee adds to this list the following obligations, which are described as 'of comparable priority':

(a) to ensure reproductive, maternal (prenatal as well as post-natal) and child health care;

(b) to provide immunization against the major infectious diseases occurring in the community;

(c) to take measures to prevent, treat and control epidemic and endemic diseases;

(d) to provide education and access to information concerning the main health problems in the community, including methods of preventing and controlling them;

(e) to provide appropriate training for health personnel including education on health and human rights.[104]

---

102 Report of the International Conference on Population and Development, Cairo, 5–13 September 1994.

103 The Committee on Economic, Social and Cultural Rights, General Comment No 14, 22nd Session, 2000, UN Doc E/C 12/2000/4; (2001) 8 IHRR 1, para 43.

104 *Ibid*, para 44.

Toward the justiciability of the right to health

Chapman proposes a complaint-based review process for ascertaining violations of ICESCR rights comparable with monitoring systems operating in many international civil and political rights instruments.[105] There are many salient grounds for reorienting the supervisory method, including the insufficient and inadequate nature of State reports, lack of co-operation from States, and the inherently circumscribed vigour of the Committee's supervisory power exercised on the basis of a 'constructive dialogue' with a State suspected of infringing the rights of its citizens. The 'violation approach' may gain valuable insight from the practices of the UN and its affiliated organs, including the ILO's procedure on trade union rights and working conditions, the procedure of the United Nations Educational, Social and Cultural Organization for dealing with rights concerning education, science and culture, as well as the procedures of the Economic and Social Council Resolution 1503 (1970).[106] The Optional Protocol to the CEDAW, which was adopted in 1999, envisages the right of individuals and groups of individuals to submit to the Committee on the Elimination of Discrimination against Women a complaint of a violation of the rights enumerated in the CEDAW, which covers substantial elements of economic, social and cultural rights.[107] Economic, social and cultural rights are already under judicial scrutiny in the revised ESC.

The conceptual foundation of the right to health is reinforced by the argument that although this right is deemed as a right of economic and social character, it encompasses certain negative duties comparable with civil and political rights. States are required not only to provide health services and medical facilities, but also to prevent any action inimical to health and welfare. Similarly, States are obliged to refrain from withholding information vital to the health and well being of the population. Such duties are more readily accepted by States as those of immediate effect or of justiciable nature. The Committee on Economic, Social and Cultural Rights emphasises that the right to health contains both freedoms from interference and entitlement to a system of health protection.[108] By re-conceptualising

---

105 Chapman, AR, 'A "violations approach" for monitoring the International Covenant on Economic, Social and Cultural Rights' (1996) 18 HRQ 23, pp 36 *et seq*. See, also, Eide, A, 'Realization of social and economic rights and the minimum threshold approach' (1989) 10 HRLJ 35–51; and Robertson, E, 'Measuring State compliance with the obligations to devote the ' maximum available resources' to realizing economic, social, and cultural rights' (1994) 16 HRQ 693–714.

106 Chapman, AR, 'A "violations approach" for monitoring the International Covenant on Economic, Social and Cultural Rights' (1996) 18 HRQ 23, p 40.

107 Optional Protocol to the Convention on the Elimination of All Forms of Discrimination against Women 1999, Art 2.

108 The Committee on Economic, Social and Cultural Rights, General Comment No 14, 22nd Session, 2000, UN Doc E/C 12/2000/4; (2001) 8 IHRR 1, para 8.

the right to health as straddling the traditional line between first and second generation human rights, this crucial right may be considered as the 'precondition for participation in social, political, and economic life', and as such precedent to the enjoyment of all other rights, civil and political or economic and social.[109] There is even a proposition that regardless of the nebulous nature of its definition and scope of application, the right to health should now be considered a norm of customary international law binding on all States. Indeterminacy in definitional content and scope of application hardly constitutes an impediment to characterisation as a norm of customary law or even as a norm 'superior' to others.[110]

Toebes' contribution to the debate on the minimum core is her linking of the elements of the 'core content' of Art 12 of the ICESCR with the question of justiciability. Obligations that entail an immediate effect are considered as capable of adjudication. In order to identify justiciable elements in the right to health, she suggests four criteria: the '*degree of clarity and concreteness* of the provision'; 'the extent to which the right created provides *programmatic obligations* for States'; the *gravity of the matter at issue*; and finally, '*unusual, exceptional circumstances*' that would warrant judicial intervention in the inadequate functioning of institutions (such as legislature's failure or inaction).[111] The first two criteria relate to the character of the norm, and the second criterion logically flows from the first proposition that those provisions couched in general and ambiguous terms are less susceptible to judicial review and enforcement. The third and fourth criteria may be combined as a single benchmark based on the nature of particular circumstances. Toebes' first criterion is consistent with the position of the Committee on Economic, Social and Cultural Rights. In its third General Comment on 'the nature of States Parties' obligations' with special reference to Art 2(1), the Committee observes that the Covenant includes 'obligations which are of immediate effect' and that among them is the undertaking to take concrete and clearly targeted steps 'within a reasonably short time after the Covenant's entry into force for the States concerned'.[112] Subsequently, in the General Comment No 14 on the right to health, the Committee recognised that the minimum core of obligations singled out in its

109 Taylor, AL, 'Making the World Health Organization work: a legal framework for universal access to the conditions for health' (1992) 28 Am JL & Med 301, p 311.

110 In this regard, see the in-depth analysis of the concept of an 'absolute right' with respect to ECHR, Art 3 (freedom from torture or other forms of ill-treatment): Addo, MK and Grief, N, 'Does Article 3 of the European Convention on Human Rights enshrine absolute rights?' (1998) 9 EJIL 510.

111 Toebes, BCA, *The Right to Health as a Human Right in International Law*, 1999, Antwerp: Intersentia, pp 238–40 (emphasis in original).

112 General Comment No 3 (1990), 'The nature of States parties' obligations' (Art 2, para 1 of the Covenant), *Committee on Economic, Social and Cultural Rights, Report on the Fifth Session, Economic and Social Council Official Records*, 1991, Supplement No 3, Annex III, 83, para 2.

disaggregation analysis helps identify the violations of Art 12 of the ICESCR.[113]

The conceptual validity of the 'violations approach' has also been upheld by the Limburg Principles on the nature and scope of obligations of States Parties to the International Covenant on Economic, Social and Cultural Rights, which provide that a State would be in breach of the ICESCR in circumstances where 'it fails to remove promptly obstacles which it is obligated to remove in order to permit the immediate fulfilment of a right', and where 'it wilfully fails to meet a generally accepted international minimum standard of achievement, which is within its powers to meet'.[114] The second circumstance noted in the Limburg Principles defends the thesis that potentially justiciable aspects can also be found as regards positive obligations (the duty to afford care and facilities for minimum subsistence).[115] With respect to positive obligations on States, resource constraints may offer some justification for non-compliance with obligations. The suggestion of the ICESCR Committee in its General Comment that the burden of proving constraints should be placed on the States[116] may relieve some obstacle to the justiciability of economic, social and cultural rights.

CONCLUSION

This analysis has attempted to provide some guidelines on interpretation and application of the right to health in international human rights instruments. The relationship between the progressive realisation yardstick and issues of justiciability is the most intractable. No effort has been spared by experts on human rights to identify elements of the minimum core content of the right to health on the assumption that those elements can be

113 The Committee on Economic, Social and Cultural Rights, General Comment No 14, 22nd Session, 2000, UN Doc E/C 12/2000/4; (2001) 8 IHRR 1, paras 46–52.

114 'The Limburg Principles on the nature and scope of the obligations of States parties to the International Covenant on Economic, Social and Cultural Rights' (1987) 9 HRQ 122; Chapman, AR, 'A 'violations approach' for monitoring the International Covenant on Economic, Social and Cultural Rights' (1996) 18 HRQ 23, pp 42–43.

115 Toebes, BCA, *The Right to Health as a Human Right in International Law*, 1999, Antwerp: Intersentia, p 300.

116 In its 14th General Comment, the Committee on Economic, Social and Cultural Rights has noted as follows:

> A State which is unwilling to use the maximum of its available resources for the realization of the right to health is in violation of its obligations under Art 12. If resource constraints render it impossible for a State to comply fully with its Covenant obligations, it has the burden of justifying that every effort has nevertheless been made to use all available resources at its disposal in order to satisfy, as a matter of priority, the obligations ...

The Committee on Economic, Social and Cultural Rights, General Comment No 14, 22nd Session, 2000, UN Doc E/C 12/2000/4; (2001) 8 IHRR 1, para 47.

characterised as embracing obligations of immediate effect. A future review process of the right to health in the ESC, subsequent to the recent operation of the complaint mechanism under the Additional Protocol to the ESC, will illuminate the practical value of human rights approaches to public health. It is desirable that the Committee on Economic, Social and Cultural Rights be equipped with enhanced supervisory power, allowing both individual and collective complaints to be submitted to its critical appraisal on a violations approach. Such a procedure will inject practical viewpoints into some unresolved conceptual questions such as the nature of the right to health, and the clear demarcation of its obligations between those that entail immediate effect and those that do not. It can assist the feasibility of the thesis that core aspects of the right to health are susceptible to judicial review, while strengthening the effectiveness of the guarantee afforded to individual entitlement to healthy living conditions.

PARTICULAR ISSUES OF PUBLIC HEALTH: REFUGEES

Sylvie Da Lomba

INTRODUCTION

Refugees constitute one of the most vulnerable groups of people worldwide. They are people whose States have failed them, compelling them to flee and seek international protection. The circumstances of their departure mean that most of them are destitute and therefore dependent upon host countries for their means of subsistence, including health care. This creates problems which are faced by the international community as a whole, and which must be addressed by the international community. The international dimension inherent in refugee matters founds the relevance of international law.

This chapter focuses on the provisions of international law in relation to refugees' health. Whilst there is no specific instrument upholding refugees' right to health, such a right may be inferred from more general international provisions on health. Before examining and appraising international law in relation to health and refugees, three preliminary issues need to be addressed. First, it is necessary to define 'refugee'. The term is commonly used to refer to people in need of international protection, but the refugee population is not uniform and it is critical to differentiate categories of refugees as their status varies with implications for entitlements in relation to health. Secondly, it is important briefly to examine what is meant by the right to health in order to determine the extent of entitlements. Finally, the significance of a right to health for refugees in international law will be examined.

REFUGEES: A COMPLEX REALITY

Refugees are usually defined as people in need of international protection, their national State – or State of residence, where the individuals concerned are stateless – having failed them. However, this definition does not reflect the diversity and complexity of the refugee population worldwide. The definitional debate regarding the concept of refugee is not and must not be confined to the theoretical sphere as categorisation has significant implications and the rights enjoyed by refugees are determined by their status. Refugees fall into five categories: Convention refugees, also referred to as recognised refugees, asylum seekers, individuals who have been conferred territorial asylum, persons who have been granted temporary protection and, finally, displaced people.

Convention refugees or recognised refugees

Convention refugees or recognised refugees are individuals who have been granted refugee status under the 1951 Convention relating to the Status of Refugees (the 1951 Convention).[1] The term 'refugee' is defined in Art 1(A)(2) of the Convention as any person who:

> ... owing to a well-founded fear of being persecuted for reasons of race, religion, nationality, membership of a particular social group or political opinion, is outside the country of his nationality and is unable to or, owing to such fear, is unwilling to avail himself of the protection of that country; or who, not having a nationality and being outside the country of his former habitual residence as a result of such events, is unable, or owing to such fear, is unwilling to return to it ...

Individuals who have been granted refugee status within the meaning of Art 1(A)(2) enjoy a status that can be considered permanent. This status is partially organised by the 1951 Convention. Its provisions cover a number of areas[2] where the treatment reserved to recognised refugees in the host country shall not be less favourable than that conferred upon other non-nationals[3] or, in some instances, identical to that enjoyed by nationals.[4] For the purpose of the Convention, the term 'non-nationals' refers to foreigners who are legally residing in the host country. The 1951 Convention is silent on the issue of health and, to be more precise, on recognised refugees' right to health in the host country. However, the permanence of the status offered by the Convention and the rights it confers contribute to the recognition of a right to health in the host country for those enjoying refugee status.

Equating all people in need of international protection to Convention refugees would give an erroneous picture of the refugee situation. A

1 1 189 UNTS 150.

2 In addition to general provisions contained in Chapter 1, the 1951 Convention contains provisions regarding the juridical status of recognised refugees (section II), gainful employment (section III), welfare (section IV) and administrative measures (section V).

3 Areas where Convention refugees enjoy a treatment that must not be less favourable than that granted to non-nationals include access to the labour market (Art 17(1)), access to liberal professions (Art 19(1)), housing (Art 21) and access to education other than elementary education (Art 22(2)).

4 Areas where Convention refugees enjoy the same treatment as nationals of the host country include rationing (Art 20), elementary education (Art 22(1)) and selected provisions of labour legislation and social security (Art 24).

significant proportion of the population in need of international protection does not enjoy refugee status for a number of reasons. These reasons do not necessarily question the 'genuine' nature of the alleged need for international protection, and the absence of refugee status should not be interpreted as necessarily negating the need for international protection.

The conferment of refugee status supposes, in the first instance, that the person concerned is in a position to leave his or her country of nationality, or residence if he or she is stateless, with a view to applying for refugee status abroad. According to Art 1(A)(2) of the 1951 Convention, refugee status cannot be sought from within. Many of those in need of international protection are not able to leave their country of nationality or residence. What has caused these people to flee is a fear of persecution emanating from the State itself or from non-State agents in the absence of State protection. Since, in most instances, the search for protection will prove to be risky, difficult and expensive, it is inevitable that some will not succeed in leaving. Others, having failed to reach a host country where they can apply for refugee status, will end up in refugee camps in neighbouring countries. While they might have been eligible, their failure to reach a State where they could apply for refugee status will deprive them from the protection offered by the 1951 Convention.

People in need of international protection may have applied for refugee status and been denied that status on the ground that they do not fall within the Convention definition of refugee. This failure does not necessarily mean that the fear of persecution is absent and the need for international protection not justified. To be entitled to refugee status, an individual has to demonstrate that fear of persecution is based on one or more Convention grounds, namely race, religion, nationality, membership of a particular social group, or political opinion. An application for refugee status based on a ground which is not articulated in the 1951 Convention will be unsuccessful, and this is often the case with applicants alleging gender-based persecution.[5] Difficulties in obtaining refugee status have also arisen from national restrictive interpretations of the Convention definition inconsistent with its spirit and object. One flagrant example relates to the way some States have confined the benefit of refugee status to individuals

5 Gender is not mentioned in Art 1(A)(2) of the 1951 Convention as a ground for persecution. Hence, some States have been eager to reject asylum claims based on gender-based persecution. Some national courts have recognised that asylum seekers who allege gender-based persecution could be considered as forming a particular social group within the meaning of Art 1(A)(2). This is, for instance, the position endorsed in Canada (see, eg, *Cheung v Canada* [1993] 2 FC 314 and *B (PV) (Re)* [1993] CRDD No 12 (QL) referred to in Carlier, J-I, Vanheule, D, Hullmann, K and Peña Galiano, C, *Who is a Refugee? A Comparative Case Law Study*, 1997, The Hague/London/Boston: Kluwer, p 209). It has been argued that the Convention definition of the term refugee should be amended in order to include gender as a ground for persecution (see, eg, Schenk, TS, 'A proposal to improve the treatment of women in asylum law: adding a "gender" category to the international definition of "refugee" (1995) Global Legal Studies Journal II, http://www.law.indiana.edu/glsj/vol2/schenk.html.

fleeing State persecution, denying this status to those persecuted by non-State agents despite the absence of such a limitation in the 1951 Convention.[6] These limiting interpretations are usually designed to reduce the numbers of refugees in host countries. A discussion of the limits and appropriateness of the Convention definition of the term refugee goes beyond the scope of this chapter.

Asylum seekers

Asylum seekers are persons who are in the course of applying for refugee status and are awaiting a final decision[7] of their asylum claim. Unlike recognised refugees, their status is not organised by the 1951 Convention and is therefore left to the States' competence. Their status is precarious and uncertain by nature, since their rights are much more limited than those granted to recognised refugees, and vary greatly from State to State. The development of increasingly restrictive asylum laws and policies in recent years in States which were seen as traditional host countries, essentially Western developed countries, has been detrimental to asylum seekers' rights including their right to health in the country responsible for examining their asylum claim.[8]

Territorial asylum

Territorial asylum is a concept inherent in the sovereignty of the State and relates to the State's discretion to confer protection in its territory to individuals who are considered to be in need of international protection. The concept of territorial asylum must be distinguished from that of

---

6 Eg, in France, the *Commission des Recours des Réfugiés* has interpreted Art 1(A)(2) of the 1951 Convention as requiring State persecution. Where persecution does not emanate from the State, the asylum seeker will need to establish that persecution was voluntarily tolerated or encouraged by the State (Conseil d'Etat, 27 May 1983, *Dankha,* referred to in Tiberghien, F, *La Protection des Réfugiés en France,* 1988, Paris: Collection Droit Public Positif, Presses Universitaires d'Aix-Marseilles, p 393). A similar approach was adopted in the Position of 4 March 1996 defined by the Council on the basis of Art K.3 of the Treaty on European Union on the harmonised application of the term 'refugee' in Art 1 of the Geneva Convention relating to the Status of Refugees (OJ L63 13.3.96, p 2).

Such a restrictive interpretation of the Convention definition of the term refugee has been expressly rejected by the Supreme Court of Canada which considers that the identity of the perpetrator is irrelevant for the purpose of refugee status (*AG of Canada v Ward, United Nations Commissioner for Refugees et al, Interveners,* 30 June 1993 [1993] 2 SCR 689).

7 The term final is designed to stress that applicants appealing against a negative initial decision are still considered asylum seekers.

8 Eg, in the UK, the Immigration and Asylum Act 1999 (1999, c 33) has been highly criticised for significantly curtailing asylum seekers' entitlements and relying on voucher schemes.

international protection conferred through refugee status. While the States which have ratified the Convention are legally bound to grant refugee status to individuals who satisfy the requirements of Art 1(A)(2), entitlement to territorial asylum remains a matter for States' domestic provisions. Territorial asylum may be regarded as a means to supplement the protection offered by refugee status. Territorial asylum is generally granted on grounds other than Convention grounds, usually referred to as humanitarian grounds. The conferment of territorial asylum amounts to recognising the need for international protection in spite of the failure to fall within the scope of the 1951 Convention. A State will grant territorial asylum where it feels that it would not be safe to return the individual concerned to his or her country of nationality or residence. In most cases, the State will also have failed to identify a safe third country, that is, a country other than the country of nationality or residence, where the person could be safely dispatched. The removal of an individual in need of international protection to a country where his or her safety would be at risk would constitute a blatant violation of the principle of *non-refoulement*. Originally enshrined in Art 33 of the 1951 Convention, this principle is now believed to be a rule of international customary law.[9] As in the case of Convention refugees, persons who have been granted territorial asylum enjoy a permanent status and thus a wider range of rights.

Temporary protection

In recent years, many traditional host countries have introduced various forms of temporary protection. This trend is particularly evident in Member States of the European Union (EU) where the development of temporary protection schemes was concomitant with conflicts in former Yugoslavia and the resulting mass influx of refugees. Temporary protection was proposed by host States as the most appropriate means to address the need for international protection of large groups,[10] because of the alleged inability of the 1951 Convention to deal with groups. It was argued that the Convention only targeted the individual asylum seeker, not groups. The view taken was that the vast majority of those fleeing former Yugoslavia were not entitled to refugee status as they were either alleging gender-based persecution or fleeing non-State persecution.[11]

9 See, eg, Plender, R, *International Migration Law*, 1988, Dordrecht/Boston/London: Martinus Nijhoff, p 427.

10 See, eg, Kerber, K, 'Temporary protection: an assessment of the harmonisation policies of the European Union Member States' (1997) 9 International Journal of Refugee Law 3, p 453.

11 See above, fns 5 and 6.

However, it can be argued that this position suffers from a number of weaknesses. In order to determine whether an individual is entitled to refugee status, the claim must be formally and properly determined. These 'official assumptions' are based on restrictive interpretations of the Convention dictated by hostile asylum policies. The introduction and development of various forms of temporary protection was driven in the main by political willingness to reduce the numbers of asylum seekers and thus recognised refugees in the EU. The status of those who have been granted temporary protection is precarious and is based on the understanding that the individuals concerned will be removed from the territory of the host country as soon as the host country judges it safe and appropriate. The precariousness of the status inherent in temporary protection is reflected in the limited numbers of rights it confers. For instance, the right to work is usually denied and entitlements to benefits curtailed. Whilst temporary protection may be suitable in certain circumstances,[12] it should not be construed by host country governments as a substitute for refugee status.

Displaced persons

Another category of individuals in need of international protection is that of displaced persons. These probably form the most disadvantaged group. Displaced persons have been driven from their country of nationality or residence as a result of that State's failure to secure their safety. They will often find themselves in refugee camps in neighbouring States, having been unable to reach a third country where they can apply for refugee status, enjoy territorial asylum, or warrant temporary protection. In some instances, these individuals may be internally displaced, compelled to move to another area of their country of origin or residence in equally distressing conditions. Displaced people who find themselves in refugee camps do not enjoy any kind of status and are entirely dependent on the 'generosity' of the international community, often relying on assistance provided by non-governmental organisations. This has particularly detrimental effects on their right to health and it can be argued that such a right is in fact denied.

12 Eg, the use of temporary protection may be justified where a prompt response to a massive need for international protection is required. This type of protection may also be contemplated where the need for international protection has a temporary nature. However, this is very difficult to foresee, and the adequacy of temporary protection decreases as the need for international protection lengthens.

THE RIGHT TO HEALTH: DEFINITIONAL ISSUES

Health as a human right has been the object of much definitional controversy and there is still disagreement amongst commentators as to terminology.[13] The most commonly used expressions are 'right to health' and 'right to health care', although other expressions are in use.[14] This definitional debate must not be overlooked, since the choice of terminology is not neutral and contributes to defining the scope of the right to health.

The author has opted for the phrase 'right to health', because at international level the expression 'right to health' is the most consistent with the wording of relevant international instruments,[15] and because it is critical to ensure that the chosen terminology does not unnecessarily restrict the right to health. The phrase 'right to health' is not confined to health care, but covers a range of rights. The expression 'right to health care' instead of 'right to health' carries the risk that some essential aspects of the right to health such as access to drinking water, adequate nutrition and housing, will be excluded. A study of the right to health of refugees under international law goes beyond issues arising from access to health care, and extends to living conditions.

THE SIGNIFICANCE OF A RIGHT TO HEALTH FOR REFUGEES

It is argued that it is critical that international law ensures refugees' right to health. The arguments underpinning this statement are threefold. First, it is vital to the well being of refugees themselves. The majority of refugees are dependent on host countries for the fulfilment of their most basic needs such as food, housing and health care. This situation is exacerbated by the fact that refugees' access to the labour market of host countries is generally very limited.[16] Serious concern has been raised with regard to refugees' health and their living conditions at large. For instance, the risk of tuberculosis transmission, which is enhanced in confined environments, may be further

---

13 Toebes, BCA, *The Right to Health as a Human Right in International Law*, 1999, Oxford: Hart-Intersentia, pp 16–20. See, also, Chapter 5.

14 The expression 'right to health protection' is also used (*ibid*, p 16). The phrase 'health rights' is also occasionally used (Tomasevski, K, 'Health rights', in Eide, A, Krause, C and Rosas, A (eds), *Economic, Social and Cultural Rights: A Textbook*, 1995, Dordrecht/Boston/London: Kluwer, pp 125–43).

15 It is also the most frequently used by United Nations sources and academics (see Toebes, BCA, *The Right to Health as a Human Right in International Law*, 1999, Oxford: Hart-Intersentia, p 16).

16 *Circulaire Ministérielle* 26 September 1991, *Journal Officiel de la République Française* 27 September 1991, p 12606.

aggravated in reception centres and other forms of accommodation designed to shelter asylum seekers.[17] The poorest conditions are generally found in refugee camps where access to drinking water, sanitation and other basic services is often insufficient. Outbreaks of infectious disease are frequently reported.[18]

Secondly, ensuring refugees' right to health is also important for the populations of host countries, as the State of refugees' health is not without consequences for the host community. This is particularly so in relation to communicable diseases. As stressed in the Preamble to the WHO Constitution:[19] '[U]nequal development in different countries in the promotion of health and the control of disease, especially communicable disease, is a common danger.' This is, for instance, the case with tuberculosis. This disease is often highly prevalent in developing countries. It has been found that tuberculosis is more common amongst asylum seekers and other categories of people in need of international protection whose status is precarious than it is amongst host country residents, including nationals and other foreigners.[20] It is in the interest of host country populations that refugees receive adequate health care in order to prevent the communication of infectious diseases. Not only is it important to ensure health care, it is also imperative that refugees' living conditions are not conducive to disease. Poor housing is very often connected with the risk of tuberculosis.

The third reason for ensuring refugees' right to health under international law relates to the very nature of refugee matters. These have an inherent international dimension that undermines the efficiency of States'

17 Van Loenhout Rooyackers, JH, 'Risk of tuberculosis in the inadequate handling of refugees seeking asylum' (1994) Ned Tijdschr Geneeskd 138, p 2496, referred to in Bollini, P, 'Asylum seekers: entitlements, health status, and human rights issues (1997) European Journal of Health Law 4, p 259.

Concern was also raised in relation to asylum seekers' access to HIV prevention programmes. Many of these programmes do not specifically target refugees and may never reach them, mainly because of language and cultural differences (Burgi, D and Fleury, F, 'A national AIDS prevention programme for migrants', in Haour-Knipe, M and Rector, R (eds), *Crossing Borders. Migration, Ethnicity and AIDS*, 1996, London: Taylor and Francis, pp 136–53, referred to in *ibid*, Bolloni).

18 See, eg, WHO, Communicable Disease Surveillance and Response (CSR), Disease outbreaks reported, 20 January 1997, 'Health situation in Rwandan refugee camp in Zaire'; WHO, Communicable Disease Surveillance and Response (CSR), Disease outbreaks reported, 6 December 1996, 'Cholera in refugees: Kigoma, Tanzania'; and Press Release WHO/18, 6 April 1999, 'Communicable diseases are main health threat to Kosovo refugees'.

19 Constitution of the World Health Organisation (WHO), 14 UNTS 186.

20 Shang, H and Desgranchamps, D, 'Tuberkulose in der Schweiz' (1995) Schweiz Rundsch Med Prax 84, p 1114, referred to in Bollini, P, 'Asylum seekers: entitlements, health status, and human rights issues (1997) European Journal of Health Law 4, p 259. However, this is not necessarily the case where health standards are generally poor in the host country.

individual initiatives in this field. Poor health conditions in refugee camps situated close to borders may have detrimental consequences for neighbouring countries in facilitating the communication of infectious disease. Refugee issues, because of their magnitude, cannot be dealt with by a single State,[21] and international co-operation is essential. A joint action of the international community must aim to ensure refugees' right to health. This need for international co-operation has been acknowledged by the Member States of the EU,[22] recognising that their laws and policies on asylum had an interdependent nature and could no longer be considered to fall within the exclusive competence of each Member State. With the adoption of the Treaty of Amsterdam of October 1997,[23] competence in asylum matters has now been transferred to the European Community (EC).[24] The need for co-operation amongst the Member States was reinforced by the integrated nature of the EC, and in particular the free movement of persons. This does not, however, undermine the international dimension of refugee issues, including health, and thus the need for an international response.

RELEVANT INTERNATIONAL PROVISIONS

In order to identify international provisions on the basis of which refugees' right to health may be established, international refugee law, international human rights law and World Health Organisation (WHO) instruments will need to be considered.

International refugee law

The first, and most obvious, field of international law to examine is that of international refugee law. The primary instrument of international refugee law is the 1951 Convention, the scope and status of which are confined to

21 This is particularly the case in situations of large numbers of refugees. Eg, neighbouring countries, on their own, would have been unable to cope with the exodus following the events in Kosovo.

22 The purpose of Title VI on Justice and Home Affairs (also known as the third pillar) of the Treaty on European Union (TEU), which came into force on 1 November 1993, was to render intergovernmental co-operation compulsory in a number of areas of 'common interest' which included asylum (Art K1(1)).

23 OJ C340 10.11.97, p 173.

24 Title IV of the Treaty Establishing the European Community (TEC) on visas, asylum, immigration and other policies related to free movement of persons. However, three Member States have, for the time being, opted out of this transfer of competence. So far as the UK, Ireland and Denmark are concerned, asylum matters remain governed by intergovernmental co-operation.

one category of individuals in need of international protection, recognised refugees.[25] The Convention does not contain provisions that guarantee recognised refugees' rights to health as such. However, a number of Convention articles may contribute towards the recognition of such a right. These articles are found in Chapter III on gainful employment and Chapter IV on welfare issues. The relevant provisions are Art 21 on housing, Art 17 on wage-earning employment and Art 24 on labour legislation and social security.[26]

Under Art 21 of Chapter IV, the host country provisions on housing must offer recognised refugees legally residing in its territory a 'treatment as favourable as possible' and this treatment must not be less favourable than that of non-nationals who find themselves 'in the same circumstances'.[27] Entitlement to adequate housing can be regarded as forming part of the right to health, as poor housing conditions are likely to have an adverse effect on heath. However, Art 21 of the Convention does not go so far as to confer a right to adequate housing upon recognised refugees, and only sets a minimum standard as an objective to be attained by the States party to the 1951 Convention. The article does not impose on States any substantive requirements as to the quality of housing, leaving the matter to the competence of those States which are party to the Convention. The extent and appropriateness of the right granted to recognised refugees by the Convention in terms of housing will depend upon the States' own provisions on housing for non-nationals who are lawful residents.

Article 17 of Chapter III on gainful employment[28] is also relevant, providing that recognised refugees who are legally residents shall be granted the 'most favourable treatment accorded to nationals of a foreign

25 Certain provisions may also apply to other categories of persons in need of international protection such as asylum seekers. However, these provisions do not relate to the status of refugees as organised by the 1951 Convention. This is the case, for instance, of Art 33 of the Convention which establishes the principle of *non-refoulement*. According to this principle, individuals shall not be returned to a country where their life may be at risk.

26 Article 20 on rationing is also relevant, providing that where a rationing system exists in the host country with a view to regulating the distribution of goods in short supply, recognised refugees shall enjoy the benefit of this system on the same basis as nationals. However, this article will only apply in exceptional circumstances. The insertion of Art 20 may be explained by the fact that the 1951 Convention was drafted in the aftermath of the Second World War, at a time where rationing systems may have still been in force or recently abrogated.

27 'For the purpose of this Convention [the 1951 Convention], the term "in the same circumstances" implies that any requirements (including requirements as to the length and condition of sojourn or residence) which the particular individual would have to fulfil for the enjoyment of the right in question, if he were not a refugee, must be fulfilled by him, with the exception of requirements which by their nature a refugee is incapable of fulfilling' (Art 6).

28 Access to gainful employment, in other words access to the labour market, is strictly confined to employment which is lawful.

country in the same circumstances'. Whilst this provision does not directly concern recognised refugees' right to health, it addresses, to a limited extent, the situation of dependency in which most people in need of international protection find themselves. Access to the labour market may enable these individuals to address their basic needs, such as food and housing, and the ability to cater for personal needs as well as those of one's family members is an important factor in preserving dignity. Living conditions that undermine refugees' dignity may have an adverse effect on their mental health and aggravate any mental health problems caused by their circumstances as refugees.

Article 17 of the 1951 Convention suffers from the same weaknesses as Art 21. The benefit is granted exclusively to recognised refugees, and the extent to which recognised refugees may access the labour market is left to States' discretion. The treatment across States will vary. Access to employment is particularly problematic with regard to individuals who do not enjoy permanent status. The precarious nature of their situation is often presented by host country governments and potential employers as an obstacle to the right to work in the host country. Whilst this reasoning may be justified in relation to short sojourns, its pertinence decreases as refugees' stays lengthen. States' reluctance further to extend the right to work for refugees is not the only reason why access to employment is limited. Refugees may face difficulties in finding employment because of language barriers, skill and qualification issues or difficulties in establishing qualifications. Employment opportunities, because of the economic situation in the host country, may be scarce.

Finally, Art 24 of the 1951 Convention is also pertinent to refugees' right to health. This article provides that recognised refugees shall receive the same treatment as nationals in respect of a number of matters including family allowances, working hours and minimum age of employment as well as rights under social security schemes.[29] Whilst Art 24 provides that refugees enjoy the same treatment as nationals, entitlements are confined to recognised refugees, and the quality of that treatment remains a matter for the laws of the States party to the Convention. Thus, although the 1951 Convention is central to the protection of refugees, its contribution to the recognition of the right to health of refugees is limited.

It is also necessary to examine the recommendations and other documents adopted by the United Nations High Commissioner for Refugees

---

29 Article 24(b)(i) and (ii) provides for limitations to recognised refugees' entitlements to social security rights. It reads that: 'There may be appropriate arrangements for the maintenance of acquired rights and rights in the course of acquisition; national laws or regulations of the country of residence may prescribe special arrangements concerning benefits which are payable wholly out of public funds, and concerning allowances paid to persons who do not fulfil the contribution conditions prescribed for the award of a normal pension.'

(UNHCR), although they lack binding effect. There is no UNHCR document that expressly recognises refugees' right to health, but UNHCR's recommendations may be useful in specifying what the right to health entails with regard to refugees. UNHCR has stressed the specific needs of particularly vulnerable individuals; for example, through the UNHCR's Guidelines on the Protection of Refugee Women.[30] These Guidelines primarily apply to refugee women who find themselves in refugee camps and emphasise the need for assistance policies designed to ensure that refugee women gain access to food, shelter, health care and clean water. UNHCR's concern has been prompted by reports from people working within refugee camps or other places of settlement, pointing out that female refugees face more difficulties than their male counterparts.[31] It has been noted that in many instances, women have not enjoyed equal access to health services and that their specific needs have often been overlooked.[32] Women's health is also considered in the context of UNHCR's Guidelines on Applicable Criteria and Standards relating to the Detention of Asylum-Seekers.[33] Guideline 8 on the detention of women provides that the special needs of female asylum-seekers who are detained must be addressed and, in particular, their need for gynaecological and obstetric services. Guideline 8 also stipulates that: '[A]s a general rule the detention of pregnant women who are in their last months as well as nursing mothers, both of whom have special needs, should be avoided.' Guideline 10(v) provides that 'asylum-seekers should have the opportunity to receive appropriate medical treatment, and psychological counselling where appropriate', and Guideline 7 considers the detention of groups of individuals deemed particularly vulnerable, unaccompanied elderly persons, torture or trauma victims and persons with mental or physical disability. Alternatives to detention must be contemplated in the case of individuals falling within these categories and where such persons are detained:

> ... it is advisable that this should only be on the certification of a qualified medical practitioner that detention will not adversely affect their health and well being. In addition there must be regular follow up and support by a relevant skilled professional. They must also have access to services, hospitalisation and medication counselling, etc, should it become necessary.

30 Information note on UNHCR's Guidelines on the Protection of Refugee Women, Executive Committee of the High Commissioner's Programme, Forty-Second Session, EC/SCP/67, 22 July 1991.

31 In its Progress Report on the Implementation of the UNHCR Guidelines on the Protection of Refugee Women, UNHCR reiterated its concern with regard to refugee women's state of health and access to health services in certain countries (EC/SCP/74, 22 July 1992).

32 Eg, it was reported that gynaecological services were often inadequate. UNHCR noted that the recruitment of additional female staff had helped, although the situation remained problematic.

33 UNHCR's Guidelines on Applicable Criteria and Standards relating to the Detention of Asylum Seekers, Geneva, 10 February 1999.

UNHCR has contributed to drawing the needs of the refugee population to the attention of the international community. In doing so, the High Commissioner has stressed the significance of health issues. However, UNHCR's interventions cannot in themselves ensure the recognition of a right to health for refugees as its role is impaired by two major factors, both of which relate to the discretion left to States. UNHCR's instruments lack legal binding effect, and their implementation is contingent on States' willingness to comply with UNHCR's recommendations and guidelines. Moreover, UNHCR often suffers from shortages of resources in that it is almost entirely funded by direct, voluntary contributions from governments, non-governmental organisations and individuals.[34] In practice, the amount of resources available to UNHCR largely depends upon States' 'generosity' and the effectiveness of UNHCR is to a large extent entrusted with States.

Whilst international refugee law must not be disregarded when examining refugees' right to health, the limits of its contribution must not be ignored and other areas of international law must be considered. These are international human rights law and WHO instruments.

International human rights law

The first instrument of international human right law that may be considered is the Universal Declaration of Human Rights (UDHR) 1948.[35] Article 25 of the Declaration reads:

> 1 Everyone has the right to a standard of living adequate for the health and well-being of himself and his family, including food, clothing, housing and medical care and necessary social services, and the right to security in the event of unemployment, sickness, disability, widowhood, old age or other lack of livelihood in circumstances beyond his control.
>
> 2 Motherhood and childhood are entitled to special care and assistance. All children, whether born in or out of wedlock, shall enjoy the same social protection.

The UDHR confers rights upon individuals regardless of their status. All persons in need of international protection should, in principle, be entitled under its provisions. The Declaration is a milestone instrument of human rights whose influence in the development of modern human rights law must not be undermined. However, its lack of binding effect renders its effectiveness problematic.

34 There is also a very limited subsidy emanating from the regular budget of the United Nations. The latter is used exclusively for administrative costs.

35 General Assembly Resolution 217A (III) 10 December 1948.

Another instrument of international human rights law that may be considered is the International Covenant on Economic, Social and Cultural Rights (ICESCR) 1966.[36] Article 12 is particularly important with regard to the right to health, providing that '[t]he States Parties to the present Covenant recognise the right of everyone to the enjoyment of the highest attainable standard of physical and mental health'.[37] Article 12 can be interpreted as requiring host countries to take reasonable steps 'to achieve the full realisation'[38] of this right enshrined in the Covenant in relation to refugees present in their territory.

Other instruments of international human rights law that may be examined are the Convention on the Elimination of All Forms of Discrimination Against Women (CEDAW) 1979[39] and the Convention on the Rights of the Child (CRC) 1989.[40] Although the scope of these instruments is more limited, their relevance in relation to refugees' right to health must not be undermined, as women and children represent a considerable proportion of the refugee population worldwide.

Article 12 of the CEDAW provides for the right to health care for women; it reads:

> 1 The States Parties shall take all appropriate measures to eliminate discrimination against women in the field of health care in order to ensure, on a basis of equality of men and women, access to health care services, including those relating to family planning.
>
> 2 Notwithstanding the provisions of paragraph 1 of this Article, States Parties shall ensure to women appropriate services in connection with pregnancy, confinement and the post-natal period, granting free services where necessary, as well as adequate nutrition during pregnancy and lactation.

Article 12 of the CEDAW is limited in its personal and material scope when compared to Art 25 of the UDHR and Art 12 of the ICESCR. CEDAW only applies to women as its primary objective is the prevention of discrimination, and focuses on equality of access to health care rather than the right to health as such. The CRC, whilst it is confined to children's rights,

---

36 UN Doc A/6316 (1966).

37 Article 12(2) of the ICESCR stipulates: 'The steps to be taken by the State Parties to the present covenant to achieve the full realization of this right shall include those necessary for: (a) the provision for the reduction of the stillbirth-rate and of infant mortality and for the healthy development of the child; (b) the improvement of all aspects of environmental and industrial hygiene; (c) the prevention, treatment and control of epidemic, endemic, occupational and other diseases; (d) the creation of conditions which would assure to all medical service and medical attention in the event of sickness.'

38 *Ibid*.

39 UN Doc A/34/46 (1980).

40 28 ILM 1448 (1989).

recognises a comprehensive right to health on the part of a child. Article 24(1) stipulates:

> States Parties recognise the right of the child to the enjoyment of the highest attainable standard of health and to facilities for the treatment of illness and rehabilitation of health. States Parties shall strive to ensure that no child is deprived of his or her right of access to such health care services.[41]

These instruments demonstrate that health is a recurrent topic in international human rights law. The obligations these instruments impose on States which are party to them as regards health may be used further to found and define their duties as host countries towards refugees.[42] However, the implementing difficulties that characterise the international legal order should not be overlooked. The absence of effective supervisory mechanisms means that sanctions for States' failures to comply with international law are often of limited effect. In the international legal order, the State very much remains the 'champion' of individual rights. In practice, this means that where a State is unwilling or unable to perform these obligations, the individuals who fall within its jurisdiction will generally be deprived of the benefit of the rights conferred by international law, including the right to health.[43]

WHO instruments

The WHO is the most important international organisation in the field of health. The WHO Constitution came into force on 7 April 1948. This instrument constitutes an international treaty which is legally binding upon

41 Article 24 of the CRC continues: '2. States Parties shall pursue full implementation of this right and, in particular, shall take appropriate measures: (a) to diminish infant and child mortality; (b) to ensure the provision of necessary medical assistance and health care to all children with emphasis on the development of primary health care; (c) to combat disease and malnutrition, including within the framework of primary health care, through, *inter alia*, the application of readily available technology and through the provision of adequate nutritious foods and clean drinking-water, taking into consideration the dangers and risks of environmental pollution; (d) to ensure appropriate prenatal and post-natal care for mothers; (e) to ensure that all segments of society, in particular parents and children, are informed, have access to education and are supported in the use of basic knowledge of child health and nutrition, the advantages of breastfeeding, hygiene and environmental sanitation and the prevention of accidents; (f) to develop preventive health care, guidance for parents and family planning education and services. 3. States Parties shall take all effective and appropriate measures with a view to abolishing traditional practices prejudicial to the health of children. 4. States Parties undertake to promote and encourage international co-operation with a view to achieving progressively the full realization of the right recognized in the present article. In this regard, particular account shall be taken of the needs of developing countries.'

42 It is acknowledged that not all States are parties to these international instruments.

43 Robertson, AH and Merrills, JG, *Human Rights in the World: an Introduction to the Study of the International Protection of Human Rights*, 1996, Manchester: Manchester UP, pp 278–82.

those States which have signed and ratified it. The right to health is set forth in the preamble to the WHO Constitution:

> Health is a state of complete physical, mental and social well-being and not merely the absence of disease or infirmity. The enjoyment of the highest attainable standard of health is one of the fundamental rights of every human being without distinction of race, religion, political belief, economic or social conditions ...[44]

In 1977, the World Health Assembly determined that: 'the major social goal of governments and WHO should be the attainment by all people of the world by the year 2000 of a level of health that would permit them to lead a socially and economically productive life.'[45] In 1981, the WHO Assembly unanimously adopted a global strategy for health for all by 2000 known as the 'Health for All by the Year 2000' programme.[46] 'Health for All' is defined as meaning that 'resources for health are evenly distributed and that essential health care is accessible to everyone'.[47]

The wording of WHO instruments suggests that the right to health is granted to 'every human being' on a non-discriminatory basis. There is no justification for excluding refugees. This view is supported by the WHO, which has expressed concern for refugees' health and remains involved in actions designed to improve it. Some of these actions have been initiated in conjunction with UNHCR.[48] However, the wording of the last sentence of the Preamble to the WHO Constitution reads that '[g]overnments have a responsibility for the health of their peoples which can be fulfilled only by the provision of adequate health and social provisions'. The words 'their people' are susceptible of restrictive interpretations by governments and there is a risk that some States may attempt to exclude non-nationals from

---

44 The Preamble to the WHO Constitution continues as follows: 'The health of all peoples is fundamental to the attainment of peace and security and is dependent upon the fullest co-operation of individuals and States. The achievement of any State in the promotion and protection of health is of value to all. Unequal development in different countries in the promotion of health and control of disease, especially communicable disease, is a common danger. Healthy development of the child is of basic importance; the ability to live harmoniously in a changing total environment is essential to such development. The extension to all peoples of the benefits of medical, psychological and related knowledge is essential to the fullest attainment of health. Informed opinion and active co-operation on the part of the public are of the utmost importance in the improvement of the health of the people. Governments have a responsibility for the health of their peoples which can be fulfilled only by the provision of adequate health and social provisions.'

45 http://www.who.int/aboutwho/en/healthforall.htm

46 WHO, *Global Strategy for Health for All by the Year 2000* (adopted in WHO Resolution WHA.34.36), 1981.

47 *Ibid*.

48 Eg, the action taken by WHO following reports of UNHCR in 1996 on a cholera outbreak in the Kigoma refugee camp in Tanzania. Measures were taken to improve, *inter alia*, water and sanitation (above, fn 18). UNHCR and WHO published *A Manual on Mental Health of Refugees* (WHO in collaboration with UNHCR, 1996). WHO initiated a project in this field which started in the WHO Programme on Mental Health in 1996.

the scope of their responsibilities in the field of health. This is particularly worrying with regard to refugees, and in particular to those who do not enjoy permanent status such as asylum seekers or persons in refugee camps. Whilst such restrictive interpretations are inconsistent with WHO initiatives, refugees as well as non-nationals at large would benefit from more precise wording that would leave no doubt as to the extent of governments' responsibilities. The words 'their people' must be construed as embracing any person residing within State territory if discrimination is to be avoided.

International law recognises a right to health for all human beings. Some instruments, such as the CRC or the CEDAW, may have a more restricted personal scope. However, these must be construed as strengthening and specifying the right to health granted by instruments such as the WHO Constitution, the UDHR and the ICESCR. It follows that refugees, irrespective of their status, have a right to health. This may be affirmed despite the absence of an international instrument expressly recognising the right to health of people in need of international protection.

THE IMPLEMENTATION OF THE RIGHT TO HEALTH FOR REFUGEES: A FAILURE

To date, the international community has failed adequately to implement refugees' right to health.[49] A number of reasons may explain this failure. They relate to the implementing difficulties inherent in the international legal order, the absence of international provisions specifically dealing with refugees' right to health, stretched resources and prejudice against refugees.

Deficient implementation mechanisms of international law

It is recognised that mechanisms for the implementation of international law are often less than satisfactory and do not offer the same degree of efficiency as in some national or regional systems.[50] This can have an adverse effect on refugees' right to health. For instance, in relation to the ICESCR,[51] Arts 16–25 of the Covenant provide for a system of periodic reports made by States. These reports are designed to monitor States' achievements and progress in relation to the rights guaranteed by the Covenant. The task of supervising the implementation of the ICESCR was initially entrusted to the

49 It is acknowledged that people in need of international protection are not the only category of people whose right to health is poorly implemented.

50 See, eg, the EC and the European Convention of Human Rights systems.

51 Robertson, AH and Merrills, JG, *Human Rights in the World: An Introduction to the Study of the International Protection of Human Rights*, 1996, Manchester: Manchester UP, p 278.

Economic and Social Council (ECOSOC) and now lies with the United Nations Committee on Economic, Social and Cultural Rights. At present, the system of international control of the ICESCR is confined to a reporting procedure, as there is no provision for individual communications. The possibility of such communications would, of course, significantly improve the implementation of the Covenant.[52] Implementation issues have also arisen in relation to the WHO. As in the case of the ICESCR, supervision takes place through a reporting procedure.[53] The WHO is also obliged to report to the ECOSOC, and now to the United Nations Committee on Economic, Social and Cultural Rights, on compliance with the relevant provisions of the ICESCR.[54] However, the WHO has only submitted one report on the implementation of the Covenant to the Committee.[55] The efficiency of reporting procedures depends to a great extent on States' goodwill and this is where their main weakness lies. The WHO has also been criticised for not placing more emphasis on the implementation of the right to health and it has been argued that the Organisation should have been more proactive in assisting and encouraging its members.[56] In particular, it has been contended that the WHO should have made greater use of its legislative powers.[57] The problems arising from the implementation of international law are exacerbated where international instruments lack legal binding effect. Such is the case with UNHCR's recommendations.

The lack of international provisions expressly recognising refugees' right to health

Various instruments of international law uphold the right to health for all, others further specify this right in relation to certain categories of individuals such as children or women. However, there are no international provisions that explicitly deal with refugees' right to health. Whilst, in principle, refugees are entitled under international law through instruments such as the UDHR, the ICESCR and the WHO Constitution as they apply to all people, it is argued that this absence of specific provisions has had an adverse effect on refugees' health. As suggested in relation to the Preamble

52 Robertson, AH and Merrills, JG, *Human Rights in the World: An Introduction to the Study of the International Protection of Human Rights*, 1996, Manchester: Manchester UP, pp 281–82.

53 According to Art 61 of the WHO Constitution, Member States of the Organisation are under the obligation to report to the WHO as regards their achievements and progress in improving peoples' health.

54 Article 18 of the ICESCR.

55 UN Doc E/1980/24.

56 Taylor, AL, 'Making the World Health Organization work: a legal framework for universal access to the conditions for health' (1992) 12 Am JL & Med 4, p 302.

57 *Ibid*, p 330. See also Chapter 4 by Yutaka Arai-Takahashi, above.

to the WHO Constitution, international provisions on the right to health may be subject to restrictive governmental interpretations and conducive to the development of laws and policies that may exclude refugees from the scope of provisions on health. This is aggravated by the fact that implementing mechanisms at international level lack efficiency.

Shortage of resources

The need for more efficient systems of control suggests that States are not fulfilling their duties under international law in the field of health. Whilst some elements of the international community may simply be unwilling to comply with their obligations, the existence of serious resource problems must be acknowledged. All States are not on an equal footing when it comes to fulfilling international obligations in relation to refugees. Some States will have greater numbers of refugees than others because of their geographical location or regional political climate. Compliance with international obligations will be burdensome where a State is both a developing country and a significant host country. In these circumstances, the difficulties encountered by States are not confined to refugee issues, but affect the local population at large. In most instances, these countries will already be facing financial hardship, poor and scarce health care facilities including shortages of qualified personnel, as well as poor access to drinking water, food and adequate accommodation. The state of destitution that characterises the situation of the majority of refugees makes matters worse not only for refugees themselves, but also for host countries. States which find themselves in such situations are dependent on direct international assistance from other States or provided through international organisations such as UNHCR and WHO and, to a considerable extent, non-governmental organisations. These international organisations, both governmental and non-governmental, also face financial difficulties.[58]

Without undermining the problems faced by developed countries in implementing refugees' right to health, it must be noted that they are not of the extent experienced by developing countries. Yet in recent years, a number of European countries have expressed concern as to their ability to 'cope' with the increase in the number of refugees following the conflicts in former Yugoslavia. In the UK, health service representatives argue that they do not have the means to address refugees' health needs.[59] They 'blame' the

58 Eg, in March 1998, UNHCR declared that it needed almost US$160 m to help hundreds of thousands of refugees in the Great Lake region of Africa (BBC News, 'UN refugee agency calls for cash', 2 March 1998, http://news6.thdo.bbc.co.uk/hi/english/world/africa/newsid_61000/61492.stm.

59 'Refugees could break NHS', http://www.news.bbc.co.uk/hi/english/uk/wales/newsid_836000/836321.stm.

current state of the National Health Service, which is already overloaded, as well as their lack of awareness of refugees' specific needs. It is claimed that refugees often have complex medical needs and that religious requirements, language barriers and the absence of medical records makes the diagnostic process very difficult.[60] The difficulties faced by developed countries are not confined to access to health care. Local councils in the UK have argued that they are unable to provide adequate accommodation for refugees, prompting government initiatives to disperse refugees across the UK.[61]

If refugees' right to health is to be improved, it is important to acknowledge the difficulties that some States may face and act upon them. However, it is also important to ensure that States do not use difficulties, actual or potential, to legitimise curtailments in refugees' entitlements.

Prejudice against refugees

A final factor that contributes to the failure of the international community to implement refugees' right to health satisfactorily lies with attitudes towards refugees in host countries. Local populations are not always welcoming, and refugees may face hostility upon arrival in the host country. Prejudice against refugees has undermined the implementation of refugees' right to health in a number of countries and governments have used and even fostered public negative perceptions of refugees in order to justify the adoption of increasingly restrictive policies and laws on asylum.[62] This is, for instance, the case in the UK with the adoption of the 1999 Immigration and Asylum Act, which has been criticised for significantly curtailing asylum seekers' entitlements.[63] It is critical to the implementation of refugees' rights, including their right to health, that governments do not encourage and use prejudice against refugees to legitimise domestic laws and policies inconsistent with their obligations under international law.

---

60 'GPs need help with refugees-report', http://www.news.bbc.co.uk/hi/english/uk/wales/newsid_218000/218100.stm

61 See, eg, Taylor, D, 'Councils hit by U-turn over asylum seekers', in *Refugees in Britain*: special report, 5 March 2000, http://www.newsunlimited.co.uk/Refugees_in_Britain/Story/0,2763,143456,00.html and 'Refugee dispersal plans attacked', BBC News, UK Politics, 1 June 2000, http://news.bbc.co.uk.

62 Amongst the 'cruel myths' about refugees is the common belief that 'only a tiny proportion of refugees are genuine and the rest are bogus' and that 'refugees only come ... for the money' (Hardwick, N, 'Cruel myths' (1999) *The Guardian*, 17 February).

63 See, eg, 'Asylum vouchers spark protests', BBC News, UK Politics, 3 April 2000, http://news.bbc.co.uk.

CONCLUSION

International law is not silent on the issue of refugees' right to health, and international provisions that recognise this right can be identified. However, to date, the situation worldwide gives the impression of a 'legal vacuum' in this area. Whilst the existence of relevant provisions is a significant step, this achievement will remain *'lettre-morte'* if implementation is not ensured. Difficulties lie primarily with deficient implementation mechanisms, and with the fact that while refugees fall within the scope of international provisions regarding the right to health, there is not an instrument which specifically upholds their right to health.

The adoption of a specific instrument could contribute to strengthening refugees' right to health. This would constitute an opportunity to determine the scope of the right by reference to relevant international instruments, while stressing the specificity of some of refugees' health needs. For instance, refugees may have mental health problems caused by having had to flee their country of origin in tragic circumstances. Moreover, as noted by Kemp: '[m]any refugees also experience environmental problems in the host country that negatively affect their mental health.'[64] Difficulties such as language barriers also need to be overcome. However, the adoption of such an instrument will not solve the problems regarding the implementation of international law. These are issues that go far beyond the scope of refugees' right to health under international law.

In enhancing refugees' right to health, the difficulties faced by certain host countries as well as international organisations must be acknowledged if implementation is to be improved. It is argued that a principle of solidarity[65] should underpin the application of international provisions on health and assistance. This may take the form of financial help or assistance in situ. The principle of solidarity rests upon a higher degree of co-operation amongst the international community. Health provision for refugees must not be perceived as an individual matter for the host country dealing with a particular group of refugees, but as a responsibility shared by the international community. More intensive co-operation is contingent on States' willingness to take such a step, but it must acknowledged that international co-operation, whatever the issue at stake, is an onerous and ambitious goal.

---

64 Kemp, C, 'Mental health issues among refugees', http://www.baylor.edu/~Charles_Kemp/refugee_mental_health.htm.

65 An application of the principle of solidarity may be found in Art 63(2)(b) of the TEC; it reads: 'The Council, acting in accordance with the procedure referred to in Article 67, shall, within a period of five years after the entry into force of the Treaty of Amsterdam, adopt ... measures ... [designed to] promot[e] a balance of effort between Member States in receiving and bearing the consequences of receiving refugees and displaced persons.'

In these circumstances, is international law the most adequate framework for ensuring refugees' right to health? In theory, the international legal order is the most appropriate framework, as it reflects the international nature of refugee issues. To be fully effective, problems need to be tackled at international level. However, the international system suffers from a number of weaknesses that, at present, prevent a satisfactory implementation of refugees' right to health. Whilst this international approach should not be abandoned as it is potentially the most effective, other frameworks may also be considered. Initiatives should be taken at regional level, particularly where co-operation is already well established. The EC provides a good example. The Treaty of Amsterdam has recently transferred asylum matters to the competence of the EC,[66] and the EC legal order has the benefit of more advanced implementing mechanisms. It is to be hoped that the measures to be adopted by the EC in the field of asylum will recognise refugees' right to health in line with international law provisions. The policies of the EC may have repercussions beyond its borders. Hence, if the EC were to fail to comply with international requirements regarding refugees' rights, including the right to health, this would send 'worrying signs' to the rest of the international community.

66 Title IV of the TEC (see fn 24).

CHAPTER 7

PARTICULAR ISSUES OF PUBLIC HEALTH: THE LEGAL FRAMEWORK OF POPULATION CONTROL

Robyn Martin and Linda Johnson

INTRODUCTION

In October 1999, the world's population was calculated to have reached 6 billion,[1] tripling the population of 1927, and by the year 2050, the population is predicted to approach 9 billion.[2]

The growing world population has, for a long time, been a public health concern in that the size of the earth's population is an important determinant of its condition and the condition of the individuals who populate it.[3] Understanding of the relationship between population density and health has evolved as sociologists have questioned scientific and mathematical models of population growth. Early studies equated increasing populations with food, water and fuel over-consumption,[4] and considered over-population as a barrier to development.[5] By the time of the second UN International Conference on Population[6] in 1984, it was accepted that population growth and economic growth were not mutually exclusive, and the greater concern was the effect of over-population on the world's environment. The 1992 Earth Summit[7] introduced consideration of sustainable development as a measure of population feasibility and at the third UN Conference on Population and Development in 1994,[8] there was recognition that relationships between population size, socio-economic development, environmental harm, health and women's reproductive rights

1 Announced by the United Nations Population Fund, reported on BBC News, 12 October 1999.

2 Worldwatch Institute, Washington DC, quoted on BBC News, 11 April 1999.

3 See Editorial (1999) 319 BMJ 931.

4 See Malthus, T (Rev), *An Essay on the Principle of Population*, 1798, and the writings of neo-Malthusians such as Paul Ehrlich; eg, Ehrlich, P and Ehrlich, A, 'Symposium on population law: the population explosion: why we should care and what we should do about it' (1997) 27 Environmental Law 1187; Ehrlich, P and Holdren, J, 'The impact of population growth' (1971) 171 Science 1212; Holdren, J and Ehrlich, P, 'Human population and the global environment' (1974) 62 Am Scientist 282.

5 See the first UN Population Conference, Bucharest, 1974.

6 Held in Mexico City.

7 UN Conference on Environment and Development, Rio De Janeiro, Brazil.

8 In Cairo.

were complex. The Malthusian assumption[9] that macro-scale over-population and micro-scale large families are causes of national and domestic poverty is now treated with scepticism. At the macro level, population growth does not necessarily hinder economic growth,[10] and at micro level people have large families because they are poor (lack of access to fertility control, need for support in old age, need for increased family production for the family to survive, children as status) rather than the other way around.[11]

Discussion of population control at international level has been complicated by other agendas. The eugenics movement was behind much early policy on population growth[12] and there is still suspicion that classism[13] and racism[14] underlie some population control policies. Diverse religious positions on birth control, and diverse cultural positions on the role and status of women make any universal approach to population control difficult to achieve. There has also been tension between the first world, characterised by low population growth and surplus resources, and the developing world, characterised by high population densities and insufficient resources.[15] Population growth policies in the Western world

---

9 Malthus, T (Rev), *An Essay on the Principle of Population*, 1798.

10 See Waternberg, B and Zuismeister, K (eds), *Are World Population Trends a Problem?*, 1984, Washington: American Enterprise Institute; Kuznets, S, 'Population and economic growth' (1967) 111 Proceedings of the American Philosophical Society 3; Boserup, E, *Population and Technological Change: A Study of Long Term Trends* 1981, Chicago: Chicago UP.

11 Doyal, L, *The Political Economy of Health*, 1981, London: Pluto; Hartman, B, *Reproductive Rights and Wrongs: The Global Politics of Population Control and Reproductive Choice*, 1987, New York: Harper and Row.

12 See, eg, Furedi, F, *Population and Development: A Critical Introduction*, 1997, Cambridge: Polity; Hodgson, D, 'Orthodoxy and revisionism in American demography' (1988) 17 Population and Development Review; and Petchesky, R, *Abortion and Women's choice: The State, Sexuality and Reproductive Freedom*, 1986, London: Verso; see also Meehan, M, 'How eugenics birthed population control' (1998) Human Life Review, 22 September, cited in Slifer, D, 'Growing environmental concerns: is population control the answer?' (2000) 11 Villanova Environmental Law Journal 111; see also Gordon, S, *The History and Philosophy of Social Science*, 1991, London: Routledge.

13 See, eg, the work of Margaret Sanger, such as her pamphlet *Family Limitation*, published in 1914, where she talks of limiting the excessive fertility of the poor, associating large families with 'poverty, toil, unemployment, drunkenness, cruelty, fighting, jails' and small families with 'cleanliness, leisure, freedom, space, sunshine'; Greer, G, *Sex and Destiny: The Politics of Human Fertility*, 1984, London: Secker and Warburg.

14 See Greer, G, *Sex and Destiny: The Politics of Human Fertility*, 1984, London: Secker and Warburg; Caldwell, J and Caldwell, P, 'The South African fertility decline' (1993) 19 Population and Development Review 225; Franks, E, 'Women and resistance in East Timor' (1996) 19 Women's Studies International 155. In 1998, testimony to the Truth and Reconciliation Commission in South Africa exposed research on the release of immunocontraceptive drugs into the water supply of black African women to induce infertility. Meanwhile, white women were given inducements to reproduce. See Bennett, T, 'Reproductive health in South Africa' (1999) 114 Public Health Reports 88.

15 Hartmann, B, *Reproductive Rights and Wrongs: The Global Politics of Population Control and Contraceptive Choice*, 1987, New York: Harper and Row.

and, in particular, policies of the United Nations and the World Bank,[16] have focused on developing world populations as threats to world resources and environments, while the developing world accuses the West of reckless consumption of resources, energy waste and pollution.[17] For all this, there is wide acceptance that unchecked population growth will result in environmental, economic and social harm, as well as decline in the quality of life and health of national populations.[18] Equally, crude methods of population control, particularly coercive birth control and contraceptive trials[19] also create public health risks.

Law at national, regional and international level has an important part to play in population control policies. Legislation and practices of population control must fall within the constitutional power of governments. Resource allocation decisions must fall within the powers of the appropriate authorities. Interference with the populations of other nations is regulated and monitored by international law, while interference with the rights and bodies of women has fallen within national law. Legal regulation will be necessary for the maintenance of standards of contraceptive and abortion devices and drugs, for research and clinical trials, for methods of distribution and for price control. International trade law will govern the movement of medical products across borders. Environmental laws will be concerned with the environmental impact of contraceptive waste and dumping, particularly chemical contraceptives containing human hormones, and laws on discrimination[20] will be needed to regulate policies of population distribution and access to health services. This chapter will focus on the international, regional and national legal framework of fertility control as a mechanism of population control.

---

16 Ringel, A, 'The population policy debate and the World Bank: limits to growth vs supply-side demographics' (1993) 6 Geo International Environmental Review 213, cited in Connell, J, 'Norplant and the new paradigm of international population policy' (1995) 2 William and Mary Journal of Women and the Law 73.

17 Eg, the US in 1990 used 195 times as much commercial energy per capita as Madagascar, 20 times that of Zambia and 13 times that of China; Ehrlich, P and Ehrlich, A, 'Symposium on population law: the population explosion: why we should care and what we should do about it' (1997) 27 Environmental Law 1187.

18 See McMichael, A, *Planetary Overload: Global Environmental Change and the Health of the Human Species*, 1993, Cambridge: CUP.

19 Eg, the trial of quinacrine as a sterilising drug on women in India. China has approved the use of quinacrine, but the drug is now proscribed in India. See (1998) 316 BMJ 955; see also http://www.hsph.harvard.edu/organizations/healthnet/Sasia/repro/bolquinacrine3.html.

20 Eg, laws preventing discrimination against pregnant woman. See *Mfolo v Minister of Education, Bophuthatswana* (1994) 1 BCLR 136 (South Africa), in which pregnant students successfully challenged exclusion from schools; see Nadasen, S, *Public Health Law in South Africa*, 2000, Durban: Butterworths.

POPULATION CONTROL VERSUS FERTILITY CONTROL

It was for a long time assumed that population control was to be achieved primarily by the promotion of fertility control. The 1927 World Population Conference organised by the American birth control activist Margaret Sanger[21] assumed that population control and fertility control were more or less synonymous. While fertility control is clearly an element of population control policies, and is often the public face of population control, there are many factors that influence population levels.

Taxation and public welfare provision have traditionally been used to manipulate population growth. Laws regulating child labour and compulsory education, making children more or less financially productive, are influential on family size, and the availability of old age protection in the form of pensions and care reduces the need to provide for old age through children. Gatekeeping of access to contraception and abortion also serves to control populations. Laws regulating marriage and divorce contribute to reproductive choices. Education of women, particularly education that values women's involvement in the economic infrastructure, enables women to make informed and practical decisions about the size of their families. Government information fed through the media can influence attitudes to reproduction in accordance with population objectives. Of enduring influence, however, are the practices and traditions centred around the family which vary across cultures and which, in the absence of social revolution, have dominated attitudes to sexual relations and reproduction, particularly in the developing world.[22]

Population is determined as much by mortality rates as by birth rates. Natural disasters can result in high levels of mortality. While the causes of disaster are often outside human control, the scale of consequences is attributable to sub-standard housing, high-density population and inadequate health care. Such disasters rarely cause such significant loss of life in the Western world. Armed conflict is responsible for high mortality in both fighting and civilian populations, again exacerbated by absence of basic resources and medical care. High infant mortality resulting from poor nutrition and poor healthcare for both mother and child curbs population growth. The spread of diseases such as AIDS is responsible for thinning populations across Africa and much of the developing world, and the Worldwatch Institute claims that rising death rates are beginning to contribute to falling population levels for the first time since famine claimed

---

21 Held in Geneva.

22 See, eg, Wilson, T, *Engendering AIDS: Deconstructing Sex, Text and Epidemic*, 1997, London: Sage, who examines the varying constructions of gender and sexuality and their necessary impact on sexual safety.

30 million lives in China in the late 1950s,[23] as a result of AIDS, water shortages and shrinking croplands.

At the same time, advancements in medical science have resulted in some decrease in mortality rates and increased life expectancy. The rapid rise in population levels in India has been attributed in part to improvements in health care introduced with British colonialism resulting in 'diffusion of death control techniques'.[24] International public health programmes funding vaccination, medicines and health training have significantly reduced disease mortality across the developing world. Large scale migration to avoid drought, starvation and war can rapidly boost national population levels. Yet, the relationship between declining mortality rates and the provision of vaccination and therapy is a complex one.[25] Research examining declining disease-specific mortality rates has found the role of medicine to be very minor,[26] and others have identified links between poverty and disease[27] and development and disease[28] as determinative. Meredeth Turshen, in her international study of public health, found social and economic relations and the gender relations they support as having the most significant impact on mortality rates.[29]

Population control is not only about population numbers, but also about population distribution. Urbanisation of populations and depleted rural populations are a population control concern. Age imbalance in the population structure is also a focus for population control. The advanced age profile of populations in the West is worrying because the economically and socially productive sector of populations will be unable to support the

---

23 Worldwatch Institute, Washington DC, as reported on BBC News, 11 April 1999.

24 Davis, K, *Population of India and Pakistan*, 1968, New York: Russell and Russell.

25 Eg, the programme to eradicate smallpox was highly effective, partly because of the nature of smallpox itself (the model for germ theory and unaffected by nutritional status) and partly because of the methods employed by the WHO to effect eradication (combining surveillance with vaccinations that did not require continuous refrigeration). Similar success has not been met with programmes to deal with more complex diseases like malaria, where clinical eradication efforts have led to mutations and drug resistance. Also, traditional healers used inoculation methods by introducing tiny amounts of the smallpox infection into the blood to create immunity before Jenner invented the cow-pox vaccine. Despite the global eradication of smallpox, global mortality rates have not declined as other diseases have continued to thrive or have emerged. See Wain, H, *A History of Preventative Medicine*, 1970, Springfield, Ill: Charles C Thomas.

26 McKeown, T, *The Role of Medicine: Dream, Mirage or Nemesis?*, 1976, London: Nuffield Trust.

27 Townsend, P, and Davidson, N, *Inequalities in Health: The Black Report*, 1982, Harmondsworth: Penguin; McKinlay, J and McKinlay, S, 'The questionable contribution of medical measures to the decline of mortality in the United States in the twentieth century' (1977) Millbank Memorial Fund Quarterly 405–28.

28 Doyal, L, *The Political Economy of Health*, 1979, London: Pluto; Panos Institute, *The Hidden Costs of AIDS: The Challenge of HIV to Development*, 1992, London: Panos.

29 Turshen, M, *The Politics of Public Health*, 1989, London: Zed.

unproductive sector. The young age profile of the developing countries is worrying because a high proportion of the population is soon to reach the age of reproduction. Population control is also concerned with migration patterns, employment patterns and brain drains from poorer to developed countries.[30]

Population control can also include polices of population increase. The Government of Singapore is concerned at shrinking birth rates which are below replacement levels, and is offering financial incentives to families who have a second child.[31] France, Germany, Italy, Japan, the Republic of Korea, the Russian Federation, the UK and the US are all developing population programmes to counter population decline and population ageing, and looking to controlled migration in order to maintain an active workforce and pay growing security costs.[32] During President Ceausescu's government of Romania, fertility control was proscribed for political reasons, including the building of a pure Romanian population,[33] and similar politically motivated pronatalist policies have operated in Germany and Japan.[34]

More disturbingly, population control can also be about population 'quality', where some sectors of society are encouraged to reproduce and others discouraged.[35] Singapore has targeted the educated ethnic Chinese population in its financial incentives for reproduction, and in Israel until recently, free contraception was available only to Palestinian women, while Jewish women were encouraged to contribute through reproduction to the building of the nation.[36] Black women have historically been targeted by South African population control campaigns[37] and the poor, black, welfare

30 Boland, R, 'Population and development: the Cairo conference and programme of action: an innovative approach to population policy or old wine in a new bottle?' (1995) St Louis-Warsaw Transatlantic Law Journal 23.

31 Reported in the Christian Science Monitor, 27 September 2000.

32 UN Population Division, 'Replacement migration: is it a solution to declining and ageing populations?' Press release, 12 July 2000, United Nations Department of Economic and Social Affairs; 'Italy looks to migrants', BBC News Report, 21 March 2000; 'Greying west needs immigrants', BBC News Report, 21 March 2000.

33 Boland, R, 'Recent developments in abortion law in industrialised countries' (1990) 18 Law, Medicine and Health Care 404.

34 See Walsh, S, 'Liquid lives and liquid laws: the evolution of abortion law in Japan and the United States' (1995) International Legal Perspectives 187; and Telman, D, 'Abortion and women's legal personhood in Germany: a contribution to the feminist theory of State' (1998) 24 New York Uni Rev of Law and Social Change 91.

35 See Boland, R, 'Symposium on population law: the environment, population and women's rights' (1997) 27 Environmental Law 1137.

36 Salzberger, L *et al*, *Patterns of Contraceptive Behaviour among Jerusalem Women Seeking Pregnancy Counselling*, 1991, Jerusalem: Hebrew University; Yuval Davis, N, 'National reproduction and the "demographic race" in Israel', in Afshar, H (ed), *Women, Nation, State*, 1989 London: Macmillan, cited in Doyal, L, *What Makes Women Sick*, 1995, Basingstoke: Macmillan.

37 Klugman, B, 'Balancing means and ends – population policy in South Africa' (1993) 1 Reproductive Health Matters 44.

supported communities are the most likely targets of family planning campaigners in Western society. Sterilisation of mentally handicapped women has been based upon eugenic ideas both in the developed as well as the developing world.[38] Controversies have emerged over recent years showing that women determined as having inadequate intelligence levels were sterilised in Sweden, Australia, the US and Denmark in the false belief that this would reduce the number of dependent adults in future years.

The relationship between population control and fertility control is complex. Population control policies will include fertility control mechanisms, but there are other freestanding public health objectives of fertility control. Access to cheap, safe and effective fertility control may be provided in order to improve the health of women and their families.[39] Informed choice in the context of family planning may be seen as an essential element of an effective, comprehensive health care system. The economic benefits of women's involvement in the productive workforce might justify provision of fertility control services. The recognition of the equal status of women and the importance of reproductive choice require access to reproductive health care. The relationship between reproductive control and economic dependence, however, is an overarching one. Women who need to reproduce in order to contribute to the welfare of their extended family are unlikely to be able to control contraception in order to limit the number or frequency of births. To do so could have implications for her family or village which, in social terms, would outweigh the harm caused to her individually.

There is no simple causal relationship between fertility control and population control. Beginning in 1952, India instituted a series of five year family planning plans. In his address to the 21st International Population Congress in September 1989, the late Prime Minister of India Rajiv Gandhi noted that 'there was inadequate causal connection between our family planning programmes and the impact of these on our birth rates' and that financial outlay on family planning had not been matched by decline in

---

38 The eugenics movement was founded in England by Francis Galton in the late 19th century and many American and European States incorporated eugenic ideas into legislation allowing for the sterilisation of the so called feeble-minded, vagrants, those with mental or physical disabilities, drunkards and others. The aim behind the eugenics movement was to produce a purer race devoid of these less than perfect examples of individuals within national populations. For discussion of Western eugenics, see Buchanan, A *et al*, *From Chance to Choice: Genetics and Justice*, 2000, Cambridge: CUP. For an example of the use of eugenic thinking in Chinese law, see Johnson, L, 'Expanding eugenics or improving health care in China: commentary on the provisions of the Standing Committee of the Gansu People's Congress concerning the prohibition of reproduction by intellectually impaired persons' (1997) 24 JLS 2, pp 199–234.

39 Eg, Rebecca Cook has argued that the number and proximity of births, together with the age of the first pregnancy are major determinants of women's health in developing countries. See Cook, R, 'Human rights and reproductive self-determination' (1995) American University L Rev 975; 'International protection of women's reproductive rights' (1992) 24 NYULJ Int'l Law and Pol 647; 'International human rights and women's reproductive health' (1973) 24 Studies in Family Planning 73.

population growth.[40] High levels of access to contraception in countries such as Costa Rica, Haiti, Zimbabwe and Peru have not succeeded in reducing birth rates to replacement level, in part because the services were not supported by education policies, or rises in the standard of living.[41]

At the 1974 UN World Population Conference in Bucharest, the developing world objected to American involvement in fertility control programmes which were part of a wider population control agenda. The American approach was seen as imperialist, particularly as American policies focused on reducing third world populations with little concern for the growing population in the US. In response, the Population branch of USAID relaxed its emphasis on fertility control as population control and opted instead for social and economic development as a population control strategy. By the time of the 1984 Mexico City International Conference on Population, the fertility control/population control link had been further weakened. The Reagan Government adopted the 'Mexico City Policy', such that the US would no longer fund any family planning programme that supported abortion, thus withdrawing funding from the main international family planning organisations. It was not that population control was no longer an American or UN objective, but rather that population control was to be managed through development policies rather than fertility control mechanisms. Ironically, the development approach was not universally supported at the 1984 conference, with many developing countries calling for restoration of international funding for family planning services because development policies needed to operate in conjunction with funded access to fertility control.

FERTILITY CONTROL AND HEALTH

The 'Mexico City Policy' was reversed by President Clinton early in his term of office, and the underlying principle of population control had evolved by the time of the 1994 Cairo population conference from development to sustainable development, with sexual and reproductive health and choice seen as essential to any population control programme. The health of women, and improvement in their economic and social status, were acknowledged as primary aims rather than as means to further population policies. Access to education and health care, particularly for women, would contribute to educated choice about family planning and infant care. Quality

40 Rao, M, 'An imagined reality: Malthusianism, neo-Malthusianism and population myth', South Asia e-journal No 1, at www.hsph.harvard.edu/organisations/healthnet/Sasia/repro/rao3.html.

41 Benagiano, G, Director General of the *Istituto Superiore di Sanita*, Rome, Italy; see (2000) 320 BMJ 1207.

of life rather than crude demographic statistics were to be used as indicators of the success of population programmes, and family planning was to be promoted not as a demographic goal, but as a health goal. Health in the context of population control policies had been virtually ignored in early UN approaches to population growth, but as a result of concerted pressure by women's movements worldwide, the 1994 Cairo conference saw a change in focus from population statistics to reproductive health services. The conference acknowledged that women's health is dependent on reproductive choice in an environment of supportive health services, and that the health of the family is dependent on the health of women.[42]

However, the rhetoric of the Cairo conference has not radically altered grass roots population control operations. President Bush has now reinstated the 'Mexico City Policy' as one of his first presidential acts.[43] Given that the US is the largest source of funding of the United Nations Fund for Population Activities, this will have a significant impact on access to fertility control programmes where they are most in demand. Underfunded family planning tends to abandon reproductive choice in favour of long term contraception, sterilisation and abortion, and to neglect the health support to these services. Reports of coercive fertility control and coercive abortion in Bangladesh, Indonesia, Peru and China suggest that the aspirations of the Cairo conference have had little effect where population size is the most serious public health concern.[44]

The relationship between fertility control and health works both ways. Access to choice of fertility control is associated with improved levels of health. But, the most effective forms of fertility control involve either invasive surgery (sterilisation, for example) or long term chemical contraceptives such as Norplant, which create health risks and reduce women's reproductive choice. Fertility control research has focused on the control of women's fertility on the premise that contraception is the responsibility of women, and some fertility control mechanisms have been responsible for harm to the health of women as well as a contributory factor to increasing population infertility. Contraceptive mechanisms (for example, Dalcon Shield and Depo-Provera) may be tested on women in the developing world before being introduced into First World countries[45] in circumstances where there is no health monitoring.

42 See Brown, S and Eisenberg, L, *The Best Intentions: Unintended Pregnancy and the Well-being of Children and Families*, 1995, Washington DC: National Academy Press.

43 Memorandum issued 22 January 2001 by President George W Bush, banning federal funds to international family planning groups that offer abortion services, counselling or referrals.

44 Connell, J, 'Norplant and the new paradigm of international population policy' (1995) 2 William and Mary Journal of Women and the Law 73.

45 Bolton, P, 'Health technologies and women of the Third World' (1989) 1 Woman and International Development Annual 57; (1998) 317 BMJ 1340.

Complications from abortion continue to constitute a public health problem, ironically more so in countries which do not recognise abortion and so are unlikely to provide post-abortion health support.[46] Fertility control that incorporates gender preference encourages late stage abortion with resultant health risks.[47] Thus, population control policies which focus primarily on fertility control can prove detrimental to health. Equally, fertility control services such as family planning clinics, which are established and funded as part of a wider population control agenda, may prioritise birth control at the expense of other values such as health, choice and women's reproductive power. Assessment of the success of fertility control measures and policies in terms of birth rate rather than in terms of improvement in health, opportunity and quality of life, emphasises population control outcomes at the expense of health outcomes and patient choice.

It is doubtful whether global reproductive health is achievable without a considerable increase in the funding committed to global development. Any commitment to establishing family planning recognising choice is open-ended, requiring access to low cost, high quality contraceptives as well as antibiotics for the control of sexual disease and infection.[48] Family planning policies are dependent on education and communication,[49] which are often excluded from the costing. Higher education levels in women tend to result in delayed marriage and more balanced power relationships within marriage, leading to increased contraceptive use,[50] but education can only be achieved with development funding which recognises the links between education and population control. Funding on an international level is complicated by issues of politics, such as the US embargo on food and medicines to Cuba, which resulted in restricting access to contraceptive supplies for Cuban women.[51] The US has control over the availability of a significant proportion of essential drugs worldwide,[52] which enables

46 Centre for Reproductive Law and Policy, *Abortion and Women's Reproductive Health: Reproductive Freedom Around the World*, 1994, New York; see also the report by Washington-based policy group Population Action International, which ranks 133 countries according to their sexual and reproductive health in 10 categories including maternal deaths, prenatal care, use of contraceptives, HIV/AIDS and teenage pregnancies. Ethiopia was identified as having the highest overall risk, followed by Angola, Chad, Afghanistan and the Central African Republic. The lowest risk countries were identified as Italy, Sweden, Finland and The Netherlands. Reuters, 9 March 2001.

47 Kulczycki, A and Potts, M, 'Abortion and fertility regulation' (1997) 347 The Lancet 1663.

48 See costing data in Potts, M and Walsh, J, 'Making Cairo work' (1999) 353 The Lancet 315.

49 Westoff, C and Rodrigues, G, 'The mass media and family planning in Kenya' (1995) 21 International Family Planning Perspectives 26.

50 See, eg, Harrison, K, 'The importance of the educated health woman in Africa' (1997) 349 The Lancet 644.

51 Kirkpatrick, A, 'Medicine and the US embargo against Cuba' (1996) 275 JAMA 1633.

52 Kirkpatrick, A, 'The role of the USA in shortage of food and medicine in Cuba' (1996) 348 The Lancet 1489.

withholding of medical supplies to be used as a political tool to the detriment of the public health of needy populations.

The director of the United Nations Population Fund, Dr Nafis Sadik, speaking at the International Conference on Population and Development in New York in 1999, strongly criticised the West for failing to fund the policies formulated at the Cairo conference, arguing that while developing countries had worked towards population growth funding targets set at Cairo, the developed countries had fallen far short of their targets.[53] There is moral pressure on the West to fund population control policies beyond their own borders on the basis that the West is ultimately responsible for the inability of the developing countries to sustain their own populations. Many of the developing nations were formally colonised under policies which depleted resources for the benefit of the colonising power, and manipulated crop production and distribution to meet the needs of the colonising power to the detriment of traditional subsistence crops. Meanwhile, the West has tightened its borders against immigration from the developing countries, so refusing to share the world's population surfeit. And the West consumes disproportionate resources such that the populations of developing countries are denied basic nutritional requirements.[54]

Despite these economic constraints, the importance of health as both a population control and a fertility control outcome is now widely acknowledged and, since Cairo, understanding of health in this context has expanded to include recognition of self-determination in relation to reproduction. Reproductive health was defined at the Cairo conference as:

> ... a state of complete physical and mental well being and is not merely the absence of disease or infirmity, in all matters relating to the reproductive system and its functions and processes. Reproductive health therefore implies that people are able to have a satisfying and safe sex life and that they have the capability to reproduce and the freedom to decide if, when and how often to do so. Implicit in this last condition is the right of men and women to be informed and to have access to safe, effective, affordable and acceptable methods of family planning of their choice, as well as other methods of their choice for regulation of fertility which are not against the law, and the right of access to appropriate health care service that will enable women to go safely through pregnancy and childbirth and provide couples with the best chance of having a healthy infant.[55]

---

53 Reported on BBC News, 29 June 1999.

54 An American consumes an average of 999 kg of grain per year, compared with 180 kg of grain for the average Indian; the average American adds 5.4 tons of carbon equivalent to the atmosphere per year, while the average Nigerian adds 0.8 tons; an American child costs 15 times more to raise than an Indian child; see Gudorf, C, 'Bioethics and law symposium deconstructing traditional paradigms in bioethics: race gender, class and culture' (1996) 15 St Louis University Public L Rev 331.

55 United Nations Programme of Action of the International Conference on Population and Development, 13 September 1995, para 7.2, UN Doc A/CONF 171/13.

The role of human rights in population control was explicitly recognised at the Cairo conference, with one chapter of the Programme dedicated to 'Reproductive Rights and Reproductive Health'.[56] An examination of the law protecting reproductive health, and fertility control in particular, must begin with an examination of the way in which the law protects reproductive rights.

THE LEGAL FRAMEWORK OF REPRODUCTIVE RIGHTS

The 1968 International Conference on Human Rights in 1968[57] recognised the right to determine 'freely and responsibly the number and spacing of children'. This right is the basic tenet of reproductive rights, but is far from sufficient as a definition. It was expanded upon in the 1974 World Population Plan of Action[58] to: '... all couples and individuals have the basic right to decide freely and responsibly the number and spacing of their children and to have the information, education and means to do so ...' The juxtaposition of 'freely' and 'responsibly' is difficult. Can a choice be freely made if it must also be responsibly made? Who determines what is responsible and by what criteria? Is it irresponsible to choose to have children in an environment of population excess, or irresponsible to refuse to procreate when the economic success of the State requires an increased workforce?

The 1994 Cairo conference added to understanding of reproductive rights the requirement that population policies must adhere to international human rights norms, and identified the objective of reproductive rights as reproductive health. The mutuality of reproductive rights and reproductive health has been supported in a number of international documents including the Declaration and Platform for Action at the World Conference on Women in Beijing.[59] However, neither the Cairo nor the Beijing declarations constitute legally binding documents, and a general statement of intent does not give rise to enforceable rights which can be the subject of human rights protection.

There is no international treaty protecting reproductive health as such. To achieve reproductive health it will be necessary to attach those factors identified as making up reproductive health to other recognised human

56 Chapter VII.

57 The Teheran Proclamation, Art 16, Final Act of the International Conference on Human Rights, UN Doc A/Conf 32/41 (1968).

58 This is not an international treaty, but a consensus policy contained in the Report of the United Nations World Population Conference.

59 Beijing Declaration and Platform for Action of the United Nations Fourth World Conference on Women, para 96, UN Doc A/Conf 177/20 (1995).

rights. Of its nature, health is more likely to fit within the so called 'second generation' human rights, which include economic, social and cultural rights. Such classification has consequences for justiciability and enforceability and it is arguable that these are the kinds of rights that are less well protected at international law.[60]

The Universal Declaration of Human Rights protects the right to 'life, liberty and security'.[61] A woman's right to life may be violated when she is denied access by State laws and practices to funded contraception and pregnancy care. Testing of contraceptive drugs and mechanisms without consent on women is in breach of this right, as are compulsory sterilisation and abortion. Laws which fail to protect against sexual violence, and which support the restriction of marriage choices and economic freedoms, threaten liberty and security. The rights of children whose lives are put at risk by repeated family pregnancies and poor maternal health are protected by Art 25 of the Declaration, which provides that: '... everyone has the right to a standard of living adequate for ... health and well being ... Motherhood and childhood are entitled to special care and assistance ...' The Declaration also confirms 'a right to a private and family life' and the 'right to marry and found a family',[62] which envisage freedom to make decisions on marriage and family size without State interference. States which fail to protect against causes of infertility such as sexually transmitted disease, defective contraceptive mechanisms and environmental causes of infertility may be in breach of this right.[63]

The International Covenant on Economic, Social and Cultural Rights also provides support for reproductive rights. Article 7 provides a right to 'the enjoyment of the highest attainable standard of physical and mental health' and goes on to provide in Art 12 that steps should be taken to reduce infant mortality and for the healthy development of the child. To be meaningful, this must require States to take steps to provide health care in accordance with the State's economic capability and in accordance with available technical and medical know-how, and to provide means for reducing maternal and infant mortality including measures which enable women to regulate reproduction. Article 15(1)(b) provides a right 'to enjoy the benefits of scientific progress and its applications', such that women in developing countries are entitled to access to refined, safer, forms of contraception. Article 13 provides a right to education to include not only the right to schooling, but also the right to information and training to enable informed health decision making.

---

60 See Chapter 5 by Yutaka Arai-Takahashi.

61 UN Doc A/810 (1948), Art 3.

62 *Ibid*, Art 12.

63 See Cook, R, 'Human rights and reproductive self determination' (1995) 44 American University L Rev 975.

The Convention on the Elimination of all forms of Discrimination Against Women[64] recognises that gender-neutral human rights do not always protect against infringements of the rights of women. The Convention specifically addresses fertility control, requiring access to educational information to ensure the health and well being of families, elimination of discrimination in health care, and assurances of appropriate services in connection with pregnancy and family planning.[65]

Not all States have become signatories to this Convention, some taking the view that these Convention rights do not accord with national cultural norms and values. What is more, the Convention operates on the principle of self-reporting, such that violations of the Convention by signatories are not centrally monitored and enforcement relies on non-government surveillance. Thus, although this Convention expresses some support for reproductive rights, it provides weak enforcement of those rights.[66]

Regional conventions may also contribute to the support of reproductive rights. The European Convention for the Protection of Human Rights and Fundamental Freedoms[67] echoes many of the rights enshrined in the Universal Declaration of Human Rights, providing mechanisms of enforcement for individuals in the case of a breach of any right by a public body. The Convention has been incorporated into the domestic law of most of its signatories, and was introduced into English domestic law by the Human Rights Act 1998. The Convention protects absolutely against infringements on right to life[68] and provides a limited right to liberty and security.[69] Article 8 provides that the State shall not interfere with a person's right to respect for private and family life: '... except such as in accordance with the law and is necessary in a democratic society ... for the protection of ... the economic well being of the country ... health or morals ...'

In the context of population policies, the Convention would not protect against national laws which for economic, health or moral reasons denied access to contraception or abortion, or which enforced the use of contraception or abortion. However, the article may arguably include an obligation to provide the services necessary for fertility control. Sexual freedom is protected by this article,[70] but subject to national law. Protection

---

64 Adopted 18 December 1979, UN Doc A/RES/34/180 (1980).

65 *Ibid*, Arts 10, 12 and 14.

66 Note, however, the adoption of the Optional Protocol to CEDAW, 1999, which would improve the enforceability of the Convention by allowing the CEDAW Committee to accept both individual and inter-State complaints when the Protocol comes into force.

67 Signed 4 November 1959.

68 European Convention on Human Rights, Art 2.

69 *Ibid*, Art 5; this applies even when the individual poses no risk to others and the detention is for her own good; see *Guzzardi v Italy* (1980) 13 EHRR 333.

70 Eg, see *Dudgeon v United Kingdom* (1981) 4 EHRR 149, *Sutherland v United Kingdom* [1998] EHRLR 149.

of 'freedom of thought, conscience and religion' are similarly subject to the limitations that the State imposes for the purposes of economic, health[71] or moral objectives,[72] as is protection of freedom of expression.[73] Freedom of expression has been held to include the right to be provided with information on contraception even where the contraception itself was not available.[74] The Convention protects the right to marry and found a family subject to national laws,[75] and protects against discrimination on any grounds.[76] The rights recognised by the European Convention, while more accessible to enforcement by individuals than rights recognised by international law, are more qualified rights, subject to a margin of appreciation in their incorporation into national law.

National laws are less likely positively to support, and more likely to impose limitations on, reproductive rights, particularly in relation to abortion. Abortion laws vary across jurisdictions from access as a matter of right at least in the first trimester,[77] abortion only with the approval of medical practitioners,[78] abortion only in extreme circumstances,[79] to complete prohibition of abortion.[80] Many laws permit abortion, but put in place hurdles to make access more difficult.[81]

---

71 Such as, eg, State provided sex education; see *Kjeldsen v Denmark* (1976) 1 EHRR 711.

72 European Convention on Human Rights, Art 9.

73 *Ibid*, Art 10.

74 *Open Door Counselling and Dublin Well Woman v Ireland* (1992) 15 EHRR 244.

75 European Convention on Human Rights, Art 12.

76 *Ibid*, Art 14.

77 The Choice on Termination of Pregnancy Act 1996 (South Africa) allows abortion at the request of the mother in the first 12 weeks; abortion between the 13th and 20th week if a medical practitioner in consultation with the mother is of the opinion that an abortion is appropriate according to criteria ranging from harm to the mother or foetal abnormality to harm to the social or economic circumstances of the mother; and abortion after the 20th week in limited circumstances. Many Eastern European countries also allow abortion on request in the first trimester, including Macedonia, which allows abortion on request until the fifth month of pregnancy (Law on the Interruption of Pregnancy 1977). Russia and the Scandinavian countries have liberal abortion laws.

78 Eg, Abortion Act 1967 (England and Wales), which allows abortion until the 24th week on a range of criteria to be decided by two medical practitioners. The criteria include 'the woman's actual or reasonably foreseeable environment' (s 1(2)). Abortion is allowed after the 24th week in limited circumstances.

79 Eg, Family Planning, the Protection of the Foetus, and the Conditions for the Termination of Pregnancy Act 1993 (Poland).

80 Eg, Offences Against the Person Act 1861, s 58 (Ireland). Malta does not allow abortion. Most Latin American countries, under the influence of the Church, have not legalised abortion despite the high mortality rates from illegal abortion, and despite attempts to reform the law. See Saylin, G, 'The United Nations International Conference on Population and Development: religion, tradition and law in Latin America' (1995) 28 Vanderbilt Journal of Transnational Law 1245.

81 Eg, House Bill 2570, Senate Bill 1211, passed 6 February 2001, Virginia, USA, which imposes a 24 hour waiting period between abortion counselling and the abortion itself.

The absence of national laws regulating reproductive behaviour does not presuppose reproductive freedom. At national and local level, administrative practice, health service policy and cultural norms will determine the extent to which individual women are accorded the human rights recognised by international conventions. Even within jurisdictions, access to contraception and abortion can vary according to the distribution of economic wealth and services, social and religious attitudes to abortion and local health policies.[82]

While few countries have criminalised contraception or sterilisation,[83] several countries have used bureaucracy to inhibit access to services. The pill is not available to women in Japan, because it has not been licensed.[84] In some Eastern European countries, access to abortion and to contraceptive services has been made more difficult as a result of increasing religious influence in the provision of hospital and primary care services. The religious 'Croatian Movement for Population' successfully lobbied for inclusion in Croatian abortion laws the requirement that the woman consult a priest before an abortion could be performed. Women's NGOs overturned the law after intervention, but hospitals, many of which are owned or administered by religious institutions, have a right of conscientious objection to abortion.[85] Ironically in countries with the most limited access to contraceptive services, in Latin America[86] for example, abortion rates tend to be highest, as abortion becomes the main method of fertility control.[87]

---

82 See Raleigh, V, 'Abortion rates in England in 1995: comparative study of data from district health authorities' (1998) 316 BMJ 1712. There was, until recently, division within Germany in relation to access to abortion. The Catholic State of Bavaria had instituted local rules restricting abortion, forcing women to travel to other parts of Germany. The German constitutional court has now declared these rules unconstitutional. See (1998) 317 BMJ 1272.

83 French law prohibits vasectomy as an act of self-mutilation; (2000) 321 BMJ 470.

84 Although the impotence drug Viagra has been approved, prompting claims of discrimination. The Central Pharmaceutical Affairs Council has delayed licensing of the pill because of concerns about sexually transmitted diseases and sexual morality, as well as concern as to health risks of the pill. Japan has a high abortion rate. See Watts, J, 'When impotence leads to contraception' (1999) 353 The Lancet 819.

85 International Helsinki Federation for Human Rights, *Women 2000*, 2000, Vienna.

86 Saylin, G, 'The United Nations International Conference on Population and Development: religion, tradition and law in Latin America (1995) 28 Vanderbilt Journal of Transnational Law 1245; see also Rich, V, 'Church condemns contraception promotion in Peru' (1995) 346 The Lancet 894. Note that the American Convention on Human Rights 1969 (applicable to the Organization of American States, to which most southern American countries belong) expressly refers in Art 4 to the right to life from 'the moment of conception'.

87 Eg, in Bulgaria, where there is no family planning policy and limited services, private abortion is the main form of birth control. The Government has adopted pronatalist policies to increase birth rates, but the abortion rate continues to exceed the live birth rate. See International Helsinki Federation for Human Rights, *Women 2000*, 2000, Vienna.

Equally, it is the case that in those countries with seemingly restricted legal access to abortion, where practice is more liberal and where facilities are available, the laws may be liberally interpreted. The requirement in English law that requires the approval of two doctors for an abortion to be performed is interpreted such that any woman seriously wishing to undergo abortion will find little difficulty in obtaining that approval. Abortion within the first trimester is, at least in practice, available almost on demand. Similarly, Hungarian law requires that pregnant woman must be 'in a severe crisis'[88] before a legal abortion can be performed, but 40% of pregnancies in Hungary are terminated and abortion is available virtually on request.[89]

The legal approach to informed consent in each jurisdiction will be an important factor in reproductive self-determination. Any treatment given without consent, such as forced sterilisation or abortion, will constitute a breach of most national laws. For consent to be real, it must be given by someone competent to make the decision, it must be willingly made, and it must be adequately informed. Definitions of capacity and competency to consent are open to interpretation and manipulation. In a disturbing series of cases, English courts developed an understanding that women in labour or even in anticipation of childbirth could be characterised as incompetent such that caesarean surgery could be performed on them without consent.[90] Although there has been some belated recognition that women might be competent in such circumstances,[91] it remains the case that it is within the discretion of the health care providers to determine in each case whether a woman is competent to make a birth decision.[92] Similar approaches have been taken in US courts.[93] Determination of willingness to consent may also be open to interpretation. At what point do economic inducements, economic sanctions, social sanctions and other forms of manipulation convert consent willingly given to consent unwillingly given?[94]

It is in the determination of 'adequately informed' that laws most vary across jurisdictions. Any consent that is obtained by deliberately misrepresenting the nature of the treatment is clearly uninformed and is

88 Protection of Foetal Life Act 1992 as amended 2000, s 1(d).

89 International Helsinki Federation for Human Rights, *Women 2000*, 2000, Vienna. See also (1998) 316 BMJ 1037.

90 Eg, *Re S* [1992] 4 All ER 671; *Norfolk and Norwich Healthcare NHS Trust v W* [1996] 2 FLR 613; *Tameside and Glossop Acute Services v CH* [1996] 1 FLR 762.

91 See *St George's Healthcare NHS Trust v S* [1998] 3 WLR 936.

92 See Bridgeman, J and Millns, S, *Feminist Perspectives on Law*, 1998, London: Sweet & Maxwell, s 6.2.

93 Eg, *Re AC* (1987) 533 A 2d 611.

94 For discussion of inducement, sanction and coercion in China and in the US, see Cirando, L, 'Informed choice and population policy: do the population choices of China and the United States respect and ensure women's right to informed choice?' (1995) 19 Fordham International Law Journal 611.

invalid.[95] But what of treatment which is recommended, but where all the risks of treatment are not disclosed, or where all the available choices of treatment are not offered to the patient, or where the information given is biased in favour of government policy? Many jurisdictions determine the adequacy of information on the basis of what information the reasonable or prudent patient would think material,[96] recognising a right on the part of the patient to self-determination in respect of her body. English law, however, determines questions of adequacy of information in terms of what the reasonable health provider thinks the patient should be told.[97] In *Blyth v Bloomsbury HA*,[98] a woman was offered the contraceptive Depo-Provera after the birth of her child. In response to questions, she was told that there were no significant side effects, and when she suffered problems, she brought a claim against the doctor for failing to respond fully to her request for information. The court found that the patient had been given as much information as the reasonable doctor would think necessary[99] and the claim failed. English law does not recognise the right of a woman to be fully informed about risks of fertility control and so does not provide the necessary protection for exercise of reproductive rights.

Even those national laws which make clear that provision of fertility control services is a responsibility of the health care system[100] do not explicitly acknowledge women's rights of access to contraception or provide any mechanism for enforcing provision. In the absence of national recognition of reproductive rights, practices which infringe those rights cannot be directly challenged. States continue to see their role as a negative one, with a responsibility only to refrain from interference, rather than a positive duty to protect against interference. The statements of intent in relation to reproductive rights and reproductive health which have been

---

95 Eg, the English case of *R v Williams* [1923] 1 KB 340.

96 Eg, the American case of *Canterbury v Spence* (1972) 464 F 2d 722; the Canadian case of *Reibl v Hughes* (1980) 114 DLR (3d) 1; the Australian case of *Rogers v Whittaker* (1992) 109 ALR 625. European civil law requires a high degree of disclosure for consent to be valid and imposes a general duty of information and advice. See, eg, Van Gerven, W, *Cases, Materials and Text on National, Supranational and International Tort Law*, 1998, Oxford: Hart, p 121, and Giesen, D, *International Medical Malpractice Law*, 1988, Dordrecht, Martinus Nijhoff.

97 *Sidaway v Board of Governors of the Bethlem Royal Hospital* [1985] AC 871, but see the dissent of Lord Scarman, who preferred an approach based on the prudent patient.

98 [1993] 4 Med LR 151.

99 In accordance with the *Bolam* test for standard of care (*Bolam v Friern Hospital Management Committee* [1957] 2 All ER 118) as applied in *Sidaway*.

100 Eg, the National Health Service Act 1977, s 5(1)(b), which imposes a duty on the Secretary of State 'to arrange to such extent as he considers necessary to meet all reasonable requirements ... for the giving of advice on contraception, the medical examination of persons seeking advice on contraception, the treatment of such persons and the supply of contraceptive substances and appliances' (England and Wales).

accepted at international level cannot be fully effective until they are reflected at national level.

REPRODUCTIVE RIGHTS VERSUS PUBLIC HEALTH

Women's bodies are essential for reproduction, and reproduction has historically been considered the primary responsibility of women. Women's bodies and women's sexuality have throughout history been seen as threatening to morality and to the social stability of society,[101] prompting religious, patriarchal, medical and political surveillance and control of women's sexual and reproductive behaviour. The sexuality of black women, particularly colonised women, was and is seen as excessive, promiscuous and threatening to white racial purity, justifying containment of both sexuality and fertility.[102]

Such control appears to violate human rights, the 'fundamental and inalienable rights that are essential for life as a human being',[103] but the language and norms of human rights have focused on the experiences of men and have not addressed the particular rights issues faced by women. Traditional human rights debate has concentrated on civil and political rights which are public in nature (torture, freedom of speech, political persecution) and has not adapted easily to interference with social rights within the private, family setting.[104] More particularly, because arguments about reproductive rights have been located almost exclusively in discussion of the rights of women within the family or social environment, issues of reproductive rights have not been seen as sufficiently pressing or indeed interesting to warrant political attention.

If the focus moves from fertility control to population control, then the debate moves from the private to the public arena. Population control measures require government intervention in line with government population policies, operated in public health care facilities, and so are ripe for human rights analysis. Yet, human rights have played little part in public health debate. Public health has traditionally been concerned with the health of communities, and public health policies and objectives work top-down to improve average or overall health. Community health interests, those that are intended to produce the greatest good for the greatest number, may

---

101 Turner, B, *Medical Power and Social Knowledge*, 1995, London: Sage, Chapter 5.

102 See Pettman, J, *Worlding Women: A Feminist International Politics*, 1996, London: Routledge; Buss, D, 'Racing populations, sexing environments: the challenges of a feminist politics in international law' (2000) 20 LS 463.

103 Johns, K, 'Reproductive rights of women: construction and reality in international and United States law' (1998) 5 Cardozo Women's LJ 1.

104 See Boland, R, 'Symposium on population law: the environment, population and women's rights' (1997) 27 Environmental Law 1137.

conflict with those of individuals, where individuals' needs are conceived as atomised and self-contained. This is particularly so in relation to reproduction. Determining population quotas and policies for the benefit of the State as a whole may involve constraint of the rights of individuals to make reproductive choices. Population control measures will be to a greater or lesser extent inducive or coercive and, therefore, potentially in conflict with individual rights, not as an issue of intra-familial relationships, but as a result of State interference with the rights of individuals to make reproductive choices. Reproductive rights in the context of population control fall clearly within human rights jurisprudence, but one of the obstacles of implementing reproductive rights is reconciliation of rights discourse with public health scholarship.

It has been argued that rights terminology is out of place in the context of public health, and particularly so in relation to population control in developing countries. Reproductive rights have been criticised as a 'bourgeois concept',[105] inappropriate in the struggle against Western population strategies which presuppose Western racial and economic superiority. Human rights jurisprudence has developed in the context of international law, which has itself sprung from European origins,[106] excluding the experiences of both developing world and the world's women. Nor do rights arguments fit easily into cultures and societies which place little value on personal autonomy or individuality. Individuals in many African societies, for example, see themselves not as isolated units, but as defined by their relationships with others, 'perceiving self-interest to lie in the welfare of the relational complex'.[107] They will prioritise values such as collective welfare, shared responsibility, co-operation and compromise over rights of self-determination for the preservation of relationships. The health interests of the community may justify some population control measures at the expense of reproductive rights, provided that these population control policies have been collectively decided and not imposed by governments, international agencies or drugs companies.

The changing position of the State through transnationalisation and the expanding scope of personal identity also have an impact here. The process of globalisation has been described as weakening the power of States over populations contained in geographical limits. As borders have become less significant in terms of trade and movement, new forms of political

105 Ubinig, F, 'Reproductive rights: a critique from the realities of Bangladesh', south asia e-journals: re/productions no 1, found at http://www.hsph.harvard.edu/organizations/healthnet/Sasia/repro/farida.html.

106 Charlesworth, H, Chinkin, C and Wright, S, 'Feminist approaches to international law' (1991) American Journal of International Law 613.

107 Harding, S, 'The science question in feminism' (1986) as quoted in Charlesworth, H, Chinkin, C and Wright, C, 'Feminist approaches to international law' (1991) 85 American Journal of International Law 613.

allegiance have developed. Nationalism has been seen as waning in importance in terms of individual identity, but at the same time new individualism has flourished. The result of this scholarship is the image of an individual no longer tied to allegiance first and foremost to the State into which she was born. Globalised markets have allowed products and services to be available across frontiers. If one is constrained in a particular jurisdiction, then a less constrained jurisdiction may attract custom. In the reproductive area, this has already occurred in the use of transnational surrogacy arrangements, adoption and reproductive technology to avoid the limitations imposed by domestic law. In the globalised environment, development issues take on a further dimension as those within the developed world are more likely to exert this type of individual freedom and governments are more likely to be constrained by it. Where freedom of movement and trade is circumscribed by economic conditions, governments are potentially freer to impose more draconian forms of regulation.

On the global stage, discussion of health in terms of rights can be misleading.[108] Negotiation of rights takes place at international level, and the results of those negotiations necessarily reflect power imbalances at international level. The focus at world population conferences, Cairo included, is on 'over-population' rather than 'over-consumption', reflecting a very Western view of a global problem, diverting attention to the developing world.[109] The 'global problem' is constructed in terms of how population levels will impinge on the West, on security, on the environment, on trade and on migration.[110] In particular, the concern is with the economic consequences of excessive populations rather than concern for environment in its own right, such that environmental harms are not seen to be as threatening for poorer nations.[111] The application of human rights jurisprudence to population control is not a consideration of rights on a neutral playing field, but rather an imposition of a Western conception of the role of rights onto a global environment in which risks and benefits are distributed in accordance with Western principles.

---

108 Buss, D, 'Racing populations, sexing environments: the challenges of a feminist politics in international law' (2000) 20 LS 463.

109 *Ibid*.

110 Eg, a Cairo+5 Report from the United States Agency for International Development, 'Making a world of difference one family at a time' (1998) 3 Global Issues: Population at the Millennium, the US Perspective 32, argues that: 'Expanding populations also undermine ... economic and social development – jeopardizing the potential for these countries to be reliable allies, good trading partners, and growing markets for US exports. And chances increase that people will migrate to the United States in search of employment and a better life.' Quoted in Buss, D, 'Racing populations, sexing environments: the challenges of a feminist politics in international law' (2000) 20 LS 463.

111 See Chapter 3 of the Cairo Programme entitled 'Interrelations between populations, sustained economic growth and sustainable development'.

Concern over individual autonomy as the premise of rights jurisprudence has also been raised in Western scholarship, particularly in the context of feminist theory.[112] Beginning with the work of Carol Gilligan,[113] there has developed an approach to behaviour and to the law regulating that behaviour which has become known as the ethics of care, and which rejects classical autonomy in favour of concepts of relational autonomy and ethical humanitarian values.[114] An ethics of care approach would frame debate about health in terms of normative responsibilities within relationships, rather than descriptive individual rights. While there has been criticism of the subjectivity inherent in ethics of care arguments,[115] they have nevertheless provided a launching ground for critique of rights analysis as it is applied to the position of women.

Parallel to ideas of relational autonomy, there also developed a communitarian movement in the 1980s which similarly challenged notions of individualism in the context of rights.[116] Communitarian philosophy has been used as a constraint on rampant individualism within judicial hearings on issues of health law. For example, in cases on abortion,[117] the right to refuse medical treatment[118] and the withdrawal of life sustaining treatment,[119] North American courts have balanced patient rights and family wishes against 'the State's interests', on the basis that society itself has a valid interest in matters such as the preservation of life, the integrity of the health service and the prevention of suicide.[120] English courts have not articulated similar claims as communitarianism, but have still made use of

---

112 See Kingdom, E, *What's Wrong with Rights? Problems for Feminist Politics of Law*, 1991, Edinburgh: Edinburgh UP.

113 Gilligan, C, *In a Different Voice*, 1982, Cambridge, Mass: Harvard UP.

114 See West, R, 'Jurisprudence and gender', in Bartlett, K and Kennedy, R (eds), *Feminist Legal Theory: Readings in Law and Gender*, 1991, Oxford: Westview; and Sevenhuijsen, S, *Citizenship and the Ethics of Care*, 1998, London: Routledge.

115 See Drakopoulou, M, 'The ethics of care, female subjectivity and feminist legal scholarship' (2000) 8 Feminist Legal Studies 199.

116 See, eg, Hekmen, S, *Moral Voices, Moral Selves*, 1995, Oxford: Polity; Sandel, MJ, *Democracy's Discontents*, 1996, Cambridge, Mass: Belknap Press of Harvard UP. Other examples of communitarian critique can be found in MacIntyre, A, *After Virtue: A Study in Moral Theory*, 1981, London: Duckworth; Williams, B, *Ethics and the Limits of Philosophy*, 1985, London: Fontana; Taylor, C, *Philosophy and the Human Sciences: Philosophical Papers*, 1985, Cambridge: CUP, Vol 2; Clinton, RN, 'The rights of indigenous peoples as collective group rights' (1990) 32 Arizona L Rev 739.

117 See, eg, *Roe v Wade* (1973) 35 L Ed 2d 147; *Planned Parenthood v Casey* (1992) 505 US 833.

118 See, eg, *Brophy v New England Sinai Hospital* (1986) 497 NE 2d 626.

119 See, eg, *Cruzan v Director, Missouri Department of Health* (1990) 110 S Ct 2841.

120 See Flamme, A and Forster, H, 'Legal limits: when does autonomy in health care prevail?', in Freeman, M and Lewis, A (eds), *Law and Medicine*, Current Legal Issues, 2000, Oxford: OUP, Vol 3.

concepts such as sanctity of life[121] and human dignity.[122] These concepts have been seen as values which all individuals have a duty to maintain, constraining individual choice, rather than supplanting it with community interests.[123]

Other critiques of reproductive rights have pointed out that conventions and laws which allocate reproductive rights to 'parents' presuppose equal bargaining power between sexes.[124] Representation of rights as gender-neutral does not reflect the exercise of reproductive rights where there are contrary economic inequalities, cultural practices, religious beliefs, domestic violence and traditional gender roles. Even in countries which purport to protect gender equality, the paucity of women in positions of political and administrative power combined with social attitudes to women create a legal and medical environment in which reproductive choice is to some extent illusory. The English Abortion Act 1967, for example, presupposes that women are insufficiently responsible to decide on the appropriateness of abortion even on grounds of economic or family desirability, and requires that two doctors, who are unlikely to be familiar with the woman's personal circumstances, make the decision on her behalf. Parliamentary debate leading to the passing of the Abortion Act assumed that doctors are (or at least were in 1967) likely to be professional males and therefore better able to decide.[125] The important point here is that law, constrained by largely written language, adopts and reproduces particular ways of seeing which are not neutral, nor are they the only way of seeing. The national legal framework that is necessary to take rights from abstraction to reality may in effect pay little attention to the rights and actual needs of women in their particular ethnic, economic, cultural, religious, or other contexts where they differ from those which are perceived as representative.

A further concern is the futility of asserting patient rights in the context of a doctor/patient relationship that is based on an imbalance of power. The medical profession has traditionally acted as a gatekeeper of medical knowledge as well as of medical facilities, drugs and treatments. Much of the developed world now has access to medical information of varying quality through libraries, the media and the Internet, but the most informed and knowledgeable patient cannot convert knowledge into treatment because doctors continue, with the support of law, fiercely to guard access to

---

121 As in *Re J (A Minor) (Wardship: Medical Treatment)* [1990] 3 All ER 930; and *Airedale NHS Trust v Bland* [1993] 1 All ER 821. See critique of sanctity of life in this context in Keown, J, 'Restoring moral and intellectual shape to the law after *Bland*' (1997) 113 LQR 481.

122 As in *Re C (A Minor) (Wardship: Medical Treatment)* [1989] 2 All ER 782.

123 On the divergence between an interpretation of individualism and communitarianism in the context of public health see above, Chapter 1.

124 See, eg, Johns, K, 'Reproductive rights of women: construction and reality in international and United States law' (1998) 5 Cardozo Women's LJ 1.

125 See Sheldon, S, 'Who is the mother to make the judgment? The constructions of woman in English abortion law' (1993) 1 Feminist Legal Studies 3.

facilities and drugs. Doctors also control access to relief from employment and benefits that are denied to those who self-certify. That power imbalance is even greater in the developing world, where poor levels of education and poor information services put the patient into a position of vulnerability when it comes to sifting and evaluating health advice. To talk of the reproductive rights of a woman who is fed limited and biased fertility control information, and offered a limited range of contraceptive services unsupported by long term health services, is nonsense. Rights can only be truly effective in the context of economic security, fully informed consent, choice and equality of power. Yet, rights do provide a useful political tool for groups to advance as a basic form of recognition or protection. They can amount to a first stage in a process of improvement, although inadequate as a solution to real problems. Just as it is necessary for individuals to form alliances by selecting aspects of their identities or values or interests behind which a collective may rally for reform, rights is a mechanism through which such groups may make themselves heard. That is not to say that each individual in the group is defined only by their membership of that group (woman, black, transsexual, gay, disabled, Jew), nor that rights are the only vehicle to assure recognition. Nevertheless, forming the group and acquiring rights may be a step towards change.[126]

Rights arguments do not fit comfortably in a public health agenda, but must not be neglected in favour of public health interests. Rights language is necessary to temper zealous public health reform, and rights analysis provides a useful platform for critiquing public health policies. The gendered and Western biases in traditional rights thinking have limited the effectiveness of human rights arguments on issues of population control, but the inclusion of women from across the world in population control debates in Cairo and Beijing has now set in motion a rethinking of both rights and public health. It is still the case that even the most basic of reproductive rights, the right of access to contraception, remains unmet in large parts of the world[127] and only a public health debate which recognises rights will be effective in achieving any measure of global reproductive health. The importance of reproductive rights can be seen in a comparison of the progress of abortion laws in the US and in South Africa. In the US, access to abortion has been determined by case law based on the constitutional right to privacy. While achieving some limited success in recognising a woman's right to a private abortion, the courts have not supported State funding of

126 This form of approach is used by, eg, Stychin, C, *Law's Desire: Sexuality and the Limits of Justice*, 1995, London: Routledge.

127 Bongaarts, J, 'Population policy options in the developing world' (1994) 28 Stud Fam Planning 182; Westoff, C and Bankole, A, 'The potential demographic of unmet need' (1996) 22 International Family Planning Perspectives 16. Less than 10% of the African population uses contraception; (1996) 313 BMJ 135.

abortion because funding is not relevant to the issue of privacy. Case law can be challenged, and so provides no security of rights.[128] By contrast, the South African Constitution of 1996 uniquely recognises a 'right to make decisions about reproduction'[129] and a 'right of access to ... reproductive health care'[130] with the consequence that legislation has been passed positively recognising the right of women to make reproduction decisions.[131] The Act gives to women the choice whether to undergo abortion in the first trimester supported by State funded abortion services. The explicit recognition of rights which are relevant to women is essential for the maintenance of women's health. Generic rights formulated to protect male values will not suffice.

PARTICULAR LEGAL ISSUES OF FERTILITY CONTROL

The three main mechanisms of fertility control are contraception, sterilisation and abortion. Infertility treatment may also be classified as a fertility control technique given that the consequence of routine provision of treatment is an increase in birth rates. State funding of infertility research and treatment in an environment where population limitation polices are in place may be difficult to support if resource allocation criteria are premised on public health objectives. A more rights-based approach which recognises positive as well as negative reproductive choice would support a public health agenda that included fertility assistance as well as fertility control.

Contraception

Before the development of modern contraceptive technologies, contraception was easily defined as an appliance or substance which served to prevent the human male sperm from fertilising the female ovum. However, many modern contraceptives work by allowing fertilisation, but inhibiting the implantation of the fertilised egg in the uterus. Such contraception, more accurately called contragestation, blurs the dividing line between contraception and abortion. Those who believe that life begins at the point of fertilisation would regard the deliberate killing of the fertilised egg as abortion and oppose it on that ground. The legal status of

128 Paltrow, L, 'Pregnant drug users, fetal persons and the threat to *Roe v Wade*' (1999) 62 Albany L Rev 999.

129 South African Constitution 1996, s 12(2)(a).

130 *Ibid*, s 27(1)(a).

131 Choice on Termination of Pregnancy Act 1997.

contragestation in jurisdictions which limit access to abortion is often unclear.

In English law, s 59 of the Offences Against the Person Act creates an offence for any person to supply or procure anything with intent to procure a miscarriage, whether or not the woman was with child. There is no definition of miscarriage. Contragestation devices have forced the law to confront the difficult determination of when life begins, for if life begins at fertilisation, then most modern forms of contraception are in fact abortifacients and fall within the requirements of the Abortion Act. The legal status of contragestation has become even more pertinent with the development of the 'morning after pill'.[132]

The debate surrounding the legal regulation of embryo research assists in determining the legal status of contragestation. The Warnock Report on human fertilisation and embryology[133] considered the development of the embryo from fertilisation onwards in order to identify a point where the embryo could be considered as identifiable human life. The Report recommended that the marker for the beginning of life should, for the purposes of legal regulation of embryo research, be at the development of the primitive streak,[134] which is presumed to take place at 14 days after fertilisation. This recommendation was incorporated into the Human Fertilisation and Embryology Act 1990.[135] If embryos younger than 14 days, 'pre-embryos' as they were called in the Report, are not human life for the purposes of embryo research, then logically they cannot be considered human life for the purposes of abortion law. English medical practice works on the assumption than any form of contragestation which works within 14 days of fertilisation is to be considered a form of contraception rather than abortion, including the morning after pill.

The morning after pill, like other forms of contraception, has until recently only been obtainable from a doctor or family planning clinic on medical advice. Research suggests that women may be afraid to approach their doctor for the morning after pill and that some doctors take a paternalistic and critical approach to women who ask for it.[136] Access to the pill across Britain is 'controversial and inconsistent',[137] such that women can

---

132 This is composed of two pills, to be taken 12 hours apart, within 72 hours of intercourse. The pills may work to prevent fertilisation, or to prevent implantation of the fertilised embryo.

133 Department of Health and Social Security, *Report of the Committee of Inquiry into Human Fertilisation and Embryology*, Cmnd 9314, 1983, London: HMSO; Warnock, M, *A Question of Life*, 1985, London: Blackwell.

134 By which time the precursor cells are in the correct position. This is the last point in time for twinning.

135 Section 3(4).

136 See, eg, (1995) 311 BMJ 762; (1997) 307 BMJ 695; (1997) *The Independent*, 11 January.

137 See (1998) 316 BMJ 149.

never be sure that their request will be met. As the morning after pill must be taken within 72 hours of intercourse, delay is a problem. In December 2000, the British Government announced[138] that to reduce the high incidence of teenage pregnancy,[139] the morning after pill would be made available, subject to conditions, over the counter. There has been opposition from the Conservative Party and from some religious groups,[140] but the pill is now available from pharmacies. Health authorities may also use school nurses to increase teenage access,[141] and some pharmacists are proposing to set up Internet sales.[142] Similar debates about the ethics and wisdom of easy access to postcoital contraception have taken place across the world with many jurisdictions opting for liberal access to curb unwanted pregnancies.[143] The increasing acceptance of the morning after pill has been followed by pressure to liberalise access to other chemical early abortion substances such as RU 486. RU 486 is considered a medically safe and effective way of ending unwanted pregnancy in the early weeks and is a safer alternative to surgical abortion. Taiwan and China both allow routine sale of RU 486,[144] it is available on prescription in the UK, Sweden, France

---

138 Following the Crown Report, *Report on the Supply and Administration of Medicines under Group Protocols HSC 1998*; see Latham, M, 'Emergency contraception' (1999) 149 NLJ 366. The morning after pill became available from pharmacists in January 2001 at a cost of £19.99 per treatment.

139 Britain has the highest teenage pregnancy rate in Western Europe, see (1998) 316 BMJ 881; (1999) 318 BMJ 894; see, also, Cabinet Office Social Exclusion Unit circular letter on teenage parenthood (1998) available at http://www.cabinet-office.gov.uk/seu/1998/teepar.htm. See also Kessler, R *et al* (1997) 154 American Journal of Psychiatry 1405 on the psychiatric consequences of teenage parenthood, and Lawson, A and Rhode, D (eds), *The Politics of Pregnancy: Adolescent Sexuality and Public Policy*, 1993, New Haven: Yale UP.

140 The main arguments against increased access were that the pill would be used as a form of routine contraception, that it would encourage promiscuity, and that it would be available to underage girls. However, the Department of Health has acknowledged that since the pill became available, there had been a low take-up, that there had been very few requests from underage girls, and that pharmacists were not dispensing significantly more pills than they had under the prescription. The British Pregnancy Advisory Board suggests that the cost of the pill over the counter was such that most women still choose to obtain the pill by prescription. See (2001) *Evening Standard*, 9 February. See, also, Kosunen, E *et al*, 'Questionnaire study of use of emergency contraception amongst teenagers' (1999) 319 BMJ 91.

141 BBC News, 8 January 2001.

142 The high street chain Superdrug is seeking approval from the authorities responsible for Internet sales.

143 Eg, Argentina, France and New Zealand. The American Medical Association approved in principle over the counter sale of emergency contraception in December 2000, but so far it has only been made available in Washington. In February 2001, Virginia passed legislation allowing over the counter sale of the morning after pill, but implementation has been delayed while the question of sale to girls under 18 is determined: *Washington Post*, 21 February 2001. See also Ellertson, C *et al*, 'Should emergency contraceptive pills be available without prescription?' (1998) 53 Journal of American Medical Women Association 226; Glassier, A and Baird, D, 'The effects of self-administering emergency contraception' (1998) 339 New England Journal of Medicine 1.

144 RU 486 may be taken within the first seven weeks of pregnancy. It works by causing the uterus to shed its lining and dislodge the fertilised embryo.

and Israel, and the American Food and Drug Administration has now approved its sale in the US.[145]

The debates surrounding access to contraception, particularly access to contraception by underage girls, reveal that attitudes to contraception are about sexual morality as much as about fertility control. Denial of access to contraception and sex information is used in an attempt to impose restrictions on the sexuality of women.[146] The moral context of contraception was particularly overt in the English case of *Gillick v West Norfolk and Wisbech HA*[147] where a mother challenged a health circular allowing doctors to give contraceptive advice and treatment to girls under the age of 16 without parental consent. Antipathy to allowing treatment, particularly in the dissenting judgments, is revealed as antipathy to sexual freedom,[148] and pregnancy is presumed to be the purpose of and justification for sexual intercourse for women.

One way of limiting women's access to contraception is to make it expensive. Contraceptive choice requires an economic environment which facilitates choice with State funding of contraceptive services. A negative side of the proposal for over the counter emergency contraception in England is that it will have to be paid for by the user, whereas contraception paid for under prescription is funded by the NHS. The coverage of contraception under health insurance schemes has been an issue of debate in the US. The Equal Employment Opportunity Commission has ruled that employers are discriminating against women when they offer health care plans that exclude contraception,[149] and legislation has been proposed requiring contraceptive coverage in line with other pharmaceutical drugs.[150] Funding of contraceptive services under State provided health services can be manipulated in accordance with population control policies.[151]

145 (2000) 321 BMJ 851.

146 Though see the study by Wellings, K *et al*, 'Provision of sex education and early sexual experience: the relation examined' (1995) 311 BMJ 417, which found no evidence to suggest early sex education led to early sexual experience.

147 [1985] 3 All ER 402.

148 'There are many things which a girl under 16 needs to practise, but sex is not one of them ... it is clear that contraception removes or gives an illusion of removing the possibility of pregnancy and therefore removes restraint on sexual intercourse.' *Ibid*, *per* Lord Templeman, p 432.

149 (2000) *Washington Post*, 14 December.

150 Rovner, J, 'Politics of abortion spread to contraception' (1998) 352 The Lancet 553.

151 Contraception and abortion in Bulgaria, while legal, had until recently to be paid for by the woman in line with a government campaign to increase the population. In Kazakhstan, where population levels are declining, access to contraception is difficult and expensive, leaving abortion as the main method of fertility control. Contraception has been removed from State funding in Croatia as a result of post-war budget cuts and is now unaffordable for most women. Contraception is expensive and not State funded in Poland. See International Helsinki Federation for Human Rights, *Women 2000*, 2000, Vienna.

International organisations such as the World Health Organisation, Red Cross and the United Nations Population Fund, and NGOs with briefs ranging from protection of children to protection of women to family planning, have intervened in some jurisdictions to provide funded fertility control services where they are not State provided,[152] but the fact remains that large sections of the world's population are denied access to contraception on grounds of expense.

Some contraceptive methods raise particular concerns. An increasingly common form of cheap and effective contraception is the long-acting drug Norplant, which is administered in the form of implantation of silastic rods beneath the skin.[153] Minor surgery is required for both implantation and removal. Norplant can work both to increase reproductive choice by allowing women to use a reliable and permanent form of contraception, and decrease reproductive choice where the drugs are administered coercively and where requests for removal are ignored. Norplant has been targeted at immigrant groups and women on benefits in the US, and offered as the only contraceptive choice in some developing countries.[154] Women in Bangladesh were used as trial subjects for Norplant allegedly contrary to research ethics and without health care back up.[155] While access to contraception is generally seen as a response to a woman's reproductive rights, Norplant raises questions of contraception as a mechanism for the control of women. American courts have offered long-acting contraception as a condition of probation on conviction of a crime,[156] and some NGOs have provided financial incentives for long-acting contraception, targeted at 'risk' groups[157] who are considered incapable of controlling their own fertility. Norplant puts back into the hands of the medical profession the power of control over female fertility, particularly where there is no guarantee of instant removal on request.[158] Norplant is also very profitable for drug manufacturers and cost effective for health providers, tempting

152 Eg, in Belarus, Georgia, Kyrgyzstan, Lithuania; see International Helsinki Federation for Human Rights, *Women 2000*, 2000, Vienna.

153 The implants give a sustained release of hormone over a period of five years.

154 Brown, G and Moskowitz, E, 'Moral and policy issues in long-acting contraception' (1997) 18(1) Annual Review of Public Health 379.

155 Ubinig, F, 'Resisting Norplant: women's struggle in Bangladesh against coercion and violence' at http://www.hsph.harvard.edu/organizations/healthnet/SAsia/repro/norplant2.html.

156 Arthur, S, 'The Norplant prescription: birth control, women control or crime control?' (1992) UCLA L Rev 1; Taylor, J, 'Court-ordered contraception: Norplant as a probation condition in child abuse' (1992) 44 Florida Law Rev 379.

157 Eg, the American NGO, CRACK, which focuses on children born with drug dependency, offers $200 cash payments to alcohol and drug abusers who participate in a Norplant programme; see http://www.cashforbirthcontrol.com.

158 Thompson, M, 'Contraceptive implants: long-acting and provider-dependent contraception raises concerns about freedom of choice' (1996) 313 BMJ 1393; see also Hardee, K *et al*, 'Contraceptive implant users and their access to removal services in Bangladesh' (1994) 20 International Family Planning Perspectives 59.

health professionals to encourage use without full disclosure of risks. Similar problems have arisen with the injectable contraception, Depo-Provera, which has the additional risk that it may be administered without the knowledge of the woman that she is being given a contraceptive drug.[159] In these circumstances, strong national laws on informed consent are necessary for legal protection against contraceptive abuse.

Many modern forms of mechanical and chemical contraceptives have raised serious health risks,[160] and drugs manufacturers have resisted compensation where users have suffered harmful side effects.[161] Most chemical forms of contraception have been targeted at women,[162] and fear of health risk explains why some women do not use contraception even when it is readily and freely available.[163] There has been litigation in many jurisdictions against doctors and health services for negligent contraceptive advice resulting in injury to the user,[164] as well as litigation against both manufacturers[165] and health providers[166] in relation to ineffective

---

159 Rajusen, J, 'Depo-Provera: the extent of the problem. A case study in the politics of birth control', in Roberts, H (ed), *Women, Health and Reproduction*, 1981, London: Routledge and Kegan Paul.

160 See, eg, Farmer, R *et al*, 'Effect of 1995 pill scare on rates of venous thromboembolism among women taking combined oral contraceptives: analysis of general practice research database' (2000) 321 BMJ 477; Jick, H *et al*, 'Risk of venous thromboembolism among users of third generation oral contraceptives compared with users of oral contraceptives with levonorgestrel before and after 1995' (2000) 321 BMJ 1352.

161 See, eg, the failed action by 275 British women under the Consumer Protection Act 1987 against Hoechst Marion Roussel, the UK distributors of Norplant, claiming compensation for side effects and difficulties of removal; (1999) 318 BMJ 485. See also Ferguson, P, *Drug Injuries and the Pursuit of Compensation*, 1996, London: Sweet & Maxwell.

162 See, however, the male pill developed by the Contraceptive Development Network at the University of Edinburgh. The pill contains progesterone, which works to prevent the production of sperm, and testosterone to sustain hormone balance. It can be taken in the form of injection or adhesive patches. There has been limited commercial interest in production of the pill. See http://www.rnw.nl/science/html/pill001120.html.

163 See 'Letters' (1995) 311 BMJ 1638.

164 See *Vadera v Shaw* (1999) 45 BMLR 162 (unsuccessful), *Coker v Richmond and Roehampton AHA* (1996) 7 Med LR 58 (unsuccessful); *Brand v Buckle* (2000) 6 Clinical Risk 86 (successful). See also Doyal, L, 'Infertility – a life sentence? Women and the National Health Service', in Stanworth, M (ed), *Reproductive Technologies: Gender, Motherhood and Medicine*, 1987, Cambridge: Polity.

165 See *Richardson v LRC Products* [2000] Lloyd's Rep Med 280 where a woman claimed unsuccessfully in relation to pregnancy resulting from a defective condom.

166 Eg, *Hayden v Barking, Havering and Brentwood HA* (1998) unreported, 20 February, where a woman was advised that she was unable to conceive naturally, but became pregnant (unsuccessful); *Greenfield v Irwin* (2000) unreported, 24 January, where a doctor administering a course of long term contraception failed to check whether the woman was pregnant (unsuccessful). Note that after the House of Lords decision in *McFarlane v Tayside HA* [2000] 2 AC 59, it is no longer possible to sue in English law for damages for the birth of a healthy but unwanted child. See also *L v M* [1979] 2 NZLR 519 (New Zealand), *Kealey v Berezowski* (1996) 136 DLR (4th) 708 (Canada), *CES v Superclinics (Australia) Pty Ltd* (1995) 38 NSWLR 47 (Australia). More generally, see Kennedy, I and Grubb, A, *Medical Law*, 2000, London: Butterworths, Chapter 12.

contraception resulting in pregnancy. English domestic law provides limited protection either for women's choice in relation to contraception or for harm from contraceptive use.[167] This is partly because of the way law determines standard of care of products and services,[168] partly because the law regulating informed consent does not require all material information to be given to users,[169] and partly because English law does not facilitate class actions.[170] Women in other jurisdictions have had some success in obtaining legal recognition of harm caused by contraception,[171] but it remains the case that women exercise fertility control at their own risk.

The allocation of fertility control risks to women results from the categorisation of contraception as a private health concern, the responsibility of individual women, even though population control is considered a matter of public health. Little research has been done on invasive contraceptives for men.[172] There has been only limited recognition that women's fertility is affected by public health issues such as smoking,[173] nutrition, stress and mental health. Sexual health in the context of reproductive health has also been considered a private health issue and the responsibility of individual patients. More recently, there have been signs of a more comprehensive approach to reproductive health. The British Government, for example, has expressed concern at the high rate of teenage pregnancies, increase in sexual disease, drug taking and the sexual risk taking culture of young people, and announced a new strategy to overcome widespread ignorance of sexual and reproductive health.[174] Education level has been identified as an important contributor to youth behaviour, along with poverty and social exclusion.[175]

---

167 See Foster, P, *Women and the Health Care Industry: An Unhealthy Relationship?*, 1995, Buckingham: OU Press.

168 The standard is that of the reasonable, competent member of that profession or trade (*Bolam v Friern Hospital Management Committee* [1965] 2 All ER 118). The Consumer Protection Act 1987 imposes strict liability on manufacturers of contraceptives in relation to defects causing physical harm (but not in relation to pregnancy) subject to the limited definition of 'defect' in s 3 of the Act.

169 Only that information which a reasonable health care professional would consider appropriate: *Sidaway v Board of Governors of Royal Bethlem Hospital* [1985] 2 WLR 480.

170 See the Norplant litigation (1999) 318 BMJ 485.

171 See, eg, *Buchan v Ortho Pharmaceutical (Canada) Ltd* (1986) 25 DLR (4th) 658, where the manufacturers of an oral contraceptive drug were held liable in Canada for failing to give adequate warning of side effects of the drug.

172 Bruce, J, 'Users' perspectives on contraceptive technology and delivery systems: highlighting some feminist issues' (1987) 9 Technology in Society 359; Doyal, L, *What Makes Women Sick*, 1995, Basingstoke: Macmillan.

173 Handler, J *et al*, 'The relationship of smoking and ectopic pregnancy' (1989) 79 American Journal of Public Health 1239; Rosevear, S *et al*, 'Smoking and decreased fertilisation rates in vitro' (1992) The Lancet 1195.

174 The Minister for Public Health, Tessa Jowell, March 1999, reported in (1999) 318 BMJ 894.

175 See, eg, McKee, M, 'Sex and drugs and rock and roll' (1999) 318 BMJ 1300; Nicoll, A *et al*, 'Sexual health of teenagers in England and Wales: analysis of national data' [contd]

There has also been recognition of the public health risks created by contraceptive use. Contraceptive chemicals that rely on oestrogens and progestins have not only caused health problems for women, but have also been responsible for wider environmental harms to which have been attributed rises in male infertility levels.[176] Sexual diseases have also impacted on men, and modern contraceptives provide no protection against sexually transmitted disease. It is recognition of these public health issues rather than concern for the health of women which has prompted political and scientific interest in alternative types of contraception. The separation of sex and reproduction, enabled by effective contraception, was welcomed at the time because issues of sexual morality and control of women[177] were removed from the reproduction debate. Now that society has begun to recognise women's right to sexual choice, the connections between sex and reproduction are being reassessed from a health rather than a moral perspective to enable a more holistic view of sexual health, and to develop a public health approach to reproduction.

Sterilisation

In the developed countries of the world today, sterilisation is not explicitly considered as part of the public health agenda, but is assumed to be an aspect of individual choice and personal treatment. As a procedure,[178] it is characterised as either a form of contraception that a person may choose out of personal need or circumstances, or as a therapy to cure or alleviate an identified medical condition. As a consequence, common law countries do not tend to have legislation to deal with sterilisation. The issue of sterilisation has been litigated before the courts as either a negligence claim or as a consent problem where the subject of the action has insufficient capacity to consent herself. Civil law jurisdictions have included provisions regarding non-consensual sterilisation in civil codes dealing with the rights and responsibilities of individuals, such as the scope of proxy decision

175 [contd] (1999) 318 BMJ 1321; Bozon, M and Kontula, O, 'Sexual initiation and gender in Europe: a cross-cultural analysis of trends in the twentieth century', in Hubert, M *et al* (eds), *Sexual Behaviour and HIV/AIDS in Europe*, 1998, London: UCL Press; Noone, A *et al*, 'Sexual health of teenagers (1999) 319 BMJ 1367; Stammers, T and Ingham, R, 'For and against: doctors should advise teenagers to abstain from sex' (2000) 321 BMJ 1520.

176 Joffe, M, 'Decreased fertility in Britain compared with Finland' (1996) 347 The Lancet 1519; Carlsen, E *et al*, 'Evidence for decreasing quality of semen during the past 50 years' (1992) 305 BMJ 609; Auger, J, 'Decline in semen quality among fertile men in Paris during the past 20 years' (1995) 332 New England Journal of Medicine 281.

177 See Litt, I, *Taking Our Pulse: The Health of America's Women*, 1997, Stanford: Stanford UP.

178 Sterilisation is generally inclusive of procedures involving both males and females. Vasectomy, full or partial hysterectomy, oophorectomy and tubal ligations are all forms of sterilisation procedure. Vas occlusion and female tubal blocking devices are potentially reversible and tubal ligations can be performed using laparoscopic surgery.

making for those with mental disabilities.[179] Sterilisation can also be seen litigated as a rights issue, the most famous example being the leading Canadian case of *Re Eve*,[180] where the Supreme Court of Canada took the view that sterilisation without consent infringed the right to reproduce unless there were exceptional therapeutic reasons for the procedure to be carried out.

This centring of concern on the individual facing sterilisation has produced a particular range of legal responses. Whether or not to allow sterilisation without consent has been treated as an issue of inviolability of the body, where the starting point has been the integrity of the individual.[181] That is, whether the particular jurisdiction has developed a rights-based approach or an approach based on the common law concept of best interests of the person, the rationale addresses the legality of interfering with a body that would ordinarily be protected from incursions. Any justification for allowing a medical procedure without consent must stem from the rights or interests of the individual herself, rather than from external concerns or the concerns of others. It is this limitation to the personal that has caused most academic debate within these jurisdictions, on the basis that to allow the concerns of other individuals, groups or the State to influence a decision to sterilise would be an abuse.

Individualism has not consistently dominated legal approaches to sterilisation, either across time or across continents. The influences of national and global population policies and of eugenics have affected the way in which sterilisation has been defined as a health issue. In China, for example, policies to restrict population growth have placed contraception, abortion and sterilisation in the context of community good.[182] Since the early 1970s, projected increases in China's population have been defined as 'a problem' by the government because of the effects of rapid population growth on economic and social development. National programmes of abortion and sterilisation have been justified on the grounds that

179 In Germany, eg, the *Betreuungsgesetz* (Carership Law) permitting proxy consent for sterilisation under prescribed circumstances was introduced in 1992 to amend ss 1896–1908i of the *Bürgerlischesgesetzbuch* (German Civil Code). See Little, GB, 'Comparing German and English law on non-consensual sterilisation: a difference approach' (1997) 5 Medical L Rev 269–93.

180 (1986) 31 DLR (4th) 1 (SCC). See, also, *Re D (A Minor) (Wardship: Sterilisation)* [1976] Fam 185 and *Department of Health and Community Services (NT) v JWB and SMB* (1992) 66 ALJR 300 (High Court of Australia). The recent English decision of *Re SL (Adult Patient) (Sterilisation)* (2000) 3 WLR 1288; (2000) 2 FLR 389 tentatively reintroduces rights into decision making on sterilisation in the English courts.

181 In *Re B (A Minor) (Wardship: Sterilisation)* [1988] AC 199; [1987] 2 All ER 206; *Re F* [1990] 2 AC 1; *Re SL (Adult Patient) (Sterilisation)* [2000] 3 WLR 1288; [2000] 2 FLR 389.

182 Greenhalgh, S *et al*, 'Restraining population growth in three Chinese villages, 1988–1993' (1994) 20 Population and Development Review 365–95; Aird, JS, *Slaughter of the Innocents*, 1990, AEI Press.

unrestricted population growth presented a threat to development. Officials have explained that China needed to develop its economy and production abilities and the demands on national income, employment, housing, education, transport, health care and so on, presented by a rapidly growing population, would have held China back.[183] As a result, China now has a demographic profile similar to the industrialised West, whilst its per capita GNP ranks it amongst the developing countries.[184]

The linkage between population growth and economy was made explicit at the Cairo conference,[185] but the uneven worldwide distribution of the implications of that linkage was not explored in any depth. The social, economic and environmental value of reproduction, or more often of limited reproduction, is seen in the international context as relevant to *some* women, rather than to women globally. The imperative of containing reproduction in jurisdictions that are developing in order for those States to follow their seemingly natural 'progressive' course was presented at Cairo as a neutral step towards globalisation, rather than as a racial and particularist policy aimed at women in the least economically 'advanced' States.[186] Such claims to neutrality within internationally led population policies has the effect of reinforcing ideas about women within developing countries as being other than women in developed States: they are unrestrained in reproduction, threatening to economic stability, sexually hedonistic, irresponsible in their lack of self-restraint.[187] The women who become the subject of sterilisation and abortion programmes are imaged as different from the women who choose sterilisation, but they are also seen as different from women categorised as irrational and who are subject to court authorised sterilisation in States characterised by modernity.[188] The particularity of the women who are sterilised is more precise, however, than would appear from an analysis that divides women into categories according to the level of development of their State. Within States, 'women' is clearly not a unified, homogeneous group and identities are composed of a multitude of dimensions. It is well established within the literature on feminisms that race, class, ethnicity,

183 See, eg, 'How China handles population and family planning: interview with Peng Yu, Vice-Minister of the State Family Planning Commission' (1994) Beijing Review 1 August, p 8.

184 Johnson, L, 'Expanding eugenics or improving health care in China' (1997) 24 JLS 2, p 206.

185 *Report of the International Conference on Population and Development, Cairo, 5–13 September 1994, Annex, Programme of Action of the International Conference on Population and Development*, A/CONF 171/13, 18 October 1994, Chapter 3.

186 Buss, D, 'Racing populations, sexing environments: the challenges of a feminist politics in international law' (2000) 20 LS 463–84.

187 Pettman, JJ, *Worlding Women: A Feminist International Politics*, 1996, London: Routledge.

188 This opposition between the images of the self in the 'West' and the Other in the 'East' was first elaborated in the work of Edward Said. See, eg, *Orientalism*, 1979, New York: Vintage.

religion, sexuality and able-bodiedness are amongst the most significant distinctions cutting across gender and that identity is complex rather than simply primary allegiance to one social group. In Brazil, for example, where female sterilisation is at 45% of the female population, it is concentrated most significantly amongst the poor, black women in the North-east of the country. Amongst this sector, the level of sterilisation is approaching 80%.[189]

Otherness, or the fear of it, was evident in early European responses to fertility control that were fed by eugenics.[190] China's population control success story is also linked with eugenics in its stated aim to produce 'fewer and better births'. The assumption that China should be populated by its fittest stock has an ample history[191] and has outlived the eugenics movement that spread throughout Europe, North America and Australasia in the early 20th century. Yet, at that time, it was the fear of national populations being diluted by the unrestrained reproduction of their less fit members that led to domestic policies and legislation for the sterilisation of the unfit in those jurisdictions.

The eugenics movement began in England in the 1880s. Francis Galton coined the word 'eugenics' in 1883 to describe a population policy to improve society by encouraging the reproduction of its fittest members whilst containing the reproduction of its weakest.[192] The movement thrived on the negative aspect of eugenics and many States introduced legislation to facilitate limitations on reproduction by sterilising those designated as less fit. These eugenic measures assumed that the worth of any society could be measured by the quality of its individual members and that 'quality' was inheritable.[193] Just as the 19th century sanitation measures were based upon the false beliefs of miasma theory, eugenics was based upon erroneous understandings of genetic theory. By 1937, around 30 American States had enacted eugenic laws[194] and immigration restrictions had been introduced to ensure that the majority of the population in the US remained of British or

---

189 Women's Feature Service, *The Power to Change*, 1992, New Delhi: Kali, pp 199–200.

190 See, eg, Reilly, P, *The Surgical Solution*, 1991, Baltimore: Johns Hopkins UP; Annas, G and Grodin, M (eds), *The Nazi Doctors and the Nuremberg Code*, 1992, New York: OUP.

191 Buxbaum, DC, *Chinese Family Law and Social Change in Historical and Comparative Perspective*, 1978, Seattle: Washington UP.

192 Galton, F, *Essays in Eugenics*, 1909, London: Eugenics Education Society. See Trombley, S, *The Right to Reproduce*, 1988, London: Weidenfeld & Nicolson.

193 In upholding the constitutionality of one of the United States' sterilisation laws, Holmes J in the Supreme Court said: 'It is better for all the world, if instead of waiting to execute degenerate offspring for crime, or to let them starve for their imbecility, society can prevent those who are manifestly unfit from continuing their kind ... Three generations of imbeciles is enough.' *Buck v Bell*, 274 US 200 (1927).

194 Different sources cite different numbers of States as having forcible sterilisation laws, but all claim that a significant percentage of all States passed such laws. See Johnson, L, 'Expanding eugenics or improving health care in China' (1997) 24 JLS 199–234, fn 12.

Northern European descent.[195] Many of the coercive provisions in these laws were never used, but by 1935, 20,000 people had been sterilised without consent and many States retained the laws until well into the 1980s.[196] Recently, controversies of non-consensual sterilisation have emerged from Australia, Denmark, Sweden and Canada. In all cases, domestic laws had been used to target the unfit[197] on the basis of their irrationality and lack of economic productivity:[198] it was the 'feeble-minded', those with inadequate intelligence, addictions or promiscuity, vagrants and gypsies who were identified as less fit.

It could be argued that the distinction between an individualised and a population approach to sterilisation is an example of the clear dichotomy between individualism and communitarianism. Sandel and others have analysed this as the difference between modern society as a mass of atomised individuals selfishly pursuing their own interests and an earlier, simpler society based upon community concerns which foster mutual care and support.[199] An alternative approach would be to see both approaches as the product of wider changes in social structures which have brought about and been sustained by internationalisation and globalisation. Global population policies have been supported by international forums and organisations like the World Bank and the United Nations have sponsored family planning services in countries where sterilisation and abortion programmes have been implemented.[200] It is not, however, simply the involvement of international organisations which link sterilisation with

195 Britain has never enacted sterilisation legislation. A recommendation by the Brock Report in 1934 to authorise sterilisation of the feeble-minded did have sufficient support but was overtaken by events in Nazi Germany. Trombley, S, *The Right to Reproduce*, 1988, London: Weidenfeld & Nicolson.

196 Sources attach a wide range of figures to the number of people actually sterilised under this legislation. A recent report in the *Washington Post* concerning litigation in Michigan by a fully competent individual who was forcibly sterilised as feeble-minded in 1944 puts the figure in excess of 60,000. Lessenberry, J, 'Scarred by sterilization' (2000) *Washington Post*, 9 March, p A03.

197 Identifying the 'unfit' was presented in this legislation as unproblematic, whereas scholarship has revealed not only the class and racial bias inherent in intelligence tests, but also the assumptions inherent in any classification system. For a discussion of the failure of English law to recognise that disability and intelligence are not simply psychological categories, see Jones, MA and Keywood, K, 'Assessing the patient's competence to consent to medical treatment' (1996) 2 Medical Law International 107–47.

198 Studies have indicated that the sterilisation laws in the US were also directed against identifiable groups in their operation, namely: women; children; the unemployed; domestic workers; institutionalised persons; Roman and Greek Catholics; those of Eastern European descent or Indian or Metis ethnicity. Law Reform Commission of Canada, *Sterilization: Implications for Mentally Retarded and Mentally Ill Persons*, 1979, pp 42–45.

199 Sandel's work and varying approaches to individualism and communitarianism are discussed above, Chapter 1 by Linda Johnson.

200 Hartmann, B, *Reproductive Rights and Wrongs: The Global Politics of Population Control and Contraceptive Choice*, 1987, New York: Harper & Row.

increased globalisation. What is perhaps more significant is the shift in eugenics from the national to the global. It was nationalism that drove eugenics in the early 20th century. The aim was to produce the fittest stock for each State that pursued that agenda. National frontiers were significant and the government was seen as acting out of some concept of responsibility to its citizenry. The Chinese Government has consistently justified its population control policy on grounds of national economy and has passed provincial and national laws to support its campaign for a fitter population. Yet, like moves in other developing countries to contain population growth, the international community has reconfigured and supported such moves on an assessment of world as well as local needs.

The events of the Second World War and the genocide it revealed signalled the demise of Galton's eugenics movement in Europe and the US. The idea of legitimating mass sterilisation programmes became untenable particularly as science had begun to recognise the fallacy of the simple links of heritability assumed by the eugenics movements. The perceived need to protect the individual from potential abuses by States which followed on discoveries of the extent of genocide in Hitler's Germany enhanced the position of the individual domestically as well as within the burgeoning international human rights arena. Decisions of courts on the sterilisation of women with intellectual disabilities in the US, Canada, the UK and Australia all came to insist on centralising the best interests of the woman herself.[201] Allusions to the interests of carers and the State have been considered insufficiently compelling to justify the invasion of privacy necessarily involved in a sterilisation procedure.[202]

Analyses of domestic regulation within these countries has, however, suggested the fallacy of this ideal of individualism. The concept of best interests of the patient has been criticised in Britain for its lack of resilience against the interests of the State and carers.[203] The first House of Lords

---

201 In Canada the leading case of *Re Eve* (1986) 31 DLR (4th) 1 (SCC) took the view that the court only had jurisdiction to consent to a sterilisation where the purpose was patently therapeutic. Decisions of the US courts and courts in the UK have been more reluctant to demarcate therapeutic from non-therapeutic cases clearly and have applied a best interests of the patient test. See, eg, the House of Lords' decisions of *Re B (A Minor) (Wardship: Sterilisation)* [1987] 2 All ER 206 and *Re F* [1990] 2 AC 1. There are, however, many cases where that distinction has been used. For an Australian example, see *Between L and GM, applicants and MM respondent and the Director General of the Department of Family Services and Aboriginal and Islander Affairs (Sarah)* (1994) FLC 92-44917 Fam LR 357 (Aust).

202 This has been most recently restated by the Court of Appeal in *Re SL (Adult Patient) (Sterilisation)* [2000] 3 WLR 1288; [2000] 2 FLR 389.

203 See, eg, Brazier, M, 'Sterilisation: down the slippery slope' (1990) 6 Professional Negligence 25; Shaw, J, 'Sterilisation of mentally handicapped people: judges rule OK?' (1990) 53 MLR 91; Keywood, K, 'Sterilising the woman with learning disabilities – in her best interests?' in Bridgeman, J and Millns, S, *Law and Body Politics: Regulating the Female Body*, 1995, Aldershot: Dartmouth.

decision on sterilisation[204] firmly stated that eugenics was not tolerable in any form and proposed some guidelines to limit sterilisation applications. There must be a real risk of pregnancy, sterilisation should only be used as a last resort and only the interests of the person to be sterilised should be taken into account. But, succeeding cases failed to treat these guidelines as rigid requirements.[205] The most recent round of cases[206] has interpreted the concept of best interests as a risk assessment exercise – specifically weighing the risk of pregnancy against the disbenefits of the procedure – and has, for the first time in English law, gone some way towards acknowledging the severity of sterilisation and its implications. These cases have produced results which have protected the women, and one man, from sterilisation, but still they do not evince an approach rigidly defensive of individual interests. It has, for example, been argued that the method of risk assessment used is highly questionable and could well be prompted by economic concerns of the State.[207] As an increasing number of patients with disabilities are being cared for in the home, responsibilities for surveillance have increased with parental or carer to patient ratios far lower than within State funded institutions. The freedom for expressing sexuality allowed in institutions takes on a different social and political agenda in the 'outside world'. Having family or carers responsible for sexual surveillance provides security not only against unwanted pregnancies, but also against the sexuality of those whose knowledge and experiences preclude its 'normality'.

What can be said about the common law cases mobilising the concept of risk in decision making on applications to sterilise is that in the context of the new public health, the distinction between public and private health is

---

204 *Re B (A Minor) (Wardship: Sterilisation)* [1987] 2 All ER 206; [1988] AC 199.

205 Eg, in *Re M* [1988] 2 FLR 497 (Bush J), eugenic considerations were taken into account; and in *Re HG* [1993] 1 FLR 587 (Peter Singer QC) sterilisation was considered lawful when there was no evidence that the woman was sexually active. The pattern of approach has remained the same, but the laxity in the interpretation of parameters on professional judgments has made the framework illusive. See Brazier, M, 'Sterilisation: down the slippery slope?' (1990) 6 Professional Negligence 25.

206 *Re LC* [1997] 2 FLR 258; *Re SL (Adult Patient) (Sterilisation)* [2000] 3 WLR 1288; [2000] 2 FLR 389; *Re A (Medical Treatment: Male Sterilisation)* [2000] 1 FCR 193.

207 This argument was also used in respect of the earlier wave of cases which made indirect references to economic concerns. In *Re P* [1989] 1 FLR 182, for example, where there was no indication of current sexual activity and no clear evidence of lack of ability to care for a child, sterilisation was allowed on the basis of uncertainty over future care arrangements. The House of Lords in *Re F* [1990] 2 AC 1 unanimously viewed the management needs of those responsible for care as a valid consideration. For discussion, see Shaw, J, 'Sterilisation of mentally handicapped people: judges rule OK?' (1990) 53 MLR 91 and, generally, Lee, R and Morgan, D, 'Sterilisation: sapping the strength of the State' (1988) 15 JLS 229. On risk and some of the recent cases, see Fenwick, A, '*Re S (Medical Treatment: Adult Sterilisation)*: Retrenching on risk – revising the lawful boundaries of sterilisation' (1999) 11(3) Child and Family Law Quarterly 313–20.

further eroded. As has been discussed in earlier chapters, risk has become increasingly significant in health care decisions and has been integrated into the discourse on public health through ideas about health promotion and lifestyle.[208] The image of the individual within this view of health care is multi-faceted, with threats to health no longer confined to the body, but inherent in many aspects of life. The individual is no longer self-contained and atomised, but is an actor within a community influenced by and influencing a wide range of relationships and negotiations in everyday life. This shift is reflected in a comparison of the English sterilisation cases before and after *Re LC*,[209] the first decision overtly to base its decision on an assessment of risk. Interestingly, the later case of *Re SL* went on to image the doctor's role as one of adviser on only one aspect of the risk equation,[210] rather than as the actor most able to gauge the appropriateness and the implications of performing a sterilisation.[211]

Otherness is also inherent within domestic treatment of applications to sterilise. This individual is presented as deserving protection, but the case law in England is riven with assumptions about disabilities, and the sexuality of those disabilities. Those assumptions have produced an idea of those with disabilities as having unrestrained sexuality. The women have repeatedly been described by the court as attractive but monstrous, affectionate but uncaring, fertile but incapable of nurturing.[212] As such, they are women who are not legitimate in their sexuality: they are imaged as lacking what is assumed to be an essential aspect of womanhood, that is, motherhood. It is this status which allows the court to consider their sterilisation and which has resonances with images of colonised women.

Whilst the image of the individual contained within the English cases is more akin to the individual within the 'new' public health discourse than the atomised individual of the Enlightenment, protections are still driven by the need to protect from invasions dominated by the interests of others.[213]

208 See, especially, Chapter 1 by Linda Johnson.

209 [1997] 2 FLR 258 (decided in 1993).

210 *Re SL (Adult Patient) (Sterilisation)* [2000] 3 WLR 1288; [2000] 2 FLR 389, *per* Thorpe, LJ: 'In deciding what is best for the disabled patient the judge must have regard to the patient's welfare as the paramount consideration. That embraces issues far wider than the medical. Indeed it would be undesirable and probably impossible to set bounds to what is relevant to a welfare determination.'

211 See, eg, *Re F* [1990] 2 AC 1.

212 All the English sterilisation cases and many of the sterilisation cases in Australia and the US describe the physical attributes of the persons to be sterilised emphasising vulnerability, attractiveness and abnormality in behaviour or demeanour. For a discussion of the court's paradoxical treatment of Jeanette as vulnerable and sexually dangerous, both justifying her sterilisation for her own protection, see Martin, N, '*Re B (A Minor)*' [1987] Journal of Social Welfare Law 369 and, for the court's assessment of F, see Shaw, J, 'Sterilisation of mentally handicapped people: judges rule OK?' (1990) 53 MLR 91.

213 See *Re SL (Adult Patient) (Sterilisation)* [2000] 3 WLR 1288; [2000] 2 FLR 389, where the Court of Appeal reiterated the view that the concerns of the carers should not determine what is in the best interests of the subject of the application.

This is demonstrated more clearly in Germany, where the Carership Law requires a carer to be appointed to deal specifically with the sterilisation issue, and requires a real and present risk of pregnancy before an application can be successful.[214] Jurisdictions using a rights approach to sterilisation have also stressed the rights of privacy of the individual. Yet, there is extensive evidence that in jurisdictions where poverty is widespread, there are patent links between high levels of sterilisation and economic concerns.[215] Sometimes, government policy has been to promote widespread sterilisation, and at other times lack of information and alternative contraception has produced similar results. There are also analyses that link the majority of 'voluntary' sterilisations within developed nations to racial groups which are also economically disadvantaged such as Black, Puerto Rican and native American women in the US.[216]

The fear of impending disaster from world over-population has been presented as justification for policies promoting sterilisation. The largest increase in population in absolute terms has taken place in Asia, and this has produced anxiety in the West over the world 'population problem'. Fears have been about emigration from Asia and of being engulfed by an Asian/African impoverished majority, even though as a gross proportion of the world population they are only just reaching their pre-European industrial revolution level.[217] These fears and their attendant strain on food, environment and other resources have been seen as sufficient to override reproductive choice through legal coercion or economic repression. As Amartya Sen has pointed out, this approach runs counter to Enlightenment faith in reason that would call for increased productivity, improved prevention and wider education.[218] Economic development has historically been linked with slower population growth[219] and, he argues, coercive population control policies are ultimately counter-productive to long term development. Yet, these fears for global security have repeatedly allowed

214 There are further procedural safeguards to bolster the inviolability of the person, such as the need to show risk to mental or physical health of the woman, the requirement of a therapeutic base and last resort. For discussion of the strictness of the operation of these provisions, see Little, G, 'Comparing German and English law on non-consensual sterilisation: a difference approach' (1997) 5 Med LR 269–93.

215 Puerto Rico, for example, has 45% of its female population sterilised, in parts of the Amazon figures have been as high as 75% and India and Bangladesh have both experienced extensive sterilisation programmes. See Doyal, L, *What Makes Women Sick: Gender and the Political Economy of Health*, 1995, London: Macmillan, pp 107–09.

216 Gerber Fried, M (ed), *From Abortion to Reproductive Freedom: Transforming a Movement*, 1990, Boston: South End.

217 See Sen, A, 'Population: delusion and reality', in Lancaster, R and di Leonardo, M (eds), *The Gender Sexuality Reader*, 1997, London: Routledge, pp 89–106.

218 *Ibid*, p 93.

219 Sen, A, 'Population and reasoned agency: food, fertility and economic development', in Lindahl-Kiessling, K and Landberg, H, *Population, Economic Development, and the Environment*, 1994, Oxford: OUP.

the sacrifice of individual choice which domestically developed countries have striven to safeguard, however imperfectly.

Abortion

It is in the legal regulation of abortion that there is the least global consensus, and the greatest ongoing debate. Abortion is a major public health issue. Where there is no legal access to abortion, there are high mortality rates from complications arising from illegal abortion.[220] Where there is legal access to abortion, many countries have not approved the safer chemical methods of abortion such as mifepristone (RU 486), continuing to rely on surgical abortion provided later in pregnancy.[221] The tension between pro- and anti-abortionists keeps abortion in the public profile, maintaining an environment of insecurity in relation to women's right to choose termination of pregnancy.

Whatever the moral arguments surrounding abortion, it cannot be denied that abortion is an important fertility control mechanism, operating alongside contraception and sterilisation to provide coverage for unwanted pregnancy. The less access to free and readily available contraception a State provides, the greater use is made of abortion services, legal and illegal.[222] Within States, groups which have more restricted access to contraception, unmarried teenage girls, for example, account disproportionately for abortion use. The contraception/abortion distinction is increasingly blurred not only by the use of abortion as a form of occasional contraception, but also by the increased use and permissibility of contragestation as contraception. Traditionally, the moral outrage prompted by abortion has not applied to contraception outside countries with a dominant Catholic influence, but the increasing conflation of contraception and abortion has worked both to heighten the opposition to abortion and contraception in some jurisdictions, and to diffuse it in others.

In the US, abortion has once again become the focus of political and social conflict. In 1973 in *Roe v Wade*,[223] the Supreme Court recognised a woman's constitutional right to privacy which protected a decision to undergo abortion within the first trimester of pregnancy, by extension from

---

220 Thonneau, P *et al*, 'The persistence of a high maternal mortality rate in the Ivory Coast' (1996) 86 American Journal of Public Health 1478; Rosenfield, A and Maine, D, 'Maternal mortality, a neglected tragedy' (1985) 2 The Lancet 83; Climent, J, 'Most deaths related to abortion occur in the developing world' (1999) 318 BMJ 1509.

221 (1999) 319 BMJ 1091.

222 Eg, The Netherlands, which provides ready access to contraception for all women regardless of age, has had an abortion rate of one-fifth of that of the US, where access to contraception is more restricted and unfunded; Jones, E *et al*, *Pregnancy, Contraception and Family Planning Services in Industrialised Countries*, 1989, New Haven, Yale UP.

223 (1973) 410 US 113.

earlier decisions which had recognised the right to privacy as protecting contraception. *Roe v Wade* did not recognise a right to abortion as such, and subsequent decisions made clear that there was no obligation on the State to facilitate abortion.[224] The strong American anti-choice lobby has maintained a protest against abortion. Ironically, it has been developments in medical science aimed at improving safety during pregnancy – in particular, screening techniques – which have enabled a renewed legal assault on *Roe v Wade* based on the constitutional right to life. The concept of foetal personhood, made more real by foetal identification techniques, has been used to pressure American legislatures and courts into extending the right to life to unborn persons.

This legal challenge to abortion began with the introduction of statutory limitation on late term abortion, emotively called 'partial birth abortion',[225] and such legislation has become increasingly restrictive.[226] The Infant's Protection Act 1999 in Missouri applied the felony of infanticide to any act causing the death of a fetus when it is outside or partly outside the womb, which covers any form of abortion by dilation or extraction carried out even within the first trimester. There is no exception to protect the life or health of the mother, nor for a damaged fetus. Women who undergo such abortions could be convicted of a crime carrying a potential life sentence.[227] The Nebraskan legislature introduced similar legislation,[228] which was later struck down by the Supreme Court on two grounds: first, that 'partial birth' abortions were performed comparatively rarely and for the safety of the mother, such that the legislation violated the mother's right to life; and secondly that the law unduly burdened the woman's right to choose as the legislation potentially applied to first trimester abortions. Nevertheless, there are concerns that the anti-abortion movement in the US is gaining ground in attempts to overturn *Roe v Wade*. The election of George W Bush, who opposes abortion, and the appointment of his anti-abortion Attorney General John Ashcroft, have prompted a rush of proposed legislation introducing waiting times between counselling and abortion, proscribing

224 See MacKinnon, C, 'Privacy and equality: beyond *Roe v Wade*', in MacKinnon, C, *Feminism Unmodified: Discourses on Life and Law*, 1987, Cambridge, Mass: Harvard UP.

225 So called because the procedure involves chemically dilating the woman's cervix over several days, partially extracting the foetus, and perforating the skull to kill the foetus. This is, in reality, not a common abortion procedure, accounting, for example, for only 0.3 % of abortions in Wisconsin, one of the States which has legislated against it. However, there are circumstances where such a form of abortion is medically necessary, eg, in the case of a hydrocephalic foetus; see (1999) 319 BMJ 1200.

226 Laws preventing late term abortion have been passed in 30 States including Wisconsin, Illinois and Missouri. The constitutionality of these laws is being challenged in many of these States.

227 (1999) 319 BMJ 874. The constitutionality of the law is being challenged.

228 The Nebraskan law included an exception where the life of the mother was endangered by the pregnancy; Annas, G, '"Partial-birth abortion" and the Supreme Court' (2001) 344 New England Journal of Medicine 2.

particular abortion procedures and restrictively regulating the activities of abortion clinics, in the expectation that a newly appointed Supreme Court will be prepared to uphold the legislation.

Less direct attacks on abortion laws have operated by focusing on the more politically disempowered women in American society, particularly women on welfare, black women and drug abusers, in the move to gain legal recognition of foetal personhood. There has been both legislative and judicial support for the detention of pregnant women whose behaviour poses a threat to the fetus, and laws on child abuse have been extended to protect unborn children[229] so that the representation of the fetus as a person with rights is increasingly apparent in law. Non-consensual drug testing of pregnant women had become routine in some American States,[230] with test results reported to the police to enable arrest and detention of the pregnant woman. The US Supreme Court has now ruled that drug testing for the purposes of prosecution, which is exercised without a valid warrant, is unconstitutional.[231] Parallel to such legal challenges have been practices of protest, picketing, harassment and violence. Attempts to protect women and health workers by the creation of harassment free 'buffer zones'[232] around clinics have been struck down by the courts as offending constitutional rights to freedom of speech.[233] Legal abortion is becoming less accessible as clinics and health workers fear further intimidation.[234]

The anti-abortion environment which has arisen from these measures has gradually extended from opposition to late term abortion to envelop early abortion techniques such as RU 486. The underlying suggestion that women need to be controlled in the exercise of their fertility has begun to overlay attitudes not only to pregnant women, but also to women who might be making a decision about pregnancy. On the issue of abortion, the US is becoming uncomfortably allied with Islamic States[235] in the fundamentalism inherent in attitudes to women's sexual behaviour,[236] as

229 Eg, *State v Whitner* (South Carolina). Following a similar case, the Wisconsin Children's code has now been redrafted to include an offence of 'unborn child abuse', defining an unborn child as a 'human being from the time of fertilization to the time of birth'. See Paltrow, L, 'Pregnant drug users, fetal persons and the threat to *Roe v Wade*' (1999) 62 Albany L Rev 999,

230 Eg, in South Carolina.

231 See *Ferguson v City of Charleston* (2001) unreported, 21 March, US Supreme Court.

232 Eg, the Federal Freedom of Access to Clinic Entrances Act 1994, Lexis-Nexis.

233 (2000) 321 BMJ 1368.

234 Kahane, L, 'Anti-abortion activities and the market for abortion services: protests as a disincentive' (2000) 59 American Journal of Economics and Sociology; Kulczycki, A *et al*, 'Abortion and fertility regulation' (1996) 347 The Lancet 1663.

235 For coverage of the Islamic approach to abortion, see Rumage, S, 'Resisting the West: the Clinton administration's promotion of abortion at the Cairo conference and the strength of the Islamic response' (1996) 27 Californian Western International LJ 1.

236 Doyal, L, *What Makes Women Sick*, 1995, Basingstoke: Macmillan, Chapter 4.

the rest of the world seeks to increase women's rights and opportunities to make reproductive choices.

Movements to restrict abortion have been generally unsuccessful in Europe. In England, Private Members' Bills attempting to proscribe 'partial birth' abortions have received little support.[237] Harassment of women and health workers outside abortion clinics has not been tolerated,[238] although courts have recognised the right to protest against abortion[239] and conscientiously to object to involvement in abortion procedures.[240] Attempts to achieve legal recognition of the fetus for the purposes of protection of the fetus against neglect or abortion have been unsuccessful.[241] Western Europe and commonwealth jurisdictions have increasingly liberalised their abortion laws and practices,[242] and as medical technology enables increasing use of chemical methods of abortion, the tendency has been to extend the categorisation of contragestation to include early abortion. Thus, the European approach, in contrast to developments in the US, has been for the liberalisation of attitudes to contraception to influence liberalisation of attitudes to abortion. Even Ireland, which has resisted pressure to recognise legal abortion despite the large numbers of Irish women who go to Britain to

---

237 Eg, the 'Partial-birth Abortion (Prohibition) Bill, introduced to the House of Lords 13 December 1995, the Termination of Pregnancy (Restriction) Bill, introduced to the House of Lords 14 May 1996 and the Partial-birth Abortion Bill, introduced to the House of Commons 4 December 1996. None of these Bills was given a second reading.

238 Criminal laws on harassment have been used to remove aggressive protesters. See (1999) 319 BMJ 1520.

239 See *Bowman v UK* (1998) 26 EHRR 1, where the prosecution of an anti-abortion campaigner was held to violate Art 10 of the European Convention on Human Rights relating to freedom of expression. See, also, *DPP v Fidler* [1991] 1 WLR 91, where verbal abuse which did not involve threats to persons approaching an abortion clinic was held not to be an offence under the Public Order Act 1986, and *DPP v Clarke* (1991) *The Times*, 27 August, where parading a picture of an aborted foetus outside a clinic was held not to be an offence under the same Act.

240 See *Barr v Matthews* (2000) 52 BMLR 217. The right of conscientious objection applies only to health personnel and not to secretaries in relation to typing abortion referrals; see *R v Salford HA* [1988] 3 WLR 1350. The right of conscientious objection is examined in Hammer, L, 'Abortion objection in the United Kingdom within the framework of the European Convention on Human Rights and Fundamental Freedoms' (1999) 6 EHLRH 564.

241 Eg, *Kelly v Kelly* [1997] 2 FLR 828, in which a child's father attempted to prevent the mother from undergoing an abortion; *Re F (In Utero)* [1988] 2 All ER 193, which concerned an attempt to take wardship proceedings in relation to an unborn child at risk from the behaviour of her mother. Both actions were unsuccessful.

242 See, eg, the English National Evidence-Based Clinical Guidelines No 7, the Care of Women Requesting Induced Abortion, Royal College of Obstetricians and Gynaecologists 2000.

obtain a legal abortion,[243] is looking at ways to reconcile religious attitudes to abortion with recognition of women's reproductive rights.[244]

Attempts by the Irish Government to prioritise the right to life such as to justify infringements of other rights have been successfully challenged at the European Court of Human Rights. In *Open Door Counselling and Dublin Well Woman Centre v Ireland*,[245] the Irish Government's ban on information on abortion was found not to be necessary for the protection of moral beliefs prevalent in Ireland favouring protection of the unborn, and as such infringed Art 10 of the European Convention on Human Rights. Other claimants have attempted unsuccessfully to use Art 2 of the Convention to challenge the existence of laws allowing abortion[246] and to challenge an individual decision to undergo an abortion,[247] and to use Art 8 in challenging the restrictiveness of abortion laws.[248] Human rights arguments of any kind in relation to abortion have met with limited enthusiasm in the European Court of Human Rights, and the tendency has been to let all but the most extreme infringements of rights in this context remain to be governed by national law.

Most Asian, South East Asian and African States, concerned about rising population levels, have become resigned to abortion as a necessary fall back position for failures in contraception programmes. Attempts to challenge South Africa's constitutional right to reproductive freedom on the basis of constitutional right to life have failed on the grounds that, by analogy with comparable constitutions, constitutional rights do not extend to unborn children.[249]

The contraception/abortion dynamic is important, and abortion is generally recognised as last resort contraception rather than as a desirable fertility control option. The ideal towards which States are working is sufficiently comprehensive contraceptive coverage, such that abortion is

---

243 One in nine pregnancies in Irish women ends in abortion, mostly carried out in Britain. Three times as many late abortions are performed on Irish women compared with British women. See (2000) 321 BMJ 1310; (1999) 319 BMJ 593; (1999) 319 BMJ 1456. See also *AG v X* [1992] 2 CMLR 277, where the Irish Supreme court lifted an injunction imposed by the High Court to prevent a 14 year old girl from travelling to England for an abortion.

244 Mary Robinson, former President of the Republic of Ireland and United Nations Commissioner for Human Rights, has called for a limited legalisation of abortion in Ireland in recognition of the number of Irish women who seek abortion in Britain. A parliamentary committee established to look at abortion has proposed possible options including a further referendum, and a package of health care measures for reducing the number of unplanned pregnancies.

245 (1993) 15 EHRR 112.

246 *H v Norway* (1990) (App No 17004/90), unreported.

247 *Paton v UK* (1981) 3 EHRR 408.

248 *Bruggemann and Scheuten v FRG* (1981) 3 EHRR 244.

249 *Christian Lawyers Association of South Africa v Minister of Health* (1999) 50 BMLR 241.

reserved only for either rare cases in which contraception has not been effective, or for medically indicated abortion. The main determinant in the balance between contraception and abortion is funding. Effective contraception requires ongoing funding combined with ongoing health care that monitors contraceptive use. Abortion, especially early chemical abortion, is a one-off provision of a comparatively cheap service. However, there are physical and potential psychological health risks associated with abortion and, in the longer term, reliance on abortion as a significant fertility control mechanism will increase overall health care costs. The contemporary importance of abortion as a primary fertility control, and indeed as a population control method, is attributable to the low level of recognition of reproductive health in resource funding allocations both internationally and nationally.

There will always be circumstances where abortion is, however, the only option. Where the fetus threatens the health of the mother, or where the fetus is sufficiently damaged, abortion is indicated on medical grounds. A difficult legal issue arises as to whether a woman has an enforceable right to an abortion such that if the opportunity for abortion is denied to her, she can recover the costs of caring for the child which results. In English law, there can be no recovery for the birth of a healthy child,[250] but the courts have recognised claims for the birth of a damaged child. In *Rand v East Dorset* HA,[251] a health authority was held to be negligent for failing to inform a woman that she was likely to give birth to a child suffering from Down's syndrome, on the understanding that the woman would not have chosen to continue with the pregnancy had she been told. The courts have also been prepared to award damages where an abortion was performed negligently such that it was unsuccessful[252] or caused damage to the fetus.[253]

The issue of consent is relevant to abortion, although surprisingly, the English Abortion Act 1967, while specifying that the abortion decision must be approved by two medical practitioners, does not formally require the consent of the woman. Common law, however, dictates that no medical treatment should be performed on a competent adult without consent. Where that consent is coerced, then the consent may not be valid. In a series of cases, women who were members of the armed forces sought damages

250 See *McFarlane v Tayside Health Board* [2000] 2 AC 59, reversing earlier decisions which had allowed such a claim. European civil law generally takes the same view; see Van Gerven, W, *Cases, Materials and Text on National, Supranational and international Tort Law*, 1998, Oxford: Hart, p 123.

251 [2000] Lloyd's Rep Med 181; French courts have awarded damages in similar circumstances; see *P v Ponnoussamy*, Cass Civ 26 March 1996, where damages were awarded in relation to a failure properly to test for rubella.

252 See *M v Calderdale and Kirklees HA* [1998] Lloyd's Rep Med 157, although this decision predates *McFarlane*. European courts have not been willing to award damages in these circumstances; see Van Gerven, W, *Cases, Materials and Text on National, Supranational and International Tort Law*, 1998, Oxford: Hart, p 125.

253 See the Canadian case of *Cherry v Borsman* (1990) 2 Med LR 396.

for the physical and psychological consequences of abortion on the basis of Ministry of Defence rules in relation to discharging any woman who became pregnant. The actions succeeded, and it was held that the cause of the abortion was the employer's policy.[254] Where the woman is not considered to be competent, her consent is not necessary and the abortion decision can be made by two medical practitioners under the Abortion Act without a court declaration.[255] This may be so even where there was risk that the abortion might result in sterility.[256] Where, however, the pregnant person is a child under the age of consent and who does not have sufficient capacity to consent,[257] a court declaration may be required, especially where other parties to the application (the mother, the local authority or medical advisers) oppose the abortion.[258]

CONCLUSION

Fertility control as a component of population control is an important public health issue. National laws regulating fertility control have operated on the premise that fertility control is a medical treatment governed by the law on therapeutic medical treatment. This medicalisation of fertility control[259] has served to focus attention on the doctor/patient relationship in the provision of fertility control services. In doing so, the important wider picture of fertility control has been ignored.

It is essential that fertility control be recognised not as a medical response to injury or disease, but rather as the provision by the State of services which protect rights to reproductive health and reproductive choice. States have accepted their obligation to provide protection for other rights incorporated into international and European conventions. Where, for example, freedom of expression is threatened, States have developed legislative[260] and judicial[261] mechanisms at national level to protect that

254 *Ministry of Defence v Pope* [1997] ICR 296.

255 See *In Re G (Mental Patient: Termination of Pregnancy)* (1991) *The Times*, 31 January.

256 *SG (Mental Patient: Abortion)* [1993] 4 Med LR 75.

257 Ie, is not '*Gillick* competent'; see *Gillick v West Norfolk and Wisbech HA* [1985] 3 WLR 830.

258 Eg, *Re L (A Minor)* (1992) 3 Med LR 78; *Re B (A Minor) (Abortion for Ward of Court)* (1991) *The Times*, 22 May.

259 See Sheldon, S, 'The law of abortion and the politics of medicalisation', in Bridgeman, J and Millns, S, *Law and Body Politics: Regulating the Female Body*, 1995, Aldershot: Dartmouth.

260 Eg, in England, see the Data Protection Act 1998 and the Freedom of Information Act 2000.

261 Such as the law on defamation.

right, using State agencies[262] and enforcement mechanisms to ensure protection. There has been no similar attempt to address legal protections in relation to freedom of reproductive decision making, because fertility control has been understood as a medical service provided by doctors to women, rather than a State response to recognised rights with the medical profession as an agency of provision. The categorisation of fertility control as a medical treatment has resulted in passing responsibility for protection of reproductive rights to doctors within the laws of informed consent and abortion legislation. It is inappropriate that the agency assigned to deliver rights protections which are the obligation of the State should also be given the power to determine the exercise of those rights. The legal framework, rather than using as its focal point the rights of the woman, works from the position of the powers of the doctors in the treatment relationship, and looks only to see whether the doctor has exceeded those powers. Legal recognition of women's right to reproductive health and freedom of reproductive decision making requires a rethinking of fertility control laws.

The legal classification of fertility control as medical treatment rather than as a public health responsibility excludes from debate the wider objectives both of fertility control as part of population control policies, and fertility control as a component of the nation's profile of health. Development of law regulating fertility control which does not recognise this wider context gives rise to the potential for breach of internationally recognised reproductive rights as well as to limitations on access to fertility control contrary to health objectives. The provision of contraception, sterilisation or abortion services to an individual woman, subject to the discretion of the individual treating doctor, is part of a much broader and more important public health issue, the availability of and access to services for women generally. The power of medical determination of access to fertility control on moral grounds in individual cases is inappropriate, just as it would be inappropriate to allow doctors to determine access to other public health services, casualty treatment for example, on moral grounds. If limitations are to be placed on health services which are fundamental to women's health and the exercise of women's rights, then those limitations must be subjected to public debate which recognises the voices of women. Much national law in the developed and the developing world would not pass human rights scrutiny, all the more so as understanding of human rights develops to recognise that while some rights are generic, others are sex-specific. It is essential that laws regulating reproduction be taken out of the medical arena and placed squarely in a public health framework.

---

262 Such as the Information Commissioner and the Information Tribunal provided for under the Freedom of Information Act.

CHAPTER 8

PARTICULAR ISSUES OF PUBLIC HEALTH: INFECTIOUS DISEASES

Linda Johnson

The international legal framework on infectious diseases was discussed by Yutaka Arai-Takahashi in his chapter above on the role of international law and the WHO in public health. Stephanie Pywell also examines the specific issue of vaccination in her chapter.

The nature of diseases is changing.[1] Between 1976 and 1999, the World Health Organisation identified that 22[2] newly emerging diseases and pathogens had been found worldwide.[3] Virulent, currently untreatable, viral and infectious diseases are becoming increasingly rampant in Western hospitals.[4] The overuse and abuse of antimicrobial agents[5] had produced mutated and new organisms resistant to the effects of the very drugs hailed as bringing the end to infectious disease.[6] Old diseases, thought to be under

---

1 This comment relates not only to the scope and nature of infectious diseases, but also to the biological properties of some pathogens. See, eg, the discussion of the pathophysiology and epidemiology of the meningococcus bacterium in Cartwright, K, *Meningococcal Disease*, 1995, New York: Wiley. There is a massive amount of information on infectious diseases available on the internet. Useful sites include: http://www.cdc.gov; http://www.cdc.gov; http://www.phls.co.uk; http://www.phls.co.uk; http://www.eurosurv.org.

2 The National Science and Technology Council Committee on International Science, Engineering and Technology (CISET) Working Group on Emerging *Infectious Diseases, Infectious Diseases – A Global Threat*, 1995, identified 29 new and 20 re-emerging infectious diseases between 1973 and 1995.

3 WHO, *Report on Infectious Diseases*, 1999. They include HIV, Legionnaires' disease, ebola, T-lymphatic virus, lyme borreliosis, hepatitis C and E, sabia virus, hendra virus, avian flu, new variant CJD, Australian bat lyssavirus, Kaposi sarcoma virus, *Cryptosporidium parvum* and herpes virus 6.

4 See the UK public health laboratory site for an account of this in the UK at http://www.phls.co.uk.

5 For discussion of the legal issues raised by threats to human health presented by the use of antimicrobials in food production see Fidler, D. 'Legal challenges posed by the use of antimicrobials in food animal production' (1999) Microbes and Infection 29–38.

6 Malaria, tuberculosis, *streptococcus pneumoniae* and *staphylococcus* all show antimicrobial resistance. WHO, *Report on Infectious Diseases*, 1999. The UK Government has produced several reports on antimicrobial drug resistance, spurred on by rapid increases in the number of reported cases of staphylococcus septicaemias caused by a methicillin-resistant *staphylococcus aureus* (in 1992, only 2% of cases, rising to 32% by 1997). See House of Lords Select Committee on Science and Technology, *Resistance to antibiotics and other antimicrobials*, 1997–1998 Session, 7th Report, 1998, London: HMSO; Standing Medical Advisory Committee Sub-group on Antimicrobial Resistance, *The Path of Least Resistance*, 1998, London: Department of Health; *Government Response to House of Lords Select Committee Report on Resistance to Antibiotics and Other Antimicrobials*, 1998, London: HMSO.

the control of medical science in industrialised countries, are re-emerging, often in more resilient form.[7] In Africa and parts of Asia, these same diseases were never really under control. To talk of them as re-emerging in this context is anathema.[8] Antimicrobial resistant diseases in animals threaten the human food chain,[9] as indeed do bacterial and viral diseases created by lack of adequate hygiene or human manipulation of animal foodstuffs.[10] In 1999, the United Nations Security Council declared the HIV/AIDS pandemic to be a threat to peace and security as destructive as any war as it continues to decimate populations, particularly in the African countries.[11]

Within the international community, infectious diseases have taken on increased significance as faster and more frequent trade and travel coupled with changes in the nature of the diseases themselves have allowed microbial agents to span the globe within incubation periods. Detecting new microbial agents often requires technology and expertise beyond the budget of many developing countries, and international agencies have placed disease identification resources in some of those countries to allow for earlier detection and containment.[12] International and European collaboration have increased to monitor, prevent and control the spread of infectious diseases. For example, a collaborative network for epidemiological surveillance and control of communicable diseases in the European Community was proposed by the European Parliament in 1998[13] and became operational in December 1999. Its remit included diseases preventable by vaccination, sexually transmitted diseases, viral hepatitis,

7 Eg, in the UK, tuberculosis has been on the increase since 1995, and *E coli* 0157 outbreaks, salmonella and other gastro-intestinal infections have grown in importance. Meningococcal infection is steadily increasing, as are chlamydia, syphilis outbreaks, influenza and antimicrobial resistant strains. See the National Centre for Disease Control site for statistics on infectious diseases in the US at http://www.cdc.gov.

8 Some diseases are, however, dramatically increasing. Tuberculosis in South Africa, for example, exacerbated by the constantly increasing number of victims of HIV/AIDS, was described in 1997 as 'one of the worst TB epidemics in the world', by which time the incidence had reached in excess of 224 cases per 100,000 and was spiralling owing to multidrug resistance. South African Department of Health, *White Paper for the Transformation of the Health System in South Africa*, 1997, Government Gazette, No 17910/667/1997, cited in Nadasen, S, *Public Health Law in South Africa*, 2000, Durban: Butterworths.

9 Antimicrobial drug use in animals is regulated through maximum limits of residue in foodstuffs set by the Sanitary and Phytosanitary measures under the World Trade Organisation and other trade agreements such as Codex.

10 For a discussion of food-borne disease control, see Käferstein, K *et al*, 'Foodborne disease control: a transnational challenge' (1997) 3(4) Emerging Infectious Diseases 503–10.

11 Security Council, 'Security Council holds debate on impact of AIDS on peace and security in Africa', press release SC/6781, 4087th Meeting, 10 January 2000.

12 The lack of such resources has exacerbated health problems as well as causing friction in international relations by, eg, locating assumed causes of disease within jurisdictions where the outbreak is first identified.

13 European Parliament and Council Decision of 24 September 1998, COM (97) 31 final, COM (96) 78 final, Decision No 2119/98/EC, L268.

food-borne diseases, diseases of environmental origin, diseases covered by the International Health Regulations, rabies, malaria and newly emerging unclassified serious epidemic diseases. This network has extended to include early warning and response systems and, by the end of 1999, provided permanent surveillance of tuberculosis, HIV/AIDS, travel-associated Legionnaire's disease, salmonellosis and *E coli* 0157.[14] Its surveillance work has progressively extended,[15] and in late 1999 included cover of influenza, hepatitis A, B and C, malaria, diphtheria, measles, mumps, sexually transmitted diseases, food- and water-borne diseases, zoonoses, cholera, Creutzfeldt-Jakob disease and antimicrobial resistant diseases.[16] In 1996, the US Department of State set up an Emerging Infectious Diseases (EID) and HIV/AIDS programme to negotiate internationally for control of the threat of infectious diseases and epidemics. It included a wide range of agencies, such as the Food and Drugs Administration, the Department of Defence and the Agency for International Development and was provided with US$50 m initial funding. The concerns behind these moves are protective of the health and economy of the developed nations. As the US Institute of Medicine has specifically stated, global responses to EIDs are necessary to protect Americans, enhance the US economy and to protect American international interests.

FEAR AND INFECTION

The fear of risk of infection has dominated responses to disease throughout the history of public health. The plagues that swept across Europe throughout the middle ages promoted a necessarily defensive response. The city of Venice had quarantine regulations as early as the 14th century and the people of Eyam in Derbyshire in 1665 chose voluntarily to confine themselves to their village, allowing no one to enter or leave, so as to stem the spread of the Plague. The British Government firmly maintained that cholera was not contagious well into the 19th century and proceeded apace with sanitation and clean water reforms which contained disease even though the reasoning upon which it was based has subsequently been discredited. The motivation behind all of these measures was to stem the

14 Commission of the European Communities, Press Release, 22 December 1999, IP/99/1033.

15 For a discussion of the work of surveillance networks in the European Union, see Weinberg, J *et al*, 'Commentary. Establishing priorities for European collaboration in communicable disease surveillance' (1999) 9(3) European Journal of Public Health 236–40.

16 Commission of the European Communities, press release, 22 December 1999, IP/99/1033.

spread of disease, despite the dearth of available knowledge on the nature or epidemiology of the threat being faced.

There are many forms of microbial life that can be responsible for infectious disease. Bacteria, viruses, fungi, parasites and, most recently, prions (an abnormal protein that infects normal proteins so as to cause illness or death, as in bovine spongiform encephalopathy (BSE)). These disease agents live in hosts that transmit them to another organism. They often have no deleterious effect on the host and can be transmitted by air, water, mixing of bodily fluids or through contact with an insect or animal intermediary or vector.

There are at least five distinct ideas about what infectious disease is and how it is caused. Germ theory places responsibility for disease on germs, so the appropriate response is to eliminate the germs or exposure to them in order to contain disease. Genetic explanations link disease with predisposition, whilst lifestyle explanations see behaviour as distributing risks of disease across populations. Both of these are individual-based, shifting moral responsibility from the State and onto the individual. The key distinction, however, is between individual choice and the potential to alter one's exposure to risk, as opposed to physical condition only manipulable with the assistance of science. Other explanations are less confined to the individual, either by taking into account environmental factors in multicausal approaches, or by placing responsibility for disease on central power relationships, such as race, class and gender. This latter approach is the most contextualised, as it sees the effect of disease agents as directly related to the distribution of food, housing, leisure, the availability of health services, and other national and international inequalities.

The rise of scientific knowledge in the 19th century, coupled with a sound belief that man had mastery over nature, brought with it the certainty that disease could be controlled with adequate man-made interference. That interference revolved around the individual. The body was perceived as the site for diagnosing and treating disease, and science was seen as the appropriate vehicle for discovering the cause of disease. This search for causes within the body of the individual was not novel to the approach to disease, but was prevalent across the social sciences applying biological and the natural sciences' methodology to the human condition. This methodology, positivism, was necessarily reductionist. It was built upon an understanding of the natural world as capable of being understood through careful and precise measurement and observation. Factors being observed were susceptible to control, so that a scientist could isolate a cause by controlling all other relevant factors. Containing those factors to the body itself made the enterprise manageable, the range of factors controllable. The image of the human form was one of a machine, with interlinking parts. The work of medical science was, in the first place, to draw up a plan of the machine and then to identify the causes of malfunction. The body could be protected from the invasion of disease by addressing the body itself; confinement or inoculation provided that protection. In earlier times, the body had also been the key to protection against disease. Spiritual explanations for disease were used by doctors or priests to rid the body of evil spirits or the effects of wrong doing visited upon the body by a divine source. Ancestor retribution on their unworthy descendants was defended by those very persons performing rituals evincing respect and supplication to their superior antecedents.

RESPONSES OF MEDICAL SCIENCE

This concentration on the body was cemented by the technological revolution that created an enduring faith in the capability of medical science to combat disease. The creation of antibiotics and vaccines has been effective in taming some infectious diseases,[17] whilst that same technology has been responsible for promoting others. The classic comparison is between the WHO's eradication of smallpox and its failure to stem the spread of malaria. Smallpox, as an acute self-limiting disease, was probably the model for germ theory.[18] It is not only unusual in its lack of relationship with nutrition, but was contained by a freeze-dried vaccine that did not require constant refrigeration to remain effective.[19] Malaria, on the other hand, has a much more complex structure, is recurrent and chronic. There are four diseases that fall under the heading of human malaria, two of them life-threatening. The disease is caused directly by a parasite that is carried by a mosquito. Once in the bloodstream, the parasite continues on a cycle of development, multiplying asexually inside the liver. Mosquitoes may re-host the parasite when ingesting human infected blood and carry it to the next victim. The campaign to eradicate malaria has concentrated on the use of anti-malaria drugs, and DDT and other pesticides used to kill the mosquitoes.[20] The effect was not eradication, but drug-resistant parasites and pesticide-resistant mosquitoes, whilst creating environmental damage.[21] Critics of this

17 The treatment of tuberculosis with streptomycin, for example, has been shown as providing only 3.2% of the total reduction of mortality from that disease in England and Wales between 1848 and 1971. McKeown, T, *The Role of Medicine: Dream, Mirage or Nemesis?*, 1976, London: Nuffield, p 82.

18 Fenner, F *et al*, Smallpox and its Eradication, 1988, Geneva: WHO.

19 Henderson, D, 'The eradication of smallpox' (1976) 235(4) Scientific American 25–33.

20 The most recent development is the creation by Imperial College of a transgenic mosquito which is no longer able to host the malaria parasite, Plasmodium and is hoped to be manipulated to introduce a substance into a human which will prompt antibodies against malaria. See (2001) *The Times Higher Supplement*, 23 March.

21 Farid, MA, 'The malaria programme – from euphoria to anarchy' (1980) 1 World Health Forum 8–33.

biomedical approach have analysed the failure as economic in serving the interests of agribusiness and containing the costs of international health reform,[22] or simply wrong. The medical historian Ackerknecht, for example, sees the eradication of malaria from Europe in the 19th century as the result of prosperity (better agricultural methods, better housing, education, urbanisation, cattle-breeding), with improved drainage and anti-malaria treatment having little direct influence.[23]

This same technological revolution created other types of opportunity for the perpetuation and proliferation of infectious diseases. Developments in telecommunications and transportation integrated national and international populations into what has been called the global village. Human contacts have continued to increase through trade and travel, creating a more homogeneous gene pool and a constant intersection between a wide range of pathogenic micro-organisms. The deeper interdependencies claimed by globalisation increase the number and the extent of contact, making the spread of disease faster and more efficient. More frequent contacts between populations increase the risk of exposing immune systems to unfamiliar pathogens.[24] In the US National Academy of Sciences, there are four key routes for the transfer of health risks internationally: (a) movement of people; (b) exchange of potentially toxic products or contaminated foodstuffs; (c) variations in occupational and environmental health and safety; (d) the indiscriminate spread of medical technologies. David Fidler[25] has elaborated this list in his analysis of the globalisation of public health. In doing so, he stresses two aspects of infectious diseases as threats to populations. The means for transmission is only one aspect, the other being the socio-economic conditions that allow the infectious disease to exist in a human population.[26]

---

22 See, eg, Chapin, G and Wasserstrom, R, 'Agricultural production and malaria resurgence in Central America and India' (1981) 293 Nature 181–85.

23 Ackerknecht, EH, *Malaria in the Upper Mississippi Valley 1760–1900*, 1945, Baltimore: Johns Hopkins.

24 William McNeill has examined how this 'confluence of disease pools' can be deliberately orchestrated as part of imperialism, as well as a necessary product of exploration and trade. Eg, smallpox and other diseases were introduced to colonies to help conquer indigenous populations. McNeill, W, *Plagues and People*, 1976, Garden City, NY: Anchor.

25 Fidler, D, 'The globalization of public health: emerging infectious diseases and international relations' (1997) 5 Indiana Journal of Global Legal Studies 11.

26 Fidler, D, *International Law and Infectious Diseases*, 1999, Oxford: Clarendon, p 9.

HIV/AIDS AND THE NEED FOR A CONTEXTUAL APPROACH

HIV provides a particularly acute example of the necessity of taking a contextual approach to disease containment and eradication. As Brandt has stated: 'AIDS makes explicit, as few diseases could, the complex interaction of social, cultural and biological forces' and 'demonstrates how economics and politics cannot be separated from disease'.[27] Yet HIV/AIDS originally prompted a biomedical response to containment. The disease was viewed as sited within the individual and, in most cases, the responsibility of the individual. Two parallel initiatives were mounted. One was to provide an effective biomedical treatment for the disease through the development of a vaccine and chemical therapies. The other was to adjust the behaviour of those identified as likely to spread the disease. The persistent emphasis on a model of individual responsibility not only produced a cost effective strategy placing the burden on individuals rather than the State, it also allowed for a moralistic and victim-blaming explanation for a disastrous epidemic for which science was not equipped to respond effectively.[28]

The campaign against HIV/AIDS has resonances with the assumptions behind the quarantine regulations of the 19th century in its supposition that HIV/AIDS could be controlled by restricting the behaviour of individuals. Quarantine was the first international initiative against infectious diseases, bringing States together in a series of conferences to produce an appropriate strategy in an environment of increasing international trade.[29] The result was a scheme of control based upon surveillance and isolation with quarantine facilities established along major trade routes. Vessels were inspected and checked for contagion with a view to preventing the importation of diseases, particularly yellow fever, plague and cholera from the non-industrialised nations. The trading nations, with their rapidly developing domestic public health systems aimed at containing disease

---

27 Brandt, A, *No Magic Bullet: A Social History of Venereal Disease in the United States since 1880*, 1985, Oxford: OUP, pp 199–204, cited by Wilton, T, *Engendering AIDS: Deconstructing Sex, Text and Epidemic*, 1997, London: Sage, p 1.

28 HIV/AIDS presents a set of problems quite unlike other epidemics: it has an extended incubation period, shows no readily recognisable outward signs and it weakens the system so dramatically as to make it severely vulnerable to other conditions, particularly pneumonia and other respiratory diseases. It has proved resistant to conventional chemical therapies. It also is communicated in circumstances likely to be private and so resistant to surveillance.

29 This history has been amply discussed in Fidler, D, *International Law and Infectious Diseases*, 1999, Oxford: Clarendon; see also Chapter 3 by Robyn Martin on the history of the WHO, which arose from these early conferences.

through sanitation and drainage systems, were anxious to minimise international quarantine measures because of their interference with trade.[30]

This *cordon sanitaire* approach to containment of disease also appears in domestic legislation in notification provisions and provisions to detain those with a notifiable disease.[31] The assumption that went hand in hand with these provisions was not only isolation of the identifiable sufferer as an effective measure to reduce the spread of disease, but also that medical treatment could alleviate or cure the condition.[32] The type of disease these forms of regulation had in mind were those which followed the germ theory model: rapid onset, contagious, showing extreme and recognisable physical symptoms, such as welts, sweats and swelling. It also included assumptions about the distinction between the healthy and the sick; that separating the latter from the former was the route to ensuring health. Isolating those with disease was a method to protect the health of the rest of the population. The isolation itself was intended as altruistic reason: not only to protect the population, but also to cure or alleviate the suffering of the sick.

In the international context, the *cordon sanitaire* also reflected ideas about the State and frontiers. Disease was identified as something which was brought into Europe from other countries. Homegrown European diseases had been the subject of public health measures and it was foreign diseases that were seen as the new threat to health. The classic idea of the State was of a geographical area within which responsibilities to citizens pertained and the citizens of the State owed their allegiance to their nation. The State had obligations to protect its citizens from invasion, and there were, in theory at least, clearly defined, relatively permanent frontiers bordering those obligations. Not dissimilar to the biomedical approach to the body, the health of the State could be assured by protecting its citizens from invading destruction and by ensuring an effective and fully functioning internal social, economic and political system. Public health law reflected this approach. National public health legislation across the Western world, at

30 As David Fidler points out, Britain was at the forefront of the resistance to quarantine regulations as it had the most advanced public health system and felt confident that disease containment could be secured domestically without the necessity of interfering with trade. See Fidler, D, '*Microbialpolitik*: infectious diseases and international relations' (1998) 14(1) American University International L Rev 1–53.

31 The UK domestic legislation is discussed in Chapter 3 by Robyn Martin.

32 In the debate in the UK in early 2001 over the containment of foot and mouth disease, the technique of isolating and burning animals, which had previously been advanced by earlier governments as a superior method to vaccination, has been brought into question. The failure of isolation, scientific developments producing better, cheaper vaccines and the political, economic and social ramifications of delays in containing the disease have caused the government to rethink. Interestingly, the disease has been traced to pig swill and the government's failure to ban pig swill despite advice from the Spongiform Encephalopathy Advisory Committee (SEAC) has added to the attribution of blame on the government. Yet, there has been an enduring need to interpret the disease as an invasion from outside, a product of smuggled meat from Zimbabwe. See, eg, (2001) *The Observer*, 25 March.

least, looked inward to drawing boundaries of protection from diseases of the world outside.

The concentration on a model of individual responsibility within responses to HIV/AIDS carried with it not only assumptions about disease and the relationship between disease and the individual, but also assumptions about sexuality. Class, race, gender, able-bodiedness, nationality, age and religion also give rise to assumptions and are all interactive with and productive of sexuality.[33] This matrix of meaning has been reinforced by and has implicated the interpretation of what HIV/AIDS is, who it affects and how it is transmitted. Before turning to a consideration of sexuality, it will be useful to set out basic information about the nature of the epidemic.

HIV is a primarily a blood-borne virus which destroys a particular type of blood cells, known as CD4+ T cells or helper cells, crucial to the normal functioning of the human immune system. After a number of years of having the virus, most sufferers will develop acquired immunodeficiency syndrome (AIDS) and whilst current chemical therapies can inhibit the speed of this process, there is no vaccine or other treatment to stop the course of the virus. The virus, like hepatitis, is communicated by blood-to-blood contact, which includes body fluids containing blood such as semen, vaginal fluids, breast milk, fluid surrounding the brain, spinal cord, bone joints and fluids supporting unborn babies. The most frequent forms of transmission, therefore, are activities which involve an individual's exposure to another's blood or blood containing fluids, such as injections with shared needles, sexual intercourse, gestation within the womb, blood transfusions, and certain medical procedures. The latter two, whilst still intimate procedures, take place within a more public environment and can be subjected to observable protective regimes to minimise risk of transmission. It is control of the most intimate forms of transmission which has not only caused greatest concern, but has been most influenced by assumptions about sexuality and cultural practices.

HIV has been inaccurately presented as one of the already stigmatised category of sexually transmitted diseases, the personal and economic consequences of which are enormous,[34] remaining epidemic in the

33 See, eg, Grosz, E, *Volatile Bodies: Towards a Corporeal Feminism*, 1994, Bloomington: Indiana UP.

34 In the US, an estimated 15.3 m new cases of STDs occur each year, about 25% amongst teenagers. American Social Health Association, *Sexually Transmitted Diseases in America: How Many Cases and at What Cost?*, 1998, Menlo Park, CA: Kaiser Family. Of the top 11 reportable diseases in the US, five are transmitted sexually: chlamydial infection, gonorrhoea, AIDS, syphilis and hepatitis B. See Centers for Disease Control and Prevention, 'Summary of notifiable diseases in the United States, 1996' (1997) 45 Morbidity and Mortality Weekly Report 1, pp 1–103. Estimated worldwide figures for the curable STDs gonorrhoea, chlamydial infection, syphilis and trichomoniasis was 333 m new cases in 1997. WHO, *World Health Report*, 1998, Geneva: WHO.

developed world.[35] Whilst measures to protect the blood supply, to reduce needle-sharing amongst street drug users and to ensure clinical safety have had an impact in reducing those forms of transmission, sexual transmission and vertical transmission between mother and baby have increased as a proportion of causes. The long asymptomatic period of HIV infection has meant that changes in epidemiology have been slow to reflect in representational practices and this, in turn, has had an intense impact on the epidemic. The prolonged characterisation of HIV/AIDS as a homosexual disease has had implications not only for the gay community and the social and political consequences of homophobic attitudes, but also for wider ideas about gender, race and sexuality and the perhaps narrower concerns of epidemiology. In the developed countries, the homosexual tag has survived despite patent evidence of the predominance of heterosexual transmission worldwide.[36, 37] Knowledge of heterosexual transmission has been interpreted through ideas about race, development and sexuality so as to rationalise maintaining an infection containment strategy based upon HIV/AIDS as a homosexual/drug-user disease.[38]

The HIV/AIDS victim has remained as Other to white, educated, heterosexuals living in developed States and ideas about what it is to be 'normal' have been enhanced by that dichotomy. For example, the apparently *abnormal* rate of heterosexual transmission in Africa has been attributed to pre-existing pathologies within African culture and social practices. Untruthfulness (black African men do engage in homosexuality, but they do not admit it because of cultural expectations of manliness),

35 The cost in the US of STDs each year is around US$10 bn, excluding HIV/AIDS, and US$17 bn overall in 1994. See the report of the US Institute of Medicine Expert Committee, Eng, TA and Butler, WT (eds), *The Hidden Epidemic: Confronting Sexually Transmitted Diseases*, 1997, Washington DC: National Academy.

36 World statistics on HIV/AIDS produced by the Joint United Nations Programme on HIV/AIDS (UNAIDS) and the WHO estimate that 21.8 m people have died of AIDS, 3 m deaths occurring in 2000. There are currently an estimated 36.1 m people living with HIV/AIDS worldwide. In 1999, it was estimated that 2.2 m died of AIDS across sub-Saharan Africa and in December 2000, 25.3 m people were living with HIV/AIDS in that region, with 3.8 m newly infected; 55% of the adults are women. Around 95% of people with HIV live in the developing world, with most therapy concentrated in the high-income countries. Statistics prepared by UNAIDS Joint United Nations Programme on HIV/AIDS, *Report on the Global HIV/AIDS Epidemic June 2000* and *AIDS Epidemic Update December 2000* available at http://www.avert.org/worldstats.

37 On world estimated statistics for HIV/AIDS, women in North America occupy around 20% of domestic levels of incidence of the disease. Yet, closer analysis of actual name-based reported HIV show women accounting for 32% in 1999, 77% of whom are Hispanic and black. In the age category 13–24, the proportion of women rises to 49%. In 1999, the statistics show a continued increase in the number of people contracting HIV/AIDS heterosexually. See US HIV and AIDS Statistics Summary (based on CDC figures) at http://www.avert.org.

38 For the first time, statistics for the actual incidence of HIV in 1999 produced by the UK Public Health Service Laboratory showed that the majority of those diagnosed were heterosexual (1,070 cases), compared to 989 cases of transmission through homosexual contact. See statistics at http://www.phls.co.uk.

violent sexuality (African men engage in heterosexual practices which are more likely to produce mixing of blood, such as anal sex or vaginal sex with abrasive herbs or violence) and promiscuity (African men frequently use prostitutes, have several wives or mistresses) have all been postulated as Otherness.[39]

Lack of understanding of local differences have exacerbated problems of applicability of 'international' responses to the epidemic. The classic example is the promotion of condom use in developing States as a form of health prevention. Health education programmes targeted at women in Africa have exhorted them to use condoms on the basis of their effectiveness in protecting them from HIV/AIDS. The assumption behind such programmes and the provision and distribution of free condoms was that if women understood the value of condoms, how to use them and the dangers of not using them, they would be empowered to protect themselves from the virus.[40] Anthropological studies have, however, shown that attitudes to sex and procreation vary across tribes and States within Africa and that they are not capable of being divorced from other economic and social conditions. Women in Rwanda, for example, are not economically dependent on marriage, but live in a society which values the mixing of fluids, particularly bodily fluids, as a necessary component of social bonds. Any obstruction or blockage is considered to be pathological and harmful not only to the individuals concerned, but to the whole community.[41] Attempts to empower Rwandan women to use condoms through education, advertising and advice have been generally unsuccessful,[42] as have laws in other parts of Africa designed to empower women, whilst failing to integrate women into the development process.[43] Whilst HIV/AIDS is necessarily a global issue, global policies including assumptions about sexuality and society have presented significant barriers to effective containment measures.

The failure to meet the needs of women in the context of HIV/AIDS has attracted a considerable literature, as has the failure to meet the needs of gay communities. There is undoubtedly a need to deconstruct the gendered nature of responses to HIV/AIDS, how they are built upon and how they reinforce particular ideas about gender and sexuality, but it is important to

39 Wilton, T, *AntibodyPolitic: AIDS and Society*, 1992, Cheltenham: New Clarion.

40 Dr Michael Merson, chief of WHO's Global Programme on AIDS, at the 10th International Conference on AIDS in Yokohama, Japan, August 1994, reported in Arbuckle, A, 'The condom crisis: an application of feminist legal theory to AIDS prevention in African women' (1998) 3(2) GLSJ, available at http://www.law.indiana.edu/glsj.

41 Taylor, C, 'Condoms and cosmology: the 'fractal' person and sexual risk in Rwanda' (1990) 31 Social Science and Medicine 1023.

42 Allen, S *et al*, 'Human immunodeficiency virus infection in urban Rwanda' (1991) 266 Journal of the American Medical Association 1657.

43 Mikell, G, 'Culture, law and social policy: changing the economic status of Ghanaian women' (1992) 17 Yale J Int'l L 225–53.

do so from the perspective of their failure to meet anyone's needs. The significant scholarship on the gendered nature of health care within feminisms has demonstrated how biomedical norms reflect unstated masculine ways of seeing, legitimate those norms by clothing them with objectivity and produce particular ideas about disease and health. These discursive processes are ultimately linked with having a negative impact on the provision of health care for women and on women's ability to maintain and protect their health. For example, the representation of HIV/AIDS as a predominantly (gay) male disease has led to little involvement of women in clinical studies of HIV and AIDS in the US. Not only has this meant that knowledge about women and the effectiveness of drugs and the health effects of the virus is limited, but also women and their offspring have a disproportionately low chance of benefiting from drug trials.[44] Where women have been included in trials, it has tended to be in relation to vertical transmission to their offspring, rather than their own experience or health effects of the virus.[45] Some writers have argued that gay men occupy the same position in HIV/AIDS discourse as prostitutes have occupied in the discourse on sexually transmitted diseases in general.[46] As the site of contagion they authenticate moral reprehension of 'illicit' sexual practices and confirm the value of conformity to heterosexual marriage. In some jurisdictions, the law has been used to punish prostitutes for their infection by detaining them or having them electronically tagged.[47] In the HIV/AIDS context, this is particularly ironic, as prostitutes are amongst the groups most willing to educate themselves about and adopt safe sex practices[48] and have been the inspiration for the most recent and promising vaccine research.[49] Women have also appeared as infected receptacles transmitting the virus to their captured offspring. As Patton has remarked: 'When women are not vaginas waiting to infect men, they are uteruses, waiting to

44 Mastroianni, AC, 'HIV, women and access to clinical trials: tort liability and lessons from DES' (1998) 5 Duke Journal of Gender Law and Policy 167.

45 *Ibid.*

46 Treichler, P, 'AIDS, gender and biomedical discourse: current contests for meaning', in Fee, E and Fox, D (eds), *AIDS: The Burden of History*, 1988, Berkeley: California UP. She also explains how initially infection from prostitutes was ruled out because of the certainty of HIV as being a homosexual disease. When women were scripted into HIV transmission it was as prostitutes, drug users and women in developing countries or ethnic minorities.

47 Panos Institute, *Triple Jeopardy: Women and AIDS*, 1990, London: Panos.

48 Wilton, T, Engendering AIDS: *Deconstructing Text, Sex and Epidemic*, 1997, London: Sage, p 68.

49 Radford, T, 'AIDS jab brings new hope' (2000) *The Guardian*, 10 January, p 5. Oxford's medical research council are producing a vaccine for clinical trials in England from DNA of the HIV virus to be delivered through the vaccinia virus used against smallpox 200 years ago. The idea came from observations of prostitutes in Kenya who appeared resistant to HIV in a community where one in five adults is infected.

infect foetuses.'[50] This is another representation of a bad woman, this time because she fails her family and the State in her role as reproducer.

Heterosexual, white men have been largely invisible in the health promotion and education literature. They have not been identified as a risk category of their own[51] and appear only in disguise as intravenous drug users, young people, users of prostitutes and haemophiliacs. They have similarly been absented from responsibility for safe sex, as women have principally been targeted for condom-use promotion. This is a reflection of what Weeks[52] has referred to as the 'hydraulic model' of male sexuality, that is, once aroused has an irresistible impulse and cannot be stopped. Concern about sexual safety would represent a dilution of masculinity, especially as risk-taking is also conceived as a masculine occupation.

Equally significant in the gendered construction of health, then, is the representation of male, gay, lesbian and heterosexual identities and the bodies and sexual practices attributed to them. In order to limit the spread of HIV/AIDS, particular representations have been reproduced and have been acted upon in order to advance preventative and health promotional measures. It is the particularity of those representations and how they reproduce images that may interfere with effective containment of the disease that requires interrogation. The purpose of such deconstruction would not be to illustrate how women, gay men, lesbians, black men, black women or particular class or racial groups are the victims of hegemonic power, but to suggest that everyone's identity is constructed and that this provides space for alternative constructions, some more helpful than others in providing effective responses to threats to health.

The strategies to prevent and contain the spread of HIV/AIDS were, in the 1980s, based upon fear and blame. Hard images of tombstones and the plague were used in an attempt to coerce individuals into behaviour modification. Homosexuality, promiscuity and drug use were all targeted as blameworthy behaviour and the disease prevention message was often directed against the activity or the people engaged in it rather than against the disease. The 'new' public health brought with it a different approach based upon community action and self-empowerment, with the British Government's *The Health of the Nation* recognising that behaviour is not simply a matter of open-ended individual choice, but a response to 'the powerful influence of the social, economic and political environments that

---

50 Patton, C, *Last Served? Gendering the HIV Pandemic*, 1994, London: Taylor & Francis.

51 According to Wilton, T, *Engendering AIDS: Deconstructing Text, Sex and Epidemic*, 1997, London: Sage, p 32, the order of perceived risk groups appears to be gay men, prostitutes, adolescents, drug users, women, populations of developing countries, bisexuals and 'the hard to reach'. See WHO, *AIDS: Images of the Epidemic*, 1994, Geneva: WHO.

52 Weeks, J, *Sexuality*, 1986, London: Routledge.

lie substantially beyond the control of the individuals who are affected by them'.[53] The strategy went on to translate this into setting targets for improvements in sexual health.[54] The stated objectives were to reduce the rate of HIV infection and sexually transmitted diseases[55] by improved surveillance and the provision of better diagnosis and treatment services.

There has been a shift in the methods incorporated into prevention programmes built upon the idea that individuals need to believe that their behaviour can be changed at reasonable 'cost' and that change will bring protection.[56] It has, however, remained individualised through the incorporation of this and other parts of the public health agenda into the health service by target-setting.[57] The main health education message has continued to be the promotion of safer sex[58] through education and condom use:

> Safer sex is premised on an awareness and acceptance of risk and, in turn, on the production of trust. In this context, trust may be understood as the solution to a specific problem of risk. In turn, this raises the question of the relationship between risk-awareness and risk-avoidance.[59]

The intention is that individuals assess their own risk in light of their own circumstances and beliefs, rather than identifying particular groups as at risk.[60] Within relationships that give rise to risk, either through sexual

53 Department of Health, *The Health of the Nation: a Strategy for Health in England*, 1992, London: HMSO.

54 Johnson, A, *HIV/AIDS in The Health of the Nation*, 1991, London: BMA.

55 There were three targets: to reduce the incidence of gonorrhoea by 20% by 1995; to reduce the proportion of drug users sharing needles from a fifth to a tenth by 1997; and to halve the rate of conceptions by the under 16s by 2000. Department of Health, *The Health of the Nation: a Strategy for Health in England*, 1992, London: HMSO.

56 Bloor, M, 'A user's guide to contrasting theories of HIV related risk behaviour' in Gabe, J, *Medicine, Health and Risk: Sociological Approaches*, 1995, Oxford: Blackwell. For a critique of the assumptions underlying this method of behaviour modification, see Cohen, M and Chwalow, J, 'The health belief model: always, sometimes or never useful in guiding HIV/AIDS prevention', in Friedrich, D and Heckmann, W, *AIDS in Europe: The Behavioural Aspects, Vol 4, Determinants of Behaviour Change*, 1994, Hallstadt, Germany: Rosch-Buch.

57 See Chapter 1 by Linda Johnson.

58 As opposed to safe sex, which Cindy Patton has summarised as: 'Don't get semen in your anus or your vagina.' Cited in Boffin, T, 'Angelic rebels: lesbians and safer sex', in Boffin, T and Gupta, S (eds), *Ecstatic Antibodies: Resisting the AIDS Mythology*, 1990, London: Rivers Oram, p 164.

59 Scott, S and Freeman, R, 'Prevention as a problem of modernity: the example of HIV/AIDS', in Gabe, J, *Medicine, Health and Risk: Sociological Approaches*, 1995, Oxford: Blackwell.

60 There are substantial problems in assessing the effectiveness of prevention programmes structured around behaviour modification, many of which are exacerbated by the nature of HIV/AIDS, the long asymptomatic period, the complexity of sexual attitudes, the lack of baseline information. See Scott, S, 'Evaluation may change your life, but it won't solve all your problems', in Aggleton, P, *Does it Work?*, 1992, London: Health Education Authority. Wellings, K *et al*, *Sexual Behaviour in Britain Study*, 1994, Harmondsworth: Penguin, was conducted to try and gain greater understanding of sexual behaviour and concluded that knowledge of sexualities was essential for devising effective strategies.

contact, pregnancy or needle-sharing, Scott and Freeman see trust as the significant determinant in safer sex practices. This must necessarily be read in the context of sexualities and gender relations as trust is a concept that is rooted in cultural practices. As such, prevention strategies have altered in terms of methodology, but have not been reconfigured so as to intercept constructed sexuality.[61]

The dominant characteristic of disease prevention and education is individualism, even when policies have voiced a preference for a community-based approach.[62] As stated by the British Government in *The Health of the Nation*, the aim of health education is 'to ensure that individuals are able to exercise informed choice when selecting the lifestyles they adopt'.[63] The earlier White Paper *Prevention and Health: Everybody's Business*, produced by the Department of Health and Social Security in 1976, had also placed public health issues including sexually transmitted diseases firmly within individual responsibility: 'the individual must decide for himself.'[64] Recognition of the diverse structural constraints on health led to the WHO's policy on health promotion, relocating it in the socio-political rather than the biomedical sphere. Yet, the official response to HIV/AIDS has largely remained dependent upon health education and whilst the dissemination of factual, significant information about the disease is essential to its containment, the impact of context on the processing of that information has been intensely significant. The epidemic has demonstrated that disease information is not simply received, but is modified through the social, political, religious, moral attitudes held by the individual. Disease education disseminated by the State has been processed differently from information disseminated by community groups, such as those perceived as related to relevant sectors of the society concerned, using language, concepts and information sympathetic to local needs.[65] Social factors, particularly gender and poverty, have interfered with health promotion of safer sex because of the contextual implications of disrupting sexuality. As a result, not only is the epidemic continuing to thrive, but unprotected sex has become romanticised as a marker of resistance to prevailing Western morality or as a badge of heterosexuality.

---

61 See, eg, the study on negotiation of safer sex by Holland *et al*, 'Pressure, resistance, empowerment: young women and the negotiation of safer sex', in Aggleton *et al* (eds), *AIDS: Rights, Risks and Reasons*, 1992, London: Falmer.

62 Naidoo, J and Wills, J, *Health Promotion: Foundations for Practice*, 2nd edn, 2000, Edinburgh: Bailliere Tindall.

63 Department of Health, 1992, London: HMSO, p 4.

64 DHSS, *Prevention and Health: Everybody's Business*, 1976, London: HMSO.

65 Such as groups identified as gay disseminating information to the gay community. See Wilton, T, *Engendering AIDS: Deconstructing Text, Sex and Epidemic*, 1997, London: Sage, Chapter 5.

LEGAL RESPONSES TO HIV / AIDS

Across Europe, legal responses to the epidemic have been described as either coercive, reflecting more traditional public health ideas, or non-coercive, supporting an approach based on behaviour change.[66] Most of Europe has adopted a non-coercive strategy, which brought along with it a lack of legislation, reliance being placed on education and individual responsibility rather than overt control. The principal legislation relating to AIDS in Britain is the Public Health (Control of Diseases) Act 1984, which consolidated a number of Victorian statutes and has been adapted through its schedule. At the beginning of the crisis, the proposition that HIV / AIDS should be included within the legislation's list of notifiable diseases was raised, but rejected. Being included on that list would have made HIV and AIDS notifiable diseases subject to a range of coercive measures designed to deal with cholera, plague, tuberculosis, smallpox, scarlet fever and other diseases prevalent in the 19th century. Instead, AIDS[67] was added to the list in a restrictive way by the Public Health (Infectious Diseases) Regulations 1988 allowing surveillance and limiting the application of the more draconian measures.[68] The AIDS (Control) Act 1987 also directs legal regulation towards surveillance rather than coercive control. The issue of compulsory testing for HIV has also been dealt with restrictively by domestic British law. Blood taken in ante-natal clinics and genito-urinary medicine clinics is routinely tested for HIV, but all of the data is anonymised and the results are only used for statistical purposes. Legal responses to issues of confidentiality and partner notification are also characterised by restraint, preferring continued reliance on professional judgment controlled by the General Medical Council to direct legal rule-making.[69]

This lack of legal regulation of control has been criticised as a 'regulatory failure' attributed to the nature of law being insufficiently flexible to deal with the complex issues raised by the epidemic. The process of categorisation inherent in law as a simplification device has been seen as inadequate to provide a framework for the administration of a system of holistic health promotion.[70] The role of human rights has, in a sense,

66 Harrington, JA, 'AIDS, public health and the law: a case of structural coupling?' (1999) 6 Journal of European Health Law 213–34.

67 The term is unlikely to include asymptomatic HIV infection and so the more coercive measures such as restrictions on movement are limited to the final stages of the disease syndrome. See Montgomery, J, *Health Care Law*, 1997, Oxford: OUP, pp 31–34 and Berridge, V, *AIDS in the UK: The Making of Policy 1981–1994*, 1996, Oxford: OUP.

68 For a discussion of these limitations see Montgomery, J, *Health Care Law*, 1997, Oxford: OUP.

69 See Brazier, M and Harris, J, 'Public health and private lives' (1996) 4 Med L Rev 171–92 and the General Medical Council guidelines available from http://www.gmc.com.

70 These issues are discussed in Chapter 1 by Linda Johnson.

supported this and has been perceived as a more appropriate guide to domestic legal measures than concepts of individualised coercion.[71] Yet, problems of definition within human rights, issues of monitoring and the assumptions about individualism on which the paradigm has been built limit its usefulness as a unitary strategy.[72] The history of infectious diseases has also demonstrated the need for domestic regulation to ensure effective health strategies within States in order for there to be effective transnational and international health regulation.[73]

There are indications that a more coercive approach may be on the horizon. In March 2001, a man with HIV infection was convicted under Scottish criminal law for deliberately infecting his girlfriend.[74] This was the first conviction of its type in Britain and signals a reprioritising of concerns away from self-surveillance and monitoring and towards intervention in sexual contact. In the same month, the High Court awarded damages to 114 claimants against the health service for infecting them with hepatitis C during medical procedures before effective screening was introduced.[75] Recent public health crises as a result of BSE and foot and mouth disease have also raised calls for increased control and effective mechanisms to ensure protection from disease.[76]

The real danger is that domestic legal regulation will develop in a piecemeal way, in response to what are perceived as intermittent political crises over health, particularly in a context of contracting available resources and an already over-burdened health system. The emergence and re-emergence of infectious diseases has alerted developed States to their vulnerability and to the global nature of risks to health. Awful diseases like ebola and HIV, virulent infective agents like the prion, together with the continuing scourges of malaria, cholera and tuberculosis, increasing incidence of microbial resistant pathogens and recurring food safety scares have all reminded governments of the resilience of the microbial world. This disease-led alarm has caused a rebirth in international diplomacy on infectious diseases that has focused on the need for worldwide surveillance

71 Human rights and health are discussed in Chapter 4 by Yutaka Arai-Takahashi. In the HIV/AIDS context, see Gostin, L and Lazzarini, Z, *Human Rights and Public Health in the AIDS Pandemic*, 1997, New York: OUP. See also Carlier, J, *The Free Movement of Persons Living with HIV/AIDS*, 1999, Luxembourg: Office of Official Publications of the European Communities, for an examination of the domestic law/international law issues raised by this issue in Europe.

72 See Fidler, D, *International Law and Infectious Diseases*, 1999, London: Clarendon.

73 *Ibid*.

74 (2001) *The Independent*, 17 March.

75 (2001) *Evening Standard*, 26 March.

76 See http://www.bse.org.uk; http://www.bse.org.uk; and http://www.maff.gov.uk for an account of the crisis and the regulations that have been passed to control the supply of beef.

and rapid responses. The model of co-operation that is emerging in this international context, however, remains dependent on effective domestic systems and capabilities[77] to provide local surveillance and health care. The primary concern in the development of such a national regulatory system should be its need to ensure that its content is directed to containing and effectively treating the diseases concerned. To do that, there must be careful reassessment of the responsibilities of States and individuals involving recognition and analysis of the complexity of social life.

77 Brownlie, I, 'The expansion of international society: the consequences for the law of nations' in Bull, H and Watson, A (eds), *The Expansion of International Society*, 1984, Oxford: Clarendon, p 368.

CHAPTER 9

PARTICULAR ISSUES OF PUBLIC HEALTH: ENVIRONMENTAL DAMAGE: PROBLEMS OF INTERNATIONAL AND EC REGULATION

Mark Wilde

INTRODUCTION

Most forms of pollution have an impact on public health, direct or indirect. Obvious examples of direct health threats include contamination of water, radiation and air pollution. Even the phenomena of global warming, which most would regard as an essentially environmental problem, could have serious public health implications. These problems have a clear international dimension in that pollution does not respect international boundaries. Pollutants can be borne over many thousands of miles by natural phenomena such as wind or currents. Furthermore, many harmful substances, including waste products, are deliberately transported between countries for treatment or reprocessing. Thus, in many respects, we are living in a 'global commons'.[1]

This chapter examines the nature of international environmental law, in a public health context, by reference to specific examples drawn from regulatory initiatives. These examples are used to demonstrate the particular difficulties associated with regulating in this area. It is argued that the health implications of many forms of pollution have been an important factor in prompting the implementation of many international environmental initiatives. However, the machinations of international politics are never far from the surface; in many cases the legal mechanisms which have been put in place appear little more than a thin veneer disguising these realities. Ultimately, the short term economic interests of States may not coincide with the health interests of their populations. As will be seen, this conflict is exemplified by the continued wrangling over the issue of climate change.

---

1 Vogler, J, *The Global Commons: A Regime Analysis*, 1995, Chichester: Wiley.

ANTHROPOCENTRISM AND INTERNATIONAL ENVIRONMENTAL LAW

It is impossible to separate international environmental law from public health issues. This is due to the fact that most environmental regulation, both at a domestic and international level, has been prompted by an anthropocentric view of environmental problems. In other words, there is a need to safeguard the environment because it has an impact on the welfare of humans.

The anthropocentric view of nature is deeply rooted in philosophy, religion and science. Gillespie[2] has traced five strands of thought running through the history of these disciplines which have resulted in this 'human chauvinistic' perspective. First, an influential philosophical tradition advocated the separation of the mental and physical worlds.[3] Enlightenment could only be attained through abstract thought in isolation from one's surroundings.[4] Nature was consigned to the physical world where it was viewed as a mere object which had tangible qualities, but could not be assigned abstract attributes.[5] This led to the second strand of thought; the notion that nature was a self-contained entity[6] which functioned in the manner of a machine.[7] As Gillespie explains:

> As a consequence of the machine metaphor humanity adopted an instrumentalist rationality. This assumes a mandate to experiment, operate, or to manipulate Earthly Nature as Humans see fit. The former image of the organic unity of Earthly Nature was replaced by the notion of the world as a machine with dimensions susceptible to measurement and control. Additionally, the inertness of matter, the asserted lack of sentience and lack of inherent value in all that is not human, absolves humanity of any guilt regarding the apparent damage that humans may inflict upon individual animals or complete ecosystems.[8]

---

2 Gillespie, A, *International Environmental Law, Policy and Ethics*, 1999, Oxford: Clarendon.

3 This can be traced to the writings of Pythagoras and Plato, who were 'distrustful of sensation and empirical observation as a source of knowledge'. In more recent times, this theme was pursued by Descartes, who divided the world into mind and matter. Nature was from the realm of matter and therefore only consisted of tangible qualities such as size and weight. See *ibid*, pp 5–6.

4 *Ibid*.

5 *Ibid*.

6 This view of the universe stemmed from the 'Atomists', who believed that all entities were solid and insular and not interdependent. Thus, humans were viewed as self-contained and individualistic beings and in no way connected with nature, which functioned as a separate entity. See *ibid*, pp 7–8.

7 A view espoused by the German philosopher Kepler; see *ibid*, p 9.

8 *Ibid*.

This led to the emergence of the remaining three strands of thought identified by Gillespie: that nature was untamed and something to be feared;[9] that it only had value to the extent that it could be put to the service of humans;[10] and that it should be controlled and subjugated.[11]

Gillespie goes on to argue that this anthropocentric view of nature has permeated much international environmental law, and he cites examples in which it is possible to detect this approach. For example, the 1968 African Convention on the Conservation of Natural Resources provides that the parties:

> ... shall undertake to adopt the measures necessary to ensure conservation, utilisation and development of the soil, water, flora and fauna resources in accordance with scientific principles and with due regard to the best interests of the people.

This view of the environment as a resource, which must be protected because of its utility to humans, is also reflected in the 1980 World Conservation Strategy where the concept of sustainable development is defined as: 'The application of human, financial, living and non-living resources to satisfy human needs and to improve the quality of human life.' In a similar vein, the 1982 World Charter for Nature stated that: 'Ecosystems and organisms, as well as the land, marine and atmospheric resources that are utilised by man, shall be managed to achieve and maintain optimum sustainable productivity.' The 1992 *Rio Declaration on Environment and Development* declared that: 'Human beings are at the centre of concerns for sustainable development.'

This anthropocentric view of the desirability of environmental protection has resulted in the adoption of 'self-interest' as a primary motivation for environmental regulation. As Gillespie succinctly puts it, 'humanity protects Nature because Nature protects humanity'.[12] Thus, action on the

---

9 Historically, the wilderness and the wild 'beasts' which inhabit it have been regarded as forming part of an evil environment into which humans should not stray. Rather, humans were expected to distance themselves from nature; as Socrates argued, the most virtuous human being is, 'the one who transcends their animal and vegetative nature'; Socrates, quoted in Eckersley, R, *Environmentalism and Political Theory: Towards an Ecocentric Approach*, 1992, London: UCL Press, p 50.

10 Eg, Locke viewed 'raw' land as without value until it had been 'improved' by, for example, being put to agricultural use. See Gillespie, A, *International Environmental Law, Policy and Ethics*, 1999, Oxford: Clarendon, p 12.

11 This was a favoured theme of Francis Bacon, who argued: 'Our main object is to make nature serve the business and conveniences of man,' thus, 'Nature must be bound into service.' The theme was continued by William Sumner, who argued in 1896: 'It is legitimate to think of Nature as a hard mistress against whom we are maintaining a struggle for existence. All our science and art are victories over her, but when we quarrel amongst ourselves we lose the fruits of our victory just as certainly as we would if she was a human opponent.' See *ibid*, pp 7–11.

12 *Ibid*, p 19.

environment has focused on the impact of environmental degradation on the welfare and prosperity of humans; clearly, this includes the effects of pollution on public health. As the United Nations Environment Programme (UNEP) stated in 1973, its primary focus was 'to anticipate and prevent threats to human health'. As will be seen in the discussion of the various international health initiatives, below, public health issues have provided much of the impetus for action.

SOURCES OF INTERNATIONAL ENVIRONMENTAL LAW

International organisations

In common with most forms of international law, environmental law stems from a multitude of conventions, treaties and protocols, each of which comprises differing supervisory bodies and enforcement mechanisms.[13] Certain organisations seek to pool technical knowledge and establish harmonised environmental standards (such as emission limits) which can either form the basis of guidelines[14] or binding obligations in conventions.[15] These standards can then be absorbed into domestic law or adduced in evidence in domestic court proceedings. On rare occasions, international agreements have served to formulate generally applicable principles of international environmental law, which have been widely adopted by individual States.[16] Other organisations primarily have a research function and generate technical information regarding potential threats to the environment and health.[17]

---

13 The United Nations has established a number of specialist agencies whose responsibilities include environmental and health issues. Notable examples include the International Maritime Organisation (IMO); the International Labour Organisation (ILO); the Food and Agriculture Organisation (FAO); the United Nations Educational, Scientific, and Cultural Organisation (UNESCO); the International Oceanographic Commission (IOC); the World Health Organisation (WHO); the World Meteorological Organisation (WMO); the International Bank for Reconstruction and Development (IBRD); the International Monetary Fund (IMF); the International Atomic Energy Agency (IAEA). Outside the umbrella of the UN, the Organisation on Economic Development and Co-operation (OECD) has been particularly active in matters relating to the environment and health.

14 Eg, the IAEA has various committees which endeavour to establish universally accepted guidelines for the handling of radioactive substances.

15 The IMO has so far promoted the adoption of 30 Conventions and Protocols.

16 A notable example includes the 'polluter pays' principle, which was developed by the OECD in 1972. This was subsequently formally adopted by the EC as a basic component of its environmental policy: see below, p 265.

17 The WHO analyses international health problems and publishes research findings. These may be utilised by other agencies in drafting international agreements or in the implementation of action programmes. Indeed, the WHO has been an [contd]

In the absence of any specific treaty or convention, recourse may still be had to custom or general principles of international law.

Enforcement of any international obligation is difficult and international environmental law is no exception. This is largely due to the fact that obligations often rely upon 'soft law' mechanisms, which are not always converted into concrete principles of domestic law. However, in Europe, the European Community has the ability to implement 'hard law' in the form of legislation binding upon Member States.[18]

The European Community

The EC has been active in the field of environmental protection for many years, although a specific environmental Title on the environment was not included in the Treaty of Rome until the passing of the Single European Act (SEA) 1987. This introduced Art 174–76 (formerly 130r, s, t), which provide a firm platform for legislative initiatives. The objectives of the EC's environmental policy are set out in Art 174(1):

> Community Policy on the Environment shall contribute to pursuit of the following objectives: (1) preserving, protecting and improving the quality of the environment; (2) protecting human health; (3) prudent and rational utilisation of natural resources; (4) promoting measures at international level to deal with regional or world-wide environmental problems.

From this, it is immediately apparent that the EC recognises that environmental factors have an impact on public health and that the two are not mutually exclusive. The interrelation between the environment and public health was emphasised in the EC Commission's framework programme for action in the field of public health.[19] This refers to a range of environmental factors that have an impact on public health and necessitate action. As noted above, polluted water, whether it is drunk, bathed in, or fished, can lead to the spread of disease. Owing to the immediate threat to public health caused by polluted water, it is not surprising that there has been considerable legislative activity in this field since the 1970s. Typically, directives set emission limits, or water quality objectives, which must be attained within a set period of time.[20] Failure to comply with the terms of a

---

17 [contd] invaluable source of information on the environmental impact on international public health for the purposes of this chapter.

18 As a result of the development of the concepts of 'direct effect' and 'indirect effect' in the jurisprudence of the European Court of Justice (ECJ). See *Van Gend en Loos v Nederlandse Administratie der Belastingen*, Case 26/62 [1963] ECR 1, and *Von Kolson and Kamann v Land Nordrhein-Westfalen* [1984] ECR 1891.

19 See *Commission Communication on the Framework for Action in the Field of Public Health*, COM(93) 559 final, Brussels, 24 November 1993, Annex II.

20 Eg, Directive 80/777/EEC on Drinking Water sets out 62 parameters relating to the abstraction of water for human consumption directly or in the manufacture of [contd]

directive may lead to enforcement action against the State by the Commission and ultimately the European Court of Justice (ECJ).[21]

Mention must also be made of the European Atomic Energy Treaty (Euratom or EAEC Treaty), signed at the same time as the Treaty of Rome. The health risks associated with nuclear energy are obvious, as demonstrated by the tragic consequences of the Chernobyl disaster. The Treaty requires Member States to keep the Commission informed of any plans to dispose of waste, or to commission new facilities where a neighbouring Member State may be at risk of contamination in the event of an accident.[22] The Commission may deliver an opinion[23] or issue a directive requiring the adoption of specific safety measures.[24] The Commission must also be informed of any plans to conduct 'particularly dangerous experiments'.[25] The issue has arisen as to whether this provision applied to French atomic weapons testing in the South Pacific.

Relationship between international obligations and EC law

The European Community is unusual as a source of supranational law in that it has the ability to pass concrete legislation binding upon Member States. Thus, the EC may serve as the conduit by which certain principles, derived from international law, enter domestic law.[26]

On a number of occasions, the ECJ has used internationally agreed guidelines as an aid to construction when interpreting Community

20 [contd] food. Eg, the guide level (GL) for aluminium is 0.05 mg/l and the maximum admissible concentration (MAC) is 0.2 mg/l. As regards microbiological parameters, the Directive provides that drinking water should contain no pathogenic organisms such as faecal coliforms or faecal streptococci.

21 Treaty of Rome, Art 226. The ECJ has adopted a strict approach regarding the application of standards set by directives. In *Commission v Germany*, Case C-198/97 [1999] ECR I-3257 concerning the failure of Germany to comply with the Bathing Water Directive (76/160/EEC), the Court stated, para 35: 'Contrary to what the German Government claims, it is not sufficient to take all reasonably practicable measures: the Directive requires the Member States to take all necessary measures to ensure that bathing waters conform to the limit values set therein.'

22 EURATOM, Art 37.

23 These opinions are published in the Community law reports. Eg, in *Re The Torness Nuclear Power Station* (87/350/Euratom) [1987] 3 CMLR 659, the Commission noted that an 'unplanned release' from the facility resulting in: 'Ground contamination ... could give rise in Ireland to potential doses which would require a temporary ban or restrictions to be imposed on the consumption of certain foodstuffs originating from the contaminated area.' Thus, the Commission concluded that the UK and Irish Governments should agree contingency plans as a 'matter of urgency'.

24 EURATOM, Art 38.

25 *Ibid*, Art 34.

26 Treaty of Rome, Arts 174(4) and 228 enable the Community to conclude agreements with international organisations.

measures.[27] For example, in *Commission of the European Communities v Kingdom of Belgium* (Case C-376/1990),[28] the Commission sought a declaration that Belgium had failed to properly implement Council Directive (1980/836/Euratom) on protection of the health of the general public and of workers against the dangers of ionizing radiation properly.[29] It was argued that Belgium had breached the Directive by stipulating dose limits for certain types of occupational exposure to radiation, which were stricter than those provided for in the Directive. The ECJ found that there was nothing in the Directive which precluded implementation of stricter dose limits. There was evidence to suggest that the Directive had been intended to implement the recommendations of the International Commission on Radiological Protection (ICRP).[30] On examining the ICRP publication, the ECJ reached the conclusion that the recommendations suggested minimum standards and that local circumstances could justify more stringent measures:

> It is apparent from the ... ICRP publication that the dose limits represent the value of dose which gives rise to consequences for the health of people exposed to ionising radiation which is just tolerable and that the choice of dose limits necessarily involves judgments which may be different in different societies (see paragraphs 153 and 169 and 170 of publication 60).[31]

APPLICATION OF INTERNATIONAL ENVIRONMENTAL LAW IN A PUBLIC HEALTH CONTEXT

A detailed analysis of all international environmental law and the manner in which it seeks to protect public health would be a vast undertaking and beyond the scope of this chapter. Instead, it is proposed to refer to some specific examples of the application of international environmental law in a public health context, with a view to identifying the key issues.

Many environmental problems which may also have an impact on public health transcend the jurisdictions of individual States and require an international response. The scale of these problems differs according to the characteristics of the pollutants and may require different regulatory approaches. Certain pollutants may affect a limited number of States in a particular region; for example, fumes from smelters in Southern Canada could affect farmland in the Northern US.[32] This type of harm is often referred to as 'transboundary pollution' and may require resolution of

27 As a result of its continental character, the ECJ adopts a teleological approach to interpretation which enables it to draw upon a wide variety of extraneous sources.

28 [1992] ECR I-6153.

29 OJ 1980 L246 15.7.80, p 1.

30 ICRP Publication 60.

31 [1992] ECR I-6153, para 24.

32 See *Trail Smelter* arbitration, below, p 268.

specific disputes between individual States or private parties within those States. Thus, in many respects, disputes of this nature have the character of neighbourhood disputes and are often settled according to principles derived from domestic private law.

However, other pollutants are caused by global economic and industrial activity and are impossible to trace to specific States. This gives rise to global environmental problems rather than specific conflicts between specific parties, and demands concerted action at a political level. Clearly, the most obvious global environmental problems facing the international community concern global warming and ozone depletion.

Finally, we are concerned with harmful substances, which are deliberately shipped between States in the course of trade. An obvious hazard is created by the shipment of waste for reprocessing or recycling; this form of economic activity has become the subject of an intricate international regulatory regime.

Transboundary pollution

Atmospheric pollution

The problem of transboundary atmospheric pollution is particularly acute where industrial activities are conducted near territorial borders. In *Trail Smelter*,[33] the US brought an action against Canada before the International Joint Commission on the grounds that property damage had been caused in Washington State by emissions of sulphur dioxide from copper and lead smelters in Canada. The decision was significant in the sense that it affirmed a principle of customary international law to the effect that:

> No State has the right to use or permit the use of its territory in such a manner as to cause injury by fumes in or to the territory of another or the properties or persons therein, when the case is of serious consequence and the injury is established by clear and convincing evidence.

However, as Birnie and Boyle point out,[34] as the rule can only be invoked in narrow interstate claims, it has had little impact on wider problems caused by atmospheric pollution. That said, the application of the principle was limited at the time of the tribunal by limited scientific knowledge regarding the reach of pollutants and their insidious effects on health. The onerous nature of the causation test applied by the tribunal, 'clear and convincing

---

33 (1939) 33 AJIL 182; (1941) 35 AJIL 684.

34 Birnie, PW and Boyle, AE, *International Law and the Environment*, 1992, Oxford: Clarendon, p 394.

evidence', meant that the tribunal was limited to consideration of tangible property damage caused by smelters in the immediate vicinity of the border. This was despite the fact that much expert evidence was adduced suggesting possible links between health problems and the fumes.[35] Modern scientific techniques mean that it is now possible to trace pollutants over much longer distances and to determine where they are deposited. Thus, the 'clear and convincing' evidence test need not serve as an obstacle to the wider application of the principle.

Nevertheless, *Trail Smelter* is still the only interstate case to have reached a final international adjudication. Birnie and Boyle[36] suggest that this is due to the fact that liability rules, designed to compensate for serious harm which has already occurred, cannot be used to implement a preventative approach. This necessitates the formulation of 'diligent control' mechanisms 'created through negotiation and international co-operation'.[37]

The only international agreement in this field is the 1979 Geneva Convention on Long-Range Transboundary Air Pollution (LRTAP) signed by over 30 parties in Western and Eastern Europe including the former Soviet Union. The language of the Convention itself appears very weak, and does not contain any firm commitments relating to the reduction of emissions. Instead, it refers to the fact that States should 'endeavour to limit' and 'as far as possible gradually reduce and prevent air pollution'. However, these less than onerous commitments have been augmented by somewhat firmer undertakings in subsequent protocols. The first protocols to be added concerned sulphur dioxide (SO_2)[38] and nitrogen oxide (NO_x)[39] emissions;[40] to this end, States were required to reduce emissions by 30% by

35 The 1939 interim arbitral award was mainly calculated on the basis of property damage. Whilst experts who submitted evidence to the Commission had no doubt that the fumes had had an adverse effect on public health, they were unable to quantify this loss or determine precisely how many people had been affected; see Dewees, D, 'Sulphur dioxide emissions from smelters: the historical inefficiency of tort law', unpublished paper, 1996, University of Toronto.

36 Birnie, PW and Boyle, AE, *International Law and the Environment*, 1992, Oxford: Clarendon, p 394.

37 *Ibid*.

38 Helsinki Protocol on the Reduction of Sulphur Emissions or their Transboundary Fluxes 1985.

39 Sofia Protocol concerning the Control of Emission of Nitrogen Oxides or their Transboundary Fluxes 1988.

40 Aside from its contribution to acid rain and its damaging affect on the environment, and subsequent indirect effects on public health, the WHO has identified a number of direct health effects associated with SO2 emissions. In its latest guidelines on air quality, the WHO refers to a number of epidemiological studies which show a correlation between deaths or admissions to hospitals and concentrations of pollutants. Other studies demonstrate associations between levels of pollutants and aggravation of symptoms displayed by patients suffering from respiratory problems including bronchitis and asthma. See WHO Air Quality Guidelines (1999), Chapter 2, para 2.1.5 and Chapter 3, para 3.1. A full transcript of the guidelines is available at: http://www.who.int/air/guidelines.

1993. The US, Poland and the UK refused to ratify the protocol, arguing that there was no conclusive evidence linking them with acid rain; this approach is hardly in the spirit of the preventative or precautionary principles. However, the EC has made commitments that will impose binding obligations on the UK via Council Directive (88/609/EEC) on the limitation of emissions of certain pollutants into the air from large combustion plants.[41] This demonstrates the ability of the EC to convert international undertakings into concrete, binding legislation. However, as regards non-EC members, the executive body[42] charged with overseeing the implementation of the Convention has few powers.[43] For example, in common with most international environmental agreements, there is no binding mechanism for dispute resolution.

More recently, further protocols have been passed; from a public health perspective the Aarhus Protocol on Persistent Organic Pollutants (the POPs Protocol) 1998 is of particular interest.[44] POPs comprise a group of organic pollutants and include chemicals such as DDT and PCBs and associated by-products such as chlorinated dioxins and furans. The latter can be produced by combustion, for example, by burning PCBs in incinerators.[45] Research has shown that these substances can be borne over a great distance by air currents before being deposited in water. Owing to the tendency for POPs to be carried from warmer to cooler climes, most evidence of contamination has been found in the Baltic, the Arctic, the North Sea and the North American Great Lakes. Once deposited in a body of water, the substances progress through the food chain until they are at their most prevalent in predators at the top of the food chain. This has had a variety of adverse effects on populations of marine animals, including reproductive failure, population decline, thyroid problems, hormonal deficiencies, reduced performance of immune systems, tumours, cancers and gross birth defects.[46]

41 OJ L336 7.12.88.

42 This comprises a committee of environmental advisers to the UN Economic Commission for Europe (ECE), which meets annually, and a secretariat provided by the ECE.

43 The executive is limited to assimilating information provided to it by the signatories pursuant to their reporting obligations under Art 8 of the Convention. On the basis of this information, it may formulate future policy or attempt to promote international co-operation in specific areas.

44 For an overview of the Protocol and its background, see Hillman, K, 'International control of persistent organic pollutants: the UN Economic Commission for Europe Convention on Long Range Transboundary Air Pollution and beyond' (1999) 8(2) RECIEL 105.

45 In *Graham and Graham v Re-Chem International* [1996] Env LR 158, the plaintiffs, who were dairy farmers, alleged that their cattle's health had been damaged as a result of digesting grass contaminated by dioxins and furans as a result of the burning of PCBs in a nearby toxic waste incinerator. The court accepted scientific evidence which demonstrated a link between the burning of PCBs and the production of the hazardous substances in question. However, the plaintiffs failed on causality grounds in that there was an alternative explanation for the symptoms, which was unrelated to the operation of the incinerator.

46 The International POPs Elimination Network (IPEN), *Background Statement and POPs Elimination Platform*, 1998, Washington DC: IPEN, p 2.

For some years, scientists have been attempting to determine the extent to which these problems have been passed on to humans through the consumption of fish and other seafood. In the 1980s, it was discovered that mothers' breast milk in Northern Canada contained excessive levels of PCBs.[47] In another study, which focused on mothers in 10 Arctic regions, it was found that blood samples taken from the umbilical cord contained levels of certain POPs which were 10 times greater than samples taken from subjects in more southerly latitudes.[48]

The POPs Protocol requires States to ban the production and use of certain POPs (annex I substances), restrict the use of others (annex II substances), and to limit the emissions of a third category (annex III substances). However, in some respects the Protocol demonstrates the extent to which international agreements are often an edifice of compromise. Not all States could agree which substances should be banned outright and which should continue in use subject to restrictions. Confusingly, this led to the inclusion of certain POPs in both annexes I and II. An example includes DDT, which many States felt unable to prohibit owing to its use in controlling diseases such as malaria and encephalitis. As Hillman observes:

> While there may have been political reasons for listing DDT in annex I, its placement there is somewhat misleading: given that the protocol permits continued but limited production and use of this substance, it would likely have been more appropriate to have it appear solely in annex II.[49]

As regards limitation of emissions, in marked contrast to the earlier SO_2 and NO_X Protocols, the POPs Protocol does not set any specific targets; instead it merely requires States to reduce their emissions. This somewhat unambitious objective is further offset by the proviso that States need only implement such measures 'insofar as it is technically and economically feasible'.

As regards ensuring compliance with Protocols, an Implementation Committee has been established by the Executive Body of the LRTAP Convention.[50] The Committee is charged with monitoring progress towards the objectives set out in the Protocols and must make periodic reports to the Executive. It may also hear complaints made by one party against another in respect of non-compliance and attempt to broker a solution. If this fails, it is required to refer the matter to the Executive, which will endeavour to achieve a diplomatic settlement.

---

47 Dewailley, E *et al*, 'High levels of PCBs in breast milk of women from Arctic Quebec' (1989) 43 Bull Environ Contam Toxicol, Ch 12.

48 *Arctic Pollution Issues: A State of the Arctic Environment Report*, 1997, Oslo: Arctic Monitoring and Assessment Programme (AMAP), pp 172–76. Countries participating in the study included Canada, Denmark, Finland, Iceland, Norway, Russia and Sweden.

49 Hillman, K, 'International control of persistent organic pollutants: the UN Economic Commission for Europe Convention on Long Range Transboundary Air Pollution and beyond' (1999) 8(2) RECIEL 105, p 108.

50 Report of the Fifteenth Session of the Executive Body, Annex III.

Atmospheric atomic weapons testing by France in the South Pacific led to a bitter dispute with Australia and New Zealand in the 1960s and early 1970s. The latter feared that atmospheric tests of French nuclear devices created a risk of transboundary pollution in the form of nuclear fall out. The health effects of fall out have been exhaustively investigated in the wake of the atomic detonations over Hiroshima and Nagasaki[51] and the Chernobyl disaster.[52] Furthermore, it is believed that decay products, left in the atmosphere as a result of many years of atmospheric weapons tests, may still augment the risk of developing cancer globally by increasing the level of background radiation. Not surprisingly, the World Health Assembly roundly condemned the continuance of nuclear tests in 1973.[53]

Australia and New Zealand commenced simultaneous actions before the ICJ[54] on the grounds:

> That the conduct by the French Government of nuclear tests in the South Pacific region that give rise to radio-active fall-out constitutes a violation of New Zealand's [and Australia's] rights under international law, and that these rights will be violated by any further such tests.[55]

In the event, and in marked contrast to the devices exploded off Mururoa Atoll, the ICJ judgment was somewhat of a damp squib. The ICJ appeared to accept that there was a *prima facie* case for asserting that the tests did raise the possibility of transboundary pollution causing damage to New Zealand and Australia.[56] However, as France had undertaken not to conduct any further atmospheric tests, the Court reached the conclusion that, since the applicant's objective had already been met, 'the claim of New Zealand no longer has any object and ... the Court is therefore not called upon to give a

---

51 In 1950, an epidemiological study known as the 'Life span study' was commenced which involved some 93,000 survivors of the actual detonations and 27,000 people who subsequently moved to the affected areas. The aim of the study is to assess the long term affects on health of the fall-out on public health. Data for the period 1950 to 1987 shows an increase in the incidence of leukaemia, and cancer of the breast, bladder, colon, liver, lung, ovaries and stomach.

52 As regards the aftermath of Chernobyl and the widespread fall-out which was caused, studies have shown an increase in the incidence of certain types of cancer; see, eg, Baverstock, K, Egloff, B *et al*, 'Thyroid cancer after Chernobyl' (1992) Nature 359, pp 21–22.

53 Twenty-Sixth World Health Assembly, Geneva, 7–23 May 1973, Resolution WHA26.57, 'Urgent need for suspension of testing of nuclear weapons'.

54 *Nuclear Tests Case (New Zealand v France)* [1974] ICJ Rep 457; *Nuclear Tests Case (Australia v France)* [1974] ICJ Rep 253.

55 [1974] ICJ Rep 457, para 11.

56 On 22 June 1973, the ICJ made an interim Order stating that it considered itself to be seized of jurisdiction on the grounds that: 'For the purpose of the present proceedings it suffices to observe that the information submitted to the Court ... does not exclude the possibility that damage to New Zealand might be shown to be caused by the deposit on New Zealand territory of radioactive fallout resulting from such tests and to be irreparable.' See [1973] ICJ Rep 135.

decision thereon'.[57] Thus, there was no discussion of the substantive issues and whether France's conduct amounted to a breach of international law.

This decision left considerable doubt regarding the nature and extent of the ICJ's powers and its ability to enforce international law.

International watercourses

International watercourses provide the other main medium by which pollutants can be borne over distances between States. Water pollution constitutes a form of environmental harm which has an immediate and direct impact on public health owing to its ability to support pathogens and other agents of disease. It is no surprise that transboundary pollution of international watercourses has been a source of disputes between neighbouring States and has resulted in attempts at international regulation.

It seems beyond doubt that there is a customary obligation on States to refrain from activities which may result in harm to their neighbours through the release of pollutants into international watercourses. There appears to be no reason why the principles enunciated in *Trail Smelter* could not apply in this context. This view was supported in various Dutch court decisions in the *Rijnwater* litigation. This long running dispute stemmed from the dumping of 12 m tonnes of salt per year into the Rhine by potassium mines in Alsace. The pollution was carried to The Netherlands, where it posed a threat to the safety of drinking water and hence public health. As a result, the Dutch Government was required to adopt expensive purification measures. Damage caused to crops eventually prompted growers to pursue civil litigation against the potassium mines. It was during the course of these actions that the Dutch courts expressed the view that the dispute was analogous to the *Trail* Arbitration. Hence, those inhabitants of a riparian State who have suffered loss as a result of unlawful emissions from another riparian State have a cause of action against the polluters in question. Even if this duty could not be said to have attained the status of a customary principle of international law, it was stated that the maxim *sic utere tuo ut alienum non laedus* (so use your property as not to injure your neighbour) could be applied as a general principle of law recognised by civilised nations under Art 38(1)(c) of the Statute of the International Court of Justice:

> If what is considered above is applied to the case postulated above, this leads to the following conclusions: [a] that the general principles of law recognised by civilised peoples are binding on citizens; [b] that it is settled that the damage is caused by the salt discharges; [c] that the injury is established by clear and convincing evidence; [d] that the discharge of the saline waste into an international river by a legal person under national law in this case constitutes

57 [1974] ICJ Rep 457, para 63.

> a violation by the latter of a general principle binding upon it, *sic utere tuo ut alienum non laedus*.[58]

Of course, reliance upon individual civil actions to enforce international obligations is subject to the same criticisms postulated against this method of enforcement in transboundary atmospheric pollution disputes. In 1992, the International Law Commission (ILC) undertook the task of codifying international obligations in this area. This resulted in the 1997 Convention on the Law of the Non-Navigational Uses of International Watercourses.[59] The Convention places obligations on watercourse States to co-operate in the utilisation of international watercourses and to refrain from causing significant harm to a neighbouring State.[60] The concept of significant harm is elaborated in Art 21 on prevention, reduction and control of pollution:

> Watercourse States shall, individually and where appropriate, jointly, prevent reduce and control the pollution of an international watercourse that may cause significant harm to other watercourse States or to their environment, including harm to human health or safety, to the use of the waters for any beneficial purpose or to the living resources of the watercourse. Watercourse States shall take steps to harmonise their policies in this connection.

To this end, the Convention establishes notification and consultation procedures which States are expected to follow before engaging in any potentially harmful activities.[61] As regards the settlement of specific disputes, the Convention is consistent with almost all existing international environmental conventions in that it relies upon mediation and conciliation.[62] The Convention contains a standard clause to the effect that individual States *may* accept the jurisdiction of the ICJ or an arbitral tribunal on a voluntary basis.[63] This raises similar enforcement concerns to those addressed above in the context of atmospheric pollution.

To date, the Convention has been signed by relatively few States; this is possibly due to the fact that, as a result of the generally more localised nature of transboundary water pollution, many riparian States have already adopted measures on a regional basis. For example, in Europe, the Rhine Commission, established in 1950, is charged with harmonisation of emission

58 *Handelskwekerij GJ Bier BV en Stichting Reinwater v Mines de Potasse d'Alsace SA* (Case 4320/74) and *Handelskwekerij Firma Gebr Strik BV en Handelskwekerij Jac Valstar BV v Mines de Potasse d'Alsace SA* (Case 3789/77) [1979] ECC 206.

59 Opened for signature in New York, 21 May 1997; to date it has been signed by relatively few States.

60 Convention on the Law of Non-Navigational Uses of International Watercourses 1997, Art 7.

61 *Ibid*, Arts 11–19.

62 *Ibid*, Art 33 provides for the instigation of a Commission to investigate disputes and prepare a report recommending a solution.

63 *Ibid*, Art 33(10).

limits and regulations between riparian States. However, to date it has only adopted two Conventions, namely, the Rhine Chemicals Convention and the Rhine Chlorides Convention. Furthermore, despite the fact that it includes a compulsory unilateral arbitration procedure, which, as we have seen, is highly unusual in international environmental agreements, the mechanism has hardly been utilised. As a result, it has been incumbent upon a private riparian to pursue polluters in cases such as *Rijnwater*. A more effective programme was prompted by the *Sandoz* incident of 1987, which resulted in the instigation of the Rhine Action Programme. Similarly, the US and Canada established the International Joint Commission (IJC) under the 1909 Boundary Waters Treaty. Whilst the IJC has the capacity to act as an arbitral body imposing binding settlements in certain cases, its jurisdiction in pollution matters is limited and, in common with the ILC New York Convention on International Watercourses, focuses on conciliation and compromise.[64]

Global environmental problems

Ozone depletion

The WHO has identified a number of adverse health effects directly associated with the problem of ozone depletion,[65] including increase in various forms of skin cancers and acceleration of the development of cataracts and other eye diseases. There is some evidence to suggest that exposure to excessive levels of UV may inhibit the functioning of the body's immune system.

Negotiations for the introduction of a Treaty on ozone depletion were commenced in 1981 by UNEP and culminated in the 1985 Vienna Convention for the Protection of the Ozone Layer. The Convention bears strong similarities to the 1979 Geneva Convention on Long Range Transboundary Air Pollution in that it is largely a broad statement of intent, which contains little in the way of binding obligations. States are merely required to take 'appropriate measures' to protect the environment and public health from the effects of ozone depletion.[66] The only firm obligations imposed by the Convention relate to exchanging information and research and making alternative technologies available to developing States.[67] However, in common with the Geneva LRTAP Convention, the Vienna

64 Boundary Waters Treaty, Art IX.

65 The WHO has instigated a major research programme into the effects of ozone depletion known as the 'Intersun Project': see http://www.who.int/peh-uv.

66 Vienna Convention for the Protection of the Ozone Layer 1985, Article 2.

67 *Ibid*, Arts 2(2)(a), 4, 5.

Convention has been augmented by a protocol (the Montreal Protocol) which contains firm commitments to eliminate or restrict the use of certain ozone depleting substances. Furthermore, the Protocol seeks to exert influence over any States that have yet to sign the Convention by restricting trade with those States in the prescribed substances.[68]

Further similarities with the LRTAP Convention occur in the manner of enforcement. Disputes are brought before an implementation committee[69] whose function is to hear the representations of the parties 'with a view to securing an amicable resolution on the basis of respect for the provisions of the protocol'. The Treaty does not require the parties to submit to compulsory arbitration or judicial settlement before the ICJ, although they may voluntarily submit to this form of dispute resolution.[70]

Once again, EC law provides the conduit by which these undertakings have been converted into binding legislation in the Community. Above, it was noted that the ECJ finds international agreements persuasive when interpreting EC legislation. This interpretative obligation is particularly evident where a Community measure has been specifically designed to implement an international agreement. In Case C-284/1995, *Safety Hi-Tech Srl v S and T Srl*,[71] an Italian contract for the supply of chemicals for use in fire-fighting equipment was frustrated by the introduction of Council Regulation (EEC) 3093/1994.[72] This banned the unconfined use of hydrochlorofluorocarbons (HCFCs) as part of a range of measures intended to slow ozone depletion. The ECJ emphasised that it was settled law that: 'Community Legislation must, so far as possible, be interpreted in a manner that is consistent with international law,[73] in particular where its provisions are intended specifically to give effect to an international agreement concluded by the Community.'[74] In this case, the relevant international agreements included the Vienna Convention of 22 March 1985 for the Protection of the Ozone Layer and the Montreal Protocol of 16 September 1987 on Substances that Deplete the Ozone Layer. The limitations imposed by the EC were more restrictive than the controls prescribed by the Montreal Protocol. The ECJ noted that the measures had to be considered in the light of Art 2(3) of the Vienna Convention which provides that: '[T]he parties to

68 Article 4. At the negotiation stage, concern was expressed that this would breach the General Agreement on Tariffs and Trade (GATT). However, it was felt that these restrictions could be justified on the basis of GATT, Art 20(b), on the protection of human, animal, or plant life, or health. See Ad Hoc Working Group, Second Session, 22, Third Session, 18.

69 Established under Decision II/5 and Annex III, UNEP Ozl.Pro.2/3 (1990).

70 Ozone Convention, Art 11.

71 [1998] ECR I-4301.

72 OJ L333 22.12.94, p 1.

73 See *Commission v Germany* (Case C-61/94) [1996] ECR I-3989, para 52.

74 [1998] ECR I-4301, para 22.

that convention may adopt more severe domestic measures provided that they are intended, having regard to scientific evaluations, to promote the use of substitutes that are less harmful to the ozone layer.'[75]

Global warming

Climate change has major public health implications, which have been the subject of extensive research.[76] Climate instability increases the incidence of freak weather conditions causing immediate casualties.[77] In the longer term, warmer and damper conditions would increase populations of insects and ticks (vectors) which transmit disease (vector-borne infectious diseases). Of these diseases, the greatest threat is posed by malaria, carried by mosquitoes.[78] Malaria is likely to spread beyond those areas in which it is currently prevalent into central Asia and Eastern Europe.[79] Certain models estimate that by the 2080s, an additional 260 to 320 m people will be at risk from the disease.[80] As regards food supplies, the WHO is concerned that, although agricultural productivity in cooler climes may benefit from some warming, the consequences would be disastrous for countries in hotter parts of the world. A shortage of rain leads to crop failure and hence famine and malnutrition.[81] In more temperate regions, the threat to water supplies and the consequences for public health are obvious. Heavy rainfall causes flooding, which contaminates fresh water supplies with sewage and provides ideal conditions for pathogens. Even developed countries, with relatively sophisticated sanitation infrastructures, have experienced serious difficulties in coping with excessive rainfall. In the UK, recent heavy rainfall has resulted in an increase in the incidence of cryptosporidiosis.[82] Hotter conditions exacerbate respiratory diseases by affecting the distribution and concentrations of particulates and ground level ozone; increases in mortality rates on particularly hot days have been well documented.[83] Finally, crop failure and natural disasters are likely to lead to population displacement

75 [1998] ECR I-4301, para 23.

76 For an overview of the main research findings and their public health implications, see the WHO report, *Climate Change and Human Health: Impact and Adaptation*, WHO/SDE/OEH/00.4, May 2000.

77 *Ibid*, 3.2; it is estimated that worldwide, 140,000 persons per year are killed as a direct result of natural disasters.

78 *Ibid*, 3.3. Other vector-borne diseases, which may increase, and their vectors include: schistosomiasis (water snail); leishmaniasis (phlebotomine sandfly); American trypanosomiasis (triatomine bug); African trypanosomiasis (tsetse fly); lymphatic filariasis (mosquito); onchocerciasis (blackfly); yellow fever (mosquito); dracunculiasis (crustacean).

79 *Ibid*, 3.3.

80 *Ibid*, 3.3.

81 *Ibid*, 3.4.

82 *Ibid*, 3.5.

83 *Ibid*, 3.6.

and an increase in the number of refugees, a group which is particularly vulnerable to health threats.[84]

Despite the tangible risks to public health caused by global warming and the grave long term environmental consequences, securing an international consensus on the issue has proved near impossible. In international negotiations, short term economic interests have prevailed over the desirability of reducing emissions of greenhouse gases.

International attempts at regulation have followed a now familiar pattern, although arguably with far less success. In 1992, the Framework Convention on Climate Change was signed at the United Nations Conference on Environment and Development in Rio. Once again, the instrument appears to be no more than a broad statement of intent and an agreement in principle that greenhouse emissions must be stabilised 'at a level that would prevent dangerous interference with the climate system'.[85] Those obligations that it does include are very general; for example, States are required to compile national inventories of anthropogenic emissions and to formulate programmes for dealing with the problem.[86] However, in common with the ozone convention, there is a firmer commitment on developed States to provide financial and technical assistance to developing economies so as to enable them to reduce emissions.[87]

In 1995, at the first conference of the parties in Bonn, it was agreed that the Convention should be supplemented by somewhat firmer obligations to actually reduce emissions. This led to the Berlin Mandate,[88] which can best be described as a framework of guiding principles for negotiating specific measures designed to reduce greenhouse gases. It was agreed that developing countries should take the lead:

> The parties should protect the climate system for the benefit of present and future generations of humankind, on the basis of equity and in accordance with their common but differentiated responsibilities and respective capabilities. Accordingly, the developed country parties should take the lead in combating climate change and the adverse effects thereof.[89]

In this statement, it is also possible to see a strongly anthropocentric view of the need to secure agreement on this issue.

---

84 WHO report, *Climate Change and Human Health: Impact and Adaptation*, WHO/SDE/OEH/00.4, May 2000, 3.7. International health issues associated with refugees are discussed by Sylvie Da Lomba, above, Chapter 6.

85 Framework Convention on Climate Change 1992, Art 2.

86 *Ibid*, Art 4(1).

87 *Ibid*, Art 4(3); those developed States to which this obligation applies are listed in Annex II.

88 Adopted by Decision 1/CP(1).

89 Berlin Mandate, Art 3(1).

Equipped with the Berlin Mandate, the parties began the process of negotiating a protocol containing specific commitments to reduce emissions by specified amounts; this culminated in the third session of the Conference of the Parties at Kyoto. As French describes, the negotiation of the Kyoto protocol was painful, slow and frustrating as States put national interests before global concerns:

> There was a strange situation whereby those States most prominent in the debate for a strong protocol were in the end desperate that any protocol, whatever its provisions, be adopted. If no text had been agreed there is a danger that the international consensus in tackling climate change would have broken down completely.[90]

Parties with similar interests formed loose coalitions.[91] Those groupings in favour of the greatest reductions included the Alliance of Small Island States (AOSIS) (which are at greatest risk from rises in sea levels); the G-77 group of developing States and China; and the European Union. Those groupings in favour of more modest reductions included the OPEC States, which have a vested interest in the burning of fossil fuels; and the JUSCANZ members comprising Japan, the US, Canada, Australia and New Zealand.[92] As the US is responsible for a staggering 23% of global emissions of carbon dioxide, an agreement to which it was not party would have served little purpose. However, the dependency of the US economy on fossil fuels and the political unacceptability[93] of seeking to reduce emissions by way of measures such as increased taxes on fossil fuels, meant it was inevitable that the US would not agree to reductions of the order proposed by G-77 and AOSIS.

Not surprisingly, the Kyoto Protocol, which emerged from the negotiations, was much less ambitious than had been hoped for and shrouded in deliberately vague terminology. States were allocated specific emission allowances[94] with a view to achieving an aggregate overall reduction of 5%, below 1990 levels, in greenhouse gases.[95] There was no

---

90 French, J, '1997 Kyoto Protocol to the 1992 UN Framework Convention on Climate Change' (1998) 10(2) J Env L 227, p 230.

91 *Ibid*.

92 It should be noted that this coalition was very loose as the motivations of the members were very different. Japan and the US wished to protect their economically dominant, fossil fuel driven industries. Australia and New Zealand, on the other hand, considered that as low net contributors, they should have the flexibility to increase emissions.

93 On the run up to the Kyoto conference, Senate informed the President that any reductions would have to apply to all States, including developing countries, irrespective of their net contribution to greenhouse gases. See French, J, '1997 Kyoto Protocol to the 1992 UN Framework Convention on Climate Change' (1998) 10(2) J Env L 227, p 231.

94 Developed States listed in Annex I are expected to attain targets listed in Annex B of the Protocol.

95 Protocol, Art 3(1).

indication of how individual targets were to be co-ordinated with this collective obligation. Further controversial provisions relate to the encouragement of 'sinks'[96] (entailing the planting forests to absorb carbon dioxide) and 'emissions trading'. The latter concept involves establishing a mechanism whereby one State can sell its emissions quota to another, an approach strongly favoured by the US.[97] To this end, Art 16 of the Protocol provides that the Conference of the Parties may 'define the relevant principles, modalities, rules and guidance' to enable this process to take place. French predicted that 'emissions trading is likely to prove one of the most controversial aspects of future negotiations'.[98] At the time of writing, this prediction has proved to be correct, as the Parties to the Sixth Conference in The Hague failed to reach agreement on this issue amid a blaze of publicity and acrimony.[99]

As regards enforcement, the Protocol merely requires the development of an appropriate procedure.[100] However, a procedure entailing binding consequences cannot be established without an amendment to the Protocol; such a development has yet to occur and would entail yet more protracted negotiations. This contrasts with the Montreal Protocol on ozone depletion, where a compliance procedure was agreed without great difficulty. Indeed, global warming, although not unconnected with ozone depletion, presents a far more difficult problem. Ozone depleting substances generally form specific components in consumer products and can be replaced with alternatives. Fossil fuels, on the other hand, drive most industrial economies and are much more difficult to substitute.

At an EC level, specific legislation has been implemented with a view to fulfilling the obligations of the Rio Convention. A system of monitoring greenhouse gases was introduced by Council Decision (93/389/EEC).[101]

---

96 Protocol, Art 3(3).

97 A system of tradable permits has already been established in the US, whereby permits to emit set quantities of pollutants are auctioned off to industries. As the total emissions must not exceed a maximum aggregate level, only a limited number of permits are available. The first auction occurred in 1993 where the Chicago Board of Trade, on behalf of the Environmental Protection Agency, auctioned permits to emit sulphur dioxide. See, 'Pollution rights go to auction' (1993) *Financial Times*, 29 March; 'Mixed start to pollution permit sale' (1993) *Financial Times*, 31 March.

98 French, J, '1997 Kyoto Protocol to the 1992 UN Framework Convention on Climate Change' (1998) 10(2) J Env L 227, p 235.

99 See Nuttall, N, 'US demands imperil global warming deal' (2000) *The Times*, 25 November, p 22. The US was accused of attempting to avoid its commitments to reduce emissions by seeking to rely heavily on emissions trading, principally with former Soviet bloc countries, and by re-forestation programmes. It argued that the creation of these 'sinks' should be set against its emissions quota; thus, it should be given an additional 100 m tonnes of carbon credits for forestry programmes and 24 m tonnes for ecological farm management.

100 Convention, Art 17.

101 OJ L167 9.7.93, p 31.

This was accompanied by a programme on energy efficiency (SAVE), implemented by Council Directive (93/76/EEC);[102] this required Member States to instigate measures to reduce energy consumption by industry and in the home. This entailed, for example, the introduction of improved insulation standards for new buildings and a system of energy audits for large scale users. Furthermore, the Alternative Energy Programme (ALTENER), implemented by Council Decision (93/500/EEC),[103] made funds available for research and development into renewable energy sources. However, proposals for a carbon/energy tax[104] have met with less success. This proposed the introduction of higher taxes on fossil fuels so as to encourage the use of cleaner sources of energy. The proposal has faced considerable political opposition as Member States are resistant to any EC intervention in the field of fiscal policy. As a tax measure, the proposal could only be passed on the basis of unanimity in Council;[105] in the light of the discord which the measure has caused, it is unlikely to be implemented in the near future.

It should also be noted that, aside from measures specifically designed to implement the Rio obligations, certain pre-existing Directives already set limits for greenhouse gases. For example, Council Directive (85/203/EEC)[106] requires Member States to set air quality standards for nitrogen dioxide.

Shipment of waste

Waste disposal and recycling constitute major risks to the environment and hence public health. Pollutants from landfill sites can leach into watercourses and contaminate public water supplies.[107] Emissions from incinerators have the potential to cause atmospheric pollution thereby posing a threat to the health of the local population.[108]

The disposal and recycling of waste is a lucrative business and has given rise to a thriving industry.[109] Under EC law, waste products are classified as

102 OJ L237 22.9.93, p 28.

103 OJ L235 18.9.93, p 41.

104 COM(92) 226 final.

105 Treaty of Rome, Art 176.

106 OJ L87 27.3.85, p 1.

107 There have been a number of successful class actions in the US brought by persons whose health was adversely affected by the leaching of chemicals from landfill sites into the public water supply. See, eg, *Ayers v Township of Jackson*, 493 A2d 1314 (NJ Sup Ct App Div 1985).

108 Health concerns associated with the operation of toxic waste incinerators have been highlighted by the English case of *Graham and Graham v Re-Chem International*, above, and the ECtHR decision in *López Ostra v Spain*, below.

109 In the UK alone, the industry is estimated as being worth between £2 bn and £4 bn per year. See Hughes, D, *Environmental Law*, 3rd edn, 1996, London: Butterworths, p 364.

goods and hence subject to the free movement provisions of the Treaty of Rome.[110] Waste is commonly exported and imported as a commodity. From an international perspective, the transfrontier shipment of waste has been a cause for concern for some time. Importing waste augments health risks already faced by communities living in close proximity to waste handling facilities. Furthermore, there is a risk of pollutants being released into the wider environment as a result of accidents in transit. A general policy has emerged in favour of dealing with waste as close as possible to the point of origin. Attempts at regulation have had to face powerful economic forces, which wish to continue the international trade in waste. There is particular concern that newly emerging private enterprises, set up in the transitional economies of Eastern Europe, have been importing waste without necessarily having the infrastructure to dispose of it or recycle it safely.[111]

The Basel Convention on the Control of Transboundary Movements of Hazardous Wastes and their Disposal 1989 seeks to limit the transfrontier shipment of waste. To this end, the Convention established a requirement of 'prior informed consent'[112] whereby, in respect of shipments between signatory States, the receiving country must be informed of any proposed shipment and give its consent. In 1995, the Convention was amended so as to prohibit exports to States *other* than parties to the Convention, OECD members, the EC and Liechtenstein.[113] This amendment was designed 'to protect developing countries from unwanted imports'.[114] This prohibition was also extended to the controversial issue of recycling hazardous waste.[115]

However, Ryland[116] has identified a number of weaknesses in the regime currently in place, particularly in respect of those provisions relating to waste recycling. There was much disagreement regarding which waste products should be considered safe for the purposes of export and recycling and which should be considered hazardous. The EC adopted the approach advocated by the OECD[117] whereby waste is classified as green, amber or red according to the extent of the risk that it poses to human health or the environment. Green list waste is not considered as hazardous and is,

110 See *EC Commission v Belgium (re Wallonian Waste)* (Case C-2/90) [1992] ECR 4431.

111 See Ryland, D, 'Regulating the transboundary movement of hazardous waste in Europe: a legislative study' (1999) 5(1) JLS 102.

112 Basel Convention, Arts 4(1)(c) and 6.

113 *Ibid*, Annex VII.

114 'Basel Convention amendment adopted on hazardous waste exports' (1996) Environmental Policy and Law, p 14.

115 The hazardous waste recycling prohibition amendment, contained in Annexes VIII and IX of the Basel Convention.

116 Ryland, D, 'Regulating the transboundary movement of hazardous waste in Europe: a legislative study' (1999) 5(1) JLS 102.

117 OECD Council Decision C (92) 39 final.

therefore, exempt from the regulatory regime introduced in the EC.[118] However, the European Parliament has noted that the green list contains certain substances known to be harmful, such as cadmium.[119]

The Parliament has also noted that the amount of waste exported from the EC to developing countries for recycling probably exceeds the capacity of those countries to deal with it. This is further evidenced by a deficit between the amount of waste exported and the amount that is returned in a recycled state; somewhere, huge quantities of waste destined for recycling is disappearing.[120] The inference is that waste is simply being disposed of without any proper control. This is possibly due to the fact that the Basel Convention does not prohibit exports to developing States where a bilateral agreement has been concluded between the countries concerned. This is subject to the proviso that the recipient State has a system of 'environmentally sound management of hazardous waste'.[121] The convention does not elaborate on this concept, nor explain what steps the authorities in the exporting State should take in order to ensure that such practices have been implemented. The OECD has admitted that it is unclear as to whether the concept is being complied with.[122] This is in marked contrast to the regime implemented within the EC as regards shipments of waste between Member States where specific controls have been stipulated by legislation.[123]

The uncertainty regarding shipment of waste for recycling leads Ryland to the conclusion that there is a 'recycling loophole' which economic interests have been able to exploit:

> The inherent economic interests in the transboundary movement of recyclable hazardous waste, and the entrenched political interests of certain developing

---

118 In the EC, the provisions of the Basel Convention have been implemented by way of the Shipments of Waste Regulation.

119 European Parliament Session Document A4-0267/95, 26 October 1995, pp 7, 13.

120 'The European Union produces some two billion tonnes of waste every year, much of which is hazardous waste from industrial production ... 40 million tonnes of waste are exported to developing countries, where, as a rule, there are few facilities for treating it in an environmentally sound manner. It is not permitted to export wastes from the European Union for disposal purposes. Nevertheless, waste which is exported for recycling, in agreement with third countries, does not return to the European Union for final disposal.' European Parliament Session Document, p 11.

121 Articles 2(8) and 11(1)(2).

122 OECD Environment and Trade Directorates, COM/ENV/TD (97) 41/final Unclassified, p 4, *Trade Measures in the Basel Convention on the Control of Transboundary Movements of Hazardous Wastes and their Disposal*, p 72.

123 Waste disposed of or recycled in Europe is subject to the Directives on Waste, Council Directive (75/442/EEC) (OJ L194 25.7.75, p 39) as amended by Council Directive (91/156/EEC) (OJ L78 26.3.91, p 32) and Hazardous Waste, Council Directive (91/689/EEC) (OJ L377 31.12.91, p 20), which impose various obligations on producers of waste and the States. Thus, for example, there must be a system in place for licensing and inspecting sites.

economies in the continuation of such practices, appear to be the motivating forces behind future debate on this issue.[124]

Once again, this example of international regulation demonstrates the difficulty of securing international agreement where powerful economic interests are concerned. There are strong similarities to be drawn with the negotiations associated with the implementation of the POPs Protocol in that economic pressures have led to resistance against a total ban on trade in certain potentially hazardous substances. This has led to uncertainty and unevenness in the application of international law. This is exemplified by disagreement regarding which waste products should be included on the green list.

ENFORCEMENT OF INTERNATIONAL OBLIGATIONS

Public enforcement

At international level, there are few formal mechanisms for resolving disputes between Member States in cases of, for example, transboundary pollution. The International Court of Justice (ICJ)[125] has no general compulsory jurisdiction[126] and very few environmental treaties require the parties to resort to binding settlement.[127] As a result, the ICJ has only dealt with State responsibility in environmental matters on very rare occasions; most notably *Nuclear Tests*. Thus, most disputes rely upon the use of political solutions and diplomacy.[128]

The *Nuclear Tests* cases cast further doubt on the effectiveness of the ICJ as a means of enforcing international obligations. The ICJ declined to address the substantive issues, or provide a remedy, on the grounds that France had already undertaken not to continue atmospheric tests. This suggests that the ICJ cannot grant prohibitory injunctions enjoining States

---

124 Ryland, D, 'Regulating the transboundary movement of hazardous waste in Europe: a legislative study' (1999) 5(1) JLS 102, p 109.

125 The UN's organ of judicial settlement.

126 According to the Statute of the International Court of Justice, Arts 36–37, the Court can only accept jurisdiction in cases referred to it by the parties or where a treaty or convention specifically provides for reference to the ICJ.

127 Rare exceptions include the United Nations Convention on Law of the Sea (UNCLOS) and the Antarctic Environmental Protocol; see Birnie, P, 'International environmental law', in Hurrell, A and Kingsbury, B (eds), *The International Politics of the Environment*, 1992, Oxford: Clarendon, p 69.

128 See Björkbom, L, 'Resolution of environmental problems: use of diplomacy', in Carroll, JE (ed), *International Environmental Diplomacy*, 1988, Cambridge: CUP, pp 123–37.

from committing future breaches of international law. In their dissenting opinions, Judges Waldock, Onyeama, Dillard and Arechaga expressed the view that the Court could make a declaratory judgment addressing the legality of atmospheric nuclear testing. Some writers have argued that a declaratory judgment in these circumstances would be equivalent to an injunction.[129] However, the majority took the view that the Court could only make a declaration, as to the correct interpretation of international law, in the context of a specific dispute.[130] As the dispute had already been resolved, through the undertakings made by France, the ICJ was not in a position to make a declaration.[131] One wonders if the Court would have reached the same conclusion had it appreciated that, notwithstanding her commitment to cease atmospheric testing, France fully intended to continue underground testing.

In addition, it is important to note that at no stage did France recognise the jurisdiction of the ICJ in this matter. Although the ICJ does not enjoy compulsory jurisdiction in interstate disputes, it regards itself as having an inherent jurisdiction to make a preliminary decision as to whether it is competent to hear the substantive issues.[132] France refused to recognise even this limited degree of so called compulsory jurisdiction and did not enter any pleadings at any stage of the proceedings.[133] Most academic authorities are agreed that the ICJ is powerless where one State consistently refuses to recognise its jurisdiction; recourse must be had to diplomatic channels. In certain cases, the ICJ appears to represent no more than a thin veneer of legal due process disguising the realities of international politics.

To some extent, the unwillingness of the ICJ to engage environmental and health issues has left an enforcement vacuum. There have been attempts to circumvent the ICJ by persuading the EC Commission to exert its

129 See Gray, C, *Judicial Remedies in International Law*, 1987, Oxford: OUP, pp 96–107.

130 [1974] ICJ Rep 457, para 31. The Court refused to consider the requests for a declaration on the status of nuclear tests under international law in isolation from the specific dispute between the parties: 'The Court is asked to adjudge and declare that the French atmospheric tests are illegal, but at the same time it is requested to adjudge and declare that the rights of New Zealand "will be violated by any further such tests". The application thus contains a submission requesting a definition of the rights and obligations of the parties. However, it is clear that the *fons et origo* of the dispute was the atmospheric nuclear tests conducted by France in the South Pacific region, and that the original and ultimate objective of the applicant was and has remained to obtain a termination of those tests ... Thus, the dispute brought before the Court cannot be separated from the situation in which it has arisen, and from further developments which may have affected it.'

131 As Gray, *Judicial Remedies in International Law*, 1987, Oxford: OUP, p 214 states, the decision suggests that: 'problems which do not involve any direct injury to a particular State but rather affect the international community as a whole cannot be dealt with by means of a bilateral claim for a declaratory judgment.'

132 [1974] ICJ Rep 457, para 23.

133 *Ibid*, paras 13–15.

influence over Member States in respect of their activities in other parts of the world. However, the Commission is reluctant to act in such cases on the grounds that it could be perceived as attempting to exercise extraterritorial jurisdiction. This circumspection is exemplified by the proceedings in *Danielsson v Commission of the European Communities*,[134] which concerned French nuclear testing in the South Seas. This also provided the subject matter of the earlier unsatisfactory ICJ judgment in *New Zealand v France (Nuclear Tests)*.

The applicants, who were residents of Tahiti in French Polynesia, challenged a decision by the Commission not to exercise its powers under Art 34 of the EAEC Treaty in respect of French nuclear weapons testing off Mururoa Atoll. It was argued that the Commission had been wrong to conclude that its assent was not required, pursuant to the second part of Art 34,[135] before the tests could proceed. The applicants sought interim relief from the Court of First Instance (CFI) requiring immediate suspension of the tests before consideration of the substantive issues.[136] Although the Commission accepted that Art 34 could apply to military, in addition to civil experiments,[137] it concluded that its assent was not required in this case as the tests did not 'present a perceptible risk of significant exposure for workers or the general public'.[138] The applicants argued that the Commission had failed properly to consider evidence relating to the effect which some 20 years of testing had had on the environment and public health.[139] In the light of these circumstances, the applicants contended that the Commission had acted in breach of Art 34 itself,[140] Council Directive

134 Case T-219/1995 R, *Danielsson, Largenteau, and Haoa v Commission of the European Communities* [1995] ECR II-3051.

135 EAEC Treaty, Art 34: 'Any Member State in whose territories particularly dangerous experiments are to take place shall take additional health and safety measures, on which it shall first obtain the opinion of the Commission. The assent of the Commission shall be required where the effects of such experiments are liable to affect the territories of other Member States.'

136 For the ECJ and CFI's powers to grant interim relief in this context, see EAEC Treaty, Arts 157 and 158, and Council Decision (93/350/Euratom, ECSC, EEC) (OJ 1993 L144 8.6.93, p 21), Art 4.

137 Not surprisingly, France disputed this conclusion; see [1995] ECR II-3051, para 33.

138 *Ibid*, para 13. This conclusion was reached despite the fact that, by the Commission's own admission, during the verification visit, carried out pursuant to EAEC, Art 35, access had been denied to certain areas on the grounds of national security.

139 It was alleged that underwater landslides, tsunamis or tidal waves, releases of radioactive materials into the sea with consequent contamination of the food chain, leakage of nuclear fission products from nuclear waste into the biosphere, and an increased incidence of cancer in French Polynesia could all be directly attributed to nuclear testing. See *ibid*, paras 35–38.

140 *Ibid*, para 42.

(80/836/Euratom),[141] the precautionary principle,[142] customary international law,[143] human rights,[144] and Art 162 of the EAEC Treaty.[145]

However, in the event, none of these substantive issues was considered in full, as the CFI determined that the applicants did not possess the requisite *locus standi* to challenge the Commission's actions. The issue of *locus standi* is a crucial aspect of the case and shall be returned to below. At this point, it is worth considering some general issues, highlighted by the decision, relating to the role of the Commission in the policing of activities in Member State territories outside continental Europe. First, the decision demonstrates the difficulty of establishing an EC dimension in disputes of this nature. The Commission argued that it could only exercise its powers under the second paragraph of Art 34 where the territory of another Member State was threatened.[146] In this case, the nearest territory of another Member State, the UK, was Pitcairn Island, some 800 km to the east-south-east of Mururoa Atoll. In the Commission's view, this was well out of harm's way, with the result that Art 34 could not apply. Secondly, the decision demonstrates the limited nature of the enforcement powers conferred upon the Commission by the EAEC Treaty. As the Commission reached the conclusion that the assent procedure, under the second paragraph of Art 34, did not apply, it was limited to delivering a non-binding opinion under the first paragraph. Furthermore, the report of the three Commission inspectors, who had conducted the verification visit pursuant to Art 35, 'stressed that [they] had not been allowed access to certain facilities and that certain information had not been made available'.[147]

Private enforcement

Owing to the difficulties associated with enforcing environmental obligations at an international level, it is worth considering the extent to which a private party may seek to rely upon obligations deriving from international law in, for example, judicial review proceedings against an organ of the State.

---

141 *Ibid*, para 43.

142 *Ibid*, para 44. As to the status of the 'precautionary principle' in law. see below, p 288.

143 *Ibid*, para 45.

144 *Ibid*, para 46.

145 *Ibid*, para 47. Article 162 states: 'Regulations, directives and decisions of the Council and of the Commission shall state the reasons on which they are based and shall refer to any proposals or opinions which were required to be obtained pursuant to this Treaty.'

146 *Ibid*, para 48.

147 *Ibid*, para 9.

Where international standards, or principles of law, have not been formally adopted at a domestic level, it can be very difficult to enforce these standards before the domestic courts or the ECJ. This problem has been demonstrated by a number of cases in which individuals have sought to establish that an activity constitutes a threat to health.

The status of the 'precautionary principle', a concept derived from international law, fell to be determined by the English courts in *R v Secretary of State for Trade and Industry ex p Duddridge*.[148] The applicants were parents of children living near the route of a new underground power cable being installed by the National Grid Company. The parents were alarmed by a BBC *Panorama* documentary, which suggested that living in close proximity to power lines could cause leukaemia in children. They formed an action group and requested the Secretary of State to use his powers under the Electricity Act 1989 to require the National Grid Company to take measures to limit the emission of non-ionising radiation from the new cable.[149] When he refused to do so, they challenged his decision by way of judicial review on the grounds that, in making his determination, he had failed to apply the precautionary principle as required by European Community law. In the High Court, Smith J accepted that there was some evidence to suggest an increased incidence of leukaemia in sample groups living in close proximity to power cables. If the precautionary principle was binding in English law, by virtue of Art 130r (now 174) of the Treaty of Rome, Smith J stated that she would be prepared to require the Secretary of State to reconsider his decision in the light of the principle. Thus, the case centred on the status of the precautionary principle in English law. It was accepted that certain Treaty articles could give rise to obligations binding upon Member States, without the need for further implementation measures. The court was satisfied that Art 130r (now 174) did not fall into this category. Smith J considered that the principle was too broad and ill defined to create obligations in itself: 'I find quite remarkable the proposition that each State should be obliged to act alone on the basis of so general a statement of objectives and considerations'.[150] The form of words suggested that the article was merely a basis for future detailed measures in the form of secondary legislation and was not intended to create free-standing

---

148 [1996] Env LR 325.

149 The Electricity Act 1989, s 3(3)(d) places the Secretary of State under a duty 'to protect the public from dangers arising from the generation, transmission or supply of electricity'. To this end, s 29(1) empowers him to: 'make such regulations as he thinks fit for the purpose of (b) protecting the public from dangers arising from the generation, transmission or supply of electricity, from the use of electricity supplied or from the installation, maintenance or use of any electric line or electrical plant; and (c) without prejudice to the generality of (b) above, eliminating or reducing the risks of personal injury, or damage to property or interference with its use, arising as mentioned in that paragraph.'

150 (1995) 7(2) J Env L 224, p 233.

obligations: 'The status of the precautionary principle would appear to be no more than one of the principles which will underlie the policy when it is formulated.'[151]

Individuals may also face difficulties in establishing that international obligations are a relevant consideration in the use of discretionary powers. This difficulty is particularly acute where the legislation in question was not intended to implement the obligations. In *R v London Borough of Greenwich ex p W (A Minor) and Others*,[152] the applicant sought judicial review of the local authority's refusal to exercise its powers under s 14(2) of the Road Traffic Regulation Act 1984. This empowers highway authorities to prohibit or limit traffic on a road where the authority is satisfied that there is a 'likelihood of danger to the public or serious damage to the road'. The applicants were children living in close proximity to a main road in Greenwich. At times of temperature inversion it was contended that traffic fumes reached levels which were injurious to the children's health and exacerbated respiratory problems such as asthma. It was argued that the s 14(2) power could be used by the highway authority in such circumstances and that the legislation should be interpreted in the light of Council Directive (85/203/EEC) on air quality standards for nitrogen dioxide. This Directive is relevant to the EC's response to its international obligations in respect of the emission of greenhouse gases. The Court of Appeal was in no doubt that the Directive was concerned with an entirely different issue, namely, overall levels of nitrogen dioxide in the atmosphere. Restricting traffic on one road would not affect these overall levels. In any case, the court was satisfied that Parliament did not have this form of harm in contemplation when the provision was drafted: '[I]t seems to me that the phrase "the likelihood of danger to the public or serious damage to the road", refers and refers only to injury or damage directly caused by motor vehicles to persons in motor vehicles or pedestrians or to the road itself.'[153]

Private actions of this nature are clearly limited in scope; international obligations rarely filter down to a privately enforceable right or duty on the part of the polluter or regulatory authority. This raises the issue of whether there exists a mechanism by which an individual could assert a publicly enforceable right in respect of the international obligations of the State.

151 (1995) 7(2) J Env L 224, p 234.

152 [1997] Env LR 190.

153 *Ibid*, p 193, *per* Leggatt LJ.

HUMAN RIGHTS ISSUES

In recent years, a number of developments have suggested the possible emergence of 'environmental rights' or, at least, the right to a safe environment.

The right to a healthy or decent environment

At an international level, there have been various assertions to the effect that humans have a right to a healthy or decent environment. In 1972, the Stockholm UN Conference on the Human Environment resolved in Principle 1 that: 'Man has a fundamental right to freedom, equality and adequate conditions of life, in an environment of quality that permits a life of dignity and well being, and he bears a solemn responsibility to protect and improve the environment for present and future generations.'

Some 20 years later, the declaration following the Rio UN Conference on Environment and Development proclaimed in Principle 1 that: 'Human beings are at the centre of concerns for sustainable development. They are entitled to a healthy and productive life in harmony with nature.' Similar sentiments can be found in Art 24 of the African Charter on Human and Peoples' Rights which provides that: 'All peoples shall have the right to a general satisfactory environment favourable to their development.'

If recognised as a fundamental human right, the principle would be enforceable at an international level before the UN Human Rights Committee or the European Court of Human Rights at a European level. It would have provided an alternative cause of action for the populations of the South Pacific to pursue in respect of French atomic testing. However, despite support for the view that such a right should be recognised,[154] the firm consensus of opinion is that it has yet to harden into a concrete and justiciable principle of international law.[155] Indeed, there is some resistance to the development of environmental protection as a human right, as it may promote an anthropocentric approach.[156] In other words, it could promote exploitation of natural resources to the extent that this does not have a discernible impact on public health.[157] This raises the issue of the extent to

154 World Commission on Environment and Development.

155 World Commission on Environment and Development.

156 See Shelton, D, 'Human rights, environmental rights and the right to environment' (1991) 28 Stanford JIL, 103.

157 Although Birnie, PW and Boyle, AE, *International Law and the Environment*, 1992, Oxford: Clarendon, pp 193–94, argue that much international environmental regulation focuses on conservation and environmental issues which may not have a direct impact on public health. A right to a healthy environment would, they argue: 'be seen as complementary to this wider protection of the biosphere, reflecting the impossibility of separating the interests of mankind from those of the environment as a whole, or from the claims of future generations, quite apart from the intrinsic merit of a healthy environment as a foundation for human survival.'

which it may be possible to utilise existing rights as a vehicle for promoting the protection of the environment and public health.

'Derivative' environmental rights

It seems that existing human rights provisions may accommodate environmental concerns, in so far as such factors have an impact on the welfare of humans. In order to bring existing human rights provisions into play, in an environmental context, it is necessary to view harm caused by pollution from an anthropocentric perspective. This would entail identifying the public health implications of an activity.

The right to life

Perhaps the most fundamental human right is the right to life itself as set out in instruments such as Art 6(1) of the UN Covenant on Civil and Political Rights 1966, the European Convention on Human Rights 1950 and the American Convention on Human Rights 1969. As Churchill[158] points out, this right could be utilised in respect of environmental disasters which have led to loss of life such as Bhopal or Chernobyl, provided that failings on the part of the States in question can be identified. One problem with this approach is that there is considerable doubt as to whether the right to life imposes positive obligations on States to 'promote life expectancy, for example by the provision of better drinking water or less polluted air'.[159] Despite support for this interpretation,[160] the right has not been successfully utilised in an environmental context. An attempt by Canadian citizens to challenge the storage of radioactive waste in their neighbourhood, under Art 6(1) of the 1966 UN Covenant, foundered when the Human Rights Committee declined jurisdiction on the grounds that not all domestic remedies had been exhausted.[161]

---

158 Churchill, RR, 'Environmental rights in existing human rights treaties', in Boyle, A and Anderson, M (eds), *Human Rights Approaches to Environmental Protection*, 1996, Oxford: Clarendon, p 90.

159 *Ibid*.

160 This view has been expressed by the Human Rights Committee: see McGoldrick, *The Human Rights Committee*, 1991, Oxford: OUP, pp 329–30.

161 See Communication No 67/1980, *EHP v Canada* (1990) Two Selected Decisions of the Human Rights Committee 20.

The right to private life, family life, and the home

At a European level, Art 8 of the ECHR on the right to respect for private and family life and the home has proved more fruitful as a source of derivative environmental rights. The article provides as follows:

1 Everyone has the right to respect for his private and family life, his home and his correspondence.

2 There shall be no interference by a public authority with the exercise of this right except such as in accordance with the law and is necessary in a democratic society in the interests of national security, public safety or the economic well being of the country, for the prevention of disorder or crime, for the protection of health or morals, or for the protection of the rights and freedoms of others.

Early attempts to utilise the right focused on the problem of noise nuisance, usually from airports. In *Rayner*,[162] the European Court of Human Rights (ECtHR) accepted the argument that Art 8 was not restricted to direct incursions by the State into the sanctity of the home. It also covered 'indirect incursions which are unavoidable consequences of measures not at all directed against private individuals'. Article 8(2) requires the Court to balance the equities by weighing the loss to the applicant against the economic utility of the enterprise. The plane movements at Heathrow airport were judged to be necessary in a democratic society for the economic well being of the country.

This left open the issue of how serious harm would have to be before it could be said to outweigh any economic benefits associated with the activity. Later decisions suggest that activities which pose a direct threat to public health, by causing injury, illness, or disease, fall into this category.

In *López Ostra v Spain*,[163] the applicant lived in close proximity to a new liquid waste treatment plant, which had been built to deal with the by-products produced by the many leather tanneries in the area. Owing to a malfunction on start up, gas fumes, pestilential smells and contamination were released which caused nuisance and health problems to those living in the area and necessitated temporary rehousing. Several scientific reports stated that levels of hydrogen sulphide, in houses situated in proximity to the plant, were in excess of statutory limits. A paediatrician reported a link between this pollutant and various adverse health affects suffered by Mrs López Ostra's daughter including nausea, vomiting and allergic reactions. It transpired that the operators of the plant, SACURSA, had not obtained a licence and that, furthermore, the regulatory authorities had not taken any steps to enforce the licensing requirements. Having met with little success in

162 Application 9310/81, *Rayner v United Kingdom* (1986) 47 D & R 5, 12–14.

163 (1995) 20 EHRR (1) 277.

pursuing SACURSA in various actions before the domestic courts, Mrs López Ostra resorted to a human rights argument against the State on the grounds that, as a result of its omissions,[164] the State had breached, *inter alia*, Art 8 of the Convention. The court held that:

> Naturally, severe environmental pollution may affect an individual's well being and prevent them from enjoying their homes in such a way as to affect their private and family life adversely, without, however seriously endangering their health.[165]

As Ureta points out,[166] this assertion is significant in that it suggests that general nuisance and annoyance, falling short of a direct threat to health, may provide sufficient cause to invoke Art 8.[167]

López Ostra was subsequently applied in *Guerra v Italy*,[168] in which the applicants, who comprised 40 Italian nationals living in proximity to a chemicals plant engaged in the production of fertilisers, challenged the manner in which the regulatory authorities had exercised their powers. Following a series of accidents, the most serious of which occurred in 1976 and resulted in the hospitalisation of 150 people with acute arsenic poisoning, production at the plant was suspended. The ECtHR accepted the applicants' argument that the authorities' failure to formulate and implement appropriate safety and civil defence measures, in the wake of these accidents, constituted a breach of Art 8. Furthermore, lack of information regarding what, if any, measures has been adopted meant that it was not possible for inhabitants to assess the risk to themselves and their families. This was also found to amount to a breach of the article.

Interestingly, there have been similar developments in Pakistan. In *Shelah Zia v Wapda*,[169] residents protested against plans to build a grid station in a district of Islamabad on the grounds that there was increasing scientific evidence to suggest that electromagnetic fields could cause cancer in children. The Supreme Court upheld their claim that the scheme breached

---

164 The European Court of Human Rights has established that, in addition to placing obligations on States to refrain from breaching human rights, the Convention places a positive obligation on States to protect human rights from interference by others. See *Marckx v Belgium* (A/31): 2 EHRR 330, para 31; *Young, James and Webster v United Kingdom*, Applications Nos 7601/76 and 7806/77, Series B, No 39, para 168; *X and Y v Netherlands* (A/91): (1986) 8 EHRR 235, para 23.

165 (1994) 20 EHRR 277, para 51.

166 Ureta, AG, '*López Ostra v Spain*: environmental protection and the European Convention on Human Rights' [1995] Env Liability 81.

167 This is certainly borne out by the Court's acceptance in principle, in cases such as *Rayner's*, that noise nuisance is actionable under Art 8, although it could be argued that noise nuisance may result in physical health problems as a result of stress, sleep deprivation, etc.

168 (1998) 26 EHRR 357.

169 Case note by Zafar, SA and Hassan, J [1995] 2 Middle Eastern Commercial L Rev A-17.

the constitutional right to life and human dignity and that, in such circumstances, the court had the power to 'grant relief to the extent of stopping the functioning of factories which create pollution and environmental degradation'. Although the court found the evidence relating to the risk of cancer induced by exposure to electromagnetic fields to be inconclusive, it decided to apply the precautionary approach enshrined in Principle 15 of the Rio Declaration. The decision has been described as 'revolutionary' on the grounds that: 'In interpreting the constitutional right to life and to human dignity, the court has said that everyone has the right to proper food, clothing, shelter, education, health care, clean atmosphere and an unpolluted environment. For the first time, the Court [Supreme Court of Pakistan] has decided that the right to life means the right to a particular quality of life.'[170]

The most interesting aspect of these decisions is that disputes which had the appearance of tort problems were converted into 'rights' issues which were pursued against the States involved. Thus, in *López Ostra*, the applicant obtained damages for the loss she had suffered as a result of the nuisance and in *Shelah Zia*, the applicants obtained injunctive relief to stay the commencement of building work on the grid station because of the potential health threat.

Procedural rights

Owing to the difficulties associated with formulating a substantive environmental right, it has been argued that attention should be focused on procedural rights. As Douglas-Scott explains:

> Such an approach [...] seeks to ensure that those who have to live with the consequences of environmental degradation will be able to have a say in how, if and when it should occur, by guaranteeing them certain rights to information, participation and review of environmental regulation. It avoids certain problems in attempting to set appropriate standards to be maintained through some substantive right, which inevitably involves subjective value judgements.[171]

It is easier to modify procedural requirements than it is to enforce a vague and nebulous environmental right. Thus, steps can be taken to ease standing

170 Case note by Zafar, SA and Hassan, J [1995] 2 Middle Eastern Commercial L Rev A-17.

171 Douglas-Scott, S, 'Environmental rights in the European Union – Participatory democracy or democratic deficit?' in Boyle, AE and Anderson, MR (eds), *Human Rights Approaches to Environmental Protection*, 1996, Oxford: Clarendon, p 112.

requirements and provide access to environmental information.[172] This is in accordance with Principle 10 of the Rio Declaration.[173]

At present, standing requirements differ according to the nature of the proceedings and the subject matter of the dispute. In some areas, NGOs and concerned individuals have made progress in establishing *locus standi* to challenge administrative decisions in an environmental context.[174] In other areas, they have been less successful; surprisingly, the European Court of Justice has proved most reluctant to liberalise standing requirements.

This was clearly demonstrated by the CFI in *Danielsson and Others v Commission of the European Communities* regarding French nuclear tests in the South Pacific. One of the substantive arguments raised by the applicants was that the alleged health threats caused by the tests constituted a violation of the fundamental right to life as enshrined in Art 2 of the European Convention on Human Rights and Art 6 of the United Nations Covenant on Civil and Political Rights.[175] The institutions of the Community are bound to: '... respect fundamental rights, as guaranteed by the European Convention for the Protection of Human Rights and Fundamental Freedoms signed in Rome on November 4 1950 and as they result from the constitutional traditions common to the Member States, as general principles of Community Law.'[176] In the preliminary proceedings before the CFI, it fell to be determined whether the applicants had sufficient standing to pursue the matter before the ECJ. Unless this hurdle could be negotiated, the substantive issues could not be considered. The applicants challenged the actions of the Commission on the basis of Art 146 of the EAEC Treaty, which provides for judicial review of the decisions of the Commission. As regards standing, the case law which has developed in the context of the equivalent article in the Treaty of Rome, Art 230, imposes fairly stringent requirements. Generally, only those persons to whom a particular decision addressed may challenge it; other persons must satisfy the *Plaumann* test, which provides as follows:

---

172 The EC has attempted to improve access to environmental information by means of the implementation of Commission Directive (90/313/EEC) on the Freedom of Access to Environmental Information (OJ L158 23.6.90). However, there have been transposition problems in that the Directive appears somewhat vague upon issues such as which bodies are under a duty to make information available and the practical measures needed for making such information available. See Douglas-Scott, S, 'Environmental rights in the European Union – Participatory democracy or democratic deficit?' in Boyle, AE and Anderson, MR (eds), *Human Rights Approaches to Environmental Protection*, 1996, Oxford: Clarendon.

173 Principle 10 provides as follows: 'environmental issues are best handled with the participation of all concerned citizens at the relevant level. At the national level, each individual shall have appropriate access to information concerning the environment that is held by public authorities ... and the opportunity to participate in the decision making process ... Effective access to judicial and administrative proceedings, including redress and remedy, shall be provided.'

174 See *R v HMIP and MAFF ex p Greenpeace* [1993] ELM 183.

175 [1995] ECR II-3051, para 27.

176 Treaty on European Union, Art 6(2).

> Persons other then those to whom a decision is addressed may claim to be individually concerned by that decision only if it affects them by reason of certain attributes which are peculiar to them or by reason of circumstances in which they are differentiated from all other persons and if by virtue of those factors it distinguishes them individually just as in the case of the person addressed.[177]

The mere fact that one is part of a population exposed to a common risk by a decision is not sufficient to satisfy the *Plaumann* test. It is necessary to demonstrate the existence of certain attributes, which distinguish the individual from the population as a whole, thereby affording them a special interest in the matter:

> Even on the assumption that the applicants might suffer personal damage linked to the alleged harmful effects of the nuclear tests in question on the environment or on the health of the general public, that circumstance alone would not be sufficient to distinguish them individually in the same way as a person to whom the contested action is addressed, as is required by the fourth paragraph of Article 146 of the Treaty, since damage of the kind they cite could affect, in the same way, any person residing in the area in question.[178]

This case demonstrates that 'environmental rights' cannot bite unless they are integrated into all areas of policy. The fact that the court took a narrow view of standing, and determined the matter within the four corners of Art 146, resulted in the inability of the applicants to advance a viable human rights-based argument.

Nevertheless, these are problems which could be resolved through the adoption of procedural modifications. Birnie and Boyle conclude that the development of rights-based approaches in international environmental law is a strand which is worth pursuing. Encouraging individual participation ensures that those affected 'on the ground' have a means of redress and 'creates additional pressure for compliance by governments with their international obligations'.[179] There is evidence to suggest that this is a theme which the European Community wishes to pursue in future.[179a]

CONCLUSION

Self-interest and the protection of public health has provided a powerful incentive for international initiatives on environmental protection.

---

177 *Plaumann v Commission* (Case 25/62) [1963] ECR 95.

178 [1995] ECR II-3051, para 71.

179 Birnie, PW and Boyle, AE, *International Law and the Environment*, 1992, Oxford: Clarendon, p 196.

179a See Communication from the Commission, *Implementing Community Environmental Law* Com (96)500 final, Brussels, 22 October 1996.

Environmental measures have largely been prompted by concerns regarding public health. By focusing attention on the impact of pollution on the welfare of humans, it has been possible to adopt rights-based arguments as an additional means of securing environmental objectives.

However, self-interest is a double edged sword; at international level, the concept has often proved an obstacle to securing agreement on vital global environmental issues. Gillespie argues that international politics is still dominated by the pursuit of self-interest and that this rarely coincides with the best interests of the environment.[180] The problem is exemplified by the difficulties which have been experienced in securing agreement on climate change. In the climate change debate, the main difficulty is that there may be 'distinct winners and losers' in the short term.[181] Whilst, for example, small island States stand to lose as a result of continued reliance on fossil fuels and its consequences, other countries may actually benefit. In certain States, milder winters will increase the growing season. States with developing economies will argue that they need fossil fuels to continue growth and should be granted leeway in this respect as, historically, their contribution to the problem has been minimal. Finally, certain developed States wish to safeguard the economically dominant positions which they have already attained through reliance on fossil fuels. The US has pursued an unashamedly self-interest motivated agenda throughout the climate change negotiations. It has exemplified the acquisitive philosophy, advocated by Machiavelli,[182] by striving for agreement on a system of emissions trading with the intention of acquiring the lion's share of the right to pollute.

Hardin[183] explained the environmental problem by way of analogy with the historic over-grazing of common pastures in the Western US. Each herdsman knows that he can increase his profits through increasing the size of his herd, as he does not have to pay for the right to use the commons or the additional burden which will be placed upon them. Thus, the size of herds is increased exponentially until the commons, which are a finite resource, can no longer sustain the cattle:

> ... man is locked in to a system that compels him to increase his herd without limit – in a world that is limited. Ruin is the destination toward which all men

---

180 Gillespie, A, *International Environmental Law, Policy and Ethics*, 1999, Oxford: Clarendon, pp 23–27. The belief that international relations should be conducted on the basis of self-interest is deeply rooted in politics and philosophy. As an example, Gillespie cites the following passage from *Leviathan* by Thomas Hobbes: 'Every commonwealth has an absolute liberty to do what it shall judge, that is to say, what that assembly that representeth it, shall judge most conducing to their benefit.' Hobbes, T, *Leviathan*, 1976, Harmondsworth: Penguin, p 189.

181 Gillespie, A, *International Environmental Law, Policy and Ethics*, 1999, Oxford: Clarendon, p 26.

182 *Ibid*, pp 23–24.

183 Hardin, G, 'The tragedy of the commons' (1988) Sanctuary 7.

> rush, each pursuing his own best interest in a society that believes in the freedom of the commons. *Freedom in a commons brings ruin to all.*[184]

In other words, the environmental problem stems from a failure to co-operate in the utilisation of natural resources. Hardin applies his commons analogy to the problem of pollution as follows:

> The rational man finds that the cost of the waste he discharges into the commons is less than the cost of purifying his wastes before releasing them. Since this is true for everyone, we are locked into a system of 'fouling our own nest', so long as we behave only as independent, rational, free-enterprisers.[185]

The atmosphere and the seas constitute a form of *global* commons in which States have been able to discharge pollutants without meeting the costs involved. Progress will not be made at an international level until there is a realisation that we are living in a *global* commons in which it is not possible for States to export or dispose of pollutants into the wider environment without suffering the consequences. By contaminating the global environment, States are 'fouling their own nest' and hence threatening the health of their own populations. Thus, the short term economic national interests[186] pursued at an international level are incompatible with the interests of the world's populations. Whilst there may be 'winners and losers' in the short term, ultimately everyone stands to lose; global warming will not differentiate between 'developed' and 'developing' States; as UNEP has stated 'humanity is conducting an unintended, uncontrolled, globally pervasive experiment whose ultimate consequences could be second only to global nuclear war'.[187]

Hardin's argument that 'freedom in a commons brings ruin to all' is no less applicable to the global environment than it is to the common pastures of the US. No system of international law can hope to solve these problems unless it is backed by firm commitments at a political level and a genuine desire to co-operate between States. As recent events in The Hague demonstrate, these elements are still sadly lacking.[188]

---

184 Hardin, G, 'The tragedy of the commons' (1988) Sanctuary 7.

185 *Ibid*, p 8.

186 Any short term economic benefits will pale into insignificance alongside the financial consequences of failure to tackle environmental problems at an international level. Insurance liabilities caused by rising sea levels are estimated as running into trillions of dollars; this could lead to the collapse of the industry. See Weever, P, 'The greening of industry – the environment is at the top of the agenda in Britain's boardrooms' (1994) *The Sunday Telegraph*, 19 June.

187 UNEP, *Proceedings of the World Conference on the Changing Atmosphere*, 1988, Toronto.

188 As the leading article in *The Guardian*, reporting on the collapse of the Hague Conference, put it: 'Unless there is a change of heart, this meeting will go down in history as the moment when governments jettisoned the concept of global co-operation when it was most urgently needed: to save the planet itself.' 'Sins of emission: the US must act on domestic pollution' (2000) *The Guardian*, 27 November, p 21.

CHAPTER 10

PARTICULAR ISSUES OF PUBLIC HEALTH: VACCINATION

Stephanie Pywell

INTRODUCTION

Public health measures vary greatly in their impact upon individuals. Some measures, such as sanitation and water filtration, are imposed upon whole populations without adverse effect. Medical interventions such as breast cancer screening are transiently uncomfortable, but not invasive. Cervical smear tests are invasive, but have no known lasting effects. Other public health measures such as water fluoridation may affect individual recipients, and the dilemma for those responsible for determination of public policy is the extent to which public health benefits justify individual risks. Vaccination is invasive, and involves the administration of pharmaceuticals to people who are well. The benefits of vaccines are prospective and to some extent speculative, and there is concern that they may occasionally have serious permanent adverse effects upon those who receive them.

It is important to define 'vaccination'. When a person is vaccinated, an infectious agent – antigen – is introduced into her body. The aim is that the immune system will respond to the antigen by producing antibodies that will protect against the disease from which the antigen was derived. This response is immunisation. Vaccination is thus the process whose desired outcome, usually achieved in at least 90% of cases, is immunisation. The term 'immunisation' is often used by politicians and others who wish to stress the intended benefits of the process to denote vaccination. The percentage of cases in which vaccination leads to immunisation is termed the vaccine efficacy. This is usually measured as the percentage reduction in the incidence of the disease in a vaccinated population compared with that in an unvaccinated population. For example, if there were 100 cases per 10,000 people in the unvaccinated population, and 10 cases per 10,000 in the vaccinated population, the efficacy would be 90%.

Vaccines fall into two broad groups. Special vaccines are administered to people who are unusually vulnerable to particular disease – travellers, for example, or persons susceptible to chest infections. Mass vaccines are those administered to as many people as possible, usually young children, in programmes recommended by the public health authority.

Vaccination has two purposes. All vaccines aim to protect vaccinees against disease. Mass vaccines are additionally aimed at eliminating infectious disease from the population. When this occurs, even unvaccinated individuals are protected via the process of herd immunity. The respective sizes of these two benefits depend upon the incidence and severity of each disease in the relevant population, and the vulnerability of the individual. Special vaccines invariably afford greater protection to the individual than to society. There are currently no realistic prospects of eliminating influenza from the UK, or yellow fever from sub-Saharan Africa, so the benefit to each person protected from those diseases is high. Most mass vaccines, if administered to sufficiently large percentages of target populations, serve both purposes.

The dual purpose of mass vaccines raises questions about whether vaccines are therapeutic. In recent years, judges in common law jurisdictions have debated, in the context of authorising medical treatment for incompetent patients, whether it is appropriate to classify treatments as therapeutic or non-therapeutic.[1] A sensible approach is to require courts to have as their primary concern the protection of patients' human rights, but this should subsume express consideration of whether the treatment was therapeutic. The physical necessity for, and outcome of, invasive treatment should form a key element of determining whether such treatment is truly best for the patient. This approach was adopted by Brennan J in *Secretary, Department of Health and Community Services (NT) v JWB and SMB* (1992).[2]

There are various definitions of 'therapeutic'. A narrow definition is 'of or pertaining to the healing of disease', defining 'heal' as 'to make whole or sound in bodily condition; to free from disease or ailments, restore to health or soundness; to cure (of a disease or wound)'.[3] Because vaccinees are required to be well at the time vaccines are given, this definition does not encompass vaccination. A textbook definition is that a therapeutic treatment is one 'intended to benefit the particular individual'.[4] This does not apply to all vaccines: a 21st century child in the developed world derives little benefit from a vaccine such as polio – which the World Health Organisation (WHO) has declared to be eradicated from the Western Hemisphere[5] – or

1 See, eg, *Re Eve* [1986] 2 SCR 388 (Canada: distinction accepted); *In Re B (A Minor)* [1988] 1 AC 199 (England: distinction rejected); *Department of Health and Community Services (NT) v JWB and SMB* (1992) 175 CLR 218 (Australia: distinction accepted as necessary).

2 (1992) 175 CLR 218.

3 *Oxford English Dictionary*, 2nd edn, 2000, Oxford: OUP. Obtained from http://dictionary.oed.com 17 October 2000.

4 Grubb, A, *Kennedy and Grubb Medical Law*, 3rd edn, 2000, London: Butterworths, p 778.

5 Schlafly, R, 'Official vaccine policy flawed' (1999) 4 Medical Sentinel 3, pp 106–08. Obtained from http://www.hacidendapub.com/vaccine.html (24 November 2000), p 2. However, seven new cases of polio were confirmed on the island of Hispaniola in January 2001, where many children had not received the recommended three doses of vaccine. If an epidemic ensues, plans to eradicate polio from the world by 2005 may be jeopardised (Radford, T, 'Polio returns to threaten world plan for eradication' (2001) *The Guardian*, 19 January).

diphtheria. A judicial view is that a treatment is therapeutic 'when it is administered for the chief purpose of preventing, removing or ameliorating a cosmetic deformity, a pathological condition or a psychiatric disorder, provided the treatment is appropriate for and proportionate to the purpose for which it is administered'.[6] Most vaccines would probably fall within the first part of this definition, but rubella for boys would not, since the primary reason for rubella vaccination is the protection of unborn children. The second part of the judicial definition, requiring proportionality, is harder to determine, because the risks of vaccines are unknown. If the benefits to the vaccinee are small, it may not be justifiable to take an unquantified risk, which would position the vaccine outside the judicial definition. There is thus an arguable case that not all mass vaccines are therapeutic.

The WHO's 1978 Alma-Ata conference identified immunisation against the major infectious diseases as one of its primary health care aims.[7] The WHO's current vision of *Health for All in the 21st Century* includes health outcomes such as substantial reduction in the incidence of tuberculosis and the global eradication of polio and measles by 2005 and 2020 respectively.[8] The WHO has consistently recommended vaccination as an important element of international public health policy, and its global vaccination programmes have been responsible for successes such as the worldwide eradication of smallpox by May 1980.[9]

This chapter will focus on mass vaccination in Britain, drawing comparisons with the position in some other Western jurisdictions.

THE ROLE OF ETHICS AND LAW IN MASS VACCINATION

An ethical dilemma posed by mass vaccination is the conflict between community benefit and respect for individual autonomy. The latter, recognising the right to control over one's own body and the right to determine one's own medical treatment, is a value central to the ethics of medical practice.[10] Medical paternalism, allowing health professionals to

---

6 Brennan J in *Secretary, Department of Health and Community Services (NT) v JWB and SMB* (1992) 175 CLR 218.

7 World Health Organisation, *Health for All in the Twenty-first Century*, undated, Geneva: World Health Organisation. Obtained from http://www.who.int/wha-1998/pdf98/ea5.pdf (11 September 2000), p 5.

8 *Ibid*, pp 24–25; Brundtland, GH, untitled, text of speech to Global Polio Partners Summit, New York, 27 September 2000. Obtained from http://www.polioeradication.org/news.html (27 November 2000), p 1.

9 Great Britain: Department of Health, Welsh Office, Scottish Office Department of Health and DHSS Northern Ireland, Salisbury, DM and Begg, NT (eds), *1996 Immunisation Against Infectious Disease*, 1996, London: HMSO, Foreword.

10 Mason, J and McCall-Smith, R, *Law and Medical Ethics*, 1999, London: Butterworths.

decide which treatment is best, is – at least in theory – no longer acceptable. There are, however, limits to autonomy. Where the autonomous decisions of one individual conflict with the autonomy or interests of others, qualifications must be placed on the right to free choice. The overriding moral obligation to respect autonomy has been challenged by those who argue that, by focusing on the rights of individuals, we neglect the needs and interests of the community as a whole. One philosophical approach underlying such challenges is communitarianism, which advocates collective welfare, collective responsibility and a shared willingness to act with those values in mind.[11] Communitarianism recognises that the interest of the community is a value to be taken into account in medical decision making. This conflict between community values and respect for autonomy is relevant to the importance given to herd immunity in vaccination policy. It is exaggerated because the vaccinees are children who are as yet unable to exercise their autonomy.

This ethical dilemma is reflected in the law regulating medical treatment. In English law, as in most Western legal systems, a competent adult patient can only be treated with her own consent.[12] On the grounds of public policy and potential harm to others, the law places some limits on what a competent adult can consent to,[13] but it is reluctant to impose treatment on an unwilling competent patient. In *Secretary of State for the Home Department v Robb*,[14] in which a prisoner was on a hunger strike, Thorpe J commented: 'It seems to me that within this jurisdiction there is perhaps stronger emphasis on the right of an individual's self-determination when balance comes to be struck between that right and any countervailing interests of the State.' English law thus purports to prioritise respect for autonomy, while some other jurisdictions have taken a more communitarian line and have recognised State interests when determining whether medical treatment should be given.[15]

The right of self-determination in English law is not, however, supported by a doctrine of informed consent. Whereas many jurisdictions recognise that a patient has the right to any information which a reasonable prudent patient might think material to decision making,[16] in English law the adequacy of information for informed consent is determined in accordance

---

11 Harris, J, *Legal Philosophies*, 1997, London: Butterworths.

12 *Re C (Adult: Refusal of Treatment)* [1994] 1 All ER 819.

13 *R v Brown* [1994] 1 AC 212.

14 (1994) 22 BMLR 43.

15 See Flamm, A and Forster, H, 'Legal limits: when does autonomy in health care prevail?', in Freeman, M and Lewis, A, *Law and Medicine*, 2000, Current Legal Issues, Vol 3, Oxford: OUP.

16 Eg, *Reibl v Hughes* (1980]) 114 DLR (3d) 1 (Canada); *Rogers v Whittaker* (1993) 175 CLR 479 (Australia).

with what the reasonable doctor would think appropriate to tell the patient.[17] In relation to a competent adult patient, therefore, although vaccination can be given only with the consent of the patient, the information given to the patient on vaccination risks may be abridged according to medical common practice. If public health objectives influence that practice, the information may understate the risks so as to maximise uptake of vaccination. It is generally agreed, nonetheless, that the requirements for legally valid consent to medical treatment are that the consent should be freely given by a person of capacity who is appropriately informed.[18]

It is arguable that in cases of non-therapeutic medical treatment, such as when the patient is taking part in a clinical trial, respect for autonomy requires that the decision to participate should be dependent on knowing all the risks and benefits of treatment.[19] Since it is arguable that at least some mass vaccines are not therapeutic,[20] there is a case for imposing a higher burden of information disclosure for participation in mass vaccination programmes than for consent to special vaccines. This is supported by parental opinion: one survey indicated that 75.9% of parents (264 out of 368) would like to receive more information about vaccines than is routinely given to them.[21]

Where the vaccinee is a child, medical practice assumes that consent may be given on behalf of the child by a proxy – the child's parent or guardian – or the State.[22] There are limits to the treatment that can be consented to by proxy: the usual requirement is that the treatment should be in the child's 'best interests'. The courts have been wary of allowing parents to consent to non-therapeutic treatments such as sterilisation, cosmetic surgery, bone marrow donation and blood tests to determine paternity, unless it can be established that the treatment fulfils this requirement in some way.[23] The interests of the community would therefore be unlikely to justify any potentially harmful invasive treatment on the child's body. If, however, it were shown that it was in the child's wider best interests to live in a community which was disease-free, and if the risks posed to the child by

17 *Sidaway v Board of Governors of the Bethlem Royal Hospital* [1985] 1 All ER 643.

18 Stauch, M and Wheat, K with Tingle, J, *Sourcebook on Medical Law*, 1998, London: Cavendish Publishing, p 115. Grubb, A, *Kennedy and Grubb Medical Law*, 3rd edn, 2000, London: Butterworths, p 592.

19 *Halushka v University of Saskatchewan* (1965) 53 DLR (2d) 436. See Mason, J and McCall-Smith, R, *Law and Medical Ethics*, 1999, London: Butterworths.

20 See pp 300–01.

21 Pywell, S, 'Vaccination and other altruistic medical treatments: should autonomy or communitarianism prevail?' (2000) 4 Medical Law International 223, p 237.

22 *Re W* [1992] 3 WLR 758.

23 See, eg, *Re H (A Minor) (Blood Tests: Parental Rights)* [1996] 4 All ER 28; *Re Y (Transplant: Bone Marrow)* (1996) 35 BMLR 111.

vaccination were small, then valid proxy consent could be given. Any such consent should, however, be fully informed. This view, too, finds support among parents: a study showed that 68% of parents (249 out of 346) desired more information before they accepted vaccines for their children than if the vaccines had been for themselves.[24]

The balance between community interests and respect for individual autonomy is a matter for national legislatures. Although their vaccine schedules differ, Britain, Canada and the US share the WHO's aim of eliminating or reducing the incidence of infectious diseases via herd immunity. This approach can be contrasted with the approach to vaccination in Japan, which prioritises the protection of individual children over benefits to society.[25] Japanese children do not receive pertussis vaccine, for example, until they are over two years old, and the eradication of the disease in this age group prevents infection in infants.[26]

Some States which favour herd immunity have laws reflecting the priority given to societal interests over individuals' rights of self-determination. In the US, for example, many States have laws requiring proof of immunity to the primary and secondary schedule diseases[27] as a condition of school entry. The laws vary, some applying only to admission to kindergarten and some to admission to every grade. Rubella vaccination is required by 50 States at school entry, but only 41 States for students in all grades.[28] Certain vaccinations are thereby effectively compulsory, and their administration can be enforced via the usual public health measures of administrative orders, penalties or injunctions.[29] Vaccination against the wishes of the individual has been upheld by the Supreme Court, even where the vaccination is not for the benefit of the individual or is refused on religious grounds.[30] France also has laws requiring children to be vaccinated against smallpox, diphtheria, tetanus, polio and tuberculosis.[31]

Vaccination is not currently compulsory in Britain. Smallpox vaccination was made compulsory in 1853 following a series of Acts 'designed to extend

24 Pywell, SM, *Compensation for Vaccine Damage*, 2001, unpublished PhD thesis, University of Hertfordshire, pages not finalised at time of writing.

25 Ueda, K *et al*, 'Aseptic meningitis caused by measles-mumps-rubella vaccine in Japan' (1995) 346 The Lancet 702.

26 *Loveday v Renton* (1982) *The Times*, 31 March; Lexis transcript, p 4.

27 These are the diseases against which vaccines are routinely offered in infancy and early childhood respectively. They are detailed at pp 308–13.

28 Reef, SE, 'Rubella', in Wallace, RB (ed), *Maxcy-Roxenau-Last Public Health and Preventive Medicine*, 1998, Stanford, Connecticut: Appleton and Lange, p 97.

29 Richards, EP and Rathburn, KC, 'Public health law', in *ibid*, pp 1148–49. See also Chapter 3 by Robyn Martin p 83 *et seq*.

30 *Ibid*, pp 1151–52.

31 *Code de la Santé Publique*, Chapître II, Arts L5–10.

the practice of vaccination'.[32] Vaccination remained compulsory until the middle of the 20th century, when statute provided that each local authority should arrange for medical practitioners to vaccinate against smallpox and diphtheria.[33] In 1977, this was amended to require only that all medical practitioners should be able to participate in vaccination.[34]

The withdrawal of legal involvement in vaccination in Britain between the mid 19th century and the late 20th century probably reflects reduced public interest in, and concern about, infectious disease. During this period, sanitary, medical and socio-economic advances hugely reduced disease-associated mortality and morbidity, and most childhood diseases are no longer considered dangerous. The same cannot be said of the developing world, where the greater urgency of disease eradication might justify more intrusive vaccination laws.

In the developed world, however, there has been considerable recent concern about the possible adverse effects of vaccines. This concern is at least partly a result of the virtual elimination of many of the diseases which posed a threat to earlier generations, such that today's parents are less keenly aware of the benefits of vaccination and very conscious of possible vaccine risks. In one study of pertussis vaccine uptake, the main threat to children's health was perceived to come from the vaccine rather than from the disease itself.[35]

In Britain, therefore, vaccination policy is now determined by practice rather than law. The only statutory involvement in vaccination is in the provision of a system of financial recompense for those who claim to have been injured by the administration of vaccines. Given that mass vaccines are by their nature administered to as many children in any age cohort as possible, the lack of related law merits brief consideration. Statute law includes substantial protection for adults in the workplace, for consumers and for personal data. It is possible to argue that these issues are of importance to law makers, who are usually healthy, financially solvent, competent (usually male) adults. A contrast can be drawn with the dearth of law protecting those who are ill. Aside from the Mental Health Acts, most medical law is case law, and most cases arise when patients need to challenge unregulated medical decisions. A body of common law has thus developed in respect of such relatively rare events as the non-consensual sterilisation of incompetent patients. The recipients of mass vaccines are

32 Vaccination Act 1853 – 'An Act further to extend and make compulsory the practice of vaccination' – 16 and 17 Vict c 100.

33 National Health Service Act 1946, s 76 and Sched 10, Pt II, which came into force in 1948.

34 National Health Service Act 1977, s 53.

35 Gill, E and Sutton, S, 'Immunisation uptake: the role of parental attitudes', in Hey, V (ed), *Immunisation Research: A Summary Volume*, 1998, London: Health Education Authority, p 13.

amongst the most vulnerable people in society, yet they are unprotected in Britain by either statute or common law. Vaccination policy is determined by population-scale health concerns, and high levels of vaccine coverage are regularly quoted in Parliament as positive indicators of public health. There is certainly scope, in such a situation, for political expediency to have a greater effect on policy than does concern for the rights of individuals.

THE ADMINISTRATIVE FRAMEWORK OF VACCINATION IN BRITAIN

One consequence of parents' reduced fear of infectious disease has been that, although more childhood vaccinations have been available from the late 1950s, uptake of vaccination has been variable. Overt political intervention came in the 1987 White Paper *Promoting Better Health*,[36] which first mooted the idea of financial incentives for GPs who achieved high levels of vaccination coverage amongst children on their patient lists. General practitioners rejected this proposal 3:1, but that did not prevent it from being given effect in the new GP contract introduced in 1990, and the maximum target payment now stands at £2,730. The success of this initiative was such that by 1992, child vaccination was no longer regarded as a key area of public health improvement because it was considered to be sufficiently established. It was, however, stated that: 'the emphasis must be on sustaining and building on progress which has been made already – such as ... childhood immunisation (for which the Government has set a target of 95% uptake by 1995, the existing target of 90% for all such immunisations having been achieved in May 1992).'[37] The GP incentive system is a primary cause of pressure on parents to consent to their child's vaccination,[38] and it is arguable that consent given under pressure is not legally valid.[39]

Official publications and statements invariably refer to the desirability of achieving high levels of vaccination uptake. Health visitors discuss vaccination with potential parents ante-natally. One study found that most health visitors view their role as promoting vaccination uptake, varying from 'mild encouragement, to pushing, and to chasing up defaulters'.[40]

36 Department of Health and Social Security, *Promoting Better Health*, Cmd 249, 1987, London: HMSO.

37 Department of Health, *The Health of the Nation: A Strategy for Health in England*, Cmd 1986, 1992, London: HMSO.

38 Pywell, S, 'Vaccination and other altruistic medical treatments: should autonomy or communitarianism prevail?' (2000) 4 Medical Law International 223, p 232.

39 See above, p 303.

40 Mayall, B and Foster, MC, *Child Health Care: Living with Children, Working for Children*, 1989, Oxford: Heinemann Nursing, quoted in Bedford, H and Kendall, S, *Immunisation: Health Professionals' Information Needs – A Review of the Literature*, 1998, London: Health Education Authority, p 15.

Another found that health professionals legitimised exerting pressure to vaccinate by their conviction that vaccination was beneficial.[41] Because many new parents are overwhelmed by their responsibilities and are very tired, they may feel unable to challenge or resist well intended pressure of this kind.

Unsolicited appointments for each of the visits required by the primary and secondary vaccine schedules are sent to children's home addresses. The appointment slips are generated by health authorities' computerised child health records. Appointments are offered at the mother's chosen venue, which is ascertained by the health visitor during a home visit 14 days after the child's birth. If two appointments are missed without reason, the child's record is suspended and a report is sent to the health visitor. She will then contact the parents to discuss the matter.[42] If she advises the health authority that a parent has refused a particular vaccine, no further appointments are sent. One result of the automated appointments procedure is that some parents believe that vaccines are compulsory, and others feel they have no real opportunity to decline vaccination.[43]

It is agreed by most public health commentators that vaccination in Britain should remain optional.[44] If this is so, all parents should be made expressly aware that they may decline vaccination for their children. They must also be confident that they will not suffer any detriment, such as being removed from a GP's patient list, if they do so. The danger of such an approach is that more parents might opt for their children to be 'free riders'. Such people benefit from herd immunity, but run none of the possible risks associated with vaccination. Herd immunity would then cease to exist, and those who cannot be vaccinated for medical reasons would become vulnerable to preventable diseases, defeating one of the principal aims of mass vaccination. Another effect of reduced herd immunity would be that people would tend to contract diseases later in life, when the effects are more serious. The balance between the objective of eliminating infectious

---

41 Alderson, P *et al*, 'Childhood immunisation: support to health professionals', in Hey, V, *Immunisation Research: A Summary Volume*, 1998, London: Health Education Authority, p 24.

42 Personal conversation with the East Hertfordshire Health Authority Child Health Department, 20 December 2000.

43 Oral and written comments made by parents interviewed during research for PhD thesis, 1999.

44 Eg, Dr David Salisbury, Principal Medical Officer, Communicable Disease branch, Department of Health, speaking at the Healthcare Forum *Vaccines and Health*, University of Hertfordshire, 10 December 1999. See also Bartlett, P, 'Doctors as fiduciaries: equitable regulation of the doctor-patient relationship' (1997) 5 Med L Rev 193, p 216; and Bradley, P, 'Should childhood immunisation be compulsory? (1999) JME 25, pp 330–34.

diseases and respecting patient autonomy is delicate. As King has remarked: '(t)he recurring challenge for public health authorities is to find the best way to communicate with the public, so that they truly are informed on the relative risks and benefits of a vaccination programme.'[45]

THE DISEASES AGAINST WHICH MASS VACCINATION IS OFFERED IN THE WEST

Diphtheria

Diphtheria is an acute respiratory infection which can lead to obstruction of the airways and death. An effective mass vaccine became available in the 1930s, and greatly reduced the incidence of the disease. The vaccine was introduced to developing countries by the WHO in the late 1970s, and global coverage is now 80%, including most countries outside Africa. This has been demonstrably successful: the number of cases reported to the WHO declined from over 70,000 in 1974 to 20,444 in 1992.[46]

The present situation is that diphtheria has been virtually eliminated from most developed countries, and is reducing in developing countries. Mass vaccination in developed countries is deemed necessary to maintain protection against infection via unimmunised immigrants. The continuing importance of mass vaccination is demonstrated in the former USSR, where there were very low levels of diphtheria from the early 1960s to the late 1980s, but 125,000 cases and 4,000 deaths between 1990 and 1995. The WHO responded by ensuring that all the States had sufficient stocks of the vaccine, and by re-emphasising the benefits of the vaccine and the risks of the disease.[47]

Tetanus

Tetanus is caused by bacilli found in soil, dust, faeces and on the skin. The toxin causes agonising muscular contractions which can lead to respiratory failure, pneumonia, malnutrition and death. The tetanus bacillus cannot be eradicated, but the disease can. A vaccine became available in the 1930s, and

45 King, S, 'Vaccination policies: individual rights v community health' (1999) BMJ 319, p 1148.

46 Vitek, C, 'Diphtheria' in Wallace, RB (ed), *Maxcy-Roxenau-Last Public Health and Preventive Medicine*, 1998, Stanford, Connecticut: Appleton and Lange, p 106.

47 *Ibid.*

has been routinely used in mass infant vaccination in Britain since 1961. Five doses are believed sufficient to confer lifelong immunity to the disease.

The disease is now uncommon in developed countries: there were no more than 10 cases in Britain in any year between 1990 and 1995.[48] In developing countries, neonatal tetanus caused by contamination of the umbilical stump caused an estimated 490,000 deaths in 1994.[49] The WHO aims to eliminate neonatal tetanus from the world.[50] This involves ensuring a high level of coverage of at least two doses of vaccine amongst women of childbearing age, to enable transplacental transfer, and ensuring that babies are delivered hygienically.

Pertussis

Pertussis (whooping cough) is a highly infectious disease characterised by a paroxysmal cough accompanied by a whooping sound. Complications, which tend to be most serious in babies under six months old, can include brain damage, lung damage and death.[51] The killed whole-cell vaccine used in Britain has been available since the 1950s, and has significantly reduced the incidence of the disease: there were previously an average of 100,000 reported cases annually in Britain, and the maximum number of cases in any year since 1988 has been 5,000. The efficacy of the vaccine is at least 80% after three doses. There were epidemics of pertussis in Britain in 1977/79 and 1981/83, when vaccine coverage fell to 35% following public concern about the safety of the vaccine.[52] The US has addressed similar concerns by developing acellular pertussis vaccine, now routinely used in the trivalent diphtheria-tetanus-acellular pertussis vaccine (DTaP). Some studies have

48 Great Britain: Department of Health, Welsh Office, Scottish Office Department of Health and DHSS Northern Ireland, Salisbury, DM and Begg, NT (eds), *1996 Immunisation Against Infectious Disease*, 1996, London: HMSO, p 206.

49 Prevots, DR and Sutter, RW, 'Tetanus', in Wallace, RB (ed), *Maxcy-Roxenau-Last Public Health and Preventive Medicine*, 1998, Stanford, Connecticut: Appleton and Lange, pp 102–03.

50 World Health Organisation, *Handbook of Resolutions and Decisions of the World Health Assembly and the Executive Board*, 3rd edn, 1993, Geneva: WHO, Vol 3, Resolution 42.32.

51 Strebel, PM, Guris, D and Wassilak, SGF, 'Pertussis', in Wallace, RB (ed), *Maxcy-Roxenau-Last Public Health and Preventive Medicine*, 1998, Stanford, Connecticut: Appleton and Lange, p 98; Great Britain: Department of Health, Welsh Office, Scottish Office Department of Health and DHSS Northern Ireland, Salisbury, DM and Begg, NT (eds), *1996 Immunisation Against Infectious Disease*, 1996, London: HMSO, p 115; Howson, C, Howe, C and Fineberg, H, *Adverse Effects of Pertussis and Rubella Vaccines*, 1991, Washington DC: National Academy Press, pp 11–14.

52 Great Britain: Department of Health, Welsh Office, Scottish Office Department of Health and DHSS Northern Ireland, Salisbury, DM and Begg, NT (eds), *1996 Immunisation Against Infectious Disease*, 1996, London: HMSO, pp 155–57.

indicated that this vaccine is associated with a lower incidence of adverse reactions than its whole-cell counterpart.[53]

Much of the decline in mortality from whooping cough in Britain had occurred before the vaccine was introduced, indicating the influence of other factors. The death rate in Britain is now around one per 100,000 cases overall, although the equivalent figure for infants under six months old is 500 in 100,000.[54] The WHO estimates that global vaccine coverage is 80%, and that there are still 39 m cases of whooping cough, leading to 350,000 deaths, annually.[55]

Haemophilus influenzae B

Haemophilus influenzae B (Hib) is an organism which can cause bacterial meningitis and other invasive diseases such as pneumonia and epiglottitis in children, 95% of whom are under five years of age. Hib-related diseases have a death rate of 3–6% in developed countries, and 20–30% of cases lead to blindness, mental retardation, seizures or hearing loss.[56] Before widespread vaccination, 0.16% of children in the Britain contracted a disease caused by Hib. The conjugate vaccine has an efficacy of 95% after three doses, and has dramatically reduced the incidence of Hib diseases in Britain, from 1,259 cases in 1989 to 39 in 1995.[57]

Poliomyelitis

Poliomyelitis (polio) is an acute viral infection of the intestines which can attack the central nervous system leading to permanent paralysis or death. The parenteral (injected) vaccine, developed in the 1950s by Salk, contains killed whole viruses and is therefore known as inactivated polio vaccine (IPV). It was largely superseded by the Sabin oral polio vaccine (OPV),

---

53 Strebel, PM, Guris, D and Wassilak, SGF, 'Pertussis', in Wallace, RB (ed), *Maxcy-Roxenau-Last Public Health and Preventive Medicine*, 1998, Stanford, Connecticut: Appleton and Lange, p 100.

54 Howson, C, Howe, C and Fineberg, H, *Adverse Effects of Pertussis and Rubella Vaccines*, 1991, Washington DC: National Academy Press, p 14.

55 Strebel, PM, Guris, D and Wassilak, SGF, 'Pertussis', in Wallace, RB (ed), *Maxcy-Roxenau-Last Public Health and Preventive Medicine*, 1998, Stanford, Connecticut: Appleton and Lange, p 99.

56 Great Britain: Department of Health, Welsh Office, Scottish Office Department of Health and DHSS Northern Ireland, Salisbury, DM and Begg, NT (eds), *1996 Immunisation Against Infectious Disease*, 1996, London: HMSO, p 77; Wenger, JD, Fraser, DW and Broome, CV, '*Haemophilus influenzae* infections', in *ibid*, Wallace, p 116.

57 Great Britain: Department of Health, Welsh Office, Scottish Office Department of Health and DHSS Northern Ireland, Salisbury, DM and Begg, NT (eds), *1996 Immunisation Against Infectious Disease*, 1996, London: HMSO, p 77.

which contains live attenuated (weakened) strains of the three types of polio virus. Polio has now been eradicated from most of the developed world, and the vast majority of cases which occur in the US and Britain are due to the infection of non-immune individuals by live vaccine in the stools of newly vaccinated infants.[58] America's routine vaccine schedule is therefore now based primarily on IPV, with OPV being used only in circumstances of unusually high risk.[59] OPV is still routinely used in Britain.

The global eradication of polio is being sought by routinely administering three doses of OPV to high percentages of infants, and additionally vaccinating young children on National Immunisation Days. In some countries – such as India, which accounted for 70% of the world's reported polio cases in January 2000 – three doses do not offer sufficient protection against the high levels of wild polio virus, and additional intensive vaccination campaigns are sometimes conducted.

Meningococcal C

Meningococcal C is the bacterium which causes one form of meningitis, an inflammation of the lining of the brain and spinal cord. The initial presentation is often very mild, but within hours sufferers can become dangerously ill. If meningitis is accompanied by septicaemia, it can lead rapidly to coma and death.[60] From July 1998 to July 1999 there were 1,530 cases of meningitis C infection in Britain, with 150 deaths. The vaccine was introduced into Britain in autumn 1999, and is discussed below, pp 318–19.

Measles

Measles is an acute viral illness whose symptoms include spots, rash, fever, conjunctivitis and bronchitis. It can have severe complications including

58 Great Britain: Department of Health, Welsh Office, Scottish Office Department of Health and DHSS Northern Ireland, Salisbury, DM and Begg, NT (eds), *1996 Immunisation Against Infectious Disease*, 1996, London: HMSO, p 178; Sutter, RW and Cochi, SL, 'Poliomyelitis', in Wallace, RB (ed), *Maxcy-Roxenau-Last Public Health and Preventive Medicine*, 1998, Stanford, Connecticut: Appleton and Lange, p 124.

59 Source: undated and anonymous *Recommended Childhood Immunization Schedule United States, January – December 2000*, received with personal communication from Centers for Disease Control and Prevention, Department of Health and Human Services, Atlanta, 12 October 2000.

60 Health Education Authority, *Meningitis C – Reduce the Risk*, 1999, London: Department of Health, p 2.

brain damage and death, although deaths from measles in the developed world had declined to virtually zero before the introduction of a vaccine.[61] Before vaccination, virtually all children contracted measles. It is highly contagious, and one sufferer can transmit the disease to 12–18 others. A live attenuated single measles vaccine was introduced in Britain in 1968, and was eventually administered to about 50% of children. This increased to 80% in 1988 when the trivalent measles-mumps-rubella (MMR) vaccine, whose measles component has an efficacy of 90–95%, was introduced. The vaccine is now given to approximately 88% of children. This is lower than the 95% coverage estimated to be required to eliminate the disease, and occasional outbreaks occur.[62]

In the developing world, where there are still one million measles-related deaths per year, the vaccine is given at nine months of age, because it is too risky to wait until children are one year old.[63]

Mumps

Mumps is characterised by parotid swelling. It is not usually serious, but its side effects can include deafness and epididimo-orchitis,[64] and in rare cases it can cause encephalitis or meningitis leading to death.[65] Single mumps vaccine was introduced into the US in 1977. The vaccine within MMR, whose efficacy is 90–95%, has been in widespread use in Britain since 1988. There were 2,021 reported cases of mumps in Britain in 1995.[66]

There is no WHO target for global elimination, because the disease has an insufficient impact on health in developing countries.[67]

---

61 Great Britain: Department of Health, Welsh Office, Scottish Office Department of Health and DHSS Northern Ireland, Salisbury, DM and Begg, NT (eds), *1996 Immunisation Against Infectious Disease*, 1996, London: HMSO, p 97; Bedford, H and Elliman, D, *Childhood Immunisation: A Review*, 1998, London: Health Education Authority, pp 50–51.

62 Boseley, S, 'Fear of epidemic as jab rate drops', *The Guardian*, 5 January 2001.

63 Orenstein, WA, Redd, SC, Markowitz, LE and Hinman, AR, 'Measles', in Wallace, RB (ed), *Maxcy-Roxenau-Last Public Health and Preventive Medicine*, 1998, Stanford, Connecticut: Appleton and Lange, pp 92–93.

64 Stratton, K, Howe, C and Johnston, R (eds), *Adverse Events Associated with Childhood Vaccines: Evidence Bearing on Causality*, 1994, Washington DC: National Academy Press, p 121.

65 Wharton, M, 'Mumps', in Wallace, RB (ed), *Maxcy-Roxenau-Last Public Health and Preventive Medicine*, 1998, Stanford, Connecticut: Appleton and Lange, p 93.

66 Great Britain: Department of Health, Welsh Office, Scottish Office Department of Health and DHSS Northern Ireland, Salisbury, DM and Begg, NT (eds), *1996 Immunisation Against Infectious Disease*, 1996, London: HMSO, pp 129–30.

67 Wharton, M, 'Mumps', in Wallace, RB (ed), *Maxcy-Roxenau-Last Public Health and Preventive Medicine*, 1998, Stanford, Connecticut: Appleton and Lange, p 94.

Rubella

Rubella (German measles) is usually a very mild disease which often has no symptoms. It has few serious complications,[68] but the disease became the subject of medical interest in 1940 when it was realised that its contraction during pregnancy could cause congenital rubella syndrome (CRS), which involves numerous birth defects. In Britain, women and teenage girls were able to receive a 97–98% effective single vaccine from 1970, and 97–98% of this population had been vaccinated by 1987. In order to eliminate CRS, the vaccine was included in the mass-administered MMR from 1988.[69] There are now usually fewer than 10 annual cases of CRS in Britain, mainly amongst mothers born elsewhere.

THE PRIMARY AND SECONDARY SCHEDULES IN THE WEST

The primary and secondary schedules consist of the vaccines that are routinely administered to children who have not yet entered full-time education.

At present, the primary and secondary schedules in Britain are as shown in Table 1:

Table 1: UK primary and secondary schedule vaccines

Age	Vaccine
2 months	Diphtheria-tetanus-pertussis-Hib (DTP-Hib)
	Polio
	Meningococcal C
3 months	DTP-Hib
	Polio
	Meningococcal C
4 months	DTP-Hib
	Polio
	Meningococcal C
13 months	Measles-mumps-rubella (MMR)
4–5 years	Diphtheria-tetanus (DT)
	MMR

68 Howson, C, Howe, C and Fineberg, H, *Adverse Effects of Pertussis and Rubella Vaccines*, 1991, Washington DC: National Academy Press, pp 19–21; Great Britain: Department of Health, Welsh Office, Scottish Office Department of Health and DHSS Northern Ireland, Salisbury, DM and Begg, NT (eds), *1996 Immunisation Against Infectious Disease*, 1996, London: HMSO, p 132; Reef, SE, 'Rubella', in Wallace, RB (ed), *Maxcy-Roxenau-Last Public Health and Preventive Medicine*, 1998, Stanford, Connecticut: Appleton and Lange, pp 95–96.

69 Bedford, H and Elliman, D, *Childhood Immunisation: A Review*, 1998, London: Health Education Authority, p 39.

This schedule was designed to be practical, and in some cases immunological perfection has been sacrificed in order to maintain simplicity and a relatively low number of visits to vaccination clinics.[70] In general, there is a sufficiently high uptake of these vaccines for herd immunity to be maintained. This is the principal aim of vaccination in Britain; in the words of a public health epidemiologist: 'the aim of mass immunisation is to improve the health of the public, the population, by preventing preventable disease.'[71]

The primary and secondary schedules recommended by the Canadian National Advisory Committee on Immunisation[72] are more complex, as shown in Table 2:

Table 2: Canadian primary and secondary schedule vaccines

Age	Vaccine
2 months	Hepatitis B
	DTP
	Polio
	Hib
4 months	Hepatitis B
	DTP
	Polio
	Hib
6 months	Hepatitis B
	DTP
	Polio (only if IPV used; not required for OPV)
	Hib
12 months	MMR
18 months	DTP
	Polio
	Hib
	MMR
4–6 years	DTP
	Polio

Territories and provinces within Canada produce their own vaccination schedules which vary from that in Table 2, but the differences are few and

70 Source: personal interview with Dr Norman Begg, Consultant Epidemiologist at the Public Health Laboratory Service, Colindale, London on 13 July 1999.

71 *Ibid*.

72 Source: http://www.hc-sc.gc.ca/hpb/lcdc/publicat/ccdr/97vol23/imm_sup/imm_e_e.html (24 November 2000).

minor. The most significant is in the timing of MMR vaccines – Prince Edward Island offers the first dose at 15, rather than 12 months, and in four schedules the second dose is given at age 4–6 years, rather than 18 months. The recommended schedule involves six vaccination visits, compared with five in Britain. The programme is designed to achieve the elimination or reduction of each infectious disease by a specified date. These goals are to be achieved by attaining specified target levels of vaccination coverage of children in particular age groups. The goals and targets were set in 1996 and reviewed in 1997.[73] Progress towards all the goals was being made by 19 June 1998 – the date when the 1997 review was last updated on the internet – but no target for 1997 had been met nationally.

The primary and secondary schedules in the US[74] are even more complex, and are shown in Table 3:

Table 3: US primary and secondary schedule vaccines

Age	Vaccine
0–2 months	Hepatitis B
1–4 months	Hepatitis B
2 months	Diphtheria-tetanus-acellular pertussis (DTaP)
	Hib
	Polio (inactivated vaccine)
4 months	DTaP
	Hib
	Polio (inactivated vaccine)
6 months	DTaP
	Hib
6–18 months	Hepatitis B
	Polio (inactivated vaccine)
12 –15 months	Hib MMR
12–18 months	Varicella (chicken pox)*
15–18 months	DTaP
4–6 years	DTaP
	Polio (inactivated vaccine)
	MMR

73 Canada: Health Protection Branch, 1997, Chapter 3, pp 1–4 and 1998, pp 4–6. No National Report on Immunisation for 1998–2000 was available via the internet on 4 December 2000, despite the published intention (December 1999/January 2000) of Canada's Population and Public Health Branch to produce the Reports annually.

74 Source: undated and anonymous *Recommended Childhood Immunization Schedule* [contd]

* Varicella is recommended only for children deemed by a health care provider to be 'susceptible', that is, those who have not been vaccinated and who lack a reliable history of chicken pox.

The aim of the American schedules has been described by a British consultant epidemiologist as: 'immunological perfection ... where vaccines are given at very prescribed intervals which are done so as to generate the best immune response.'[75] The US Vaccines for Children (VFC) programme provides for vaccines to be purchased federally and made available to children who are Medicaid-enrolled, not covered by health insurance, covered by health insurance which does not include vaccination, or who are American Indian or Alaskan Native. The aim of VFC is to 'combine the efforts of public and private providers to help accomplish and sustain vaccine coverage goals'.[76] The public funding available to VFC indicates the priority given to vaccination in a jurisdiction where much health care is necessarily to be privately funded.

ONE-OFF VACCINATION CAMPAIGNS

Two one-off mass vaccination campaigns took place in Britain between 1994 and 2000. The campaigns are of interest because they illustrate a number of legal and ethical issues.

In October 1994, all children aged five to 16 years were offered the opportunity to be vaccinated with a divalent measles-rubella (MR) vaccine. The primary schedule had, since 1988, included a dose of MMR vaccine, administered at around 15 months of age. It was known that not all children had received this, and that the measles component of the vaccine had an efficacy of about 90%. The belief that 14% of schoolchildren in England and Wales were therefore not immune to the disease, coupled with an epidemic of 5,000 cases in Scotland in 1993–94, led to official fears of a measles epidemic. The decision to offer to vaccinate all schoolchildren against the disease was made public via an advertising campaign which aimed to make parents fear the potentially serious side effects of measles – 'blindness, brain damage, and even death'[77] – even though these were then extremely uncommon in the developed world.

---

74 [contd] *United States, January – December 2000*, received with personal communication from Centers for Disease Control and Prevention, Department of Health and Human Services, Atlanta, 12 October 2000.

75 Source: personal interview with Dr Norman Begg, Consultant Epidemiologist at the Public Health Laboratory Service, Colindale, London on 13 July 1999.

76 USA: Centers for Disease Control, *Vaccines For Children (VFC) Program Overview*, undated. Obtained from http://www.cdc.gov/nip/vfc/about.htm (24 November 2000), p 1.

77 Quotation from television advertisement shown in Britain in 1994.

Vaccines were administered at schools to all children whose parents had not expressly withheld consent – non-response to the notification of the campaign was taken to indicate consent. The leaflet sent to parents stated that the potential epidemic 'will happen next year unless we immunise children now'. It stated that side effects from the vaccine were likely to be 'uncommon ...very mild [and] likely to disappear quickly', although the leaflet sent to health professionals indicated that up to 25% of adolescent girls could develop joint pains. Parents who withheld consent have reported being subject to considerable pressure to accept the vaccine, and one child recalls being the only one in her class who did not receive it.[78] The vaccines were administered by school nurses. It was reported that one vaccine was administered every 30 seconds, reducing the cost per child to 62 pence.[79]

This campaign was strongly criticised in the Bulletin of Medical Ethics. A series of articles disputes the reality of the predicted epidemic and questions why rubella vaccine was included. The accuracy of the information given to parents is criticised. The author – apparently Dr Richard Nicholson, the journal's editor – questions the propriety of the tendering method applied in the awarding of the contracts for vaccine supply.[80] He also asserts that the campaign constituted research because the divalent vaccine had not been used anywhere else in the world. Two doses of the trivalent MMR vaccine were already in routine use in other jurisdictions, but the omission of the mumps component was unprecedented.

One of the British Government's advisers has publicly agreed that the leaflet sent to parents before the campaign was less than ideal: '[C]ertainly leaflets can be improved. I myself think there was a problem with the 1994 leaflet. It should have had more information about other sources of information ...'[81] It breaches medical ethics to understate vaccine risks and to overstate disease risks in order to maximise uptake of a vaccine whose value is unproven. The official report into adverse events attributable to the campaign identified 530 serious reactions from over 7 m vaccinees.[82] The statement that no child died as a result of the campaign is inconsistent with the payment by the Vaccine Damage Payments Unit of two statutory awards in respect of deceased children.[83]

---

78 Personal oral accounts from individuals whose anonymity is respected.

79 Anonymous, 'News' (1994) Bulletin of Medical Ethics 102, pp 3–5; Roberts, J, 'A horrendous gap in research in this country' (1995) *The Independent*, 7 October.

80 Anonymous, 'News' (1994) Bulletin of Medical Ethics 102, pp 3–5; Anonymous, 'UK measles campaign' (1995) Bulletin of Medical Ethics 104, pp 3–4; Anonymous, 'Measles and deception' (1995) Bulletin of Medical Ethics 110, pp 3–9; Anonymous, 'Measles and rubella again' (1996) Bulletin of Medical Ethics 114, pp 13–23.

81 Dr Robert Aston, a member of the Joint Committee on Vaccination and Immunisation, speaking on BBC Radio Four, *File on Four*, 9 December 1997.

82 Bedford, H and Elliman, D, *Childhood Immunisation: A Review*, 1998, London: Health Education Authority, p 35.

83 BBC Radio Four, *File on Four*, 9 December 1997.

In autumn 1999, a campaign began to vaccinate everyone under 19 years of age with meningococcal C vaccine. This bacterium is responsible for one strain of meningitis, the disease which probably holds the greatest fear for 21st century parents in the developed world. The first groups to receive the vaccine were those at highest risk: babies, toddlers and young people aged 15 to 17 years. During 2000, the vaccine was offered, at school, to all children.[84] Consent forms were required to be returned before a child was vaccinated. This requirement for active, rather than passive, consent was ethically appropriate for a non-essential medical intervention. In the case of at least one school, however, parents were unaware of the campaign until their 10 and 11 year old children told them they had been vaccinated.[85] Such vaccines were administered unlawfully because there was no valid consent.

The success of the vaccine in preventing 75–85% of predicted cases of meningitis C is marred by reports of relatively large numbers of adverse reactions to the vaccine. In 1999–2000, there were 16,527 reported adverse events apparently associated with about 15 m doses of vaccine – an adverse event reporting rate of one per 1,000 doses.[86] This is much higher than the equivalent published figure for any other vaccine. The Department of Health has pointed out that many of the reactions were minor, and has detailed the causes of the 11 deaths apparently associated with the vaccine.

This vaccine was, as is usual, tested on a relatively small number of people whose possible adverse reactions were monitored for a period of four weeks before being licensed for use in the general population.[87] The novelty of the vaccine was heralded by the Secretary of State for Health – 'the NHS will be the first health care system in the world to have the use of this new vaccine'[88] – yet the publicity leaflet for the vaccine included the statement that: 'the vaccine has been thoroughly tested on children of all ages and provides good protection with very few side effects ... The new vaccine has been tested carefully and has proved to be safe.'[89] Within a year of its

84 Health Education Authority, *Meningitis C – Reduce the Risk*, 1999, London: Department of Health, p 2.

85 Personal oral account from individual whose anonymity is respected.

86 Kelso, P, 'Meningitis vaccine cuts cases by up to 85%' (2000) *The Guardian*, 4 September.

87 For a detailed critique of vaccine pre-licensing trials, see Wakefield, AJ and Montgomery, SC, 'Measles, mumps, rubella vaccine: through a glass darkly' (2000) 19 Adverse Drug React Toxicol Rev 4, pp 265–83. This article was unusual in that its referees' comments were also published. The Department of Health's response, *Combined Measles, Mumps and Rubella Vaccines: Response of the Medicines Control Agency and Department of Health to Issues Raised in Papers Published in 'Adverse Drug Reactions and Toxicological Reviews, Volume 19 No 4, 2000'*, 2001, was obtained from http://www.doh.gov.uk/pdfs/mmrresponse.pdf on 1 February 2001. Both these are critically reviewed in Pywell, S, *Compensation for Vaccine Damage*, unpublished PhD thesis, 2001, University of Hertfordshire.

88 HC Deb Col 983, 20 July 1999.

89 Health Education Authority, *Meningitis C – Reduce the Risk*, 1999, London: Department of Health, p 5.

launch, the new vaccine had been given to a large percentage of schoolchildren in Britain. These children comprised the first population-wide cohort to receive it, but their parents had not been told that they were to be research subjects.

The MR and meningococcal C vaccination campaigns raise serious ethical questions because the targeted diseases were not currently causing epidemics. The MR campaign was in response to an epidemic predicted by a disputed mathematical model, and the meningococcal C campaign dealt with a disease which was rare, but greatly feared.

If there is a present or imminent risk of a large scale epidemic of a very serious disease, known vaccine risks to individuals may be justified by the potential benefit to the health of a community. At such times, public perceptions of the risk/benefit ratio alter. There was, for example, an epidemic of smallpox in New York in 1947. Five million people were vaccinated against the disease in six weeks, resulting in 45 known cases of encephalitis and four deaths due to the vaccine. This was felt to be an acceptable casualty level because the vaccine campaign averted thousands of deaths.[90] This situation contrasts with the 19th century riots against compulsory smallpox vaccine which occurred in Leicester because there was a low incidence of smallpox in the city.

It is generally accepted that normal ethical constraints may be waived when there is an immediate and serious risk to the health of large numbers of a population – such derogations exist in, for example, the European Convention on Human Rights.[91] Normally, however, medical ethics require that the autonomy of patients should be respected by obtaining fully informed consent to any medical procedure. Without respect for autonomy, it is inevitable that individual rights will be sacrificed in favour of the accumulation of the happiness of the majority. Neither law nor medical ethics sanctions such an approach, even for the achievement of worthy public health goals. Since the children receiving primary and secondary schedule vaccines are unable to give their own legally valid consent, this respect for autonomy should be transferred to their proxies who, in the great majority of cases, are the parents. For parental consent to be legally and morally valid,[92] parents should be neutrally presented with as much information as possible before deciding whether to accept vaccines for their infant children.

---

90 Last, JM, 'Ethics and public health policy', in Wallace, RB (ed), *Maxcy-Roxenau-Last Public Health and Preventive Medicine*, 1998, Stanford, Connecticut: Appleton and Lange, p 37.

91 Eg, Art 5, the right to liberty and security, which provides (para 1(e)) that persons may lawfully be detained 'for the prevention of the spreading of infectious diseases ...', and Art 8, the right to respect for private and family life, which provides (para 2) for interference with the exercise of the right 'for the protection of health or morals ...'

92 *Op cit*, fn 18.

THE COSTS AND BENEFITS OF VACCINES

The vision of a world free of preventable infectious diseases has to be considered in the context of the expense of vaccination. In January 2000, a further $300 m was believed to be required to achieve certified global eradication of polio by 2005,[93] and the sum had risen to $450 m by September 2000.[94] Although individual vaccines are cheap, politicians and public health authorities who decide vaccination policy must continually assess costs and benefits. Many have argued that it is inappropriate to place a value upon human life and health, but hard choices must be made in the pragmatic context of limited resources.[95] The costs of vaccines must be demonstrably justified, and this is most likely to occur if they are seen to result in herd immunity.

The main financial benefit of vaccines is derived from the reduced costs of treating people affected by disease. The average cost of treating a hospitalised person with meningitis C, for example, is £3,200. The vaccine is believed to have cut cases by about 75% of the previous figure of 1,530 in its first year of use, representing an estimated saving of £3.6 m.[96] The total cost of the campaign was not disclosed, but £9 m was made available to health authorities administering the campaign, and the vaccine was centrally purchased and supplied free of charge to the authorities.[97] The net expenditure was thus £5.4 m, plus the cost of the vaccine itself. This sum prevented an estimated 112 deaths and 337 cases of permanent brain damage – a cost per potential victim of over £12,000. The 1998–99 figures suggest that one case of meningitis C was avoided by roughly every 1,000 vaccines given in 1999–2000, coincidentally, the same ratio as that for reported adverse reactions to the vaccine.

Another example of a mass vaccine with a high dose-to-avoidance ratio in Britain is Bacillus Calmette-Guérin (BCG), which has an efficacy of 70–80% in protecting against tuberculosis (TB). The vaccine was introduced in Britain in 1953, and has played a major role in significantly reducing the disease. It was calculated in 1984 that 2,200 doses of BCG vaccine were

93 Brundtland, GH, *Final Push for Polio Eradication in Year 2000 – Every Child Counts*, text of speech given in New Delhi, 6 January 2000. Obtained from http://www.polioeradication.org/news.html (27 November 2000), pp 2–3.

94 Brundtland, GH, untitled, text of speech to Global Polio Partners Summit, New York, 27 September 2000. Obtained from http://www.polioeradication.org/news.html (27 November 2000), p 2.

95 See, eg, *R v Cambridge HA ex p B (A Minor)* [1995] 2 All ER 129, CA, p 137, where Sir Thomas Bingham MR said: '[d]ifficult and agonising judgments have to be made as to how a limited budget is best allocated to the maximum advantage of the maximum number of patients.'

96 HC Written Answers Col 53W, 19 June 2000.

97 HC Written Answers Col 143W, 11 January 2000.

required to prevent a single case of TB. The Department of Health still recommends routine administration of BCG vaccine to all children aged 10–14 years who give a negative result to a skin test.[98] This policy is not, however, complied with in all areas, and there have recently been supply problems which have meant that the vaccine has only been available to the groups at highest risk of TB.[99] There have been small annual increases in notified cases of the disease since 1985, notably among recent immigrants from countries where the disease is still common, and in inner city areas.[100]

Vaccines sometimes have unexpected beneficial effects in addition to reducing the incidence of infectious disease. A meta-analysis of two case-control and 10 cohort studies of measles vaccine in the developing world showed that the vaccine was associated with a greater number of avoided deaths than would be expected from acute measles infection.[101]

Vaccines can also have unexpected negative effects. As mentioned above, three doses of polio vaccine leave children in India susceptible to the disease, and polio paralysis has been triggered in the limbs of children injected with DTP vaccine. The introduction of the WHO's recommended three-dose programme of DTP has therefore caused polio paralysis in hundreds of thousands of children.[102]

There are other, currently unverified, studies which have linked certain vaccines with some kinds of long term injury. The most notable of these, published in Britain in February 1998, postulated a link between MMR vaccine, inflammatory bowel disorders and autistic spectrum disorders. This was a small scale study of 12 cases, and was published as an 'early report'. The paper itself notes the study's methodological limitations, and states: '[W]e did not prove an association between measles, mumps, and rubella vaccine and the syndrome described' before concluding '[f]urther investigations are needed to examine this syndrome and its possible relation to this vaccine.'[103] This paper came to the attention of the media, some of which misreported it, and public confidence in the safety of MMR vaccine fell. The Government's response was to convene a meeting of 37 experts

---

98 Bedford, H and Elliman, D, *Childhood Immunisation: A Review*, 1998, London: Health Education Authority, p 57.

99 HC Written Answers Cols 143–44W, 11 January 2000.

100 Great Britain: Department of Health, Welsh Office, Scottish Office Department of Health and DHSS Northern Ireland, Salisbury, DM and Begg, NT (eds), *1996 Immunisation Against Infectious Disease*, 1996, London: HMSO, pp 219 *et seq*.

101 Aaby, P *et al*, 'Non-specific beneficial effect of measles immunisation: analysis of mortality studies from developing countries' (1995) 311 BMJ, p 481.

102 Mudur, G, 'Flawed immunisation policies in India led to polio paralysis' (1998) 316 BMJ, p 1261.

103 Wakefield, AJ *et al*, 'Ileal-lymphoid nodular hyperplasia, non-specific colitis, and pervasive developmental disorder in children' (1998) 351 Lancet, 637, p 641.

who decided, a month after the study's publication, that parents should continue to accept the vaccine for their children.

Two major studies, published in June 1999, were used by the Chief Medical Officer to reassure parents about the safety of MMR. One of these collated parental accounts of the ages at which their children had first exhibited signs of autistic spectrum disorders, and compared these with the ages, if any, at which they had received MMR vaccine. There was a statistically significant clustering of cases with a five month interval, but this was dismissed as an artefact. Without these cases, the study showed no evidence for a causal association between MMR and autism.[104] The study was strongly criticised for omitting these cases from analysis, but its authors defended their decision. The second study collated information about apparent adverse effects following MMR or MR vaccine. A total of 531 reports were received, and all but 12 were disregarded on various specified grounds before final analysis. This study found that the information available did not support the suggested causal associations between the vaccines and bowel or autistic disorders, and noted its own methodological limitations.[105] Numerous other papers and letters have been published on this subject, and there is as yet no agreement on whether the postulated causal link exists.

It is certain, however, that there are in the Western Hemisphere today diseases which manifest themselves in childhood and are much more common than ever before. No link has been established between any of these and vaccines, but there is much speculation about what has caused so many children to suffer from autistic spectrum disorders, learning difficulties and asthma. It is probable that the increases are due at least in part to improved diagnostic techniques, but a greatly increased number of vaccines in early childhood is one of many factors which may be contributing towards changes in patterns of children's health. Much more research is needed into the possible causes of these disorders, ideally via prospective double-blind cohort studies in which one group of children would be exposed to various possible risk factors while another, similar, group would not be so exposed. The health outcomes of both groups would be monitored, and any significant differences could then reasonably be attributed to the risk factor in question.

One problem with such studies is that it is very difficult to isolate each risk factor – some environmental allergens, for example, are virtually omnipresent. Investigating vaccines in this way also poses ethical

104 Taylor, B *et al*, 'Autism and measles, mumps, and rubella vaccine: no epidemiological evidence for a causal association' (1999) 353 Lancet, pp 2026–29.

105 Committee on Safety of Medicines, 'The safety of MMR vaccine' (1999) Current Problems in Pharmacovigilance 25 June, pp 1–3. *Report of the Working Party on MMR Vaccine* obtained from www.open.gov.uk (21 June 1999), p 2.

difficulties. Given the generally held belief that vaccines are, on balance, a beneficial influence on children's health, it is unreasonable to expect 50% of a given population to agree that their children should receive placebos instead. It has been suggested that some parents would probably be willing to defer their children's vaccinations, but this would not be useful if the possibly linked diseases do not manifest themselves for many months, as is often the case with bowel and psychological disorders. The best study design realistically available is, therefore, the case control method. This involves starting with people who have the health problem under investigation. The difficulties with this are that detailed access to health records is required, subjects are frequently self-selecting, and no suitable comparison group is available.[106] The importance of vaccines, however, makes it necessary to surmount these difficulties. If parents are not convinced of vaccine safety, then fewer children will be vaccinated, with potentially serious consequences for public health. Governments need to identify common features in parents' anecdotal reports, and fund appropriate large scale investigations into these possible links.

In societal terms, the number of children apparently damaged by vaccines is greatly outweighed by the number protected from childhood diseases, so the cost-benefit ratio is considered acceptable. The official attitude to risks and benefits is exemplified in the history of the link between bovine spongiform encephalopathy (BSE) and variant Creutzfeldt-Jakob Disease (v-CJD). When the possibility of the association was first mooted in Britain, the Government responded that beef was completely safe to eat. It is not difficult to see the potential political problems following any official acknowledgment of a possible risk that was likely to do irreparable harm to the farming industry. Pharmaceuticals, including vaccines, were also realised to be possible sources of v-CJD infection, but this was not admitted publicly because of the official belief that it was imperative to maintain high levels of vaccine coverage. Kenneth Clarke MP, then Secretary of State for Health, told the BSE Inquiry of 'the needless death of infants' when 'mothers had been induced not to vaccinate their children'. It had been necessary to avert a similar situation:

> The difficulty is if you said, as we all believed, that the risk from vaccine was remote, that unless you say there is absolutely no risk or 110% certain that there is never any risk, it is terribly easy for somebody to go haring off starting another vaccine scare.[107]

---

106 Taylor, CW and Last, JM, 'Epidemiology', in Wallace, RB (ed), *Maxcy-Roxenau-Last Public Health and Preventive Medicine*, 1998, Stanford, Connecticut: Appleton and Lange, p 19.

107 Transcript of Day 87 of the BSE Inquiry, p 111, lines 2–18. Obtained from: http://www.bse.org.uk/transcripts/tr981127.txt (13 May 1999).

This is an admission from a former Cabinet minister that a deliberate decision was taken to overstate the true level of official confidence in vaccine safety. Guidelines against the use of British bovine serum in vaccines were issued in 1989, yet four vaccines which did not comply with the guidelines were not withdrawn. It was believed at the time that the stocks would last until late 1990–91. In the event, the affected MMR vaccine was never licensed, so the problem applied to one measles vaccine, one Tuberculin and one line of DTP.[108]

Volume 1 of *BSE Inquiry*, 2000, concludes with 'Lessons to be learned'. Two of these seem particularly applicable to current doubts about vaccine safety: '[a]n advisory committee should not water down its formulated assessment of risk out of anxiety not to cause public alarm' and '[a]lthough likelihood of a risk to human life may appear remote, where there is uncertainty all reasonably practicable precautions should be taken.'[109] Norman Baker MP has described the Government's attitude to possible vaccine risks as 'a terrible averting of eyes', and its response to the BSE risk as 'sweep[ing] it under the carpet'.[110] Doubts about vaccine safety must be identified and investigated if the beneficial effects of vaccines are to be maximised.

LEGAL REDRESS FOR THE ADVERSE EFFECTS OF VACCINES

In Britain, there are two possible routes to financial recompense for a child who may have been injured by the administration of a mass vaccine: the common law and the statutory Vaccine Damage Payments Scheme (VDPS).

There has been no successful common law claim for vaccine damage in England or Wales. The leading case is *Loveday v Renton*,[111] which was heard to determine whether in principle the pertussis vaccine could cause brain damage in young children. Stuart-Smith LJ concluded that the claimant had failed to prove on the balance of probabilities that this general causative link existed. No case has since reached the English courts. The Irish case of *Best v Wellcome Foundation*,[112] in which the claimant was awarded £2.75 m for damage caused by a faulty batch of vaccine, was based on exceptional facts and is unlikely to provide a useful precedent.

108 BSE Inquiry, *BSE Inquiry, The Report*, 2000, obtained from http://www.bseinquiry.gov.uk/report (15 November 2000), Vol 7, para 6.227.

109 BSE Inquiry, *BSE Inquiry, The Report*, 2000, obtained from http://www.bseinquiry.gov.uk/report (15 November 2000), Vol 1, paras 1275 and 1283.

110 Meikle, J and Clark A, 'BSE risk in polio vaccine revealed' (2000) *The Guardian*, 21 October.

111 [1990] 1 Med LR 117.

112 [1994] 5 Med LR 81.

A group of children whose parents believe they have been damaged by the MMR vaccine are claimants in an impending multi-party action against vaccine manufacturers[113] framed under the strict liability provisions of the Consumer Protection Act 1987. The claimants will argue that a 'defective' vaccine for the purposes of the Act was one that is capable of causing, however rarely, the injuries from which they are suffering.[114] By May 2001, several case management hearings had been held, but no date had been set for a full hearing. The claimants' research into issues of causation is being funded by over 700 individual legal aid certificates and one generic certificate.

It has long been recognised that the slow adversarial processes of the civil courts are unsatisfactory as a means to compensation for vaccine damage. Because of this, and in recognition of the social desirability of universal vaccination, the VDPS was established under the Vaccine Damage Payments Act 1979. Initially claimants received one-off payments of £10,000 if they could show that they had been at least 80% disabled by one of the vaccines recommended by the State for mass administration. The time limit for instituting the claim was six years from the later of the claimant's second birthday and the date of vaccination. The VDPS remained almost unchanged, except for three increases of £10,000 in the statutory sum, for over 20 years. In June 2000, major changes to the scheme were announced in Parliament.[115] The statutory sum has now been increased to £100,000.[116] All former recipients of VDPS awards have received top-up payments to increase their awards to the new level. Primary legislation will be required to lower the disability threshold from 80% to 60% and to increase the limitation period to any time preceding the claimant's 21st birthday. No mention of such legislation was made in the Queen's Speech at the State Opening of Parliament on 20 June 2001.

These changes, although substantial, will not solve the significant problems underlying the present scheme, which has granted awards to very few claimants in recent years.[117] Politicians are unanimous that the statutory payment does not constitute compensation, and it is clear that a payment under the scheme does not preclude a future common law action for damages. This contrasts with the equivalent scheme in the US, the Vaccine Injury Compensation Program. This no-fault scheme was introduced in October 1988, and one of its objectives is the avoidance of litigation, so recipients of awards are debarred from bringing a court action in negligence.

---

113 *Sayers and Others v SmithKline Beecham plc and Others* [1999] MLC 0117.

114 The High Court's judgment in *A and Others v National Blood Authority* (2001) *The Times*, 4 April, which was handed down after this chapter was written, appears likely to increase the claimants' chances of winning this action.

115 HC Deb Cols 719–27, 27 June 2000.

116 SI 2000/1983.

117 Pywell, S, 'A critical review of the recent and impending changes to the law of statutory compensation for vaccine damage' (2000) 4/00 Journal of Personal Injury Law, pp 246–56.

Claims under the American scheme are twice as likely to succeed as claims under the British scheme.[118]

In Britain, parents who believe their children to have been damaged by vaccination are unlikely to receive any financial recompense to cover the medical and social costs of raising a damaged child. Their main difficulty is the paucity of evidence of a causal link between vaccines and their alleged adverse effects. Government-funded research is, therefore, the key not only to safer vaccines, but also to fairer treatment of those who bear the risks of vaccines for the benefit of the community. Moral considerations suggest that the burden should lie with the benefit, and therefore that society should be prepared to pay when necessary for the disease immunity and protection which results from mass vaccination.

CONCLUSION

Vaccines are constantly being developed and improved. Investigations are currently under way into the possibility of DNA-based vaccines, and into vaccines against diseases including cancer and human immune deficiency virus (HIV). The WHO has initiated an Immunisation Safety Priority Project whose 'ultimate goal is to enable national immunisation programmes to prevent, early detect and quickly respond to adverse events in order to minimise their negative impact on health and on national immunisation programmes'.[119] The project includes ensuring that vaccine delivery systems are safe and that all national regulatory authorities will have access to adverse event monitoring systems by the end of 2002. Although commendable, this initiative does not deal with the problem that passive surveillance systems, such as the US Vaccine Adverse Events Reporting System and Britain's Yellow Card system, are thought to capture only very low percentages of suspected adverse reactions. The WHO has not advocated improving such systems, although adequate and accurate recording is a prerequisite of any project to improve vaccine safety.

Globalisation has affected patterns of disease. If populations were less mobile, it is likely that diphtheria and polio vaccines could safely be discontinued in the Western Hemisphere. CRS, too, could probably be eradicated from developed countries if there were no cases being imported from elsewhere. National strategies for disease eradication must, therefore, be devised in the context of global initiatives. There are instances, however, as India's experience with polio caused by DTP vaccine illustrates, when

118 UK data obtained from personal communication with Vaccine Damage Payments Unit, 7 December 1999. US data provided by letter from the Department of Health and Human Sciences, Rockville, Md.

119 World Health Organisation, *Health for All in the Twenty-First Century*, undated, Geneva: WHO. Obtained from http://www.who.int/wha-1998/pdf98/ea5.pdf (11 September 2000), p 1.

global policies can be fully effective only if they are modified to take account of local conditions. There is no room for complacency: TB, which is largely preventable, is increasing in Britain and elsewhere, and diphtheria has increased in the former States of the USSR.[120] The European Committee of Ministers considers it unnecessary to devise a pan-European vaccination policy because the Member States already co-operate within the WHO's programme.[121] Such reliance makes it imperative that the WHO's strategies are effective in the eradication of infectious disease.

Equally importantly, the WHO must ensure – via the instigation and careful monitoring of appropriate long term studies – that vaccines are not inadvertently causing some public health problems while solving others. Parents need to be justifiably confident that vaccines are not going to injure their children in any way. If this can be achieved, the maximum possible benefit will be derived from immunisation, which has been described as 'the single most cost-effective form of prevention and a positive health benefit to children'.[122]

---

120 See p 308.

121 Council of Europe, Committee of Ministers, 1997, Item 6.2, para 4.

122 Mayon-White, R and Moreton, J, *Immunizing Children: A Practical Guide*, 2nd edn, 1998, Abingdon: Radcliffe Medical, p 1.

CHAPTER 11

PARTICULAR ISSUES OF PUBLIC HEALTH: MENTAL HEALTH LAW AND INTERNATIONAL PUBLIC HEALTH

Gill Korgaonkar

INTRODUCTION

It is estimated that approximately 500 m people throughout the world suffer from some form of neurological or psychiatric illness.[1] Five of the ten leading causes of disability worldwide, in both developed and developing countries, are major psychiatric illnesses.[2] Such illnesses are estimated to account for almost 12% of deaths and lost productivity due to all diseases and injuries globally and, without urgent action, it has been predicted that this figure could, by 2020, rise to 15%.[3] Suicide, for example, is believed to account for 400,000 lives each year.[4]

It is not only the widespread incidence of such illnesses that is a major public health concern. The stigma that attaches to psychiatric disease is regarded as 'the central obstacle we have before us if we want to achieve anything in (psychiatric) treatment'.[5] A possible consequence of stigmatisation is that, even in established market economies with well developed health care systems, many sufferers still go untreated, despite increasing availability of improved treatments.[6] A recent study of schizophrenia in a rural community in China concluded that the problem of non-treatment 'lies in unfavourable attitudes to mental illness, rather than lack of available resources'.[7] Lack of access to treatment, whether caused by resource problems or discrimination or a combination of the two, is, not surprisingly, much worse in developing countries. One-third of the global population have no access to the WHO list of essential drugs (including

1 WHO press release, WHO/67, 12 November 1999.

2 Depression, schizophrenia, bipolar disorders, alcohol dependence and compulsive disorders; *Global Burden of Disease*, 1990, Geneva: WHO.

3 Bruntland, GH, 'WHO's global strategies for mental health' (1999) 12 November, Beijing.

4 WHO press release, WHO/67, 12 November 1999.

5 Prof Norman Sartorious Annual Meeting, Royal College of Psychiatrists International Conference, June 2000, Edinburgh. 'Raising awareness, fighting stigma, improving care', WHO press release, WHO/67, 1999.

6 Cooper, J (2001) 178 British Journal of Psychiatry 159.

7 Bruntland, GH, 'WHO's global strategies for mental health' (1999) 12 November, Beijing.

psychotropic drugs). In rural areas of Africa, such drugs are rarely available.[8] The serious implications of these statistics have led the World Health Organisation to launch a new 'Global Strategies for Mental Health' initiative aimed at 'improving the population, coverage and quality of psychiatric and neurological care throughout the world, particularly in developing countries'.[9] To facilitate this, a Mental Health Survey 2000[10] has been commissioned by the WHO in 19 countries to collect data on mental and physical disorders and disability, work loss, risk factors, provision and use of services and availability and use of medications.

To place the scale of the problem in a domestic context, the Department of Health in the UK[11] estimates that one in six adults suffer from mental illness in Britain per year, and depression alone will affect approximately 50% of women and 25% of men before the age of 70. In the 15–24 year age group, suicide is the second leading cause of violent death after road traffic accidents.[12] This is regarded as an important public health concern. The Government's current target[13] is to reduce the rate by 20% by 2010. The incidence of suicide both in prisons and on psychiatric wards is worryingly high and the implications of Art 2 of the European Convention on Human Rights to this problem is well recognised.[14] The European Union Health Commissioner also supports the introduction of a suicide prevention target.[15]

The total cost to the National Health Service of prescriptions dispensed in the community in 1998 was £4,701 m. £717 m was for drugs that impacted on the central nervous system. £279 m was for anti-depressant medication and some 3 m prescriptions were issued for drugs containing fluoxetine hydrochloride (an anti-depressant).[16]

---

8 *Primary Prevention of Mental, Neurological and Psychosocial Disorders*, 1998, Geneva: WHO.

9 'Raising awareness, fighting stigma, improving care', WHO press release, WHO/67, 1999.

10 *WHO Mental Health Survey*, 2000, Geneva: WHO.

11 See *The Health of the Nation: A Strategy for Health in England*, 1992, London: Department of Health; *Modernising Mental Health Services: Safe, Sound and Supportive*, 1998, London: HMSO.

12 *Saving Lives: Our Healthier Nation*, 1999, London: Department of Health; *National Health Service Frameworks for Mental Health* (HSC/1999/223).

13 McClure G, 'Changes in suicide in England and Wales, 1960–1997' (2000) 176 British Journal of Psychiatry 64.

14 It is estimated that at least 60 patients in acute psychiatric wards commit suicide each year and Louis Appleby, National Mental Health Director, has said: 'This rate must be reduced to zero by March 2002': DoH press release, 9 October 2000.

15 'EU aims to reduce suicides' (2000) 321 BMJ 852.

16 *Statistics of Prescriptions Dispensed in the Community 1988–1998*, DoH Statistical Bulletin, June 1999. See, too, Lacey, R, *The Complete Guide to Psychiatric Drugs*, 1996, London: Vermillion.

THE CONCEPT OF A MENTAL DISORDER

The statistics quoted are necessarily predicated on the basis that mental illness can be reliably diagnosed by reference to internationally accepted criteria. Whilst the WHO is rightly concerned about the incidence of mental illness as a public health issue, the labelling of certain forms of behaviour as 'mental illness' is still subject to controversy surrounding not only the identification of mental disorder, but whether mental illness exists at all. There is also concern as to the use of mental illness by States as a convenient method of coercion against opponents of the prevailing political regime.[17] Among the foremost critics of recognition of mental illness is Thomas Szasz, who has written recently: '... mental illnesses, like ghosts, are non-existent entities and ... psychiatry, like slavery, rests on coercing individuals as non-persons.'[18] Szasz is concerned about the profound consequences that a diagnosis of mental illness can have for the individual. It can lead to the deprivation of liberty and the imposition of treatment without consent, even when the individual is legally competent and poses no threat to third persons.[19] Social exclusion is often a result. Physical illnesses do not normally attract the same antipathy.

Misuse of psychiatry does not, however, necessarily lead to the conclusion that mental illness is a myth which has been created solely as an agent of social control. Many observers agree that illness and, consequentially, disease, are value laden concepts,[20] but this is as true for physical illness as it is for mental illness. From classical times, there has been recognition that the mind may be affected by illnesses which impact on a person's ability to behave responsibly. Exponents of the medical model of mental illness argue that the mentally ill have as much a right to effective treatment as do the physically ill. For them, intervention is justified on a 'best interests' basis in the same way that physical treatment for incompetent adults is justified.[21] Thus, for example, the WHO[22] has produced a guide to the recognition and management of mental health problems in refugees as a result of the growing awareness of the impact that trauma, fear, loss and bereavement may have on a person's mental well

17 See, eg, the writings of Foucault, M, *Madness and Civilisation: A History of Insanity in the Age of Reason*, 1973, Howard, T (trans), New York: Random House, and 'The dangerous individual', in Kritzman, L (ed), *Michel Foucault: Politics, Philosophy, Culture: Interviews and Other Writings*, 1988, London: Routledge.

18 Szasz, T, 'Mental incapacity, legal incompetence and psychiatry' (1999) 23 Psych Bull 9, p 517.

19 See, eg, the provisions of the Mental Health Act 1983.

20 Fulford, K, *Moral Theory and Medical Practice*, 1989, Cambridge: CUP.

21 *F v West Berkshire HA* [1989] 2 All ER 545.

22 *Guidelines for the Primary Prevention of Mental, Neurological and Psychosocial Disorders*, 1996, Geneva: WHO.

being. Furthermore, it is argued that to deny sufferers effective treatment is inhumane and a derogation of a civilised society's obligations.[23]

Mental disorder – an international consensus?

The ongoing problem for psychiatry is the fact that the symptoms exhibited by the sufferer are those of behaviour rather than of physical abnormality, and the cause is generally unknown. As a result, such symptoms do not easily lend themselves to a disease model, as objective tests are often unavailable. One of the consequences of the absence of scientific evidence to support a given diagnosis is that there is considerable scope for controversy even among adherents to the medical model both nationally and internationally. There are two distinct classification models in use. The first, used primarily in North America, is the *Diagnostic and Statistical Manual of Disorders*, 4th edn (DSM-IV), published by the American Psychiatric Association. The second, used in most of the rest of the world, is the World Health Organisation's International Classification of Diseases and Related Health Problems, in which mental disorders are classified in Chapter 5.[24] Whilst the two classifications have much in common, some important differences remain, which undoubtedly reflect cultural and possibly political issues.[25] Considerable controversy has, for example, centred around the inclusion in DSM-IV of pre-menstrual dysphoric disorder and self-defeating personality disorder, which are perceived by some commentators to pathologise women.[26]

The primary objectives of these classifications are to provide a common language for use by professionals in research and diagnosis and for the standardisation of diagnosis and classification of psychiatric disorders. They are not designed to determine the appropriateness of *legal* intervention.

Cultural variations in the concept of mental illness, however, undoubtedly exist,[27] and because psychiatric diagnosis is primarily determined by evidence of behaviour rather than physical symptoms, the scope for misdiagnosis as a result of lack of understanding of significant cultural variables is considerable. Thus, for example, the rate of diagnosis of

---

23 Leff, J, 'Comment on crazy talk: thought disorder or psychiatric arrogance by Thomas Szasz' (1993) 66 British Journal of Medical Psychology 77.

24 The book is a product of worldwide research involving 700 clinicians, 110 institutes and 40 countries with the aim of improving psychiatric diagnosis.

25 Kendell, R, 'The relationship between DSM-IV and the ICD-10' (1995) 1000 Journal of Abnormal Psychology 297.

26 See, eg, Caplan, P, *They Say You're Crazy: How the World's Most Powerful Psychiatrists Decide who's Normal*, 1995, Massachusetts: Addison-Wesley.

27 See, eg, Davis and Guarnaccia, 'Wealth, culture and the nature of nerves' (1989) 11 Medical Anthropology 15.

schizophrenia in the US is twice the rate in the UK.[28] There is also considerable concern in the UK about the over-representation of Afro-Caribbean men in psychiatric hospital compulsory admission rates.[29] A recent study by the Institute of Psychiatry[30] has demonstrated that African-Caribbeans are six times more likely to be diagnosed as schizophrenic than whites despite the fact that the incidence of schizophrenia in the Caribbean was identical to that of the white population in the UK. Black people are also more likely to be perceived as 'dangerous', and are similarly over-represented in the prison statistics.[31] A comparable problem has been identified in the US, where black people also are more vulnerable to discriminatory treatment.[32] 'Labelling' often denies and obscures 'the psychological consequences of social inequality among patients'.[33]

It is not only the link between race and mental illness that is controversial. The inter-relationship between mental illness and gender is similarly problematic. Whilst men are more likely to be diagnosed as suffering from schizophrenia and alcoholism, women are more likely to suffer depression, as well as pre- and senile dementia and neurotic disorders. More men are now the subject of compulsory admissions than women, although women are over-represented in the informal admissions statistics.[34] The causal connection between patriarchy and mental disorder is well documented.[35] Historically, evidence of the use of psycho-surgery, primarily on women, to regulate women's behaviour so that it conforms to man's expectations, is well documented.[36] Furthermore, ECT statistics in the UK demonstrate that one of the most controversial forms of treatment used in psychiatry is used disproportionately on women.[37]

---

28 Barbato, A, *Nations for Mental Health: Schizophrenia and Public Health*, 1998, Geneva: WHO.

29 See, eg, 'UK life blamed for ethnic schizophrenia', BBC, 14 July 2000.

30 'Breaking the circles of fear: a review of the treatment of black and Afro-Caribbean users of the mental health service' (2000) Sainsbury Centre of Mental Health and Institute of Psychiatry.

31 Home Office Prison statistics published annually by the Home Office Research, Development and Statistics Directorate.

32 Loring, M and Powell, B, 'Gender, race and DSM-III' (1988) 29 Journal of Health and Social Behaviour 1.

33 Dame Fiona Caldicott, Royal College of Psychiatrists, Edinburgh International Conference, June 2000.

34 DoH statistics on in-patients formally detained in hospitals under the Mental Health Act 1983 (1989/90–1999/2000), Bulletin 2000/19.

35 See, eg, Fegan, A and Fennell, P, 'Feminist perspectives on mental health law', in Sheldon, S and Thompson, M (eds), *Feminist Perspectives on Health Care Law*, 1998, London: Cavendish Publishing.

36 Sargant, W and Slater, E, *Introduction to Physical Treatments in Psychiatry*, 5th edn, 1972, Edinburgh: Livingstone, pp 105–06.

37 *Electro-convulsive Therapy: Survey Covering Period January–March 1999*, DoH Bulletin 1999/22.

Whilst such statistics are undoubtedly worrying, they cannot necessarily be used as evidence to support a proposition that mental disorder is wholly determined by the prevailing cultural *mores*. On the contrary, there is a well respected body of research which demonstrates that feelings of mental distress do indeed cross cultural barriers.[38]

The causes of many major mental disorders remain unknown. Treatments often merely relieve symptoms rather than cure. Controversy exists over the part played by biological, psychological and socio-cultural issues in any major mental illnesses and similar controversies surround what constitutes appropriate treatment. This is not true, however, for some mental disorders. Mental retardation, which affects some 100 m people worldwide, can be caused by a variety of factors; these include genetic (for example, Down's syndrome), pre-natal factors (for example, rubella, alcohol abuse), infections (for example, meningitis) and poor nutrition (for example, iodine deficiency). Similarly, one of the causes of epilepsy, which affects some 50 m people throughout the world, is infectious and parasitic disease from which the poor suffer disproportionately.[39] Half the world's population lives in poverty (that is, some 3 bn people live on less than US$3 per day, of which a third live in absolute poverty – that is, on less than US$1 per day). Poverty is undoubtedly a major obstacle to mental health and clearly has implications both for the susceptibility of contracting some mental illnesses as well as for the availability of treatment. In the UK, one quarter of all NHS prescriptions are for drugs that affect the central nervous system, that is, to alter mood, state of mind and/or behaviour.[40] Whilst expensive medicines may be beyond the reach of the poor in countries where there is no State funded healthcare, the cost of prevention can be much less than the cost of treatment.[41]

The statistics for treatment rates for illnesses such as schizophrenia, not surprisingly, show wide disparity throughout the world. In India, it is estimated that only 20% of sufferers receive treatment (with a similar percentage rate for epilepsy), compared with an 80% treatment rate in developed countries.[42] The cost to the State in England and Wales per patient year of schizophrenia is estimated to be some £22,000. Sufferers of

---

38 Lexicon of cross-cultural terms in mental health, 1997, Geneva: WHO. This WHO publication aims to assist cross-cultural research in mental illness by encouraging 'the reliable and consistent use of terms that are, by their culture-specific nature, particularly susceptible to misunderstanding'.

39 *Guidelines for the Primary Prevention of Mental, Neurological and Psychosocial Disorders*, 1996, Geneva: WHO.

40 *Statistics of Prescriptions Dispensed in the Community 1988–1998*, DoH Statistical Bulletin, June 1999.

41 Statistical Bulletin 1999/17 DoH, 1999, ISBN 1841820571.

42 Professor Norman Sartorious Annual Meeting, Royal College of Psychiatrists International Conference, June 2000, Edinburgh.

depression are even less likely to receive treatment. In sub-Saharan Africa, it is estimated that only 5% of sufferers have some form of treatment compared with 35% in countries with well developed health care systems.[43]

Gross inequities continue to exist despite the commitment given, some 10 years ago, by the United Nations General Assembly, to improving the protection afforded to sufferers of mental illness and to the improvement of mental health care.[44]

For many commentators, the paramount concerns for the international community in the 21st century should be a commitment to reduce poverty, to invest in primary prevention measures and work towards the eradication of 'social stigma, misconceptions and discrimination'[45] associated with mental illness. In other words, education has an equally important role to play. How, then, can human rights laws best be used to promote the interests of sufferers of mental illness?

MENTAL ILLNESS AND ENGLISH LAW

Since the 14th century, the crown has assumed jurisdiction over persons 'who happen to fail their wit' although the care of the mentally disordered largely fell outside legislative control until the 18th century. 'Asylums' were originally under the control of Justices of the Peace and indeed, until 1959,[46] the power to detain compulsorily was exercised by them. Furthermore, it has only been since 1930[47] that 'voluntary' admission to psychiatric hospitals was possible. Even then, voluntary patients had to sign a written application to be admitted to hospital and were required to give 72 hours' notice of their intention to leave. When this requirement was swept away in 1959, English mental health law was hailed as being 'one of the most liberal in the world'.[48] Today, some 90% of all admissions to psychiatric facilities are voluntary admissions, that is, the person has either consented to the admission or, if incapable of consenting, does not evidence an objection.[49]

43 WHO press release 1999/67, Geneva.

44 UN General Assembly: Principle for the protection of persons with mental illness and for the improvement of mental health care 1991.

45 See, eg, the Mental Health Foundation's survey on people's experiences of stigma and discrimination as a result of mental distress, 'Pull yourself together', April 2000, London.

46 Mental Health Act 1959. For a detailed analysis of current mental health legislation, see Hoggett, B, *Mental Health Act*, 1998, London: Butterworths.

47 Mental Treatment Act 1930.

48 See Hoggett, B, *Mental Health Act*, 1998, London: Butterworths.

49 DoH statistics on in-patients formally detained in hospitals under the Mental Health Act 1983 (1989/90–1999/2000), Bulletin 2000/19.

The current statutory provisions are contained in the Mental Health Act 1983. This legislation allows for the *civil* detention and compulsory treatment of mentally disordered persons, irrespective of whether they have capacity[50] and irrespective of the fact that they may pose no threat to third parties. The judiciary are not involved with the admission process; responsibility is placed in the hands of approved social workers[51] or nearest relatives[52] on the recommendation of either one or two doctors (dependent on the duration of the proposed detention).[53] Detention is, in broad terms, determined by evidence that the person is (a) suffering from a mental disorder *and* (b) it is of a nature or degree[54] which warrants detention *and* (c) that s/he ought to be detained for his/her own safety or for the protection of others. As the Court of Appeal in *St George's Healthcare NHS Trust v S*[55] made clear, detention must only be used for assessment and/or treatment of a mental disorder. The Mental Health Act cannot be used to detain and treat people for medical conditions just because their views about treatment are contrary to those of the majority of the population. In the year 1999–2000, of the 250,000 people who received in-patient psychiatric treatment, some 26,700 people in England were subject to compulsory admission under the Act. Of this figure, 89% were admitted under the civil detention provisions.[56]

Mental disorder is defined[57] as meaning 'mental illness, arrested or incomplete development of mind, psychopathic disorder and any other disorder or disability of mind'. Whilst the Act provides specific definitions of mental impairment, severe mental impairment and psychopathy, it provides no guidance as to what constitutes mental illness. Given that over 90% of people detained for treatment under s 3[58] are categorised as mentally ill, presumably medical judgment is preferred to legal definition. Case law[59] on the matter is equally unsatisfactory. The Act does, however, make it clear[60] that 'promiscuity or other immoral conduct, sexual deviancy or dependence on alcohol or drugs' alone cannot be taken to imply the

50 See Mental Health Act 1983, Pt IV.

51 See *ibid*, s 13.

52 *Ibid*, s 26.

53 See *ibid*, Pt II.

54 See, eg, admission for assessment (s 2) and admission for treatment (s 3).

55 [1998] 2 FLR 728.

56 DoH statistics on inpatients formally detained in hospitals under the Mental Health Act 1983 (1989/90–1999/2000), Bulletin 2000/19.

57 Mental Health Act 1983, s 1.

58 DoH statistics.

59 See, eg, *W v L* [1974] QB 711 where Lawton LJ said: 'The words (mental illness) have no particular medical significance.' The DoH memorandum (1998), on the other hand, states that the term's usage 'is a matter for clinical judgement in each case'.

60 Mental Health Act 1983, s 1(3).

existence of mental disorder. Thus, such behaviour, on its own, cannot be used to justify the use of the compulsory powers.

The Act also allows for the detention and compulsory treatment of mentally disordered persons who are suspected of or who are convicted of the commission of a criminal offence.[61] There are approximately 1,300 people detained in high security psychiatric hospitals. During the period 1988–1998, there has been a threefold increase of patients sentenced to a restriction order by the courts.[62] Offenders subject to restriction orders are detained in hospital without limit of time and the power to discharge is exclusively in the hands of Mental Health Review Tribunal and the Home Secretary.[63] Such offenders are liable to be detained for a longer period of time than offenders convicted of the same offence who have not been subject to the provisions of the Mental Health Act. In other words, the diagnosis of mental disorder can have significant implications for individual freedoms. The statistics also demonstrate that black people are twice as likely as white people to be subject to compulsory detention. Over the last 10 years, there has been a disproportionate rise in the admission of younger men under the civil detention powers, probably reflecting safety fears. Women, however, are more likely to be over-represented in the older age group. Single people and the homeless are also over-represented in these statistics.

The functions of our mental health law have long been the subject of debate. Diagnosis of mental illness can quite clearly be used as an agent of social control, but it has less stringent procedural safeguards to prevent the wrongful deprivation of liberty than exist within the criminal law. It can, of course, be used to offer protection for the oppressed and to afford treatment to those who need it. Whether it is ever ethically and legally justifiable to impose medical treatment on a person who refuses to consent to such treatment and who is not a potential danger to other people is hugely controversial. Utilitarian philosophers think not. John Stuart Mill has stated that: '[T]he only purpose for which power can be rightfully exercised over any member of a civilised community, against his will, is to prevent harm to others. His own good, either physical or moral, is not sufficient warrant.'[64] A more recent criticism is pertinent. 'One unfortunate feature of the present system of civil detention is the running together of paternalistic and protectionist considerations in the easy phrase "for the health or safety of the patients or for the protection of others". It is our view that very different considerations come into play when detention is for the protection of others.'[65]

61 Mental Health Act 1983, Pt III.

62 DoH statistics.

63 Mental Health Act 1983, s 73.

64 Mill, J, *On Liberty* (Regney (ed)), 1959, Oxford: OUP.

65 Campbell, A and Heginbotham, C, *Mental Illness: Prejudice, Discrimination and the Law*, 1991, London: Dartmouth.

There are two major concerns about existing mental health law. The first concern is whether it complies with the obligations contained in the Human Rights Act 1998[66] and the second is the alleged danger posed to society by dangerous, severely personality disordered people.[67] The current proposals for reform are contained in a Government White Paper.[68] The primary objective of these reforms is to strike an appropriate balance between the legitimate need to protect the public from harm and the obligation to prevent the violation of an individual's human rights.

Even though the Mental Health Act makes provision for compulsory detention and then goes on to regulate such detention, the recent decision by the House of Lords in the *Bournewood* case[69] makes clear that the common law retains an important role in this area of law. The case involved consideration of whether an incapacitated, compliant patient could be admitted voluntarily to a psychiatric hospital, and whether a patient admitted in these circumstances is 'detained' by the hospital authorities even when he makes no attempt to leave. The Mental Health Act gives statutory protection to people detained under its provisions. Although this protection may, on occasions, fall short of our international obligations, the protection it does give, both in relation to the imposition of treatment without consent and the right to challenge the continued lawfulness of the detention, is not available to 'voluntary' patients.

The concept of 'voluntariness' in relation to psychiatric patients is particularly controversial. Voluntary patients are, theoretically, in the same position in hospital as physically ill patients, that is, they can discharge themselves at any time, they can accept and refuse treatment for their mental disorder if they are adjudged to have sufficient capacity,[70] but the reality may be different. Section 5(2) and (3) gives doctors a 'holding power' over voluntary patients which allows for their emergency detention for up to 72 hours where the doctor thinks that an application under s 2 or s 3 should be made. A nurse has similar 'holding power' under s 5(4) that is limited to six hours' duration. The threat to use these provisions may be sufficient to compromise autonomy.

66 DoH and Home Office, *Reforming the Mental Health Act*, Cm 5016-I, 2000, London: HMSO.

67 Home Office/Department of Health, *Managing Dangerous People with Severe Personality Disorder: Proposals for Policy Development*, July 1999.

68 DoH statistics.

69 *R v Bournewood Community and Mental Health NHS Trust ex p L* [1998] All ER 319.

70 *Re C (Adult Patient)* [1991] 3 All ER 866.

Treatment for mental disorder

The mentally ill have the same basic right to self-determination as the physically ill in respect to medical treatment.[71] This principle is emphasised in the Law Commission's report on Mental Incapacity (No 231) and in the Mental Health Act Code of Practice,[72] which stress the necessity of providing patients with sufficient information to enable them to 'understand the nature, purpose and likely effect of the treatment'. The test of capacity to consent to treatment was outlined in *Re C*[73] and, despite recommendations by the Law Commission, has not been incorporated into statute. The mentally ill are not presumed to be incompetent, either at common law or under the Mental Health Act. The use of compulsory powers is not dependent on establishing incapacity, even when no risk to third parties is posed. The Code of Practice states that: '(a) person suffering from a mental disorder is not necessarily incapable of giving consent. Capacity to consent is variable in people with mental disorder and should be assessed in relation to the particular patient, at the particular time, as regards the particular treatment proposed.'[74]

If a mentally disordered voluntary patient fails the test of capacity, the patient may be treated for his mental disorder in accordance with the 'best interests' test developed at common law.[75] The treatment will be in the patient's best interests if 'it is carried out to save lives or ensure improvement or prevent deterioration in their physical or mental health'.[76]

The common law principles also apply to patients detained under the Mental Health Act except where they are specifically displaced by the provisions in Part IV. Part IV provides specific statutory authority for the imposition of certain forms of medical treatment for mental disorder in the absence of consent, in certain defined circumstances and with certain safeguards. Section 145 defines medical treatment for mental disorder as including 'nursing and care, habilitation and rehabilitation under medical supervision' to alleviate or prevent a deterioration of the patient's mental disorder which includes drug therapy, electro-convulsive therapy (ECT) and psychotherapy. What constitutes 'treatment for mental disorder' has been beset with controversy. The courts have held that force feeding a patient suffering from anorexia nervosa[77] and the performance of a caesarean

---

71 *F v West Berkshire HA* [1989] 2 All ER 545.

72 DoH, *Mental Health Act Code of Practice*, 1999, London: HMSO.

73 DoH and Home Office, *Reforming the Mental Health Act*, Cm 5016-I, 2000, London: HMSO.

74 DoH, *Mental Health Act and the Code of Practice*, 1999, London: HMSO, para 15.11.

75 *Re F (Mental Patient: Sterilisation)* [1990] 2 AC 1.

76 *Ibid*, *per* Lord Brandon, p 55.

77 *B v Croydon HA* [1995] 1 FLR 470.

section on a patient suffering schizophrenia who lacked capacity to consent[78] constituted 'treatment for mental disorder'. The Mental Health Act Commission's advice on what constitutes treatment for mental disorder states:

> Having considered the legal, pharmacological and medical advice received, the Commission concludes that the administration of medical treatment under Part IV of the Mental Health Act includes such measures as are necessary and appropriate to ensure that medicine is administered efficaciously and in accordance with good medical practice.[79]

The taking of blood samples to monitor drug dosage (for example, lithium and clozapine) would seemingly fall within this guidance.

Some controversial forms of treatment for mental disorder have special safeguards attached to them.[80] Psycho-surgery and the surgical implantation of hormones for the reduction of the male sex drive cannot be carried out on either an informal or detained patient without the patient's consent and that of a second opinion approved doctor (SOAD). The SOAD is required to consult the patient's doctor, a qualified nurse and another health professional, for example, social worker, involved in the patient's care before approving the request. Such treatments, thus, cannot, in any circumstances, be given to patients who lack capacity to consent.

Section 58 controls the use of ECT and drug treatment beyond three months. Such treatments can only be given if *either* consent is obtained or a second opinion (SOAD) is obtained. Patients detained under the emergency provisions[81] and restricted patients who are conditionally discharged[82] are not subject to these provisions and can only be treated under the common law. The Mental Health Act Commission Guidance states that 'informed consent' is required for ECT,[83] but, whether this creates, as a matter of law, a greater entitlement to information compared with other treatments is unclear and untested in the courts. The value of second opinions in protecting patients against unwarranted treatments has been challenged.[84]

The procedures in ss 57 and 58 do not have to be complied with in cases of emergency where the treatment falls within one of the following categories:

---

78 *Tameside and Glossop Acute Services Trust v CH* [1996] 1 FLR 762.

79 *Practice Note (No 1)* (June 1993).

80 Mental Health Act 1983, s 57.

81 *Ibid*, ss 4, 5, 35, 37, 135 and 136.

82 *Ibid*, s 42, 73 and 74.

83 MHAC Guidance (DHSS, 1984, para 14).

84 See, eg, the Mental Health Act Commission Biennial Reports, which highlight problems with the operation of the second opinion scheme.

- it is immediately necessary to save the patient's life; or
- it is immediately necessary to prevent deterioration of his condition (provided that it is not irreversible); or
- it is immediately necessary to alleviate serious suffering (provided it is not irreversible or hazardous); or
- it is immediately necessary and represents the minimum interference necessary to prevent the patient from behaving violently or being a danger to himself or others.

The scope of s 62 is, therefore, limited to that which is 'immediately necessary' and the 'minimum necessary'.[85] It is most often used for ECT pending an SOAD visit.[86]

Section 63 provides for a range of other forms of treatment that can be given without consent, including psychological and social therapies. It is unlikely that they can be carried out without active co-operation of the patient. The section has, however, been used to justify force feeding of anorexics and perform caesarean sections.[87] The treatment for physical disorder under Part IV is only justified if 'it can reasonably be said that the physical disorder is a symptom or underlying cause of the mental disorder'.[88] The use of restraint and seclusion is subject to guidance in the Code of Practice.[89] Both raise human rights concerns, which are considered below.[90]

PSYCHIATRY AND THE PROTECTION OF HUMAN RIGHTS

Human rights law at both the European and international level has become increasingly concerned with the problems that the treatment of the mentally ill generate, particularly in relation to compulsory treatment. The European Convention on Human Rights has, since the 1970s, become an important and, at times, an effective instrument for affording protection in this field. The United Nations adopted, on 17 December 1991, Principles for the Protection of Persons with Mental Illness and for the Improvement of Mental Health Care. The Director General of the World Health Organisation is committed to using the 10th anniversary of these UN Principles to

---

85 *Devi v West Midlands AHA* [1980] 7 CL 44.

86 Fennel, P, *Treatment Without Consent: Law, Psychiatry and the Treatment of Mentally Disordered People since 1845*, 1996, London: Routledge.

87 Dolan, B and Parker, C, 'Caesarean section: a treatment for mental disorder?' (1997) 314 BMJ 1183–87.

88 DoH, *Mental Health Act Code of Practice*, 1999, London: HMSO, para 16.5.

89 Paragraphs 19.14 and 19.23.

90 See European Convention on Human Rights, Art 2. See also *Buckley v UK* [1997] EHRLR 435.

campaign for an International Convention on the Rights of Persons with Mental Disorder.[91] The Council of Europe has also been active in this field. On 10 February 2000, a White Paper on the human rights and dignity of people suffering from mental disorder was published.[92] Some of the important implications of these instruments for the mentally ill are considered below.

MENTAL HEALTH AND EUROPEAN HUMAN RIGHTS LAW

The European Convention on Human Rights, which came into force in 1953 and which the UK was one of the first countries to ratify, was incorporated into English law by the Human Rights Act 1998 with effect from 2 October 2000. The Act imposes important obligations on courts, tribunals and public bodies to ensure that the rights set out within the Convention are complied with. Courts and tribunals are required to construe existing statutes in accordance with the Convention provisions (s 3(1)) and public authorities (which includes courts and tribunals) must act compatibly with Convention rights. Thus, ECHR case law must be taken into account when considering the development of the common law. Section 4(2) allows for a declaration of incompatibility.

It is predicted that the Human Rights Act will have a major impact on the development of English mental health law and practice. The potential application of the Convention to detained psychiatric patients has been recognised since the 1970s. The decision of the European Court in *X v UK*[93] in 1981 led directly to the reform of the Mental Health Act 1959. An analysis of some of the important case law which has already emanated from Strasbourg helps underline the significance for psychiatry of the Human Rights Act. It is important to remember that the Convention is a 'living instrument' which is required to be interpreted in accordance with present day conditions and the prevailing standards of Member States. The case law does not constitute binding precedent. Because acceptable practices in psychiatry will change significantly over relatively short periods of time, the developing case law must reflect this.

---

91 *Principle for the Protection of Persons with Mental Illness and for the Improvement of Mental Health Care*, 1991, Geneva: UN General Assembly.

92 Committee of Ministers of Council of Europe, *Addendum on the Protection of the Human Rights and Dignity of People Suffering from Mental Disorder, Especially those Placed as Involuntary Patients in a Psychiatric Establishment*, 2000, Strasbourg.

93 (1991) 4 EHRR 188.

The right to liberty

To date, the most significant area of impact has been in relation to the right to liberty. Article 5(1) provides that: 'Everyone has the right to liberty and security of person. No one shall be deprived of his liberty save in the following cases and in accordance with a procedure prescribed by law.' Paragraph (e) goes on to provide for 'the lawful detention of ... persons of unsound mind ...'. The term 'unsound mind' is not defined in the Convention, as the term 'mental illness' is not defined in s 1 of the Mental Health Act 1983. The proposals for reform of the Mental Health Act advocate a broad definition of mental disorder to cover 'any disability or disorder of mind or brain, whether permanent or temporary, which results in an impairment or disturbance of mental functioning'.[94]

The landmark case is *Winterwerp v Netherlands*.[95] The Court held that Art 5 requires that psychiatric detention can only be justified where the individual can reliably be shown to be of 'unsound mind' which is established by 'objective medical expertise'. Furthermore, the disorder must be of a nature or degree warranting compulsory confinement and the validity of continued confinement is dependent on the persistence of the disorder. 'Unsoundness of mind' was described by the Court as 'a term whose meaning is continually evolving as research in psychiatry progresses, as increasing flexibility in treatment is developing and society's attitudes to mental illness change, in particular so that greater understanding of the problems of mental patients is becoming more widespread'. The Court went on to emphasise that Art 5(1)(e) does not sanction the detention of people merely because their views or behaviour deviate from the prevailing norms of any particular society.

The implications of the *Winterwerp* decision can be seen at the domestic level. Whilst the important civil and criminal detention provisions cannot be activated without 'objective medical expertise', ss 135 and 136 of the Mental Health Act do allow for the removal of people who are suspected of suffering from a mental disorder to places of safety without the involvement of such medical expertise. However, given the short duration of such detentions (up to 72 hours) and the emergency nature of the detention, it is probable that these provisions will not offend Convention rights.

Of particular significance, however, is the impact of Art 5(1) on the way in which mentally abnormal offenders are dealt with by both the health and criminal justice systems. Jurisprudence in the Commission[96] and Court of Human Rights has demonstrated several areas of concern.

---

94 DoH, *Proposals for Reform of the Mental Health Act*, December 2000, Chapter 3.3.

95 [1979] 2 EHRR 387.

96 Before November 1998, the European Commission on Human Rights considered the admissibility of complaints from individuals who claimed their rights had been violated. This screening process was abolished by Protocol 11.

First, it is incompatible with *Winterwerp* for detention to continue once it is established that the detained person is no longer suffering from a mental disorder. The Court has made it clear that in these circumstances, discharge should not be 'unreasonably delayed'. Section 72 of the Mental Health Act requires a Mental Health Review Tribunal to discharge a patient if it is satisfied that he no longer suffers from a mental disorder. Section 73 prevents the absolute discharge of a patient subject to a restriction order unless it is satisfied that the patient should not be liable to recall. Thus, the person remains a 'patient' even though he is not currently suffering from mental disorder. In *R v Merseyside Mental Health Review Tribunal ex p K*[97] in 1990, the Court of Appeal held:

> At the time the offender is detained under a hospital order he is a patient within the interpretation in Section 145 (MHA). By Section 41(3)(a) a restricted patient continues to be detained until discharged under Section 73 and in my judgement remains a patient until he is discharged absolutely, if at all, by the tribunal. Any other interpretation of the word 'patient' makes a nonsense of the framework of the Act and the hoped-for progression to discharge of the treatable patient, treatability being a prerequisite of his original admission.[98]

In *Stanley Johnson v UK*,[99] SJ was awarded £10,000 compensation as a result of a successful challenge to his continued detention after the Mental Health Review Tribunal accepted the evidence of his psychiatrist that he was no longer suffering from a mental disorder. He was not conditionally discharged until some three and a half years after this because suitable arrangements were not made for him to be allocated supervised accommodation in the community. The delay was deemed unreasonable and the Government's arguments that he needed rehabilitation and was liable to relapse after discharge were not deemed adequate defence to the breach of Art 5. The law has not, as yet, been amended.

Section 42(3) of the Mental Health Act 1983 allows the Home Secretary to recall to hospital a restricted patient who has been conditionally discharged. There is no requirement under the current provisions to obtain objective medical evidence prior to the recall. In *Kay v UK*,[100] the Court held that the detention of a patient who was recalled to hospital and had to wait 10 weeks before a medical report was obtained constituted a breach of Art 5.

Somewhat surprisingly, perhaps, the Court has made it clear that a person detained on the grounds that he is of 'unsound mind' does not have an enforceable right to treatment under the Convention. In *Ashingdane v UK*,[101] it was argued that the patient's continued detention in a special

97 [1990] 1 All ER 694.

98 *Ibid*, *per* Butler-Sloss LJ, p 699.

99 [1997] EHRLR 105.

100 [1998] 40 BMLR.

101 (1985) 7 EHRR 528.

hospital when he should have been transferred to a regional unit constituted a breach of Art 5 as there was evidence that his health was being adversely affected. The Commission held that Art 5 does not make any requirement as to the actual manner in which the detention is effected; treatment and environment are not protected by Art 5 (and are unlikely to be a breach of Art 3). The decision has been criticised by Gostin:

> ... if the government is to deprive a person of liberty not on the grounds of dangerous behaviour but because of the person's need for treatment, then it must be incumbent upon [it] to provide a minimally adequate standard of treatment so that the person's mental health does not deteriorate, but can actually improve.[102]

However, a person must be detained in an 'appropriate institution', that is, one authorised to care for people with mental disorder. In *Aerts v Belgium*,[103] the applicant was detained in a prison psychiatric wing. This was not considered to be a therapeutic environment and, as no medical attention was available to him and his health was adversely affected, the Court considered there to be a breach of Art 5(1)(e). In the UK, we have seen in the last decade the decline in the number of mental hospital beds and an increase in the prison population. Incarceration may be preferred to hospitalisation because of public panic about the danger of people with mental disorder. Prison costs are lower than those of mental hospitals, and given that many psychiatrists regard such severely disordered people as untreatable, incarceration is the easy option.

A recent survey undertaken by the Maudsley Hospital in London[104] concluded that almost one-quarter of all adult male prisoners required psychiatric treatment in prison, but only 7% received it. Of women prisoners, 43% needed treatment and only 15% received it. The human rights implications are obvious.

Article 5(2) provides: 'Everyone who is arrested shall be informed promptly, in a language which he understands, of the reasons for his arrest and of any charge against him.' A failure to give an adequate explanation cannot effectively challenge the lawfulness of his detention. Although s 132 of the Mental Health Act requires that detained patients be given certain information as soon as practicable after their detention has begun, this is limited to information on the provisions under which detained, the effect of the provisions, and the right to appeal to a Mental Health Review Tribunal. There is no statutory requirement for the *reasons* for the detention to be provided. The Mental Health Act Code of Practice,[105] however, does state

---

102 Gostin, L, *Mental Health Services, Law and Practice*, 1986, London: Shaw, para 20.29.

103 [1998] EHRLR 777.

104 Gunn, J, 'Are prisons replacing mental hospitals?' (2000) *The Guardian*, 16 June.

105 DoH, *Mental Health Act Code of Practice*, 1999, London: HMSO, para 13.

that patients should be informed of the reasons and should be given access to trained interpreters where applicable, although these provisions are not legally binding.

Although reasons for the recall of a restricted patient are required to be given within 72 hours of the event and the patient has the right to challenge that recall to a Mental Health Review Tribunal, the delays that exist in convening a hearing probably breach Art 5.

The Convention also requires (Art 5(4)) that where a person is deprived of his liberty, he is entitled to be able to challenge the lawfulness of the detention in a court with power to order his discharge. *In X v UK*,[106] the Court held that:

> ... a person of unsound mind compulsorily confined in a psychiatric institution for an indefinite or lengthy period is in principle entitled, at any rate where there is no automatic periodic review of a judicial character, to take proceedings at reasonable intervals to put in issue the lawfulness of his detention, whether that detention was ordered by a civil or criminal court or by some other authority.

Article 5 is often used to challenge delays in convening such reviews. In *Barclay-Maguire v UK*,[107] a delay of 18 weeks was held by the Commission to be a breach of Art 5(4); and in *E v Norway*,[108] eight weeks' delay was deemed not to be a 'speedy determination':

> The Convention requires ... Contracting States to organise their legal systems so as to enable the courts to comply with its various requirements ... It is incumbent on the judicial authorities to make the necessary administrative arrangements, even during a vacation period, to ensure that urgent matters are dealt with speedily and this is particularly necessary when the individual's personal liberty is at stake.

Current Mental Health Review Tribunal statistics[109] reveal that waiting times for hearings still exceed the eight weeks target time for unrestricted cases and 20 weeks for restricted cases.

As has already been noted, the Mental Health Act 1983 does not displace the common law doctrine of 'necessity', and it is thus possible to admit and treat an incompetent but compliant patient without the safeguards of the legislation being met. The question arises as to whether such admissions, which are commonplace in England – it is estimated by the department of Health that some 44,000 people fall within this category[110] – constitute

---

106 [1981] EHRR 188.

107 [1981](App No 9117/80).

108 [1990] EHRR 30.

109 *Mental Health Review Tribunals for England and Wales, Annual Report 1997–98*, DoH, May 2000, p 43.

110 See DoH, *Reforming the Mental Health Act*, Cm 5016-I, December 2000, Chapter 1.

detention and are thus affected by Art 5. Two of the five Law Lords agreed in *Bournewood*[111] that Mr L was detained, but had no recourse to a Mental Health Review Tribunal since its jurisdiction is purely statutory. Whether the public law remedies of judicial review and/or habeas corpus provide adequate alternative remedies sufficient to comply with Art 5(4) is unlikely. The nature and scope of such reviews do not give the courts the authority to examine whether the substantive reasons given for the detention continue to subsist and thus the Convention provisions cannot be met.[112] The proposals for reform of the Mental Health Act[113] advocate the introduction of legal safeguards for this group of patients. The remit of the proposed new Commission for Mental Health, which will replace the current Mental Health Act Commission, will include a duty to ensure that care and treatment are provided in accordance with these patients' best interests. They will also be given a right to apply to the proposed new Mental Health Tribunal 'to challenge any detention and for a review where there are concerns about the quality or nature of the patient's care or treatment'.[114]

Article 5(4) has also been interpreted to require effective legal representation as an essential part of the 'special procedural guarantees' required in mental health cases.[115] Whilst legal aid is available for legal representation at Mental Health Review Tribunals, it is arguable that access to legal advice must be arranged even in the absence of the patient requesting it. In *Megyeri v Germany*,[116] the Court was required to consider the applicability of Art 5(4) to the situation of a person suffering from diminished mental capacity who was detained in connection with the commission of alleged criminal offences. His mental incapacity meant that he could not, in law, be held responsible for those criminal acts, and thus should have had legal assistance made available to him without his specifically requesting it.

The proposals for reform of the Mental Health Act contain a commitment to extend the provision of a specialist advocacy service for compulsorily detained patients so that they and their carers 'are better able to understand the purpose and scope of the legal powers that affect them'.[117] The proposed new Commission for Mental Health will be charged

---

111 For a critique of the *Bournewood* case, see Fennell, P, 'Doctor knows best? Therapeutic detention under the common law, the Mental Health Act and the European Convention' (1998) 6 Med Law Rev 6, pp 322–53.

112 See, eg, the discussion in Bartlett, P and Sandland, R, *Mental Health Law: Policy and Practice*, 2000, London: Blackstone, Chapter 5.

113 DoH, *Proposals for Reform of the Mental Health Act*, December 2000, Chapter 4.

114 *Ibid*, 6.4.

115 See *Winterwerp* [1979] 2 EHRR 387, and *X v Belgium* (1984) 3 DR 13.

116 [1992] 11 BMLR, pp 110–18.

117 DoH, *Proposals for Reform of the Mental Health Act*, December 2000, para 2.24.

with the responsibility of monitoring the quality and overseeing the operation of the advocacy service.

The current procedural rules that apply when a detained person seeks to challenge the lawfulness of his detention place on the detainee the burden of proving that the criteria for continued detention are no longer met. It is possible that this burden contravenes the Convention. If the proposals in the White Paper are adopted,[118] the doctor responsible for the patient's care and treatment will, as far as the civil detention provisions are concerned, have a statutory duty to discharge the care and treatment order where its conditions are no longer met.

Care in the community

Following the Report of the Inquiry into the Care and Treatment of Christopher Clunis,[119] the Mental Health (Patients in the Community) Act 1995 created a statutory power of supervised discharge.[120] These provisions do not, however, provide for the compulsory treatment of such persons as they are not detained as 'in-patients'. The Government's view is that the existing law does not allow sufficient flexibility in the use of compulsory powers to fit with patients' changing needs. At the moment, clinicians have to wait until patients in the community become ill enough to need admission to hospital before compulsory treatment is given. This prevents early intervention to reduce risk to both patients and the public.[121] The proposals for reform include the introduction of compulsory care and treatment orders in the community.[122] Concern has been expressed as to whether such orders would violate Art 5. In *W v Sweden*,[123] the complainant was provisionally discharged subject to the condition that he took medication and attended hospital appointments. He argued that the conditions infringed his right to liberty. The Commission concluded that they were not so severe as to constitute a deprivation of liberty and thus Art 5 had not been violated. The proposals in the White Paper are therefore likely to satisfy *Winterwerp*. They are also unlikely to infringe Art 8 if they are imposed with the aim of protecting health.

118 DoH, *Guidance on the Discharge of Mentally Disordered People and their Continuing Care in the Community*, 1994, HSG (94)27.

119 HMSO, 1994.

120 Mental Health Act 1983, s 25.

121 DoH, *Proposals for Reform of the Mental Health Act*, December 2000, 2.15.

122 *Ibid*, 3.51.

123 *W v Sweden* [1988] 59 DR 158.

Dangerous people with severe personality disorders

The Government has become particularly concerned about the risk to society posed by people with severe personality disorders whom psychiatrists have often rejected as 'untreatable'. The civil detention for treatment provisions set out in Pt II of the Mental Health Act 1983 (s 3) require, where the patient is suffering from a 'psychopathic disorder' (the term 'personality disorder' is often used interchangeably), evidence that medical treatment will alleviate or prevent deterioration in the condition. Controversy surrounds such persons' treatability and thus many are not detained until they have committed a criminal offence.[124] The Government have estimated that there exist around 500 people who fall within the category of 'dangerous' with 'severe personality disorder' whom it would be better to detain before they have the opportunity to commit a crime of violence. Around 40 homicides a year are committed by people who have had recent contact with psychiatric services.[125] The need for law reform was originally highlighted in *Managing Dangerous People with Severe Personality Disorder*.[126] The current proposals, if implemented, would permit the indeterminate but reviewable detention of such people and are highly controversial.

It is likely that, if these proposals become law, their compatibility with Art 5(1)(e) will be tested. Of particular relevance will be whether the diagnosis of 'dangerous severe personality disorder' satisfies the strict requirements of the *Winterwerp* decision in relation to 'objective medical expertise'.[127] Some commentators would argue that disorders of personality do not have the same status as those which psychiatry has traditionally considered as mental illness.[128]

The right not to be subjected to torture or inhuman or degrading treatment

Article 3 states that 'No one shall be subjected to torture or to inhuman or degrading treatment or punishment'. This provides an absolute right that cannot be derogated from by States in any circumstances, even in the event of public emergency.[129] It enshrines what the drafters of the Convention

124 See the controversy surrounding the case of Michael Stone, convicted of the murders of two people: *R v Stone* (2001) TLR, 22 February.

125 DoH, *Proposals for Reform of the Mental Health Act*, December 2000.

126 Home Office, *Proposals for Policy Development*, July 1999, London: HMSO.

127 Szmukler, G, 'A new Mental Health (and Public Protection) Act' (2001) 727 BMJ 2.

128 American Psychiatric Association, *DSM of Mental Disorders*, 4th edn, 1994, Washington: American Psychiatric Association.

129 *Ireland v UK* [1978] Series A, No 25, para 162.

regard as a right of fundamental value in all democratic societies. To fall within Art 3, the treatment must attain a 'minimum level of severity' which is determined by reference to such factors as the length of the treatment, its physical and mental effects and, in some cases, the sex, age and state of health of the victim.

In *Herczegfalvy v Austria*[130] a patient was force-fed, sedated against his will, handcuffed and secured to his bed. The Austrian Government's argument that his treatment was justified as a therapeutic necessity by reference to prevailing psychiatric standards was accepted and thus there was no violation of Art 3. The Court, did, however, state that:

> While it is for the medical authorities to decide, on the basis of the recognised rules of medical science, on the therapeutic methods to be used, if necessary by force, to preserve the physical and mental health of patients who are entirely incapable of deciding for themselves and for whom they are therefore responsible, such patients nevertheless remain under the protection of Article 3.

It is questionable now, in the light of more recent case law, whether the treatment in the *Herczegfalvy* case would be acceptable today. 'The increasingly high standard being required in the area of protection of human rights and fundamental liberties correspondingly and inevitably requires greater firmness in assessing breaches of the fundamental values of democratic societies.'[131]

In *Grare v France*[132] it was held that psychiatric treatment that may have unpleasant side effects is not a violation of Art 3. The administration of ECT without the informed consent of the patient could, in the future, be held to be inhuman and degrading despite its current accepted therapeutic value.[133] As more sophisticated drug therapies become available, the justification for the use of ECT will almost certainly decrease. The National Institute of Clinical Excellence has been asked by the Department of Health 'to develop guidance on the treatment of resistant depression and as part of this to clarify the role of ECT and other treatment choices'.[134] Further legislative safeguards may result from this guidance.

Patients held in seclusion or under restraint may also be the victims of Art 3 violations. In *A v UK*,[135] the Commission approved a friendly settlement in a case involving a Broadmoor patient who alleged his five week seclusion was inhuman and degrading. The White Paper issued by the

130 [1993]15 EHRR 437.

131 *Selmouni v France* [2000] 29 EHRR 403.

132 [1993] 15 EHRR CD 100.

133 See Public Information Leaflet, *ECT*, 2000, London: London Royal College of Psychiatrists.

134 DoH, *Proposals for Reform of the Mental Health Act*, December 2000.

135 [1981] Series A, No 46; [1996] 4 EHRR 188.

Council of Europe to: '... ensure the protection of the human rights and dignity of people suffering from mental disorder, especially those placed as involuntary patients in a psychiatric establishment' states that seclusion and restraint 'should be used only on the express order or under the supervision of a medical doctor or immediately brought to the knowledge of a medical doctor for approval, the reasons and duration of these measures should be mentioned in a proper register and in the patient's personal file.'[136]

Consideration has also been given to the question of whether the refusal to treat a person suffering from mental disorder constitutes a violation of Art 3. If so, Art 3 would be relevant to cases involving decisions made by health authorities concerning the allocation of funds between competing demands. In *North West Lancashire HA v A, D and G*[137] it was argued that the health authority's policy decision to categorise the treatment of transsexuals (gender identity dysphoria) as of low priority was unreasonable, because medical judgment was not reflected in the policy. Although the application for judicial review was successful on the facts, the Court of Appeal held that there was no breach of either Art 3 (despite the fact that transsexualism is a recognised mental disorder) or Art 8 (Art 8 does not impose an obligation to provide treatment).

The right to a private and family life

Article 8(1) states that 'Everyone has the right to respect for his private and family life, his home and his correspondence'. The objective of Art 8 is to protect against arbitrary action by public authorities. It covers a wide range of areas that affect people's daily lives. Whilst Art 8 is not an absolute right, the State has the burden of justifying any interference within Art 8(2):

> There shall be no interference by a public authority with the exercise of this right except such as in accordance with the law and is necessary in a democratic society in the interests of national security, public safety or the economic well-being of the country, for the prevention of disorder of crime, for the protection of health or morals, or for the protection of the rights and freedoms of others.

In *JT v UK*,[138] the applicant had been detained under s 3 of the Mental Health Act 1983. Her mother, in accordance with the provisions in s 26, was deemed to be her 'nearest relative'. Under current legislation, nearest relatives are afforded considerable powers both in relation to admission (s 11) and discharge (s 23). JT claimed that Art 8 had been violated because

136 Committee of Ministers of Council of Europe, *Addendum on the Protection of the Human Rights and Dignity of People Suffering from Mental Disorder, Especially Those Placed as Involuntary Patients in a Psychiatric Establishment*, 2000, Strasbourg, p 6.

137 [1999] Lloyd's Rep Med 399.

138 [2000] App No 26494/95.

she wished to replace her mother as nearest relative and she was precluded from doing so by the operation of the Act. The Commission unanimously upheld her claim. The UK Government has accepted that the legislation should be amended. The proposals in the White Paper[139] provide for the replacement of the nearest relative by a 'nominated person' whom a patient can identify in an advance agreement where this is applicable.[140]

In *Y v UK*,[141] the Commission considered whether the prohibition on sending a telegram by a Broadmoor patient constituted a breach of Art 8.

Section 134 of the Mental Health Act permits the interception of incoming and outgoing mail of detained patients in certain circumstances. The Code of Practice[142] also provides guidance on its operation. The Mental Health Act Commission has statutory authority[143] to review the decisions of managers of special hospitals to withhold the correspondence of detained patients and it is thus unlikely that the current provisions are a breach of Art 8.

More recently, the Court of Appeal has considered whether the proposed closure of a nursing home in which a person had been promised 'a home for life' constituted a breach of Art 8.[144] The court held that Ms Coughlan had a 'legitimate expectation' that the promise would not be breached. The Convention created a free standing ground of review of the decision. 'The more substantial the interference with human rights, the more the court required by way of justification before it could be satisfied that the decision was reasonable or fair.' The public interest did not justify the breach of promise or the right to respect for her home and thus the public authority had no legitimate defence.

The right to life

Article 2 provides:

> (1) Everyone's right to life shall be protected by law. No one shall be deprived of his life intentionally save in the execution of a sentence of a court following the conviction of a crime for which this penalty is provided by law.

139 DoH, *Proposals for Reform of the Mental Health Act*, December 2000.

140 *Ibid*.

141 [1977] 10 DR 37.

142 Para 24.15.

143 Mental Health Act, s 121(7).

144 *R v North and East Devon HA ex p Pamela Coughlan and Secretary of State for Health* [1999] TLR 20/7/99.

(2) Deprivation of life shall not be regarded as inflicted in contravention of this article when it results from the use of force which is no more than absolutely necessary:

(a) in defence of any persons from lawful violence;

(b) in order to effect a lawful arrest or to prevent the escape of a person lawfully detained;

(c) in action lawfully taken for the purposes of quelling a riot or insurrection.

The article has been construed as imposing a positive obligation to safeguard life as well as refraining from the intentional and unlawful taking of life. As has been noted earlier, Art 2 almost certainly applies where death occurs in custody and where this could and should have been prevented. This will include the suicide of patients whilst undergoing in-patient psychiatric care. In *Keenan v UK*,[145] the Commission considered the possible liability of the prison authorities for the suicide of a prisoner with a history of serious mental disorder. Whilst the Commission held, on the facts, that there had been no violation of Art 2, it did make clear that prison authorities have a positive obligation to take steps to safeguard the lives of the people in their care.

In *Osman v UK*[146] the Court was asked to consider whether the failure of the authorities to protect the life of a schoolchild from the child's former teacher constituted a violation of Art 2. Whilst it was established that the authorities knew that the teacher had developed a 'disturbing attachment' to the child (the murderer was removed as a teacher from the school), it was argued that they could not have known the magnitude of the risk posed. Whilst, again on the facts, the Court held that there had been no violation of Art 2, liability could be incurred if:

(a) the authorities knew or ought to have known at the time of the existence of a real and immediate risk to the life of the identified individual or individuals from the criminal acts of a third party; and

(b) that they failed to take measures within the scope of their powers which, judged reasonably, might have been expected to avoid that risk.

It could be argued, therefore, that in certain circumstances, such as when serious risk to self or others is demonstrated, there exists an internationally protected legal right to health care for the mentally disordered.

145 [1998] EHRLR 648.

146 [1997] EHRLR 105–08.

The right to marry and found a family

Article 12 provides for the right to marry and found a family. In *X and Y v Switzerland*[147] and, more recently, in *ELH and PBH v UK*,[148] the Commission held that Art 12 was not violated by the refusal of prison authorities to provide facilities for the exercise of conjugal rights. The restrictions were considered necessary 'for the prevention of disorder or crime'. A general prohibition, however, in psychiatric institutions, could contravene Art 12.

Prohibition of discrimination

Article 14 provides that: 'The enjoyment of the rights and freedoms set forth in this Convention shall be secured without discrimination on any ground such as sex, race, colour, language, religion, political or other opinion, national or social origin, association with a national minority, property, birth or other status.' Whilst the promotion of equality has a prominent place in all international human rights documents,[149] Art 14 is, on the face of it, more restrictive in scope than comparable anti-discrimination provisions.[150] This is because it does not create a free standing right, but provides protection against discrimination only in relation to the rights and freedoms set out elsewhere in the Convention. Furthermore, it seems not to promote equality in a positive sense, but rather to prohibit discriminatory treatment, although the wording of Art 14 makes the grounds on which discrimination is prohibited open-ended.[151] Neither does Art 14 prevent a State from taking positive measures to promote the interests of a disadvantaged group.[152]

The problem of access to employment of the disabled (which includes the mentally disordered) has been a long standing concern for civil rights campaigners.[153] The Disability Discrimination Act 1995, which came into effect in December 1996, provides measures to outlaw discrimination against the disabled in the workplace. A person is regarded as being disabled 'if he

---

147 [1979] DR 13.

148 [1997] 25 EHRR CD 158.

149 See, eg, UN Declaration of Human Rights, Art 2.

150 Compare ICCPR, Art 26, which provides comprehensive protection against discrimination in all those activities which the State chooses to regulate by law.

151 The grounds listed in Art 14 are expressed in a non-exhaustive manner – 'any ground such as ...' and 'or other status'.

152 For an example of reverse discrimination, see *DG and DW Lindsay v UK*, No 11089/84 (1984) 49 DR 181, where a tax advantage for married women was justified objectively to encourage married women back to work.

153 Disabled people account for nearly one-fifth of the working population, but account for only 12% of people in employment. Furthermore, disabled employees earn on average only two-thirds of the wages of non-disabled employees (Labour Force Survey 1999).

has a physical or mental impairment which has a substantial and long term adverse effect on his ability to carry out normal day to day activities'.[154] Mental illness, however, only counts as a mental impairment if it is a 'clinically well-recognised illness'.[155]

Whilst the Act is subject to considerable criticism[156] it does, for the first time, place on employers certain positive obligations towards both potential and existing employees. This is expressed as a duty to make 'reasonable adjustments'[157] which includes time off work for rehabilitation, assessment and treatment.[158] How significant these provisions are in improving the rights of the mentally disordered in the workplace is questionable, but scope for interpretation of Convention rights as applied to the interests of psychiatric patients is potentially far reaching. It is certain that any new legislation will be subject to considerable judicial scrutiny.

THE COUNCIL OF EUROPE AND THE MENTALLY DISORDERED

The Council of Europe has demonstrated particular concern for the rights of the mentally disordered for some time.[159] In 1994, the Parliamentary Assembly of the Council of Europe adopted a Recommendation[160] which resulted in the establishment of a Working Party on Psychiatry and Human Rights. The result of the Working Party's deliberations is the present White Paper on the Protection of the Human Rights and Dignity of People suffering from Mental Disorder, especially those placed as involuntary patients in psychiatric establishments.[161] This is designed, subject to public consultation, to provide guidelines for a new legal instrument of the Council of Europe. The important areas in which the Council of Europe are seeking responses include the following:

154 Disability Discrimination Act 1995, s 1.

155 Sched 1, para 1(1). The EAT stated, in *Goodwin v Patent Office* (1999) IRLR 4 that, in the event of doubt as to whether a mental illness falls within the definition, it would be advisable for an Employment Tribunal to consult the WHO's ICD.

156 See Smith, I and Thomas, G, *Industrial Law*, 7th edn, London: Butterworths, pp 309–20.

157 Disability Discrimination Act 1995, s 6.

158 This can include attendance at therapy or counselling sessions: *Kapdia v London Borough of Lambeth* [2000] IRLR 14.

159 *Recommendation No R (83)2 on the Legal Protection of Persons Suffering from Mental Disorder Placed as Involuntary Patients*, 1983, Geneva: UN.

160 No 1235 (1994).

161 Council of Europe White Paper CM(2000)23 Addendum, 10 February 2000.

- Should the grounds for civil detention be restricted to situations where (*inter alia*) the person is a *danger* to himself or others, and if so, how should 'danger' be defined?
- Should the grounds for criminal detention be based on different criteria to that of civil detention (which is not the case under English legislation at present)?
- Should family members be involved in detention and involuntary treatment?
- What safeguards are necessary in emergency situations?
- What safeguards are necessary for the administration of ECT, psychosurgery and hormone implants?
- How should minors be protected?
- What safeguards should be provided to govern restraint or seclusion of patients?
- What concrete measures should Member States be expected to take to reduce discrimination?

Whilst a detailed analysis of the provisions are beyond the scope of this chapter, the questions for consultation cited above highlight the constant themes arising in the area of human rights law. One of these themes is that of discrimination. The Committee of experts feels that 'Member States should take measures to eliminate discrimination against people suffering from mental disorder, including within health services'. The document cites some important examples such as 'the incorrect and stigmatising use of terms such as schizophrenia in the media, discriminatory practices concerning employment of patients or former patients, discriminatory practices concerning insurance'.[162] This is further evidence that international bodies are concerned that the treatment and quality of life of sufferers from mental disorder are severely compromised by public attitudes.

THE UNITED NATIONS AND THE PROTECTION OF THE MENTALLY DISORDERED

The UN Declaration of Human Rights recognises 'the inherent dignity' and the inalienable rights of 'all members of the human family'.[163] It further provides: 'Everyone has the right to a standard of living adequate for the health and well-being of himself and his family including food, clothing,

162 Council of Europe White Paper, para 12.

163 UN Declaration of Human Rights, Art 1.

housing and medical care and necessary social services.'[164] The implications of these provisions for the rights of the mentally ill were not immediately recognised. The first important step came in 1977 when concern was expressed by the United Nations Commission on Human Rights about the consequences that advances in the field of neuro-surgery, biochemistry and psychiatry may hold for the protection of human personality and its physical and intellectual integrity. But it has taken the UN a very long time to move from recognition of the human rights problems to a declaration of intent. Even now, no internationally enforceable legal protection exists. The concern expressed by the Commission on Human Rights in 1977 led to the establishment of a Sub-Commission which, in 1983, published a Final Report. Years of consultation with governments, the World Health Organisation and interested Non-Governmental Organisations finally resulted, in 1991, in the adoption by the General Assembly of the United Nations of an International Human Rights document. The 'Principles for the protection of persons with mental illness and for the improvement of mental health care' contains 25 important principles.

The principles do not have the legal status of a treaty; that is, they are not legally enforceable. They are intended as a 'guide to governments, specialised agencies, national, regional and international organisations, competent Non-Governmental Organisations and individuals to stimulate a constant endeavour to overcome economic and other difficulties in their adoption and application'. They represent minimum UN standards for the protection of fundamental freedoms and human and legal rights of persons with mental illness. They are aimed at providing a framework on which all nations should base their mental health legislation. The UN's goal is to encourage the incorporation of new international norms into national law. They are aimed at reinforcing the commitment to the inherent dignity and inalienable rights of every person.

No international organ is charged with monitoring its implementation, nor its application, at the national level. There is no procedure by which individual complaints can be received. But, arguably, they do act to reinforce rights and freedoms and many commentators see the Principles as having symbolic strength, incorporating as they do a moral ideal and providing member nations with the political goal of enhancing the respect for the mentally disordered. A detailed analysis of the Principles is outside the scope of this chapter. Of particular relevance, however, are the non-discrimination and consent to treatment provisions and their implications for reform of English mental health law.

164 UN Declaration of Human Rights, Art 25.

Non-discrimination

The Principles are based on the recognition that 'persons with mental illness are especially vulnerable and require particular protection. It is essential that their rights be clearly defined and established in accordance with the International Bill of Human Rights':

> Principle 1: There shall be no discrimination on the grounds of mental illness but ... special measures solely to protect the rights and secure the advancement of the mentally ill are not deemed discriminatory.

As has already been noted, there is a worldwide problem of discrimination and stigma attaching to mental disorders. But, discrimination in the document is defined in vague and general terms and arguably recognises the right to intervene rather than protect against discriminatory intervention. A key aim of the proposals for reform of the Mental Health Act is to end discrimination and stigma[165] against the mentally disordered. Standard One in the Mental Health Service Framework provides that health and social services should 'combat discrimination against individuals and groups with mental health problems and promote their social inclusion'.[166] It is easier to state in general terms a commitment to non-discrimination than it is to draft legislation that makes this a reality. Nowhere can this be seen more starkly than in the comparable rights of psychiatric patients and physically ill patients to consent to or withhold consent to medical treatment. Treatment for *physical* conditions can be refused where capacity exists, but not for mental disorder where the patient is detained under the Mental Health Act.[167] How much further forward do these Principles take the debate?:

> Principle 11: No treatment shall be given to a patient without his informed consent except as provided for in paras 6, 7, 8, 13 and 15 of the present principle.

The *Travaux préparatoires*[168] highlighted the classic controversy that exists about the rights of the mentally ill. The proposals for reform of the Mental Health Act 1983 in England have been influenced by a similar debate. Does or should the psychiatric patient have the same rights of informed consent as the physically ill patient?

The problems inherent in this debate surround the traditional tensions that exist between paternalism and autonomy. Paternalists subscribe to the

---

165 DoH, *Proposals for Reform of the Mental Health Act*, December 2000.

166 DoH, *NHS Frameworks: Mental Health*, 2000, London: HMSO.

167 In *Re C (Refusal of Medical Treatment)* (1994) 1 FLR 31, the Court of Appeal held that, at common law, a competent patient with capacity had the right to refuse surgery even where that refusal might lead to death. The same person did not have a right to refuse consent to treatment for his mental disorder.

168 See, eg, UNDOC E/CN.4/sub.2/1988/WG3/WP3, 1988, Geneva.

commonly held view that a person diagnosed as being mentally ill is, by definition, incapable of exercising his or her right to consent. Refusal to accept treatment is often the trigger to involuntary detention and involuntary admission is often used to determine incapacity in both law and practice. The refusal is viewed as a symptom of the illness and the failure to treat a denial of that person's 'right to treatment'. Voluntary patients have, in law, the same rights as any other patient in any other field of medicine, the involuntary patient's admission and treatment are justified by reference to the fact that it is in the patient's 'best interests' to be treated, irrespective of capacity.

The alternative argument is, however, that the values of autonomy and equality apply universally. Psychiatric patients are not necessarily rendered incompetent to exercise consent merely by the diagnosis of a psychiatric illness or involuntary admission. The law should not presume that refusal is a consequence of mental disorder; the right to treatment and the right to refuse treatment are not mutually exclusive. Adherents to this school sought specific norms governing the right to consent to treatment of patients admitted compulsorily. Whilst Principle 11, on the face of it, looks to support autonomy over paternalism, it is doubtful whether in reality this is the case.[169]

What is meant by 'informed consent'?

The definition in para 2 comprises two elements: the right to information and the right to make a decision freely without threats or improper inducements. There is no reference to capacity as a precondition. But Principle 11(6) provides that the informed consent of an involuntary patient is not necessary if either the patient lacks capacity *or* he *unreasonably* withholds consent having regard to his own safety or the safety of others *and* an independent authority is satisfied that the proposed plan of treatment is in the patient's best interests. This principle has been criticised on the grounds that it contradicts the value of autonomy and consecrates a particular medical approach to human rights.[170] Is it designed for therapeutic purposes or to ensure social control? Are doctors being given the supreme right of intervention to pursue 'improvement of mental health care'? Are the provisions thus not inherently discriminatory and in

169 Gendreau, G, 'The rights of psychiatric patients in the light of the principles announced by the United Nations: a recognition of the right to consent to treatment?' (1997) 20 Int'l J of Law and Psychiatry, pp 259–78.

170 Rosenthal, E and Rubenstein, L, 'International human rights advocacy under the "Principles for the Protection of Persons with Mental Illness"' (1993) 16 Int'l J L and Psychiatry 257, pp 291–300.

contravention of the most important internationally protected human right, the right not to be discriminated against? In English law, at least, the adult, competent physically ill person who refuses medical treatment cannot have his decision challenged on the grounds that it is 'rational or irrational, unknown or even non-existent'.[171]

Paragraph 4 goes on to require that the patient who refuses treatment or who demands the cessation of treatment be explained the consequences of such refusal, but it is arguable that this acts as an encouragement to gain consent rather than a recognition of an inherent right to refuse.

Whilst Principle 8(2) provides that 'every patient should be protected from harm including unjustified medication', the over-use of tranquillising medication in psychiatric wards and prisons has long been a cause of concern.[172] Drug treatments which exceed the BNF recommended doses and the use of polypharmacy appear commonplace. Lack of patient involvement in choice of medication is also criticised. A recent survey conducted by the National Schizophrenia Fellowship, the Manic Depression Fellowship and MIND revealed that some 62% of people with severe mental illness were denied a choice of drug treatment by their doctor.[173] Cheaper drugs with more adverse side effects are often prescribed in preference to newer ones with fewer side effects which are, unfortunately, more costly.[174]

CONCLUSION

Whilst non-discrimination is a fundamental aim of all human rights instruments, for the mentally disordered it remains illusive in practice. Words alone are not enough. Positive measures to end stigma and discrimination will almost certainly improve the quality of life of the millions of sufferers of mental disorder. The law is a blunt instrument; political will is also required.

171 *Per* Lord Donaldson in *Re T (An Adult) (Consent to Medical Treatment)* [1992] 2 FLR 458, p 473.

172 See, eg, Fraser, K and Hepple, J, 'Prescribing in a special hospital' (1992) 3 J of Forensic Psychiatry 2, p 311; and *Report of the Inspector of Mental Hospitals for the Year Ending 31 December 1999*, Dublin: Government of Ireland.

173 *A Question of Choice*, December 2000.

174 (1999) 5 Effective Health Care 6.

CHAPTER 12

PARTICULAR ISSUES OF PUBLIC HEALTH: FROM TELEMEDICINE TO E-HEALTH – SOME LEGAL IMPLICATIONS

Diana Tribe

TELEMEDICAL PRACTICE

Telemedicine is a 20th century concept which can be broadly defined as the linking of any two or more sites by interactive television, telephone or computer as a vehicle for the exchange of clinical information, the purpose of which is to facilitate the delivery of patient care. The term tends to be used generically to include a wide range of health care activities which use telecommunication technology to provide clinical information and services via electronic imaging equipment,[1] transferring information from one site to another either in 'static' or 'dynamic' form.

'Static' imaging involves the one way transmission of high resolution still-frame images and is used primarily in radiology and pathology utilising teleradiology and telepathology equipment. This is often referred to as a 'store and forward' procedure, because an image is taken using a digital camera ('stored') which is then sent ('forwarded') to another location. It is used typically for non-emergency situations when a diagnosis or consultation may be made in the next 24–48 hours and then sent back. 'Dynamic' imaging involves the two way transmission of full motion videos via interactive video conferencing equipment. It is used for patient care from a distance and for remote physician consultation. This two way interactive television (IATV) is based upon the availability of videoconferencing equipment at both locations, thus allowing a 'real time' consultation to take place between health professionals or between health professionals and patient. The majority of telemedicine programmes employ a combination of dynamic and static imaging.

A transmission medium, or network, is needed to link sites within a telemedicine programme. This could be as simple as an analogue phone line and a modem (for static imaging), or as complex as a satellite-leased line hybrid network (for 'high bandwidth' dynamic imaging). Simple examples of a telemedical exchange are those involving the linking of two sites, which may be as close as two adjacent buildings or as far apart as ships in different

1 Stanberry, B, *The Legal and Ethical Aspects of Telemedicine*, 1998, London: Royal Society of Medicine Press, p 97.

oceans. It has been utilised during space exploration, and for patients in ocean going vessels, deep-sea mining ships and oceanographic laboratories. In the US, it has been used to benefit isolated under-served populations that do not routinely attract clinical services, such as prison inmates, the armed forces, disaster relief and housebound patients.[2] It can provide very simple aids to the transmission of clinical information such as details of foetal heart rate, which can be monitored by a remote paediatric cardiologist via a facsimile machine. It can be used to assist a midwife attending a rural delivery, or more simply still, message systems may be employed rather than humans to inform a patient of test results by telephone.

At the other end of the scale, computers could become active participants in planning and performing surgery. Telepathologists can view cross-sections of tissue samples and access computer network databases to facilitate diagnosis, and then transmit findings to the patient's consultant. Indeed, telesurgery may routinely be possible and 'scalpelless' surgery using a 'gamma knife' which focuses radiation to excise brain tissue, for instance, might be guided across national boundaries rather than from within operating theatres. In all these examples, the doctor may still be said to be 'practising medicine', albeit from a distance.

Telemedicine began as a technique for facilitating medical practice. Developments in technology have enabled the use of telemedicine as a public health tool and it has been commented that public health has an electronic future.[3] Electronic networks for research and teaching in public health have been established across the world, including in Australia, Israel, Canada, Norway and Hungary.[4] Telemedicine facilitates access to sophisticated and specialist health care in geographical areas which until now have been physically, economically and even culturally remote from all but the most rudimentary health services.[5] There have been public health programmes devoted to increasing access to health information in

---

2 About 2,000 non-military telemedical consultations were performed in the US in 1993, while the armed forces have established satellite connections for clinical education, diagnosis, triage and treatment to more than 70 remote locations throughout the world. Teleradiology Associates, whose HQ are in Durham, North Carolina, is linked to 45 hospitals in 20 States and reads up to 20,000 studies per annum, providing a service to practitioners in rural settings; Troy, A, 'Roadblocks on the information superhighway: removing the legal and policy barriers to telemedicine', in *National Information Infrastructure Testbed – Vision Becomes Reality*, 1995, http://www.naf.edu/readingroom/books/wpn3, p 46.

3 'Global health and the information superhighway: epidemiologists are using the internet' (1994) 309 BMJ 736.

4 Ostbye, T, Bojan, R *et al*, 'Establishing an international computer network for research and teaching in public health and epidemiology' (1991) 2 European Journal of Epidemiology 34.

5 See Lown, B, Bukachi, F and Xavier, R, 'Health information in the developing world' (1998) 352 The Lancet 34-8S.

developing countries,[6] but there remains a problem with the 'digital divide'.[7] Telemedicine makes it possible for simultaneous mass distribution of knowledge and expertise, improving communication of public health advocacy and public health information, but is dependent on the receiving technology of the beneficiaries of knowledge. Internet access in Africa, India and South America is significantly lower than in the Western world,[8] and the funding of improved access is a significant global public health objective.[9] Through telemedicine, patients can explore alternative sources of health information and alternative sources of diagnosis and treatment which will change the whole face of health care provision once access problems have been solved. Telemedicine has revolutionalised the preparation and use of health databases, facilitating public health surveillance and improving the quality and accuracy of health prediction.

Using telemedical techniques, issues of medical treatment can be expanded to reach mass populations at limited expense and requiring limited personnel, such that contemporary public health practice is making increasing use of technology as an integral part of its operation. The development of telephone access to the internet, the increasing sophistication and accuracy of web search engines and the monitoring of health websites will all contribute to the integration of electronic information into public health practice. This will result in more than just a change in the kind of technology used by health professionals; it will result in a change in the culture of public health. Use of electronic information by professionals and patients is not just a passive exercise. Technology enables input as well as output, such that users can influence through the internet the direction of public health.[10] The whole face of public health will, over the next decade, be altered by the injection of technology into traditional public health measures, and the importance of telemedicine and e-health in this context cannot be underestimated.

---

6 Such as the Satellife project which uses a low orbit satellite to provide health information to heath professionals across Asia and Africa. See Groves, T, 'Satellife: getting relevant information to the developing world' (1996) 313 BMJ 1606.

7 Tan-Torres, T, 'Disseminating health information in the developing countries: the role of the internet' (2000) 321 BMJ 797.

8 Tan-Torres (*ibid*) notes the report of the United Nations Development Programme that there are more internet hosts in New York than in continental Africa, more hosts in Finland than in Latin America and the Caribbean, and many villages in India still lack a working telephone. See United Nations Development Programme, Report of the Meeting of High-level Panel of Experts on Information and Communication Technology, April 2000, New York.

9 However, many development organisations have concentrated resources on infrastructural projects rather than on improving information dissemination. See 'Global information flow' (2000) 321 BMJ 776.

10 See Zielinski, C, 'New equities of information in the electronic age' (1995) 310 BMJ 1480.

History

The first recorded use of telemedicine dates back to a 1957 Nebraska project that allowed doctors and patients to interact over a closed circuit television link. In another early and notable telemedicine project, STARPHAC, health care was delivered to residents in the Papago Indian Reservation in the US. The STARPHAC project was eventually discontinued on the grounds of organisational problems,[11] although other difficulties experienced include the reluctance of the Medicare health insurers to reimburse physicians for technologically mediated consultations,[12] an issue resolved in 1997. In the 1970s and 1980s,[13] other limited telemedicine projects were developed in the US and Canada. With the exception of the 20 year old telemedical project at the Memorial University of Newfoundland, St John's, which was based on the telephone network as the core technology supporting audio conferencing and the transmission of electro-encephalograms, none of the programmes commenced before 1986 appears to have survived.

In Texas, telemedicine is currently being used in the prison system where patients are examined by use of videoconferencing equipment by doctors located at urban hospitals. In Oregon, a project is being developed for dermatology consultations to be performed by transferring images from a clinic in rural areas to a specialist in Portland. It played an important role in the Los Angeles Olympics by providing athletes and visitors access to clinical centres across the US. The US Navy had its own telemedicine links between Zagreb and the National Naval Clinical Centre in Bethesda to support UN forces in Croatia.[14]

NASA has been involved in the development of high data-rate satellite communications to reach distant areas and has developed an Advanced Communication Technology Satellite, the world's first processing Ka-band satellite, to develop new initiatives in communication technology for the telemedicine industry. ACTS allows the use of small, low-cost, portable antennae that provide affordable high data rate transmission of clinical records and live video.[15] The Spacebridge project links seven clinical sites across the US and Moscow, and the NASA Langley Research Centre has developed a prototype internet access model which allows a whole local

11 Preston, J, Brown, F and Hanley, B, 'Using telemedicine to improve health care in distant areas' (1992) 43 Hospital Community Psychiatry 25.

12 Bergman, L, 'Letting telemedicine do the walking in hospitals and health networks' (1993) IO 47.

13 Richards, B, 'Telephone triage cuts costly ER visits' (1995) *Wall St Journal*, 25 October, B1.

14 (1996) 13 Health Law Update 20.

15 Beller, A, 'A vote for telehealth' (1996) 4 Telemedicine Today 1, p 3.

area network (LAN) of computers to connect to the internet using only a standard analogue telephone line.

In Europe, the Telemedicine in Norway project, which was centred on the University Hospital of Tromsö, combined geographical inaccessibility with an advanced digital telecommunications structure and ran successful pilot studies of remote diagnosis in dermatology, cardiology, pathology, radiology and endoscopy of otorhinolaryngology patients. The European Commission's research and development in advanced technologies in Europe (RACE) project funded the Telemed project from 1988 to 1992, which evaluated pilot studies of applications in remote radiology, reference database management and psychiatry. The RGIT Survival Centre in Aberdeen has developed a system called Camnet, which allows transmissions of vital signs and video and audio pictures from a remote paramedic to a secondary care centre.[16]

In Hong Kong, an audiovisual systems network has been installed between the CUHK Clinical Science Building and the Prince of Wales Hospital which allows for integrated consultation, teaching and demonstrations of medicine, surgery, and diagnostic and interventionist radiology and endoscopy. A link between this hospital and a district hospital without neurosurgical coverage provides triage of head injury patients as they are admitted.[17]

From 1996 onwards, there have been a wide variety of telemedicine projects together with their respective applications operating across the UK. Staff at the Royal Free Hospital, London, have investigated the effectiveness of telemedicine in improving communication between primary and secondary care providers.[18] The University of Cambridge has been running a European funded internet project to predict birth outcomes using a telemedical technique. Other examples include the ongoing paediatric cardiology project at Brompton Royal and Harefield NHS Trust Hospitals, the home telecare system currently running at Bristol Royal Infirmary and the emergency videotelemetry project for pre-hospital care at the University of Bath.

Telemedical objectives

Rapid development of technology to support telemedical initiatives has been driven by desire on the part of governments and others for cheap, yet

16 McLaren, P and Ball C, 'Telemedicine lessons remain unheeded' (1997) 310 BMJ 1390.

17 Ko, P, 'Telemedicine in Hong Kong', http://telemedicinetoday.com/articlearchive/articles/telemedicinehongkong.htm

18 Harrison, R, Clayton, W and Wallace, P, 'Can telemedicine be used to improve communication between primary and secondary care?' (1996) 313 BMJ pp 1377–80.

nonetheless high quality clinical advice and treatment, regardless of location. The procedures are perceived as providing a cost efficient form of delivery, eliminating hours of 'windshield time' for circuit riding doctors.[19] It is also believed that telemedicine may lead to reduced expenditure by allowing patients to be treated earlier when their illness is less serious rather than waiting until a condition has reached a more advanced, critical stage.[20] These developments have been facilitated by recent advances in technology, such as digital compressed video, and telecommunications. Manufacturers of videoconferencing, imaging, computer, clinical and multimedia equipment have all been attracted to the telemedicine market.

E-HEALTH RECORDS

An important and secondary outcome of the technology of telemedecine has been the development and transmission of electronic patient records. What is often termed 'e-health' has been described by some as a broader application of telemedicine and includes recording the assessment, treatment and monitoring of patients between remote locations and multiple personnel.[21] Various strategies have been employed worldwide. In some cases, patients themselves have internet access to their own health records and can themselves insert data on their private health treatment (for example, osteopath, chiropractor, acupuncturist). At the other extreme, these records are simple records with data entry and access only available to a limited number of health professionals.

LEGAL IMPLICATIONS OF TELEMEDICINE AND E-HEALTH RECORDS

The practical advantages of telemedicine and electronic patient records are considerable, and increasingly sophisticated technical developments are making such activities more reliable and accessible. There are undoubtedly, as with all technological developments, legal problems arising from the use of this technology which are only slowly being addressed. These include questions as to jurisdiction and choice of law, as to confidentiality and data protection and as to licensure to practice across State and national boundaries.

19 Little, A, 'The unfinished business of the NIIT' (1996) 119 National Information in Health Care, pp 211–13.

20 Richards, B, 'Telephone triage cuts costly ER visits' *Wall St Journal*, 25 October 1995, B1.

21 Grigsby, J, 'Current status of domestic telemedicine' (1995) 19 J of Clinical Systems 1, p 19.

It would appear that telemedicine and e-health can be divided into three broad categories. The first consists of patient consultation and diagnosis (telemedicine) by means of real time transmission of 'static' and 'dynamic' video images, and patient treatment through the dynamic control of clinical hardware by use of virtual reality tools. Such distant consultation and treatment may give rise to all the normal clinical issues of liability, together with product liability where there are technological faults causing patient injury. The most commonly held view is that a telemedicine link 'transports' the doctor to the patient, although an equally valid argument could be made for treating it the other way, thus reflecting real life practice. If it is assumed that the doctor is transported to the patient, it will be important for the doctor to know something of the private international law rules of the patient's jurisdiction as to choice of law, and the legal rules that would be applied on consent and malpractice.

The second category comprises remote expert systems and online databases that provide aids to self-diagnosis and treatment, such as the web-based system, Bandolier, and NHS Direct.[22] It is clear that potential privacy risks arise from the traces that must inevitably be left when any individual uses the internet. These traces would allow a personal profile to be built up of an individual's medical history or interests which would be of commercial value to insurers or pharmaceutical manufacturers. Similarly, where a GP in the UK utilises a system such as PRODIGY,[23] a computer software system which gives prescribing advice to GPs, there is a possibility of invasion of a patient's privacy for the commercial benefit of outsiders, 'although undesired use of personal medical information can be prevented by opting for anonymous access to and anonymous use of services'.[24] Privacy enhancing technologies, the harmonised use of smart cards for assessing the internet and best practice in electronic health services are among the key elements of the European Union action plan, eEurope 2002, of June 2000.[25]

The third category covers individual patient information and records, collected and transmitted between sites using electronic records (either

22 A 24 hour nurse-led Helpline offering triage information to patients.

23 Prescribing Rationally with Decision Support in General Practice, commissioned in 1995 by the NHS; see Harpwood, V, 'The manipulation of medical practice', in Freeman, M and Lewis, A, *Law and Medicine*, Current Legal Issues Vol 3, 2000, Oxford: OUP, pp 57–58.

24 Roscam Abbing, H, 'Internet, the patient and the right to care for health', 7 European Journal of Health Law, p 224.

25 Anonymity of users looking for health related information and the confidentiality of information exchanged fall under the right to privacy and secrecy of correspondence as guaranteed by Art 8 of the European Convention on Human Rights.

electronic patient records or electronic health records). The UK Government has developed an ambitious programme to enable the electronic delivery of government services, announced by the Prime Minister in March 2000, committing public agencies such as the NHS to making 100% of their services electronically available to citizens and businesses alike by the year 2005. This policy is based on the assumption that health records should be readily accessible to health professionals wherever the patient is being treated in order to provide what has been described as 'fast and seamless care to patients'. Here, there are serious legal problems relating to the protection of data and its confidentiality.

Meanwhile, the systems in use today for telemedicine and e-health records largely remain reliant on adaptations of teleconferencing or desk top computer systems. These were neither designed nor evaluated for their ability to provide accurate diagnostic information and confidential records. They require the involvement of technicians and other personnel who have specialist non-clinical training in the operation of the systems and in the transmission of telemedical information together with the health professional.

JURISDICTION

Where telemedicine is practised within one country and clinical negligence has been identified, problems of 'forum shopping' and conflicting rules of law do not arise. Where telemedicine operates across State and/or national boundaries, difficulties have arisen in identifying the location of the consultation for jurisdiction purposes. It is not always easy to identify exactly where a tort was committed for the purposes of determining jurisdiction, and this is undoubtedly the case with telemedicine in which medical treatment and advice might be administered by health personnel in one country through the agency of practitioners of different nationalities to a patient in another country.

The Brussels and Lugano Conventions[26] specify that where the defendant is domiciled in a Contracting State of the European Community,

26 The Brussels Convention on Jurisdiction and the Enforcement of Judgments in Civil and Commercial Matters 1968 was drafted with the intention of harmonising rules on jurisdiction within the European Community. The Lugano Convention on Jurisdiction and the Enforcement of Judgments in Civil and Commercial Matters 1988 is a parallel Convention negotiated in countries which were then members of EFTA (Iceland, Austria, Finland, Norway, Switzerland and Sweden). Austria, Finland and Sweden have since joined the EC and are now governed by the Brussels Convention. Issues of jurisdiction may also be governed by the Modified Convention of the Brussels Convention which adapts the Convention for operation in the UK. These Conventions are given effect in English domestic law by the Civil Jurisdiction and Judgments Act 1982.

jurisdiction in relation to an action in law is primarily determined by the domicile of the defendant. In some circumstances, the claimant may have a choice of where to bring proceedings, and may choose instead to bring proceedings in the State where the wrong was committed. The scope of these Conventions is confined to civil and commercial matters. Where the Brussels and Lugano Conventions are inapplicable, that is, when the defendant is not domiciled in a Contracting State, and when the matter at issue does not fall within the civil and commercial scope of the Conventions, then national law will govern jurisdiction.

Choice of law

UK law

The European Union has not yet enacted rules as to the choice of law in tort/delict so that neither EC legislation nor international agreement replaces the existing English common law. There has been no reported judicial examination under English law of whether parties can choose the law to govern their liability in tort. However, it would appear that prior to 1995, when the Private International Law (Miscellaneous Provisions) Act was passed, English choice of law rules for claims in tort were based upon the ancient case of *Phillips v Eyre*,[27] in which Willes J laid down that:

> As a general rule in order to found a suit in England for a wrong alleged to have been committed abroad, two conditions must be fulfilled. First, the wrong must be of such a character that it would have been actionable if committed in England ... Secondly the act must not have been justifiable by the law of the place where it was done.

This was known as the 'double actionability' rule, and subsequent case law made clear that a claimant was required to establish that a tort was actionable both under the *lex fori* (the law of the land where the question of law is being considered, in this case English law) and under the *lex loci delicti* (the law of the land where the tort was committed),[28] subject to limited exceptions where justice was seen to dictate the application of English law.[29] The double actionability rule gave 'the predominant role to English law, even though the tort was committed abroad, and regardless of whether either party was English'.[30] The Chairman of the English Law Commission, Brooke J, referred to the English rule as being a 'double whammy' in favour

27 *Phillips v Eyre* (1870) LR 6QB.

28 *Boyes v Chaplin* [1971] AC 356 926, HL.

29 *Red Sea Insurance v Bouygues SA* [1995] 1 AC 190.

30 Clarkson, C and Hill, J, *Jaffey on the Conflict of Laws*, 1997, London: Butterworths, p 256.

of defendants, and as being virtually unique in all systems of law which had a European foundation, being 'anomalous, unjust and uncertain'.

This rule has now been abolished by the Private International Law (Miscellaneous Provisions) Act 1995, which was drafted to provide clarity and certainty in the law in relation to acts and omissions giving rise to claims in tort/delict after May 1996. Given the relatively new development of telemedicine, it is likely that the majority of claims arising from this practice will fall under the new legislation.

The Act establishes that the applicable law in relation to claims relating to a tort occurring in a single country is *prima facie* that of the place of occurrence of injury, damage or death. A medical procedure administered in England will give rise to proceedings in England, regardless of the nationality of the doctor or patient. Where the events constituting the tort occur in different countries ('multi-country' torts), as could well be the case in claims based upon telemedical practice, the rules are more complex. However, s 11(2) identifies applicable law for a cause of action in respect of personal injury or death, as being that of the country where the individual was when he sustained the injury. This has significant implications for medical practitioners who might find themselves subject to foreign civil law with which they are unfamiliar and for which they have no insurance cover. The clear intention of the Act is to allow claims based on causes of action or heads of damage that were previously unfamiliar to English law. However, it remains possible for an English court to disapply the applicable law under s 14(3) if 'it would conflict with principles of public policy'.

This legislation accords with the choice of law rules applicable in most European systems, and is likely to correspond to the reasonable expectations of parties involved in the tort or delict. The legislation is expected to promote uniformity and discourage forum shopping. If an English court would not recognise an issue as being one of tort, the court will not hear the action (s 9). Alternatively, the courts may invoke the ground of public policy, as provided by s 14, in order to disregard the provisions. The Act also provides for an exception by s 12, which is to be applied in any case where upon comparing the significance of the factors connecting the tort with a country whose law would be applicable under the general rule, it appears substantially more appropriate for the applicable law to be that of another country. This exception has the effect of applying the law of another country in the same way as the common law position in *Boyes v Chaplin* and the *Red Sea* case. It would be invoked where there was no single territory or country in which the most significant elements in the sequence of events occurred, or where it would be most substantially appropriate that the other law should apply.

The wording of s 12 would appear to indicate 'that those seeking to rely on it will face an uphill task'.[31] However, the section has since been applied in *E v Simmonds*,[32] where the most significant factors (that is, those relating to the parties, to any of the events which constituted the tort or delict in question, and any of the circumstances of consequences of those events) were applied. In this case, it was held that an accident in Spain, in a Spanish vehicle which was owned and insured by a Spanish company and which was involved in an accident with a Spanish driver driving a vehicle owned and insured in Spain, should nonetheless fall to be determined under English law. This decision would imply that the courts are likely to be generous to those seeking to rely on s 12 of the Act.

The abolition of the double actionability rule has been a welcome development and the *prima facie* choice of law in personal injury cases under s 11 of the Act constitutes a positive step towards greater clarity and certainty. However, until such time as the courts have developed a clear preference for the flexibility offered by s 12 (displacement of the general rule) or the greater certainty rules under s 11, the overall impact of the legislation cannot be assessed. The passage of time and an accumulation of tort cases should lead to greater clarity.

An issue which remains to be resolved in the context of telemedicine is whether issues of choice of law can be resolved in advance, through the use of consent forms agreed by patients, prior to consultation. This may be possible in respect of private patients where the relationship between doctor and patient is contractual. Where contracting parties are free to choose the proper law of a contract, the principles which will guide an English court on the question of the proper law of contract are now well settled. It is the law that the parties intended to apply. Their intention will be ascertained by the intention expressed in the contract, if any, which will be conclusive. If no intention is expressed, the intention will be presumed by the court from the terms of the contract and the relevant surrounding circumstances.[33] There is no reported case of an English court striking down a choice of law clause, unless there are statutory rules in the *lex fori* which override the choice of the parties, such as in the Employment Protection (Consolidation) Act 1978 and the Unfair Contract Terms Act 1977. Choice of law in contract is now covered in the European Union by the Convention of Rome, which has been incorporated into English law by the Contracts (Applicable Law) Act 1990. Under Art 3(1), 'A contract shall be governed by the law chosen by the parties. The choice must be express or demonstrated with reasonable certainty by the terms of the contract or the circumstances of the case. By

31 O'Brien, J, *Smith's Conflict of Laws*, 1999, London: Cavendish Publishing, p 463.

32 *E v Simmonds* QBD WL1629608, 4 October 2000 (Westlaw).

33 *Per* Lord Atkin, in *R v International Trust for the Protection of Bondholders* [1937] AC 500, p 529.

their choice parties can select the law applicable to the whole or a part only of the contract.'

Under English law, there is no contractual relationship in relation to patients treated under the National Health Service. Here, the duty of care is founded only in the law of tort, to which the Private International Law (Miscellaneous Provisions) Act 1995 applies.

United States

The historic dependence of English courts on the *lex fori* has not been shared by other legal systems. In *Babcock v Jackson*,[34] a New York court held that:

> Justice, fairness and the 'best practical result' may best be achieved by giving controlling effect to the law of the jurisdiction which, because of its relationship or contact with the occurrence or the parties, has the greatest concern with the specific issue raised in litigation.[35]

This view has now been accepted in some 26 States of the US,[36] whilst being rejected in another 10. Quite frequently, the application of the appropriate law by American courts has simply meant that they have indulged a preference for using American law rather than that of other countries.

Other jurisdictions

Most of the world outside of the US and legal systems strongly influenced by English law, apply the *lex loci delicti* to questions of choice of law in tort. This seems a sensible strategy, since litigants will normally expect that the law of the country where the accident took place will apply.

However, there is support in Germany[37] and in The Netherlands for freedom to choose the law which will govern tort liability. In 1976, in the leading case before the European Court of Justice on jurisdiction over tort claims under Art 3 of the Brussels Convention on jurisdiction and enforcement of judgment, the parties' choice of Dutch law was upheld.[38] Swiss private international law also confers an express, but limited freedom of choice in tort cases, allowing parties at any time after the tort was committed to choose the application of the law of the forum, in that case Swiss law.[39] The Supreme Court of Canada has abandoned the rule in *Phillips v Eyre* for all intra-provincial intra-Canadian cases embracing a rigid

---

34 *Babcock v Jackson* (1963) 191 NE 2d 279.

35 *Per* Fuld J.

36 See *Camporeses v Port Authority of New York and New Jersey* (1979) 415 NYS 2d 28.

37 Kahn-Freund [1974] III Hague Receuil 139–341, n 44.

38 *Bier BV v Mines de Potasse de Alsace SA* [1976] ECR 1735 Case 21/76.

39 North, P, *Essays in Private International Law*, 1992, Oxford: OUP, p 228.

lex loci delicti approach with no flexibility, and asserting that such a rule accorded with the territorial principle of international law, the practical concerns of certainty, ease of application and the expectations of ordinary people and the majority of other States.[40]

The effect of choice of law on clinical negligence claims

So far, there are no reported decisions regarding the wide range of legal issues arising from the use of technology for telemedical purposes. There have been but a handful of (unreported) claims to the American Physicians' Association following alleged negligent telemedicine practices.[41] This may be because telemedicine consultations are likely to be more thorough than traditional examinations (on the basis that two or more heads are better than one) or because practitioners with access to databanks of clinical records are more likely to diagnose uncommon ailments resulting in better patient outcomes.

There is, however, a more general view that as clinical technology has increased, so have malpractice claims, although there is no evidence as to a causative link between these two developments. In the UK, the tide of clinical litigation is increasing incrementally[42] and patients now seem to expect more precise diagnoses and more positive clinical outcomes. Yet, new technologies require doctors to learn new skills, and deficiencies or failures in telemedicine equipment or practice may give rise to claims in negligence. The fact that the public perceives the manufacturers of technical equipment as having 'deep pockets' may make this even more likely, as manufacturers may be joined as third parties in litigation. At the same time, it may be possible to offer a higher standard of protection for doctors against negligence claims in telemedicine, since records of each session can be incorporated within patient files. Recording may, of course, prove a two edged sword, since this would clearly document mistakes, and is of course discoverable by a patient claimant.

An important question to which there is as yet no clear answer concerns vicarious liability for a doctor practising via telemedical links. If the doctor is acting as an employee of a hospital, will that hospital be vicariously or personally liable for the treatment or advice offered over a telemedical link, despite the fact that the patient is located within another hospital (or indeed

40 Walker, J, 'Choice of law in tort: the Supreme Court of Canada enters the fray' (1995) 111 LQR 397.

41 Telephone conversation with Lois Bartholomew of the American Physicians' Association.

42 White, P (1995) MDU Annual Reports 1965–90; Mann, R and Harvard, J, *No Fault Compensation In Medicine*, 1997, London: Royal Society of Medicine.

another country)? Will that doctor be covered by his insurance? Normally, insurance policies assume single country (or State) practices, so presumably a doctor giving advice across national (or State) borders must arrange additional private insurance cover.

NEGLIGENCE ISSUES ARISING FROM TELEMEDICAL PRACTICE

Medical treatment through the medium of telemedicine will be subject to the same legal rules as to duty and standard of care as traditional medical treatment. Under English law, the test for standard of clinical care was originally laid down in 1957 in *Bolam v Friern Barnet Hospital Management Committee*[43] and subsequently interpreted in *Bolitho v City and Hackney HA*.[44] The test in *Bolam* required a doctor to conform to the standards of an ordinary skilled man exercising and professing to have that particular skill which the defendant held himself out as possessing. An examination of the standards imposed by the law upon doctors in the performance of their therapeutic and diagnostic functions revealed the isolated and defensive attitudes of judges to doctors except in the most unusual cases. Expert evidence enjoyed virtually exclusive status in determination of standards. In *Bolitho*, Lord Browne-Wilkinson sought to correct what he believed had been a misinterpretation of *Bolam*, stating that ultimately the courts are the only arbiters of what constitutes reasonable care. In other words, doctors cannot be judges in their own courts. It has been commented that this, together with the recent decision in *Marriott v W Midlands HA*,[45] 'the establishment of the National Institution of Clinical Excellence and the Law Commission's proposals relating to the treatment of mentally incapacitated patients are just some of the practices which we contend will in many cases ensure that the courts can no longer blindly accept assertions of good practice, but evaluate that practice'.[46]

In most other countries, under both common and civil law,[47] courts have held that the determination of clinical standards, whilst being informed by expert clinical evidence, is ultimately and exclusively a judicial function. As was indicated in the Australian case of *Rogers v Whittaker*:[48] '[I]f a court merely followed the path apparently pointed out by expert evidence with no

43 *Bolam v Friern Barnet Hospital Management Committee* [1957] 1 WLR 582.

44 *Bolitho v City and Hackney HA* [1993] 4 Med LR 393.

45 *Marriott v W Midlands HA* [1999] Lloyd's Clinical Reports 23.

46 Brazier, M and Miola J, 'Bye-bye *Bolam*: a medical litigation revolution?' (2000) 8 Med Law Rev 1, p 86.

47 Eg, Austria.

48 *Rogers v Whittaker* (1992) 109 1 ALR 625.

critical consideration of it and other evidence, it would abdicate its duty to decide on the evidence whether in law a duty existed and had not been discharged.' Similarly, the Canadian courts have recognised that there are questions relating to medical practice that will fall within the comprehension of a layman:

Coyne J's remarks in *Anderson v Chasney* in the Canadian Supreme Court are interesting. He said that ... a group of professionals could legislate themselves out of liability for negligence to the public by adopting or continuing what was an obviously negligent practice, even though a simple precaution, plainly capable of obviating the danger which might result in death, was well known.[49]

NO FAULT / STRICT LIABILITY

Some countries have introduced a system of 'no fault' liability for acts of clinical negligence, for example, in Sweden, Finland, and some Australian and American States. Doctors practising across State boundaries need to be aware of these differences before undertaking consultations. No fault liability for death and personal injury arising from tort means that a claimant is not, as in England and many other jurisdictions, required to identify negligence. All that is required is for the claimant to show that any injury was *caused* by the defendant regardless of whether he was at fault.

Those practitioners who are accustomed to a fault-based system of liability need to be fully aware of the consequences of telemedical consultations with clients from no fault legal systems. These systems are superficially attractive, in that where a patient is injured, there is no requirement for investigation of the defendant's clinical skill and expertise against a standard set by law. On the other hand, in such jurisdictions it may be easier to prove liability, and doctors' insurance arrangements should take this possibility into account.

French and German legal systems both impose strict liability for which there is no State insurance cover, so unless the country in question will compensate the victim from a State insurance fund (as would be the case in New Zealand and Sweden), liability could prove onerous indeed.[50]

---

49 Lord Woolf's Inaugural Lecture in the Provosts Lecture Series at University College London, 17 January 2001.

50 Kahn-Freund [1974] III Hague Receuil 139–341, n 44.

PRODUCT LIABILITY

Telemedical procedures operate on a range of telecommunication and information technology equipment together with software products, and use of the internet and/or intranet (for example, NHSnet) technologies. These procedures depend upon equipment manufactured by third parties who may or may not be in a contractual relationship with health professionals, or who may owe a duty of care to the patient under tort/delict or relevant statutory provisions.

Part I of the Consumer Protection Act 1987 represents the British interpretation of the EC Product Liability Directive[51] and results predominantly from the difficulties experienced by victims of the thalidomide disaster in sustaining an action against the pharmaceutical suppliers of the drug.[52] The purpose of the Act was to impose strict liability upon a producer of a defective product. Section 1 of the Act defines a product to include medical treatment products such as surgical instruments, catheters, needles, intra-uterine devices, pacemakers and drugs, and would undoubtedly cover telemedical technology. Section 2 seeks to impose strict liability against producers or suppliers of the product. Providing it can be proved that a product caused the injury complained of, a claimant can seek compensation under the Act without having to prove negligence on the part of the manufacturer or supplier, although causation problems still remain to be solved.

Section 3(1) defines a defect in terms of safety so that 'if the safety of the product is not such as persons are generally entitled to expect', then the product is defective. Section 3(2) explains that what people are actually entitled to expect is to be determined by reference to a range of factors. First, the manner in which, and purposes for which the product has been marketed, its get-up, and any instructions or warnings, will be relevant. Although the Act is presented as imposing strict liability, its provisions concerning 'warnings' and 'instructions' would seem refer to negligent warnings and failures to warn only. Secondly, the court will consider what might reasonably be expected to be done in relation to the product, and thirdly, the time when the product was supplied by its producer will be relevant.

What actually constitutes a defect is likely to be the subject of complex litigation, particularly in respect of telemedical equipment. A PC used for office purposes which has a known adverse failure rate of 10% might be considered 'safe' for office or academic use, whilst a similar failure rate would be 'unsafe' when used by health professionals for telecardiology or teleradiology.

51 85/374/EEC.

52 See, also, the recommendations of the Pearson Commission, Cmnd 7054, 1978.

Section 4(1) appears to remove much of the effect of strict liability for certain States, including the UK, by allowing for the 'development risks' defence. It is a defence for a manufacturer to show that 'the state of scientific or technical knowledge at the relevant time was not such that a producer of products ... might be expected to have discovered the defect if it had arisen in the products'. This was a provision available to Member States in derogation from the EEC Directive on Product Liability (85/374). However, as Lord Scarman commented in the House of Lords debate: '(i)f you introduce the state of the art defence, you are really introducing negligence by the back door.'[53] This was thought to mean that the claimant damaged by information technology products after 1987 would be in no better position now than the claimants in the thalidomide, Opren and Debendox actions.

Moreover, the Act does have the effect of reversing the burden of proof and imposes on a defendant the task of making out a defence. The defendant cannot plead how expensive or difficult it would have been to eliminate the defect, that the product was manufactured to a national or international standard or that it was manufactured in accordance with traditional industrial practices.

By s 4(1)(d), a manufacturer or supplier can use the defence that the defect did not exist at the time that a product was manufactured or supplied. With computer equipment, defects can arise from the mishandling of products, making NHS trusts and general practitioners potentially liable for defects in equipment used for telemedical purposes. Imposition of liability would depend upon whether the technical fault lay at the doctor's or the patient's end of the telemedicine link, and the ability of a claimant to identify the manufacturer or producer within the EU of the faulty link. Where images are of poor quality and are alleged to have given rise to errors of diagnosis or treatment, the potential defendants will be the consulting doctor, the supporting technician, the manufacturer or provider of the hardware or software, the purchaser of the equipment, the doctor or his employer. There have so far been no cases where product liability has been considered in relation to use of IT equipment by health professionals.

However, in *A and Others v National Blood Authority*,[53a] claimants who had been infected with hepatitis C as a result of blood transfusions were successful in proving that the blood was defective within the meaning of Art 6 of the Council Directive 85/374 and that the defendants were strictly liable under Art 6 despite the absence of fault. In his judgment, Burton J held that the question of availability of the harmful characteristic, the impracticability of taking precautions and the benefit of the product to society were not factors which the court was required to consider under

53 HL Deb Vol 414 Col 1427.

53a [2001] Lloyd's Rep Med 157.

Art 6. Moreover, Art 7(e) did not afford a defence when it was known that a particular product could have harmful consequences.

CONSENT TO THE USE OF TELEMEDICAL PROCEDURES

Where a doctor is to use telemedical procedures in the diagnosis and or treatment of a patient, then the legal rules on consent will apply.[54] These vary from jurisdiction to jurisdiction.

The experimental nature of some telemedical procedures may require a doctor to disclose the novel nature of the consultation or treatment, and any uncertainty as to risks. At present, many telemedicine applications are delivered on a demonstration basis, which suggests some levels of uncertainty. Factors that may be important in determining the experimental nature of treatment would include analysis of the quality of data obtained from the same procedures conducted traditionally, analysis of the outcomes of telemedicine in comparison with traditional procedures, and analysis of how the technology of the telecommunications process may skew or enhance data.

English law on consent

Almost uniquely, English law imposes a standard of care in relation to consent to treatment, based not on the informational needs of the patient, but rather upon the judgment of a reasonable doctor as to what information should be disclosed to the patient. This is known as the 'English rule' on consent. In *Sidaway v Bethlem Royal Hospital Governors*,[55] the claimant argued that her doctor had been negligent in failing to inform her of the small element of risk inherent in a surgical procedure to which she had agreed. She argued that had she been aware of the risk, she would not have given her consent. The House of Lords held that the proper test to determine whether the doctor had met the required standard of care was the *Bolam*[56] test. Importantly, Lord Bridge added that there might be circumstances where '(t)he disclosure of a particular risk was so obviously necessary to an informed choice on the part of the patient that no reasonably prudent clinical man would fail to make it'. The possibility of 'grave adverse consequences' should always be revealed to a patient unless there were some 'cogent clinical reason why the patient should not be informed'. Lord

54 It is assumed for the purposes of this discussion that the patient is a competent adult. The laws on consent across jurisdictions in relation to minors and adults without capacity is complex, and beyond the remit of this chapter.

55 *Sidaway v Bethlem Royal Hospital Governors* [1985] 1 AC 582.

56 *Bolam v Friern Barnet Hospital Management Committee* [1957] 1 WLR 582.

Templeman gave an example of such a clinical reason: because 'some information might confuse, other information might alarm, a particular patient, a doctor might not consider it to be in the patient's best interests to reveal it'.

Thus, in English law and in those common law jurisdictions which continue to apply the English rule, the question of extent of information to be offered to a patient would still appear to be balanced between the medical professions and the courts. Where telemedical procedures are to be used in the treatment of a patient, it will be of particular importance to explain this to the patient and seek consent to the procedure.

The position where the patient asks specific questions of his doctor about a proposed procedure is less clear. In *Sidaway*, Lord Bridge was of the view that those questions must be answered 'both truthfully and as fully as the questioner requires'. However, two years later, in *Blyth v Bloomsbury HA*,[57] Kerr LJ appeared to disagree with Lord Bridge when he stated that:

> The question of what a plaintiff should be told in answer to a general enquiry cannot be divorced from the *Bolam* test any more than when no such enquiry is made ... indeed I am not convinced that the *Bolam* test is irrelevant even in relation to the question of what answers are properly to be given to *specific* enquiries, or that Lord Bridge or Lord Diplock intended to hold otherwise.

The American approach to informed consent

In the US, about half the States[58] apply an 'informed consent' rule, known as the American rule, in which the emphasis lies on the rights of the patient to information. Following *Canterbury v Spence*,[59] a doctor in these States must reveal to the patient those material risks of which a reasonably prudent patient would wish to be informed, subject to the defence of 'therapeutic privilege' by which a doctor may decline to disclose a risk on the grounds that disclosure was clinically contraindicated.

A similar test is applied in Canada,[60] New Zealand,[61] South Africa[62] and civil jurisdictions such as Germany, Switzerland and Austria.[63] In these jurisdictions, a patient oriented approach to consent is adopted, under which the doctor must consider the informational needs of the individual

---

57 *Rogers v Whittaker* (1993) 4 Med LR 79 (Cth).

58 Those American States that have not adopted the American rule on consent, adhere to the English approach.

59 *Canterbury v Spence* (1972) 464 F2d 772, DC.

60 *Reibl v Hughes* (1980) 114 DLR (3d) 1 (Can Sup Ct).

61 *Smith v Auckland Hospital Board* [1965] NZLR 191, CA.

62 *Castell v De Greef* (1994) (Case No 976/92), Sup Ct of S Africa, Cape of Good Hope, Provincial Division, *per* Ackerman J.

63 See Giesen, D [1995] Med LR 34.

patient in determining what level of information and consent must be obtained.

The Australian High Court considered the issue of consent in the case of *Rogers v Whittaker*.[64] Here, the doctor failed to reveal to the plaintiff that there was a 1 in 14,000 chance of sympathetic opthalmia developing in the 'good' left eye as a result of an operation on her right eye. The Australian High Court declined to follow the English *Bolam* test as applied in Sidaway, and found that the defendant had been negligent in failing to warn the claimant of the risk to her 'good' eye. The question was not whether the defendant's conduct accorded with normal clinical practice, but rather whether it conformed to the standard of reasonable care which the law requires. This was a question of law to be decided by the courts rather than a question of fact to be decided by the profession. The court held, approving *F v R*,[65] that the test for the disclosure of information was that all material risks to which the 'reasonably prudent patient' would attach significance, should be revealed. As King CJ had stated in *F v R*:

> Professions may adopt unreasonable practices. Practices may develop in professions, particularly as to disclosure, not because they serve the interests of the clients, but because they protect the interests or conveniences of members of the profession. The court has an obligation to scrutinise professional practices to ensure that they accord with the standard of reasonableness imposed by the law ... This is a question for the court and the duty of deciding it cannot be delegated to any profession or group in the community.

Thus, in Australia, the doctrine of informed consent is applied. This was defined in *Rogers v Whittaker* as a duty on the doctor to:

> Warn a patient of a material risk inherent in the proposed treatment; a risk is material if, in the circumstances of the particular case, a reasonable person in the patient's position, if warned of the risk, would be likely to attach significance to it or if the clinical practitioner is or should be reasonably aware that the particular patient, if warned of the risk, would be likely to attach significance to it.

This may mean that patients should also be warned of the risks which are integral to the use of information technology and audiovisual equipment. However, it might be unreasonable to expect the doctor to have sufficient technological information to understand the technical glitches that can occur in telemedical communications and their necessary effect upon telemedical practice.

Where treatment is innovative, the duty owed by the doctor to inform of the novelty is arguably even greater. A leading Canadian case[66] held that the 'duty is at least as great if not greater than the duty owed by the

64 (1993) 4 Med LR 79.

65 *F v R* (1983) 33 SASR 543.

66 *Halushka v University of Saskatchewan* (1965) 53 DLR (2d) 436.

ordinary physician or surgeon to his patient ... The subject of clinical innovation is entitled to the full and frank disclosure of all the facts, probabilities and opinions which a reasonable man might be expected to consider, before giving his consent'.[67] Telemedical treatment will for some time be experimental or novel in nature, and it would appear that under North American law at least, the duty of care owed to patients in respect of that treatment will be correspondingly higher.

LICENCE TO PRACTISE

Whether a doctor is required to obtain a clinical licence to practice in each country with which he may undertake telemedical consultations is unclear. Interstate telemedicine practitioners in the US are concerned about licensing, and suggestions have been made to develop a national licensing system.[68] Currently, each American State has a Clinical Practice Act that defines the process and procedures for granting a health professional licence, renewing a licence and regulating clinical practice within the State. Historically, interstate physician to physician communications including the mailing of x-rays, clinical histories, pathological and laboratory specimens for evaluation and interpretation, oral and written inquiries to an out of State physician involved in the patient's care, and specific consultations requesting advice, have not been subject to licensing requirements. In these interstate communications, the physician consulted is normally regarded either as practising medicine within his or her own home State or as being exempt from the licensure requirements under the 'consultation exception' in the patient's own State.

Over the past few years, 20 States[69] have enacted legislation governing licensure of out of State clinical practitioners, and another 10 States have telemedicine licensure bills pending.[70] All but one (California) have required the out of State doctor to obtain a full and unrestricted licence to practise before consulting directly with patients. Other States are expected to adopt similar measures. The clinical boards of another seven States[71] have interpreted State licensing arrangements to require out of State telemedicine practitioners to license within their own States. Only Mississippi permits out

67 *Per* Hall J, pp 616–17.

68 For a general discussion of State licensure statutes in regulations in a telemedical context, see Young, H and Waters, R, 'Licensure barriers to the interstate use of telemedicine' (1995) Newsletter Arent Fox, Washington DC, Issue 1, available on http://www.arentfox.com/telemed.5.html.

69 Kansas, Nevada, California, Connecticut, Indiana, Oklahoma, S Dakota, Tennessee and Texas.

70 Gobis, L, 'An overview of State laws and approaches to minimise licensure barriers', Telemedicine Today, Vol 5, p 6 and Vol 6, p 1.

71 Arizona, Florida, Iowa, Maine, Massachusetts, Pennsylvania and Virginia.

of State doctors to practise without further licence.[72] The American courts have not to date ruled on the issue of whether a State has jurisdiction over an out of State professional offering telemedicine services to a patient located in that State. A State may have jurisdiction over a defendant so as to require him to defend himself in that State whilst at the same time not having jurisdiction over the defendant to regulate his professional activities.[73]

Some American States recognise 'consultative' exceptions, which permit out of State practitioners to consult on a 'one off' basis. This exception is usually limited in duration and often requires the presence of a licensed practitioner from the home State. Some States allow 'emergency' exceptions under the 'good Samaritan' rules. However none of these exceptions accommodate telemedical applications by out of State practitioners. American States have primary responsibility for regulating health, and most have regulations and statutes (often antiquated) governing licence to practise. It would probably be necessary to license in any States where telemedicine is to be performed, and the same is even more likely to be true of cross-border activities.

Perhaps the most significant barrier to worldwide telemedicine service is this traditional system of licensing practitioners. A draft model Act to regulate the practice of telemedicine across US State lines has been developed by the Federation of State Clinical Boards, and several States have proposed requirements similar to those contained in the draft Act. The definition of the 'practice of medicine' varies very much from State to State and from country to country. Thus, a doctor who is licensed to practise in various States or countries may be subjected to inconsistent or conflicting disciplinary and practice standards.

There are alternative approaches that might be adopted to licensing doctors to practise across State or national boundaries. One possibility is consulting exemptions, which allow for the practice of telemedicine but prohibit the doctor from opening an office or receiving calls from within the State. There might be a process of endorsement, where other States or countries are perceived to have equivalent standards. Mutual recognition has been proposed where licensing bodies voluntarily enter into an agreement to legally accept the policies and processes of a licensee's home State or country. This practice has been adopted by the European Community and by Australia to enable cross-border practice of medicine. There might be reciprocity of relationship between two States or countries

---

72 Letter from the office of the AG of Mississippi to P Doyle Bradshaw, Executive Officer of the State Board of Clinical Licensure, 8 December 1995 (Miss AG LEXIS 867 (8 Dec 1995)).

73 *Quill Corporation v N Dakota* (1992) US 298, pp 320–21.

where each gives agreed reciprocal privileges. A registration system could be established under which a doctor licensed in one State would inform the authorities of another State of intention to practise in that State and, by so registering, submit to the State's legal jurisdiction. Health professionals would not be required to meet entrance requirements, but would be accountable for breaches of professional conduct. The State of California has enacted legislation which would authorise registration, but has not to date implemented it. Finally, there is the possibility of limited licence to practise, allowing the delivery of specific services for a specific time and under specific circumstances.

ELECTRONIC PATIENT RECORDS

A practical and immediately useful function of new technology is the provision by electronic patient records of easy access to health information by health professionals, patients and any third party entitled to access. Such access can improve the quality and efficiency of health care, health research, public health surveillance and intervention providing that it does not result in unacceptable risks to patient confidentiality.

Examples of Electronic Patient Health Records programmes around the world include St Mary's Hospital, Fukoaka, Japan, which has recently installed a sophisticated US-based system to provide for unified patient centred health records. The Forest General Hospital in Mississippi, US, has also implemented a state of the art patient information system to create a paperless environment which enables information to be shared simultaneously between accident and emergency departments, the hospital pharmacy, hospital laboratories and all wards. Multiple procedures such as ordering drugs from the pharmacy prior to surgery and radiology can be co-ordinated. The strategy is used to develop patient care pathways, and doctors can review and update a complete patient record from any ward workstation, laptop, home or surgery PC. They no longer have to wait for reports to be transcribed or recalled from records, and by coupling wireless technology, they now have a real time longitudinal patient record available anywhere in the world.

The University Health Network in Toronto, Canada also has a community wide integrated health care delivery service handling over 800,000 patient visits per year. Research indicated that doctors were spending up to one-third of their time searching for patient information that had been recorded in several locations. Now there are 4,000 networked workstations from which detailed patient records are made available electronically to all health professionals working with a patient, reducing the time spent in acquiring data from records.

It has become clear, from observation of European developments, that availability of patient records could be substantially improved through the effective use of informatics.[74] This would enable the development of computer-based record systems with powerful physical attributes which make them ideal for data capture, and storage systems which allow multiple individuals to read a record simultaneously. Traditional manual records may be incomplete, illegible, inaccurate and sometimes missing completely.[75] Electronic health data must be created, used, transmitted, aggregated and abstracted in ways and in environments that maintain data security and accuracy. Most importantly, inadvertent or accidental release of records must be prevented, as must use by unauthorised users, and unauthorised use by authorised users.

The UK's National Health Service now has access to a mass of patient information that is not always accessible at the time when it is required, such as where patients are admitted to casualty following accidents or on GP referral. Periods of intense activity may make the recording of events impossible and the accuracy and completeness of recording may vary. New technologies have extended the ability electronically to record, store, transfer and share clinical data, and an automated record with automated methods of tracking records via a computer database, bar codes and readers could potentially eliminate problems by improving the speed and accuracy of recording file movements. Whilst these new advances have the potential to improve health care delivery, they also create serious questions about who may have access to information, and how information can be protected. Unlike standard clinical records, in which a doctor may use his discretion to record findings selectively, most interactive telemedicine consultations are recorded *in toto*. This record is maintained as a part of the documentation of that consultation and doctors have less discretion to remove sensitive items. The patient will not be able to see who else is physically viewing a telemedical consultation or reading the patient record.

The UK Government has developed an ambitious programme to enable electronic delivery of health records required to be readily accessible to health professionals wherever the patient is being treated. Funds to develop pilot projects pioneering online health records have been allocated to four NHS areas, which are investigating the use of Electronic Patient Records (EPRs) to enable the sharing of patient information across health and social services communities jointly.[76] This programme is at the heart of the modernising agenda as set out in *The New NHS*,[77] and is the basis for

74 Waegmann, C, 'On the creation of a European Health Record', Centre for the Advancement of Electronic Health Records Conference, November 2000, London.

75 Byrne, A, Sellen, A, Jones, J (1998) 80 British Journal of Anaesthesia 1, p 58.

76 ERDIP press release (2000) *The Times*, 17 April.

77 *The NHS, Modern, Dependable*, Leeds, 1997 NHS Executive.

Department of Health plans to have a patient held health record available by 2004[78] and full EPRs in place in the NHS by 2005. The National Health Service Information Authority has initiated and selected pilot sites for the development and has collaborated with the College of American Pathologists to commence work on a thesaurus of clinical terms to be used internationally in patient records. A new NHS online service (nhs.uk) has been developed together with a national electronic library for health (NeLH). By March 2000, over 98% of NHS trusts and 50% of general practitioners were connected to the NHS networks.[79]

An EPHR will represent a patient's total clinical record derived from many sources, and will be integrated with secure, web-enabled technology. The ultimate goal is a shared record between the patient and all relevant health care professionals, whether they be GP, dentist, optician, hospital doctor or even acupuncturist. This will represent significant opportunities in terms of speeding the availability of patient information between health professionals.

Various possibilities have been suggested as to the technical basis on which these records could be maintained, by 'smart card', a web-based personal record into which inputs could derive from sources including the patient himself, or a floppy disk or CD-ROM. Meanwhile, the Electronic Record Development and Implementation Programme (ERDIP) has been established within the NHS Information Authority to work with the NHS to assist in development of EPHRs in support of the Information for Health Targets.[80] This is designed to ensure implementation of EPHRs throughout the NHS covering primary care, community and secondary care and the sharing of patient information across the health professional communities. It is anticipated that the work of ERDIP will lead to a lifelong electronic record for every patient in the UK, a system known sometimes as 'sperm to worm' or 'cradle to grave', providing round the clock access to patient records together with information about best clinical practice, and 'seamless' patient care throughout the NHS.

The argument underlying these developments is that the traditional paper patient record permits sharing of information in very limited form. It does, however, allow health professionals to document patient events and findings in lay language integrated with specialised clinical vocabulary. Additionally, the use of diagrams allows the expression of complex ideas with brevity and clarity. Thus, the key requirement for these newly created electronic records is to capture information in a way that is 'unambiguous, reproducible and durable'.[81] For example, anaesthetic records include notes

78 NHS plan 2000.

79 NHS Information Authority Annual Report 2000, Department of Health.

80 NHS Executive, *Information for Health*, 1998, London: HMSO.

81 Clinical Standards for the Electronic Health Record TEHRE 2000 Conference proceedings.

of the pre-operative interview and examination, laboratory data, details of anaesthetic procedures, drugs, events and physiological data. This information then provides the basis for hands-on information to recovery staff and on the ward following recovery. These records may subsequently be retrieved for case review or audit and may also be used as evidence in the event of litigation. Any EPHR proposed must fulfil all these requirements, whilst at the same time meeting the needs of the clinical fraternity by providing accurate data to a universal standard which is, above all, secure and confidential. It is this last requirement which is the most difficult to achieve and which necessarily gives rise to legal considerations. Patient data confidentiality is essential. Where electronic records are concerned, it depends upon the integrity of the 'firewalls' which provide barriers to data access, and upon encryption, the science of scrambling the text of messages, to provide data security to prevent eavesdropping on data traffic and the making of unauthorised copies of data.

Legal implications of EPHRs

Such records, while undoubtedly of potential benefit to patients and practitioners, give rise to problems in ensuring confidentiality of information. Traditionally, the Hippocratic Oath imposed upon clinical practitioners the duty to maintain the confidentiality of patient information: 'What I may see or hear in the course of treatment or even outside of the treatment in relation to the life of men, which on no account must be spread, I will keep to myself ...' More recently, the International Code of Clinical Ethics has restated a doctor's duty to maintain patient confidentiality: '(t)he doctor owes to his patient complete loyalty; a doctor shall preserve absolute secrecy on all he knows about his patient because of the confidence entrusted in him'[82] and 'I will respect the secrets which are confided in me even after the patient has died'.[83]

In England, the General Clinical Council's 'Blue Book',[84] drawn up under the provisions of s 35 of the Clinical Act 1983, contained strict rules which oblige a doctor to refrain from disclosure of any information obtained by him regarding a patient in a professional capacity. The English courts and most common law jurisdictions have recognised this duty of confidentiality, which is so strong that a legal duty is imposed upon

82 The International Code of Clinical Ethics.

83 Declaration of Geneva.

84 GMC, *Professional Conduct and a Discipline: Fitness to Practise.* Three GMC publications advise doctors regarding their obligations to patients to maintain confidentiality: *Good Medical Practice,* which sets out the basic principles of good practice; *Confidentiality,* which sets out the GMC's principles in more detail; and *Serious Communicable Diseases,* which expands on the advice given in the earlier publications.

clinicians to maintain confidences unless this obligation is overridden by public interest issues.[85] 'The doctor is under a duty not to (voluntarily) disclose, without the consent of the patient, information which he, the doctor, has gained in his professional capacity.'[86]

The challenge for telemedicine/e-health policy makers lies in ensuring that the unique combination of patient data, video imaging and electronic clinical information that is generated between distant sites during a telemedicine consultation, together with any subsequent record keeping, remains confidential. Where there is an electronic transfer of patient records, whether by computer, or computer and satellite, or on the internet, the patient's legal right to limit the dissemination of clinical information must be considered.[87] Traditional record keeping protocols will need to be redrafted to clarify who is responsible for retaining a consultation record, how the records are to be created, updated and archived and who is physically responsible for these tasks. It will need to be determined how access to these records is to be restricted. Will records be available to non-health professionals who provide the necessary technical support to the health profession?

Controls

Computer encryption and other techniques are utilised to protect the confidentiality and integrity of records. However, stories of 'hackers' breaking into hospital computer systems to alter or acquire patient data are common. There is a growing market for sale of personal health data, access to which can affect an individual's ability to secure credit, insurance, or employment.[88] *R v Department of Health ex p Source Informatics*[89] raised the question of what duty of confidence is owed by pharmacists to patients to whom they dispense prescribed drugs, and, does their duty of confidence to patients prevent pharmacists from using the material contained in the GP's prescription forms for whatever purposes they wish? In reaching his

85 Eg, *W v Egdell* [1969] 1 All ER 8.

86 *Hunter v Mann* [1974] QB 767.

87 Darley, D *et al*, *How to Keep a Clinical Confidence*, 1994, London: HMSO; Directive of the European Parliament and the Council adopted by the Council on 24 July 1995 on the protection of individuals with regard to the processing of personal data and on the free movement of such data; Information technology security evaluation criteria, EU document COM(90) 314.

88 'Hacker attacks can be hazardous to health' (1990) 16.7 Computer World 31; Report to Senate by the USA Congress Office Centre of Democracy and Technology, *Protecting Privacy in Computerised Clinical Information*, 1993.

89 *R v Department of Health ex p Source Informatics Ltd* [2000] 1 All ER 786.

decision that the pharmacists were not in breach of the duty of confidentiality to patients, Latham LJ stated that:

> ... participation in Source's scheme by doctors and pharmacists would not expose them to any serious risk of successful breach of confidence proceedings by a patient (any more than were a prescribing doctor, asked by a manufacturer's representative what medicine he ordinarily prescribes for a given condition, to answer candidly on the basis of his current practice). If the Department continue to view such schemes as operating against the public interest, then they must take further powers in this already heavily regulated area to control or limit their effect. The law of confidence cannot be distorted for the purpose.

Despite this decision, there is undoubtedly a duty to maintain patient confidentiality at a time when there are reports of blackmail attempts following access to GP computer databases. Software bugs, viruses and hardware failures occasionally re-route data flow, and routine practice is to send laboratory results via non secure email messages. It may be that efforts to ensure clinical confidentiality will create obstacles to developing EPHR systems, especially bearing in mind that even now, paper and computer systems do not necessarily achieve confidentiality.

Legislative regulation of patient records

Some countries such as Spain and Portugal have, for some time, recognised the right to privacy within their constitutions. In Spain, Art 18 of the Act of Civil Protection of Honour, Personal and Family Privacy and One's Likeness 1982 permits a plaintiff to obtain compensation for a breach of privacy even where the plaintiff has suffered no quantifiable loss.[90] Article 20 recognises the right to freedom of speech and establishes that this right will be limited by the former one. There is also a legal right to privacy in the North American and French Constitutions.

However, the UK has recognised no such general right to privacy.[91] English law has relied instead upon common law forms of action such as libel, malicious falsehood, trespass, nuisance and passing off which have developed quite separately and in an *ad hoc* fashion. The Data Protection Act 1984 has also provided individuals with some protection in relation to information about themselves which was held upon a computer, and the Access to Health Records Act 1990 gave individuals some rights in relation to personal health records.

90 Possibly the most famous case is one concerning the death of a famous bullfighter, Paquirri, who was injured during a bull fight and died shortly afterwards. His pain and suffering were broadcast on television and subsequently recorded and sold on video tape. The widow of the bullfighter sued the video company for invasion of privacy and was awarded damages by the Constitutional Court, reversing the judgement of the Supreme Court (Tca S, 2 December 1988).

91 *Malone v Metropolitan Comr of Police* [1979] 1 Ch 344, *per* Sir Robert Megarry VC, p 360.

There is inevitably conflict between concerns about protection of privacy of information, and recognition of the importance of freedom of information. Freedom of information laws had been established in many States of the US before the US Federal Freedom of Information Act in 1966. Sweden[92] was the only European country with legislation until the latter part of the 20th century, when Finland adopted a freedom of information law in 1951, followed by Norway[93] and other European States.[94] Although the European Court of Human Rights has interpreted Art 10 of the European Convention as not requiring freedom of information legislation, the Parliamentary Assembly and the Committee of Ministers of the Council of Europe have adopted recommendations endorsing such measures.[95]

In 1995, the EU Directive on the Protection of Individuals with Regard to the Processing of Personal Data and on the Movement of Such Data[96] was adopted, for implementation by 1998, 'to protect the fundamental rights and freedoms of natural persons and in particular their right to privacy with respect to the processing of personal data'. Telemedical links which store clinical data identifying individuals domiciled in the European Union must now conform to the relevant EU requirements.

This has had a significant impact on the confidentiality of patient records in the UK. The Data Protection Act 1998, designed to bring into effect the European Data Protection Directive, supersedes and repeals the Data Protection Act of 1984 other than in its provisions for the rights of personal representatives to the records of a deceased patient. The new legislation covers a more extensive list of users of data than was the case with the old Act. The Data Protection (Processing of Sensitive Data) Order 2000, which came into force in March 2000, provides detailed conditions under which it is lawful to process patient health information and applies to both computerised and manual data. The new Data Protection Commissioner, who will become the Information Commissioner under the terms of the Freedom of Information Act 2000, will determine the purposes and manner of processing personal data. The UK Government intends there to be greater openness concerning NHS administrative records,[97] and it needs to be determined whether this is feasible under the new legislation.

---

92 Freedom of the Press Act 1809, Chapter 2.

93 Act No 69 of 19 June 1970 amended by Act No 437 of 11 June 1982.

94 France, 1978, Law No 78-753 and 79-587; The Netherlands, 1978 and 1991, Art 110 of Law No 65/78; Austria, 1987, Art 20 of the Constitution; Spain, 1992, Administrative Procedure Act, November 1992; Portugal, 1993, Art 268 and Law No 65/93; Belgium, 1994, Art 32 of the Constitution; and Ireland, 1997. The laws of Greece and Italy might also be said to include Freedom of Information Acts.

95 Peers, P (2000) 10(2) CP Rev 57; Lord Irvine of Lairg, 'Constitutional reform and Bill of Rights' (1997) 5 EHRLR 483.

96 95/46/EC.

97 Cm 3818, December 1997.

The Data Protection Act 1998

The Act covers personal data, that is, data that can lead to the identification of an individual. The Act came into force in March 2000 and with application to fully automated data from October 2001. Separate provisions apply to manual data which are covered from October 2001, and between October 2001 and 2007 there is to be a further exemption in relation to manual data which was actually in the data controller's possession as of October 1998. This exemption does not relate to subject access to data.

Of especial importance in the field of public health law is the sub-category of 'sensitive personal data' that includes information as to the 'physical or mental health and condition' of the data subject and which may be held either manually or electronically. The Act regulates the processing of this data, which may include organising, consulting, using, disclosing or destroying information. Data may only be processed in accordance with the 'data protection principles'.[98] Thus, it may only be processed 'fairly and lawfully' (principle 1), it must be adequate, relevant and not excessive (principle 3), it must be accurate and kept up to date (principle 4) and it must not be kept for any longer period that that for which it was processed (principle 5).

Most importantly, perhaps, the seventh and eighth principles aim to protect personally sensitive data which would include patient records. These principles require that adequate technical and organisational measures are taken both to ensure that there is no unlawful or unauthorised processing of the data, and to prevent loss or damage of data. The data controller must ensure that there is security appropriate to the harm that might result from unauthorised or unlawful processing or loss or damage. Employees must be reliable and adequately trained, and must act in accordance with a written contract that requires them to comply with the seventh data protection principle. Further schedules set out the circumstances that must exist before 'sensitive personal data' can be processed. Processing requires the 'explicit consent' of the data subject, or an assurance that such processing is 'vital to the interests of the data subject' where the data subject cannot give consent or where the data controller cannot reasonably obtain consent. The information on which the data is based must have been made public as a direct result of steps taken by the data subject, and the processing of this information must be necessary either for clinical purposes, including preventative or diagnostic treatment and research, or for legal purposes.

Moreover, the information must have been obtained by a health professional owing a duty of confidentiality to the patient or by someone

98 Data Protection Act 1998, s 4 and Sched 1, Pt 1.

who owes a duty of confidentiality similar to that of a health professional. The term 'health professional' may include a registered clinical practitioner, a dentist, an optician, a pharmaceutical chemist, a nurse, midwife or health visitor, an osteopath, a chiropractor, a psychologist or child psychotherapist and a speech therapist.[99]

The 'data subject' has a range of rights under the Act including the right to access his own personal data, and a right to prevent processing of the data where it is likely to cause damage or distress[100] or where it may be used for the purposes of direct marketing. Where a data subject believes that data are inaccurate, a high court or county court judge may order the 'rectification, blocking, erasure or destruction of those data'.[101] Any individual who suffers distress or damage as a result of contravention by a data handler of any of the requirements of the Act is entitled to compensation, subject to the defence that the data handler had taken such care as was reasonable in all the circumstances to comply with the relevant requirements.[102]

The effects of this statute on the development of electronic records in general, and the UK Government's recent plans in particular, are unclear. There are concerns about the use by UK doctors of email and internet (GPnet), and it has been suggested that the scheme to link family doctors via the National Health Service network may be insufficiently safe to meet the requirements of the seventh and eighth principles. All health records are now governed by the new Act, which provides no specific rights for third party access to records. Difficulties may well arise in relation to parents of young children or adult children of elderly parents who request access to their children's/parents' health records. Since the Data Protection Act gives no right to applicants who are not data subjects, request for access from third parties must be based on non-statutory grounds in which the courts will seek to balance the public interests of the parties.[103]

If data is to be transferred overseas, then the eighth data protection principle must be observed. Personal data shall not be transferred to a country or territory outside the European Economic Area unless that country ensures an adequate level of protection for the rights and freedoms of data subjects in relation to the processing of personal data.[104]

---

99 Data Protection Act 1998, s 69.

100 *Ibid*, s 7.

101 *Ibid*, s 14.

102 *Ibid*, s 13.

103 As in *W v Egdell* [1990] 1 All ER 835.

104 The EEA consists of the EU Member States together with Iceland, Norway and Liechtenstein.

Human Rights Act 1998

The Human Rights Act 1998 incorporated into UK domestic law, from October 2000, the European Convention for the Protection of Human Rights and Fundamental Freedoms and certain of the Protocols to the Convention,[105] affecting a patient's rights to privacy in respect of health care records. The most relevant provision is Art 8, the Right to Respect for Private and Family Life, Home and Correspondence, which has significant implications for clinical confidentiality and is likely to affect the development of electronic health records. By s 1(1) of the Act, the Convention rights are now available in a 'qualified form' in the UK.[106] This has the effect of protecting patients' rights to the privacy of their clinical records within the NHS, although this is not an absolute right, since para 2 of Art 8 states that public authorities may interfere with this right. The term 'public authority' undoubtedly includes NHS trusts and health authorities. Under s 6 of the Act, it is unlawful for a public authority to act in a way which is incompatible with Convention rights.

Whilst the European Court has confirmed the importance of preserving the confidentiality of clinical records in *Z v Finland*,[107] the possibility of avoiding this obligation has been recognised by courts throughout the European Union. In *Z v Finland*, the applicant was a Swedish national married to X, whom she had met in Africa. During an investigation of X for a number of sexual offences, it was discovered that he was HIV-positive. He was tried on several grounds, including attempted manslaughter. As it was not clear that he had knowledge of his condition at the time of commission of the assaults, the issue at trial was when he had obtained such knowledge. Because Z had invoked her legal right not to give evidence, orders were issued obliging the doctors treating both X and Z to give evidence, and police seized clinical records relating to Z. X was convicted on several counts of attempted manslaughter and the Court of Appeal disclosed both the applicants' identity and her clinical condition in the course of the judgment. Local courts had ruled that confidentiality should be maintained for at least 10 years, and the applicant claimed that there had been a breach of her rights under Art 8 relating to the seizure of her clinical records, and disclosure of her identity and clinical data. Surprisingly, the Court held that here had been no breach of Art 8 in requiring her doctors to provide the necessary clinical evidence, since there were important public interest considerations in the trial. Neither was there a breach of Art 8 in the seizure of the applicant's clinical records.

---

105 Rome, 4 November 1950; TS (1953) Cmnd 8969.

106 (2000) 5 Woogara J Health Law 8, p 1.

107 *Z v Finland* (1998) 25 EHRR 371.

Similarly, in *MS v Sweden*[108] the applicant had made a claim for compensation from the Social Insurance Office which was alleged to have arisen from a back injury incurred whilst at work. The Office acquired the patient's records without her consent from a clinic where she had been treated for a long standing back condition, and on this basis the office rejected the patient's claim. The European Court held that there had been an interference with the patient's rights under Art 8 of the Convention, but that the interference had been justified since it had served a legitimate objective, the protection of the economic well being of the State, and thus was in the public interest.

In *McGinley v UK*,[109] the refusal by the UK Government to disclose clinical records to the alleged victims of nuclear weapons testing in the 1950s was held not to be in breach of Art 8, as was the UK refusal to amend its records of registered births to allow postoperative transsexuals to record their new identity (*Sheffield v UK*).[110] The UK courts have also considered Art 8 in a claim regarding the introduction of random health testing for prisoners, holding that there was no breach,[111] and in relation to a health authority's refusal to disclose clinical records, in which it was also held that there was no breach.[112] Only in *R v North and East Devon HA ex p Coughlan*,[113] on the closure of a nursing home for the severely mentally disabled, has the court decided that there was a potential breach of Art 8.

Regardless of the legislation, it will always be difficult to maintain and enforce a high level of confidentiality, given the large number of personnel who may legitimately handle patient records. In many cases, records are maintained in both written and computer form, and are to be found in many locations within the NHS (GP's surgery, A&E Dept, ward notes, paraclinical records, etc). Initially, the Access to Health Records Act 1990 (now repealed in part) and the Data Protection Act (DPA) 1984 (now DPA 1998) were enacted to create checks and balances within a system necessarily prone to error. Now, following the incorporation of Art 8 into UK law, it is anticipated that with the existing legislation[114] and the common law,[115] a

108 *MS v Sweden* (1999) 28 EHRR 313.

109 *McGinley v UK* (1999) 27 EHRR 1.

110 *Sheffield v UK* (1999) 27 EHRR 163.

111 *R v SoS for the Home Department ex p Tremayne* (1996) unreported, 2 May, QBD.

112 *R v Mid Glamorgan Family Health Services ex p Martin* [1995] 1 WLR 110, CA.

113 [1999] Lloyd's Rep Med 306.

114 The NHS Venereal Diseases Regulations 1974 as amended in 1991; the Access to Health Records Act 1990; the Human Fertilisation and Embryology Act 1990 as amended by the Human Fertilisation and Embryology (Disclosure of Information) Act 1992; the Abortion Regulations 1991; the Data Protection Act 1998; the Data Protection: Processing of Sensitive Data Order 2000.

115 *AG v Guardian Newspapers (No 2)* (1988) 3 All ER 545.

patient's right to privacy of recorded information has become an even more significant and important legal issue.

Caldicott guardians

Within the NHS there has been a response to the need for privacy of patient records. It had already become clear by 1995 that a number of NHS databases that were under construction or already in use held health information about identifiable patients without their knowledge or consent. For example, the Hospital Episode Statistics (HES) system at the Department of Health contains records of all hospital treatments, in which patients are identified by their date of birth and postcode. This combination is sufficient to identify some 98% of the UK population.

Professional organisations, led by the BMA, objected that identification was both unethical and unnecessary. The statistics which these systems were supposed to provide, such as referral patterns and readmission rates, are also supplied by private sector health informatics companies using properly de-identified data. For example, data collected by private firms to monitor hospital performance statistics use a patient number, which only the hospital trust can link to the patient's name. Age data is restricted to year of birth and address to postcode sector. This is sufficient to identify age cohorts and deprivation index, but not enough to identify individuals.

The UK Department of Health's response was to set up the Caldicott Committee to review all flows of personal health information other than for patient care, research and statutory notification. Unsurprisingly, perhaps, the Committee, whose membership was heavily weighted with NHS managers, found in 1997 that all information flows that it identified were for 'justifiable purposes'. The Committee recommended that where personal health information was to be used outside the context of immediate care, the NHS number should replace the patient's name and address. However, this will provide little anonymity, as the new NHS tracing service enables NHS staff to find out names and addresses corresponding to numbers.

Caldicott was also emphatic that both date of birth and postcode should be retained 'to reduce the risk of error to an acceptable level'.[116] This is a curious argument, as the NHS number already contained a check digit, as with bank accounts. If further protection were felt necessary, then one would have expected a competent system designer to use an error correction code or cryptographic authentication methods. The retention of postcode and date of birth has the effect that most patients will continue to be easily identifiable in records used by HES and other systems.

116 Caldicott Report, 1997, 4.6.4.

The proposals for the NHS Tracing Service also give rise to concern. This system will be the first database to contain up to date information on the whereabouts of every man, woman and child in the country. Existing databases, such as those run by the DVLA or the National Insurance system, do not cover the whole population and typically have many out of date addresses. The proposed security measures are unconvincing, as the wide uptake of the NHS number envisaged by Caldicott will mean that large numbers of health care professionals will need daily access to these records. On past experience, it is possible that some staff may be misled into providing patient information to those not entitled to receive it and who might be able to profit financially from the information. In addition, the data flows endorsed by Caldicott may well be *ultra vires* in a number of cases, such as where the content of records is covered by the more stringent confidentiality provisions applying to sexually transmitted disease, human fertility and embryology and mental health.

The Caldicott Committee recommended that NHS organisations be held accountable through clinical governance procedures for continuing to improve confidentiality and security procedures governing access to and storage of personal information. A Health Service circular[117] was issued in January 1999 for action by chief executives of all health authorities, special health authorities, NHS trusts and primary care groups, to implement key recommendations of the Caldicott Report. The circular advises on the appointment of 'Caldicott guardians' to oversee access to patient-identifiable information. Ideally, the guardians will be at Board level and will have been appointed as senior health professionals with responsibility for promoting clinical governance within the organisation. They will be required to ensure that the strategy by which the NHS handles and protects patient information is effective and in line with government requirements. The circular outlines the first year's work programme for improving the way each organisation handles confidential patient information and identifies resources, training and other support for guardians who will be central to the development of a new framework for handling patient information in the NHS. In particular, they will develop local protocols governing the disclosure of patient information to other organisations, restrict access to patient information within each organisation by enforcing 'need to know' principles, regularly review and justify use of patient information and improve organisational performance across a range of related areas.

To date, there is no information available about the effectiveness of the appointment of Caldicott guardians. However, it is hoped that the implementation of these proposals will have the necessary effect in protecting electronic patient records from unethical use by third parties.

117 HSC 199.012.

CONCLUSION

Health services and health professionals the world over are faced with a challenging and exciting task in harnessing communication technology to improve patient care by utilising e-health developments through the use of 'health informatics'. Proposals for integrated electronic health systems have emerged in Australia, Canada, New Zealand and the UK, whose proponents almost universally describe these proposals as facilitating an 'individual' or 'consumer' focus in health care. However, its use should ideally support, and must certainly not be in conflict with, fundamental medical ethical principles of beneficence, non-malfeasance and respect for patients' autonomy.

Telemedical developments will certainly permit technology to be deployed to help physicians provide care to patients from whom they are separated either by distance or by availability, and will hold out potential solutions to many of the limitations of current health provision. An additional effect of telemedicine practices will be to bring together data items and patient records and will facilitate the planned electronic health records.

All of these developments will, however, give rise to complex medical legal issues in terms of responsibility, standards and control. Security, confidentiality and data protection issues are crucial and must be addressed as an integral part of the projects currently being developed, perhaps in collaboration with medical insurers. In addition, training of health professionals will be required to be enhanced to include IT skills so that clinicians can use the technology effectively and with confidence to meet the necessary standards of care.

In the UK, where there is a growing fear that the privacy of patients' medical data may be compromised by these developments. The Health and Social Care Act 2001 makes provision under s 60 for the protection of confidential patient information and sets up a Patient Information Advisory Group (s 61(1)) to advise the Secretary of State on 'matters connected with the processing of patient information'. The Act aims to control all patient information 'however recorded' that 'relates to the physical or mental health or condition of an individual, to the diagnosis of his condition or to his care or treatment' so that it cannot be used for commercial purposes. However, a recent review of a New Zealand attempt to introduce the electronic integration of health records warns:

> The substantial changes to existing medical record systems will place a vast amount of additional information about the health care of identifiable

> individuals in the hands of various agencies which have not previously had such information in any usable form,[118]

which in turn may have the effect of damaging the doctor/patient relationship that depends heavily upon confidentiality.

Perhaps the most significant comment to be made to date on these developments comes from the Canadian Privacy Commissioner, when he reported that these developments involved making:

> ... available the health information of virtually the entire population online for armies of health professionals, bureaucrats and researchers. A leak from a doctor's office is damaging enough; maintaining a trusted relationship with the health system's cast of thousands is quite another.[119]

118 Stevens, R, *Medical Record Databases. Just What you Need?*, Report prepared for the Privacy Commissioner, New Zealand 1998; available at:
http://www.privacy.org.nz/people/mrdep.html.

119 Privacy Commissioner of Canada, 1997–98 Annual Report. Ottawa: Minister of Public Works and Government Services Canada, 1998: see
http://www.privcom.gc.ca/02_04_06_e.htm.

INDEX

D

I

N

O

P

S

Y

Z